Private Life and Privacy in Nazi Germany

Was it possible to have a private life under the Nazi dictatorship? It has often been assumed that private life and the notion of privacy had no place under Nazi rule. Meanwhile, in recent years historians of Nazism have been emphasising the degree to which Germans enthusiastically embraced notions of community. This volume sheds fresh light on these issues by focusing on the different ways in which non-Jewish Germans sought to uphold their privacy. It highlights the degree to which the regime permitted or even fostered such aspirations, and it offers some surprising conclusions about how private roles and private self-expression could be served by, and in turn serve, an alignment with the community. Furthermore, contributions on occupied Poland offer insights into the efforts by 'ethnic Germans' to defend their aspirations to privacy and by Jews to salvage the remnants of private life in the ghetto.

Elizabeth Harvey is Professor of History at the University of Nottingham. She has published extensively on Weimar and Nazi Germany, particularly on gender history, the history of youth and the history of photography. She is the author of *Women and the Nazi East: Agents and Witnesses of Germanization* (2003) and is currently working on the history of gender and forced labour in occupied Poland during the Second World War.

Johannes Hürter is Head of the Research Department Munich at the Leibniz Institute for Contemporary History Munich – Berlin and Adjunct Professor of Modern History at the University of Mainz. He is a leading expert on the political and military history of Weimar Germany and the Third Reich. His works include *Hitlers Heerführer: Die deutschen Oberbefehlshaber im Krieg gegen die Sowjetunion 1941/42* (2006) and he has most recently edited, with Elizabeth Harvey, *Hitler: New Research* (2018).

Maiken Umbach is Professor of Modern History at the University of Nottingham. She is co-director of Nottingham's Centre for the Study of Political Ideologies, and Principal Investigator of the AHRC-funded project 'Photography as Political Practice in National Socialism'. She has published extensively on the relationship between subjectivity, identity politics and ideology in modern European history. Her works include *Authenticity: The Cultural History of a Political Concept* (2018) and *Photography, Migration, and Identity: A German-Jewish-American Story* (2018).

Andreas Wirsching is Director of the Leibniz Institute for Contemporary History Munich – Berlin and Professor of History at the Ludwig Maximilian University of Munich. He has published extensively on European political history in the nineteenth and twentieth centuries and on the history of the European Union. His most recent works include *Hüter der Ordnung. Die Innenministerien in Bonn und Ost-Berlin nach dem Nationalsozialismus*, edited with Frank Bösch (2018).

Private Life and Privacy in Nazi Germany

Edited by

Elizabeth Harvey
University of Nottingham

Johannes Hürter
Leibniz Institute for Contemporary History Munich – Berlin

Maiken Umbach
University of Nottingham

Andreas Wirsching
Leibniz Institute for Contemporary History Munich – Berlin

and

CAMBRIDGE
UNIVERSITY PRESS

University Printing House, Cambridge CB2 8BS, United Kingdom

One Liberty Plaza, 20th Floor, New York, NY 10006, USA

477 Williamstown Road, Port Melbourne, VIC 3207, Australia

314–321, 3rd Floor, Plot 3, Splendor Forum, Jasola District Centre, New Delhi – 110025, India

79 Anson Road, #06–04/06, Singapore 079906

Cambridge University Press is part of the University of Cambridge.

It furthers the University's mission by disseminating knowledge in the pursuit of education, learning, and research at the highest international levels of excellence.

www.cambridge.org
Information on this title: www.cambridge.org/9781108484985
DOI: 10.1017/9781108754859

© Cambridge University Press 2019

This publication is in copyright. Subject to statutory exception and to the provisions of relevant collective licensing agreements, no reproduction of any part may take place without the written permission of Cambridge University Press.

First published 2019

Printed in the United Kingdom by TJ International Ltd, Padstow Cornwall

A catalogue record for this publication is available from the British Library.

Library of Congress Cataloging-in-Publication Data
Names: Harvey, Elizabeth, editor. | Hürter, Johannes, editor. | Umbach, Maiken, editor. | Wirsching, Andreas, editor.
Title: Private life and privacy in Nazi Germany / edited by Elizabeth Harvey, Johannes Hürter, Maiken Umbach, Andreas Wirsching.
Description: Cambridge, United Kingdom ; New York, NY, USA : Cambridge University Press, 2019. | Includes bibliographical references and index.
Identifiers: LCCN 2019008392 | ISBN 9781108484985 (alk. paper)
Subjects: LCSH: National socialism – Social aspects – Germany. | Interpersonal relations – Germany – History – 20th century. | Privacy – Germany – History – 20th century. | Germany – Social conditions – 1933–1945. | Germany – Social life and customs – 20th century.
Classification: LCC DD256.6 .P75 2019 | DDC 943.086–dc23
LC record available at https://lccn.loc.gov/2019008392

ISBN 978-1-108-48498-5 Hardback

Cambridge University Press has no responsibility for the persistence or accuracy of URLs for external or third-party internet websites referred to in this publication and does not guarantee that any content on such websites is, or will remain, accurate or appropriate.

Contents

List of Figures	page vii
Notes on Contributors	ix
Acknowledgements	xiv
List of Abbreviations	xv

I Interpreting the Private under National Socialism: New Approaches   1

1 Introduction: Reconsidering Private Life under the Nazi Dictatorship   3
ELIZABETH HARVEY, JOHANNES HÜRTER, MAIKEN UMBACH AND ANDREAS WIRSCHING

2 A Particular Kind of Privacy: Accessing the 'Private' in National Socialism   30
JANOSCH STEUWER

3 Private Lives, Public Faces: On the Social Self in Nazi Germany   55
MARY FULBROOK

4 Private and Public Moral Sentiments in Nazi Germany   81
NICHOLAS STARGARDT

5 (Re-)Inventing the Private under National Socialism   102
MAIKEN UMBACH

II The Private in the *Volksgemeinschaft*   133

6 Private Life in the People's Economy: Spending and Saving in Nazi Germany   135
PAMELA E. SWETT

7 'Hoist the Flag!': Flags as a Sign of Political Consensus and Distance in the Nazi Period 156
KARL CHRISTIAN FÜHRER

8 The Vulnerable Dwelling: Local Privacy before the Courts 182
ANNEMONE CHRISTIANS

9 Walther von Hollander as an Advice Columnist on Marriage and the Family in the Third Reich 206
LU SEEGERS

III The Private at War 231

10 Personal Relationships between Harmony and Alienation: Aspects of Home Leave during the Second World War 233
CHRISTIAN PACKHEISER

11 Working on the Relationship: Exchanging Letters, Goods and Photographs in Wartime
ANDREW STUART BERGERSON, LAURA FAHNENBRUCK AND CHRISTINE HARTIG 256

12 Love Letters from Front and Home: A Private Space for Intimacy in the Second World War? 280
CORNELIE USBORNE

13 'A Birth Is Nothing Out of the Ordinary Here...': Mothers, Midwives and the Private Sphere in the 'Reichsgau Wartheland', 1939–1945 304
WIEBKE LISNER

14 Transformations of the 'Private': Proximity and Distance in the Spatial Confinement of the Ghettos in Occupied Poland, 1939–1942 331
CARLOS A. HAAS

Bibliography 353
Index 383

Figures

5.1 'Should I gaze into the deep valley, or the sea of clouds?' Holiday album page, anon., Mondsee, Austria, 1944, from the author's collection. *page* 117
5.2 'The young Mozart ... and his admirers'. Holiday album page, anon., Mondsee, Austria, 1944, from the author's collection. 118
5.3 'The Honeymoon'. Line drawing from the Diary of Gisela R., Deutsches Tagebucharchiv Emmendingen, reproduced by kind permission. 121
5.4 Hiking in the Alps. Line drawing from the Diary of Gisela R., Deutsches Tagebucharchiv Emmendingen, reproduced by kind permission. 123
5.5 Holiday in Munich. Line drawing from the Diary of Gisela R., Deutsches Tagebucharchiv Emmendingen, reproduced by kind permission 124
5.6 Long-distance phone calls to Bialystok. Line drawing from the Diary of Gisela R., Deutsches Tagebucharchiv Emmendingen, reproduced by kind permission. 125
5.7 Death and bomber attacks. Line drawing from the Diary of Gisela R., Deutsches Tagebucharchiv Emmendingen, reproduced by kind permission. 126
5.8 Preparing the home for Kurt's home leave. Line drawing from the Diary of Gisela R., Deutsches Tagebucharchiv Emmendingen, reproduced by kind permission. 127
5.9 Outdoor fun. Line drawing from the Diary of Gisela R., Deutsches Tagebucharchiv Emmendingen, reproduced by kind permission. 128
5.10 Reunion after the end of the war. Line drawing from the Diary of Gisela R., Deutsches Tagebucharchiv Emmendingen, reproduced by kind permission. 129
11.1 Roland in uniform, autumn 1940, *Trug und Schein* (T&S) Ff2.16, reproduced by kind permission of the family. 263

11.2 Mosque, Plovdiv, Bulgaria, probably 5 April 1941. T&S Ff4.13, reproduced by kind permission of the family. 274
11.3 Mountain climbers, Plovdiv, Bulgaria, probably 5 April 1941. T&S Ff4.8, reproduced by kind permission of the family. 277

Notes on Contributors

ANDREW STUART BERGERSON is Professor of History at the University of Missouri–Kansas City. He has also served as a guest professor and researcher in Austria, France, Germany and Taiwan. He is an ethnographic historian of modern Germany with a particular interest in the history of everyday life. Among his publications are *Ordinary Germans in Extraordinary Times* (2004, German version forthcoming in 2019), *The Happy Burden of History* (2011) and *Ruptures in the Everyday* (2017). Since 2011, he has been one of the project leaders of *Trug und Schein* (www.trugundschein.org), an intermedial public-humanities project focusing on the letters of an ordinary German couple before, during and after the Second World War.

ANNEMONE CHRISTIANS is Research Associate and Lecturer at the Chair of Modern and Contemporary History at the Ludwig Maximilian University of Munich. Her interests focus on social, legal and cultural history in National Socialist Germany as well as on the history of science and economics in twentieth-century Europe. Her publications include *Amtsgewalt und Volksgesundheit: Das öffentliche Gesundheitswesen im nationalsozialistischen München* (2013) and *Tinte und Blech: Eine Pilotstudie zu Fritz Beindorff (1860–1944)* (2018).

LAURA FAHNENBRUCK is Assistant Professor at Leiden University and works as a historian and cultural scientist in German Studies in the teacher education programme. She is one of the project leaders of the public history project *Trug und Schein* (www.trugundschein.org). Her most recent publications are *Ein(ver)nehmen. Sexualität und Alltag von Wehrmachtsoldaten in den besetzten Niederlanden* (2018) and *The 'Private' Gaze in the Public Sphere: Photographic Self-Fashioning by German Soldiers in the Netherlands in Visual Context* (forthcoming).

KARL CHRISTIAN FÜHRER is Adjunct Professor of History at the University of Hamburg. He has published widely on the history of twentieth-century Germany. His publications include *Medienmetropole*

Hamburg: Mediale Öffentlichkeiten 1930–1960 (2008), *Die Stadt, das Geld und der Markt: Immobilienspekulation in der Bundesrepublik 1960–1985* (2016) and *Gewerkschaftsmacht und ihre Grenzen: Die ÖTV und ihr Vorsitzender Heinz Kluncker* (2017).

MARY FULBROOK is Professor of German History at University College London. A graduate of Cambridge and Harvard, she has taken the German Democratic Republic as one of her major research areas; she has also published on German national identity, on historical theory and on overviews of German and European history, and was Founding Joint Editor of *German History*. Among her publications are *Dissonant Lives: Generations and Violence through the German Dictatorships* (2011, two vols, 2017), the Fraenkel Prize-winning *A Small Town near Auschwitz: Ordinary Nazis and the Holocaust* (2012) and *Reckonings: Legacies of Nazi Persecution and the Quest for Justice* (2018).

CARLOS A. HAAS is Research Associate at the Leibniz Institute for Contemporary History in Munich. He holds a PhD in history from the Ludwig Maximilian University of Munich. Among his research interests are Holocaust studies and the history of National Socialism, as well as the history of Central America and its entanglements in the twentieth and twenty-first centuries. His dissertation, *Privacy in the Ghettos*, is due to be published in 2020.

CHRISTINE HARTIG is Research Associate at the Institute for the History of Medicine of the Robert Bosch Foundation in Stuttgart and an associated member of the Institute for the History of the German Jews in Hamburg. She received her PhD in 2014 from the University of Erfurt and has published on the topics of German–Jewish history, the history of Nazi Germany and the history of medicine. She is one of the editors of *Montagen zur Herrschaftspraxis in der klassischen Moderne: Alltagshistorische Perspektiven und Methoden* (2013).

ELIZABETH HARVEY is Professor of History at the University of Nottingham. She has published extensively on Weimar Germany and Nazi Germany, particularly on gender history. She is a Co-Investigator of an AHRC-funded project on 'Photography as Political Practice in National Socialism'. Since 2013 she has been a member of the Independent Historians' Commission on the history of the Reich Labour Ministry in the period of National Socialism. Among her publications are *Women and the Nazi East: Agents and Witnesses of Germanization* (2003, German edition 2010) and most recently *Hitler: New Research* (*German Yearbook of Contemporary History*, vol. 3), edited with Johannes Hürter (2018). She is currently working on the history of gender and forced labour in occupied Poland during the Second World War.

JOHANNES HÜRTER is Head of the Research Department Munich at the Leibniz Institute for Contemporary History Munich – Berlin and Adjunct Professor of Modern History at the University of Mainz. His research focuses on the political and military history of Germany in the twentieth century and his publications include *Wilhelm Groener: Reichswehrminister am Ende der Weimarer Republik (1928–1932)* (1993), *Hitlers Heerführer: Die deutschen Oberbefehlshaber im Krieg gegen die Sowjetunion 1941/42* (2006), *Notizen aus dem Vernichtungskrieg: Die Ostfront 1941/42 in den Aufzeichnungen des Generals Heinrici* (2016) and *Hitler: New Research* (*German Yearbook of Contemporary History*, vol. 3), edited with Elizabeth Harvey (2018).

WIEBKE LISNER is Research Associate at the Institute for History, Ethics and Philosophy at Hannover Medical School. She received her PhD in history from the Leibniz University Hannover in 2004. Her current research focuses on German, Polish and Jewish midwives and mothers and biopolitics in Western Poland from 1918 to 1945. Among her publications are the monograph *Hüterinnen der Nation? Hebammen im Nationalsozialismus* (2006) and the articles 'German Midwifery in the "Third Reich"', with Anja Peters (2014), and 'Midwifery and Racial Segregation in Occupied Western Poland 1939–1945' (2017).

CHRISTIAN PACKHEISER is Research Associate at the Leibniz Institute for Contemporary History in Munich. He holds a PhD in history from the Ludwig Maximilian University of Munich. Among his research interests are interactions between society, political institutions and the military, as well as the history of the transitions between dictatorship and democracy. His dissertation, *Home Leave and Aspects of Privacy during the Second World War*, is due to be published in 2020.

LU SEEGERS is Lecturer at the University of Hamburg as well as Managing Director of the Schaumburger Landschaft, Bückeburg. Her research focuses on twentieth-century German history, in particular urban history, media history and memory cultures. Among her publications are the monographs *Hör zu! Eduard Rhein und die Rundfunkprogrammzeitschriften (1931–1965)* (2003) and *'Vati blieb im Krieg': Vaterlosigkeit als generationelle Erfahrung im 20. Jahrhundert – Deutschland und Polen* (2013) and the article 'Hanseaten und das Hanseatische in Diktatur und Demokratie: Politisch-ideologische Zuschreibungen und Praxen' (2015).

NICHOLAS STARGARDT is Professor of Modern European History and Fellow of Magdalen College Oxford. His research has focused particularly on how people experienced the Second World War under Nazi rule. *Witnesses of War: Children's Lives under the Nazis* (2005) offered the first social history of Nazi Germany in the Second World War through the eyes of children. His latest book, *The German War: A Nation under Arms, 1939–45* (2015), explores how ordinary Germans understood and experienced the Second World War and what they thought they were fighting for.

JANOSCH STEUWER is Senior Lecturer at the University of Zurich. He has worked on the social history of National Socialism and on the history of diary writing in the twentieth century. Currently he is engaged in research on social debates on the far right since the 1960s in Western Europe. He is author of *'Ein Drittes Reich, wie ich es auffasse': Politik, Gesellschaft und privates Leben in Tagebüchern 1933–1939* (2017) and *Selbstreflexionen und Weltdeutungen: Tagebücher in der Geschichte und der Geschichtsschreibung des 20. Jahrhunderts*, edited with Rüdiger Graf (2015).

PAMELA E. SWETT is Professor of History at McMaster University in Canada. She has published articles and books on daily life and its intersections with political and commercial developments in Weimar and National Socialist Germany, including *Selling under the Swastika: Advertising and Commercial Culture in Nazi Germany* (2014) and *Neighbors and Enemies: The Culture of Radicalism in Weimar Berlin, 1929–1933* (2004). She is also a co-editor of the German Historical Institute Washington's online collection *German History in Documents and Images*.

MAIKEN UMBACH is Professor of Modern History at the University of Nottingham. She has published widely on the relationship between visual culture and ideology in different historical moments. Her books include *German Cities and Bourgeois Modernism, 1890–1930* (2009); *Authenticity: The Cultural History of a Political Concept*, with Mathew Humphrey (2018); and *Photography, Migration, and Identity: A German-Jewish-American Story*, with Scott Sulzener (2018). She is currently Principal Investigator of an AHRC-funded project on 'Photography as Political Practice in National Socialism'.

CORNELIE USBORNE is Professor emerita of History at Roehampton University and Senior Research Fellow at the Institute of Historical Research in London. She has published works on modern German social and cultural history, including *Cultures of Abortion in Weimar*

Germany (2007) and the article 'Female Sexual Desire and Male Honor: German Women's Illicit Love Affairs with POWs during World War II' (2017), and she has co-edited the forum *At Home and in the Workplace: Domestic and Occupational Space in Western Europe from the Middle Ages* (2013).

ANDREAS WIRSCHING is Director of the Leibniz Institute for Contemporary History Munich – Berlin and Professor of Modern History at the Ludwig Maximilian University of Munich. His research covers German, French and British political history in the nineteenth and twentieth centuries and the history of the European Union. Among his publications are *Vom Weltkrieg zum Bürgerkrieg? Politischer Extremismus in Deutschland und Frankreich 1918–1933/39. Berlin und Paris im Vergleich* (1999), *Abschied vom Provisorium: Geschichte der Bundesrepublik Deutschland 1982–1990* (2006), *Der Preis der Freiheit: Geschichte Europas in unserer Zeit* (2012), *Weimarer Verhältnisse? Historische Lektionen für unsere Demokratie*, edited with Berthold Kohler and Wilhelm Ulrich (2018), and *Hüter der Ordnung: Die Innenministerien in Bonn und Ost-Berlin nach dem Nationalsozialismus*, edited with Frank Bösch (2018).

Acknowledgements

As editors we owe a great debt of thanks to the organisations and institutions which supported the work leading to this book. Firstly, we thank the Leibniz Gemeinschaft for its generous funding of the research project 'Das Private im Nationalsozialismus', based at the Leibniz Institute for Contemporary History Munich – Berlin. The project ran from 2013 to 2017 as a collaboration with the German Historical Institute Warsaw and the University of Nottingham. We also thank the University of Nottingham International Collaboration Fund and the German History Society for co-funding the conference in Nottingham in June 2016 from which many of the contributions for this volume arose.

We would also like to record our thanks to others who have helped make the volume possible, first and foremost all our contributors for their efforts and their cooperation. We would also like to thank those participants and commentators who attended the Nottingham conference who do not appear as authors in this volume but whose presentations and contributions to discussion gave us valuable insights. We are very grateful to our translators, Paul Bowman and Kate Tranter, whose names appear at the start of the respective chapters for which they were responsible. We would also like to acknowledge the capable and efficient support of editing assistant Manuela Rienks of the Leibniz Institute for Contemporary History in Munich. Finally, we would like to thank Liz Friend-Smith at Cambridge University Press very warmly for her support and encouragement and Natasha Whelan, Mathivathini Mareesan and Ami Naramor for all their help during the production process.

Abbreviations

a.d.S.	an der Saale
AHRC	Arts and Humanities Research Council
a.M.	am Main
AOK	Armeeoberkommando
APK	Archiwum Państwowe w Katowicach
APŁ	Archiwum Państwowe w Łodzi
APP	Archiwum Państwowe w Poznaniu
APW	Archiwum Państwowe we Włocławku
ARG	Archiwum Ringelbluma
Az.	Aktenzeichen
BArch	Bundesarchiv
BArch-MA	Bundesarchiv, Abteilung Militärarchiv Freiburg/Breisgau
BDM	Bund Deutscher Mädel
BGB	Bürgerliches Gesetzbuch
BIZ	Berliner Illustrierte Zeitung
DAF	Deutsche Arbeitsfront
DFW	Deutsches Frauenwerk
DRZW	Das Deutsche Reich und der Zweite Weltkrieg
DTA	Deutsches Tagebucharchiv Emmendingen
Flak	Flugabwehrkanone
FZH-Archiv	Forschungsstelle für Zeitgeschichte Hamburg, Archiv
GDR	German Democratic Republic
Gestapo	Geheime Staatspolizei
HA	Hamburger Anzeiger
H.Dv.	Heeresdruckvorschrift
HHL	Harvard Houghton Library
IfZ	Institut für Zeitgeschichte München – Berlin
IPN	Instytut Pamięci Narodowej
KdF	Kraft durch Freude
KLV	Kinderlandverschickung
KPA	Kempowski Biographien-Archiv, Berlin

List of Abbreviations

KPD	Kommunistische Partei Deutschlands
KSSVO	Kriegssonderstrafrechtsverordnung
LAB	Landesarchiv Berlin
L.Dv.	Luftwaffendruckvorschrift
MadR	Meldungen aus dem Reich: Die geheimen Lageberichte des Sicherheitsdienstes der SS, 1938–1945
M.Dv.	Marinedruckvorschrift
MfK-FA	Museum für Kommunikation Berlin, Feldpostarchiv
NARA	National Archives and Records Administration, Washington, DC
n.d.	no date given
NKVD	(Soviet) People's Commissariat for Internal Affairs
n.p.	no place given
Nr.	*Nummer* (number)
NSDAP	Nationalsozialistische Deutsche Arbeiterpartei
NSF	Nationalsozialistische Frauenschaft
NSV	Nationalsozialistische Volkswohlfahrt
NWDR	Nordwestdeutscher Rundfunk
OKH	Oberkommando des Heeres
OMGUS	Office of Military Government for Germany (the United States)
RAF	Royal Air Force
RfG	Reichsstelle für Getreide, Futtermittel und sonstige landwirtschaftliche Erzeugnisse
RGBl.	Reichsgesetzblatt
RGZ	Reichsgericht in Zivilsachen
RK	Reichskanzlei
RM	Reichsmark
RMdI	Reichsministerium des Innern
SA	Sturmabteilung
SD	Sicherheitsdienst
SFN Wien	Sammlung Frauennachlässe am Institut für Geschichte der Universität Wien
Sopade	Exile organisation of the SPD
SPD	Sozialdemokratische Partei Deutschlands
SS	Schutzstaffel
StAM	Staatsarchiv München
StdA	Stadtarchiv
SuStB	Staats- und Stadtbibliothek
Ufa	Universum Film AG

USAAF	United States Army Air Forces
USHMM	United States Holocaust Memorial Museum, Washington, DC
VB	Völkischer Beobachter
VZ	Vossische Zeitung

I

Interpreting the Private under National Socialism

New Approaches

1 Introduction
Reconsidering Private Life under the Nazi Dictatorship

Elizabeth Harvey, Johannes Hürter, Maiken Umbach and Andreas Wirsching

To begin with, two snapshots, one from 1933 and one from 1941. In November 1933 'Elisabeth from Berlin' had problems with her parents, but knew where to turn: she wrote to the magazine *Die junge Dame* (*The Young Lady*) for advice.[1] She presented herself as a committed fan of the magazine, who would read its contents aloud to the BDM group (*Bund Deutscher Mädel*, League of German Girls) that she led. Her parents, she complained, insisted that she be chaperoned everywhere she went. The published editorial response took Elisabeth's side, congratulated her on winning over new readers via her BDM group and suggested that if she was responsible enough to lead a BDM group, she was also responsible enough to be trusted out on her own: 'Tell them that a girl who leads a group of young girls must know what she wants.'[2] This episode casts an interesting light on the history of the private. As elsewhere, in Nazi Germany, personal aspirations and conflicts featured as topics of interest, entertainment and discussion in the media, which provided a public audience for seemingly private concerns: one of many instances of blurred boundaries between supposedly distinct 'spheres'. And in Nazi Germany, as in many other modern societies, norms and expectations about privacy and personal autonomy within families were anything but uniform. But there are specificities here too that related to the newly installed Nazi regime. The magazine legitimated Elisabeth's bid for private autonomy through her political achievements; Elisabeth in turn regarded the magazine – with its emphasis on self-realisation, celebrity chat, film stars, beauty and 'personal problems' – as a resource to sustain the attention of her group within a Nazi youth organisation in which

---

[1] See 'Elisabeth aus Berlin', *Die junge Dame* 1/23 (1933), 5 Nov. 1933, 22 On the magazine, see Sylvia Lott, *Die Frauenzeitschriften von Hans Huffzky und John Jahr. Zur Geschichte der deutschen Frauenzeitschrift zwischen 1933 und 1970* (Berlin, 1985), 94–311; see also Chapter 9 by Lu Seegers in this volume.
[2] 'Machen Sie ihnen klar, daß ein Mädel, das eine Gruppe junger Mädchen führt, wissen muss, was sie will.'

membership was still voluntary.[3] Private self-optimisation, this suggests, could be mobilised for a regime that promised not just to change the political system but also to revolutionise German lifestyles.

The second snapshot: the author Jochen Klepper, recording in his diary the progress of his Wehrmacht unit through Ukraine, captured a peaceful moment on a sunny Sunday, 3 August 1941, in his quarters in the village of Pestchana, a few kilometres behind the front line. He evoked an idyllic, homely scene, a private moment with a few comrades in the shade of a pear tree in a big garden run to wild, where they sat reading letters from home and then laid a table for coffee, decorating it with flowers and serving the 'good honey' they had secured. 'Then we all sat sewing or reading the newspaper at the garden table, with our steel helmets lying next to us giving a distinctive touch to our little group, because an enemy bomber was circling our village. But nothing happened.'[4] Klepper's bucolic and domestic scene emphasised how he and his comrades preserved and performed their private identity as husbands and fathers within the military collective, and a couple of weeks later he noted how it was the done thing to show family photos to comrades. He was initially reluctant to do the same, but was then amused by reactions to photos of his wife, Hanni ('she cannot be older than 25!').[5] In October 1941 Klepper was forced to leave the Wehrmacht because his wife was Jewish. His desperate efforts in the course of 1942 to enable his wife and stepdaughter to emigrate came to nothing, and in December 1942 the three of them committed suicide in their Berlin flat.[6] Thinking about Klepper's diary and its context suggests further motifs and questions for a history of the private under Nazism. On one hand, Klepper is deliberately highlighting his own family role and the importance of private life for men in the Wehrmacht. For all the propagandistic manipulation of the connection fostered between home front and fighting front by *Feldpost* (the forces postal service) and home leave, Klepper's diary entry underlines the private importance of letters as a focus of time off duty, and

---

[3] On the history of the *Bund Deutscher Mädel* see Dagmar Reese, *Growing Up Female in Nazi Germany* (Ann Arbor, MI, 2006).

[4] Jochen Klepper, *Überwindung: Tagebücher und Aufzeichnungen aus dem Kriege* (Stuttgart, 1958), 124.

[5] Entry on 24 Aug. 1941, 'Ich bin sehr vorsichtig mit dem Vorzeigen von Bildern von [zu] Hause: aber bei den Landsern spielt das eine solche Rolle, daß man Frau, Kind und Haus nicht geheimhalten kann. Diese Begeisterung über Haus und Garten, Renate. Aber der 22jährige Unteroffizier Werner Kurz war heute nicht minder begeistert von Hanni, die doch "höchstens 25 Jahre alt sein kann".' Ibidem, 161.

[6] See Markus Baum, *Jochen Klepper* (Schwarzenfeld, 2011); Harald Seubert, *'Auch wer zur Nacht geweinet': Jochen Klepper (1903–1942). Eine Vergegenwärtigung* (Wesel, 2014); see also Nicholas Stargardt, *The German War: A Nation under Arms, 1939–1945* (London, 2015), 262–3.

family photos as a marker of status within a male environment. It also suggests how the privilege of a 'normal' private life served to integrate German men into National Socialism and its devastating war. Yet the subsequent story of the Klepper family reminds us how precarious private life was under a racist dictatorship: the regime destroyed the private lives of those who did not conform to National Socialist norms, before eradicating their very existence.

These two examples point to the complexities of exploring the private under National Socialism, but perhaps also to a hint of what is to be gained. Recent years have seen a growth of interest in the private life of leading Nazis, evident in the recent scholarly edition of Himmler's private correspondence[7] and a study of Hitler at home,[8] as well as older popular works such as *Die Frauen der Nazis*.[9] The wider historiography on Nazism since around 2000 too has been informed by a concern to explore – alongside mechanisms of community formation, group bonding and collective mobilisation – the leeway that the Nazi regime allowed for individual self-realisation and the pursuit of private satisfaction.[10] At the same time, new research has also shed further light on how the regime eroded and destroyed the private sphere of those it persecuted on political and 'racial' grounds.[11] In this volume, we suggest that these two are best understood as two sides of the same coin. The regime was eager

---

[7] See Katrin Himmler and Michael Wildt (eds.), *Himmler privat: Briefe eines Massenmörders* (Munich, 2014).

[8] See Despina Stratigakos, *Hitler at Home* (New Haven, CT, London, 2015).

[9] See Anna Maria Sigmund, *Die Frauen der Nazis* (Vienna, 1998), critically discussed in Johanna Gehmacher, 'Im Umfeld der Macht: Populäre Perspektiven auf Frauen der NS-Elite', in Elke Fritsch and Christina Herkommer (eds.), *Nationalsozialismus und Geschlecht: Zur Popularisierung und Ästhetisierung von Körper, Rasse und Sexualität im 'Dritten Reich' und nach 1945* (Bielefeld, 2009), 49–69.

[10] See Andrew Stuart Bergerson, *Ordinary Germans in Extraordinary Times: The Nazi Revolution in Hildesheim* (Bloomington, IN, 2004); Peter Fritzsche, *Life and Death in the Third Reich* (Cambridge, MA, 2008); Mary Fulbrook, *Dissonant Lives: Generations and Violence through the German Dictatorships* (Oxford, 2011); Moritz Föllmer, *Individuality and Modernity in Berlin: Self and Society from Weimar to the Wall* (Cambridge, 2013); most recently: Stargardt, *The German War*; Janosch Steuwer, *'Ein Drittes Reich, wie ich es auffasse': Politik, Gesellschaft und privates Leben in Tagebüchern 1933–1939* (Göttingen, 2017).

[11] See Beate Meyer, 'Grenzüberschreitungen: Eine Liebe zu Zeiten des Rassenwahns', *Zeitschrift für Geschichtswissenschaft* 55 (2007), 916–36; Andrea Löw, Doris L. Bergen and Anna Hájková (eds.), *Alltag im Holocaust: Jüdisches Leben im Großdeutschen Reich 1941–1945* (Munich, 2013). The volumes of the multivolume document edition *Die Verfolgung und Ermordung der europäischen Juden durch das nationalsozialistische Deutschland* contain numerous items documenting the erosion and destruction of the private lives of Jews in the 'Greater German Reich' and in occupied Europe. The volumes will begin appearing in English translation from 2019, www.edition-judenverfolgung.de/neu/index.php?option=com_content&view=article&id=55&Itemid=27 [accessed 25 Oct. 2017].

to enable and to showcase private happiness as an expression of one's status as a 'good Nazi'; by the same token, it would conspicuously deny the right to private happiness to those deemed politically and racially 'undesirable': the loss of a fulfilling private life would cement their formal exclusion from the *Volksgemeinschaft*.

Many of the findings presented in this book were developed as part of a collaborative research project on the private under National Socialism ('Das Private im Nationalsozialismus') begun in 2013, which was led by the Leibniz Institute for Contemporary History Munich – Berlin, in collaboration with historians at the University of Nottingham, and funded by the Leibniz Foundation.[12] The project set out to test the hypothesis that dictatorship and war made private life and pleasures all the more prized, and that the regime knowingly channelled and manipulated Germans' aspirations to a 'normal private life', even as it destroyed, for millions, the chances of achieving it. Indeed, by holding out the prospect of private life as a privilege for those deemed politically worthy and racially acceptable, the regime underscored its promise of integration into a newly cohesive national community. The project also addressed the destruction of the private lives of excluded groups: critics and opponents of the regime and victims of antisemitic persecution. We have examined the consequences of Nazi rule for courtroom battles over the private sphere of the German *Volksgenossen*, the ideas and practices relating to soldiers' home leave in the Second World War, and the way in which the Jewish inmates of ghettos in Nazi-occupied Poland sought to defend their remnants of privacy as a last remaining psychological lifeline.[13] In this volume, the results of our research are placed alongside other new research on related issues, which we brought into a dialogue at an international conference in Nottingham in 2016.

Defining the Private

The private is not a neutral analytical concept. How we understand its role under National Socialism is deeply embedded in how we define the private, which is itself a political question. Some scholars have seen the

---

[12] See www.ifz-muenchen.de/no_cache/aktuelles/themen/das-private-im-nationalsozialismus/print/ja/print.html [accessed 25 Oct. 2017].

[13] See Annemone Christians, 'Das Private vor Gericht: Verhandlungen des Eigenen im Zivil- und Strafrecht 1933–1945' (manuscript, publication forthcoming 2020); Christian Packheiser, 'Heimaturlaub: Soldaten zwischen Front, Familie und NS-Regime' (PhD, Munich, 2018, publication forthcoming 2020); Carlos A. Haas, 'Das Private im Getto: Transformationen jüdischen privaten Lebens in den Gettos von Warschau, Litzmannstadt, Tomaschow und Petrikau 1939 bis 1944' (PhD, Munich, 2018, publication forthcoming 2020).

private as a realm under threat from intrusions by modern states, enabled by new technologies. As early as 1890, Harvard law professors Louis Brandeis and Samuel Warren defended the 'right to be left alone', an intervention occasioned by concern over camera technology and the new press photography with its potential to capture people's images without their permission.[14] Other scholars, meanwhile, have been wary of the way in which the private itself has 'colonised' other spaces, and diagnosed a tendency to judge even that which ought to be properly public by the values, affects and emotions associated with private life and identity; thus, for Richard Sennett, in the course of the twentieth century the private became a substitute for the political, which undermined the proper functioning of a public sphere.[15] Underpinning such seemingly contradictory concerns are different definitions of the private itself. What is clear is that these are themselves a product of history. Even the most universal claims of what constitutes an appropriate division of the private and the public spheres are rooted in particular historical conditions. The private is not so much an a priori feature of human life which is then manipulated, appropriated or destroyed by political power; instead, the private itself is the product of historically specific imaginaries and forms of power. This is also clear from interdisciplinary work on the private and privacy, which shows how contemporary understandings of and concerns about privacy have been provoked by new forms of state surveillance and the risk of exposure through social media.[16] That is not to say that private life is not marked by certain traits that occur across chronological and cultural divides. Anthropologists have identified beliefs and practices concerning solitude, seclusion and disclosure in relation to bodily and personal habits, intimacy and family life that appear in many different cultures and periods.[17] Historical scholarship, however, has suggested that the *concept* of the private as a distinct sphere of human activity and the formation of selfhood, which is set in opposition to public life and identities, is rooted

---

[14] See Daniel Solove, *Understanding Privacy* (Cambridge, MA, 2008), 15–18; Helen Nissenbaum, *Privacy in Context: Technology, Policy and the Integrity of Social Life* (Stanford, CA, 2010), 19.

[15] See Richard Sennett, *The Fall of Public Man* (New York, NY, 1977).

[16] For examples of recent literature, see Beate Rössler and Dorota Mokrosinska (eds.), *Social Dimensions of Privacy: Interdisciplinary Perspectives* (Cambridge, 2015); Sandra Seubert and Peter Niesen (eds.), *Die Grenzen des Privaten* (Baden-Baden, 2010); Karin Jurczyk and Mechthild Oechsle (eds.), *Das Private neu denken: Erosionen, Ambivalenzen, Leistungen* (Münster, 2008); Nissenbaum, *Privacy in Context*; Solove, *Understanding Privacy*.

[17] See Jean Bethke Elshtain, 'The Displacement of Politics', in Jeff Weintraub and Krishan Kumar (eds.), *Public and Private in Thought and Practice: Perspectives on a Grand Dichotomy* (Chicago, IL, London, 1997), 166–81, here 168–70; Solove, *Understanding Privacy*, 50, 53–4, 66.

in distinctive historical traditions, notably the Enlightenment challenge to autocracy, and liberal notions of citizenship that emerged in the nineteenth century.[18] In this political tradition, a polity that is based on political participation is imaged as rooted in a conceptual distinction between a realm of 'the public', characterised by open political debate outside the organs associated with executive power, which is clearly separated from the private sphere.

An implied juxtaposition between this ideal typical liberal distinction between the private and public realms and its alleged antithesis in twentieth-century 'totalitarian' regimes, which respected no separation of private and public identities, has long shaped the way historians have approached the history of the private under National Socialism. Yet before we analyse such interpretations, it is important to recall that the liberal conception of the private was itself deeply embedded in the exercise of power. In insisting on the distinction between the proper scope of state authority and a private sphere, liberals portrayed the private as the repository of positive and politically relevant human qualities. Within it, individuals – historically assumed to be men – were thought to develop their personalities and to nurture the human qualities and values that enabled them to act as mature citizens in a revitalised public sphere.[19] Expectations and norms concerning the private – both as a protected refuge from the outside world and as a site of personal fulfilment and self-cultivation[20] – evolved in close correlation with the new forms of political authority that were based around notions of 'expertise', and that were exercised by a broadly urban bourgeoisie.[21] Such ideas of authority were predicated on the notion of disinterested knowledge and judgement exercised by rational, self-determined, deliberating individuals, who had cultivated such virtues in a private capacity. Valverde suggested that the notion of liberal rule was based on a conception of self-rule and 'intellectual maturity', which she traces from its Enlightenment origins, particularly the philosophy of Immanuel Kant, to twentieth-century formulations of democratic citizenship in a rational public sphere, as articulated, for instance, by Jürgen Habermas. For Valverde, 'liberal governance [...] is constituted by a binary opposition between nature and freedom, passion and reason, that continually reproduces despotism

---

[18] See Jeff Weintraub, 'The Theory and Politics of the Public/Private Distinction', in Weintraub/Kumar (eds.), *Public and Private*, 1–42, here 1–2.
[19] See Raymond Geuss, *Public Goods, Private Goods* (Princeton, NJ, 2001), 1–4; Maiken Umbach, *German Cities and Bourgeois Modernism, 1890–1924* (Oxford, 2009), 6, 23.
[20] See Krishan Kumar and Ekaterine Makarova, 'The Portable Home: The Domestication of Public Space', in Jurczyk/Oechsle (eds.), *Das Private neu denken*, 70–3.
[21] See Umbach, *German Cities and Bourgeois Modernism*.

Introduction 9

within rational autonomous self-rule'.[22] It also offers an object lesson in the patriarchal quality of liberalism, where the private sphere was based on the supposedly natural subordination of women to men, who were deemed less capable of rational deliberation.[23] It is therefore perhaps less surprising than it appears at first glance that, in our first snapshot, Elisabeth would draw on an explicitly anti-liberal political ideology to challenge conventional limitations of her right to full personal autonomy.

Liberal definitions of the private were not, of course, homogenous. The boundaries between 'public' and 'private' in broadly liberal societies have been drawn in very different ways, and both terms acquired multiple and overlapping meanings in the process. The contrast between public and private may commonly function to demarcate 'public life' – broadly encompassing government, the economy and the associational life of civil society – from the 'private', denoting the realm of the individual, the family, domestic life and friendship networks. But it can also distinguish the public sector as the realm of governance and collective interests from the private sector, based on the market and on particular interests; or mark the difference between public law (relating to government actors and institutions) and private law (resolving disputes between individuals or private institutions such as corporations).[24] Broadly, the public/private distinction differentiates the public as that which pertains to the state or society in general from particular interests and property ownership, the 'closed circles' within society and the personal matters that are classed as private. But no single and straightforward cleavage exists: there is 'no single clear distinction between public and private but rather a series of overlapping contrasts'[25] or 'a family of oppositions'.[26]

The related notion of privacy too has been much contested. Sociologists, political scientists and legal scholars have suggested that legal norms safeguarding the legitimately 'private' in modern liberal societies are required to protect individuals from interference from the state and from third parties. In this view, individuals ought to have control over personal information and communication and to be allowed a degree of physical and psychological seclusion, and freedom from unwanted attention.[27] This notion of personal seclusion applies within the home but also in public spaces, for example, in the expectation that one can

---

[22] Mariana Valverde, 'Despotism and Ethical Liberal Governance', *Economy and Society* 25/3 (1996), 357–72, quote 326.
[23] See Carole Pateman, *The Disorder of Women: Democracy, Feminism, and Political Theory* (Stanford, CA, 1990), 118–40, esp. 121.
[24] See Nissenbaum, *Privacy in Context*, 90. [25] Geuss, *Public Goods*, 6.
[26] Weintraub, 'The Theory and Politics of the Public/Private Distinction', 3.
[27] See Beate Rössler, *Der Wert des Privaten* (Frankfurt a.M., 2001).

walk down a street without being pestered.[28] Privacy may thus be defined in terms of a claim, or even a right, to limit and control access to personal information, property, space and time, where these things are vital to an individual's sense of security and integrity. But claims to privacy can also relate to individual autonomy, dignity and capacity for self-expression, for instance the power to make decisions ('decisional privacy') about personal preferences, leisure and consumption, and in relation to one's own body, intimate relationships, sexuality and reproduction.[29] Those who advocate legal claims to privacy present such entitlements as being of general value: society thrives if individuals feel that their innermost thoughts and personal affairs are secure from the intrusion of others.[30] But again, the seemingly universal language of such claims is deceptive. In practice, the right to privacy has often cemented existing power relations. In this sense, privacy in Western societies can be seen as a 'privileged condition of freedom and control'.[31] As already noted, the private realm could shield patriarchal domination: as Catherine McKinnon provocatively put it, privacy can mean the right of men 'to be let alone to oppress women one at a time'.[32] The idea of a right to privacy has also been used to preserve bourgeois dominance over other social groups, unable or unschooled in the 'proper' exercise of privacy. One tangible result of this was a social stratification of urban space based on 'proper' and 'improper' practices of private life, and the associated question of sensory order and disorder. Thus, Otter suggests that the 'liberal city' consists of different spatial configurations that correspond to a hierarchy of different sensory perceptions.[33] For emerging liberal elites, the senses of proximity, such as smell and touch, which interfered with the proper exercise of privacy, were replaced by a new discipline with which 'the respectable mastered their passions in public spaces conducive to the exercise of clear, controlled perception: wide streets, squares and parks.

---

[28] See Solove, *Understanding Privacy*, 18–24; Nissenbaum, *Privacy in Context*, 67–71; Anita Allen, 'Privacy', in Alison M. Jaggar and Iris Marion Young (eds.), *A Companion to Feminist Philosophy* (Oxford, 1998), 456–65, here 459.

[29] See Allen, 'Privacy', 460; Solove, *Understanding Privacy*, 24–34; Nissenbaum, *Privacy in Context*, 81–5. There are disagreements over this dimension of the definition: Wacks disagrees with what he calls the 'promiscuous extension of privacy to [...] so-called "decisional" issues and its conflation with freedom and autonomy'; see Raymond Wacks, *Privacy: A Very Short Introduction*, 2nd edn (Oxford, 2015), xiv.

[30] See Nissenbaum, *Privacy in Context*, 85–7.

[31] Patricia Meyer-Spacks, *Privacy: Concealing the Eighteenth-Century Self* (Chicago, IL, 2003), 1.

[32] McKinnon cited in Solove, *Understanding Privacy*, 82.

[33] See Chris Otter, 'Making Liberalism Durable: Vision and Civility in the Late Victorian City', *Social History* 27/1 (2002), 1–15.

Introduction   11

In their homes, separate bathrooms and bedrooms precluded promiscuity and indecency.'[34]

These insights can help situate the private under Nazism within longer-term developments in modern German history and other twentieth-century European societies. They can illuminate some of the norms and expectations concerning the private that were upheld, or denied, by the National Socialist regime after 1933. And they can help answer the question whether and how the personal and the private, as is often said, 'became political' or 'were politicised' in new ways under Nazism.

Points of Departure: Historiographical Perspectives on the Private in Nazi Germany

One particular reading of private life under Nazism casts a long shadow: this is the interpretation contained in texts written in the 1950s by liberal critics of totalitarianism, such as Hannah Arendt and Carl J. Friedrich. With National Socialism and Stalinism as their points of reference, these texts had a particular political urgency, fuelled by the Cold War, in portraying the all-pervasive presence of the totalitarian state, underpinned by terror, reaching into individuals' private lives and crushing personal autonomy and freedom. They stressed the overwhelming power of the terror apparatus, 'the power nucleus of the country, the superefficient and supercompetent services of the secret police',[35] generating a universal fear of the knock on the door, coupled with the creation of an all-pervasive climate of fear and mutual suspicion.[36] Contrasting 'tyrannical' regimes that nevertheless still left private life intact with totalitarian regimes that destroyed it, Arendt declared that '[w]e know that the iron band of total terror leaves no space for such private life and the self-coercion of totalitarian logic destroys men's capacity for experience and thought just as certainly as his capacity for action'. The other assumption of this analysis was its normative construct of a free liberal order, characterised by a particular relationship between the public and the private, that was destroyed by totalitarianism: in Carl J. Friedrich's words, 'only an individual free to shape his own life and that of his immediate human relations is capable of fulfilling the crucial function of a citizen in a democratic community'.[37]

---

[34] Ibidem, 3.
[35] Hannah Arendt, *The Origins of Totalitarianism* (Cleveland, OH, New York, NY, 1966), 420.
[36] See ibidem, 430.
[37] Carl J. Friedrich, *The Pathology of Politics: Violence, Betrayal, Corruption, Secrecy and Propaganda* (New York, NY, 1972), 186; see also Carl J. Friedrich and Zbigniew Brzezinski, *Totalitarian Dictatorship and Autocracy* (Cambridge, 1956).

There were elements in Arendt's account of the use of terror against opponents and the operation of concentration camps which captured important dimensions of the workings of Nazi rule. Nevertheless, critiques of her interpretation subsequently emerged from different angles. Some questioned its emphasis on the pervasiveness of surveillance by the organs of the security apparatus.[38] Others pointed out that totalitarianism theorists understated the intrusions into the private sphere in modern liberal and democratic polities, setting up a false contrast in terms of a supposed public/private divide between democratic and dictatorial states.[39] From this debate, new perspectives emerge that can illuminate both a history of the private under Nazism and, more broadly, the use of the private as a category when writing a political history of modern Germany. One is a comparative approach to the history of the private under non-liberal regimes. Paul Betts, arguing the case for the importance of the private under state socialism in the GDR, observes that the private sphere also played a role in the Nazi regime, and his suggestion that 'it may have been the very erosion of the public sphere in the GDR that made the private sphere so important and particularly potent' is not only a spur to investigate the scope and meanings of private life under Nazism but also to ask what, if anything, remained of a public sphere.[40] At the same time, the insight that the politicisation and penetration of the private sphere in Germany was not solely brought on by Nazism turns the spotlight onto longer continuities from the Kaiserreich to the Weimar Republic and beyond 1933.[41] Like their counterparts in other countries, the German middle classes, or *Bürgertum*, fashioned notions of private life that emphasised the capacity for self-discipline, quiet contemplation and rational decision-making as a way of legitimating their cultural, social and, increasingly, political hegemony[42] – albeit one that evolved, at least initially, in primarily local and municipal settings.[43] Subsequently, the

---

[38] Robert Gellately, *The Gestapo and German Society: Enforcing Racial Policy 1933–1945* (Oxford, 1990), 6, voices criticism but also acknowledges Arendt's insights.

[39] See Krishan Kumar, 'The Promise and Predicament of Private Life at the End of the Twentieth Century', in Weintraub/Kumar (eds.), *Public and Private*, 204–36, here 229.

[40] Paul Betts, *Within Walls: Private Life in the German Democratic Republic* (Oxford, 2010), 11, 3; see also Chapter 4 by Nicholas Stargardt in this volume.

[41] See Paul Nolte, 'Öffentlichkeit und Privatheit: Deutschland im 20. Jahrhundert', *Merkur* 60 (2006), 499–512.

[42] See Geoff Eley, 'German History and the Contradictions of Modernity: The Bourgeoisie, the State, and the Mastery of Reform', in Geoff Eley (ed.), *Society, Culture, and the State in Germany, 1870–1930* (Ann Arbor, MI, 1997), 67–103; and Maiken Umbach, 'The Civilising Process and the Emergence of the Bourgeois Self: Music Chambers in Wilhelmine Germany', in Mary Fulbrook (ed.), *Un-civilising Processes: Excess and Transgression in German Society and Culture* (New York, NY, 2007), 175–202.

[43] See for example Jennifer Jenkins, *Provincial Modernity: Local Culture and Liberal Politics in Fin-de-Siècle Hamburg* (Ithaca, NY, 2003); Jan Palmowski, *Urban Liberalism in Imperial*

welfare policies of the Weimar Republic and the rise of professional social work sought to engineer the moral and material welfare of working-class families in the image of these politically charged notions of how a 'proper' private life was to be conducted.[44] There were also concomitant efforts to connect private households with the fate of the nation through moulding and channelling domestic practices and families' private consumption in line with patriotic priorities.[45]

What, then, was distinctive about the relationship between private and public concerns under National Socialism? Traditional 'totalitarianism' interpretations have tended to focus on the structures and actions of the state bearing down on the private in ways that were distinctive, and often more overtly violent and coercive, than those employed by previous and subsequent governments and regimes. In the 1970s and 1980s, by contrast, a strand of historical research emerged, often termed the history of everyday life, or *Alltagsgeschichte*, that was more concerned with the view from below, examining popular responses to the Nazi dictatorship, and tracing the impact of coercion and propaganda on families and individuals, peer groups and friendship and neighbourhood networks at the grass roots.[46] This inevitably complicated Arendt's assumption of a singular 'experience' of totalitarian rule, and revealed both the wide variety of political persecution and new mechanisms people developed for defending spaces for relative autonomy, or, in Lüdtke's famous phrase,

---

Germany: Frankfurt am Main, 1866–1914 (Oxford, 1999), as well as Jan Palmowski, 'Mediating the Nation: Liberalism and the Polity in Nineteenth-Century Germany', *German History* 19/4 (2001), 573–98; and Kevin Repp, *Reformers, Critics, and the Paths of German Modernity: Anti-Politics and the Search for Alternatives, 1890–1914* (Cambridge, MA, 2000).

[44] See Nolte, 'Öffentlichkeit und Privatheit'; Young-Sun Hong, *Welfare, Modernity and the Weimar State 1919–1933* (Princeton, NJ, 1998); David Crew, *Germans on Welfare: From Weimar to Hitler* (Oxford, 1998).

[45] See Maiken Umbach, 'Made in Germany', in Hagen Schulze and Etienne François (eds.), *Deutsche Erinnerungsorte*, vol. 2 (Munich, 2003), 405–38; see also Jennifer Jenkins, 'Introduction: Domesticity, Design and the Shaping of the Social', special issue of *German History* 25/4 (2007), 465–89.

[46] See Timothy W. Mason, *Arbeiterklasse und Volksgemeinschaft: Dokumente und Materialien zur deutschen Arbeiterpolitik, 1936–1939* (Opladen, 1975); Timothy W. Mason, *Sozialpolitik im Dritten Reich: Arbeiterklasse und Volksgemeinschaft* (Opladen, 1977), English edition: *Social Policy in the Third Reich: The Working Class and the 'National Community'* (Providence, RI, 1993); Detlev Peukert and Jürgen Reulecke (eds.), *Die Reihen fast geschlossen: Beiträge zur Geschichte des Alltags unterm Nationalsozialismus* (Wuppertal, 1981); Alf Lüdtke (ed.), *Alltagsgeschichte: Zur Rekonstruktion historischer Erfahrungen und Lebensweisen* (Frankfurt a.M., 1989); Michael Wildt, 'Die alltagsgeschichtliche Wende der Zeitgeschichte in den 1970er und 1980er Jahren', in Forschungsstelle für Zeitgeschichte in Hamburg (ed.), *Zeitgeschichte in Hamburg* (Hamburg, 2011), 42–54.

Eigensinn.[47] The notion of public/private boundaries or of 'private life' did not always feature explicitly as the focus of enquiry within this historiography. Nevertheless, for anyone searching for evidence on underground youth gangs seeking to evade and to subvert the Hitler Youth, covert meetings of leftist networks in private flats or allotment huts or the intrusions of the local Party into urban neighbourhoods and apartment blocks, there are vivid flashes and rich insights to be teased out about the scope remaining to individuals to shield aspects of their lifestyle and personal behaviour from the attention of Party and state.

While *Alltagsgeschichte* saw itself as an alternative perspective to that of 'totalitarianism', there was ambivalence in how some of its exponents interpreted private life.[48] Was there such a thing as a private sphere under National Socialism, how far did it persist as a 'refuge', how far was it eroded and undermined? This tension was evident in Detlev Peukert's influential *Volksgenossen und Gemeinschaftsfremde* and his treatment of the theme of private life in relation to the regime's drive to forge consensus among those designated *Volksgenossen* while excluding and persecuting opponents and those branded ethnic and 'community aliens'.[49] Peukert identified a central contradiction in the way the regime combated, through its pressure to participate in organised activities in the workplace and in leisure time, individual desires to stand aside or to withdraw to a private sphere; yet at the same time it promoted a vision of domestic security and prosperity – the *kleinbürgerliche Idylle* – as an achievable goal for worthy members of the *Volksgemeinschaft*. Peukert also found complexity and ambiguity in individual responses to the pressures to conform and to participate. The attempt to withdraw to a private sphere, or what remained of one, may have been a gesture of refusal, but it could also serve to stabilise the existing National Socialist order.[50]

The categories of public and private and the gendered nature of these supposedly complementary spheres were meanwhile fundamental to the emerging field of feminist historical research in the 1970s, in Germany as in other countries, and questions about continuities and changes in the way in which gendered spheres of activity were constructed after 1933

---

[47] An excellent overview of the gains of *Alltagsgeschichte* in understanding the German experience of National Socialism is the forum 'Everyday Life in Nazi Germany', *German History* 27/4 (2009), 560–79.
[48] See Steuwer, '*Ein Drittes Reich, wie ich es auffasse*', 499.
[49] See Detlev Peukert, *Volksgenossen und Gemeinschaftsfremde: Anpassung, Ausmerze und Aufbegehren unter dem Nationalsozialismus* (Cologne, 1982), English edition: *Inside Nazi Germany: Conformity, Opposition, and Racism in Everyday Life* (New Haven, CT, and London, 1987).
[50] See Riccardo Bavaj, *Der Nationalsozialismus: Entstehung, Aufstieg und Herrschaft* (Berlin, 2016), 112–34 ('Die eigenen vier Wände').

constituted an important dimension of the work of women's and gender historians on National Socialism. For practitioners of women's and gender history, understanding the public/private divide meant analysing the gendered asymmetries of power bound up with the notion of the two spheres and critiquing the ascription of particular gendered qualities to the private sphere. This was typically equated in bourgeois thinking about the private with the domestic sphere, the space of home and family life: whatever other connotations might be attached to 'the private' and 'privacy', home life could always appear as its irreducible core. If 'the private' in modern Western societies had come to signify a haven from the demands of public life and the world of employment, it had also become coded as the 'smaller world' created by the emotional and practical efforts of the housewife.

In addressing questions relating to the private sphere under National Socialism and its place in the regime, historians of women, gender and sexuality have considered the topic from a number of angles. Important studies from the 1970s and 1980s on motherhood and family life under National Socialism highlighted the proliferating interventions of state and Party authorities into family life. Local health and welfare authorities triggered compulsory sterilisation proceedings; the new marriage loans scheme in 1933 drew thousands of couples into the net of eugenic screening; applications for the Mother's Cross from 1939 could lead to damning verdicts of feckless housekeeping; midwives were instructed to report on the birth of 'defective' babies.[51] Wartime crackdowns on allegedly promiscuous behaviour by women and the policing and punishment of forbidden sexual liaisons with foreigners added to the mechanisms for enforcing the double sexual standard in the name of protecting the 'German family'.[52]

A perspective of gender history thus reveals both the disruptive and sometimes devastating reach of the regime into private life and the specifically gendered way in which women's bodies were targets of regulation and control. At the same time, historians of gender and sexuality have also addressed the stigmatisation of 'unmanly' men and the murderous drive

[51] See Gisela Bock, *Zwangssterilisation im Nationalsozialismus: Studien zur Rassenpolitik und Frauenpolitik* (Opladen, 1986); Gabriele Czarnowski, *Das kontrollierte Paar: Ehe- und Sexualpolitik im Nationalsozialismus* (Weinheim, 1991); Irmgard Weyrather, *Muttertag und Mutterkreuz: Der Kult um die 'deutsche Mutter' im Nationalsozialismus* (Frankfurt a.M., 1993); Wiebke Lisner, *'Hüterinnen der Nation': Hebammen im Nationalsozialismus* (Frankfurt a.M., 2006).

[52] See Birthe Kundrus, *Kriegerfrauen: Familienpolitik und Geschlechterverhältnisse im Ersten und Zweiten Weltkrieg* (Hamburg, 1995); Birthe Kundrus, 'Forbidden Company: Romantic Relationships between Germans and Foreigners, 1939 to 1945', in Dagmar Herzog (ed.), *Sexuality and German Fascism* (New York, NY, 2005), 201–22; Silke Schneider, *Verbotener Umgang: Ausländer und Deutsche im Nationalsozialismus: Diskurse um Sexualität, Moral, Wissen und Strafe* (Baden-Baden, 2010).

against male homosexuals.[53] There have been, however, also other perspectives emphasising the scope for individual initiative and self-gratification under National Socialism for 'worthy' Germans of both sexes and how this was used to pursue, in gender-specific ways, self-interest and private pleasures. These include studies showing how wartime wives navigated regulations on wartime allowances to secure material benefits for themselves or to accumulate resources for the future needs of their households,[54] and how soldiers pursued opportunities for sexual encounters ranging from rape to consensual sex in occupied territories.[55] Much scope remains, however, for exploring further the private sphere, the realm of the home and the domestic under National Socialism as a potential source of power and pleasure for women as well as a site of subordination and exploitation.[56] Meanwhile, important insights on men in relation to their domestic life, their role as fathers and husbands and their masculine identities as played out in patterns of private sociability can be gained from a study of the experiences of Wehrmacht soldiers on leave.[57]

The Private as Personal Experience and Testimony

Over the past decades, the insights and approaches derived from *Alltagsgeschichte* and from research on women, gender and sexuality have continued to evolve, and given rise to new questions and methodological trends that illuminate private life in Nazi Germany, informed in turn by new cultural histories of Nazism.[58] These have examined how Germans living under Nazism appropriated, expressed and acted out key elements of Nazi ideology both in public and in their private lives, and emphasised consent and self-mobilisation as constitutive elements of the regime.[59] Such works

---

[53] See Stefan Micheler and Patricia Szobar, 'Homophobic Propaganda and the Denunciation of Same-Sex-Desiring Men under National Socialism', *Journal of the History of Sexuality* 11/1–2 (2002), 95–130; Susanne zur Nieden, *Homosexualität und Staatsräson: Männlichkeit, Homophobie und Politik in Deutschland 1900–1945* (Frankfurt a.M., 2005).
[54] See Kundrus, *Kriegerfrauen*; Nicole Kramer, *Volksgenossinnen an der Heimatfront: Mobilisierung, Verhalten, Erinnerung* (Göttingen, 2011).
[55] See Regina Mühlhäuser, *Eroberungen: Sexuelle Gewalttaten und intime Beziehungen deutscher Soldaten in der Sowjetunion, 1941–1945* (Hamburg, 2010).
[56] See Elizabeth Harvey, 'Housework, Domestic Privacy and the "German Home": Paradoxes of Private Life during the Second World War', in Rüdiger Hachtmann and Sven Reichardt (eds.), *Detlev Peukert und die NS-Forschung* (Göttingen, 2015), 115–31.
[57] See Chapter 10 by Christian Packheiser in this volume.
[58] See Frank Bajohr, Neil Gregor, Johann Chapoutot and Stefan Hördler, 'Podium Zeitgeschichte: Cultural Turn und NS-Forschung', *Vierteljahrshefte für Zeitgeschichte* 65 (2017), 219–72.
[59] See Martina Steber and Bernhard Gotto (eds.), *Visions of Community in Nazi Germany: Social Engineering and Private Lives* (Oxford, 2014); for an overview of the literature, see

Introduction 17

have built on a more extensive and systematic evaluation of 'ego-documents' in the form of private letters and diaries and have brought to light a large body of evidence illuminating complicity, involvement and self-alignment. Some of the research on the active formation of a Nazi community through self-mobilisation has focused on collective bonding processes, notably reconstructing the ways in which groups launched an onslaught of humiliating and violent acts directed above all against Jews, acts which were amplified in their impact by the presence of onlookers.[60] Other studies concerned with the Nazi project of reconstituting German society as a politically mobilised and racially exclusive *Volksgemeinschaft* have focused on the role of individual behaviour and the private sphere. This historiography has several sub-strands. First, the literature on denunciation serves as a reminder that the private is not only a space for intimacy and trust but also a site of close observation, and, at times, of betrayal and revenge. The system of repression that was constantly on the alert for enemies and opponents opened the floodgates to denouncers eager to get the better of business rivals, neighbours or ex-partners; gestures of disapproval by the police and the Party condemning political denunciations out of private motives did nothing to halt the trend.[61] A second body of work has traced the process of political surveillance by Party officials at the level of the building, street or block through which individuals came under scrutiny. Party records reveal both the readiness of many who had formerly been critics of Nazism to make the crucial everyday gestures of political loyalty (Hitler greeting, donations to Party collections) that helped cement the façade of a unified national community. But such records also reveal those holding out against making such gestures. Negative Party reports on the reputation of individuals labelled secretive or furtive (*nicht offen*) indicate how some sought to uphold their privacy and, in the words of one report, 'throw a veil over their political beliefs'.[62] Thirdly, studies of the Party in wartime have suggested how it

---

Janosch Steuwer, 'Was meint und nützt das Sprechen von der "Volksgemeinschaft"? Neuere Literatur zur Gesellschaftsgeschichte des Nationalsozialismus', *Archiv für Sozialgeschichte* 53 (2013), 487–534.

[60] See Michael Wildt, *Volksgemeinschaft als Selbstermächtigung: Gewalt gegen Juden in der deutschen Provinz 1919 bis 1939* (Hamburg, 2007).

[61] See Gellately, *The Gestapo and German Society*; Gisela Diewald-Kerkmann, *Politische Denunziation im NS-Regime oder Die kleine Macht der 'Volksgenossen'* (Bonn, 1995); Christoph Thonfeld, *Sozialkontrolle und Eigensinn: Denunziation am Beispiel Thüringens, 1933 bis 1949* (Vienna, Cologne, Weimar, 2003); Vandana Joshi, *Gender and Power in the Third Reich: Female Denouncers and the Gestapo (1933–45)* (Basingstoke, 2003).

[62] Quote from Dieter Rebentisch, 'Die "politische Beurteilung" als Herrschaftsinstitut der NSDAP', in Peukert/Reulecke (eds.), *Die Reihen fast geschlossen*, 107–28, here 109 (character 'nicht offen') and 124: 'Über einen Geschäftsmann, der noch keine drei Monate in Neu-Isenburg lebte, räsonierte man, dass er streng katholisch und politisch ein höchst unsicherer Zeitgenosse sei "wenn er auch mit viel Geschick einen Schleier über seine politischen Ansichten zu breiten versucht"'.

presented itself as a source of aid for 'deserving' Germans in their private lives, providing not only emergency assistance to the bereaved or bombed out but also advice and support on private matters. The corollary of this, it has been suggested, is that individuals willingly opened up their private lives to Party officials in the hope of securing individualised help.[63]

Another significant trend in recent research shedding light on the private under Nazism takes diaries, letters, personal photos and other forms of contemporary personal narratives (such as the autobiographical essays written for the 1939 Harvard competition on 'My life before and after the 30 January 1933') as a starting point for reconstructing experiences and subjectivities under Nazism.[64] Much of this material can illuminate the experiences of those who were excluded and persecuted by the regime: indeed, the very term 'ego-document', now used increasingly routinely, was coined by the Dutch researcher Jakob Presser in 1958 to characterise the testimonies of Jewish Holocaust survivors.[65] Many of the best-known diaries published in recent decades have enabled insights into Jewish private life and experiences of persecution after 1933 in Germany and later within 'Greater Germany' and in the wartime occupied territories.[66] Goebbels cynically proclaimed in 1934 that Jews would be left alone if they 'withdraw quietly and modestly into their four walls'.[67] The regime's exclusion of Jews from public life did indeed tend to force them into a mode of life increasingly segregated and focused on the home and private networks, even if their 'invisibility' to non-Jewish

---

[63] See John Connelly, 'The Uses of *Volksgemeinschaft*: Letters to the NSDAP Kreisleitung Eisenach, 1939–40', *Journal of Modern History* 68/4 (1996), 899–930; Kramer, *Volksgenossinnen*; Armin Nolzen, 'The NSDAP's Operational Codes after 1933', in Steber/Gotto (eds.), *Visions of Community*, 87–100; Kerstin Thieler, '*Volksgemeinschaft' unter Vorbehalt: Gesinnungskontrolle und politische Mobilisierung in der Herrschaftspraxis der NSDAP-Kreisleitung Göttingen* (Göttingen, 2014).

[64] On the Harvard competition essays, see Christian Meyer, 'Semantiken des Privaten in autobiographischen Deutungen des Nationalsozialismus 1939–1940' (PhD, Bielefeld, 2015, publication forthcoming 2019).

[65] See Kaspar von Greyerz, 'Ego-Documents: The Last Word?', *German History* 28/3 (2010), 273–82, here 277.

[66] On diaries written by Jews and by the non-Jewish spouses of Jews, see Beate Meyer, '"Ich schlüpfe unbeachtet wie eine graue Motte mit durch": Die Wandlungen der Luise Solmitz zwischen 1933 und 1945 im Spiegel ihrer Tagebücher', in Frank Bajohr and Sybille Steinbacher (eds.), *Zeugnis ablegen bis zum letzten: Tagebücher und persönliche Zeugnisse aus der Zeit des Nationalsozialismus und des Holocaust* (Göttingen, 2015), 61–80; Susanne Heim, '"Beim Schreiben habe ich immer noch einen Funken Hoffnung": Tagebücher und Briefe verfolgter Juden', in Bajohr/Steinbacher (eds.), *Zeugnis ablegen*, 81–99; Alexandra Garbarini, *Numbered Days: Diaries and the Holocaust* (New Haven, CT, 2006).

[67] Karl Christian Führer, '"Guter Lebenskamerad, nichtarisch, zw. Ehe ersehnt": Heiratsanzeigen als Quelle für die jüdische Sozial- und Mentalitätsgeschichte im nationalsozialistischen Deutschland 1933–1938', *Historische Anthropologie* 18/3 (2010), 450–66, here 451.

eyes should not be overstated.[68] At the same time the regime systematically set about the incremental destruction of the material basis of Jewish private life through measures to exclude Jews from the economy and through the seizure of homes and property.

What has the literature on the *Selbstzeugnisse* of Germans who were not excluded or persecuted revealed about private life under Nazism? There was an influential trend in post-war West Germany to use private diaries and letters as evidence of political and psychological refusal and rejection of the regime: here, the private sphere appeared as a site of 'inner emigration', of resilience and integrity in the face of dictatorship. While diaries clearly existed recording an individual's determination to document at every step their dissent and disagreement from regime policy – Friedrich Kellner's recently published diary is one example – other studies have examined a wider range of personal documentation stemming from the German majority population in which protest and refusal were far from being the norm: instead, forms of accommodation with the regime were prevalent.[69] These texts and materials – letters, diaries, personal photos – often seem to offer an authentic glimpse of private worlds, emotions and intimate relationships, and it is hard to imagine investigating the private in Nazi Germany without them. That said, any reading of such sources has to be tempered with an understanding that producing them was a social practice. Writing involved an initial filtering of impressions and views of events: in this process, what individuals wrote was shaped by prevalent ideologies and forms of widely accepted knowledge, social customs, conventions of writing and visual representation, and the agendas of the Party, state and Wehrmacht.

Since the 1980s, the extraordinary volume of wartime correspondence to and from members of the Wehrmacht (*Feldpost*) has emerged from its earlier neglect as a source for historians to become a major focus of research.[70] Resourced as a priority by the Wehrmacht, monitored and

---

[68] On the continuing 'visibility' of Jews in the press, see Führer, 'Guter Lebenskamerad'; on the enforced turn towards private life, see Marion Kaplan, *Between Dignity and Despair: Jewish Life in Nazi Germany* (New York, NY, 1998), 33, 45, 50–1.

[69] See for example Sven Keller (ed.), *Kriegstagebuch einer jungen Nationalsozialistin: Die Aufzeichnungen Wolfhilde von Königs 1939–1946* (Berlin, Boston, MA, 2015).

[70] See Ortwin Buchbender and Reinhold Sterz (eds.), *Das andere Gesicht des Krieges: Deutsche Feldpostbriefe 1939–1945* (Munich, 1982); Martin Humburg, 'Feldpostbriefe aus dem Zweiten Weltkrieg: Zur möglichen Bedeutung im aktuellen Meinungsstreit unter besonderer Berücksichtigung des Themas "Antisemitismus"', *Militärgeschichtliche Mitteilungen* 58 (1999), 321–43; Klaus Latzel, *Deutsche Soldaten – nationalsozialistischer Krieg? Kriegserlebnis – Kriegserfahrung 1939–1945* (Paderborn, 1998); contributions to special issue of *WerkstattGeschichte* 22 (1999) 'Feldpostbriefe': Klaus Latzel, 'Kriegsbriefe und Kriegserfahrung: Wie können Feldpostbriefe zur erfahrungsgeschichtlichen Quelle werden?', 7–23, Martin Humburg, 'Siegeshoffnungen und "Herbstkrise" im Jahre 1941:

censored to ensure a channel of essential emotional and material support for its soldiers, 'field post' served many purposes for the millions of Germans who engaged in correspondence: maintaining or initiating intimate relationships, requesting and exchanging parcels and photos, and reassuring family members and friends that the writer was safe, well and in good spirits. Censorship and the ban on defeatist messages meant their value as evidence about the wartime experience and actions of soldiers was correspondingly limited.[71] To be reassuring, after 1941, often meant telling lies. Moreover, self-censorship on the part of the men – out of consideration for the feelings of the recipient, out of an urge to preserve self-respect, out of shame or despair – contributed to notable silences regarding actions of Wehrmacht troops amply documented in other sources: forcible sexual encounters, terror perpetrated against conquered populations and involvement in mass murder. As documentary evidence about Germans' wartime experiences and what ordinary Germans knew about terror perpetrated in the occupied territories and the deportation and murder of the Jews, *Feldpost* has obvious limits. However, it can illuminate how individuals constituted their 'private sphere' through the practice of letter writing (snatching a moment of peace at the kitchen table or in the bunker) as well as through the content of the correspondence.[72] Maintaining the illusion of a continuing normality in the midst of war meant, for many writers, continuing to perform accustomed gender roles, as fathers to their children, as loving husbands or fiancés to their partners and as sons to their parents. For many couples, bonding through long absences sometimes took the form of erotic suggestions, conjuring up kisses, embraces or even intercourse, coupled with intense memories of past intimacies.[73] In order to bridge the physical distance and to combat the sense of life on hold, couples often exchanged future visions of private

---

Anmerkungen zu Feldpostbriefen aus der Sowjetunion', 25–40, Inge Marszolek, '"Ich möchte Dich zu gern mal in Uniform sehen": Geschlechterkonstruktionen in Feldpostbriefen', 41–59, Ulrike Jureit, 'Zwischen Ehe und Männerbund: Emotionale und sexuelle Beziehungsmuster im Zweiten Weltkrieg', 61–73; Gerald Lamprecht, *Feldpost und Kriegserlebnis: Briefe als historisch-biografische Quelle* (Munich, 2001); Veit Didczuneit, Jens Ebert and Thomas Jander (eds.), *Schreiben im Krieg – Schreiben vom Krieg: Feldpost im Zeitalter der Weltkriege* (Essen, 2011).

[71] Alternative sources for illuminating wartime experiences are offered by the transcripts of secretly taped conversations between prisoners in British and American captivity, see for example: Sönke Neitzel, *Abgehört: Deutsche Generäle in britischer Kriegsgefangenschaft 1942–1945* (Berlin, 2005); Sönke Neitzel and Harald Welzer, *Soldaten: Protokolle vom Kämpfen, Töten und Sterben* (Frankfurt a.M., 2011); Felix Römer, *Kameraden: Die Wehrmacht von innen* (Munich, 2012).

[72] Humburg, 'Siegeshoffnungen und "Herbstkrise"' contains statistics on which categories of soldier wrote most frequently, length of letters etc.

[73] See Jureit, 'Zwischen Ehe und Männerbund'; see also Chapter 12 by Cornelie Usborne in this volume.

Introduction   21

security and prosperity as a counter-world to the current deprivations and losses afflicting the nation as a collective.

Letter writing and diary writing particularly in wartime often went hand in hand, and when postal services became increasingly unreliable at the end of the war diaries could take the place of letters that could not be sent. For all that, diaries remain a distinctive form of personal writing and the genre associated most closely with the private sphere.[74] However, studies of diary writing under National Socialism have since the 1990s challenged the older idea prevalent in notions of a 'Literatur des Kerkers' ('literature of the dungeon') that writing a diary in the Third Reich necessarily signalled an urge to turn away from the regime and to preserve a sense of a private, authentic self in opposition to the claims of Party and state. For all that Nazi propaganda promoted the virtues of community, institutionalised myriad forms of enforced communal training and 'service' and denigrated the cultivation of the solitary self as bourgeois, it did not discourage the writing of diaries. Rather the reverse: as a genre that could capture the immediacy of an experience and the emotions aroused by it, the diary was promoted to National Socialists as a means to record their personal experience of the 'historic events' accompanying and following the Nazi takeover, of their time in communal training or service camps, at Party Congresses or at the Olympic Games. Concerns over military secrecy and security limited diary writing in theory, but rarely in practice – even senior commanders, such as General Gotthard Heinrici, kept remarkably detailed diaries.[75] And during the war, the Berlin city archive appealed to residents of the city to send in diaries to document how bravely Berliners were coping during the war.[76] Even once the era of quick victories was past, diaries were not necessarily repositories for the expression of private doubts or protest. As Susanne zur Nieden observed in her pioneering study of diaries by German girls and women in the Second World War, the records they produced of these years did not evoke a refuge from the outside world so much as the interpenetration of public and private, and they show – along with gestures of partial distancing – much evidence of individual accommodation with Nazism and the war.[77]

---

[74] See Janosch Steuwer and Rüdiger Graf, 'Selbstkonstitution und Welterzeugung in Tagebüchern des 20. Jahrhunderts', in Janosch Steuwer and Rüdiger Graf (eds.), *Selbstreflexionen und Weltdeutungen: Tagebücher in der Geschichte und der Geschichtsschreibung des 20. Jahrhunderts* (Göttingen, 2015), 7–36.
[75] See Johannes Hürter (ed.), *Notizen aus dem Vernichtungskrieg: Die Ostfront 1941/42 in den Aufzeichnungen des Generals Heinrici* (Darmstadt, 2016); also Felix Römer, *Die narzisstische Volksgemeinschaft: Theodor Habichts Kampf 1914 bis 1944* (Frankfurt a.M., 2017).
[76] See Susanne zur Nieden, *Alltag im Ausnahmezustand. Frauentagebücher im zerstörten Deutschland 1943-1945* (Berlin, 1993).
[77] See ibidem, 98.

A related but as yet relatively unexplored form of ego-documents were personal photographs, taken extensively both in peacetime and during the war years, on the home front and at the fighting fronts alike; many of those, in turn, were arranged in albums, captioned, or combined with other printed materials, such as postcards, advertising brochures or newspaper cuttings, as well as home-made artefacts, such as drawings, poems or pressed flowers. Older historiography looked to soldiers' photographs primarily as evidence of actions, and especially atrocities, in which particular units were implicated.[78] More recent work has also considered the relationship between the taking of such photographs and soldierly identities, sense of selfhood and a 'private' practice of making sense, individually, of shared and collective experience.[79] At the same time, historians have also turned their attention to photos and album making amongst women and young adults, either at home or in various Nazi organisations, auxiliary services and even on holidays. In such work, private photography emerges as part of the process of self-fashioning identities, and the intermingling of public and private identities, aspirations and fears, under National Socialism.[80]

Interpreting diaries, letters and collections of personal photos always has to confront the challenge of establishing what was typical, less typical or exceptional. Given the regime's overwhelming pressure on Germans to conform outwardly, debates about the extent of inner distancing

---

[78] The 1995 *Verbrechen der Wehrmacht* exhibition relied heavily on photographs to document atrocities committed by ordinary Wehrmacht soldiers in World War II. The subsequent controversy is discussed in Frances Guerin, *Through Amateur Eyes: Film and Photography in Nazi Germany* (Minneapolis, MN, 2012), 37–92; see also Anton Holzer (ed.), *Mit der Kamera bewaffnet: Krieg und Fotografie* (Marburg, 2003); Kathrin Hoffmann-Curtius, 'Trophäen und Amulette: Die Fotografien von Wehrmachts- und SS-Verbrechen in den Brieftaschen der Soldaten', *Fotogeschichte* 78/20 (2000), 63–76.

[79] Both the factual and the emotional significance of soldiers' private photographs are discussed in Petra Bopp, *Fremde im Visier: Fotoalben aus dem Zweiten Weltkrieg* (Bielefeld, 2012); Willi Rose, *Shadows of War: A German Soldier's Lost Photographs of World War II*, ed. by Thomas Eller and Petra Bopp (New York, NY, 2004); Bernd Boll, 'Das Adlerauge des Soldaten: Zur Photopraxis deutscher Amateure im Zweiten Weltkrieg', *Fotogeschichte* 85–86/22 (2002), 75–87.

[80] A collaborative research project on 'Photography as Political Practice in National Socialism' is currently under way at the University of Nottingham; see www.nottingham.ac.uk/history/research/projects/photography-as-political-practice-in-national-socialism.aspx [accessed 20 Nov. 2017]. Some of the ideas to be explored in the project are discussed in Elizabeth Harvey and Maiken Umbach (eds.), *Photography and Twentieth-Century German History*, special issue for *Central European History* 48/3 (2015); see also Timm Starl, *Knipser: Die Bildgeschichte der privaten Fotografie in Deutschland und Österreich von 1880 bis 1980* (Munich, 1995); Marianne Hirsch, *Family Frames: Photography, Narrative and Postmemory* (Cambridge, MA, 1997); Miriam Y. Arani, *Fotografische Selbst- und Fremdbilder von Deutschen und Polen im Reichsgau Wartheland 1939–1945*, 2 vols. (Hamburg, 2008).

compared to private self-alignment inevitably continue – and, unsurprisingly, different positions can be found in the contributions to the current volume.

New Directions: Questions and Hypotheses

The chapters in this volume aim to build on the historiography and approaches we have outlined here, bringing new sources into play, and challenging some established interpretations. The questions and hypotheses about private life and privacy under National Socialism they tackle can be grouped roughly into three groups; some chapters touch on more than one of these. The first group examines privacy under the Nazi dictatorship as something that was precarious, above all for alleged critics and opponents, for racial 'others' and for conquered populations in occupied territories; yet even here, they suggest, the private was, at least in some instances, open to contestation and negotiation. The second group examines the idea of a 'normal private life' as a promise through which the regime sought to legitimate itself and to mobilise popular support. The private, as a source of happiness, strength and sense of purpose, was presented as a privilege enjoyed by members of the *Volksgemeinschaft*, whose private lives would now be unencumbered by the crises and conflicts of the Weimar years.[81] In such contexts, our authors suggest, the private as political promise and reward represented an opportunity structure for living out personal aspirations for many. Finally, a third group of chapters turns this question around and asks how far the Nazi political system was constituted and upheld by particular configurations of the private and by emerging patterns of personal self-positioning and individual interaction. They ask what happened to the public/private divide under dictatorship in relation to expressions of political loyalty and the repression of opposition. This entails exploring recent views on the relationship between the private and the Nazi political system, asking whether it is possible to assert the existence of a 'public sphere' during the Third Reich, and what might be meant by the 'politicisation of the private'.

In relation to the first theme outlined earlier in this chapter, many of the chapters deal with the issue of privacy as something to be asserted or defended, exploring how the idea of an entitlement to be 'left alone' was

---

[81] See Andreas Wirsching, '*Volksgemeinschaft* and the Illusion of "Normality" from the 1920s to the 1940s', in Steber/Gotto (eds.), *Visions of Community*, 149–56; Andreas Wirsching, 'Privacy', in Winfried Nerdinger et al. (eds.), *Munich and National Socialism: Catalogue of the Munich Documentation Centre for the History of National Socialism* (Munich, 2015), 439–45.

perceived both by the regime and by ordinary Germans living under Nazi rule. Claims to privacy, as we have defined them, were rarely respected by the regime as a 'right'. With the Reichstag Fire Decree of 28 February 1933, the Nazi regime abolished at a stroke the basic entitlements (*Grundrechte*) of privacy as upheld in the Weimar Constitution of 11 August 1919: personal freedom (*persönliche Freiheit*) (Artikel 114), the security of one's private dwelling (*Unverletzlichkeit der Wohnung*) (Artikel 115), the privacy of private correspondence (*Briefgeheimnis sowie Post-, Telegraphen- und Fernsprechgeheimnis*) (Artikel 117) and freedom of speech (*freie Meinungsäußerung*) (Artikel 118).[82] Similarly, with the *Heimtückegesetz* of 20 December 1934, private communications judged to be subversive were made subject to criminal proceedings.[83] But what happened in actual practice? Answering this requires reference not only to decrees and legislation but also to legal and courtroom practice, and variations in practice such as those relating to the secret ballot in Nazi elections/plebiscites.[84] One can also ask what Germans after 1933 understood to be the changed situation, what room for manoeuvre they felt they had, and by what means they sought to assert their sense of entitlements to privacy. Take, for example, a feature in the *Berliner Tageblatt* from Christmas 1935: the editor posed the question whether amidst the new regime's drive for a community ethos, it was not time to re-emphasise the significance of the private; invited individuals responded with their thoughts on private life and privacy under the new regime.[85] The answers were wildly divergent. While the Nazi educationalist Alfred Bäumler dismissed in a one-line response the idea of a private sphere altogether, another correspondent – a student – expounded the classic bourgeois liberal theory of the private sphere as a repository of individual self-development, the foundation of European culture and a bulwark against Bolshevism.[86]

---

[82] See Thomas Raithel and Irene Strenge, 'Die Reichstagsbrandverordnung: Grundlegung der Diktatur mit den Instrumenten des Weimarer Ausnahmezustandes', *Vierteljahrshefte für Zeitgeschichte* 48 (2000), 413–60.

[83] See Bernward Dörner, *'Heimtücke': Das Gesetz als Waffe. Kontrolle, Abschreckung und Verfolgung in Deutschland 1933–1945* (Paderborn, 1998).

[84] See Steuwer, *'Ein Drittes Reich, wie ich es auffasse'*, 476–81.

[85] See 'Die private Sphäre', *Berliner Tageblatt* 64 (1935), Nr. 608, 25 Dec. 1935, Morgen-Ausgabe, 4. Beiblatt.

[86] See Alfred Bäumler, 'Ich bin so sehr Gegner der privaten Sphäre, dass ich mich überhaupt nicht dazu äußere.' Hans Behrens, Student: 'Wollte man die Private Sphäre überhaupt und gänzlich aufheben, das Niederreißen ihrer legitimen Grenzen würde nicht nur zu einer seelischen Enteignung im großen führen, sondern auch zu einer Überschwemmung, einer Zersetzung des Beruflich-Amtlichen durch das Private, die für das Bestehen des Ganzen ohne Zweifel noch viel gefährlicher wäre. Im kommunistischen Rußland scheint die Private Sphäre durch Staatsgewalt beseitigt, in den demokratischen USA zum Teil durch die "Öffentliche Meinung" aufgesogen. Es ist die Frage,

As the contributions to this volume by Annemone Christians and Karl Christian Führer show, there was room for doubt and uncertainty concerning the extent and the limits of privacy and private self-expression after 1933 despite the formal abolition of basic individual rights, including the local private sphere of the home. As Führer's contribution demonstrates, individuals could use the ritual of putting out flags to signal their own particular, sometimes idiosyncratic position with regard to the regime. Others – including Jews, until they were explicitly banned in 1935 from 'showing the flag' – precisely used the conformist gesture of hoisting the 'correct' flag to protect their own private sphere and to keep the Party at arm's length. Christians uses court cases to explore how ideas about the private were treated in the judicial system. Regardless of such notorious pronouncements such as that by Labour Front leader Robert Ley that 'there are no longer any private individuals in National Socialist Germany',[87] courts grappled with the complexity of individual disputes and came up with contradictory views over whether private conversations based on an assumption of trust and confidentiality should be regarded as incriminating or disregarded as harmless.

A further dimension of attempts to negotiate and to defend both 'decisional' and 'spatial' privacy against the odds emerged in the context of conquest, occupation, racial policy and antisemitic persecution. Two contributions to this volume deal with occupied Poland. Wiebke Lisner explores the efforts on the part of expectant 'ethnic German' (*volksdeutsche*) mothers in occupied Poland to choose their midwife regardless of regulations on boundaries of 'race' and nationality and to retain control over how and in whose presence they would give birth. She argues that establishing trust between mother and midwife was a vital ingredient in the preservation of a private sphere in the situation of childbirth, and that the decisions taken by mothers in order to uphold such a sphere could collide with the regime's biopolitical and Germanising agenda. In Carlos Haas's contribution, the notion of spatial privacy is in the foreground. He investigates the drive of Jewish inmates of the ghettos of Warsaw and Tomaschow to assert and to defend their dwindling space in order to maintain some room for intimacy and some sense of control over their immediate living environment amid murderously cramped and insanitary conditions.

The second angle opened up by chapters in this volume relates to the expectations aroused by the regime that it would secure, through

---

ob sich ein eigenes Kulturleben im europäischen Sinne auch ohne Private Sphäre gestalten kann.'

[87] For further discussion of Ley's statement and its context, see Chapter 2 by Janosch Steuwer in this volume, and Steuwer, '*Ein Drittes Reich, wie ich es auffasse*', 518.

restoring the employment of breadwinners, providing support to married couples and delivering on its promises to solve the housing problem, the basic conditions under which the mass of Germans could secure a 'normal private life', defined conventionally in terms of employment, a stable family structure, the sexual division of labour and consumption.[88] The potency of such a promise is clear given the obstacles to achieving such 'normal' goals created by the successive crises of inflation, rising unemployment in the late 1920s, and full-blown social and economic disaster in the Depression with mass lay-offs, business collapses and the slashing of the social welfare budget by increasingly right-wing conservative governments. But it also evoked what was for anti-feminists a prospect of reversing the real but fiercely contested women's rights fought for by liberals and above all by the left during the Weimar Republic, and crushing the nascent movement for homosexual rights. The promise of 'normal family life' implied the restoration of masculine authority in the public sphere as well as patriarchal relations in private life.

The regime appeared to deliver on some of its promises to secure the material basis of 'normal' private life, and for many Germans looking back in the decades after 1945, the peacetime years under Nazi rule could seem as a brief window when 'private normality' appeared within their grasp.[89] The rearmament drive secured full employment, and certain mass-produced consumer goods like radios became more affordable. But the acute shortage of housing, one of the most basic preconditions for a full experience of private life, was never overcome, and the housing crisis only escalated in wartime.[90] During the war, the regime expanded its promises to secure private life for Germans by conjuring up fantasies of German settler homes flourishing across the conquered territories of Eastern Europe.[91] Such promises were hollow from the outset, as the conflict not only wrecked the lives of non-Germans across occupied Europe through conquest, terror and genocide, but also left millions of

---

[88] See Ulrike Haerendel, *Kommunale Wohnungspolitik im Dritten Reich: Siedlungsideologie, Kleinhausbau und Wohnraumarisierung am Beispiel München* (Munich, 1999); Karl Christian Führer, 'Das NS-Regime und die "Idealform des deutschen Wohnungsbaues": Ein Beitrag zur nationalsozialistischen Gesellschaftspolitik', *Vierteljahrschrift für Sozial- und Wirtschaftsgeschichte* 89/2 (2002), 141–66; S. Jonathan Wiesen, *Creating the Nazi Marketplace: Commerce and Consumption in the Third Reich* (Cambridge, 2011).

[89] Ulrich Herbert, 'Good Times, Bad Times: Memories of the Third Reich', in Richard Bessel (ed.), *Life in the Third Reich* (Oxford, 1987), 97–110.

[90] See Karl Christian Führer, *Mieter, Hausbesitzer, Staat und Wohnungsmarkt: Wohnungsmangel und Wohnungszwangswirtschaft in Deutschland 1914–1960* (Stuttgart, 1995).

[91] See Elizabeth Harvey, *Women and the Nazi East: Agents and Witnesses of Germanization* (New Haven, CT, London, 2003).

German soldiers and civilians dead, missing or physically and mentally disabled. Yet suffering also fuelled the wartime media's portrayal of home as a private place in which the energies and spirit of the 'fighting community' would regenerate, in moments of domestic stillness and inwardness, and especially during Christmas as a family festival – coupled with promises that consumer wishes would be granted once victory came.[92] Such representations became more persistent, brazen and cynical as the war dragged on.

The contributions to this volume that re-focus attention on the motif of a private 'normality' consisting of family life and consumption as a reward and a privilege for worthy Germans provide an important counterweight to accounts of the regime that focus overly on the regime's prioritisation of the common good over the interests of the individual (*Gemeinnutz geht vor Eigennutz*), mass organisation and mass spectacle. Moreover, they open up avenues of enquiry both into the material and the psychological conditions for the private. Pamela Swett's chapter in this volume, on saving and spending, confirms that the regime sought to uphold consumer aspirations even while managing them. Even into the war years, Germans were encouraged to hold onto their private plans for securing their future through saving, and calls to make sacrifices for the sake of the *Volksgemeinschaft* were accompanied by hints that individuals could also hope – in some unspecified future – to realise their dreams of consumption. The chapter by Andrew Bergerson, Laura Fahnenbruck and Christine Hartig also picks up the theme of consumption, focusing here on consumption as a private pleasure for couples in wartime. Conquest opened up opportunities for Germans to acquire treats – at the expense of occupied populations – to share with one another.

Other chapters focus on the psychological dimension of managing and maintaining private life and relationships. In the contributions by Cornelie Usborne and by Bergerson et al., this theme is explored from the point of view of the couples themselves. Both contributions explore wartime correspondence between couples, examining the meanings of letter writing as a social practice. For Bergerson et al., the examination of one couple's correspondence reveals the entanglements between private rituals of exchange and their commitment to the *Kriegsgemeinschaft* (war community) of Germans in wartime. For Usborne, wartime letters offer a window into the history of sexuality and private emotions in wartime. Other contributions add to our understandings of private life and the quest for personal fulfilment by examining external forms of intervention,

---

[92] On the Nazi celebration of Christmas, see Joe Perry, *Christmas in Germany: A Cultural History* (Chapel Hill, NC, 2010), 189–238.

influence and advice. Christian Packheiser's contribution reveals how the Wehrmacht and the Nazi Party sought to manage the morale of soldiers through the institution of home leave. Party efforts focused on measures to 'look after' married soldiers on home leave or to act as an 'introductions bureau' for unmarried men in the Wehrmacht: here, private life was regarded as a resource to be harnessed to the goal of victory. Lu Seegers, meanwhile, examines the media as a channel purveying advice for the psychological management of private matters. Her focus is the common-sense wisdom about how to tackle personal and marital problems that was purveyed in popular magazines and bestselling novels by the evergreen Walther von Hollander, whose career as an 'agony uncle' spanned the decades from the Weimar Republic through the Third Reich into the post-war Federal Republic. The seemingly unpolitical promise carried by the popular media of happiness through self-optimisation chimed well with the regime's message that individual aspirations could be realised in harmony with the values of community.

If the two approaches just outlined illuminate how the repressive policies and promised benefits of the dictatorship shaped and distorted the conditions of private life, the third explores the implications for the political system of 'private life' after the abolition of political pluralism and the proclamation that Nazism would bring about a far-reaching revolution in the German way of life. The regime called on all Germans, insofar as they were not a priori targeted for exclusion from the *Volksgemeinschaft* on grounds of 'race', to take up a position 'for or against' National Socialism: standing on the sidelines was not to be an option, and keeping one's political views to oneself was regarded as a telltale sign of subversive intent. Moreover, from 1933 onwards the realisation of all life chances, professional opportunities and personal prospects could only take place within the framework set by the regime, and from 1939 onwards this framework was that of war, conquest and occupation.

The effects of the Nazi takeover on what remained of the 'public' (which was no longer a public sphere in the liberal sense of the term, a forum for pluralist exchange) and the private were full of paradoxes. As Janosch Steuwer in particular has argued, what 'being a Nazi' meant during the period 1933–1945 was slippery.[93] Individuals had no option but to express their opinions using the formulae and slogans of National Socialism, while they still sought to assert different versions of what a Nazi

---

[93] See Janosch Steuwer and Hanne Leßau, '"Wer ist ein Nazi? Woran erkennt man ihn?" Zur Unterscheidung von Nationalsozialisten und anderen Deutschen', *Mittelweg 36* 23/1 (2014), 30–51.

line on a particular question should be. Moreover, since outward conformity became the rule wherever visible gestures were required, coupled with tacit assent to the measures of exclusion and persecution introduced by the regime, many Germans asked themselves who was a 'genuine Nazi' and assumed many were not. What were the implications of all this for private behaviour? Steuwer's reading of private diaries leads him to argue that for many, the private was not so much a place of refuge and escape from politics but a space within which Germans positioned themselves consciously vis-à-vis the new regime. In that sense, 'the private' was a potential resource for the political system.

The challenge for historians is to make sense of the evidence for inward self-alignment as opposed to outward conformity, and – as already mentioned – there is room for different takes on the problem, including within this volume, particularly between the contributions of Mary Fulbrook, Nicholas Stargardt, Janosch Steuwer and Maiken Umbach. Using very different sources, Steuwer and Umbach both emphasise the degree to which private self-positioning in relation to National Socialism could confirm and stabilise core beliefs of official ideology. Steuwer argues that many Germans did not see the regime as a threat to private life but as an opportunity to pursue their own interests within the new system. Umbach focuses less on explicit political opinions in ego-documents, and looks instead to the importance of emotion and seemingly trivial everyday pursuits documented in recorded conversations, illustrated diaries and photo albums produced by women in fostering an affective alignment with elements of Nazi ideology. She also suggests, however, that in turn, such private appropriations could gradually hollow out Nazi ideology from within, rather than opposing it directly. Stargardt examines how Germans in wartime, confronted with the evidence of terror and genocide, agonised in private diaries and letters about the stance they should adopt in the face of these revelations. Fulbrook discusses evidence of a widespread dissonance between 'private selves' and 'public faces', and develops the argument that this dissociation between public and private selves generated the fateful inertia that made Germans stand by as the stigmatisation and persecution of the Jews escalated into mass murder. But however one regards the degree of 'dissonance' involved in Germans' loyalty to the regime, particularly demanded and tested in wartime, the idea that a continuing practice of self-positioning in private helped to secure the outward conformity that the regime demanded does shed light on the ease with which Germans disengaged from Nazism after 1945. If a privately harboured set of reservations and critiques had always accompanied and enabled the performance of loyalty, such reservations now loomed into the foreground for Germans who now claimed that they had always been sincerely opposed to the regime.

2 A Particular Kind of Privacy
Accessing the 'Private' in National Socialism

Janosch Steuwer

This scene is world famous. A man comes home, but he is not alone. As soon as he walks into the stairwell, he is confronted by threatening posters announcing 'Big Brother is watching you'. When he steps into his room, which doubles as a living room and a bedroom, he can hear a voice quoting official statistics. They come from the 'telescreen', a device on the wall, which constantly broadcasts propaganda but at the same time observes everything that happens in the room. These telescreens are installed in every room and, together with other surveillance devices, they ensure that everyone constantly has to live with the assumption that not only in public spaces but also inside their homes, 'every sound you made was overheard, and, except in darkness, every movement scrutinized'. As a result, occupants set their 'features into the expression of quiet optimism, which it was advisable to wear when facing the telescreen', even when they are in private, so that they do not become victims of the 'Thought Police'.[1]

The man experiencing this horror story of total control by the state is Winston Smith; his creator was George Orwell. Orwell conjured up this dystopian scene in his novel *Nineteen Eighty-Four*, which he completed in 1948, as the starting point for its plot, which evolves around a slight anomaly in Winston Smith's flat: for some reason, it has an alcove, which the telescreen is unable to observe. It is partly this unusual geography of the room that gives the protagonist the idea with which the novel begins. Hidden in his alcove, Winston starts a diary.[2] This is extremely dangerous, but in writing it, he is, for the first time, able to develop his own ideas, become aware of his real emotions and desires, and embark upon a project for which he will be relentlessly hunted down and punished: a so-called Thoughtcrime, namely to develop an autonomous self not defined by external influences. The conversation with himself that he begins in his diary is his first step towards that personal development, and pits him against the dictatorship. Further steps follow, which lead to

(Translated from German by Kate Tranter)
[1] George Orwell, *Nineteen Eighty-Four* (New York, NY, 1949), 4, 6. [2] Ibidem, 7.

Winston becoming the target of state terror and ideological re-education, finally resulting in him and his desire to resist being totally destroyed. By the end of the novel, deprived of all his true emotions and opinions, Winston accepts the ideology prescribed by Big Brother as his own thoughts and feelings: Winston has 'won the victory over himself'.[3]

Nineteen Eighty-Four is a work of dystopian literature, the plot of which is set in a fictitious regime of the future. However, it also reflects a past reality, namely everyday life in the ideological dictatorships of National Socialism and Stalinism. Peter Fritzsche has recently reiterated the book's transformative impact on 'our everyday speech [being] steeped in the vocabulary of imagined totalitarian worlds. We use the adjective "Orwellian" to describe "Big Brother", the "Thought Police", "doublethink", "Newspeak" and other menacing attributes found in George Orwell's classic dystopian novel Nineteen Eighty-Four'. According to Fritzsche, this is one of the key texts that 'have given subsequent generations a vocabulary with which to discuss and imagine totalitarianism'.[4] The role of 'the private' in a totalitarian dictatorship was central to this impact. It is not by chance that the novel begins in Winston's flat, and it is not by chance that I have used this scene to begin my reflections to respond to the questions posed by the editors in the introduction to this volume, about how academic research should approach the private in National Socialism. The first part of this chapter argues that there has been a specific interpretation of the private when it is subject to an unrestrained political system, and that this interpretation still has a crucial influence on historiographical discourse today. Research on National Socialism has on the whole distanced itself from the principles of the theories of totalitarianism, on which Orwell based his dystopia of complete and utter state control in 1948. However, a closer examination of the historiography of the private in the Nazi dictatorship and the theories developed since the 1950s relating to its politicisation reveals a surprising degree of persistence of this Orwellian trope.

My analysis provides an opportunity to step out of the long shadow of the Orwellian interpretation, and to develop an alternative approach to the private in the Nazi dictatorship, whose main features are presented in the second part of this chapter. The main argument is that researchers should be less concerned with searching for the remnants of a bourgeois notion of privacy, which was shaped during the Weimar Republic, and which may have evaded the Nazi claim to total power. They should,

---

[3] Ibidem, 300.
[4] Peter Fritzsche, 'Introduction', in Thomas Riggs (ed.), *Histories of Everyday Life in Totalitarian Regimes*, vol. 2: *Effects of Totalitarianism* (Farmington Hills, MI, 2015), xiii–xvi, here xiii, xvi.

rather, be pursuing the idea that the private in National Socialism is of its own particular kind, determined by different dynamics and limits than George Orwell and others believed. Although the private in National Socialism was no longer protected by any legal restrictions, there were still limits to how far the state could extend its grasp. The Nazi regime may have aspired to total rule, but this did not mean that individuals simultaneously lost most of their power. Overall it was not the case, as is presented in *Nineteen Eighty-Four*, that in the Nazi dictatorship the political was configured as the antithesis of the private. On the contrary, I argue, the political was now the prerequisite for private life.

Fixed Points and Pitfalls: Four Observations on *Nineteen Eighty-Four* and the Private in National Socialism

There is indeed good reason to consider Orwell's *Nineteen Eighty-Four* as still one of the most influential books on the question of the private in the (Nazi) dictatorship, precisely because its view is by no means original. While he was writing, Orwell referred to reports and assessments of numerous contemporaries.[5] Others, including various historians, also found their ideas of life under National Socialism and Stalinism confirmed in Orwell's writing. At the beginning of the 1980s, for example, Karl Dietrich Bracher praised *Nineteen Eighty-Four* for preserving an important 'recent historical experience' for the present. And in his 'New History' of the Third Reich, Michael Burleigh calls *Nineteen Eighty-Four* 'possibly the most compelling vision of a developed totalitarian society' ever.[6] In this chapter, I therefore treat Orwell's novel not as a singular work, but as one which can help to demonstrate an interpretation of the private whose popularity reaches far beyond that of the novel itself. Its characteristics are particularly clearly articulated in the fictional form of Orwell's dystopia, but, as I hope to show, they have also been influential in shaping the approach taken by historiography to the private in National Socialism more broadly. I focus on four points, which seem helpful in finding an approach to studying the private in National Socialism and at the same time reveal pitfalls to avoid and fixed points that are useful as orientation.

In a first step, we can treat Orwell's novel and its opening scene as a reminder that the question of the private in the Nazi dictatorship is anything but new, even if 'very little empirical work on the private sphere in non-

---

[5] On Orwell's literary and historical sources, see William Steinhoff, *George Orwell and the Origins of 1984* (Ann Arbor, MI, 1975).
[6] Karl Dietrich Bracher, 'Die totalitäre Utopie: Orwells 1984', *Psychosozial* 22 (1984), 31–48, here 45; Michael Burleigh, *The Third Reich: A New History* (London, 2000), 16.

liberal regimes' exists to date.[7] It is the central topic of the novel, which in this respect develops the story of a historical experience into a dystopian future. However distant Orwell's fictional surveillance techniques may (still) have been in the mid-twentieth century, the effects of the total control depicted in the novel, particularly in the private sphere, for Orwell were merely the culmination of the 'perversions' of modern societies, 'which have already been partly realised in Communism and Fascism'.[8] So in some ways, works such as this volume, which turns its attention to the private in National Socialism with renewed vigour, are in fact following an established tradition of thought that began before Orwell and *Nineteen Eighty-Four*. Reports and analyses by German writers, politicians and journalists who had fled abroad at the beginning of the Nazi dictatorship also often focused specifically on the private.[9]

Looking at the private became a central element of academic research into National Socialism in the first post-war decade in the context of discussions of the theory of totalitarianism, in which Orwell's novel was firmly embedded. Political scientists attempted to discover what was new and unique about the kind of power that had emerged in National Socialism and Stalinism, by comparing it systematically with previously known forms of government. What they diagnosed was an invasion of the private sphere by the state. For many, the decisive feature indicating that a dictatorial regime had become 'totalitarian' was the fact that those in power strove not only to control political and public life but also to exert complete control over private life, to the extent of destroying the private sphere completely.[10] One reason why this idea persisted was that in the context of the beginning of the Cold War, it did not remain within the confines of academic discussion. As Paul Betts stresses, in the confrontation between the Eastern and Western Blocs, 'a free private life' became a 'very marker of liberal democracy' in public discourse The global success of *Nineteen Eighty-Four* contributed to the popularity of this conviction to no small degree.[11] The inviolability of the private sphere

---

[7] Paul Betts, *Within Walls: Private Life in the German Democratic Republic* (Oxford, 2010), 6.
[8] George Orwell, 'Letter to Francis Henson', in Sonia Orwell/Ian Angus (eds.), *The Collected Essays, Journalism and Letters of George Orwell, vol. 4: In Front of Your Nose, 1945–1949* (London, 1968), 502.
[9] See Christian Meyer, '"…nichts war mehr Privatangelegenheit": Zur Semantik von Politisierungsprozessen in autobiographischen Berichten aus der Zeit des Nationalsozialismus', in Willibald Steinmetz (ed.), *'Politik': Situationen eines Wortgebrauchs im Europa der Neuzeit* (Frankfurt a.M., New York, NY, 2007), 395–416.
[10] For an overview, see Wolfgang Wippermann, *Totalitarismustheorien: Die Entwicklung der Diskussion vor den Anfängen bis heute* (Darmstadt, 1997); Eckhard Jesse (ed.), *Totalitarismus im 20. Jahrhundert: Eine Bilanz der internationalen Forschung* (2nd edn.) (Baden-Baden, 1999).
[11] Betts, *Within Walls*, 7.

became the touchstone for assessing the difference between Western democracies and their supposed antithesis, coercive totalitarian systems.

This was the premise that lent the theory of totalitarianism its most lasting influence, including on academic research into National Socialism. It is true that many studies by early historians of the Nazi period that were committed to this theory did not employ its comparative classifying method.[12] Nevertheless, the fundamental concept of the private as 'the natural and exclusive offspring of liberalism' was also shared by many of those historians who had criticised the methods and classifications of comparative research into totalitarianism that emerged from the 1960s.[13] For example, although he had very little time for the concept of totalitarianism itself, Ian Kershaw, like many others, was nevertheless convinced that by striving for total control of German society, the Nazi regime had caused the total breakdown 'even in theory [...] of any differentiation between the public and the private sphere, the state and society'.[14] The idea that the Nazi regime had occupied the private sphere was deeply inscribed into historical writing, and led to the paradoxical situation that research into National Socialism still faces today. That is to say that one of the most significant features of National Socialism is still considered to be the extent to which it exerted its power over the private sphere, but as this has been taken as 'self-evident', it is rarely the subject of specific investigations of the kind found in this volume.

This brings into play a second dimension, in which Orwell's novel demonstrates that within the tradition of thought discussed earlier in this chapter, the concept of 'the private' relating to the Nazi dictatorship does not simply refer to an empirical phenomenon, but to a particular historical problem. This is clear in the opening scene of *Nineteen Eighty-Four*. It is set in Winston Smith's private rooms, but its topic is more specific: it tackles the penetration of the state into an area that ought to be well outside its reach. The telescreen (which not only monitors the protagonist but also wakes him at a time prescribed by the state and urges him to improve his performance in collective early morning exercise), the flying police patrols that can see through the windows of flats on the upper stories to monitor them, the constant obligation to participate

---

[12] See Clemens Vollnhals, 'Der Totalitarismusbegriff im Wandel', *Aus Politik und Zeitgeschichte* 56/39 (2006), 21–6, here 26.

[13] Betts, *Within Walls*, 5. For an overview of the critique of the concept of totalitarianism, see Wippermann, *Totalitarismustheorien*, 35–44; Ian Kershaw, *Der NS-Staat: Geschichtsinterpretationen und Kontroversen im Überblick* (4th edn.) (Reinbek bei Hamburg, 2006), 63–9.

[14] Ian Kershaw, 'Nationalsozialistische und stalinistische Herrschaft: Möglichkeiten und Grenzen des Vergleichs', in Jesse (ed.), *Totalitarismus im 20. Jahrhundert*, 213–22, here 216.

A Particular Kind of Privacy

in 'communal recreation' in the 'community centre', the social control exerted by neighbours and informers – all of these details portrayed in the novel demonstrate how the all-powerful state is able to invade the private sphere of its main character. This is a further aspect in which *Nineteen Eighty-Four* is typical of many other texts.[15] They address the topic of the private within political deliberations on National Socialism and thus focus on one systemic issue: the question of whether within the Nazi political system, any limits were set on state intervention, and if so, which ones.

This focus is still of interest to the current discussion. It distinguishes between the category of the private and that of the everyday. The latter was the category with which academic research on Nazism of the late 1970s first ventured into the history of private life under National Socialism in empirical studies. The concept of 'everyday life' focused on 'ordinary' people. Its purpose was to see and to understand how they had suffered from history, to understand their actions as an integral part of historical development, and thus to restore them to their rightful place in historical narratives.[16] The concept of the private, by contrast, focuses on understanding political systems. As a basic category of political theory, it is firmly established in the analysis of political systems in the social sciences. There, it defines the sphere which sits outside the limits of state intervention. The purpose of this sphere, which is guaranteed by the constitutional state and is beyond the reach of 'politics', is to allow individuals to form their own opinions of the world, without political interference.[17]

However, it was for precisely this reason that the concept of the private was problematic for the history of everyday life in the 1970s and 1980s. This first attempt to study the history of National Socialism not from the point of view of its decision-making structures and instruments of power, but in terms of its impact on 'the experiences and behaviour of ordinary people' was met with bitter opposition.[18] The only way to counter such criticisms was for the protagonists of the history of everyday life to declare

---

[15] See as one example among others Reinhard Koselleck, 'Terror and Dream: Methodological Remarks on the Experience of Time during the Third Reich', in Reinhard Koselleck (ed.), *Futures Past: On the Semantics of Historical Time* (Cambridge, MA, 1985), 205–11.

[16] See contributions to Alf Lüdtke (ed.), *Alltagsgeschichte: Zur Rekonstruktion historischer Erfahrungen und Lebensweisen* (Frankfurt a.M., 1989).

[17] For an overview, see Jeff Weintraub and Krishan Kumar (ed.), *Public and Private in Thought and Practice: Perspectives on a Grand Dichotomy* (Chicago, IL, London, 1997).

[18] See the colloquium at the Institute for Contemporary History in Munich (IfZ): *Alltagsgeschichte der NS-Zeit: Neue Perspektive oder Trivialisierung?* (Munich, 1984) (Quote: Martin Broszat, in ibidem, 12).

that by examining the 'everyday life' of National Socialism, they were trying to gain 'new and more precise insights into its exercise of power and mechanisms of rule'.[19] In this context, a concept like 'the private', which referred to the complete opposite of everyday life and politics, was anything but attractive, and received correspondingly little consideration.

Looking at it from the current status of research on Nazism, however, the concept of 'the private' seems to have the potential to become a central category of the 'new political history of National Socialism'.[20] From the very outset of research on the everyday history of National Socialism, numerous studies made quite clear that the political system of National Socialism cannot only be explained by the internal power struggles within the Nazi leadership.[21] What also has to be considered are the diverse relationships between the Nazi regime and German society – a society that was, on one hand, excluded from any political decision-making, but was on the other hand closely involved in the realisation of National Socialist policies. Submitting these empirical findings to a rigorous conceptual analysis, however, proved more difficult. Various recent suggestions to describe the character of National Socialism as a 'compliant', 'participatory' or 'consensual' dictatorship are hardly adequate.[22] While they do succeed in emphasising the importance of a society's support for and participation in the antidemocratic Nazi regime, the precise mechanisms of how individual approval of and active cooperation with National Socialism developed into overall political support are still relatively unclear. Many questions remain: How did contemporaries' everyday conformist behaviour under the Nazi regime lead to its political legitimisation? How did their support for the government develop into collective collaboration in a political system that insisted that legitimacy required no formal mechanisms?

A lack of clarity around these questions has become the basis for fierce criticisms of much recent social historical research on National Socialism. It was summed up in Ian Kershaw's pertinent question to what extent it is 'meaningful to talk about a consensus when those who oppose what is

---

[19] Ibidem, 12–13.
[20] Michael Wildt, *Geschichte des Nationalsozialismus* (Göttingen, 2008), 90.
[21] This concern unites the opponents in the dispute between 'intentionalists' and 'functionalists'. See the contributions to Gerhard Hirschfeld and Lothar Kettenacker (eds.), *'Führer State': Myth and Reality. Studies on the Structure and Politics of the Third Reich* (Stuttgart, 1981).
[22] Frank Bajohr, 'Die Zustimmungsdiktatur: Grundzüge nationalsozialistischer Herrschaft in Hamburg', in Forschungsstelle für Zeitgeschichte in Hamburg/Josef Schmid (eds.), *Hamburg im 'Dritten Reich'* (Göttingen, 2005), 69–121; Sven Reichardt, 'Faschistische Beteiligungsdiktaturen: Anmerkungen zu einer Debatte', *Tel Aviver Jahrbuch für deutsche Geschichte* 42 (2014), 133–60; Götz Aly, *Hitlers Volksstaat: Raub, Rassenkrieg und nationaler Sozialismus* (Frankfurt a.M., 2005), 36.

happening are locked up or coerced into silence'.[23] The category of the private, taken from political theory, opens up opportunities for a more detailed analysis of these questions. It is a concept that draws attention to the interface between politics and everyday life, and demands an explanation of the relationships and dynamics that make up this interface. As a relational category to the public and to the political, the private represents one side of the 'grand dichotomy', which shapes modern society in general.[24] It is therefore a good starting point for a systematic conceptualisation of National Socialism as based on the numerous interactions between society and politics that defined the regime.

However, the analytical potential of this concept can only be exploited if, in a third step, we accept that for Orwell and others, the private does not only refer to a specific set of problems, but is at the same time an important means of interpretation. This can also be seen in the novel, most clearly in the trappings of the 'classical' bourgeois ideal of privacy, which are constantly referenced in the text. Winston's diary plays a particularly central role. Orwell's inspiration for this came from the Soviet writer Yevgeny Zamyatin, who had created a shocking vision of a collectivist society without a private sphere at the beginning of the 1920s.[25] His novel *We* also uses diary entries to portray everyday life in the coercive collectivist system of a 'united state' at some point in the future. However, Zamyatin uses diary entries as a simple stylistic tool to portray both the individualist desires of the first-person narrator and his final reintegration into the collective. Orwell gave his protagonist's diary itself the status of an icon of a bourgeois identity. Winston writes in 'a peculiarly beautiful book', whose 'beautiful creamy paper deserved to be written on with a real nib'.[26] Both of these items have to be found in dubious antique shops, because such objects have not been produced for a long time. He writes the diary secretly, and keeps it hidden. In Orwell's novel, the diary is the individualist counterpart of the collective dictatorship: in it, Winston finds himself and becomes aware of the thoughts and feelings that set him apart from 'collectivism', seen by Orwell as the quintessence of totalitarian rule.[27]

---

[23] Ian Kershaw, '"*Volksgemeinschaft*": Potential and Limitations of the Concept', in Martina Steber and Bernhard Gotto (eds.), *Visions of Community in Nazi Germany: Social Engineering and Private Lives* (Oxford, 2014), 29–42.

[24] Jeff Weintraub, 'The Theory and Politics of the Public/Private Distinction', in Jeff Weintraub and Krishan Kumar (eds.), *Public and Private in Thought and Practice: Perspectives on a Grand Dichotomy* (Chicago, London, 1997), 1–42.

[25] See Robert Russell, *Zamiatin's We* (Bristol, 2000).

[26] Orwell, *Nineteen Eighty-Four*, 7, 8.

[27] Orwell's review of F. Borkenau, 'The Totalitarian Enemy', in Sonia Orwell and Ian Angus (eds.), *The Collected Essays, Journalism and Letters of George Orwell, vol. 2: My Country Right or Left 1940–1943* (London, 1968), 24–6, here 25.

What Orwell mobilised in his novel was the classic image of a diary, which embodies the bourgeois ideal of privacy in miniature, that is, a space where a person is protected from outside view, and can be him- or herself. This device served his political purpose well. His plot was set in the future, so if he wanted the book to be understood as a political warning rather than as a fantasy story, he had to connect it somehow to the contemporary experiences of his readers. The bourgeois model of privacy is the main means of achieving this in the novel, since it throws the threat of totalitarianism into sharp relief. However, a historically grounded understanding of privacy under National Socialism cannot be uncovered via Orwell. If the bourgeois conception of privacy is taken as a norm, as it is by Orwell, privacy under National Socialism is reduced to that which fits this conception, and will always be restricted to this singular meaning ascribed to it in *Nineteen Eighty-Four*.

When research on Nazism has used the concept of privacy as a means of interpretation in this way, it has naturally focused on remnants of the private sphere from the Weimar Republic, and interpreted them as evidence for opposition. Much of the debate, particularly in the 1980s, used the German concept of *Resistenz* (a refusal to accept or to internalise political demands) to determine whether private life under National Socialism could be considered as a type of (proto-) resistance; in doing so, it took a bourgeois norm of privacy to be a universal one.[28] This led to findings such as that, by 'withdrawing into privacy', people at that time had wanted to 'erect a wall to protect themselves against the totalitarian demands of the Nazi state'.[29] The private can also be frequently found as an interpretative tool in current research on Nazism, where it is used as an indicator to gauge whether a person should be considered a Nazi or not.[30] A similar approach rests on the unspoken assumption that the 'real opinions' of contemporary actors are located 'in the private', for example in their diaries.[31] It is for this reason that reflecting on the private has such powerful potential to lead to new insights in research on Nazism. It

---

[28] For a summary, see Peter Fritzsche, 'Where Did All the Nazis Go? Reflections on Resistance and Collaboration', *Tel Aviver Jahrbuch für deutsche Geschichte* 23 (1994), 191–214.

[29] For a summary, see Riccardo Bavaj, *Die Ambivalenz der Moderne im Nationalsozialismus: Eine Bilanz der Forschung* (Munich, 2003), 78–81.

[30] See Janosch Steuwer and Hanne Leßau, '"Wer ist ein Nazi? Woran erkennt man ihn?" Zur Unterscheidung von Nationalsozialisten und anderen Deutschen', *Mittelweg* 36 23/1 (2014), 30–51.

[31] E.g. Heidrun Kämper, 'Telling the Truth: Counter-Discourses in Diaries under Totalitarian Regimes (Nazi Germany and Early GDR)', in Willibald Steinmetz (ed.), *Political Languages in the Age of Extremes* (Oxford, 2011), 215–41.

challenges scholars to rethink the often implicit assumption that privacy and National Socialism stood at opposite ends of a spectrum.

The bourgeois ideal of privacy not only restricted Orwell's and others' view by elevating privacy to an indicator of not being National Socialist. In a fourth step, we might understand it as a basis for the overall interpretation of totalitarian systems, which *Nineteen Eighty-Four* and any studies of the private under dictatorships frequently favour. Orwell's original title points to this. The novel was to be called *The Last Man in Europe*, since this is how Orwell saw his protagonist Winston Smith. In contrast to his fellow human beings who were totally controlled by Big Brother, Winston had not yet become a 'man of paralyzing stupidity, a mass of imbecile enthusiasm'.[32] As long as Winston can withdraw into what remains of his privacy, the alcove in his room and his diary, he is able to remain 'sane' and secretly to preserve 'the human heritage'.[33] These remnants of privacy are the grounds for his hope that the dictatorship 'can't get inside you' and that, in spite of the adverse circumstances, he will be able to remain 'human', 'even when it can't have any result'.[34] But when Winston is arrested and deprived of his space to withdraw to, he is no longer able to lead a self-determined human life. Without an opportunity for private reflection, Winston is totally at the mercy of torture and re-education. He has to watch the dictatorship worming its way further and further into his 'inner self', obliterating personal memories and finally rendering him as stupid as his neighbours.

This interpretation too is based on a bourgeois model of privacy. For the bourgeoisie of the eighteenth and nineteenth centuries and its conception of political and social order, having a space free from the influence of others where a person could be him- or herself was considered essential for them to be able to become aware of their own opinions, desires and emotions.[35] This private sphere was to be particularly protected from the authorities so that citizens could develop their own personalities, free from political influence. This was also thought to make it possible for them to represent their own interests in public and to act autonomously. In the bourgeois model, the existence of private space provided the necessary basis for self-awareness and autonomous living, and Orwell expressly confirmed the validity of this equation in dystopian reversal. If the state destroys private space, an autonomous private life is no longer possible.[36]

---

[32] Orwell, *Nineteen Eighty-Four*, 23. [33] Ibidem, 28, 29. [34] Ibidem, 167.
[35] For a longer discussion of the evolution of the bourgeois notion of privacy in the eighteenth and nineteenth centuries, see the relevant paragraphs in the Introduction to this volume.
[36] The authoritative work on this is still Jürgen Habermas, *The Structural Transformation of the Public Sphere: An Inquiry into a Category of Bourgeois Society* (Cambridge, MA, 1989).

The bourgeois model of privacy was, of course, even in the eighteenth and nineteenth centuries, no more than that: a model, which in many aspects did not correspond to reality. Research on the bourgeoisie has repeatedly characterised the idea of a private space free from politics and power relations as an ideological construct and pointed out, for example, that the gender order was particularly effective in the private sphere, allowing men and women to be anything but 'themselves'.[37] The private has always been political, but the idea that there should be a space for individual self-development inaccessible to politics was an ideological construct with particularly lasting effects. Even today, the word 'private' still denotes spatial arrangements in which the individual is protected from any interventions by others, as well as a sphere of action and responsibility in which the individual is supposed to be able to follow their own personal inclinations.[38] This bourgeois model of privacy has also been firmly embedded in the interpretation of National Socialism. Based on their observations of the Nazi regime's unlimited access to what was previously considered a private sphere, historians, in the same way as Orwell, developed wide-ranging theories about the way people's everyday lives and their ideas of their own personality changed after 1933. This meant that the interest in the private gained a further dimension, besides the question of the limits of the Nazi state. The concept of the private focused attention on the role of subjectivity in National Socialism, and with it a question about the scope, or lack thereof, for living an individual, autonomous life under the dictatorship.

There have, however, been very few empirical studies on this 'subjective dimension of Nazism'.[39] The bourgeois model of privacy seems to have explained the effects of state intrusion into private space even for those historians who did not share Orwell's theories of totalitarianism. In this context, their arguments show a surprising continuity. The theory of the 'withdrawal into the private' put forward by historians of everyday life reproduces in many ways what had been formulated since the 1950s in the debates on so-called inner emigration: both suggest that National Socialism was unable to invade private life completely, and that there were still opportunities to withdraw – whilst at the same time cautioning that even where this withdrawal stemmed from a rejection of the Nazi dictatorship, in the end, it amounted to no more than passive compliance.[40] The theory of the

---

[37] See e.g. Rebekka Habermas, *Frauen und Männer des Bürgertums: Eine Familiengeschichte (1750–1850)* (Göttingen, 2002).
[38] See Beate Rössler, *The Value of Privacy* (Cambridge, 2005), 9–10.
[39] See Moritz Föllmer, 'The Subjective Dimension of Nazism', *Historical Journal* 56/4 (2013), 1107–32.
[40] Detlev Schmiechen-Ackermann, *Nationalsozialismus und Arbeitermilieus: Der nationalsozialistische Angriff auf die proletarischen Wohnquartiere und die Reaktion in den sozialistischen Vereinen* (Bonn, 1998), 490. For an overview of the theses of the history of everyday life,

'atomisation of everyday life', which Detlev Peukert used at the beginning of the 1980s to bring together the results of research into the history of everyday life, was taken directly from the theory of totalitarianism. Hannah Arendt and Carl J. Friedrich were equally convinced that the aim of the Nazi regime to gain total control and its penetration into the private sphere had robbed each individual of their established social relationships and pitted the individual 'as a single atom' against 'the monolith of the totalitarian state'.[41] In the same way, Peukert argued that under National Socialism, 'even in the ultimate refuges of private life [...] the need for self-control, for caution vis-à-vis one's surroundings' existed, which made it impossible for individuals in a society 'ruined [...] in respect of its social bonds' to 'be themselves'.[42] Likewise, the theory that people 'learned to form distinctions between what they saw as their "private" and presumably "authentic" selves, and their public behaviour', and the notion that a 'divided reality' under National Socialism also led to a 'divided consciousness' amongst the Germans can be traced back to the early post-war years.[43] At the beginning of the 1960s, for example, Hans Buchheim was convinced that the 'essence and features' of 'totalitarian rule' could be found in the 'fusion [...] of the old natural and the new artificial actuality' created by Nazi ideology, and that this had led to the fact that 'of necessity many forms of behaviour and expression must be ambiguous'.[44] What was clear to him too was that this meant that 'artificiality, repression and confusion' had become 'characteristic of life under totalitarian rule', and that those who had made themselves 'the object of ambitious self-education' in National Socialism had merely been 'erecting an artificial personality around their true individuality'.[45]

From the late 1970s, research into everyday life and the social history of the Nazi period recorded its 'seizure of the power over the private' far more precisely than earlier research.[46] In the wake of the groundbreaking research projects 'Bayern in der NS-Zeit' and 'Lebensgeschichte und

---

see Bavaj, *Die Ambivalenz der Moderne*, 62–9, 73–7. For a summary of the debate on 'inner emigration', see Ralf Schnell, *Literarische innere Emigration 1933–1945* (Stuttgart, 1976).

[41] Carl J. Friedrich, *Totalitäre Diktatur* (Stuttgart, 1957), 250; see Hannah Arendt, *Elemente und Ursprünge totaler Herrschaft* (10th edn.) (Munich, Zurich, 2005), 971–9.

[42] Detlev Peukert, *Inside Nazi Germany: Conformity, Opposition and Racism in Everyday Life* (New Haven, CT, London, 1987), 239, 241.

[43] Mary Fulbrook, *Dissonant Lives: Generations and Violence through the German Dictatorships* (Oxford, 2011), 163; Hans Dieter Schäfer, *Das gespaltene Bewußtsein: Über deutsche Kultur und Lebenswirklichkeit 1933–1945* (Munich, Vienna, 1981), 164–7.

[44] Hans Buchheim, *Totalitarian Rule: Its Nature and Characteristics* (Middletown, CT, 1968), 39, 41.

[45] Ibidem, 103–4.

[46] The programmatic formulation can be found in Gisela Bock, *Zwangssterilisation im Nationalsozialismus: Studien zur Rassenpolitik und Frauenpolitik* (Opladen, 1986), 79.

Sozialkultur im Ruhrgebiet', numerous historians discovered various mechanisms by which Party officials, police stations and other official bodies of the regime attempted to intrude into the private sphere.[47] These studies revealed the extent and effect of the Nazi claim to power in many different arenas of everyday life. They documented the great extent to which the Nazi regime was dependent on the approval and active participation of large sections of German society. Overall, they succeeded in identifying National Socialist policies as a 'social practice', in which those who were ruled were also active participants as a consequence of their private behaviour. Cumulatively, this research corrected the picture painted by Orwell of an individual forced to submit to total control and regulation by the state.[48] However, the resulting interpretation of the effects of politicisation on the chances of living an individual life and of contemporaries' views of themselves fitted surprisingly well into the familiar interpretations of earlier decades. For example, Hans-Ulrich Thamer's study of everyday life, 'Seduction and Violence', was praised even by older historians for 'clearly' showing 'how the National Socialist regime in the space of a few years implemented the level of totalitarianism that caused Robert Ley to exclaim in 1938 [sic] that "in the 'Third Reich' the only thing that was still private was sleep"'.[49]

It seems appropriate to challenge a theory on which so many different research efforts have converged, notably that National Socialism had destroyed 'not just the "public sphere", but also the idea of an authentic self'[50] – and not only because of its weak empirical basis. The argument is also not logical in itself. On one hand, it emphasises the fact that under National Socialism, the private was comprehensively politicised and transformed by the intrusion of the state, if not totally destroyed. On the other hand, the bourgeois model of the private is supposed to have remained influential and intact. Why should this be the case? Is it not just as likely and (more probable) that the relationship between private opportunities to withdraw and self-determined ways of life had also changed? Might not these theories of the 'atomisation of society' and the 'divided consciousness'

---

[47] Martin Broszat et al. (eds.), *Bayern in der NS-Zeit*, 6 vols. (Munich, 1977–83); Lutz Niethammer et al. (eds.), *Lebensgeschichte und Sozialkultur im Ruhrgebiet*, 3 vols. (Berlin, Bonn, 1983–5).

[48] For an overview of the research, see Bavaj, *Die Ambivalenz der Moderne*; Janosch Steuwer, 'Was meint und nützt das Sprechen von der "Volksgemeinschaft"? Neuere Literatur zur Gesellschaftsgeschichte des Nationalsozialismus', *Archiv für Sozialgeschichte* 53 (2013), 487–534.

[49] Klaus Hildebrandt, 'Die Gewöhnlichkeit des Monströsen: Das Doppelgesicht des "Dritten Reiches"', *Frankfurter Allgemeine Zeitung*, 4 Dec. 1986, 27–8.

[50] Bernd Weisbrod, 'The Hidden Transcript: The Deformation of the Self in Germany's Dictatorial Regimes', *German Historical Institute London Bulletin* 34/2 (2012), 61–72, here 72.

of Germans have to address the gap that emerges when the bourgeois model of the private and the assumptions about self-determined private behaviour connected with it are applied to the history of the Nazi era? In order to pursue these questions, historical research should adopt an approach towards the private in National Socialism which opens itself to ways of understanding the dynamics and contexts of private space and private ways of life other than those thinkable within the bourgeois ideal of the private.

My reflections on Orwell's novel *Nineteen Eighty-Four* and its interpretation of the private in a totalitarian dictatorship have uncovered both useful starting points and traps to avoid. On one hand, historical research can continue to build upon the approach outlined earlier in this chapter, taking from it useful ideas on how to approach the private as an empirical problem. This can be done, for example, by looking at the limits to the scope of state intervention, even in a dictatorship, and asking how the expansion of state power affected the ability of the individual to lead an autonomous life based on self-knowledge. On the other hand, new research should try to avoid the blind spots in the traditional approaches, by consistently subjecting the private to empirical examination, rather than seeing it as an a priori category of interpretation. Instead of trying to find bourgeois privacy in the Nazi era, research should begin with the hypothesis that in National Socialism, we are dealing with a peculiar kind of privacy, whose specific dynamics and modes of operation can be discovered by means of empirical studies. This would mean, for example, testing whether in the 1930s and 1940s, people really did only express their true opinions in private. It would mean asking whether the politicisation of the private affected German society uniformly or not, and then asking to what extent the war and its consequences transformed the private yet again. But above all, it would mean not assuming unquestioningly that private space and private life were interdependent in the way postulated by the bourgeois ideal model. They need to be regarded separately in order to reconstruct their dynamics and their relation to each other empirically.

Dynamics of the Private in the National Socialist Dictatorship

To write a new history of the private under National Socialism, we cannot rely on the records of state institutions alone, which mainly expose the invasion of private space by the political bodies of the Nazi regime. We also have to base our inquiry on materials that make it possible to analyse the private as a sphere of individual action and decision-making. One possible option is to explore diaries and letters from the 1930s and 1940s. This is not because they reveal the 'true' private opinions of the

Germans,[51] but rather, because they record how individuals strove to shape their private sphere, and how they reflected on changes to it. The advantage of diaries and letters over retrospective ego-documents such as autobiographies and oral history interviews is that they are not influenced by subsequent events. This does not only address the key methodological question about the value of personal reminiscences as sources. It is particularly relevant to the private in National Socialism, because the retrospective interpretation of National Socialism through the lens of a bourgeois model of privacy was by no means restricted to academic research. It also included the personal appraisal of individuals of their own Nazi past after 1945, when many people distanced themselves from the regime, asserting that they had continued to live their own private lives.[52] This meant that the bourgeois model of privacy became integrated into retrospective interpretations of lives, which is why these records can often be misleading for any attempt to analyse the operation of the private during the Nazi years. An example of this problem is Ulrich Herbert's much quoted thesis, based on the evaluation of oral history interviews, that between 1933 and 1945, people had banished 'politics to areas outside their own field of perception'.[53] This claim captures one of the central *topoi* in the discussion about National Socialism in the post-war period, but it hardly describes the true relationship between politics and the private in the 1930s and early 1940s.

Diaries and other contemporary ego-documents can disclose something different. They make the politicisation of the private after 1933 quite clear, but they also show that this followed different dynamics to those normally assumed. The Nazi authorities could not simply occupy every private space, nor did they intend to do so. Most Germans were, therefore, not exposed to unrestricted intervention by the Nazi state, disempowering them and depriving them of their awareness of their own personality. On the contrary, diaries record the active role that individuals inevitably assume in the politicisation of the private, and

---

[51] On the value of diaries as sources see Janosch Steuwer and Rüdiger Graf, 'Selbstkonstitution und Welterzeugung in Tagebüchern des 20. Jahrhunderts', in Janosch Steuwer and Rüdiger Graf (eds.), *Selbstreflexionen und Weltdeutungen: Tagebücher in der Geschichte und der Geschichtsschreibung des 20. Jahrhunderts* (Göttingen, 2015), 7–36.

[52] See Moritz Föllmer, *Individuality and Modernity in Berlin: Self and Society from Weimar to the Wall* (New York, NY, 2013), 185–211; Steuwer/Leßau, 'Wer ist ein Nazi?', 44–9.

[53] Ulrich Herbert, '"Die guten und die schlechten Zeiten": Überlegungen zur diachronen Analyse lebensgeschichtlicher Interviews', in Lutz Niethammer (ed.), *'Die Jahre weiß man nicht, wo man die heute hinsetzen soll': Faschismuserfahrungen im Ruhrgebiet* (Berlin, Bonn, 1983), 67–96, here 91.

through which politics becomes the foundation of private life, rather than its antithesis.[54]

In the period after 1933, diaries mention political topics far more frequently and in far more detail than in the final years of the Weimar Republic. Seasoned diarists who had previously only written about their everyday lives began to speak of political topics. In addition, immediately after the beginning of the Nazi dictatorship in spring 1933, many people felt the need to start writing a diary because they wanted to document the 'momentous historical events' that they were experiencing, or because they were seeking a means of orientation after the dramatic events of spring 1933. One of these people was the teacher Hans Maschmann, born in 1887. He had kept a diary throughout his youth and vocational training, but stopped in the middle of the 1920s. He completed two entries in 1928 but did not take the diary out again until 1933. 'I am retreating to my diary' is how he began the first entry after a break of more than four years. After that he kept the diary almost daily, but his numerous entries were almost entirely restricted to one topic – his observations of political events and defining his own position towards them.[55] How explicit this engagement with National Socialism was is also recorded in other diaries after 1933, where headings such as 'Thoughts on National Socialism' can be found.[56]

The final years of the Weimar Republic had also been turbulent, and would have provided enough food for thought in diaries. Yet it was not until Hitler was appointed *Reichskanzler* that the widespread politicisation of diary entries began. This was not merely the expression of a particularly dramatic political situation, but also of the new and far-reaching demands that the Nazi regime was making on what had previously been private ways of living. From the start, the regime insisted that the Germans should organise all their thoughts and actions according to new ideological categories, so that people felt compelled to define their attitude towards National Socialism in private – for instance in diaries.[57]

---

[54] For more detail and further evidence on the following, see Janosch Steuwer, *'Ein Drittes Reich, wie ich es auffasse': Politik, Gesellschaft und privates Leben in Tagebüchern 1933–1939* (Göttingen, 2017), esp. 493–548; and Peter Fritzsche, *Life and Death in the Third Reich* (Cambridge/London, 2008); Föllmer, *Individuality and Modernity in Berlin*.

[55] Archiv der Akademie der Künste (Berlin), Kempowski-Biografienarchiv, 5965/1, 31.3.1933.

[56] Mecklenburgisches Landeshauptarchiv, 10.9 – S/8, 13 April 1934.

[57] For more detail, see Janosch Steuwer, '"Ein neues Blatt im Buche der Geschichte": Tagebücher und der Beginn der nationalsozialistischen Herrschaft 1933/34', in Frank Bajohr and Sybille Steinbacher (eds.), *Zeugnis ablegen bis zum letzten: Tagebücher und persönliche Zeugnisse aus der Zeit des Nationalsozialismus und des Holocaust* (Göttingen, 2015), 42–60; Fritzsche, *Life and Death in the Third Reich*, esp. 25–8.

The new rulers made no secret of their unbounded political demands. Hermann Göring, the Prussian Interior Minister and Reich Aviation Minister (*Reichsluftfahrtminister*), for example, in 1935 announced quite openly that the National Socialist state, in contrast to the preceding 'vanquished epoch', was not determined by 'the ideas of a night-watchman state, in which the state had nothing better to do than to ensure that every individual was perfectly safe and sound in their own strictly demarcated private sphere'. Instead of that, the National Socialist state was based on a 'completely different, more natural perception of life and of the state' in which 'it was not the individual but the community of all members' (*die Gemeinschaft aller Volksgenossen*) that was of 'primary importance'.[58] In this way, the demands on the private were comprehensive. But they affected different people to different degrees. Göring and the Nazi regime were not only endeavouring to extend the limits of the state. They were also challenging political categories. According to the Nazi ideology of the community (*Gemeinschaft*), state intrusion into the private differed substantially according to whether this involved the majority, those deemed to belong to the community (the so-called *Volksgenossen*), or those minorities excluded from it.[59]

For those considered its 'enemies' or 'opponents', the state saw space for private retreat as a potential threat, because it might enable conspiracies and the persistence of anti-Nazi attitudes. So the regime quickly tried to gain control over this space by means of its security forces. Only four weeks after Hitler's appointment as *Reichskanzler*, with the introduction of the 'decree on the protection of the people and the state' (*Reichstagsbrandverordnung*), the Nazi state 'suspended until further notice' the basic rights of the Weimar Republic. In the past, these rights had set strict legal limits on the power of state institutions to invade the private sphere, which had included the right to free speech, the privacy of correspondence, whether by letter or telephone, and the inviolability of the home. Now house searches could also be authorised 'outside their legally defined guidelines' and therefore without any means of constitutional control. The same was true for the opening of personal correspondence.[60]

In spring 1933, the regime frequently used its new powers to defeat the labour movement. Thousands of the homes of members of the Communist Party (KPD), the Social Democratic Party (SPD), of trade union officials

---

[58] Hermann Göring, *Die Rechtssicherheit als Grundlage der Volksgemeinschaft* (Hamburg, 1935), 5–6.
[59] Frank Bajohr and Michael Wildt (eds.), *Volksgemeinschaft: Neue Forschungen zur Gesellschaftsgeschichte des Nationalsozialismus* (Frankfurt a.M., 2009).
[60] Verordnung des Reichspräsidenten zum Schutz von Volk und Staat, quoted from: Reichsministerium des Innern (ed.), *Reichsgesetzblatt*, Jg. 1933, Teil I, Berlin 1933, 83.

A Particular Kind of Privacy

and political opponents, were searched and wrecked by the SA, now acting as the auxiliary police (*Hilfspolizei*). In Hamburg alone, police carried out 850 raids between April and July 1933 in working-class areas of the city.[61] The diaries and letters of the victims often talk of the consequences of this intrusion into the private sphere, of the restless panic that it caused and of the often vain attempts to resist. One powerful example is documented in the diary of a young Social Democrat from the Odenwald, Wilhelm Scheidler. It records how in 1933 its author began 'to lock the door of my room (at night) because I was afraid of violent attacks by the local Nazis'.[62] By this time, he had already hidden his 'party political books and important documents' outside his flat, so that they would not be found if a house search was carried out.[63] He had also expressed his fears in his diary, portraying several dreams which also involved Nazi thugs invading his home. 'I dreamt that my father had been shot by the Nazis. I saw a horribly mutilated body on our sofa at home, and when I woke up, I was still horrified by the image.'[64]

This terrifying vision of the state breaking violently into one's home became reality for German Jews, especially during the pogroms of November 1938. The spread of antisemitic violence into people's homes was the reason why the pogroms cut so deeply into Jewish lives in Germany. There had been antisemitic violence before on several occasions, but in the earlier phase, it had only occurred in public spaces, so that many German Jews had hoped to be able somehow to adjust to the increasingly harsh antisemitic Nazi policies and retreat into their private lives.[65] But their ruined homes proved conclusively that this hope was an illusion. The damage to their homes forced the Jews to move in with other Jews whose homes were still intact, thus often pre-empting the official establishment of 'Jew houses' (*Judenhäuser*). During the war, German Jews were forced to live in these tenements in cramped conditions under constant surveillance by the Gestapo and with practically no private space to withdraw to – a situation that persisted and worsened dramatically after deportation to the camps and ghettos.[66] Pictures of homes ruined in the pogroms give

---

[61] See Schmiechen-Ackermann, *Nationalsozialismus und Arbeitermilieus*, 411. On violence in 1933 see Richard Bessel, *Political Violence and the Rise of Nazism: The Storm Troopers in Eastern Germany 1925–1934* (New Haven, CT, London, 1984).
[62] Archiv der Gedenkstätte KZ-Osthofen, 2/27/2, 14 April 1933.
[63] Ibidem, 10 March 1933.
[64] Ibidem, 18 March 1933. Similarly 14 March, 11 April, and 13 April 1933.
[65] On anti-Jewish violence and the takeover of public space see Michael Wildt, *Volksgemeinschaft als Selbstermächtigung: Gewalt gegen Juden in der deutschen Provinz 1919 bis 1939* (Hamburg, 2007).
[66] On *Judenhäuser* see Ulrike Haerendel, *Kommunale Wohnungspolitik im Dritten Reich: Siedlungsideologie, Kleinhausbau und Wohnraumarisierung am Beispiel Münchens* (Munich, 1999), 395–405.

a chilling impression of the way the Nazi state invaded the private space of those Germans they regarded as 'enemies' and 'opponents'.

However, most people would 'at no point' have had to 'live in constant fear of the knocking on the door in the early hours'.[67] The question of the existence of private space and the right of the state to intrude into it was completely different for those whom the Nazi regime regarded as *Volksgenossen* and wanted to integrate into their grand socio-political project. In May 1936, for example, a woman in Ulm complained angrily to the district leader (*Kreisleiter*) of the NSDAP, Eugen Maier, that the state had intruded into her private affairs. The woman lived next door to the building occupied by the district administration and had received a letter addressed to her by an NSDAP official which had been '*opened* in the district offices and put into a *different* envelope'. The incident resulted from a mistake: the number of the house on the letter was wrong, and so it had been delivered to the district administration and opened routinely with the other post. When the error was noticed, the member of staff responsible had put the letter into a new envelope with the correct address and had it delivered to the neighbour. She, however, was extremely annoyed by what had happened. 'This kind of minor error in an address happens every day,' she wrote to the district leader. 'But it gives no one the right to open other people's letters and put them in a different envelope and deliver them.' As she maintained, 'there is a law about the privacy of the post that every child knows about. I request the gentleman involved to offer me an apology, and request the district leader to inform me of what steps are being taken in this case.'[68]

Even three years after the *Reichstagsbrandverordnung*, which had also suspended the privacy of correspondence, people could still believe that they had a legally guaranteed right to their own private sphere. The woman from Ulm reinforced this conviction by adding at the end of the letter that she reserved the right to take further legal action against the district leader. It was not necessarily blindness to the violence against 'enemies' and 'opponents' and the destruction of their privacy that lay behind this letter. The woman may well have internalised the distinction between *Volksgenossen* and those outside the *Volksgemeinschaft* (*Gemeinschaftsfremde*), which was the sphere where the Nazi state really did discriminate in its dealings with the private. At

---

[67] E.g. An early study: Richard Grunberger, *Das zwölfjährige Reich: Der Deutschen Alltag unter Hitler* (Vienna, Munich, Zurich, 1972), 32. More recent studies on the surveillance of German society have a similar emphasis; see Robert Gellately, *Backing Hitler: Consent and Coercion in Nazi Germany* (Oxford, 2001); Eric A. Johnson, *Nazi Terror: The Gestapo, Jews and Ordinary Germans* (New York, NY, 1999).

[68] For this and the previous quote see Staatsarchiv Ludwigsburg, PL 502/32 I Bü 117, letter by E. A. to the NSDAP Kreisleiter, Ulm, 28 May 1936. Emphasis in the original.

A Particular Kind of Privacy 49

any rate, the letter that she received a few days later confirmed her expectations of greater respect for her personal privacy. The Party official who had opened the letter explained the error again and insisted that 'there [could be] no question of her letter having been opened on purpose', and so her reference 'to the privacy of correspondence' was irrelevant. The letter closed with the words 'we, too, know what is to be done', with no reference to the fact that official bodies of the Nazi regime were indeed permitted to open personal correspondence, and that 'privacy of correspondence' had not been legally guaranteed since spring 1933.[69]

Even if there were no longer any legal restrictions to protect the private from the intrusion of political bodies in the Nazi dictatorship, there were still restrictions on how far the political system could encroach upon the private. These resulted from the specific political approach that the Nazi regime adopted with respect to those Germans considered *Volksgenossen*. The regime was anxious for those who declared themselves supporters of the new government to buy into their project of the 'renewal of the German people'. The socio-political vision of the *Volksgemeinschaft*, which the regime had elevated to its overarching aim, was to be realised by individual Germans adapting their idea of themselves and their everyday behaviour to new political goals. This could not be achieved by force. Force could be used to uphold the National Socialist claim to leadership, and to achieve the 'cleansing' of society of 'enemies' and 'opponents'. But in order to mobilise the so-called *Volksgenossen*, other means were necessary – which included accepting the existence of private space into which to withdraw.

This is clearly demonstrated by a quote usually put forward by researchers as evidence of the regime's aim to completely destroy the private sphere.[70] In 1937, the director of the German Labour Front (*Deutsche Arbeitsfront*) and chief organiser of the Reich (*Reichsorganisationsleiter*) of the NSDAP, Robert Ley, had declared in a speech that 'there are no longer any private individuals in National Socialist Germany. It is only possible to be a private person when you are asleep. As soon as you go into everyday life, into your daily life, you are a soldier of Adolf Hitler.'[71] Hannah Arendt quoted this as key evidence for her interpretation of unhindered penetration of privacy, and numerous historians adopted it and her interpretation.[72] However, what

---

[69] Ibidem, letter from Kreisgeschäftsführung to E. A., 5 June 1936.
[70] See e.g. Richard J. Evans, *Das Dritte Reich*, vol. II/1: *Diktatur* (Munich, 2006), 134; Paul Ginsborg, *Die geführte Familie: Das Private in der Revolution und Diktatur 1900–1950* (Hamburg, 2014), 513.
[71] Robert Ley, 'Unser Volk soll jung bleiben', in Robert Ley (ed.), *Soldaten der Arbeit* (2nd edn.) (München, 1939), 121–38, here 125.
[72] It can be seen that the popularity of this quote stemmed from the fact that when it is quoted in German-language studies, it is not usually in the original but in Arendt's German translation of *Elemente und Ursprünge*, 723.

Ley was saying was not a threat aimed at eliminating the private. If it is read in the context of the whole speech, it becomes clear that it is related to Ley's call for every individual to participate in daily 'physical exercises', which he believed should be an everyday personal contribution towards maintaining and reinforcing the 'strength' of the 'people' (*Volk*). Immediately before the much-quoted passage, Ley had demanded that 'every single individual must do their part', showing that his purpose was not to eliminate private space. By contributing to the aims of the Nazi regime in their private lives, people were to become 'soldiers of Adolf Hitler', and no longer 'private people'.[73]

Thus the regime did not take over the private sphere of those Germans considered *Volksgenossen* by violent state intrusion into their homes or into their private correspondence. This project was carried out, instead, by appeals to a National Socialist way of life, in the manner formulated in Ley's speech. It was manifest in the intensity of the Party's efforts to educate Germans to adopt a National Socialist self-conception and way of life.[74] This became intrusive when, in the first years of the Nazi dictatorship, NSDAP organisations at local level were required to implement a comprehensive 'duty of care' (*Betreuungsauftrag*). After Hitler was appointed *Reichskanzler*, the NSDAP's original purpose became obsolete: it found a new focus of activity in 'caring', which in effect meant interfering in the private lives of the German people. Local NSDAP offices were converted into 'contact points' 'not only for Party members, but for all *Volksgenossen*'. They were 'responsible at all times for practically any question the people wanted to ask, and were to signal by their presence that people could turn to the Nazi Party in their village or district with their problems at all times'.[75] This meant that local minor Party officials, from the NSDAP district leader down to the individual neighbourhood leaders (*Blockleiter*) of the various Nazi organisations, were given the task of ensuring that their contemporaries were leading a National Socialist life – even in private.

The amount of effort put into this task of 'caring' for the people makes clear how important the Nazi regime considered the mobilisation and political education of Germans for the realisation of their socio-political

---

[73] Ley, 'Unser Volk soll jung bleiben', 125.
[74] For more detail, see Steuwer, '*Ein Drittes Reich, wie ich es auffasse*', 185–202.
[75] Carl-Wilhelm Reibel, *Das Fundament der Diktatur: Die NSDAP-Ortsgruppen 1932–1945* (Paderborn et al., 2002), 274. On the following also see Kerstin Thieler, '*Volksgemeinschaft' unter Vorbehalt: Gesinnungskontrolle und politische Mobilisierung in der Herrschaftspraxis der NSDAP-Kreisleitung Göttingen* (Göttingen, 2014); John Connelly, 'The Uses of *Volksgemeinschaft*: Letters to the NSDAP Kreisleitung Eisenach, 1939–1940', *Journal of Modern History* 68/4 (1996), 899–930; Detlev Schmiechen-Ackermann, 'Der "Blockwart": Die unteren Parteifunktionäre im nationalsozialistischen Terror- und Überwachungsapparat', *Vierteljahrshefte für Zeitgeschichte* 48/4 (2000), 575–602.

aims. The fundamental orientation of Nazi politics towards political education meant that the private sphere became an important political arena, but not one in which the Nazi regime could act ruthlessly. The district office in Ulm in 1936 was not alone in realising that in their efforts to win the support of the people in their 'territory', they had to accept that where people required it, they were entitled to a private sphere to which to retreat. Other local NSDAP officials also realised how easily they could be drawn into 'private disputes', and made quite clear that 'we cannot be involved in purely family matters'.[76]

Training materials for minor Party officials warned them again and again not to behave like 'commanders', but more like 'pastors'. One *Blockleiter*, for example, was to 'take extreme care not to be suspected of keeping *Volksgenossen* under surveillance, and only to make things difficult for them if they disagree in some way with our professed *Weltanschauung*'. The aim was to gain people's confidence and win them over to National Socialism, so 'officious behaviour' was only likely to have 'a damaging effect'. 'There are people who may be reluctant to allow a third party access to their domestic circumstances, but this does not necessarily mean that they are politically suspect or unwilling to integrate into the community.'[77]

The Nazi regime clearly recognised that, with respect to those Germans they considered *Volksgenossen*, they were dependent on how people reacted to the demands made on them. It endeavoured to make the 'care' attractive by ensuring that its officials behaved tactfully, or that 'care' delivered material advantages. The fact remained that in their attempts to politicise the private within the *Volksgemeinschaft*, Nazi authorities had to rely on the Germans turning to the regime in private affairs, or at least not rejecting its interference. It is for this reason that it is important not to examine the private from the perspective of the state, but as a space where individuals have the freedom to act and to take decisions, and to explore how people at the time reacted to the appeals, demands and attempts to educate and care for them to which they were subjected.

Diaries disclose many different reactions. Some people accepted various 'offers of care' and so exposed private spaces and private affairs to the regime. This was not only the case for those numerous Germans who turned to their local NSDAP centres in the 1930s and 1940s in return 'for every conceivable sort of aid', and thereby allowed them insight into and

---

[76] Connelly, 'The Uses of *Volksgemeinschaft*', 919, 922.
[77] Manuscript 'Aufgabe des Blockleiters sowie des Blockwartes', n.d. (probably 1937), quoted from Thieler, *Volksgemeinschaft unter Vorbehalt*, 162–3.

influence over their private affairs.[78] People were prepared to adapt their private ways of life to the ruling order during the Nazi dictatorship not only in return for material gain. This also occurred when people strove to 'combine *Weltanschauung* with their own individual self', and explored their own ability to be part of the community (*Gemeinschaftlichkeit*) in Nazi education camps.[79] Others attempted to trace their ancestry with the help of special courses in genealogy (*Ahnenkunde*) to assert 'for themselves their racial status as Aryans'.[80] In similar ways, many diaries show how people grappled with the regime's expectations of unreserved political support, for example when their authors wrote that they were trying to find the reason why they could 'not believe unconditionally'.[81]

Many Germans did not see the Nazi regime, with all its demands for a 'National Socialist way of life' and the related attempts to influence the private, as a threat. They saw it instead as an opportunity to realise their own notions of their private lives or identities.[82] In these cases, diaries show again that their authors did not simply comply with the demands of the regime. On the contrary, they considered very carefully where they felt their own personal interests could be furthered by the regime. They tried to live a self-determined private life supported by National Socialism, not separated from it.

Other people, by contrast, were still trying to retain the classic division between public and private even under the Nazi dictatorship, and rejected the invasion of their private lives by political institutions. This was different from the retreat into 'inner emigration' that many people professed after 1945. The diaries of people who attempted to continue living their lives in tune with the bourgeois model of privacy often displayed a remarkable preoccupation with the politics of the regime. Although Hans Maschmann spoke of 'retreating' to his diary in his first entry after resuming writing it in March 1933, during the subsequent period of the Nazi dictatorship, he hardly mentioned anything other than political events and his own personal assessment of them. This was similar in the case of Daniel Lotter, a gingerbread baker from Fürth, who began to write a diary on the first anniversary of the Nazi seizure of power in order to record his views on political events.[83] Diarists like Hans Maschmann and

---

[78] Connelly, 'The Uses of *Volksgemeinschaft*', 902.
[79] Janosch Steuwer, '"Weltanschauung mit meinem Ich verbinden": Tagebücher und das nationalsozialistische Erziehungsprojekt', in Steuwer/Graf (eds.), *Selbstreflexionen und Weltdeutungen*, 100–23.
[80] Fritzsche, *Life and Death in the Third Reich*, 77.
[81] For more detail, see Steuwer, *'Ein Drittes Reich, wie ich es auffasse'*, esp. 378–96 (quote at 395).
[82] Also emphasised by Föllmer, *Individuality and Modernity in Berlin*, esp. 101–31.
[83] See Deutsches Tagebucharchiv Emmendingen, 1315, 30 January 1934.

Daniel Lotter were not escaping into an area away from politics. What they were trying to reactivate was the political function of the private, i.e. a space in which an individual could explore their own stance towards the politics of the day without state interference, and in which people could meet each other as 'private individuals' regardless of their different political views.

The distinction between insisting on one's own private space and buying into the offers of the Nazi regime is an ideal-typical one which describe the outer poles of a spectrum of action. In individual cases, the relationship between the political system and the private sphere did not have to correspond to one of the two poles, and the insistence on private retreats with simultaneous recourse to individual regime offers was probably most widespread. However, the two modes of behaviours were only possible if there was no doubt about these people's political affiliation. This is a further reason why the distinction between those who readily opened up their private sphere to the Nazi regime and those who wanted to keep to the traditional separation of private and public was not a distinction between supporters and opponents of the regime. In contrast to the 'enemies' and 'opponents' of National Socialism, whose privacy was constantly threatened by violent intrusion by the state, these people considered themselves supporters of the Nazi government in principle. However critical Hans Maschmann was of the policies of the Nazi regime, he repeatedly stressed how important the 'national uprising' of National Socialism was to him. And in spite of all the problems that the Nazi regime had created for him, which he recorded in his diary, Daniel Lotter also repeatedly confirmed that as a 'good German', he did not want the Nazi government to fail.[84] Neither of them considered themselves opponents of National Socialism. All they wanted was to preserve their own private sphere.

Diaries like these demonstrate particularly clearly the underlying paradox of the politicisation of the private in National Socialism. The regime wanted there to be no space where the principles of National Socialism were not applied, so any such space was constantly under the threat of regime violence. However, if space was designated as 'belonging' to the *Volksgemeinschaft*, whether by the fact that its occupants were members of Nazi organisations, by flags being displayed on Nazi public holidays or in any other way, the Nazi authorities were limited to the extent they could intervene, because they wanted to mobilise and to educate the inhabitants rather than to coerce them. So even when citizens insisted on the

---

[84] Ibidem, 15 April 1934. For more detail, see Steuwer, *'Ein Drittes Reich, wie ich es auffasse'*, 98–104.

authorities respecting their private space, politics did not become the antithesis of a self-determined private life, but its premise.

Conclusion

The ideas developed here can be no more than a rough sketch of the dynamic of the private in National Socialism, which need verification and expansion based on further studies. They do show, however, how inadequately Orwell's image captures this dynamic. Perhaps it can be seen as a fictional exaggeration of state intrusion into the private lives of those Germans considered 'enemies' or 'opponents' of the regime. But in the case of the majority of Germans, those considered *Volksgenossen*, the Nazi regime did not destroy their private sphere. Rather, they were put under intense pressure to shape the politicisation of the private individually. This was a decision that Germans were compelled to make because of the manifold attempts by the regime to impose the validity of its political principles, even in private. However, the style of politics in National Socialism, whose aim was to mobilise and to educate the Germans, allowed individuals some scope for interpretation, which could be exploited in different ways to further their own interests – whether by accepting or rejecting state agents.

In this way, the private in National Socialism certainly had one overarching characteristic: it was not uniform. One reason for this was that the limits of the political system were determined by the way people acted in each individual case, rather than by general principles of the rule of law. This meant that in everyday encounters, there was frequently a discrepancy between perceptions of what significance should be attributed to the political demands of the regime or to traditional concepts of privacy.[85] After 1933, Germans had to come to their own conclusions about the validity of the political demands of the Nazi regime and the scope of its influence, not only when dealing with political institutions, but also amongst themselves. The politicisation of the private was not only achieved as a result of the power of an omnipotent state. It was to a large extent dependent on the self-politicisation of Germans.

---

[85] This is particularly evident in the context of denunciations. For more detail, see ibidem, 532–42.

3 Private Lives, Public Faces
On the Social Self in Nazi Germany

Mary Fulbrook

The biggest crime in German history, in which millions of innocent victims were rounded up, deported and murdered, with the participation, collaboration and knowledge of innumerable people along the way, did not produce a mass outcry of rage or refusals to cooperate. As Ian Kershaw once commented: 'The road to Auschwitz was built by hate, but paved with indifference.'[1] This pithily summarises the distinction between the makers, shapers and drivers of Nazi policies, and the millions who turned a blind eye.

Those fuelled by hate have been in the spotlight for decades. Yet the social production of indifference has not as yet received the attention it deserves. This chapter argues that interactions in private life helped to create a 'bystander society' that paved the road to Auschwitz.[2] In this era more than any, the private was also, inevitably and inextricably, political. What was possible in 1942 would have been unthinkable in 1932.

Theoretical Approaches

Definitions of what constitutes privacy or the private sphere vary widely across societies and over time, as Norbert Elias has reminded us.[3] Historians' practices also differ. Some historians pragmatically treat the private sphere as a residual category, encompassing what remains beyond organisations, institutions, movements or events of historical significance. Archival practices also make pragmatic distinctions in light of personal data protection considerations to restrict access to sources concerning individuals' private lives. A quite different theoretical approach contrasts 'private' with the 'public sphere', defining it as an arena beyond the reach of public

---

[1] Ian Kershaw, *Popular Opinion and Political Dissent in the Third Reich: Bavaria 1933–1945* (Oxford, 1983), 277.
[2] What follows is necessarily brief, and relates to a book I am currently writing under the provisional title *Bystander Society*.
[3] See Norbert Elias, *The Civilizing Process, vol. 1: The History of Manners* (Oxford, 1978; first published in German 1939), 278–9.

debate, including private clubs and associations, private schools and private networks for the exchange of ideas, goods or money.[4] This approach is primarily interested in transformations in the 'public sphere' in bourgeois societies, and the freely accessible exchange of views on matters of common interest, even what defines 'common' interest.

Everyday life understandings of what is 'private' are particularly interesting. 'Private' is frequently seen as that which is or should be chosen freely and is purely personal. There are of course always wider constraints and implications – evident, for example, in debates over same-sex marriage – and some argue that inevitably 'personal problems are political problems', as Carol Hanisch put it in a 1969 feminist essay entitled 'The Personal Is Political'.[5] Even so, this is not how most people most of the time see things. People come to naturalise distinctions between private and public. Of particular interest, then, are moments when everyday assumptions about what is or should be 'purely personal' come into conflict with an interventionist state.

The Nazi assumption of power brought a sudden intrusion into what people had previously considered to be their 'private lives'. They were confronted with new constraints, challenges and opportunities that required rapid adjustment and accommodation. Transgressions or failure to conform could attract penalties ranging from informal social ostracism to severe punishments. Previous assumptions about private lives came under attack in a state seeking to construct a *Volksgemeinschaft* or 'national community' in pursuit of collective goals.

This may serve to cast a new light on the history of everyday life in Nazi Germany. Approaches to this topic have shifted significantly. Conceived as an ethnographically informed 'history from below', *Alltagsgeschichte* initially developed as a reaction to traditional political, diplomatic, institutional and organisational history, as well as the history of social and political movements, and even the structural societal history associated with the Bielefeld school. The most sophisticated and influential theoretical statements were those of Alf Lüdtke, but there were many variants.[6] In works ranging from

---

[4] See Jürgen Habermas, *Strukturwandel der Öffentlichkeit: Untersuchungen zu einer Kategorie der bürgerlichen Gesellschaft* (Frankfurt a.M., 1990; orig. 1962).

[5] See Carol Hanisch, 'The Personal Is Political', www.carolhanisch.org/CHwritings/PIP .html [accessed 19 June 2016].

[6] See Alf Lüdtke, *The History of Everyday Life* (Princeton, NJ, 1995); see also for example Lutz Niethammer, 'Anmerkungen zur Alltagsgeschichte', in Klaus Bergmann and Rolf Schörken (eds.), *Geschichte im Alltag – Alltag in der Geschichte* (Düsseldorf, 1982), 11–29. For a detailed discussion and a review of key works informed by *Alltagsgeschichte* approaches at that time, see Geoff Eley's review essay, 'Labor History, Social History, "Alltagsgeschichte": Experience, Culture, and the Politics of the Everyday – A New Direction for German Social History?', *Journal of Modern History* 61/2 (1989), 297–343.

the Bavaria project under Martin Broszat's direction at the Munich Institute for Contemporary History to the lay explorations of local history in the History Workshop movement, ordinary people were brought back into history. Agency was cast largely in terms of self-interest in pursuit of personal goals, obstinacy, stubborn resistance and small refusals, within a wider meta-narrative of high politics, power structures and official policies. The linguistic turn further heightened historians' sensitivity to shifting meanings and cultural interpretations.

These approaches were controversial. In characteristically lively polemics, the doyen of societal history Hans-Ulrich Wehler critiqued what he cast as a predominantly amateurish, left-leaning, a-theoretical, romanticist bunch of historians who tended to idealise small communities and the 'little people' of a pre-industrial past. He accused them of being incapable of developing historical syntheses, of being intrinsically opposed to modernisation theory and lacking in rational conceptual clarity.[7] In more measured tones, Jürgen Kocka conceded that structural social history could be complemented by a history of experience and subjectivity, but he too critiqued a widespread lack of conceptual clarity and theoretical rigour.[8] *Alltagsgeschichte* was widely attacked for leaving out the larger picture, ignoring 'politics' and being incapable of explaining historical change, with ethnographic methods suited to small, relatively static communities. Methodologically, some of the research techniques associated with *Alltagsgeschichte* also attracted criticism: the use of oral history interviews, for example, was cast as a naïve and unscientific way of seeking to access a past 'as it really was'.

The complicity of the many tended to be downplayed in an approach that frequently sought to identify small resistances and dissent in everyday life. As far as the most contentious period of German history was concerned, these critiques intersected with the debate between Broszat and Saul Friedländer over the risk of 'normalising' a past which, from the perspective of its victims, could never be viewed in the same way as any other period of history.[9] Only in the heated controversies in the 1980s among female historians of Nazi Germany over the roles of women, who

---

[7] See for example Hans-Ulrich Wehler, 'Königsweg zu neuen Ufern oder Irrgarten der Illusionen? Die westdeutsche Alltagsgeschichte: Geschichte "von innen" und "von unten"', in Hans-Ulrich Wehler (ed.), *Aus der Geschichte lernen?* (Munich, 1988), 130–51.

[8] See Jürgen Kocka, 'Sozialgeschichte zwischen Strukturgeschichte und Erfahrungsgeschichte', in Wolfgang Schieder and Volker Sellin (eds.), *Sozialgeschichte in Deutschland*, vol. 1 (Göttingen, 1986), 67–89; Jürgen Kocka, *Sozialgeschichte: Begriff, Entwicklung, Probleme* (Göttingen, 1986), 132–76. See also Peter Borscheid, 'Alltagsgeschichte – Modetorheit oder neues Tor zur Vergangenheit?', in Wolfgang Schieder and Volker Sellin (eds.), *Sozialgeschichte in Deutschland*, vol. 3 (Göttingen, 1987), 78–100.

[9] See the contributions by Martin Broszat and by Saul Friedländer in Peter Baldwin (ed.), *Reworking the Past: Hitler, the Holocaust, and the Historians' Debate* (Boston, MA, 1990).

were variously cast as either accomplices or victims, did debates over everyday complicity become a little more complex.[10] Such critiques have subsequently been addressed, with everyday lives incorporated into wider narratives. Marion Kaplan, for example, explored the impact of Nazi policies on those who were excluded and persecuted; she speaks of their subjection, their excommunication from the 'legitimate social or moral community' and their 'relegation to a perpetual state of dishonor'.[11] Moreover, a focus on lower levels of administrative and political structures, and on local circumstances, has emphasised the importance of grassroots contexts in understanding major historical developments.[12]

Curiously, however, despite this maelstrom of approaches, those who were neither persecuted nor mobilised in support of Nazism have remained somewhat out of focus, beyond the lens of the historian's gaze – and this even when it is precisely the *Volksgemeinschaft* or 'national community' on which historians have focused.

In some respects, debates on the *Volksgemeinschaft* appeared to promise a way of bringing together everyday experiences and Nazi racial politics. The 'ethnicised' variant of the *Volksgemeinschaft* concept became a key term in Nazi visions of the future and attempts at social transformation. Historians have explored cultural meanings and social practices in everyday life, emphasising 'self-empowerment' in everyday practices.[13] They have also drawn attention to consensual aspects of the Nazi dictatorship, which some felt had been downplayed in previously dominant emphases on terror, repression and coercion. The significance of denunciations in assisting the work of a relatively understaffed Gestapo, for example, or the apparent lack of fear in people's memories of life in the Third Reich as recounted in the 1990s, seemed to support a renewed emphasis on

---

[10] See for example Claudia Koonz, 'A Tributary and a Mainstream: Gender, Public Memory and Historiography of Nazi Germany', in Karen Hagemann and Jean H. Quataert (eds.), *Gendering Modern German History: Rewriting Historiography* (New York, NY, 2007), 147–69; Adelheid von Saldern, 'Victims or Perpetrators? Controversies about the Role of Women in the Nazi State', in David Crew (ed.), *Nazism and German Society, 1933–45* (London, 1994), 141–65.

[11] Marion Kaplan, *Between Dignity and Despair: Jewish Life in Nazi Germany* (Oxford, 1998), 5.

[12] See also for example Andrew Stuart Bergerson, *Ordinary Germans in Extraordinary Times: The Nazi Revolution in Hildesheim* (Bloomington, IN, 2004); Peter Fritzsche, *Life and Death in the Third Reich* (Cambridge, MA, 2008).

[13] Frank Bajohr and Michael Wildt (eds.), *Volksgemeinschaft: Neue Forschungen zur Gesellschaftsgeschichte des Nationalsozialismus* (Frankfurt a.M., 2009); Michael Wildt, *Hitler's* Volksgemeinschaft *and the Dynamics of Racial Exclusion: Violence against Jews in Provincial Germany* (New York, NY, and Oxford, 2011).

consent, conformity or even enthusiasm rather than coercion, repression and the defeat of opposition and resistance.[14]

These debates continue. As far as the *Volksgemeinschaft* approach is concerned, historians fundamentally disagree both about the heuristic value of adopting a term used by contemporaries as an analytic concept, and about what it may have signified for the Third Reich in practice. There are also theoretical differences. Scholars critiquing the *Volksgemeinschaft* approach emphasise political, economic and social structures, and argue that this approach over-emphasises consensus at the expense of terror. The debate has also drawn attention to moral implications, in that it risks making all who were not persecuted in some sense complicit.[15] Moreover, there are difficulties in defining 'residues' after 1945, given changes in terminology and ideologies in divided Germany.

For all the critiques, these debates clearly address an area that requires further exploration: that of the attitudes and actions of those who were neither excluded nor in positions of power.

The 'Bystander Society': A Relational Approach

In place of the *Volksgemeinschaft* approach to the Third Reich, I would propose for further discussion a more abstract notion, that of a 'bystander society'. This does not place specific attitudes and opinions – for or against the regime, support or opposition to particular policies, commitment or otherwise to the idea of a *Volksgemeinschaft*, degrees of enthusiasm for Hitler and so on – but rather social behaviours and relationships at its centre. It is not specific to the analysis of the Third Reich, but rather can be used – as a concept or 'ideal type' – for analysis of a wide range of situations.

---

[14] See for example Robert Gellately, *Backing Hitler: Consent and Coercion in Nazi Germany* (Oxford, 2001); Eric A. Johnson, *The Nazi Terror: Gestapo, Jews and Ordinary Germans* (London, 2002; orig. 1999).

[15] For an overview of debates, see Detlef Schmiechen-Ackermann, '"Volksgemeinschaft": Mythos der NS-Propaganda, wirkungsmächtige soziale Verheißung oder soziale Realität im "Dritten Reich"? – Einführung', in Detlef Schmiechen-Ackermann (ed.), *'Volksgemeinschaft': Mythos, wirkungsmächtige soziale Verheißung oder soziale Realität im 'Dritten Reich'? Zwischenbilanz einer kontroversen Debatte* (Paderborn, 2012), 13–53; Martina Steber and Bernhard Gotto, '*Volksgemeinschaft*: Writing the Social History of the Nazi Regime', in Martina Steber and Bernhard Gotto (eds.), *Visions of Community in Nazi Germany: Social Engineering and Private Lives* (Oxford, 2014), 1–25, particularly 13–14. For critiques, see for example Ian Kershaw, '"Volksgemeinschaft": Potenzial und Grenzen eines neuen Forschungskonzepts', *Vierteljahrshefte für Zeitgeschichte* 59 (2011), 1–17; Michael Wildt's response, '"Volksgemeinschaft": Eine Antwort auf Ian Kershaw', *Zeithistorische Forschungen* 8 (2011), 102–9.

It is important to highlight the distinction between this and the more conventional category of 'bystanders'. The notion of bystanders as part of an analytic triad, alongside victims and perpetrators, is theoretically problematic.[16] It is an inherently unstable category, defined primarily not in terms of its own identity but of its location in relation to others: by proximity to or knowledge of a conflict in which others are the direct protagonists, the perpetrators and victims. Inaction, once such a conflict is registered, will soon fade into complicity through failure to challenge the perpetrator; action, on one side or the other, will soon lead the initial bystander into other roles, from rescuer or resistance fighter on one side to accomplice, beneficiary or even perpetrator on the other. The situation is very different in places where the dominant political and social authorities condemn the acts of violence and can be turned to for assistance by bystanders, and in circumstances where, by contrast, the authorities themselves are inciting or directly initiating the acts of violence. Moreover, who can be included in this category poses major problems in practice. In his key work on this topic, Raul Hilberg defined the concept of bystander so broadly as to be, in the end, almost meaningless, and certainly conceptually imprecise; for Hilberg, it was primarily a means of castigating widespread failure to intervene effectively, to engage in rescue attempts or to oppose the persecution of European Jews at a time when this still might have helped.[17] Other historians have tended rather to focus on the involvement of local communities around places where extreme violence was concentrated, as in regions where concentration camps or euthanasia centres were situated or where round-ups, deportations and mass killings took place.[18] Often, again, such involvement reveals a wide spectrum, including, at one end, plundering, benefitting and assisting the perpetrators, or, at the other, engaging in acts of rescue and hiding of fugitive victims. In cases of systemic, state-ordained or state-sanctioned violence which persists over a significant period of time, it is hard to identify locations and roles which are genuinely 'outside' the immediate dynamics of violence.

---

[16] See Mary Fulbrook, 'Bystanders: Catchall Concept, Alluring Alibi or Crucial Clue?', in Mary Fulbrook (ed.), *Erfahrung, Erinnerung, Geschichtsschreibung: Neue Perspektiven auf die deutschen Diktaturen* (Göttingen, 2016), chapter 5.

[17] See Raul Hilberg, *Perpetrators, Victims, Bystanders: The Jewish Catastrophe 1933–1945* (New York, NY, 1993).

[18] See for example Gordon J. Horwitz, 'Places Far Away, Places Very Near: Mauthausen, the Camps of the Shoah, and the Bystanders', in Michael Berenbaum and Abraham J. Peck (eds.), *The Holocaust and History: The Known, the Unknown, the Disputed, and the Reexamined* (Bloomington, IN, 1998), 409–20; Gordon J. Horwitz, *In the Shadow of Death: Living Outside the Gates of Mauthausen* (New York, NY, 1990).

What is, by contrast, a 'bystander society'? It is one in which, for a wide range of reasons, people will tend to err on the side of not intervening on behalf of the direct targets of persecution. They will often, moreover, not even register what is going on. Collective identities are defined and others stigmatised in invidious ways, such that it is possible to ignore or to turn a blind eye to the sufferings and fates of those excluded from the dominant 'community of empathy'.

The notion of a 'bystander society' explores patterns of behaviour in the face of state-sanctioned violence, rather than support for a particular vision of society as in the *Volksgemeinschaft* approach. It is important to note that passivity and conformity in a repressive regime may arise as much from fear and terror as from 'self-empowerment' or ideological support for the regime's goals. Ideology might be important for some groups and generations, shifting over time – a younger generation being particularly influenced by socialisation under Nazism – but passive and conformist behaviour could also mask a sense of inner distance or dissent. The spectrum informing conformist behaviours can run from genuine enthusiasm, through a gamut of careerist and conformist considerations, to hostility and opposition tempered by fear of the consequences of stepping out of line. The bystander analysis does not inherently tend, therefore, in the direction of proposing a 'consensus dictatorship'.

The approach directs attention to changes over time in patterns of social relations, changing identities and perceptions and redefinitions of the situation. It seeks to understand the growing divide between the included and the persecuted, including even the growing distance between non- and anti-Nazis who ended up in the category of bystanders and those who were victims of Nazism.

It directs attention also to the changing contexts of action, as perceived by contemporaries. This does not mean using contemporary accounts to find out 'how it really was', but rather to explore how people saw and thought about the situation, taking into account experiences and wider knowledge at the time, and how they reflected on the likely consequences for themselves and others of particular courses of action that they might be considering. One of the key questions here is what it would take to stand out and act on behalf of victims, and what would tend to militate against any action on their behalf. This would entail understanding contemporary perceptions of opportunities and threats, and calculations of the benefits and risks, potential costs or outcomes of different types of action.

The approach is not, however, limited to exploring the ways in which people's social identities or evaluations of circumstances changed. It incorporates also the wider context. Key here, for example, is the changing social composition of the wider community and perceptions of how other people will act – or who is no longer there to act. This is significant, for example, in decisions about resistance, political opposition, daring to stand out or choosing not to intervene because no one else or too few others are likely to assist. This sort of consideration is evident not only among political activists but also among other citizens.

A 'bystander society' develops over time. There are many aspects: identification and stigmatisation of salient differences; the introduction of informal as well as formal rewards and penalties relating to conformity; rehearsals and day-to-day performances of new scripts, learning to enact new roles and to play by new rules; the tearing apart of previous bonds and emotional ties; the dulling of sensitivities, forgetting former relationships and minimising or disregarding compromises made along the way. Notably, this transforms not only those who are excluded – as already described quite extensively for Jewish Germans – but also, and to date far less well explored, those who remain on the side of the dominant community.

Underlying this analysis is a conception of the 'relational self'. People's social selves are formed through their interactions in particular configurations. There is also a dramaturgical aspect, as analysed by Erving Goffman: people present themselves in a certain light, 'performing' a particular image or role that they project to others. This includes not only the expressions and (witting and unwitting) impressions 'given off' by the actor, but also settings and props (the 'front'), 'routines', parts played by other members of the 'team' in any given performance and interactions with particular audiences. Impressions created through behaviour, gestures and speech may be more or less at odds with other elements of appearance, expression, front and teamwork – notably in the case of the confidence trickster whose act goes awry, but to some degree in all social interactions, even among what Goffman calls 'sincere' rather than 'cynical' performers. Aspects of identity may also be perceived as 'damaging' a person's status, stigmatising them as 'inferior': awareness may affect performance and self-presentation in having, for example, to 'outperform' others who fit the stereotype of 'normal' or have the desired characteristics.[19] Goffman's approach is derived from analysis of only slowly changing societies, and is most easily applied in small-scale settings. It needs to be extended and adapted to assist in understanding changes over time and under more extreme political conditions.

---

[19] Again a key early text is by Erving Goffman, *Stigma: Notes on the Management of Spoiled Identity* (Englewood Cliffs, NJ, 1963).

Even if Nazi policies did not effect the proclaimed transformation in social and economic structures, or build a compelling and widely acknowledged sense of 'national community', they certainly had a major impact on the construction of social identities and role expectations. For many people, it was not so much a matter of an autonomous self inhabiting different roles in overlapping, mutually compatible, even concentric circles, but rather of finding that the previous balance of roles and personal preferences was challenged, tipped, overturned or transformed. Furthermore, in Goffman's examples, however constrained by professional codes of conduct or social expectations, individual actors have considerable leeway in choosing strategies and ends; but in Nazi Germany, imperatives were more extreme and potential penalties far more severe. Even so, individual aims were often not congruent with the puppet masters' intentions, and double meanings had to be conveyed. Often too, people improvised. They pre-emptively adopted patterns of social interaction that were in line with what the regime was trying to achieve, but acted in advance of actually needing to, and on occasion for purposes other than the official ones.

What is remarkable about Nazi Germany is the speed with which everything was transformed – and particularly the speed with which people across Germany not merely 'fell into line', conforming to policies handed down from above, but also, apparently almost spontaneously, started behaving in their everyday social relations – even in private – in ways that began to enact the desired society.

Much attention has been paid to how people behaved when they could be observed in public: mass rallies, enthusiastic raising of hands and saying 'Heil Hitler', use of flags and so on. However valuable they are, Sopade and SD reports on general patterns of mood, opinion and behaviour do not allow much access to the inner conflicts of individuals. Diaries of observers such as William Shirer have been mined for observations about behaviours and imputed mentalities; more broadly, ego-documents have largely been used to illustrate events and happenings beyond the self.[20] Few scholars have to date used such material to look at the impact of changing relationships on individuals over time.[21]

How far did intimate social relations change when there was no one else to observe, or only oneself and intimate and trusted others? How far did behaviour conform to new norms where there was no obvious pressure or official policing of social life? What did people choose to do, or not to do,

---

[20] See William Shirer, *Berlin Diary* (New York, NY, 1942).
[21] See Nicholas Stargardt, *The German War: A Nation under Arms, 1939–1945* (London, 2015).

when they had a degree of choice? And how did people reflect on their own behaviour and the behaviour of others, as social relations changed under the new regime? The private sphere may give us some clues as to the extent to which Nazism penetrated people's hearts and minds – and transformed them in the process.

In what follows, I take just a few examples from a unique source to explore some of the key transformations in the private sphere in the peacetime years. These not only illuminate how society in the Third Reich was transformed 'from within', as well as 'from above'; they also illustrate the kind of approach I believe is a necessary complement to analyses of wider political and structural developments in trying to understand the social genesis of genocide.

Lives 'Before' and 'After': Enacting New Selves

In summer 1939, well aware that something extraordinary was going on in Germany under Hitler's rule, and also in different ways deeply concerned at a personal level, three Harvard professors decided to explore further by soliciting accounts of personal experiences of life in Germany before and after 1933. The young sociologist Edward Y. Hartshorne had written on German universities and spent time in Germany in the mid-1930s; the senior historian Sidney B. Fay – who was also Hartshorne's father-in-law – had written both on Germany's role in the origins of the First World War and on eighteenth-century Prussia; and the psychologist Gordon Allport had interests in the ways in which personality was affected by current circumstances. Propelled in large measure by Hartshorne's drive, and assisted by external funding, they set up a competition soliciting autobiographical essays under the title 'My Life in Germany before and after 1933'.[22] The competition was announced in the *New York Times* as well as German-language and exile newspapers published outside the expanded German Reich.[23] It offered a very attractive first prize of $500, a significant sum for impoverished refugees at the time, in addition to other prizes of smaller amounts, totalling $1,000 in all. The Harvard professors on occasion went well beyond their academic brief, seeking to secure support for some of those in severe difficulties; one

---

[22] See Harry Liebersohn and Dorothee Schneider, 'Editors' Introduction', in Harry Liebersohn and Dorothee Schneider (eds.), *'My Life in Germany before and after January 30, 1933': A Guide to a Manuscript Collection at Houghton Library, Harvard University* (Philadelphia, PA, 2001).

[23] The competition announcements in the *New York Times* and in German-language newspapers are reproduced as figures 1 and 2 in Uta Gerhardt and Thomas Karlauf (eds.), *Night of Broken Glass: Eyewitness Accounts of Kristallnacht* (Malden, MA, 2012), 12 and 14.

essay writer, for example, received a payment of $2.50 to help him to survive; others were put in touch with relief agencies or individuals to supply affidavits to assist in getting out. Several received personal letters indicating sympathy and regretting they could not provide assistance. This was an intervention that clearly went beyond the normal boundaries of purely scientific academic research.

Many of the stories are heart-breaking, and written under conditions of sheer desperation. Not all writers conformed to the requirements of the competition with regard to length: some essays are simply short accounts of pain and pleas for practical help in gaining affidavits, financial support or assistance in getting away from the engulfing storm; others are ten times longer, providing detailed accounts across a considerable time span, even well back before the First World War. Nor is there any particular genre or style that could be said to be characteristic across the whole collection. Some more educated writers were clearly influenced by their reading of other memoirs, short novels or novellas, seeking to endow their accounts with some literary merit; others tended to ramble, organising anecdotes and memories in roughly chronological fashion; some authors incorporated or reproduced selections from diaries or contemporary letters; a few, as indicated, were simply cries for help, concentrating on only a few key moments or agonising incidents. Some make for far more gripping reading than others.

The published selections of excerpts from these essays have concentrated on those written by Jewish exiles who provide vivid depictions of scenes from their lives in Germany and Austria before and under Nazi rule, and the ways in which they were stigmatised, excluded and eventually forced out of their homeland.[24] The archival collection includes not only these harrowing tales but also accounts by non-Jewish individuals,

---

[24] Selections from these accounts have been published in Margarete Limberg and Hubert Rübsaat (eds.), *Sie durften nicht mehr Deutsche sein: Jüdischer Alltag in Selbstzeugnissen 1933–1938* (Frankfurt a.M., New York, 1990); with a reduced selection of these in English translation in Margarete Limberg and Hubert Rübsaat (eds.), *Germans No More: Accounts of Jewish Everyday Life, 1933–38* (New York, NY, Oxford, 2006); Margarete Limberg and Hubert Rübsaat (eds.), *Nach dem 'Anschluss': Berichte österreichischer EmigrantInnen aus dem Archiv der Harvard University* (Vienna, 2013); Gerhardt/Karlauf (eds.), *Night of Broken Glass*. Uta Gerhardt unearthed the extraordinary story of the Harvard sociologist Edward Hartshorne, who had originally selected and edited these excerpts and had intended to publish them under the title *Nazi Madness*. Hartshorne was unable to complete this project since he was murdered in Bavaria while in the midst of denazification work on behalf of the OMGUS: he was shot in the head in late August 1946 while driving on the autobahn from Munich to Nuremberg – an incident which remains unresolved. See also related materials in Andreas Lixl-Purcell (ed.), *Women of Exile: German-Jewish Autobiographies since 1933* (Westport, CT, London, 1988); Monika Richarz (ed.), *Jüdisches Leben in Deutschland*, vol. 2: *Selbstzeugnisse zur Sozialgeschichte im Kaiserreich*, vol. 3: *Selbstzeugnisse zur Sozialgeschichte, 1918–1945*

including visitors to Germany from other countries, some of whom were remarkably uninhibited in discussing what they saw as the 'positive' aspects of Nazism. Among those who were sympathetic to Nazism, there was little of the later defensive self-censorship that would characterise post-war accounts of former Nazi sympathisers. The essays, we have to remember, were written at a time when the height of persecution seemed to have been reached with the events of 9–10 November 1938, the so-called 'night of broken glass', often followed by incarceration in concentration camps and enforced emigration. Few at this time could have predicted how very much more murderous the policies would become after the outbreak of war, and particularly from 1941 onwards with the mass shootings in the east and the establishment of dedicated extermination camps.[25]

One of the most striking features noted by these writers is the way in which people first learned who was 'other', and then sought to apply this in everyday life. There are numerous semi-humorous stories about 'racial science' lessons at school where a teacher would pick on a particularly 'Aryan'-looking blonde, blue-eyed student and ask about her heritage, only to be told that the student in question was of Jewish descent. Conversely, there are stories about passengers on public transport being mistaken for people of Jewish descent and being asked to give up a seat in a crowded carriage. Such episodes were part of a wider process in which people learned about allegedly visible characteristics and developed new self-identifications in 'racial' terms.[26]

Clearly in public there were social pressures to conform. In official roles, regulations were generally enforced, and incidents in which people chose to circumvent rules were deemed worthy of comment. On occasion personal relations took precedence over official regulations, but such moments were rare. There was a sort of mutual recognition when a person in authority was secure enough to bend the rules for another; it was a measure of mutual respect and trust. More interesting for present purposes, however, is the question of whether people adapted their private behaviours to the new categories. For many the process of adjustment required a considerable element of play-acting, in which distinctions between what was 'performance' and what was 'real' were sometimes enacted explicitly. Multiple

(Munich, 1982); English edition: *Jewish Life in Germany: Memoirs from Three Centuries* (Bloomington, IN, 1991).

[25] See also Saul Friedländer, 'Foreword', in Gerhardt/Karlauf (eds.), *Night of Broken Glass*, x–xi; Richard J. Evans' review of *The Night of Broken Glass*, The Guardian, 11 April 2012, available at: www.theguardian.com/books/2012/apr/11/night-broken-glass-kristallnacht-review [accessed 6 August 2018].

[26] See for example Mary Fulbrook, *Dissonant Lives: Generations and Violence through the German Dictatorships* (Oxford, 2011), 100–20.

simultaneous audiences could attract a performance that was appropriately multifaceted – but not always without costs and contradictions.

Consider, for example, the case of a prominent Hamburg businessman, a grain importer whom I shall call Jansen (not his real name). We know about his activities from an account by a young Danish man, Borge N., who came to Germany to work for him.[27] Jansen's business fell on hard times after Hitler came to power, so Jansen joined the NSDAP to try to ingratiate himself. This did not at first yield the desired results. Then further misfortune, as he saw it, struck the Jansen household: his daughter fell in love with a Jew. Jansen told her to break it off – not, as he was hasty to reassure her, because he had anything personal against her fiancé, but rather because such a liaison would be terrible for his business. Much in love with her Jewish boyfriend, the daughter refused to give him up. Jansen then issued an ultimatum: if she decided to stay with 'her Jew' he would break off all connections and cast her out of his house and family. She refused to give up her love, happiness, and future life for the sake of her father's business.

So far, so similar to innumerable stories found in communities that believe in endogamy and exert massive pressures to sustain invisible community borders by not 'marrying out'. But the private had wider ramifications in the Nazi context.

Jansen decided to go public and to exploit this development for his own purposes. According to Borge's account, Jansen placed a big notice in the newspaper 'announcing that from now on he would not recognise his daughter anymore on account of her acquaintanceship with a jew [sic]. His wife, who had been against him all the time, never forgave him this and also many of his former friends disliked his attitude. Even some of his friends who were 100% Nazis told me that although it was a big mistake of his daughter to have anything to do with a jew [sic], it was not necessary for him to treat her as he did.'[28] Even so, Jansen achieved his ends. The newspaper announcement came to the attention of NSDAP bigwigs who formed the view that here they had a 100 per cent Nazi whom they could trust: one who was even prepared to break with his daughter because of her Jewish fiancé and to declare this in public. As a result Jansen's business was regarded favourably in ruling circles, and he gained a big government grain-importing contract. By 1936, according to Borge, Jansen was 'the leading controller in Hamburg for the [...] Government's grain and feeding stuff department', the RfG [Reichsstelle für Getreide, Futtermittel und sonstige landwirtschaftliche Erzeugnisse].[29] Meanwhile

---

[27] See Harvard Houghton Library (hereafter HHL), b MS Ger 91 (167), Borge N., 8–10.
[28] HHL, b MS Ger 91 (167), Borge N., 9.   [29] HHL, b MS Ger 91 (167), Borge N., 10.

Jansen's daughter had gone to Denmark to marry her fiancé, since it was forbidden for a Jew and an 'Aryan' to marry in Germany, but they were also not allowed to stay in Denmark because the Jewish husband was only granted a visa for a short visit.[30] We do not know what subsequently became of them, but Borge's account tells us a great deal more about how Jansen now maintained his act.

This act had multiple audiences. Borge relates that Jansen did 'nice work as an actor', and if he 'was so successful in dealing with the Nazi government it certainly was not because he really was a 100% Nazi (neither I nor any of his business friends thought of him as such). However, he was a good actor and a smart business man.'[31] His act included saying 'Heil Hitler' very loudly on the phone when the RfG called from Berlin. He also had a large radio brought into his office, along with coffee and cakes, and employees were gathered to listen to Hitler delivering a two-hour speech while he periodically interjected words 'to show his appreciation of Hitler's speech'. Moreover, at the beginning and end of the speech 'Mr. Jansen always yelled out in the air "My Führer, my beloved Führer" so as to make clear to everybody that he was a good Nazi'. Yet at the same time as performing the good Nazi, Jansen would provide additional subtle clues to ensure that all present knew he was simply play-acting. As Borge commented: 'It was always very amusing to me to listen to his remarks and a couple of times when I looked at him I seemed to see a twinkle in his eyes as if he enjoyed his own words. A few of his employees, I am sure[,] had the same impression as I. But that was none of our business, of course, and nobody could prove what was only a supposition.'[32] Indeed, Borge wondered 'many times [...] whether he really was a 100% Nazi or he was just acting'.[33] For present purposes, it matters less whether Jansen was or was not 'really' a Nazi than that he was able to present multiple faces in public, performing both the convinced supporter and the self-distancing actor, according to context and calculation of personal benefits.

Jansen was not the only person in Nazi Germany to present a public face while providing subtle indications of the element of acting involved. Verena H. was an 'Aryan' whose husband was Jewish and whose children were, as 'Mischlinge' (of mixed descent), suffering discrimination at school. When the family decided to emigrate, Verena went to say goodbye to friends and acquaintances, including the local theatre director. She found him to be doing very well, since, as he told her, he was now

---

[30] See ibidem. [31] HHL, b MS Ger 91 (167), Borge N., 11, 10.
[32] HHL, b MS Ger 91 (167), Borge N., 11–12.
[33] HHL, b MS Ger 91 (167), Borge N., 11.

financially supported and able to expend vast sums of money in the interests of the Nazi cause; with 'a little wink', he added that 'we theatre people are used to changing our character, we do it every evening, it becomes second nature'.[34] Another acquaintance told Verena about a brother who, as director of a hospital, had to attend Nazi lectures which he found distasteful: he hated this, but 'found it somewhat easier if he pretended to himself that he was going voluntarily'.[35] In different ways, the jokey self-distancing and the uncomfortable attempt at self-persuasion were strategies for dealing with the dissonance between new behaviours and inner views that remained somewhat at odds with the performances that were now required.

Everywhere, it seems, people were putting on an act – and were widely aware of it. On one occasion Ernst R., a convinced Christian and anti-Nazi, met an acquaintance wearing an SA uniform. The latter recounted how he had been commanded to maltreat 'Marxists' who had been arrested; he told Ernst how he had complied with this order, 'despite it making him feel quite sick'.[36] Again, it matters less whether the acquaintance in an SA uniform was putting on an act for Ernst to maintain an appearance of humanity in the eyes of an anti-Nazi, or genuinely registering his feelings when acting the Nazi thug; the key point is that multiple performances were necessary in a situation when selves were fractured and presentations of self were mutually inconsistent and facing in different directions for different audiences.

Another of Ernst R.'s acquaintances, a Protestant community worker, had the temerity to express her regrets about 'the destruction of Jewish apartments' during the 'night of broken glass' of November 1938. She was arrested by an apparently sympathetic SS man who marched her off to the police station. On the way he said to her: 'You can think anything you like! Just don't say anything!' and let her go free.[37] This injunction to present the appropriate outward expression, whatever was going on inside, was illuminating. And in the absence of the eyes of colleagues, this particular representative of Nazi law and order was able momentarily to drop his own act and to behave in a friendly manner to an erring compatriot. Such a switch would have been unlikely, however, had she not been a member of his own 'national community'.

Uniforms made a difference to the ways in which people acted. Ernst noted on his journeys through Germany that ever more people were wearing Party badges or uniforms of one sort or another. Even if they were what Ernst called 'forced members' and behaved one way when in

---

[34] HHL, b MS Ger 91 (93), Verena H., 32. [35] HHL, b MS Ger 91 (93), Verena H., 34.
[36] HHL, b MS Ger 91 (181), Ernst R., 21. [37] HHL, b MS Ger 91 (181), Ernst R., 23.

sight of colleagues and another when out of sight – as in the example just quoted – they were, as Ernst put it, serving a party 'whose goal it was to destroy spiritual Germany (*das geistige Deutschland*)'.[38] Just to wear a uniform, however one actually performed the act, was to participate in a wider national performance.

Such play-acting affected the private lives and conceptions of self of those who were on the receiving end of Nazi persecution. One young Jewish woman, Gerta P., felt how the prevalence of people in uniform affected her own sense of self and her own behaviour: 'I trembled before every new person. [...] In uniform people were totally changed. It boosted their self-confidence and in this Hitler costume (*Hitlertracht*) they dared to be far meaner than when wearing civilian clothing.'[39] Gerta also felt there were significant differences in the extent to which people were aware of enacting new roles, or simply accepted everything unthinkingly. When, for example, a friend whom she often met in a restaurant took to reading out loud from newspapers in a heavily ironic style, the wit was not noticed by others sitting nearby, who were 'mostly dumb'. For some, silence was presumably because of fear, but others took every official pronouncement as 'God given'.[40]

Play-acting a new public self may have been context-dependent and enacted only in front of certain audiences. But it had an effect on the people involved – on both sides, not only among victims. And it could take place even in the most intimate of private spheres.

From 'Cynical' to 'Sincere' Performers: Public Faces in Private Places

The family was seen as the vehicle for the procreation of the 'Aryan race', and subjected to massive state control, with both prohibitions and prescriptive practices affecting people on both sides of the 'racial' divide, as well as those not conforming to the heteronormative standards of the Nazi ideal. Leading a genuinely 'private' life became well-nigh impossible.

The difficulties for a young Jewish man with a non-Jewish girlfriend were described vividly by Hans K.[41] Hans was, eventually, the casualty of his girlfriend's acting skills and her transformation, over a period of months, from a 'cynical' to a 'sincere' performer. Hans' story is one of trust betrayed and intimacy severed.

---

[38] HHL, b MS Ger 91 (181), Ernst R., 17. [39] HHL, b MS Ger 91 (177), Gerta P., 20.
[40] HHL, b MS Ger 91 (177), Gerta P., 23.
[41] See HHL, b MS Ger 91 (118), Hans K. (aged 34), writing from Shanghai, China, 27 March 1940.

Even before Hitler came to power, relationships between Jewish and non-Jewish Germans were frowned upon in some circles. But Hans experienced increasing difficulties after 1933; he noted that while members of the older generation generally remained decent, the younger generation was typically more susceptible to Nazism.[42] Hans enjoyed an intimate relationship with a non-Jewish workmate by the name of Trude, but this now came under threat.[43] They experienced difficulties in meeting and in making marriage plans, and he was living in an increasingly nervous state. Nevertheless, 'blinded by passion', they did not give up their relationship.[44] In the summer of 1934, they went on holiday together to Switzerland, where people could hardly believe the difficulties they were experiencing in Germany.[45] In autumn 1934, however, their relationship entered a crisis.[46] A new employee, a member of the SS by the name of Koch, began to take an interest in Trude. At first Trude complained, but Hans could do nothing about it. Then he began to fear that Trude was actually enjoying the attentions of Koch; she, however, claimed she was only behaving 'as if' so as not to betray their relationship. The issue finally came to a head in January 1935.[47] Hans went away to attend his brother's wedding prior to the latter's emigration to Palestine. He returned to find that Trude had slept with Koch following the New Year's Eve celebrations. On being confronted, Trude claimed she was still true to Hans and was only having a relationship with Koch to protect Hans. Even so, it came to a showdown. In front of Koch, Hans had to ask Trude if she would marry him, and in the presence of this particular audience, SS man Koch, Trude said no, again allegedly only to protect Hans. For Hans, however, the whole thing had become increasingly unbearable.[48] In the end (like many others at this time), he chose to marry a Jewish friend: although this was not a passionate love affair, the two were partners in distress. Just before the outbreak of war, they managed to escape to China, from where Hans wrote about his experiences in March 1940.

Performance and behaving 'as if' in this way deeply affected the most intimate of relationships – it sowed the seeds of distrust in previously loving relationships, where mutual trust should be at the heart of the intimacy. Whether or not Trude was a 'weak character' (as Hans thought), whether she was personally attracted to Koch or was genuinely

---

[42] See HHL, b MS Ger 91 (118), Hans K., 20–1.
[43] See HHL, b MS Ger 91 (118), Hans K., 17.
[44] HHL, b MS Ger 91 (118), Hans K., 23.
[45] See HHL, b MS Ger 91 (118), Hans K., 24.
[46] See HHL, b MS Ger 91 (118), Hans K., 25.
[47] See HHL, b MS Ger 91 (118), Hans K., 26. [48] See ibidem.

trying to protect Hans, the relationship was clearly unsustainable under the new circumstances. Intimacy was broken off, since sexual relations across 'racial' fault-lines became too problematic and the 'Aryan' partner began to believe her new act.

In other cases, people of the 'national community' entered marriages precisely because of official encouragement and pressure. Borge again provides interesting examples of male colleagues who were – for reasons he is too sensitive to intimate explicitly – effectively pressured into feeling they must marry. One such was Erich M., aged forty-one.[49] Erich claimed he had to join the Party because he was 'a supervisor with one of the big oil concerns in Hamburg', with responsibility for a staff of 120, and would otherwise lose his job.[50] Erich had to make a little pro-Nazi speech every morning to the men, and usually just recycled material from Nazi leaders' published speeches. But as far as his private life was concerned, the compromise seems to have been of a somewhat larger order. Erich was not married and, as Borge delicately put it, 'did not want to either'.[51] But the NSDAP and the oil concern's management put pressure on him to marry. Borge commented: 'I felt sorry for him, because he was the type that will never be happy in marriage. But he realised he would have to marry sooner or later if he wanted to keep his job.'[52] Compromises in private life seem to have been outweighed by the professional benefits.[53] Not everyone who shared the apparent sexual inclinations of Erich made this compromise, however – and many paid a heavy penalty in terms of arrests and incarceration.[54]

Borge provides another interesting portrait, this time of a young colleague motivated more by conviction than professional concerns. Borge had read that 'the Mayor of Stettin had announced that no male person over 25 years of age would be allowed a municipal job unless he was married and that all male persons over 25 years of age who already had such a municipal job without being married would have to marry within three months or lose their jobs'. Borge asked his colleague 'if it really was the case that a mayor could pair his employees as if they were animals'. He continued: 'This question made my friend so angry that he could hardly say a word. He finally managed to collect himself and he told me, his face still red, that he would not discuss anything with me because I did not

---

[49] See HHL, b MS Ger 91 (167), Borge N., 71ff.
[50] HHL, b MS Ger 91 (167), Borge N., 72.
[51] HHL, b MS Ger 91 (167), Borge N., 73.
[52] HHL, b MS Ger 91 (167), Borge N., 74.
[53] See HHL, b MS Ger 91 (167), Borge N., 75.
[54] Explored in more detail in Mary Fulbrook, *Reckonings: Legacies of Nazi Persecution and the Quest for Justice* (Oxford, 2018).

understand National-Socialism and the wonders it had done to the German people.'[55] In Borge's view, 'his attitude was typical for most of the young Nazis with whom I tried to discuss the value of National-Socialism. Their only argument seemed to be "you do not understand the greatness in Nazism." Or they used what they considered a stronger argument namely: "Even if we realise you are Arisch the many jews [sic] and communists in your country [Denmark] have already influenced you to such an extent that you are an enemy of National-Socialism."'[56]

The notion of what constituted 'sexual relations' broadened, as accusations of 'racial defilement' (*Rassenschande*) became ever more widespread and the definition of what this meant became ever more diluted. Fascinating details are provided by Max P., a Jewish lawyer who had managed to leave his native Germany and was living in Palestine.[57] He reported how Nazi regulations expanded what was included under 'sexual relations'. Judges extended the phrase to mean any supposedly inappropriate behaviour between Jewish and non-Jewish Germans, including even just a glance.[58] Sexual relations that crossed 'racial' boundaries were considered a deeply political matter and were treated with severity, although the length of sentences varied in different regions.[59] Transgressions in private were hard to prove, but this was of little help to those accused.[60] Moreover, accusations were often made purely for petty personal gain. Ernst R., for example, recounts how a female customer tried on a pair of shoes in a Jewish-owned shoe shop, then suddenly accused the shop owner of having touched her legs. She 'grabbed the shoes and left the shop without paying', certain that the trader would not dare to pursue her for fear of being accused of 'racial defilement'.[61]

It is clear that intimate relations in the 'national community', supposedly rooted in common ethnic descent, would be targets for state intervention. What is less obvious are the ways in which people began to enact the racial state in areas of their private lives that were less easy to regulate. One of the most interesting areas in this connection is that of the ill-defined sphere of friendship. It is also one of the most significant, viewed from the perspective of the formation of a 'bystander society' in which bonds of affection and empathy are severed.

---

[55] HHL, b MS Ger 91 (167), Borge N., 15.
[56] HHL, b MS Ger 91 (167), Borge N., 15–16.
[57] See HHL, b MS Ger 91 (178), Max Moses P.
[58] See HHL, b MS Ger 91 (178), Max Moses P., 92–3.
[59] See HHL, b MS Ger 91 (178), Max Moses P., 95.
[60] See HHL, b MS Ger 91 (178), Max Moses P., 97.
[61] HHL, b MS Ger 91 (181), Ernst R., 22.

Severing Bonds of Friendship: From Integration to Indifference

An old Polish joke, circulating under communist rule, encapsulated the meaning of friendship. When asked whether the Russians were their brothers or their friends, Polish people would reply: 'Our brothers of course! Your friends you can choose.'

Friendship is a difficult concept to define precisely. Historically, friendship has different meanings and functions, encompassing kinship ties and utilitarian relations as well as bonds of affection. In the twentieth century (and earlier) the notion of friendship primarily referred to an emotionally warm relationship between people who are not necessarily related in other ways. Colleagues may be friends, but friends are not necessarily colleagues; relatives may or may not also be friends. Friends are people you want to spend time with, to 'socialise with'. Even this is not an entirely personal matter: structural, cultural and contextual factors influence those designated as appropriate candidates for friendship; and utilitarian considerations often play a role, as in the notorious 'connections' (*Beziehungen*, 'Vitamin B') in the GDR that were vital to 'organising' scarce goods and services in a shortage economy. So friendship, like so much else, is never a purely personal matter.

Even so, friendship is an area that is hard for any state to define or to regulate. And in early 1930s Germany it was largely a matter of social bonds of mutual affection, more likely to be shaped by class than 'racial' considerations. There were many informal friendships between Jews and gentiles in pre-Nazi Germany. This is not to say that there were no distinctions: families might not want their offspring to marry across community boundaries, including not only Jewish but also Protestant, Catholic and status group or class boundaries. Even so, mixed marriages were not uncommon: in 1935 there were around half a million Jews in Germany, and around a quarter of a million people of mixed background. Stereotypes and prejudices existed, and could be whipped up under circumstances of economic distress and political instability. But informal friendships were widespread.

If the road to Auschwitz was paved with indifference, then there was an earlier road to be travelled from integration to indifference. A lack of empathy with the targets of persecution was not only created by official policies; it was also proactively created in the private sphere. Some indifference was of course simply based on ignorance, on lack of personal relationships. Many Germans – particularly in rural areas – barely knew any Jews personally, and were unlikely to be personal friends with casual business acquaintances. But where there were significant populations of

Jews, as in Berlin, Frankfurt or Hamburg, there were also many non-Jewish friends – and these were people who should not have been indifferent to their fate.

Yet one of the most striking features already in the first years of Nazi rule is the way in which 'Aryans' dropped friendships with those to be excluded from the *Volksgemeinschaft*. This was not a matter of official regulation; friendship was supposedly a private matter. Many ego-documents record the breaking of friendships as one of the most painful experiences they had gone through. George K., for example, chose this as the sole focus of his essay. He had wanted to write about his experiences at greater length, but chose to single out the loss of his closest childhood friend as the key issue on which to focus.[62] Following the Nazi takeover, his closest school friend gave up Catholicism and became a Nazi, and 'no longer dared to hang out with a Jew'.[63] Both George and his friend were somewhat ashamed and embarrassed when they subsequently met by chance on the street. They would both act as though they 'purely coincidentally happened to be looking in a different direction'.[64] In this way, they could avoid any awkwardness and pretend they had not seen each other. This was an early moment in practising the art of 'not seeing' that was later to become so important in a 'bystander society'. This story is typical of many.

There seem to have been a variety of motives for dropping friendships: careerism and opportunism, new ideological convictions, social pressures for conformity and fear of possible penalties. Ideological convictions were certainly important in some cases, particularly among young people. Gerhard M., for example, recalled one former friend who was still concerned for his well-being and warned him about the boycott in April 1933, but soon after this joined the NSDAP, breaking off the friendship in a perfectly cordial manner, if justified in racist terms.[65] Soon afterwards, Gerhard had much the same experience with another friend: 'We had a long discussion and came to the conclusion, that our friendship was no longer possible.'[66] Many friendships were broken off less out of conviction than for reasons of performance and presenting a particular version of the acceptable social self in public. Those who felt at risk of being labelled oppositional were particularly concerned. Fearing disadvantage at work, as Gerhard recalled, some former friends 'did not dare to meet us openly and when one of them came up to us we had to take the strongest

---

[62] See HHL, b MS Ger 91 (119), George K., letter dated 15 January 1940.
[63] HHL, b MS Ger 91 (119), George K., 3.
[64] HHL, b MS Ger 91 (119), George K., 4.
[65] See HHL, b MS Ger 91 (158), Gerhard M., 3.
[66] HHL, b MS Ger 91 (158), Gerhard M., 7.

possible precautions so that nobody saw him'.[67] Economic considerations could become significant in quite different ways. Borge, the young Danish man in Hamburg, observed that his landlady's son only broke off one friendship as late as 1937 because he 'had borrowed several hundred Marks' from this friend 'and a break came, therefore, rather handy'.[68] Social pressures for conformity, for not being seen as different, were also important, although the question often arises as to who was actually doing the 'social policing'. Often fear simply of being labelled a '*Judenknecht*' ('servant of the Jews') seems to have been more important than any real penalties. And if friendship is based on affection, it is based also on a degree of mutual trust. Alongside the severance of friendship ties was the growth of mutual mistrust, registered in many accounts.[69]

Minor differences of political opinion could relatively easily be bridged and friendships sustained where there were no 'racial' issues complicating matters. Borge reported several incidents that demonstrated how prior friendships within a relatively narrow social group, a Hamburg sailing club that he frequented, could take priority over political considerations. Even when one member overstepped the mark in political critiques, he was safe among friends, 'because everybody knew each other and had been friends for so many years that they would not betray each other. The younger people of my own age seldom attended these discussions, and those of the older ones that were 100% Nazis always pretended they were not listening, and if they found it advisable they just left our table and joined some other party.'[70] But this was friendship within a particular social group with common leisure interests. It was not across 'racial' lines, where sticking with one's friends was a far more serious matter.

The transformation of friendship relations is a good barometer of the ways in which Nazism got 'inside' people and of how the new norms affected everyday behaviours in settings that were beyond formal regulation. The changing social topography of friendship may provide clues to the rapid, radical development of a 'bystander society' over a relatively short period. And the apparently spontaneous disentangling of ties of friendship was one of the many steps on the path to genocide, ensuring the progressive social isolation of Jewish (and other minority) communities.

Even so, some non-Jewish Germans had the courage to refuse to break off with their Jewish friends. Individual cases provide some indication of the pressures to conform and the personal price that could be paid for resisting the wider tidal wave engulfing German

[67] HHL, b MS Ger 91 (158), Gerhard M., 12.
[68] HHL, b MS Ger 91 (167), Borge N., 65.
[69] See for example HHL, b MS Ger 91 (18), Elisabeth B., 11–12.
[70] HHL, b MS Ger 91 (167), Borge N., 58.

society.[71] Often, however, people did not have command over sufficient resources to resist, and simply had to keep their heads down and conform. For many, the embarrassment and shame that might be occasioned by informal encounters across the newly instituted racial ravines of German society could only be avoided by 'not seeing' and 'not knowing'. Many stories suggest that it was easier to resolve moments of tension by turning away, by pretending not to see, not to know, not to have heard.

If clandestine visits were not paid to friends in the ever more restricted privacy of the home – under increasing surveillance of neighbours and block wardens – then it would be easy enough to lose former friends from sight, metaphorically as well as physically. To comment on the privacy of the home without also discussing who was not invited, who was now excluded, would be to lose sight of the enormous significance of this aspect.

Many later oral history interviewees recall, when pressed, that they did indeed remember one or two Jewish friends from schooldays but then 'lost contact' with them, or they 'left' the neighbourhood, and the interviewee simply registers that they 'did not know' what became of them. The severance of ties of friendship did not loom so large in the memories of these bystanders as it did in the early accounts of those who had been ousted from the dominant 'national community'.

Conclusions

How does this approach to private lives help us to understand the 'big' historical questions of the time? Or, looked at another way: can we now ask not only how Nazism had an impact on people's private lives but also how transformations in the private sphere had an impact on the way the Nazi regime developed? And what can it tell us about the longer-term reverberations of this period?

If we analyse the social topography of transformations of the self, we can discern distinct generational patterns.[72] The apparently most 'sincere' performers can be found disproportionately among younger generations. Those who were older – who had, in effect, already internalised other scripts – were less likely to believe their own acts, more likely to engage in knowingly 'cynical' performances, aware of the ends they were seeking to achieve in the process.

---

[71] I have explored one such case in Mary Fulbrook, *Subjectivity and History: Approaches to Twentieth-Century German Society* (London, 2017).

[72] See further Fulbrook, *Dissonant Lives*.

Further factors need to be brought into play. Differences in command over material and cultural resources affected the extent to which people had the capacity to make choices, as well as the consequences of their decisions. Moral positions (political, religious and ethical) and personal attributes affected how specific individuals chose to respond to common challenges in particular positions and situations. Some accommodated themselves early and easily, as we have seen in the case of Jansen, who cast out his daughter in favour of his business interests. Some, who capitulated out of fear or in pursuit of favour, became used to their new acts and learned how to lead double lives, or even switched sides, as in the case of Trude.

Not all who conformed were necessarily convinced by what they were doing. The 'bystander society' was far from being a consensual *Volksgemeinschaft*, even in times of peace when Hitler's popularity was at its height. But the emergence of a 'bystander society' allowed the relatively easy removal of the newly 'unwanted' from the heart of their former communities with barely a whisper of protest. And it eased the passage into far more dangerous waters. Nazi policies were frequently designed to maximise distress, humiliation and degradation of people as human beings. This was very obviously the case in shaming people by bearing boards announcing their guilt in 'racial defilement', or the shaving of Jewish men's beards, or forcing Jews to scrub streets with small brushes, or making communities in the annexed territories of Poland and in the General Government witness public hangings a few weeks before their own deportation to death. All such practices served to enact the Nazis' claims to superiority and power, while reducing capacity for resistance on the part of victims. Once we get into the period of war and genocide, the rehearsals of scripts and performances that had taken place over the peacetime years would play a significant role in the self-mobilisation and participation of many on the side of the perpetrators.

Some who were sincere performers found that their selves were so bound up with the performance of Nazism that they could not conceive of a liveable life after the end of this era. This was not only a matter of fearing retribution for roles played in a murderous regime, although many did indeed commit suicide to evade post-war justice. There were also many cases where people simply could not envisage lives after the collapse of the 'thousand-year Reich'.

Others had, however, maintained a greater sense of distance between their conceptions of self and their commitment to the regime. Many could no longer recognise their former selves in what they had written at the time. Those who had been largely 'cynical performers' often managed to split what they saw as their 'authentic' selves from the public roles that they had played. In this way, they could later seek to assuage any nagging sense of guilt, or deflect potential criticism, by saying they had never 'really' been Nazis.

The diffuse burden of discomfort, if not actually acknowledgement of guilt, that hung over post-war Germany was a direct consequence of the knowledge that the roles people had played in their private lives had also had significant consequences for events on the public stages of history. People did not need to have pulled a trigger in order to have been complicit in creating the preconditions for genocide. The wider story, of having seen, heard and known 'nothing about it', was rooted in an experienced past in which people had chosen to cross the road, to turn a blind eye, to precisely not recognise a former friend; in which people had, in their private lives, helped to prepare the ground for the path to genocide. An awareness of past complicity in the social production of the indifference that paved the road to Auschwitz lay behind later avowals of ignorance and innocence. At the same time, the knowledge that they had to some extent been putting on a public face, engaging in a social performance, meant that people also felt there was an authentic 'inner self' that had remained in some sense genuinely innocent; that they need not, as individuals, bear responsibility for their outer behaviours and actions, and hence need feel no personal guilt.

We cannot, then, write a separate 'history of the private' for Nazi Germany, in some way sealed off from knowledge of the genocide that this state unleashed, since the private was so deeply, intrinsically and inevitably also political, in both the ways it was shaped and what it made possible. The transformation of the private sphere was an integral part of the persecution of excluded groups, as well as, eventually, helping to create the preconditions for mass murder. The initiators, policy makers and practitioners of physical violence were essential to the course and direction that history took under Nazi rule, but to treat 'the people' as having been simply coerced or enticed into cooperation with the regime is to miss a whole dimension of the ways in which Nazi society functioned and the wider social transformations that it inaugurated.

We cannot look only at selected elements of the interplay between different communities of experience; a focus solely on the principal perpetrators and the victims of persecution is insufficient to understand the fuller import of this period. Among the wider bystander community, there were thinking and acting individuals who negotiated the emergent constraints and opportunities of the new regime to develop new social performances; in the process, they became new types of social self, capable of very different kinds of action and inaction under altered circumstances. They saw, and did not see, in different ways.

The enactment of certain roles – the putting on of certain public faces – itself changed social relations. Fear certainly played a role for some who accommodated themselves and conformed; it was integral to their performance. For others, enticements and lures, from the petty to the more significant, affected their changing relations with compatriots who were now to be excluded. We need, then, to develop an approach which addresses the private sphere not as a set of discrete, possibly even marginal, topics of relevance only to those who are interested in issues such as consumption or sexuality, but rather as an essential and integral part of a comprehensive approach to history.

Historians now need to recognise and to constitute as a significant historical subject the myriad ways in which social relations and private lives came to constitute the kind of 'bystander society' that allowed the Holocaust to happen. Such an approach can serve to challenge post-war tales of innocence and to clarify the widespread patterns of complicity and capitulation that helped to make mass murder possible.

4 Private and Public Moral Sentiments in Nazi Germany

Nicholas Stargardt

During the past twenty years, historians have turned increasingly to exploring subjective sources in order to understand how far 'ordinary Germans' identified themselves with the Third Reich. This has led to a historiographic shift from looking for nonconformity and dissent to finding consensus and self-mobilisation. That 'tipping point' into a new normality of how to write history came in the late 1990s, at about the time that a generation of young scholars like Klaus Latzel, Ulrike Jureit and Martin Humburg started reading family letters from the Second World War. Several years earlier, Susanne zur Nieden and Ingrid Hammer had given impetus to this approach by publishing a collection of private diaries.[1] But it is too great a shift in awareness to be located around any single intervention or interpretative schema. In the mid-1990s, Christopher Browning and Daniel Goldhagen were both trying to explain why 'ordinary' reserve policemen became willing perpetrators, and this voluntaristic 'turn' influenced much subsequent research on the Holocaust. They in turn were building on studies of the Gestapo, which showed that policing at home depended on multiple forms of social cooperation and not just terror, and the turn to thinking of the Third Reich more broadly as a 'racial state'.[2] That emphasis on the importance

---

[1] See Martin Humburg, *Das Gesicht des Krieges: Feldpostbriefe von Wehrmachtssoldaten aus der Sowjetunion 1941–1944* (Opladen, Wiesbaden, 1998); Klaus Latzel, *Deutsche Soldaten – nationalsozialistischer Krieg? Kriegserlebnis – Kriegserfahrung 1939–1945* (Paderborn, 2000); Ulrike Jureit, 'Zwischen Ehe und Männerbund: Emotionale und sexuelle Beziehungsmuster im Zweiten Weltkrieg', *WerkstattGeschichte* 22 (1999), 61–73; Ingrid Hammer and Susanne zur Nieden (eds.), *'Sehr selten habe ich geweint': Briefe und Tagebücher aus dem Zweiten Weltkrieg von Menschen aus Berlin* (Zurich, 1992); Susanne zur Nieden, *Alltag im Ausnahmezustand: Frauentagebücher im zerstörten Deutschland 1943 bis 1945* (Berlin, 1993).

[2] See Christopher Browning, *Ordinary Men: Reserve Police Battalion 101 and the Final Solution in Poland* (New York, NY, 1993); Christopher Browning, *Nazi Policy, Jewish Workers, German Killers* (Cambridge, 2000), chapter 6; Daniel Goldhagen, *Hitler's Willing Executioners: Ordinary Germans and the Holocaust* (London, 1996); Ulrich Herbert, *Best: Biographische Studien über Radikalismus, Weltanschauung und Vernunft 1903–1989* (Bonn, 1996); Michael Wildt, *Die Generation des Unbedingten: Das Führungskorps des Reichssicherheitshauptamtes* (Hamburg, 2002); Jürgen Matthäus et al. (eds.), *Ausbildungsziel Judenmord? 'Weltanschauliche Erziehung' von SS, Polizei und Waffen-SS im Rahmen der 'Endlösung'* (Frankfurt a.M., 2003); Klaus-

of consent and consensus, race and self-transformation has continued in more recent work on how German society coped with the air war or how far people felt 'empowered' within the *Volksgemeinschaft* by participating in the new violent rituals of exclusion meted out to Jews and later to Poles.[3] Cumulatively, historical scholarship has moved a long way from Martin Broszat's notion of *Resistenz* as the principal feature of society's relationship to the regime, or even from Detlev Peukert's characterisation of society as 'atomised' by the later stages of the war.[4]

Much of the evidence for the newer historiography comes from the patient and thoughtful sifting of private sources. I do not want to argue against this development – indeed, it is one to which I have also contributed – but it does raise a new set of problems in its turn, around what Peter Fritzsche provocatively called 'Germans into Nazis'. His answer to his own question was to go on and to work on private diaries, showing how even people who thought of themselves in some way or other as non- or anti-Nazi were also not immune to the cultural and political norms of the

---

Michael Mallmann and Gerhard Paul, 'Omniscient, Omnipotent, Omnipresent? Gestapo, Society and Resistance', in David Crew (ed.), *Nazism and German Society, 1933–1945* (London, 1994), 166–96; Robert Gellately, *The Gestapo and German Society: Enforcing Racial Policy, 1933–1945* (Oxford, 1990); Nikolaus Wachsmann, *Hitler's Prisons: Legal Terror in Nazi Germany* (New Haven, CT, 2004); Günther Grau, 'Persecution, "Re-education" or "Eradication" of Male Homosexuals between 1933 and 1945', in Günther Grau (ed.), *Hidden Holocaust? Gay and Lesbian Persecution in Germany, 1933–1945* (London, 1995), 1–7; Saul Friedländer, *Nazi Germany and the Jews: The Years of Persecution, 1933–1939* (London, 1997); Alexandra Przyrembel, *'Rassenschande': Reinheitsmythos und Vernichtungslegitimation im Nationalsozialismus* (Göttingen, 2003); Elizabeth Harvey, *Women and the Nazi East: Agents and Witnesses of Germanization* (New Haven, CT, London, 2003). The term 'racial state' comes from the synthetic overview by Michael Burleigh and Wolfgang Wippermann, *The Racial State: Germany, 1933–1945* (Cambridge, 1991).

[3] See Michael Wildt, *Volksgemeinschaft als Selbstermächtigung: Gewalt gegen Juden in der deutschen Provinz 1919–1939* (Hamburg, 2007); Dietmar Süß, *Death from the Skies: How the British and Germans Survived Bombing in World War II* (Oxford, 2014); Nicole Kramer, *Volksgenossinnen an der Heimatfront: Mobilisierung, Verhalten, Erinnerung* (Göttingen, 2011); Martina Steber and Bernhard Gotto (eds.), *Visions of Community in Nazi Germany: Social Engineering and Private Lives* (Oxford, 2014); Birthe Kundrus and Patricia Szobar, 'Forbidden Company: Romantic Relationships between Germans and Foreigners, 1939 to 1945', *Journal of the History of Sexuality* 11/1–2 (2002), 201–22; Maren Röger, *Kriegsbeziehungen: Intimität, Gewalt und Prostitution im besetzten Polen 1939 bis 1945* (Frankfurt a.M., 2015); Gerwin Strobl, *The Swastika and the Stage: German Theatre and Society, 1933–1945* (Cambridge, 2007); Shelley Baranowski, *Strength through Joy: Consumption and Mass Tourism in the Third Reich* (Cambridge, 2004); Kristin Semmens, *Seeing Hitler's Germany: Tourism in the Third Reich* (Basingstoke, 2005).

[4] See Martin Broszat, 'Resistenz und Widerstand: Eine Zwischenbilanz des Forschungsprojekts', in Martin Broszat, Elke Fröhlich and Atina Grossmann (eds.), *Bayern in der NS-Zeit*, vol. 4 (Munich, 1981), 691–709; Detlev Peukert, *Inside Nazi Germany: Conformity, Opposition and Racism in Everyday Life* (London, 1987), 236–42.

Third Reich.[5] It has proved a very fruitful research strategy. It also cannot fully answer the question which those charged with monitoring the 'public mood' asked themselves at the time: how could they tell the difference between true believers and performative opportunists? To the Nazi leadership, with its belief that the defeat of 1918 was down to a failure of nerve, this question mattered acutely. Partly because they greatly underestimated the burdens which German civilians had put up with in the First World War and overestimated the power of enemy propaganda, the Nazi leaders feared that what Hitler called 'this chicken-hearted nation' would fail the ultimate test of war again.

Within a contemporary historiographic frame, this problem re-emerges around how much resonance we should give to individual voices and subjective experience. Were these opinions 'private' or 'public'? How far should the 'private' still be defined in contrast, or even opposition, to the 'public'? Does the distinction even matter, if private sentiments seemed to reinforce, rather than resist, public ones? What these questions reveal is that how we define and understand the 'public' has only partly kept pace with our growing sophistication in interpreting private sources. Whereas historians like Susanne zur Nieden started drawing our attention in the early 1990s to the ways that public slogans were taken up and echoed in private diaries, their findings have not been played back in reverse. If private opinions were shot through with Nazi propaganda, what does that say about 'public opinion'? Although some historians have started to use the term 'public opinion' tentatively for Nazi Germany, even to talk about a limited 'pluralism' of publishable and tolerated views, this remains an under-theorised area. Indeed, it is one place where the dominant construction still comes from the older historiography. Back in 1970, Marlis Steinert stipulated that historians should avoid using the term 'public opinion' because the Nazis established their dictatorship precisely by destroying the institutions and practices associated with a liberal public sphere. Without such a heuristic space, there could be no free debate in which public opinion could develop. Without an independent civil society, there could be only propaganda on one side and 'popular opinion' on the other.[6]

---

[5] See Nicholas Stargardt, 'Children's Art of the Holocaust', *Past and Present* 161 (1998), 192–235; Nicholas Stargardt, *Witnesses of War: Children's Lives under the Nazis* (London, 2005); Nicholas Stargardt, *The German War: A Nation under Arms, 1939–1945* (London, 2015); Peter Fritzsche, *Germans into Nazis* (Cambridge, MA, 1999); Peter Fritzsche, *Life and Death in the Third Reich* (Cambridge, MA, 2008).

[6] See Marlis Steinert, *Hitlers Krieg und die Deutschen: Stimmung und Haltung der deutschen Bevölkerung im Zweiten Weltkrieg* (Düsseldorf, 1970), 17–48; Ian Kershaw, *Popular Opinion and Political Dissent in the Third Reich: Bavaria, 1933–1945* (Oxford, 1983), 4. Richard Evans, *The Third Reich in Power* (London, 2005) adopts the same approach.

Yet deploying 'popular' instead of 'public' opinion, to encompass all the independent and critical views which were articulated in everyday life, has not established a particularly robust and rigorous construct. What has limited the utility of the notion of 'popular opinion' was that it does not really deal with the question it was designed to side-step. Drawing on the underground reports of the exiled Social Democrats and the monitoring of the 'popular mood' by the secret police, it was clear that people often felt entitled to disagree with the official message.[7] But it was no clearer how 'popular opinion' was formed, spread or articulated in a dictatorship which had crushed 'public opinion'. Was it bound up with pre-Nazi sets of values and mental worlds or was it self-reproducing within the fabric of the Third Reich? And how far did it reach? Was popular opinion always plural rather than singular, limited by the local reach of word of mouth? What happened if critical rumours and views were articulated across the Reich at the same time and gained real force? At what point would such a situation signal a reinvention of 'public opinion', despite – or perhaps even in conjunction with – the best efforts of the regime's propagandists? Does the current emphasis on core Nazi ideas like the *Volksgemeinschaft* take away too much cultural initiative from German society? And how can we test the limits of self-identification?

Self-reflection, a quest for authenticity by cultivating a self-aware moral interiority or *Innerlichkeit*, was itself of course a well-established cultural practice. Indeed, for many educated Germans it furnished an essential measure of their own moral and cultural sophistication. Broszat even famously claimed that such interiority served as a space in which Germans conducted a process of silent self-denazification in the second half of the war. But he did not investigate the moral issues and dilemmas people actually pondered in private during this time.[8] This is what I propose to do here, and I want to argue that even highly critical private moral thinking remained shot through with public legitimations. Conversely, private moral sentiments also coloured public opinion in

---

[7] See *Deutschland-Berichte der Sozialdemokratischen Partei Deutschlands (Sopade) 1934–1940*, 6 vols. (Frankfurt a.M., 1980); Heinz Boberach (ed.), *Meldungen aus dem Reich: Die geheimen Lageberichte des Sicherheitsdienstes der SS 1938–1945*, 17 vols. (Herrsching, 1984), 1–13 (hereafter, *MadR*); Steinert, *Hitlers Krieg und die Deutschen*; Kershaw, *Popular Opinion and Political Dissent*; Ian Kershaw, '*Volksgemeinschaft*: Potential and Limitations of the Concept', in Steber/Gotto (eds.), *Visions of Community in Nazi Germany*, 29–42.

[8] See Martin Broszat, Klaus-Dietmar Henke and Hans Woller, 'Einleitung', in Martin Broszat, Klaus-Dietmar Henke and Hans Woller (eds.), *Von Stalingrad zur Währungsreform: Zur Sozialgeschichte des Umbruchs in Deutschland* (Munich, 1988), XXV–XLIX; Nicholas Stargardt, 'The Troubled Patriot: German *Innerlichkeit* in World War II', *German History*, special issue on 'Ego Documents', 28/3 (2010), 326–42.

ways which the regime found unacceptable but which, in historical hindsight, scarcely make it look less Nazified.

To get at these questions, we need issues which laid bare core Nazi values and forced a wider public to engage with them. In this chapter, I try to show that the opinions uttered in public both followed media prompts and, on important issues, also challenged the propagandists' spin. As Gerwin Strobl has shown, propagandists did not simply pick themes and images to act as transmission belts for their key ideological messages.[9] Rather, like good advertisers, they treated their domestic audience as a sophisticated and plural one, whose existing values and beliefs had to be played upon selectively if any consensus was to be forthcoming. Managing public opinion, in other words, forced propagandists into a dialogue – and that indeed was the use that Goebbels made of the weekly digests of the public 'mood', as he tweaked the message in order to maintain control over several different public conversations. There were two aspects to this process which made dialogue particularly unpredictable and fraught. The first was the character of moral sentiments: which arguments would really convince people and which would merely precipitate critical public discussion. Propagandists could not predict what the response would be. The second difficulty was the unforeseeable character of wartime events, as military crises threatened to lead to communication breakdowns. It is precisely the pathological character of such crises which allow us to probe the underlying logic of the relationships involved. This is a non-linear, episodic form of analysis, but precisely because they were abrupt, unrehearsed and unpredictable, wartime crises had a percussive force which broke through the veneer and revealed many more layers of opinion formation than we would be able to uncover otherwise. These moments of relative loss of regime control offer analytical openings that seemed closed off even to the regime's own observers in more 'ordinary' pre-war times.

If it is core values and moral sentiments that matter here, let us start with the ultimate moral transgression: the murder of the Jews. Long assumed to be a taboo topic in Nazi Germany, this subject brings us first to those diarists who were so agitated by the enormity of genocide that they felt compelled to put pen to paper in order to work out what they thought about it. We need access to both the private and public here, in order to understand what may have been emotionally and morally at stake for the individual participants, and in what way the understandings people displayed in their public conversations created something recognisable as 'public opinion' or even proved enduring enough to be worth

---

[9] See Gerwin Strobl, *The Germanic Isle: Nazi Perceptions of Britain* (Cambridge, 2000).

calling a 'mindset'. I start with private reflection and then turn to conversations in public.

***

Wilm Hosenfeld was a devout Catholic and a veteran of the First World War. He was also a *Volksschullehrer*, from Thalau in Hesse, where he had joined first the SA and then the Nazi Party in order to bring sport and the 'national revolution' to his village in Hesse. During the 1939 invasion of Poland, Wilm Hosenfeld was sent to guard prisoners of war in Pabianice, where soon he witnessed the wave of violence unleashed against local Jews. He confessed that 'I'm outraged by the harsh treatment.' A strange Nazi – who had been horrified by the pogrom against the Jews in November 1938 – he was again deeply disturbed a year later. Instead of dying down once the military campaign was over, German violence increased greatly, as the SS started its campaign to eradicate the Polish elites and educated classes. On 10 November 1939, Hosenfeld wrote home to his wife, 'This is not about reprisals. It looks like a desire to exterminate the intelligentsia following the Russian example.' He was astonished, and had no idea how accurate his guess was. He also felt both powerless to stop it and contaminated with responsibility: 'How gladly I became a soldier, but today I'd like to tear the field-grey uniform into shreds.' Was he to help hold 'the shield behind which these crimes against humanity can occur'?[10]

During this emotional upheaval, Germany's Catholic prelates provided no spiritual guidance for men like Hosenfeld, preferring to remain completely silent about the executions – including those of Polish clerics. Hosenfeld went on serving loyally in occupied Poland. He learned to ride and drew on his teaching skills and love of sport to carve out a niche in the Warsaw garrison. He also continued to judge things according to his own standards, choosing fellow officers with whom he could discuss and strengthen his increasingly critical views of the Nazi Party he had joined in 1935. As soon as the mass deportations to Treblinka started in July 1942, he immediately registered their full import and, on the second day of the deportations, wrote to his wife that the 'ghetto with its half million Jews is to be emptied' on Himmler's orders: 'History has no real parallel. Perhaps, cave men ate each other, but to simply butcher a nation, men, women, children, in the twentieth century, and that it should be us, who are waging a crusade against Bolshevism, that is

---

[10] Wilm Hosenfeld, *'Ich versuche jeden zu retten': Das Leben eines deutschen Offiziers in Briefen und Tagebüchern*, ed. by Thomas Vogel (Munich, 2004), 250: Wilm to Anne Marie Hosenfeld, 10 Nov. 1939, 286.

such a dreadful blood-guilt as to make you want to sink into the ground with shame.'[11] Each detail he learned over the following weeks about the death camp called 'Triplinka' deepened that sense of shame. Finally, he attended a private dinner on 25 September, four days after the last train to Treblinka. One of the other guests was an SS major, Dr Gerhard Stabenow, who 'talks of the Jews', Hosenfeld noted in his diary, 'as if they were ants or other pests. Of the "resettlement", that is of the mass murder, as of the eradication of bedbugs when disinfecting a house.' Hosenfeld was horrified and revolted, asking himself afterwards what he was doing eating at the 'richly laden table of the wealthy, while all around it the greatest poverty and the soldiers go hungry. Why is one silent and does not protest?'[12]

The unanswered question of personal responsibility which had gnawed at Wilm Hosenfeld since the first autumn of the war continued to prompt him. In 1943, following the final destruction of the Warsaw ghetto, he sheltered two Jews in the Wehrmacht sports school which he ran and created a cover identity for one of them. For Wilm Hosenfeld – First World War veteran, Catholic schoolteacher, sometime storm trooper and member of the Nazi Party – helping to hide two Jews in Warsaw was a natural response, the kind of moral action his sense of powerlessness and shame finally demanded. But it did not compete with his own patriotism, let alone make Hosenfeld wish for the only outcome which might secure the hidden Jews' survival, namely Germany's defeat. After loyally participating in crushing the Warsaw uprising in the summer of 1944, he helped to hide another Polish Jew. During the last months of occupation, Hosenfeld regularly brought food to the pianist Władysław Szpilman, who hid in the attic of a house which served as a command post for the German garrison. Once again, Wilm Hosenfeld did not waver in his sense of overriding military duty, and rejoiced at moving back to a position of active service and taking command of an infantry company.[13]

It is worth pausing here over Hosenfeld's twin roles and allegiances. His personal courage in deciding finally to act to save at least three Jews from

---

[11] Hosenfeld, 'Ich versuche jeden zu retten', 628: 23 July 1942.

[12] Hosenfeld, 'Ich versuche jeden zu retten', 657–8: diary, 26 Sept. 1942. SS-Untersturmbannführer Gerhard Stabenow, born 26 Jan. 1906 in Halle, had a PhD and a doctorate in law, and was still alive to be interviewed in 1950: *Der Spiegel*, 31 Aug. 1950, 35/ 1950. He wrote two short books: *Ostreparationen: Inaugural-Dissertation* (Halle a.d.S., 1934); *Die Olympiaberichterstattung in der Deutschen Presse unter besonderer Berücksichtigung der Provinzpresse und die Entwicklung der Sportberichterstattung in der Provinzpresse 1936 bis 1940* (Halle a.d.S., 1941).

[13] See Hosenfeld, 'Ich versuche jeden zu retten', 849 and 856–73: 20 Sept., 5 Oct.–17 Nov. 1944; Władysław Szpilman, *The Pianist: The Extraordinary Story of One Man's Survival in Warsaw, 1939–45* (London, 1999), 177ff.

Treblinka lends gravity and conviction to his earlier admissions of outrage and shame. In autumn 1939, at the start of the German occupation, Hosenfeld had made a point of walking or riding through the Jewish district, scattering sweets for the children: however little the gesture could undo what was being done, he needed to do something, to show that there was a different kind of German, even if the principal witness remained himself. The very candour with which Hosenfeld wrote home to his wife about feeling that he was being made into an accomplice to atrocity in November 1939 – 'the shield behind which these crimes against humanity can occur' – already suggested the direction he would take later on. Taking the plunge and facing his moral dilemma head on did lead to meaningful individual action.

In this sense, Wilm Hosenfeld was both a very unusual German officer and exemplified what historians hoped to find when they first elevated the private as a moral refuge and the foundation of a spiritual resistance to Nazism. But this was only one aspect of Hosenfeld's commitment. During the great deportation of the Warsaw Jews, Hosenfeld's own activities had focused on the sports school he ran for the Wehrmacht. He organised a week-long sports competition, which drew in 1,200 competitors and an audience of thousands – a resounding success for military morale, after which he was allowed to take his wife on a week of leave in Berlin.[14] Having unburdened himself in several letters to his son Helmut about the deportations from Warsaw, Hosenfeld told him how the resilience of German troops from North Africa to the Arctic 'make one proud to belong to this nation. One may disagree', he added – probably referring to the anti-Jewish action – 'with this or that, but the inner bond to the essence of one's own people lets one overlook the flaws'.[15] Helmut was now serving on the Eastern Front, but Hosenfeld's sense of patriotic duty went far beyond that of a loving father. Despite his increasing horror at Nazi genocide, already by 7 August 1942, just two weeks into the deportations from Warsaw, he was squaring his own conscience as he told himself that the 'National Socialist idea [...] is only tolerated, because it is currently the lesser of two evils. The greater is to lose the war.' Rather than indulging in anti-Nazi activity which – if successful – could only lead to national defeat, Hosenfeld seems to have been intent on fulfilling all the public demands made on him with real enthusiasm and commitment. His private moral gestures helped him to redeem himself,

---

[14] See Hosenfeld, *'Ich versuche jeden zu retten'*, 637–8, 645–7, 650–1 and 656–7 and 25–27 Aug., 1 and 7 Sept. 1942.
[15] Ibidem, 659, 637, 641–3 and 660: diary, 1 Oct. and 7 and 18 Aug. 1942.

but they did not compete with his patriotic duty: rather, they showed that it was possible to perform a better, purer national service.[16]

As far as I can tell, few letter writers and diarists expressed similar moral anguish on the page, and even fewer felt impelled to act in the same way as Wilm Hosenfeld. It is here that it helps us to listen for silence. Lapsing into silence and interrupting themselves before they had finished, with thoughts broken off in mid-articulation, alert us to different ways in which Germans expressed and also censored their sense of moral affront and private quandary. What I mean by this is illustrated in the correspondence of two young high school graduates from the Münsterland. Both were fascinated by art and wanted to find aesthetic models for expressing their strongly Catholic and romantic yearnings. Imbued with Ernst Jünger's post-1918 heroic prose about the 'war as inner experience', Hans Albring had written lengthy word pictures from France revelling in the sharp, 'expressionist' contrasts of war. One moment they were baking potato cakes and drinking old Bordeaux; the next they passed a field full of rotting animals lying on their backs, 'legs in the air like wooden rocking horses' – and 'everywhere [there are] crosses with steel helmets on fresh graves'.[17] After the campaign, Albring spent his free time admiring the frescoes in the ancient baptistry in Poitiers, grieving at the loss of so many stained glass windows and haunting a bookshop where he spent his money on prints of the old masters.

At the start of the Soviet campaign, he wrote about the raw 'natural world' he could see from his signals van: 'pine forests stretching into the distance and few huts. Nature'. His old school friend Eugen Altrogge was enjoying a prized posting to Paris, and sympathised with Albring's bleak account of the barbaric land where 'Europe ends' and the villages where 'Hebraic German' was spoken. Like Hosenfeld in Warsaw, the two young Catholics were incensed by radical Nazis' attacks on the Church at home in the summer of 1941. Albring also fumed against Bolshevik atheism, the destruction of the Catholic churches and vandalisation of the Orthodox ones – uniting both his moral and aesthetic judgements in one telling phrase: 'Käthe Kollwitz's spiritual homeland'.[18] The two young Catholics were searching for a kind of deep, religious purity, which they believed modern commercial civilisation had destroyed in the West. As he encountered the faith of the Ukrainian peasants, he thought he had found it. In a wonderfully self-contradictory gesture, Albring turned himself into

---

[16] See ibidem, '*Ich versuche jeden zu retten*', 637: diary, 7 Aug. 1942.
[17] Museum für Kommunikation Berlin, Feldpostarchiv (MfK-FA), 3.2002.0211, Albring to Altrogge, [n.d.] May 1940.
[18] MfK-FA, 3.2002.0211, Albring to Altrogge, 8 July 1941.

a representative of the very Western 'commerce' for which he blamed the demise of such primitive faith in the West, and began buying up icons.

In August 1941, Hans Albring found himself witnessing the execution of a group of suspected partisans. They were led to a ditch near a small watermill one at a time, shot in the back of the neck and booted into the ditch. Albring stood close enough to see the exit wound in the head and to see the Russian in the ditch who had to shovel calcium chloride over the corpses. Having described all this to Eugen in detail, he clearly felt the need to conclude with a justificatory gloss. 'It is a hard but just end,' he explained to Eugen, 'if you know what led up to it and however much one may dispute the method, which bears the sign of the times', adding this last phrase in Latin with all the distancing effect of an educated Westerner abroad in a barbarous land. Albring's fascination, his desire 'to see everything, in order to know everything and to reckon with everything', as he put it, centred not on the war, the victims or the logic of reprisal, but on the ahistorical mystery of death itself. 'What is that which we hang onto and which is snuffed out and gone in a fraction of a second?' he asked. It was the same question which George Orwell recollected asking himself when he witnessed a prison hanging in Burma while serving in the colonial police. And it was a question that only those not menaced by the deed could pose.[19]

Reflecting on the metaphysical dimensions of his war experience was something that Albring had expected from the start. Whereas war in France had been exhilarating and stimulating, full of vivid and contrasting scenes, perfect for the visual imagery of a would-be young artist, the murderousness of the war in the Soviet Union was overwhelming. As he tried to describe to his friend Altrogge what he witnessed, he clawed at the religious metaphors and artistic role models he knew, which would allow him to continue their joint project of drawing out the aesthetic and moral significance of their war experience:

Just to be alive still seems like a gift of God and I don't just want to give thanks with words if we survive this man- and life-eating ogre Russia with all our limbs and senses intact. The sight of bestially mutilated corpses which wear the same uniform as you cuts into your whole mental map of where you are. But also the staring faces of the hanged. The pits full of the shot – pictures darker than the darkest of Goya – oh, Eugen, you can never forget it, even if you want to. And in such proximity it takes away our sense of being carefree and [...] gives us something instead of the harried creature, of the pitiful, impoverished man. Our path here is strewn with some kind of self-portraits, whether they have lost their lives or are still

---

[19] See MfK-FA, 3.2002.0211, Albring to Altrogge, 30–31 Aug. 1941; George Orwell, 'A Hanging', *The Adelphi* (Aug. 1931), in www.george-orwell.org/A_Hanging/0.html [accessed 16 Aug. 2017].

living, you find yourself in them. It is just like those who sit by the path in the Gospels, plagued by this and that, until the Saviour comes. I have not yet found a poem which encompasses what is happening here – much must remain forever unsaid, saved up for the hour when it is handed down to people without any mediation.[20]

Nothing had prepared him for this. The 'bestially mutilated corpses' of German soldiers, the 'staring faces of the hanged' and the 'pits full of the shot' – Russians and Jews – interspersed with a cascade of metaphors – the land as an 'ogre', man a 'harried creature' sitting by the path instead of questing resolutely onwards, praying to God for deliverance, already turning them into images 'darker than the darkest of Goya' and hoping they might somehow be communicated 'to people without any mediation', before admitting defeat and condemning what he had just written to remaining 'unsaid'. Albring's words skidded across the page, unable to find their billet, unable to create an imaginary structure which could hold what he had seen. They showed how far he had strayed from the programme of romantic modernism with which he had gone to war, and how impossible it was becoming to render a full account of the 'war as inner experience'. By January 1942, Albring referred to the Jews as 'these people who are doomed to die'. He was close enough to the rear of Army Group Centre to have had other opportunities to witness the mass executions being conducted there, but he mentioned just one further incident to Eugen, this time after being sent to fill a gap in the front line. On 21 March, he noted that '[t]he corpses which used to be thrown without order onto a heap have been sorted out as well as possible and lime has already been scattered over the half a thousand Jews who were shot'. He added uneasily, '[t]his isn't the place to go into detail about what happened here'. Hans Albring did not write about the subject again.[21]

Albring's path to this half-apologetic but, as it turned out, enduring act of self-censorship took more than nine months of campaigning, including the first terrible winter in which Army Group Centre was nearly destroyed. His emotional and moral adaptation to the new murderous norms of Army Group Centre was not unusual. It was part of a well-chronicled and general transformation of the military culture around him.[22] What was less common was that Albring persisted so long and against his own profound unease in his idealist aestheticism, his mission

[20] MfK-FA, 3.2002.0211, Albring to Altrogge, 28 Oct. 1941.
[21] MfK-FA, 3.2002.0211, Albring to Altrogge, 1 Jan. and 21 March 1942.
[22] See Christoph Rass, *'Menschenmaterial': Deutsche Soldaten an der Ostfront. Innenansichten einer Infanteriedivision 1939–1945* (Paderborn, 2003); Felix Römer, *Der Kommissarbefehl: Wehrmacht und NS-Verbrechen an der Ostfront 1941/42* (Paderborn, 2008);

to chart the war as a spiritual experience. We cannot know for sure what made Albring turn away from describing what he witnessed and felt. But there is a suggestive pattern here which reveals something striking and problematic about the capacity – and limits – of private moral reflection. We are dealing here with a kind of silence that is neither entirely involuntary, like someone in the grip of extreme trauma, nor is it tacit, like the highly coded way in which German couples wrote to each other about sex.[23] Rather, this lapse into silence seems like a kind of moral and emotional self-interruption, a breaking off in mid-sentence and mid-thought. It is as if the implications of the half-shaped thoughts which stretched ahead were so alarming that instead of Albring's setting them down on the page, his mind went into reverse and he started to censure and to admonish himself, without actually erasing what he had already written.

The third case of private writing which I want to explore about the murder of the Jews also involves a lapse into silence, but of a different and temporary kind. This lapse was not lasting. Lieselotte G. was fifteen and living with her parents in Berlin when her mother told her about the murder of the Jews. She did not immediately commit it to her personal diary, but, after grappling with this knowledge, on 31 August 1943, she did: 'Mummy told me recently most of the Jews have been killed in camps, but I can't believe it.' Checking her own sense of shaken moral proportion, she continued: 'It's good that they're gone from Germany, but actually to murder them!'[24] What was it that she could not believe? Was the fact too implausible or the transgression too enormous? Or did this moment of disbelief merely register the initial sense of shock, before it gave way to acceptance of the fact? We cannot know for sure because this was all she wrote – for now.

After nearly twenty months of silence, Lieselotte suddenly broached the subject again, on 12 April 1945, in a diary entry which fleetingly denounced 'the whole Nazi brood, these war criminals and Jew-murderers'. Although her parents were generally hostile to the regime, Lieselotte was not reacting to Allied revelations about the death camps – Majdanek had been liberated the previous July, Auschwitz in January. Rather, she had just heard the news on German radio announcing that the garrison commander of Königsberg had been sentenced to death in

---

Christian Hartmann, *Wehrmacht im Ostkrieg: Front und militärisches Hinterland 1941–42* (Munich, 2009).

[23] See Latzel, *Deutsche Soldaten*, 332 and 337–9; Ingrid Bauer and Christa Hämmerle, *Liebe schreiben: Paarkorrespondenzen im Kontext des 19. und 20. Jahrhunderts* (Göttingen, 2017).

[24] Lieselotte G., in Hammer and zur Nieden, *'Sehr selten habe ich geweint'*, 278–9: 31 Aug. 1943.

absentia for surrendering to the Red Army after a siege lasting months. She was appalled by this staggering verdict:

> His family is to be arrested. Is that not the rule of terror? Oh, how can the German people and our *Wehrmacht* bear it. Because the brave officer did not want to sacrifice all his soldiers, they hang him and his whole family who are sitting at home ignorant of it all. To hang a German, a Prussian officer![25]

Lieselotte was so outraged that for the first time she swore, cursing 'the whole Nazi brood, these war criminals and Jew-murderers, who now drag the honour of the German officer into the dirt'. She may have been unable to fully comprehend the news that Jews were being murdered in the camps back in August 1943, but by some process this information had become a certainty in the almost two years of diary silence since then. The knowledge had lain dormant, ready – in her current mood of outrage and despair – to burst out again.

Although Lieselotte came from an old Social Democratic family, it was not her parents' anti-Nazism but her own Prussian patriotism which goaded her into this passing admission of what she had repressed. And it was the same patriotic commitment which had served as a counterweight to Lieselotte's shock when she had first articulated what she knew in the summer of 1943. Through the bombing of Berlin, Lieselotte had drawn comfort by reciting the prayer from her confirmation during the air raids and, above all, by modelling her demeanour on how she imagined her German teacher, Frau L., would compose herself. Although she harboured far stronger reservations about the Führer than one might have expected of a teenage member of the BDM, she listened as eagerly as the rest of the home front to Hitler's broadcast speech on 8 November 1943. Echoing Hitler's own obsessive reiteration that the capitulation of 1918 must never be repeated, Lieselotte took private refuge in apocalyptic public sentiments: 'And even if all should go down in defeat, there will not be another 1918. Adolf Hitler, I believe in you and the German victory.' Above all she was buoyed up by the promise of turning the tide: 'Hitler has given me faith in victory again, he has spoken of a landing in England and of retaliation for the terror bombing.'[26]

By January 1944, the continued air raids had become so frightening that Lieselotte had had a serious conversation with her father about the future. He had remained true to his pre-1933 Social Democratic convictions and tried to convince her that Germany had lost the war and the best to be hoped for would be an American occupation. She was not ready for such a message and chose a different role model. Frau L., her German

---

[25] Ibidem, 309: 12 Apr. 1945.   [26] Ibidem, 282: 8 Nov. 1943.

teacher at school, married to a Prussian officer, had become her model of the perfect German woman as well as the focus of a full-scale teenage crush. Pushing aside the sobering conversation with her father, Lieselotte took refuge in myth: '"If victory is no longer to be had, then there is still honour," shouted Teja the Ostrogoth, still fighting as he fell. Can one not shout to Germany's enemies: "you can murder me, but you cannot kill me, for I am eternal!"'[27]

In the relative quiet of evacuation in Saxony, these choices had receded again, only to re-emerge in much starker and more realistic form when she returned to Berlin in April 1945. With the Red Army poised to cross the Oder fifty miles away, Lieselotte could see that further fighting served no rational or strategic purpose. As she looked at the street barricades being erected in Berlin, she jotted down the joke going the rounds: 'The Russian tanks will stand at the entry of Berlin for 2 hours splitting their sides with laughter, then drive over them in 2 minutes.' Yet even now in her new, resolutely anti-Nazi mood, she could not resist the emotional pull of the heroic death, of a final resistance whose futility and certain failure only increased its grandeur in her eyes. Confronting the prospect that her brother Bertel would soon be fighting with the *Volkssturm* in the battle for Berlin, she wrote, 'I'm terribly afraid for Bertel, because it would be so dreadful for mummy. I myself,' she confessed candidly, 'would be ready to sacrifice him, Frau L. sacrificed her Life's joy after all'. Would Bertel's death make her equal with her teacher, now a war widow? Two days later, on 19 April, seventeen-year-old Lieselotte stood and watched the boys of the *Volkssturm*, most of them younger than herself, cycling through Friedrichshagen to defend Münchehofe. Her feelings were still mixed. 'I am so proud of our boys, who are now throwing themselves against the tanks when the order comes,' she wrote the next day, adding, without a trace of personal responsibility for supporting their patriotic act, 'but they are being hounded to their deaths'. It would take defeat and occupation before she decided that their sacrifice had been in vain.[28]

This pattern of admission, repression and readmission of a greater knowledge which had silently grown on other information in the interim is not a pattern unique to one teenage girl. The schoolmaster and commandant of a prisoner of war camp August Töpperwien traced an identical trajectory. He first faced the enormity of the genocide of the Jews in November 1943, and – after four days of private reflection – explicitly acknowledged to himself that '[w]e are not just destroying the Jews fighting against us, we literally want to exterminate this people as such!' Having set down this momentous admission on the page, Töpperwien

[27] Ibidem, 289–90: 2 Jan. 1944.   [28] Ibidem, 307–10: 12 and 17 Apr. 1945.

promptly dropped the subject again. Like Lieselotte, he did not pick it up again until spring 1945. Like her, he did so at a time when he was assailed by doubt, offsetting German and Allied atrocities against each other, in order to dissolve German transgression in a more universal guilt:

> A humanity wages war like this which has become godless. The Russian barbarities in the German east – the terror attacks of the Anglo-Americans – our struggle against the Jews (sterilisation of healthy women, shootings of infants to old women, gassing of Jewish transport trains)![29]

But like his Catholic contemporary Wilm Hosenfeld in Warsaw or the young Lieselotte G. in Berlin, the Protestant August Töpperwien did not draw defeatist conclusions from this consciousness. Like Lieselotte in Berlin, Töpperwien's return to the murder of the Jews came at a time when he chose to face the fact that Germany could not win the war any longer. For her, the test was when the Red Army would cross the Oder. For him, it was the British and American crossing of the Rhine. Yet even this did not uproot his commitment to patriotic sacrifice. Three weeks later, on 15 April 1945, he was still consoling himself with the thought that 'the clash of arms can only lead to *defeat with honour*.' If this final residue of Protestant nationalism persuaded Lieselotte that it would be worth sacrificing her brother Bertel, for August Töpperwien, it was his son Karl-Christoph who was being readied with his *Volkssturm* unit to face American tanks near Hannover. For Karl-Christoph, his 'baptism by fire' as he turned eighteen promised to be a double coming of age, and the last line of the patriotic poem his father sent him for his birthday vowed, '[w]e are storming heaven's gate'.[30]

***

If we only had such diaries and personal letters to go on, it would be tempting to assume that the moral battle being fought out on the page was between private knowledge of the murder of the Jews pitted against the public, patriotic virtues of self-sacrifice. In many respects, this would not be wrong. Writing did offer a safe space to start to articulate individual moral shock about supporting a war of mass murder. But we are already a long way from the private sphere as some kind of moral refuge from Nazism. For the question which preoccupied all four of these writers was

---

[29] Hubert Orłowski and Thomas F. Schneider (eds.), *'Erschießen will ich nicht!' Als Offizier und Christ im Totalen Krieg. Das Kriegstagebuch des Dr. August Töpperwien 3. September 1939 bis 6. Mai 1945* (Düsseldorf, 2006), 247 and 338: 18 Nov. 1943 and 17 March 1945; Stargardt, 'The Troubled Patriot'.

[30] Orłowski/Schneider (eds.), *'Erschießen will ich nicht!'*, 342, 347 and 344–5: 26 March, 15 and 10 April 1945.

in fact a public one. It was the question of legitimacy: how to square morally repugnant means with a laudable end; the murder of the Jews with the goal of what they saw as Germany's national defence. And commitment to German patriotism did serve to contain how far even Wilm Hosenfeld – the only one of our writers to move from words to actions – was prepared to go in thinking through the moral dilemma. As he put it so succinctly, '[t]he greater [evil] is to lose the war'. But even this way of formulating the problem does not do justice to the intersection of public and private here.

In fact, by the summer of 1943, speaking about the murder of the Jews was not a clandestine event. In the weeks immediately preceding and following Lieselotte's diary entry of 31 August 1943, Germany was full of conversations in public places about the murder of the Jews. The conversations had a consistent theme and pattern, as people equated the 'treatment of the Jews', as the Security Police euphemistically paraphrased it, with the Allied 'terror' bombing of German civilians. In Hamburg, it was noted 'that the common people, the middle classes, and the rest of the population make repeated remarks in intimate circles and also in larger gatherings that the attacks count as retaliation for our treatment of the Jews'. In Schweinfurt in Bavaria, people were saying exactly the same thing: 'The terror attacks are a consequence of the measures carried out against the Jews.' After the USAAF's second raid on the town in October 1943, people complained openly 'that if we hadn't treated the Jews so badly, we wouldn't have to suffer so from the terror attacks'. Over the summer and autumn of 1943, as the 'area bombing' raids continued and evacuees from all over northern and western Germany brought their tales to the south and east of the country, similar sentiments were amplified across the Reich. Such views were reported to the authorities in Berlin, not just from all major German cities, but even from quiet Franconian backwaters like Rothenburg ob der Tauber. By this point, references to the bombing and German 'measures taken against the Jews' had spread to parts of the Reich which had little or no direct experience of the bombing itself.[31]

Comparing what had been done to the Jews with the Allied air attacks seems to have been a conversation which was so widespread and compelling because it was driven by a sense of having been engulfed by a critical

---

[31] See Otto Dov Kulka and Eberhard Jäckel (eds.), *Die Juden in den geheimen NS-Stimmungsberichten, 1933–1945* (Düsseldorf, 2004), 3693, SD Außenstelle Schweinfurt, n. d. [1944], and 3661, NSDAP Kreisschulungsamt Rothenburg ob der Tauber, 22 Oct. 1943; Nicholas Stargardt, 'Speaking in Public about the Murder of the Jews: What Did the Holocaust Mean to the Germans?', in Christian Wiese and Paul Betts (eds.), *Years of Persecution, Years of Extermination: Saul Friedländer and the Future of Holocaust Studies* (London, 2010), 133–55.

crisis. The need to talk openly arose spontaneously under the impact of something so momentous and frightening that it escalated the air war to a whole new level of intensity and called all prior expectations into question. In a series of air raids from 25 July to 2 August, Germany's second largest city, Hamburg, was engulfed in a firestorm of unprecedented proportions. Half the city was destroyed and 34,000 people were killed. The 800,000 people who fled or were evacuated brought stories of the devastation wherever they went. On the first day of the raids, Mussolini was toppled from power in Italy and German civilians quickly drew the parallel: if this could happen after governing for twenty years, then 'National Socialism could be got rid of even more quickly after a ten-year rule'. According to the weekly confidential reports on 'popular sentiment' compiled by the SD, hope was growing that a military dictatorship along the lines of the one just installed in Italy offered Germany 'the best', or possibly even 'the last', way of reaching a 'separate peace' with the Western Allies.[32]

Such open and widespread talk of regime change was unprecedented in Nazi Germany, and the crisis rocked the dictatorship. On 6 August, Goebbels confessed that 'the air war is a sword of Damocles hanging over our heads' and that since the raids on Hamburg, 'a large part of the Continent is gripped by a panic-struck terror of the English air force'. Himmler instructed the police not to clamp down on public dissent until the credibility of the regime had been restored. Only after instituting a programme of mass evacuations and occupying most of Italy in early September did the regime dare to carry out selective and exemplary repression for public expressions of 'defeatism'.[33]

What makes this short-lived crisis so interesting is the range of common-sense assumptions and moral sentiments which people revealed as they struggled to make sense of their own dire predicament. If this was hardly an 'ideal speech situation', this eruption of hostile public opinion nonetheless defied official control. The massive scale of destruction visited on Hamburg created a pervasive and acute sense of vulnerability, which also sparked public self-questioning about how culpable Germans had also made themselves. This was a convulsive process, a desperate need to rethink, as existing expectations about the war were shattered. But it did not create a *tabula rasa*: the sense people constructed both closely followed and, crucially, inverted propaganda. From the regime's

---

[32] See Malte Thießen, *Eingebrannt ins Gedächtnis: Hamburgs Gedenken an Luftkrieg und Kriegsende 1943 bis 2005* (Munich, 2007), 46–51; *MadR*, 5560–9, 5573–4 and 5620–1: 2, 5 and 16 Aug. 1943.

[33] See Elke Fröhlich (ed.), *Die Tagebücher von Joseph Goebbels, Teil II: Diktate 1941–1945*, vol. 9 (Munich 1993), 226, 6 Aug. 1943; Stargardt, *The German War*, 370–80.

point of view, regret for what had been done to the Jews and the – however impossible – wish to reverse the mass deportations and murder of 1941–2 were infuriating. They threatened exactly the kind of 'defeatism' which the Nazi regime, with its belief that the First World War had been lost because of a civilian loss of nerve, had feared from the beginning. But the regime was still uncertain about how to manage public discussion. Newspapers carried editorials to steer the conversations back towards approved conclusions, arguing that anyone who believed that 'if National Socialist Germany had not solved the Jewish Question so radically, international World Jewry would not be fighting us today' was a 'senile fool'.[34] But this was a risky tactic, which only served to confirm to a wide readership how widespread such conversations and criticism in fact were. Such schoolmasterly chiding – and its failure – also demonstrates that in Germany propaganda did not work along such pedagogic lines.

The problem for the Nazi regime was that the wave of public criticism drew on themes put in the public domain by the propagandists themselves. Whereas the mass deportations from Germany, occupied western Europe and Poland of 1942 had been accompanied by media silence, during the late spring and summer of 1943, this taboo was broken by the propagandists themselves. Goebbels set the tone in *Das Reich* which reiterated the Führer's 'prophesy' about the Jews and confirmed that his threat of extermination was being enacted:

[I]f World Jewry succeeded in provoking a Second World War, it would lead not to the destruction of Aryan humanity but to the extinction of the Jewish race. This process is of a world historic significance and, given that it will probably entail unavoidable consequences, it also takes time. But it can no longer be halted.

Goebbels insisted that this was a reason of state, not a matter of '*Ressentiment*' or 'naïve plans of revenge', but of a 'world problem of the first rank'. When the Jews, Goebbels concluded, 'laid their plan against the German people for their complete destruction, they signed their own death sentence. And here too world history will be a world court.'[35]

The traditionally conservative Berlin daily, the *Deutsche Allgemeine Zeitung*, carried an editorial on 29 May reminding its readers that 'we have carried out our antisemitic campaign systematically'. Within the week, this was followed up by a report from an SS unit serving in the

---

[34] *Der Führer*, 3 Sept. 1943; Peter Longerich, *'Davon haben wir nichts gewusst!' Die Deutschen und die Judenverfolgung 1933–1945* (Berlin, 2006), 292–6; David Bankier, *The Germans and the Final Solution: Public Opinion under Nazism* (Oxford, 1992), 149–51.

[35] Goebbels, *Das Reich*, 9 May 1943; Longerich, *'Davon haben wir nichts gewusst!'*, 267–81 and 271–2.

east, which explained that now was 'not yet the time to open the reports which cover the operations of the Security Police and the SD. Much will certainly remain unsaid, since it is not always advisable to reveal one's strategy.' This tactic of ostentatiously omitting details in order to remind readers of what they already knew privately continued. In May and June 1943, newspapers drip fed allusions to what their readers knew about how the 'Jewish problem had been solved' in discussions of kindred topics, such as the incompleteness of Slovak measures against their Jewish population or the need to tackle the 'gypsy question' in south-eastern Europe.[36]

This was a new and risky public relations tactic on the regime's part. In March 1943, in response to the defeat at Stalingrad and the start of the mass bombing of the Ruhr, Goebbels had hoped, as he explained to Göring, to help to stiffen German resolve to fight the war to the finish by letting people know what had been done to the Jews.[37] These themes were openly discussed in part because they had been sanctioned and encouraged by the media in the preceding four months, with the Allied bombing of German cities and the mass grave of Polish officers shot by the NKVD recently unearthed in the Katyn forest serving as visceral portents of what 'the Jews' had in store for the German population as a whole. But legitimating open public reflection on the kind of war that Germany itself was fighting did not guarantee what conclusions people would draw. The dialogic character of this relationship became clear in a minor way in May. Goebbels was surprised to discover that calling the RAF's 'dam-buster' raids 'Jewish terror bombing' prompted much criticism even in the Ruhr itself, where more than 1,000 people had been killed as a result of the raids. 'The population is of the opinion,' the *Gauleiter* reported back to Berlin in late May, 'that of course dams, locks and installations count as important military targets.' Overall, people were saying that 'the destruction of the dams is an extraordinary success of the English and the falsification of a legitimate attack on an important military target into a pure terror attack is not understood'.[38]

Goebbels could not simply shift meanings and metaphors as he pleased. In popular parlance, the power and meaning of 'terror bombing' and its attribution to the annihilatory aims of the 'Jewish lobby' in

---

[36] See Longerich, *'Davon haben wir nichts gewusst!'*, 278–80.
[37] See Fröhlich (ed.), *Die Tagebücher von Joseph Goebbels*, vol. II/7 (Munich, 1993), 454, 2 March 1943; Longerich, *'Davon haben wir nichts gewusst!'*, 263–7.
[38] Fröhlich (ed.), *Die Tagebücher von Joseph Goebbels*, vol. II/8 (Munich, 1993), 337: 21 May 1943; *MadR*, 5277, 5285 and 5290: 23 and 30 May 1943; Kulka/Jäckel (eds.), *Die Juden in den geheimen NS-Stimmungsberichten*, 3595, NSDAP Parteikanzlei II B 4, Bericht Munich, 23–29 May 1943.

London and Washington were circumscribed and could only refer to the indiscriminate bombing of civilians. It was the very illegitimacy of this escalation in warfare which made Goebbels' introduction into the media of the parallel logic of a Jewish and a German war of annihilation both plausible and, as he would find out a few months later, morally unstable. By then, much of the public discussion drew all the wrong conclusions from the regime's point of view. And yet, by attributing the terror bombing to the annihilatory aims of the Jewish lobby in Washington and London, people were turning Nazi propaganda into the building blocks of their own common sense. Critical, humanitarian and 'defeatist' sentiments – all of which the regime found profoundly threatening – played as important a part in creating this view of the war as one of mutual annihilation. In the immediate context of the Hamburg firestorm, this was an apocalyptic perspective. But it also established axioms about the air war which did not disappear once the political crisis after Hamburg died away, or indeed even with the final defeat of the Nazi dictatorship. To cite one example among many, in June 1945, a Catholic priest in Münster told Allied investigators how many people believed that their wartime bombing represented 'the revenge of world Jewry'.[39]

The media opened up and pushed topics to the fore. Media reports presented an associative underlying explanatory framework, but the regime could still neither predict nor always shape what sense people constructed out of them. In other words, however successful the media had been in lodging fundamental building blocks in the public mind – the Jewish conspiracy, bombing as annihilatory and 'Jewish' – that success was constrained by its own logic. Far from establishing a 'totalitarian' monopoly over meaning, the regime found that its very success in having key ideas accepted as common-sense axioms also meant losing control over how people deployed them. They appeared in public discussion episodically thereafter, sometimes in response to Goebbels turning up the volume of antisemitic propaganda in the media, sometimes sparked by events: herding Budapest's Jews into a ghetto was greeted in May 1944 as erecting a human shield against air attack; the American occupation of Aachen five months later prompted many people to say that they expected to be collectively punished for what had been done to the Jews, a pattern repeated more widely in May 1945.[40]

Conversely, the very importance of writing in private about moral quandaries shows that the space which was being created here was not 'outside' Nazi Germany at all. The problems, dilemmas and the terms in

[39] Süß, *Death from the Skies*, 292–3; Stargardt, *The German War*, 'Epilogue'.
[40] See Stargardt, *The German War*, 417 and 546.

which they were formulated were common to that society. However critical they may occasionally have been of the regime itself, they were also part of a social process of self-transformation, not so dissimilar to the personal one which the young soldier Hans Albring charted in his letters to his friend. Part of what made the private sphere a simultaneously fertile and constrained space for moral self-reflection in Nazi Germany was precisely because of this 'bleed through' between the public and the private. If we are to understand the often self-limiting range of private moral reflections, we need to grasp how much the moral demands of the Third Reich were sustained by cultural values – especially when it came to wartime patriotism – which were older than the regime and which became increasingly deeply contaminated by the most extreme characteristic of Nazism, namely the genocidal war Germans were waging.

Although the triggers for public discussion and private reflection differed, both shared the same episodic quality. If the difficulties of private reflection cast any light on the pattern of long silences in between, it is to suggest that knowledge only grew in the intervals between Lieselotte G.'s and August Töpperwien's diary entries. In their cases, the brake on reflection concerned their inability to assimilate genocide into their panoply of idealist, patriotic, self-sacrificial moral sentiments. This moral difficulty may also help to account for the fact that the public discussion of the murder of the Jews so often was circumscribed by an apparently pragmatic, utilitarian calculus of escalation and the threat of mutual destruction. It was both easier and more imperative to discuss it this way. If only minorities really embraced the justification and rationale offered for the annihilation of the Jews by the Nazi regime, the very flow of ideas and information through German society forced private and public discussions to assimilate the accomplished fact of genocide into their prognoses of the future course of the war. This also made it impossible to disown.

5 (Re-)Inventing the Private under National Socialism

Maiken Umbach

Introduction

The interest in the private identities of 'ordinary' Germans living through the Nazi regime began under the regime itself: it was, this chapter suggests, an important reason for the production of the kind of sources under discussion here. Certainly, since then, the rise of *Alltagsgeschichte*, the history of everyday life, from the 1970s,[1] critiques of the older interpretative model of 'totalitarianism' that gave rise to more polycentric approaches to Nazi rule,[2] new methods cultivated under the 'cultural turn'[3] and, last but not least, a particular boom in 'perpetrator studies' in the 1990s and 2000s,[4] have all contributed to a richer and more nuanced scholarship on the role of private identities and individual subjectivities in both supporting and resisting key tenets of Nazi policy and ideology. Most of these studies rely, at least in part, on ego-documents, in other words, contemporaneous sources in which individuals reported on their

---

[1] For a debate on the conceptual gains made by *Alltagsgeschichte*, as well as its limitations, for understanding Nazi Germany, see the forum 'Everyday Life in Nazi Germany', with contributions by Andrew Stuart Bergerson, Elissa Mailänder Koslov, Gideon Reuveni, Paul Steege and Dennis Sweeney, *German History* 27/4 (2009), 560–97, as well as the introduction to this volume.

[2] A useful summary of the limits of the totalitarianism paradigm for understanding National Socialism is Ian Kershaw, *The Nazi Dictatorship: Problems and Perspectives of Interpretation* (London, 2000), esp. 45–6. For a fuller discussion of recent critiques of totalitarianism, see also the introduction to this volume.

[3] For a new overview, see the 'Podium Zeitgeschichte: *Cultural Turn* und NS-Forschung', with contributions by Johannes Hürter, Thomas Raithel, Jürgen Zarusky, Frank Bajohr, Neil Gregor, Johann Chapoutot and Stefan Hördler, *Vierteljahrshefte für Zeitgeschichte* 65/2 (2017), 219–72.

[4] The literature on perpetrator studies, fuelled in part by debates around the works of Daniel Goldhagen and Christopher Browning, is vast. A useful overview is Olaf Jensen and Claus-Christian Szejnmann (eds.), *Ordinary People as Mass Murderers: Perpetrators in Comparative Perspectives* (Basingstoke, 2008).

experience in a private rather than an official capacity.[5] They have also drawn on records of conversations, which took place either during the Nazi regime or retrospectively, in which witnesses spoke about their personal experience of life under Nazi rule.

In this chapter, I argue that such sources do not only offer historians insights into the private, but that they themselves were methods for producing this concept in the first place. Sources that narrate, stage and perform a notion of private selfhood under the conditions of Nazi rule and the war need to be read as part of a project to redefine 'the private' under the dictatorship, in which millions of Germans took part. This is not to say that there was a radical break between meanings of the private before and after 1933. Constructions of private identities typically draw on older conventions and habits, which help render them 'authentic'.[6] After 1933, such traditions were not discarded, but they were modified and adapted to changing political contexts, often capitalising on opportunities to stake out private identities that could be politically expedient, or offer mechanisms for creating distance from a regime that was either hostile to one's identity, or, especially during the final war years, when this regime was no longer perceived to be delivering on its promise of private happiness, either for individuals or for the nation at large.

To elucidate the operations of the private during National Socialism, this chapter offers a close reading of some exemplary sources which employ different narrative methods and images to represent the experience of life in Nazi Germany. The chapter begins with an analysis of the observations of a foreign visitor to Germany, the British educationalist Amy Buller, who recorded numerous private conversations with Germans in search of authentic insights into the reach and limitations of Nazi ideology into the private sphere. In the following section, I compare this account to two different kinds of ego-documents, both capturing, in words and images, the experiences of young German women during the war years. The first of these is a photo and poetry album that chronicled the travels of three young women through Austria in 1944. The second is an illustrated diary that charted the private life and romantic fantasies of a German woman between 1942 and 1945. Through this analysis, I aim to uncover the political agendas at work in performances of private lives and sense of self under the Nazi regime. In addition, I trace how the

---

[5] On ego-documents in the historiography of modern Germany, see Mary Fulbrook and Ulinka Rublack, 'In Relation: The "Social Self" and Ego-Documents', *German History* 28/3 (2010), 263–72.

[6] On the importance of authenticity in the making and contesting of individual and collective identities, see Maiken Umbach and Mathew Humphrey, *Authenticity: The Cultural History of a Political Idea* (Basingstoke, 2018).

private was constructed, at least in part, out of building blocks that relied heavily on the official political language, imagery and imaginaries of the Third Reich.

Sources such as those analysed here have traditionally been viewed as a strategy for asserting the significance of private voices against the all-pervasive language of National Socialism. Victor Klemperer's famous *Lingua Tertii Imperii*, or *LTI* for short, is a case in point: his incisive analysis of official language in the Third Reich, with its proliferation of acronyms (which Klemperer's title mocks) and the inflationary use of terms such as 'heroism', contrasts sharply with Klemperer's own, emphatically personal use of language describing his increasingly beleaguered existence as a Jew in Germany married to an 'Aryan' wife.[7] And yet more recent scholarship has shown that the prolific production of ego-documents during the Nazi years was not always associated with distance from public discourse. Indeed, it often served the opposite purpose. In Steuwer's account, for many Germans, writing detailed diaries became a way of pulling elements of National Socialist ideology into a narrative about their private sense of selfhood.[8] This process, to be sure, had different ideological inflections. For some, National Socialism was a vehicle for ascribing a renewed sense of purpose or significance to their private life. For others, it prompted personal reflection on what that purpose should be, which could combine elements of ideological alignment with official discourse and some critical distance, for example, by distinguishing between Hitler as an inspirational national leader, and less agreeable ideologues such as Himmler, who were seen as embodiments of less savoury aspects of 'race theory'.[9] In some diaries and letters, such as those of August Töpperwien, as analysed by Nick Stargardt, such reflections had explicitly moral undertones, focusing on the question of which elements of National Socialism were compatible with their Christian faith.[10] Stargardt's book *The German War* pulls together many such cases.[11] Like other historians at the forefront of uncovering the history of subjectivities under National Socialism, Stargardt looked to ego-documents for explicit moral reflections about the ethical failings of the regime and its murderous war. Such an approach tends to privilege

---

[7] See Victor Klemperer, *Lingua Tertii Imperii: Notizbuch eines Philologen* (Berlin, 1947), translated as *Lingua Tertii Imperii: The Language of the Third Reich* (London, 2001).
[8] See Janosch Steuwer, *'Ein Drittes Reich, wie ich es auffasse': Politik, Gesellschaft und privates Leben in Tagebüchern 1933–1939* (Göttingen, 2017).
[9] The point was first made by Kershaw's seminal study *Popular Opinion and Political Dissent in the Third Reich: Bavaria 1933–1945* (Oxford, 1983).
[10] Nicholas Stargardt, 'The Troubled Patriot: German *Innerlichkeit* in World War II', *German History* 28/3 (2010), 326–42.
[11] Nicholas Stargardt, *The German War: A Nation under Arms, 1939–1945* (London, 2015).

ego-documents (in his case, both diaries and private letters) that were shaped by a long-standing tradition of diary writing in Germany, which had its historical roots in confessional writing of the late eighteenth and nineteenth centuries, most importantly, the Pietist or evangelical 'conversion narrative'.[12] Indeed, a disproportionate number of such ego-documents were produced by authors steeped in Christian traditions of writing, many of them members or sons of the German clergy.[13] To some extent, one of the sources in this chapter, the book by Amy Buller, written by a leading figure in the Student Christian Movement in interwar Britain, has a similar selection bias. And yet, as we see in what follows, Buller's account also showcases a very different dimension of subjectivity formation under National Socialism, which, in a variation of Hannah Arendt's famous phrase, we might characterise as the banality of Nazism in the private sphere. In focusing on moments of cosiness, in reducing one's role in public life to questions of emotion and affect, and sometimes downright kitsch, Buller's observations, like the two diaries by young women this chapter analyses, illuminate an aspect of the private under National Socialism that was not about moral introspection. Rather, such accounts configure the private as a sequence of momentary experiences and the associated emotions, such as joy, excitement and sometimes anxiety.

In analysing such accounts, it is important to note the constitutive role of such experiences and emotions in defining the private in the first place. In liberal discourses of the nineteenth century, the private was an ideal type that demarcated the absence of public, formal or official agency. Private ownership was defined in contradistinction to public property; to act in a private capacity was not to speak in an official or public role. The term *privacy* was defined as a state in which one is not observed or disturbed by other people. Nevertheless, it is important to note that the private was always more than an absence: it had its own defining rituals, habitus and language. In volume 5 of the *History of Private Life* series, Antoine Prost and Gérard Vincent described the advent of modernity in terms of the emergence of distinctly private spaces, bodily habits and emotions:

---

[12] See Jonathan Strom, 'Pietist Experiences and Narratives of Conversion', in Douglas H. Shantz (ed), *A Companion to German Pietism, 1660–1800* (Leiden, 2015), 293–318.

[13] The same applies to General Heinrici, a notable diarist from the German military elite in this period. See Johannes Hürter, *A German General on the Eastern Front: The Letters and Diaries of Gotthard Heinrici, 1941–1942* (Barnsley, 2014); new German edition: Johannes Hürter (ed.), *Notizen aus dem Vernichtungskrieg: Die Ostfront 1941/42 in den Aufzeichnungen des Generals Heinrici* (Darmstadt, 2016).

[P]roductive labor shifts from the home to an impersonal public setting. [...] Zoning laws segregate industrial and commercial areas from residential neighborhoods, which are [...] an assemblage of aloof and anonymous individuals or families. Homes are marked by elaborate spatial subdivisions; privacy is now possible even among one's own family. Men and women are obsessed with health, fitness, diet, and appearance as the body becomes the focal point of personal identity. Mirrors, once a rarity, are ubiquitous. In the search for sexual and individualistic fulfilment, romantic love becomes the foundation of marriage.[14]

In this account, new physical infrastructures and new consumer goods shape and define what a society understands by privacy. It is unsurprising, therefore, that in a bid fundamentally to redefine the role of the private in relation to the political, the Nazi regime paid particular attention to consumption and leisure.[15] But there is a third dimension at work in constituting the meaning of private: the experience and cultivation of private emotions. Prost and Vincent touched on this when they described romantic love as foundational to modern ideas of the private.

If the private is something that is constituted, importantly, in the sphere of *emotions*, then it is problematic to associate it only with particular spaces, such as domesticity, or with particular times of day, i.e. leisure hours. True, in particular moments, emotions that define our private selves may require private moments and spaces, which shield intimacy and confidentiality, but also scenes of personal conflict, from the prying eyes of neighbours, colleagues or the authorities. But these emotional lives do not cease to be private when they take place in public contexts. What makes the private distinctive is thus not, or at least not necessarily, its physical or temporal distance from public life, but a particular language – verbal, visual and embodied – which demarcates particular human experiences as private, no matter when or where they occur. The private, thus understood, is part of the history of selfhood – but it is not divorced from politics and ideology. Public discourses, such as advertising, which rely heavily on associating particular products with particular emotions, and indeed propaganda itself, which mobilises supporters by invoking hope, aspiration, longing and so forth, all provided templates for experiencing and articulating emotions that link this realm of the private inextricably with the public. The Nazi regime capitalised on this. Indeed, it was particularly outlandish in its claims not only to deliver better political solutions for people's social and economic problems, but

---

[14] Antoine Prost and Gérard Vincent (eds.), *A History of Private Life: Riddles of Identity in Modern Times*, vol. 5 (Cambridge, MA, 1998, paperback edition, translated by Arthur Goldhammer), summary of the argument on the back cover.

[15] A useful overview is Pamela E. Swett, Corey Ross and Fabrice d'Almeida (eds.), *Pleasure and Power in Nazi Germany* (Basingstoke, 2011).

to transform all aspects of life for those included in the *Volksgemeinschaft* in a way that would give their private lives deeper meaning and purpose, and thus profound and genuine joy. 'Strength Through Joy' was not just the title of the Nazi organisation that coordinated leisure activities, holidays and beautification of the workplace schemes, but also a ubiquitous trope in the political propaganda of the time.[16] The phrase expressed a fundamental belief that failure or success of political leadership were symptoms of the underlying moral and spiritual well-being of the imagined racial community. In making this argument, National Socialists drew on a political discourse that had taken root in the 1920s, which framed the experience of the Weimar years as the expression of a fundamental 'crisis', against a new future characterised by both personal happiness and collective 'joy'.[17] To trace performances of selfhood that engage with such templates for experiencing, even celebrating, the private, we have to look to genres beyond the reflective diary of highly educated citizens writing in a Christian or *bildungsbürgerlich* idiom. The three examples analysed in this chapter, representing three different types of sources, all focus on precisely such emotions, and draw on them to perform and to record notions of private selfhood.

Buller and the Performance of 'Private Conversations'

Amy Buller's *Darkness over Germany*, which was first published in 1943, is a compendium of personal conversations Buller held with Germans on her visits to that country between 1933 and 1939.[18] Buller's travels formed part of a series of official 'dialogues' between delegations of educational professionals and other intellectuals from Germany and the United Kingdom to promote 'mutual cultural understanding' and an exchange of pedagogic ideas. Each chapter of the book, however, is devoted to a 'private' conversation with Germans she met outside the official remit. As Buller herself admitted in the introduction to her volume, her interlocutors were not a representative cross-section of the German population at large: the *dramatis personae* of *Darkness over Germany* are schoolteachers, headmasters, university professors, Protestant and Catholic clergy and

---

[16] See Shelley Baranowski, *Strength through Joy: Consumerism and Mass Tourism in the Third Reich* (Cambridge, 2004); Hasso Spode, 'Die NS-Gemeinschaft "Kraft durch Freude" – ein Volk auf Reisen', in Hasso Spode (ed.), *Zur Sonne, zur Freiheit: Beiträge zur Tourismusgeschichte* (Berlin, 1991), 79–93.
[17] See Moritz Föllmer, *Ein Leben wie im Traum: Kultur im Dritten Reich* (Munich, 2016).
[18] See Amy Buller, *Darkness over Germany* (original edition: London, 1943; all citations here are to the new edition published by Arcadia Books: London, 2017).

some officers serving in the Wehrmacht. Working-class voices are largely absent, as are those of people who held higher offices in the Party or the state. Buller did not aim to chronicle public opinion at large. She was, instead, interested in those private selves that she assumed lingered behind the façade of collective beliefs in Nazi Germany.

To underscore this emphasis on the private, Buller's account gave most room to citing, in the first person, the voices of Germans she encountered. We cannot verify how accurately Buller recorded what was said to her. Yet in the immediate aftermath of the book's first publication in 1943, and again in the debates surrounding its republication in 2017, *Darkness over Germany* derived much of its impact from appearing to offer authentic access to 'private experience', seemingly unadulterated by academic analysis or explicitly political commentary.[19] Buller's own interventions, as she recorded them, were little more than prompts, inviting people to tell their own stories, to discuss experiences and expectations. She was also at pains to present her case studies in such a way as to showcase a wide range of different stories and experiences, of those who benefitted from the Nazi regime and those who felt oppressed by it, describing strategies for accommodation and the experience of living in fear.

In her analysis of British travellers to Nazi Germany, Schwarz classified Buller as one of a group of observers sceptical of the Nazi regime, who nevertheless approached Germans with 'sympathy'.[20] Yet it was not just sympathy that was at work in Buller's accounts. Her demonstratively private interactions with Germans were supposed to showcase them in their individuality, focusing the readers' attentions on their private emotions and thoughts. To do so, Buller herself adopted a private persona when conducting her conversations – in ways that chimed with her interlocutors, and referenced a shared set of assumptions about the moral legitimacy, indeed superiority, of private voices over official speech. In keeping with this persona, Buller did not judge, categorise or attempt to analyse the positions she encountered: except for some brief concluding thoughts, her own voice in the book is restricted to some scene setting and questioning. She did, however, convey much about the atmospheric and emotional markers that designated her dialogues with Germans as

---

[19] The reception history of the book's first appearance is described by Kurt Barling, 'Foreword' to Buller, *Darkness*, 2017, xxvi–xxvii. Cumberland Lodge has since organised several public debates around the new edition of the book; see, for example, 'Open Society under Threat: A Warning from History', in St Paul's Cathedral on 16 May 2017; a full recording at www.stpaulsinstitute.org.uk/videos/2017/may/16/open-society-under-threat-a-warning-from-history [accessed 24 Oct. 2017].

[20] Angela Schwarz, *Die Reise ins Dritte Reich: Britische Augenzeugen im nationalsozialistischen Deutschland (1933–1939)* (Göttingen, 1993), 121; Buller appears in a category of observers who were simultaneously critics of National Socialism, yet 'germanophile'.

authentically 'private'. Space was one important aspect of this. Each chapter begins by describing where Buller met her interlocutors. For example, she recorded how Dr Schuster, a German teacher whom Buller prompted to discuss the role of racial teachings in the classroom, 'rose and looked over the balcony' on which they were seated before replying to her: 'It would probably be alright to talk here but one never knows, so let's talk of other things till we go inside later.'[21] Looking over one's shoulder and postponing the discussions of sensitive issues until they can be conducted in an interior, domestic space here became both practical and symbolic acts, underscoring how the private settings enabled sincere and authentic conversations. Like Dr Schuster, Buller first met many of her interviewees in a public place, such as a park or a café, but when difficult topics, disconcerting experiences or moral dilemmas emerged, these conversations continued in more secluded spaces, such as living rooms; in some instances, Buller even noted that her interlocutors also disconnected their telephone lines to ensure their talks were not overheard.[22]

Private spaces and settings were only one constitutive aspect of privacy. Another important component were rituals of hospitality, and an emphasis on 'relaxation'. Buller's conversations often involved drinking, smoking and sitting on 'comfortable' furniture. On Dr Schuster again: 'As darkness fell we entered the maisonette and closing all doors and windows, he drew across thick curtains, unconsciously anticipating nights of blackout in Europe. Then offering me a glass of good Saxon cherry brandy, he settled down with his own glass of beer, saying: "I would like to tell you of the kind of position I find myself in."'[23] The thick curtains not only provided visual and acoustic protection from the gaze of the outside world. They also served as symbolic markers of the living room becoming an exclusively private sphere. Buller went on to describe how Dr Schuster lit a cigarette, which underscored the relaxed attitude he took to their exchange, before musing on whether Buller would truly be able to understand his experience. He concluded with the words: 'Anyhow, it will help me clear my mind if I may talk to you.' To which she replied simply: 'Go ahead.'[24]

Buller was interested in body language, facial expression, gestures and the rhythm at which people walked or drank their tea when talking: all of these conjure up ideas of private authenticity. She noted when her interlocutors appeared to be feeling confident, uncomfortable, anxious or defiant. Sometimes, such feelings were made explicit; for example, she described that Dr Schuster accompanied some of his critical observations

[21] Buller, *Darkness*, 5. [22] See ibidem, 34. [23] Ibidem, 5. [24] Ibidem, 6.

about Nazi rule in everyday life with 'a grunt of disgust'.[25] At other times, the symbolism was more subtle. Buller noted that when Elizabeth, a schoolteacher and Dr Schuster's cousin, entered the same living room, she appeared 'tall, fair and very handsome' – a physical description which sets the scene for Buller's portrayal of this young woman as a paragon of quiet, inner resistance.[26] Later, when Elizabeth walked Buller back to her hotel, they encountered a gathering of SS men 'laughing in a coarse, unpleasant way' – again, a habitus that to Buller is indicative of a particular moral position – to which Elizabeth responded, according to Buller, 'with a look [...] half of anger and half of pity'.[27]

Buller's interest in the private feelings of Germans was not ideologically neutral. It was a strategy that served political purposes. *Darkness over Germany* was intended to caution Buller's British compatriots against a view that all Germans were 'Nazis', brainwashed into adopting an official ideology, mere pawns of an evil regime. Her perspective conjured up a world inhabited by individuals with whom her readers might identify: not because all her characters were sympathetic, but because, even in their flaws, they seemed to be people 'like you and me'. Portraying political actors as private individuals, Buller believed, would help to nurture a meaningful dialogue between German and British citizens after the end of the war, which could underpin a more just and enduring peace than that created after the end of the First World War, which she regarded as the very trigger for the rise of National Socialism in the first place.

The emphasis on privacy and individuality also served Buller's religious agenda. Her role as Christian leader and educationalist shaped both the topics of her conversations with Germans and the manner in which she relayed them to her readers. This is most evident when Buller talked to members of the German clergy, such as Dr Heim, a Catholic priest in Bavaria.[28] Because Dr Heim was already being observed by local Nazi officials, according to Buller, for his refusal to abandon the traditional Bavarian greeting 'Grüss Gott!' for 'Heil Hitler!', he decided to meet Buller away from the town altogether. In her account, 'we left the car in a wood and climbed a hill. Here we were really free to talk as we looked across a valley with fruit trees in full blossom, in the midst of which rose the spire of the church.'[29] The harmony of nature conjured up in such phrases, and the church spire's symbolically charged location amongst blossoming trees, served to naturalise the conversation, as one coming from the heart, seemingly unimpeded by public considerations. As in many other meetings Buller recorded, she and Dr Heim then explored

[25] Ibidem, 6.   [26] Ibidem, 9.   [27] Ibidem, 16.   [28] See ibidem, 17–23.   [29] Ibidem, 19.

whether accommodation with the regime's supposedly anti-clerical outlook and 'pagan' values was compatible with following Christian teachings in one's private life. Dr Heim felt a tension between the two, but like most of Buller's German interlocutors, he also suggested that a degree of compromise in public life would be more conducive to the survival of a private Christian ethic than public political opposition. Lay Germans too spoke to Buller about the tension between their religious beliefs and their understanding of official Nazi doctrine. Buller welcomed such confessions. The important role of personal faith in Germans' private identities would, Buller believed, facilitate a recovery from what she saw as the core problem of National Socialism: an irrational belief in Hitler, or 'Hitlerism', which she understood as a substitute religion.

The Germans to whom Buller spoke not only willingly collaborated in these conversations: most of them seemed delighted to seize an opportunity to articulate their sense of selfhood in 'private' terms, fashioning themselves as thinking, feeling individuals who took pride in their own strategies for making sense of the world they inhabited and their place within it. Gender played an important role in these performances. Women, for Buller, were almost by definition private beings. By focusing on their personal appearance, indeed beauty, their seemingly more natural 'fit' in domestic spaces and their apparent distaste for male-dominated public gatherings, the German women in Buller's account appear as unadulterated private selves. This did not mean that Buller portrayed them as insulated from public pressures: more than once, she described her female interlocutors as subject to a pernicious combination of generic male bullying and the masculine nature of official Nazi doctrine. But that very fact served to underscore the sense that women were somehow 'out of place' in the public performance of adherence to the Nazi regime. This representational strategy featured prominently in Buller's account of Elizabeth's response to the SS gathering. It also surfaced in her conversations with a Bavarian teacher named Frau Otto, and a gathering of seven mothers, also from Bavaria, both Catholic and Protestant, who struck Buller as 'extremely intelligent' and 'united in [...] a friendship based on common suffering and a determination to try to find ways of preventing their children's minds being crippled by Nazi philosophy' only a few minutes into their conversation.[30] Buller described the ways in which such women mobilised private attributes and identities subtly to subvert, rather than openly to confront, the regime. Some of her favourite anecdotes involve female teachers who, rather than refusing to teach Nazi racial science, opt to teach these subjects in ways that would make them 'boring' to their pupils,

---

[30] See ibidem, 52–4.

while they pour personal enthusiasm and charm into those topics they deem morally unproblematic and in which they want to enthuse their students.[31]

Yet when conversing with German men, too, a conscious performance of traditional gender roles was decisive in bringing the private to the fore. From the perspective of a reader in the early twenty-first century, the chatty, at times almost trivial, tone of Buller's account is difficult to digest; it stands in a disconcerting contrast to the seriousness of the subject matter. Yet it was instrumental in producing the conversations that Buller recorded. Although the narrative of the published book casts Buller as an educationalist – she is recounting her stories to six young female students in Liverpool while they are on fire-watching duty during an air raid – when conducting her interviews, Buller's turns of phrase are more reminiscent of that of a young woman who writes her first diary than of a seasoned political observer. The role of the naïve, young woman asking questions apparently without prejudice allowed Buller to put aside obvious political differences and to form 'human connections' that encouraged her interlocutors, including men, to speak relatively freely in front of a stranger from a different country with different political values: her feminine persona lessened the threat of such interrogations. What Buller elicited often had a confessional undertone, yet her prompts were less those of a priest than those of a student, whose feminine innocence and curiosity conjured up a seemingly 'safe space' in which confidences could be shared. Buller did not approach her interlocutors as a journalist, opinion pollster, anthropologist or politician. As her motive, she cited, to her interviewees as well as to her readers, personal curiosity and a desire to understand the perspective of others who are 'like her', but who find themselves living in a radically different political situation. This private pitch allowed Buller to raise difficult questions with people who, albeit often plagued by some moral qualms, broadly supported or at least did not resist a regime that was about to go to war with Buller's own country.

Gender performances thus reinforced the private settings of the conversations. Buller recorded the drinks that she shared with her hosts, the garden chairs or sofas on which they sat, the walks they enjoyed together, the glances they exchanged; she recorded the way in which people sipped their tea, enjoyed their beer and gazed pensively into landscapes, how they sat or walked with straight backs or with their heads bent down. Buller also paid attention to physical appearance and expression: men's faces are characterised as 'serious', 'thoughtful' and sometimes 'pained',

---

[31] Ibidem, 11.

those of women often as 'handsome': Buller is evidently very taken with their looks as well as their personalities.[32] Variation was a key component of this construction of private encounters: each conversation had its own, distinctive choreography, traversing the whole spectrum of emotions and attitudes that people experienced as they shared their life stories with Buller. The resulting book therefore reads more like a personal diary or a letter one might send to a close friend about new experiences and social encounters than a scholarly analysis or a political text.

In reality, Buller was by no means inexperienced in national and international politics. Born in 1891, she spent much of her youth in South Africa, then moved to the United Kingdom. One of only a handful of women to graduate from Birkbeck College in 1917, she was unusually academically accomplished for a woman of her generation. She was a skilled political operator, able to deal with the authorities in Nazi Germany and winning the support of senior figures of the British establishment, including the later Archbishop of Canterbury William Temple and the king and queen.[33] Yet little of this political skill and experience is visible in *Darkness over Germany*. In her private persona, Buller's questions never referenced prior knowledge of politics. In 1938, Buller met Herr von Bretten, a German officer whom, in an effort to invoke the moral dilemmas he faced, she described as 'looking tired and strained'.[34] Von Bretten explained to Buller that an alliance between Nazis and military leaders was a necessary evil to lead Germany out of a crisis, because 'we are in such a mess now that it is difficult to get out without several more disasters. I see no hope of going from the Nazis straight on to anything resembling a form of government that would be good and permanent. There must be this transition stage during which there is a strong control.'[35] Throughout this prolonged conversation, Buller never offered a different political interpretation: her only interventions are reminding the officer of remarks he had made in another conversation with her a few years earlier, in which he had been more sceptical of Hitler's agenda. Buller noted her own sense of dismay that many Germans 'did not begin to realize the danger of the whole Hitler business until it was too late' in the published version of the book.[36] Yet in her conversation with von Bretten, her remarks only convey emotional reactions, and further questions, for example, when her reply to a long speech by von Bretten about

---

[32] Ibidem, 9.
[33] The publication of *Darkness over Germany* propelled Buller to fame and influence; shortly afterwards, Queen Elizabeth and King George VI granted Buller the use of the former royal residence Cumberland Lodge to set up her own educational foundation. See Kurt Barling, 'Foreword' to Buller, *Darkness*, xxvi–xxvii.
[34] Buller, *Darkness*, 33.   [35] Ibidem, quote 32.   [36] Ibidem, 37.

the need to focus on his military duties rather than politics, are confined to the sentences: "'You certainly made me feel there is no way to escape war,' I said, 'but what then?'"[37] In other conversations, too, Buller never challenged her interlocutors directly, except by communicating incomprehension: a technique that played effectively on conventions of feminine innocence and naïveté. The same performance of gender is evident in encounters with German women, whose confidence she gains by bonding with them over matters ranging from personal appearance to feeling intimidated by the hypermasculine mannerisms of the SS. A shared sense of visceral distaste for such aggressive male posturing seemingly circumvented the need for any further political analysis, and Buller's female interlocutors felt at ease in her 'private' company.

Ego-Documents and the Privatisation of Nazi Aesthetics

The performative conflation of femininity and privacy appears to have resonated with many of the Germans Buller met. And it is a theme which also shaped the performance of the private in many German ego-documents of the time. Women played an active role in the production of diaries, letters, photo albums and documents which traversed all three of these genres during the Nazi regime. In fact, women were, in many ways, the dominant group in shaping such media for representing and staging the self. There were certainly diaries by men, including soldiers serving on the front and in the occupied territories. Men wrote personal letters, and men also took photographs, and some soldiers even made personal photo albums documenting their experiences, especially when hundreds or thousands of miles away from home.[38] Yet the surviving evidence suggests that it was often women who kept diaries of predominantly private content, reflecting on their personal experiences and emotions, as well as chronicling the daily lives of their families. Women also took countless photographs, and women were typically those who arranged photos taken by all members of a family, including those by serving soldiers, into 'family albums', which they often embellished with

---

[37] Ibidem, 35.
[38] See, for example, Petra Bopp, *Fremde im Visier: Fotoalben aus dem Zweiten Weltkrieg* (Bielefeld, 2012); Willi Rose, *Shadows of War: A German Soldier's Lost Photographs of World War II*, ed. by Thomas Eller and Petra Bopp (New York, NY, 2004); Bernd Boll, 'Das Adlerauge des Soldaten. Zur Photopraxis deutscher Amateure im Zweiten Weltkrieg', *Fotogeschichte* 85–86/22 (2002), 75–86; Anton Holzer (ed.), *Mit der Kamera bewaffnet: Krieg und Fotografie* (Marburg, 2003); Kathrin Hoffmann-Curtius, 'Trophäen und Amulette: Die Fotografien von Wehrmachts- und SS-Verbrechen in den Brieftaschen der Soldaten', *Fotogeschichte* 78/20 (2000), 63–76.

captions, commentary, drawings, poems, pressed flowers and cuttings from newspapers or other media.[39] As part of a wider project on 'Photography as Political Practice in National Socialism', my collaborators and I have been analysing the ubiquitous practice of personal album making between 1933 and 1945.[40] We have argued that photography in this period was 'a quotidian practice that could forge and sustain private identities, communicate and reinforce ideologies, and, last but not least, pre-emptively capture events and emotions for future viewers'. Photography, we have suggested, was 'not just [...] a window onto history: it produces and transforms the very practices that constitute history'.[41] In another article, I have analysed how many of the photos displayed in such albums take up, reflect and re-code the official pictorial culture of the regime, as well as older iconographic traditions, in order to perform subjective experience and emotion under the specific conditions of Nazi rule.[42]

What such albums reflect is a picture not entirely different from that conveyed by Amy Buller: German responses to the regime and the war were certainly more than replications of a singular Nazi ideology, yet also more varied than the genre of the (Protestant) moral reflections of writers such as Töpperwien suggest. Album making was inflected by a vast range of different individual dispositions and personal experiences. Indeed, the very vagueness of Nazi ideology itself meant that many Germans saw it less as a political orthodoxy they needed to adhere to than as an opportunity structure for furthering their personal ambitions and aspirations or to cope with their own anxieties. Referencing Nazi slogans and images could lend legitimacy, purpose and gravitas to what were often very particular personal concerns and objectives. The regime in turn encouraged this practice. A variety of albums were officially produced and distributed by the regime to encourage individuals to create authentically personal records of their service in the armed forces, in the Reich Labour

---

[39] There is as yet no systematic account of the private practice of album making in Nazi Germany, but the subject is discussed in various more general histories of private photography in this period, for example, Marianne Hirsch, *Family Frames: Photography, Narrative and Postmemory* (Cambridge, MA, 1997); and, on Jewish photo albums, see Leora Auslander, 'Reading German Jewry through Vernacular Photography: From the Kaiserreich to the Third Reich', *Central European History* 48/3 (2015), 300–34.

[40] After several completed pilot projects, this is now the topic of a three-year AHRC-funded project (2018 to 2021) directed by Maiken Umbach at the University of Nottingham; for details, see www.nottingham.ac.uk/history/research/projects/photography-as-political-practice-in-national-socialism.aspx [accessed 25 Oct. 2017].

[41] Elizabeth Harvey and Maiken Umbach, 'Photography and Twentieth-Century German History', special issue for *Central European History* 48/3 (2015), 287–99, quote at 299.

[42] See Maiken Umbach, 'Selfhood, Place, and Ideology in German Photo Albums, 1933–1945', *Central European History* 48/3 (2015), 335–65.

Service and in other auxiliary organisations, as the ready-made title pages with decorative embossed metal lettering suggested.[43] Similar albums with a more civilian focus were produced and heavily marketed during the Nazi years as commercial products to sell to Germans who might wish to create their own albums documenting 'historic' events, such as the 1936 Olympic Games. People not only purchased countless such albums and filled them with their photographs and other artefacts. They also created their own albums drawing on such ready-made templates, often adorned with elaborate title pages that framed a particular holiday or the birth of a child as a momentous event that called for careful documentation.[44]

Some albums focused on the personal experience of performing official service, including that by women, for example, in the *Reichsarbeitsdienst*; the majority of images in them, however, show moments of relaxation, taking time off, 'having a break' or enjoying leisure activities with friends and co-workers. In other words, they frame their protagonists as private individuals. Other albums were devoted entirely to moments of private pleasure, often to holidays, most typically walking holidays in mountains. One such album, from 1944, documented a walking holiday in Austria.[45] The creator of the album and her two friends, who are depicted in many of its photos, were three young women, respectively, from Vienna, Berlin and Stuttgart, who had met in the *Reichsarbeitsdienst*, but were now enjoying a time of leisure away from official duties. Correspondingly, the focus is on private experiences and sentiments. Photos and captions frame Alpine settings as picturesque and uplifting; many captions end in multiple exclamation marks to express an almost childlike sense of enthusiasm about a particular vista or the sounds and smells of nature (Figure 5.1).

The young women also photographed one another walking or resting in the landscape, proudly showing off their new *Dirndl* dresses and posing as admirers of Mozart in front of his sculpture in Salzburg (Figure 5.2).

Similar scenes would have been perfectly thinkable in the 1920s. Yet continuing such conventions under the radically different circumstances of the final war year meant that the ostentatious display of private pleasures,

---

[43] On the materiality of albums designed for soldiers, see Bernd Boll, 'Vom Album ins Archiv: Zur Überlieferung privater Fotografien aus dem Zweiten Weltkrieg', in Holzer (ed.), *Mit der Kamera bewaffnet*, 167–81. On soldiers' photographs during the Second World War, see also Chapter 11 by Andrew Bergerson, Laura Fahnenbruck and Christine Hartig in this volume.

[44] Examples are discussed in Umbach, 'Selfhood, Place'.

[45] This album, a hard-bound book that comprises fifty-two pages in slightly smaller than A4 format, most of which contain between one and three photographs, belongs to the author's personal collection.

Figure 5.1 'Should I gaze into the deep valley, or the sea of clouds?' Holiday album page, anon., Mondsee, Austria, 1944, from the author's collection.

especially in a setting which in itself featured so prominently in Nazi aesthetics, now acquired distinctly political undertones. Austria itself of course was an auspicious setting: at the very moment when the Third Reich was nearing its final collapse, the album celebrated the unity of Germany and Austria created by the *Anschluss* of 1938. The amateur poetry in the album underscored the ideological resonances of the setting and endowed the aesthetic appreciation of the Alps with political gravitas (undiminished by the poor aesthetic quality of the poetry itself). One example:

> Proud you stand, enveloped in sun-gold
> In your beauty, and splendour
> Jagged you are, yet in closed rank
> United is, in you, power and glory![46]

Such ecstatic admiration spoke at once of private pleasures and an affective alignment with Nazi propaganda. The poem's diction, like the aesthetics of the photographs, appropriate official aesthetic templates: we find similar tropes in the ubiquitous publications on Hitler's life at the *Berghof*, but also in some of the most popular films produced under the auspices of the

---

[46] This is the author's translation of the German original: 'Stolz steht ihr da, vom Sonnengold umflossen/ In Eurer Schönheit, Eurer Pracht/ Zerklüftet seid ihr, doch geschlossen/ Vereint in Euch ist Kraft und Macht!'

Figure 5.2 'The young Mozart ... and his admirers'. Holiday album page, anon., Mondsee, Austria, 1944, from the author's collection.

regime, the so-called *Bergfilme*, not least the oeuvre of Nazi star filmmaker Leni Riefenstahl.[47] And yet albums such as this do not just replicate official propaganda. Rather, enjoying the Alpine setting was here transformed into a celebration of authentic, lived experience and private joy. It is therefore unsurprising that in many similar private photo albums of the time, depicting relaxation and the joyous experience of nature featured alongside photos and texts that placed one's own biography in the context of the national narrative of struggle and sacrifice; and often, moments of enjoyment and relaxation in nature are described as a spiritual 're-fuelling' that enabled dutiful citizens to carry on with their national duties.

After the end of the war, such attitudes left a certain affective vacuum behind. The album of the mountaineering girl-poet concludes with a postscript from 1946, entitled 'In Memoriam', that praises 1944 as a time of 'happiness' that still offers spiritual nourishment for the present:

---

[47] A classic example of this genre was the lavishly illustrated coffee table book *Hitler in seinen Bergen: 86 Bilddokumente aus der Umgebung des Führers* (Berlin, 1935), edited and with photographs by Heinrich Hoffmann, Hitler's personal photographer of choice. On Hoffmann's role in the Nazi regime, see Rudolf Herz, *Hoffmann und Hitler. Fotographie als Medium des Führer-Mythos* (Munich, 1994). On Alpine aesthetics in Nazi films, see Christian Rapp, *Höhenrausch. Der deutsche Bergfilm* (Vienna, 1997).

When you are tired from the day's toil and labours
When you have had enough of people and of life
Pick up this album, and cast a glance inside
And instantly the world is filled with sunshine
Happily I recall those times
My little Ilse, and the joys of Mondsee![48]

What emerges from such accounts is that seemingly private experiences of joy and happiness were rendered 'meaningful' by the wider political narrative which, implicitly and at times explicitly, framed private experience: correspondingly, the loss of the political frame renders the album into a document that compensates for this 'loss' through sentimental nostalgia for the 'good old days'. While such sentiments were widely held, this particular album gave them a gendered reflection: neither the photos nor the poetry display any pretensions to being professional. Rather, their apparent authenticity was constituted by their dilettantism, the sense of naïve enthusiasm, and occasionally sheer gigliness, with which this young German woman performed her participation in the zeitgeist of Nazi Germany, whilst locating her experience firmly within a relatively traditional understanding of a girl's holiday experience.

Everyday Life, Fantasy and Nazi Ideology

One area of private life rarely appeared in photo albums: the more quotidian rhythms of everyday life and the emotional experiences associated with the absence of loved ones. Photos, even in the age of cheap cameras, were usually taken on special occasions. Many document being away from home: on holiday, on weekend outings, or when placed in new environment by official duties, during *Kinderlandverschickung* (KLV) (the state-run child evacuation programmes from cities hit by aerial bombardment), in the Nazi auxiliary services and as part of a military occupation or at the front. At home, photos were usually taken to commemorate momentous occasions, such as birthdays, christenings or weddings, or sometimes to capture the acquisition of a new house or car. Most captured or staged moments of happiness and joy. Photos of everyday chores, conversations amongst family members or sociability with friends, except on special occasions such as weddings or birthdays, however, are exceedingly rare; so are photos that record moments of doubt, uncertainty or anxiety of the kind that Buller captured in many of her conversations.

---

[48] Author's translation of: 'Bist Du mal müde von des Tages Müh und Last/ Von Mensch und Leben Du genug dann hast/ Nimm dieses Buch, werf einen Blick hinein/ Gleich ist die Welt von Sonnenschein/ Froh denk ich dann an jene Zeit zurueck/ Ans Ilslein und ans Mondsee-Glück!'

And yet such moments also feature in ego-documents of the time. The example to which I now turn is from an album that contained no photographs. Written and illustrated between 1942 and 1946 by a young German woman called Gisela R., resident in a suburb of the city of Heilbronn in south-west Germany, this album is a montage of short diary entries and countless drawings, plus paraphernalia such as theatre tickets and official documents, assembled in two consecutive volumes. In many ways, the absence of photos, and the associated semi-public acts of posing for images, developing them commercially and then sharing them with others, gave Gisela's album an even more emphatically private feel than most photo albums of the time. The focus of her account are her private feelings about friends and family, primarily her romantic relationship with her fiancé, and from April 1942 husband, Kurt. Although the album makes no overt mention of any outward signs of status or success, it is important to bear in mind when interpreting it that both Gisela and Kurt were members of an elite that was particularly highly prized in Nazi Germany. The marriage permit included in Figure 5.3 identifies Gisela's husband as Captain, later Major and Wing Commander, Kurt N., a member of the airborne Kampfgeschwader 4 'General Wever' in the German Luftwaffe, stationed for most of the duration of the diary in Bialystok, in the eastern part of what before the war had been independent Poland. In April 1944, he was moved from Bialystok to Budapest. As an officer in the air force, Kurt was an exemplar of what Nazi propaganda frequently portrayed as a new 'heroic' soldierly elite. Gisela in turn was the daughter of an officer, which would have entailed being socialised during the interwar years into a particular understanding of the dutiful army wife: a role, which, as we see in what follows, shaped her own understanding of her identity, although her emotional experiences often departed from official expectations.[49]

Gisela's illustrated diary was dedicated, literally and metaphorically, to her feelings for Kurt. One of the earliest pages in the first volume features, at the top, a telegram from Kurt announcing the date of the wedding and his arrival from the front, and at the bottom, the official marriage permit (Figure 5.3). Between the two, Gisela drew her first self-portrait in the album – seated, in a skirt and short-sleeved top and simple shoes – her handwritten text explains that this was her final day at work as a seamstress

---

[49] The role of army wives has been explored, for example, by Birthe Kundrus, *Kriegerfrauen: Familienpolitik und Geschlechterverhältnisse im Ersten und Zweiten Weltkrieg* (Hamburg, 1995). For a more general argument on the gendered performance of marriage under National Socialism, see Claudia Koonz, *Mothers in the Fatherland: Women, the Family and Nazi Politics* (New York, NY, 1987), who argues that the 'feminine home sphere' was an integral and enabling part of the masculine world of Nazi brutality.

(Re-)Inventing the Private under National Socialism 121

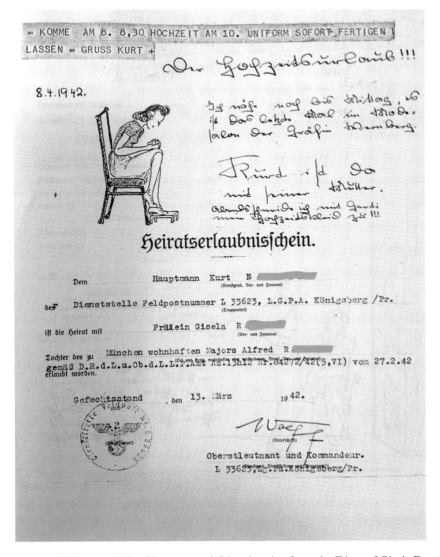

Figure 5.3 'The Honeymoon'. Line drawing from the Diary of Gisela R., Deutsches Tagebucharchiv Emmendingen, reproduced by kind permission.

in the fashion salon of Countess Wernberg. It was, presumably, in this role that Gisela learnt to sketch: the style of her drawings throughout the diary betrays a degree of professional skill in representing poses and items of fashionable clothing. As Gisela noted on the same page, on the evening of the same day, she made preparations to make her own wedding dress. Throughout the album, her pride in making her own, fashionable clothes is a recurrent theme. The title of the page, however, also points towards an exciting future: the title, 'The Honeymoon', is adorned with three exclamation marks.

Subsequent pages feature highlights from the honeymoon and later trips the couple undertook together while Kurt was on home leaves. They include the inevitable Alpine hike, showing the couple in sturdy outfits admiring the view (Figure 5.4), while 'everything is beautiful'. The text on the page ends, however, with the rather mundane statement that, while Kurt was telling war stories in the evening, Gisela was 'off to bed!'.

Another page, which also includes printed matter, recounts an evening the couple spent together in Munich, in October 1942 (Figure 5.5). The couple watched *Andreas Schlüter*, a Ufa propaganda film released in the same year, which featured the baroque architect as a visionary if pained artistic genius, whose creations are depicted in the film in dramatically illuminated shots that suggested parallels with Albert Speer's architectural oeuvre. Gisela pasted the cinema ticket stubs into the album. She also included a postcard from the *Grosse Deutsche Kunstausstellung*, the premier propaganda exhibition of desirable 'German art', which the couple visited in Munich; the postcard chosen featured Wilhelm Sauter's pathos-laden oil painting *Rheinübergang bei Breisach*, which was first exhibited in the same year.[50] This was a typical pattern in photo albums from the same time: private leisure time was given an air of added topicality and significance by showing the protagonists as enthusiastic consumers of the cultural offerings of the regime.

Most of Gisela's album pages, however, focused on domestic life. The cover page of the second volume, starting in 1944, dedicates the book to 'my beloved husband'. From now on, each page number is encircled by a little heart. Gisela made numerous sketches of herself looking after the house, raising their young son Jörg, visiting and hosting friends, celebrating parties in her own home and shopping. Kurt was

---

[50] See Wolfgang Schmidt, 'Maler an der Front: Zur Rolle der Kriegsmaler und Pressezeichner der Wehrmacht im Zweiten Weltkrieg', in Rolf-Dieter Müller and Hans-Erich Volkmann (eds.), *Die Wehrmacht: Mythos und Realität* (Munich, 1999), 635–84. This particular painting is discussed on page 658; page 673 features a colour reproduction.

Figure 5.4 Hiking in the Alps. Line drawing from the Diary of Gisela R., Deutsches Tagebucharchiv Emmendingen, reproduced by kind permission.

mostly absent, but his memory is constantly present and is the leitmotif of the narrative, as well as of many illustrations. Gisela sketched their empty marital bed, and even added a drawing depicting Kurt and herself talking on opposite ends of the telephone line while he was in Bialystok (Figure 5.6).

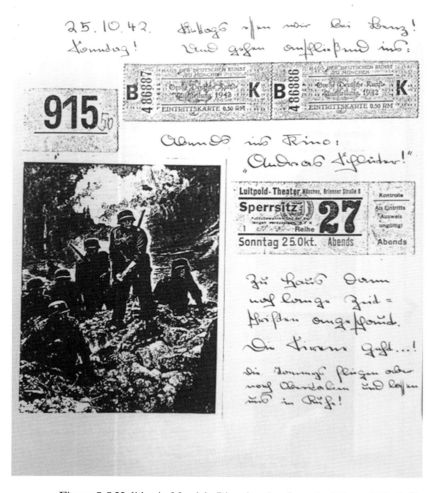

Figure 5.5 Holiday in Munich. Line drawing from the Diary of Gisela R., Deutsches Tagebucharchiv Emmendingen, reproduced by kind permission.

However, Gisela's portrayal of Kurt's absence was not always that of a dutiful Nazi wife. On one occasion, Gisela noted, with an undertone of disappointment, that Kurt was 'swanning off' back to active duty, while she was ill in bed with jaundice. When drawing their long-distance

Figure 5.6 Long-distance phone calls to Bialystok. Line drawing from the Diary of Gisela R., Deutsches Tagebucharchiv Emmendingen, reproduced by kind permission.

telephone conversation, she noted that Kurt was 'too busy to write to me because he is celebrating too many parties' – a complaint that sat oddly alongside the fact that she depicted herself spending many evenings partying with friends, noting the different types of drinks and delicacies consumed on such occasions.

The album is not free of anxiety either. Gisela noted the names of family members and acquaintances missing on the Eastern Front under

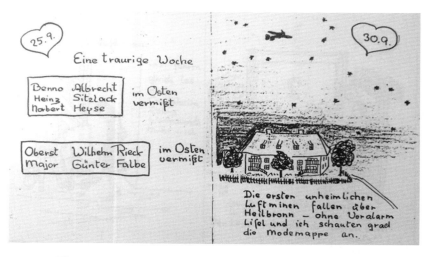

Figure 5.7 Death and bomber attacks. Line drawing from the Diary of Gisela R., Deutsches Tagebucharchiv Emmendingen, reproduced by kind permission.

the caption 'a sad week' (Figure 5.7), and included drawings of bombs falling on the city of Heilbronn. Yet she also wrote that, at the moment she first heard the bombs beginning to fall, she was leafing through a fashion magazine, which was one of her favourite pastimes. Horrific news about the war and the eventual arrival of Allied troops, as well as the fact that two of her close female friends were raped by Allied soldiers, featured in this diary alongside comments on the weather and drawings of the garden and of flowers she has arranged in a vase.

Particularly striking in terms of Gisela's interpretation of her own femininity is a drawing of her cleaning the house when she receives notification of Kurt's next home leave in March 1944 (Figure 5.8). She noted that she was 'overjoyed' ('*selig*') by the news and drew herself preparing the home for Kurt's arrival, with broom, bucket, dustpan and rolled-up sleeves – but nevertheless wearing one of her elegant dresses.

Other drawings show mother and son celebrating daddy's birthday by lighting a candle; shortly afterwards, Gisela created and drew a flower arrangement to commemorate her and Kurt's third wedding anniversary. On the same page, she depicted the cellar in which she has created a second bedroom, for her and Jörg to spend the nights safe from aerial bombardments. Gisela's ostentatious devotion to the absent soldier-husband did not, however, distract her from drawing herself on cycling

(Re-)Inventing the Private under National Socialism 127

Figure 5.8 Preparing the home for Kurt's home leave. Line drawing from the Diary of Gisela R., Deutsches Tagebucharchiv Emmendingen, reproduced by kind permission.

tours, sketching landscapes and showcasing the many cakes she baked for visiting guests, the parties she hosted and even an attractive young man whom she met one afternoon at the local swimming pool, to whom she referred as her 'swimming pool acquaintance' (Figure 5.9). The same drawing shows Gisela in a revealing bikini, and the caption notes that she went swimming with this new friend on several subsequent occasions.

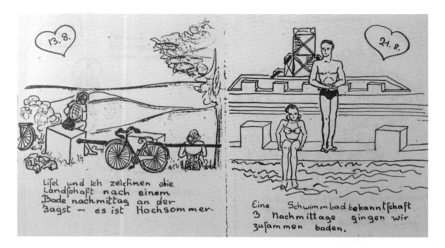

Figure 5.9 Outdoor fun. Line drawing from the Diary of Gisela R., Deutsches Tagebucharchiv Emmendingen, reproduced by kind permission.

The album ends with Kurt's returning to the marital home, after serving a brief stint in a prisoner of war camp near Heilbronn in June 1945 – the reunion of the couple is celebrated with much visual fanfare and numerous exclamation marks (Figure 5.10).

But the story did not end there. The final page of Gisela's album contains a postscript written in 1946. Gisela noted that in June 1945, she had 'thought, hoped and expected that married life would now begin for real. But unfortunately, it was in fact the beginning of the end. We discovered that we each had totally different expectations of our life together, and we separated within a year.'

Gisela and Kurt's attempt to actually lead a life together ended in immediate failure. This almost instantaneous dissolution of the carefully staged romantic bond to the heroic soldier on active duty, which had formed the narrative core of Gisela's account of her private self between 1942 and 1945, suggests that, in some ways at least, this story was a fiction. This is not to say that Gisela's portrayal of her emotions was an act of deliberate deception. It appears, rather, that the experience of romantic love which motivated Gisela's loving construction, upkeep and beautification of the marital home, as well as her careful self-fashioning as an attractive, well-dressed and emphatically feminine young woman, was a meaning-making template that she picked up and then quickly discarded again, in much the same way as her apparent attachment to Nazi cultural

(Re-)Inventing the Private under National Socialism

Figure 5.10 Reunion after the end of the war. Line drawing from the Diary of Gisela R., Deutsches Tagebucharchiv Emmendingen, reproduced by kind permission.

products such as *Andreas Schlüter*, the *Grosse Deutsche Kunstausstellung*, majestic Alpine landscapes or even the images in her fashion magazines. In her portraying the most intimate dimensions of her private life, Gisela used what the zeitgeist had to offer – role models, ways of being and imagining the self – that suited her own emotional aspirations at the time. We have no reason to doubt the sincerity of these sentiments, and yet they also proved eminently changeable when the circumstances changed. Gisela's account of the collapse of the Third Reich was laconic. Her diary contains few explicit political value judgements, but in the final weeks of the war, she recounted conversations at parties in her house in which guests asked each other: 'Who still believes in the final victory??' When the war ended, she noted that that everything 'has gone to pieces', and drew a burning swastika flag with no evident sign of regret. Her brief comments on the fact that her life with Kurt 'never really started' once the longed-for opportunity to live together finally arrived, seem equally laconic. What 'went to pieces' was not so much a lived reality as a vision of the private self. The attendant, politically sanctioned templates for endowing this private life with meaning and heroic significance turned out to be quite fleeting. They could perhaps be more accurately understood as a sketch of a possible future self which was aspirational but never fully 'inhabited' in the present. When it vanished, together with the Nazi regime that had helped her to frame such aspirations, the sense of loss was therefore relative.

Conclusion

There was no singular model for Germans' narrating their private selves, to themselves or to others, during the Nazi years. Their accounts are as varied as their experiences and their attitudes towards the many facets of National Socialism they witnessed, experienced or took part in. What is clear, however, is that there was no fixed a priori definition of private identity which was then acted upon by the state or official ideology. Nor was there a sense that the private was, in and of itself, separate from or opposed to the political. Instead, the examples analysed in this chapter suggest that private life during the Nazi years is best thought of as something that was co-produced by individuals and discursive, pictorial and embodied templates of meaning-making, in which elements of Nazi ideology intermingled with commercial culture, technological innovation and fashion. Buller was right in suggesting that her interviews showed that ordinary Germans were not simply brainwashed into believing Nazi ideology. Yet, in a sense, she was asking the wrong question. What her conversations, and different kinds of ego-documents produced at the time, tell us is not so much what National Socialism did *to* Germans, but what Germans did *with* National Socialism. Official ideology, state-sponsored advertising and new lifestyle offerings, but also the fateful story of a nation at war, provided a framework in which private experiences, sentiments and desires could be imagined as possessing a sense of historical significance. National Socialism helped to valorise the private as a significant category both of identity and of experience. This is the important flip side of the more commonly known story of the regime's erosion of the private sphere in the pursuit of ideological conformity. In their aspirational nature, conjuring up perfect worlds and brighter futures, accounts of private selves produced during the Nazi years often mirror official propaganda's propensity for promising an exciting new age. The regime was heavily invested in 'marketing' this promise through consumer goods such as KdF cars and holidays, even if it rarely succeeded in delivering them.[51] This obsession with projecting oneself into a future

---

[51] See Baranowski, *Strength through Joy*; Kristin Semmens, *Seeing Hitler's Germany: Tourism in the Third Reich* (Basingstoke, 2005); Wolfgang König, *Volkswagen, Volksempfänger, Volksgemeinschaft: 'Volksprodukte' im Dritten Reich. Vom Scheitern einer nationalsozialistischen Konsumgesellschaft* (Paderborn, 2004); Bernhard Rieger, *The People's Car: A Global History of the Volkswagen Beetle* (Cambridge, MA, 2013); Silke Horstkotte und Olaf Jürgen Schmidt, 'Heil Coca-Cola! Zwischen Germanisierung und Re-Amerikanisierung: Coke im Dritten

defined by joyous, hopeful emotions and fantasies was embraced by many. But that did not mean that such parallels necessarily reinforced what we might describe as National Socialist ideology itself. In the process of inscribing itself into private stories, performances and states of mind, the specific politics of National Socialism became, in a sense, rather elusive. In extending ideology well beyond the boundaries of the public sphere, the Nazis had made specific political content oddly marginal to the aspirations of many members of their *Volksgemeinschaft*. This in turn enabled many Germans simply to clutch onto the next available ideological templates after 1945, once again projecting their sense of self into an imaginary future of collective joy, excitement and affluence, without ever questioning or rethinking the fundamental coordinates of their private identities, aspirations or political ethics.

Reich', in Heike Paul and Katja Kanzler (eds.), *Amerikanische Populärkultur in Deutschland* (Leipzig, 2002), 73–87.

II

The Private in the *Volksgemeinschaft*

6 Private Life in the People's Economy
Spending and Saving in Nazi Germany

Pamela E. Swett

The first images that come to mind when we think of life in Nazi Germany are collective ones – perhaps the Nuremberg Party rallies or a Hitler Youth camping expedition, or maybe the crowds of the 1936 Olympics or columns of soldiers marching to war. And while it is the case that National Socialist ideology prioritised the nation over the individual, it did not entirely forsake the private lives of those deemed worthy.[1] Even the Führer was expected to need time for pleasure, reflection and regeneration beyond the reaches of his public responsibilities.[2] The belief that privacy nurtured the life of the mind and familial intimacy was central to the bourgeois ideals that still held great sway in the 1930s. By this period, however, private lives in Western Europe and North America were also increasingly shaped by desires for and possession of consumer goods – a trend which ran counter to the economic policies of the German dictatorship as it readied for war. Beyond the practical limitations to consumer goods in this production-minded economy, some National Socialists discounted material wants as 'Jewish' materialism, decadent and selfish. This chapter seeks to tease out where personal property and desires for possessions fit within a dictatorship that claimed to support the private lives of its citizens, as sites of pleasure and personal aspiration, but also downplayed, even suppressed, opportunities to fulfil dreams through individual consumption.[3]

---

[1] I would like to thank Jonathan Zatlin for his many thoughtful comments on an early draft of this chapter, and to the editors of this volume for later suggestions. Any shortcomings remain wholly my own.

[2] See Despina Stratigakos, *Hitler at Home* (New Haven, CT, London, 2015). Hitler's promotional team highlighted their boss's love for his mountain retreat and his possessions as signs that he was a cultured, introspective person with good taste and wholesome desires.

[3] In the introduction to his study of private life in the GDR, Paul Betts implicitly reminds readers of the importance of consumer goods to the experience of the private. When asked about their definitions of private life, he explains, his East German interviewees generally cited their weekend cottages, books, radios, automobiles, hobbies and family celebrations and holidays as key symbols and moments. One can assume that family celebrations and

Keeping in mind that ideology and policy shaped consumer habits in the Third Reich, this chapter takes up the charge presented by the editors in the Introduction to explore the ways the regime 'co-produced the private'. First, I examine the regime's uneasy relationship with the idea of individual consumption. This section illustrates the extent to which it was accepted and welcomed by the state as part of a National Socialist ethic, and offers evidence of the ways those in the consumer products sector sought to navigate the line between the regime's wishes and the public's interest in material goods as the means to shape personal identity. The second section explores the issue of personal savings. I maintain that the regime's recognition of the link between consumer items and private happiness led officials to encourage saving as the mobilisation of individual wealth towards the attainment of private wishes. Even after the war began, the calls to save emphasised individual goals rather than primarily as a duty to serve national aims, despite the regime's use of deposits to fund the war. The two phenomena spending and saving, therefore demonstrate how 'Aryan' citizens and their leaders worked together to imagine private abundance, while maintaining the state's long-range military goals.

Spending

Those scholars interested in the private lives of Germans during the National Socialist era have generally focused on experiences rather than relationships to goods, which is understandable. The regime emphasised spectacles over things in its own offerings, most of which were group activities, though scholars have investigated the private aspects of group endeavours. Shelley Baranowski's important work on Strength Through Joy tourism, for example, provides a window into personal perceptions of the German and foreign landscapes and German vacationers' feelings towards the regime, its travel programme and other holiday makers while they attended the packaged trips.[4] Neil Gregor is interested in the experience of listening to symphonic concerts in the Nazi era, an activity that, as today, was enjoyed alongside others and within the closed confines of the private mind and body.[5] Many contemporary diarists also focused in their

---

holidays also regularly included some manner of gift-giving. Paul Betts, *Within Walls: Private Life in the German Democratic Republic* (Oxford, 2010), 3.

[4] See Shelley Baranowski, *Strength through Joy: Consumerism and Mass Tourism in the Third Reich* (Cambridge, 2004).

[5] See Neil Gregor, 'Listening as a Practice of Everyday Life: The Munich Philharmonic Orchestra and Its Audiences in the Second World War', in Christian Thorau and Hansjakob Ziemer (eds.), *Oxford Handbook of the History of Music Listening in the 19th and 20th Centuries* (New York, NY, 2019).

writing on this complicated intermingling of the private and the public – the self within the group. Sebastian Haffner's reflection on his time at a camp for young jurists is an obvious, if not singular, example.[6] Moritz Föllmer's work on individuality in the Third Reich adds greatly to our understanding of the value placed on the private in these years by providing evidence of 'Aryan' Germans who resisted intrusions into their private lives – arguments, demonstrates Föllmer, that appealed in some cases to Party officials, as in the story of Fritz K., who was fired from his job for taking his holiday on a week that did not suit the company with a woman who was not his wife. The Nazi Party's German Labour Front defended the former Schering employee, insisting that no one (not even a corporate pharmaceuticals giant) had the right to intervene in his private life.[7]

Each of these examples, however, focuses on the private life of emotions. The activities involved – experiencing travel and new sights, cultural events and spending time with loved ones – are not devoid of the objects of material culture, but the emotional responses to these activities have been considered far more central to the experience than any objects that may have been involved. But the regime and National Socialists more generally did not reject objects out of hand as contributors to private life. As one advocate explained in the autumn of 1933:

> Whoever buys something must not be seen exclusively as a money-spender, rather he also has a right as a supporter of the economy through his purchase to have the psychological wish fulfilled that he seeks to fulfill with that purchase. Whatever it may be, the consumer always makes the purchased object a part of his personal life. At the moment when the object is taken out of the milieu of the store or factory and brought into the personal sphere of the consumer, it becomes a piece of the life of the purchaser. The psychological component lies in the recognition that every object has a spiritual meaning, that each object helps decidedly to influence the cultural picture of the individual's life as well as the life of the whole nation.[8]

It could be argued that this example, authored by a professional within the retail sector, simply reflected the wishes of someone struggling to find a raison d'être in the face of economic depression and regime change. While those pressures undoubtedly played a role in motivating the author, the perspective was one that gained traction in the years that followed. The point was that individual consumption had a place in the 'new

---

[6] See Sebastian Haffner, *Defying Hitler: A Memoir* (New York, NY, 2000), 258–68.
[7] See Moritz Föllmer, *Individuality and Modernity in Berlin: Self and Society from Weimar to the Wall* (Cambridge, 2013), 105–6.
[8] 'Die psychologischen Voraussetzungen der deutschen Wirtschaftswerbung', *Die Reklame* 26/15 (1933), 449; see further Pamela E. Swett, *Selling under the Swastika: Advertising and Commercial Culture in Nazi Germany* (Stanford, CA, 2014), 51.

Germany' – first as a stimulant to the economy, particularly during the first two years as job creation had been a campaign promise of the NSDAP. Beyond this practical consideration, individual consumption had a private side as well. While the 'whole nation' was drawn into the author's argument about the cultural value of objects, the individual was most directly affected (psychologically and spiritually) by the acts of purchase and possession.

Such understanding did not signal an ideological acceptance of unbridled consumption. Individuals were encouraged by Party and state organs to consume rationally, which meant that the racial prescriptions of the new Germany were to be followed. So-called German goods and retailers were acceptable as objects of desire and sites of transaction. Retailers and manufacturers who were deemed to be 'Jewish' by local officials, and the goods and services they provided, were rejected. Excluding Jewish businesses from the economy served multiple purposes.[9] It led to the economic ruin of countless Jewish families, speeding up social isolation and emigration. It enriched 'Aryan' businesses by siphoning off customers and encouraging the sale of struggling 'Jewish' firms. Differentiating between purchases made at 'Aryan' firms and those bought at 'Jewish' businesses also lent further legitimacy to those items and services purchased from approved 'Aryan' vendors. Individuals could feel good about bringing 'German' products into their private lives.

According to National Socialist ideologues, however, the task was still greater than simply eliminating firms demonised as 'Jewish' from the marketplace. Certain types of individual consumption were still frowned upon. 'Crass materialism' was to be avoided as beneath the dignity of ideal 'Aryan' Germans, even though the nation's elite, particularly its political leaders, lived lives of increasingly lavish spending.[10] Göring, Bormann and others amassed massive art collections among other private luxuries, and Hitler himself enjoyed multiple residences that benefitted from costly renovation and careful interior design.[11] And yet at all levels

---

[9] For the most in-depth recent study of this process, see Christoph Kreutzmüller, *Final Sale in Berlin: The Destruction of Jewish Commercial Activity, 1930–1945* (New York, NY, 2013); also important is the work of Frank Bajohr, *Arisierung in Hamburg: Die Verdrängung der jüdischen Unternehmer, 1933–1945* (Hamburg, 1997), and Avraham Barkai, *Vom Boykott zur 'Entjudung': Der wirtschaftliche Existenzkampf der Juden im Dritten Reich, 1933–1945* (Frankfurt a.M., 1988).

[10] See Emil Endres, 'Die neue Gesinnung in der Werbung', *Die Reklame* 26/12 (1933); quoted also in Corey Ross, 'Visions of Prosperity', in Pamela E. Swett, S. Jonathan Wiesen and Jonathan Zatlin (eds.), *Selling Modernity: Advertising in Twentieth Century Germany* (Durham, 2007), 52–77, here 69.

[11] See Fabrice d'Almeida, *High Society in the Third Reich* (Cambridge, 2008); Jonathan Petropoulos, *Art as Politics in the Third Reich* (Chapel Hill, NC, 1996); Stratigakos, *Hitler at Home*.

of the state and Party apparatus, there was an insistence that individual consumption had the potential to enrich private lives by increasing pleasure, which would in turn contribute to national well-being.

Officially, this goal would be achieved by educating consumers to make proper decisions, which meant not only rejecting 'Jewish' firms and the 'Jewish' materialistic world-view, but to recognise good taste over kitsch. Taste was defined not as 'high class', even if the regime's leaders and the nation's elite continued to live well beyond the means of the rest of society. Rather, good taste (in public discourse) was defined by the product's level of authenticity, while kitsch was the cheap replica that falsely claimed quality or singularity.[12] Indeed, many in advertising believed that all people (at least all 'Aryans') had a natural 'desire for beauty and purity of form'.[13] And we should not assume that this discussion was motivated solely by a romanticisation of a pre-modern craft tradition. Technology and mass production could provide high-quality, authentic goods, if function and form were appropriate. And personal decisions about one's purchases mattered, because the tchotchke kept on the mantel may be private, but the damage done to that consumer who 'wasted' her money and did nothing to enrich the culture bled into her family and the community beyond the home.

Since private spending decisions had far-reaching consequences, according to National Socialists, education was critical. Two avenues were targeted. The first was personal finance, which played an increasingly important role in the latter 1930s and into the war years, as consumers' disposable income grew and available goods declined. I turn to a discussion of saving in the next section. The other avenue for educating consumers was through the efforts of a 'reformed' advertising industry. Advertisers and retailers were thrilled that the new regime and its Ad Council, founded in 1933 under the authority of Goebbels' Ministry of Propaganda, recognised the usefulness of commercial ads in the new Germany.[14] There were those who advocated for an end to all advertising now that the 'liberal economy', or as one antisemite put it, 'the Jewish

---

[12] See Gustav Bischoff, 'Was ist eigentlich "Kitsch"?', *Seidels Reklame* 11 (1933), 366.

[13] Education (through ads and other venues) was still necessary, however, to reinforce and protect this natural inclination: see Ch. Lebahn, 'Werbemittel als Ausdruck der Zeit und als Geschmacksbildner!', *Seidels Reklame* 11 (1936), 379.

[14] See Swett, *Selling under the Swastika*; Uwe Westphal, *Werbung im Dritten Reich* (Berlin, 1989); Hartmut Berghoff, '"Times Change and We Change with Them": The German Advertising Industry in the Third Reich – Between Professional Self-Interest and Political Repression', *Business History* 45/1 (2003), 128–47; Gerulf Hirt, *Verkannte Propheten? Zur 'Expertenkultur' (west)deutscher Werbekommunikatoren bis zur Rezession 1966/67* (Leipzig, 2013).

salesmania' had been overcome.[15] But these fanatics failed to realise that the movement's leadership did see a role, as has been presented here, for individual consumption as a contributor to private happiness and the nation's cultural capital. What was more, Nazi leaders assumed that if consumers could be educated to make rational, tasteful choices in their spending, the sort of companies that would flourish (once Jews were also pushed out of the market) would be those that sought to make all ('Aryan') lives better, leading to a decrease in class-based inequality, if not a disappearance of class.[16] As the future president of the Ad Council Heinrich Hunke declared in 1936: '[National Socialism] is not about the socialisation of goods, it is about the socialisation of people.'[17]

The Ad Council's task, therefore, was to serve as a mediator between businesses and the state and to help to build a new 'German advertising' that prioritised truthfulness as a principle of 'a clean, morally healthy economy'.[18] A truthful appraisal of a product's merits would educate the audience and help them to discern for themselves whether the product had value/taste. This 'healthy' advertising was predicated first upon the removal, via a race-based licensing system, of Jewish advertisers and those who had been active on the political left. Beyond this forced expulsion, which directly affected thousands of men and women in the industry, we do not see significant censorship of ad content or design. Those who staffed Goebbels' Ministry did not feel it necessary. If consumers learned to trust the messages within advertisements, because their experiences with products reflected the promotional slogans, they were more likely to make rational choices with their money, spending or saving as appropriate. In other words, it was assumed that the state's aims and those of consumers were ultimately aligned.

Jonathan Wiesen has alerted us to the importance of trust (*Vertrauen*) in the marketing and public relations campaigns of the era. He refers to the example of Bayer pharmaceuticals which relied on the slogan 'the mark of trust' alongside their iconic Bayer cross logo. Wiesen explains that 'building confidence in merchandise and services merged with the aims of

---

[15] Fritz Nonnenbruch, *Völkischer Beobachter*, 9 Sept. 1939, as quoted in Dr Hans Jacobsen-Fauluck, 'Marktordnung in der Werbewirtschaft', *Die Deutsche Werbung* 33/5, 6 (1940), 148; see also Swett, *Selling under the Swastika*, 50. The reference to the end of a liberal economy can be found in numerous sources, including Werbe-Sed [nom de plume, PS], 'Wo endet die Aufgabe der Gemeinschafts-Werbung?', *Seidels Reklame* 2 (1934), 64.

[16] For a concise statement on the goal of undermining class difference, see Heinrich Hunke, 'Menschen gestalten die Wirtschaft', *Die Deutsche Volkswirtschaft* 11 (1935), 329–30.

[17] Heinrich Hunke, 'Kernfragen der Wehrwirtschaft', *Die Deutsche Volkswirtschaft* 1 (1936), 19–21, here 21. Hunke was also the president of the Ad Council and the editor of the Nazi economics periodical *Die Deutsche Volkswirtschaft*.

[18] Werbe-Sed, 'Wo endet die Aufgabe der Gemeinschafts-Werbung?', 64.

building trust in professionals, the state, its leaders, and Germany's seemingly humanitarian mission'.[19] The only element missing in this insightful formulation is that the idea of building trust implies a level of confidence also in consumers – that they will understand the value of the goods on offer. Consumers were becoming more sophisticated in Germany, as elsewhere, in the interwar period, and the Nazi regime and business leaders banked on that growing confidence. State and economic elites believed German consumers would see their best interests (even their most private desires) mirrored in the political aims and commercial slogans of the day.

For example, one article from 1934 in the popular advertising trade journal *Seidels Reklame* discussed the efficacy of 'the family as an ad-argument'. The article began by noting that copy writers and designers always needed to keep the psychological 'essence and habits' of the targeted consumers in sight. He implied that the skilled advertiser must be ready to recognise such common customs and beliefs, but also that these change over time. One such 'sphere of interest', claimed the author, which had allegedly fallen out of favour in the recent republican era that cared little for 'intimacy and honesty', was now ready to be brought back to centre stage, owing to 'the changes underway in the public and private lives of the *Volk*'. That basic value was 'the family and its harmonious configuration'.[20] The author proceeded to provide examples of how to create ads that support 'the burning desire of most housewives' to keep their husbands home by creating a 'comfy and cosy house'. One furniture ad ran the headline: 'My husband rarely goes out!' thanks to the relaxing and tasteful décor. Another appealed to the mother of teenagers under the headline: 'Our youngster always says' that his home is 'a thousand times nicer than his pals''. The ad copy worked on multiple levels. It appealed to the female consumer's desire to create the same sort of setting for her loved ones. It also appealed to her pride by promising results that would outshine the homes of neighbours and friends. Finally, parents' wishes to prepare their children for adulthood is also at play: 'Already in the consciousness of a young person lies the vision of a nice home and parents must see the caring for and strengthening of this impulse as a valuable educational task. A nice home lifts self-confidence.'[21]

---

[19] S. Jonathan Wiesen, *Creating the Nazi Marketplace: Commerce and Consumption in the Third Reich* (Cambridge, 2011), 89–90.
[20] Carl Schnell-Koch, 'Die Familie als Werbe-Argument', *Seidels Reklame* 3 (1934), 92.
[21] Sample advertisements for Möbelhaus Norwest in Schnell-Koch, 'Die Familie als Werbe-Argument.'

Such ad copy is not Nazified in any overt way. We can imagine similar advertisements appearing in other Western, democratic societies in the same era – perhaps even in our lifetimes. And that is my point. The National Socialist government did not need to strong-arm advertisers or consumers, nor did it wish to do so. Rather advertisers were supported in their attempts to look for pre-existing sentiments that seemed to speak to contemporary desires and fears. One prominent commentator referred to advertisements as 'in their aim and content another form of news'.[22] Advertisers sought to tap into what people wished for and were concerned about in their private lives. In this case, the author of the *Seidels Reklame* article believed that most Germans living in the Third Reich could relate to the guiding principle behind the furniture store's ad: 'The family as germ cell of the state is the fertile soil for all cultural endeavours.' In doing so, consumers were brought in as partners to the relationship of trust that commercial leaders and the state sought to forge.

Those connected to the consumer goods industry and to the Ad Council liked to claim that these efforts were a great success. As the prominent ad-man Hanns Brose wrote in 1934:

The brand name good [*Markenartikel*] has taught the individual to systematically care for the face and hands, the whole body [. . .] in doing so it has played its role in the bridging of social difference. [. . .] The brand name article has made it possible for the individual to dress better, in a more dignified way, and in accordance with their own taste, which has increased pleasure and performance [. . .]. The brand name good has turned amateur photography into a mass sport, music into a people's art, and radio into a mass experience, which has expanded, deepened, and enriched the world of the mind and cultural world for countless members of the *Volk*.[23]

These examples do not seem to square with our understanding of the regime's efforts to suppress consumption in the years leading up to the onset of war. Adam Tooze has demonstrated convincingly that German consumer purchasing power remained low and shortages of certain consumer items remained common throughout the entire pre-war period.[24] But what has been presented here does not necessarily contradict such evidence. Rather this chapter maintains that individual consumption had a role in the National Socialist world-view that recognised and upheld the

---

[22] O. F. Döbbelin, 'Ausblick auf die Markenartikel-Werbung von 1940!', in Döbbelin (ed.), *Archiv für Markenartikel-Propaganda* (Berlin, 1935), 23 (Manuscript).
[23] Hanns Brose, *Götterdämmerung des Markenartikels? Neue Wege zu neuen Käufern* (Schwarzenberg, 1934), 19–20.
[24] See Adam Tooze, *The Wages of Destruction: The Making and Breaking of the Nazi Economy* (New York, NY, 2006), 141–3.

importance of private life. It is the case that there were limits to its tangible realisation, but we should not forget that inexpensive purchases remained part of daily life and that planning for larger ones intensified in these years, as Germans began to see their incomes grow towards the end of the 1930s thanks to the rapid expansion of the economy owing to rearmament. In concert with the implementation of the Four-Year-Plan, beginning in 1936, however, consumer choice was on the decline as imports dried up and existing raw materials went towards preparations for war. German consumers, therefore, were increasingly left to postpone purchases for the future.

Saving

Like with consumer spending, National Socialists had a somewhat fraught relationship to banking. National Socialists frequently lambasted Germany's large private banks as part of the international Jewish conspiracy that preyed upon the German nation. As the Nazi economist Gottfried Feder saw it in 1933, '[t]he idea to control a people through money and with money accords perfectly with the mentality of the Jews'.[25] The Banking Crisis of 1931 had deepened mistrust in broad sectors of society and brought calls for reform that would eventually be implemented by the National Socialists. In December 1934 a new federal regulatory law was passed.[26] However, according to Tooze, the three largest private banks (Deutsche, Dresdner and Commerzbank) were the chief 'losers' of the crisis and the recovery that accompanied rearmament under Hitler's government. The total assets held by the big three only increased by 15 per cent between 1932 and 1939. But theirs is not the entire story of banking during these years. The growth of the Sparkassen system (communal savings banks) far outpaced these giants, rising by 102 per cent over the same period.[27] For National Socialists, these local

---

[25] Gottfried Feder, *Die funktionelle Bedeutung des Geld- und Kreditwesens* (Berlin, 1933), 6; for another example of the same sort of praise for the history of public banking in Germany, in contrast to 'Jewish' private banking, see Arthur Herrmann, *Zweihundert Jahre öffentliches Bankwesen* (Berlin, 1935); on Jewish participation in the development of European banking, see among others Derek J. Penslar, *Shylock's Children: Economics and Jewish Identity in Modern Europe* (Berkeley, CA, 2001), 128–9.

[26] See Jens Piorkowski, *Die deutsche Sparkassenorganisation 1924 bis 1934* (Stuttgart, 1997), 121–26.

[27] See Tooze, *Wages of Destruction*, 110. For a brief overview of the place of German banks within the Nazi economy, see Dieter Ziegler, '"A Regulated Market Economy": New Perspectives on the Nature of the Economic Order of the Third Reich, 1933–1939', in Hartmut Berghoff, Jürgen Kocka and Dieter Ziegler (eds.), *Business in the Age of Extremes: Essays in Modern German and Austrian Economic History* (Cambridge, 2013), 139–52. On the Sparkassen see Paul Thomes, 'German Savings Banks as Instruments of Regional

savings institutions were an authentic manifestation of *Volksgemeinschaft*. On 1 July 1933, the NSDAP leadership announced that the banking for the regional Party administration (*Gauwaltungsapparat*) would be handled through public banks like the Sparkassen, and a number of the Party's affiliated associations followed suit.[28] When Interior Minister Wilhelm Frick referred to frugality and industry as the 'most noble of German virtues' in 1933, he congratulated the Sparkassen for fostering and protecting these virtues.[29] To those like Frick and Feder, the Sparkassen offered a counterweight to the 'liberal economic mind-set' that motivated the owners of the large private banks. Indeed Feder believed the Sparkassen to be 'the oldest and proudest bearer; one can go so far as to call them the cornerstone of the German credit system.'[30] Local branches fostered this image by marking the anniversaries of their founding with *völkisch* festivities and commissioning commemorative poetry.[31]

Feder's antisemitism may have been particularly virulent, but many Germans shared his age-old prejudice that Jews were 'the agents of the creative destruction characteristic of capitalism' and embraced the public savings banks as civic-minded 'German' institutions.[32] By the end of the 1930s, almost every German household possessed at least one savings account, and a large proportion had more than one. These accounts, made visibly tangible by the booklets that identified the account owners and tracked deposits and withdrawals, speak to a number of issues related to the concept of 'the private' in Nazi Germany. First, the accounts themselves represented the private earnings of the individual whose name graced the cover. Second, those savings often reflected the private aspirations of the account holder. Whether she was saving for a holiday or a child's school expenses, a new hat or the possibility of a medical crisis, the plan was likely her own or made in concert with her loved ones. Third, as with spending, saving had a public mandate as well as a private one. During the Third Reich, Germans were constantly being told what to do with their money. The government issued frequent refrains to contribute to a host of collection boxes, alongside the required fees associated with

---

Development', in Youssef Cassis, Gerald Feldman and Ulf Olsson (eds.), *The Evolution of Financial Institutions and Markets in Twentieth-Century Europe* (Aldershot, 1995), 143–62, here 144; Piorkowski, *Die deutsche Sparkassenorganisation*, 65.

[28] See Hans Pohl, *Wirtschaft- und Sozialgeschichte der deutschen Sparkassen im 20. Jahrhundert* (Stuttgart, 2005), 151.

[29] BArch Berlin, NS6/492, Special edition of the *Deutsche Sparkassen-Zeitung*, 3 Oct. 1933.

[30] Feder, *Die funktionelle Bedeutung des Geld- und Kreditwesens*, 11.

[31] Nuremberg's Oberbürgermeister was the editor of one such collection: Willy Liebel, *Kleines Lesebuch vom Sparen: Eine Dichtergabe für jung und alt* (Nuremberg, 1941).

[32] Jerry Z. Muller, *Capitalism and the Jews* (Princeton, NJ, 2010), 16, 60–1.

membership in Nazified social and professional organisations. They were also encouraged, as we see in what follows, to deposit 'excess' cash into their Sparkassen accounts – and deposit it they did. As Adam Tooze and others have explained, the billions that were poured into the nation's savings banks created a massive reservoir of capital that was central to the 'silent' financing of the war.[33] In this context of mobilising private funds to achieve the public agenda of the state, which was chiefly the preparation for and waging of war, there was no more significant factor than the deposits Germans made into their accounts in the country's communal savings banks. However, in contrast to the resentment that often accompanied the calls for donations, most Germans seem to have accepted the encouragement to save their money.

Beyond the macroeconomic issues, historians have tended to be interested in the savings habits of Germans to demonstrate either the coercive nature of the dictatorship or citizens' trust in and consent for national aims. For example, in his 1995 essay on savings bank advertisements, Peter Borscheid argues that 'nationalist thinking dominated Sparkassen advertising from 1933 on', including the overt militarisation of the discourse and reliance on Nazi ideological tropes such as 'homeland and race, blood and soil, mother and child'.[34] In his reading, then, the language around saving was almost exclusively focused on the public good – thrift and sacrifice for the homeland. A second look, however, at the exhortations to save in state propaganda and among Sparkassen promotional materials demonstrates that these were far more varied than Borscheid contends. Instead of motivating savers solely (or even predominantly) with images of national unity, duty or destiny, officials also encouraged saving as a way of realising personal dreams – the same dreams that turn up in writing about and advertisements for consumer goods. What is the significance of this observation? The main point – and it is one that reinforces the assertions of the first section of this chapter – is that the population participated in the rethinking of the relationship between personal and communal [*eigen/gemein*] via their deposits into the communal Sparkassen just as they did through their negotiation of how individual consumption fit into this evolving society. The culture

---

[33] Tooze, *Wages of Destruction*, 354–5. This moniker, which was first used by regime officials, is somewhat inaccurate. While the siphoning of individual savings was less direct than war bonds or special taxes, citizens knew their funds were being used to support the war effort.

[34] Peter Borscheid, 'Sparsamkeit und Sicherheit. Werbung für Banken, Sparkassen und Versicherungen', in Peter Borscheid and Clemens Wischermann (eds.), *Bilderwelt des Alltags* (Stuttgart, 1995), 316–25, here 318.

around saving and spending, around an acceptable 'private' life, then, was co-produced by the regime and the 'Aryan' population.

The tradition of public banking dates back to the nineteenth century, but the new government had cast the tradition as National Socialist first during the Depression, as a communal way to fight unemployment, and Germans responded positively. The discourse changed mid-decade, as discussed later in this chapter, but Germans continued to save. Indeed, money became far more concentrated in the savings economy, as spending continued to decline on the eve of war. The war years intensified this process further. Wages were coming home during the war and were moving into savings accounts at astounding rates. However, late in the war, Germans no longer rushed to deliver their money to the Sparkassen. This shift is most often described as a rupture, the moment in which Germans finally chose their self-interest over national interest. Ideology and personal economic aims no longer appeared to converge sometime in late 1942, and so Germans were faced with a decision. But when we think about the place of spending and saving together within this society, the rupture becomes less prominent. The regime had always made room for Germans to think of their funds as their own, particularly after the crisis of the Depression was overcome. In this sense, withholding money was less about rejecting the Nazi world-view. Rather Germans continued to safeguard their dreams of private life, as they had been encouraged to do by their leaders for years. The problem was one of the dictatorship's own making.

This nineteenth-century tradition, in which the Sparkassen were lauded as communal institutions, was most apparent during the dictatorship's early years of economic depression and political revolution. Nazi advocates of a greater role for the Sparkassen during the 'national reawakening' focused on the role individuals could play in helping their unemployed 'national comrades' by depositing excess earnings in the public banks, which, it was argued explicitly, would stimulate job creation by funding capital projects initiated by municipal governments and providing credit to local businesses hoping to expand or to withstand the difficult times. With the receding importance of job creation by mid-decade, the language coming from the regime changed, even though the desire to promote saving was stronger than ever before and must be considered in conjunction with the simultaneous emergence of a National Socialist discourse (by state actors, the private sector and consumers) on individual consumption.

On one hand, the funds were now needed to finance rearmament. The government ensured deposits would be used this way by forcing the Sparkassen to buy high levels of Reich debt. On the other hand, the government also sought to remove excess funds from the pockets of its citizens, because with the shift to arms manufacturing, the level of consumer items available for purchase had fallen dramatically. Advertisers would continue to promote daily-use items and consumers would continue to purchase and judge the merits of those products available to them. However, given that men and women still desired consumer goods that were unavailable, the language used to promote saving now emphasised that the practice was the rational, responsible way to attain (at a future date) the things one most wanted.[35]

This is an area where my findings diverge from those of Borscheid and others: despite the work done by the Reich government to dampen consumer spending, there were no prohibitions on advertisements for consumer goods, as discussed in the first half of this chapter, nor were there bans on ad copy that encouraged saving by embracing the goals of consumption. In 1938, for example, slogans such as 'Saving makes buying easy', 'Save in order to buy', and 'First save, then buy' were common.[36] Moreover, Germans were encouraged to value the *process* of saving, and in doing so state and bank officials promoted the private intimacy between savers and the dreams embodied in their bank accounts. Promotional materials extolled the comfort the individual could draw from one's account booklet, like a personal diary that recorded the ups and downs of life: 'By diligent saving the saver sees the accumulation of his wealth, sees how [...] he has achieved goals, and sees ultimately how [his wealth] rebounds after it has been spent rationally. His own production, success, bad times and good, come to light to him through his savings book.'[37]

In order to channel savings in ways the regime could manage and even take credit for, certain purchases were prioritised. The Party's Strength Through Joy office famously ran savings programmes for holiday travel and the

---

[35] The need to wait for a time in the future without shortages is discussed quite plainly in writings about saving; see for example, Der Deutsche Sparkassen- und Giroverband (ed.), *Das Gefolgschaftssparen: Ein Handbuch für die Sparkassenpraxis* (Berlin, 1939), 7. The granting of credit to small businesses and communities by the Sparkassen fell overall between 1933 and 1939, owing to the political and economic prioritisation of rearmament. Personal credit remained flat before 1939 and declined markedly after the onset of war. New mortgages also declined throughout the decade. See Pohl, *Wirtschaft- und Sozialgeschichte der deutschen Sparkassen*, 212–22. Interest rates at the Sparkassen decreased over time in this era. In 1933–4, the average interest rate was 3.5 per cent. In the remaining pre-war years, it dropped to 3 per cent, and once the war began it fell under 2 per cent by 1941 for short-term deposits, though those willing to leave their money in the account for more than twelve months could still earn just over 3 per cent. See *Statistisches Jahrbuch für das Deutsche Reich* (Berlin, 1943), 480–1, for the last Nazi-era volume, which provides data through 1941.
[36] Norbert-Christian Emmerich, *Die Deutsche Sparkassenwerbung, 1750–1981* (Stuttgart, 1983), 170.
[37] Ernst Hochrein, *Die deutschen öffentlichen Sparkassen* (Berlin, 1938), 18.

Volkswagen. In the case of the former, Germans made regular small contributions towards holiday travel packages, amounting to 15.18 million RM in 1937 (a drop in the bucket when compared to the hundreds of millions going into regular Sparkassen accounts).[38] But the rhetoric of private wish fulfilment through saving for desired goods was much more widespread than these well-known projects.[39] Common goals for saving were dowries, education expenses, Christmas presents or simply establishing a safety cushion in case of family crisis. A small number of middle-class Germans also still planned for the purchase of other larger-ticket items, like household appliances. In other words, people saved in order to fulfil their individual desires, as encouraged by the state and Party, and not in order to donate money to the national war chest. The fact that the two aims – consumer abundance and military victory – were linked is far more apparent to us than it would have been to most Germans before the autumn of 1939.

Another promotional focus of long-term saving was the goal of home ownership. Germany had been facing a housing crisis for decades with overcrowding and substandard living conditions common in urban areas. Conditions had deteriorated further during the Depression, leading to the establishment of large encampments on the outskirts of many cities. The economist and Nazi Ad Council official Heinrich Hunke argued that the republican era's rent freezes were responsible for the extreme shortage of new building.[40] He advocated policies that would affirm the place of property ownership in National Socialist Germany, because 'it means for the individual a home [*Heimat*] born out of effort and work'.[41] Germans who had money to invest seem to have agreed and the regime was happy to see money go into accounts earmarked for this purpose.[42]

---

[38] See Rudolf Schraut, 'Das Kleinsparwesen – eine bedeutsame Quelle fuer die Sammlung nationalen Sparkapitals', *Die Deutsche Volkswirtschaft* 15 (1938), 581. See also Bernhard Rieger, 'The "Good German" Goes Global: The Volkswagen Beetle as an Icon in the Federal Republic', *History Workshop Journal* 68 (2009), 3–26.

[39] For further reading on Strength Through Joy travel programmes and the *Volksprodukte*, including the Volkswagen, see Baranowski, *Strength through Joy* and Wolfgang König, *Volkswagen, Volksempfänger, und Volksgemeinschaft: 'Volksprodukte' im Dritten Reich. Vom Scheitern einer nationalsozialistischen Konsumgesellschaft* (Paderborn, 2004). See also Rieger, 'The "Good German" Goes Global'. On the private sector's attempts to remain profitable in this period, see Swett, *Selling under the Swastika*; Wiesen, *Creating the Nazi Marketplace*.

[40] Tooze, *Wages of Destruction*, 157–61. The rent controls implemented during the hyperinflation to stave off mass evictions had meant that apartment construction was very unattractive to private investors. Publicly subsidised construction, however, went some way towards filling the gap.

[41] 'Der nationalsozialistische Eigentumsbegriff', *Die Deutsche Sparkassen-Zeitung* 13 (1935), 3.

[42] The number of new accounts earmarked for future building projects grew annually from 1939 until 1943. There was some drop off in 1944 before the complete collapse in 1945. See diagram 22 in Philipp Kratz, 'Sparen für das kleine Glück', in Götz Aly (ed.), *Volkes*

However, while saving for future construction increased dramatically in the 1930s, home construction was in sharp decline, as the regime sought to limit private investment in construction and to put dramatic limits on publicly funded housing starting in 1938.[43] Public and private funds were, therefore, again made available to fund the German war machine.

The Sparkassen also 'created savings-opportunities for the everyman'.[44] In 1936, three quarters of all savings books were attached to accounts that held less than 300 RM, and remarkably more than 50 per cent of accounts held between 20 and 100 RM.[45] While most accounts were small, savings books were held by about 35 million German men, women and children in 1938, or roughly half the population.[46] Deposits increased annually, and the positive trends in bank balance sheets were magnified by a decrease in the number of withdrawals as opportunities for spending dried up.[47]

Everyone, young and old, rich and poor, was urged to nurture his/her dreams through saving, but housewives were especially targeted as the keepers of the family's finances. Sparkassen and state officials presented how-to pamphlets and exhibits aimed at the 'clever housewife'; free budgeting books and small coin banks were handed out; print ads were run in magazines – even clocks that would only run for twenty-four hours and required a coin deposit to get restarted were made available.[48] While we know the DAF prodded workers aggressively, savings banks also veered towards coercion by assigning employees the work of visiting outlying homes on a weekly or monthly basis to pick up deposits from families who could not readily visit the branches in town.[49] In these ways, we certainly do see attempts to influence private decisions about savings. What is worth emphasising, however, is that this intervention was

---

Stimme: Skepsis und Führervertrauen im Nationalsozialismus (Frankfurt a.M., 2006), 59–79, here 67.
[43] On the failed Nazi settlement programme and *Volkswohnungen*, see Tooze, *Wages of Destruction*, 157–61.
[44] T. Heckmann-Schwege, 'Vertrauen', *Die Deutsche Sparkassen-Zeitung* 19 (1935), 3.
[45] See Thomes, 'German Savings Banks', 148. For the breakdown of these data, see the table in Schraut, 'Das Kleinsparwesen', 581.
[46] Hochrein, *Die deutschen öffentlichen Sparkassen*, 10.
[47] See 'Deutsche Sparkassen', *Die Deutsche Volkswirtschaft* 10 (1938), 348, which includes a table that sums up these findings between 1934 and 1937.
[48] Advertising for banks was regulated by the Nazi Ad Council as was the case for all types of advertisements. See for example the rules about ads to mark the annual *Spartag*, or national savings day in 1936 in Hunke Nachlass, Landesarchiv Nordrhein-Westfalen, Abteilung Ostwestfalen-Lippe, Karton 7–2. The 'saving-clock' is mentioned in Schraut, 'Das Kleinsparwesen', 581–2; on advertising public banks more generally, see Emmerich, *Deutsche Sparkassenwerbung*, 156–75, as well as Borscheid, 'Sparsamkeit und Sicherheit'; Pamela E. Swett, 'Mobilizing Citizens and Their Savings: Germany's Public Savings Banks, 1933–1939', in Mary Lindemann and Jared Poley (eds.), *Money in the German-Speaking Lands* (New York, NY, 2017), 234–49.
[49] See Ernst Joachim Haas, *Stadt-Sparkasse Düsseldorf, 1825–1972* (Berlin, 1972), 242.

about increasing the level of deposits and not about harmonising the motivations for deposits.

By the time the war began in September 1939, the Sparkassen had played their role, safely siphoning 'excess' funds towards financing the preparations for war, and this strategy would continue.[50] Adam Tooze calculates that 8 billion RM from Sparkassen savings was redirected towards the war effort in 1940 alone – a figure that climbed to 12.8 billion RM in 1941.[51] Members of the security apparatus understood well that the stability of the savings system underpinned the war economy, and there were rumours in early 1940 that the SD and/or Gestapo kept lists of those making sizeable withdrawals from savings accounts.[52] By the end of the war, 60 million savings books were in circulation.[53] Throughout the conflict, official statements made direct connections between duty, savings and military victory.[54] However, the strident calls for ever greater saving also still framed the decision as a personal one, rather than solely as a question facing the nation. For example, when Fritz Reinhardt of the Reich Ministry of Finance announced the regime's new flagship saving plan, *Eisernes Sparen*, in a national radio broadcast in October 1941, he began: 'It does not matter that the private wishes of individuals cannot be fully fulfilled during the war. [...] The soldier at the front expects that the home front will think of him first and not themselves.' However, Germans were not asked to sacrifice those 'private wishes', in terms of their total surrender or destruction. Instead, Reinhardt added: 'Each [individual] must strive to lay aside the largest part of his income for the time after the war. The time will come, when the restrictions on the market will fall away. Then everyone will be able to catch up on the purchases which he had to forgo during the war.' To convince listeners, Reinhardt did not rely on nationalist fervour or fear of defeat. Rather he spoke to the individual about safeguarding his/her own money so that it was not lost

---

[50] See 'Die Kriegsfinanzierung Deutschlands', *Deutsche Sparkassen-Zeitung* 95 (1940).
[51] See Tooze, *Wages of Destruction*, 354–5, including figure 15 on 355.
[52] See BArch Berlin, NS25/17, Akten-Vermerk, Betr: Zusammenarbeit des SD mit den Sparkassen-Reichsgruppe Banken, Stuttgart, 21 Feb. 1940. This memo includes a debate about whether lists of account holders who had made withdrawals shortly after the onset of war were being collected by the SD or the Gestapo.
[53] See Kratz, 'Sparen für das kleine Glück', 63. The author estimates these 60 million booklets were held by two-thirds of the population.
[54] Walther Funk declared, for example, in October 1940, that 'every war requires substantial financial means. [...] Every German must be aware of this: that saving in this grand hour is a serious duty to the fatherland, and that each Mark put aside helps attain victory.' Funk, Speech on the occasion of the second 'Kriegsspartag' in *Deutsche Sparkassen-Zeitung* 125 (1940), 1.

(*verloren geht*). 'Whoever puts his money in a shoebox, in his wallet, or elsewhere, runs the risk of losing it.' And if that didn't work, he added for good measure: 'Whoever holds back money without justifiable reasons, also runs the danger of being arrested.'[55]

Germans continued to see saving as their means to achieving personal goals and that contributed directly to the failure of the *Eisernes Sparen* system. This new programme created tax-free accounts that required the holder to select a regular predetermined amount to be deducted from his wages or salary, but it did not allow for withdrawals of funds until after the conclusion of the war. Introduced in October 1941, the plan failed to win over Germans, which was a bitter disappointment for the regime. Officials in the Reich Ministry of Finance had forecasted that the new scheme would raise 4–5 billion RM of additional funds per year, but when it was rolled out, months before Germany's military fortunes turned decidedly negative, there was no rush to sign up.[56] In September 1944, *Eisernes Sparen* deposits only comprised 1.76 per cent of total Sparkassen savings.[57] The state may have increased the likelihood for failure itself by employing an advertising campaign for *Eisernes Sparen* that stressed the private reasons for signing up. One ad that ran in Goebbels' weekly newspaper, *Das Reich*, in May 1942, carried the headline 'We all save with *Eisernes Sparen*!' Below that slogan three Germans were pictured: the first image was a saleswoman from Hannover who declared that she could only deposit 12 RM per month, but even so she would have a large dowry saved by the end of the war; the second image featured a bookkeeper from Hamburg who explained that he was 'the father of three children' and was using *Eisernes Sparen* 'to save for apprenticeship training'; and the third was a farm labourer in Bavaria who was saving to buy himself land and 'increase his income'.[58]

Nowhere in the ad copy are Germans encouraged to save to help achieve victory or to donate to the national cause. Focusing on the private plans for savings may have slowed enrolment in the programme, because potential savers knew that there were restrictions on withdrawals. *Eisernes Sparen* was in reality a direct contribution to the war effort, even if it was not marketed as such. Germans could not square the circle of saving for a dowry or land purchase through a system that put off those purchases indefinitely. Poor enrolment results immediately led to internal state and

---

[55] Fritz Reinhardt, 'Rundfunkrede: Eisernes Sparen', Oct. 1941, 9–10.
[56] See LAB, Rep. A 219, Nr. 74, Deutscher Sparkassen- und Giroverband an alle Sparkassen, Verbände und Stammgirozentralen, Betr: Eiserne Sparkonten, 31 Oct. 1941.
[57] See Kratz, 'Sparen für das kleine Glück', 77.
[58] 'Wir alle Sparen eisern!', advertisement in *Das Reich* 5 (10 May 1942).

Party discussions about making *Eisernes Sparen* accounts mandatory, but these suggestions were rejected by superiors as bound to incite widespread resistance to *Zwangssparen* (forced saving).[59]

And so the regime continued on its path of highlighting the individual benefits of savings accounts. In early 1943, for example, banks and local officials were still urging people to save for home construction. Restrictions on commercial advertisements were extensive by this point, but not when it came to saving. While encouraging Germans to invest in the future, potential savers were, however, also reminded that new building would not start immediately on the cessation of the conflict, that mass-produced materials would need to be used and that 'biological and social' standards would be employed to determine who would build where.[60] In May of the same year, when Funk spoke to a large audience of business leaders alongside representatives of the Party, state and military, his concluding remarks repeated the familiar refrain about saving. However, his choice of words also hinted at a new awareness that account holders were beginning to doubt the security of their money. In response, Funk highlighted the need 'to stabilise the belief that money saved today will later be applied to the goods economy, meaning that the one who saves in war, will be able to buy something with this money in peace time, and he will buy cheaper and better than today'.[61]

Stories of individuals who had chosen to safeguard their money at home only to subsequently lose those funds were circulated among savings banks staff, presumably in order to be passed on as words of warning to customers. In one story titled 'Bad luck with the stroller' printed in the national trade journal for Sparkassen employees during the spring of 1943, a woman who carried her savings in a heavy envelope hidden under her infant's stroller linens was featured. For some time her strategy worked just fine, the periodical reported, but one day she left the stroller outside the store she entered. When the baby became upset, a nearby man whose attention was drawn to the carriage by the baby's cries attempted to calm the child down, and in the process saw the envelope. Guessing the nature of its contents, he grabbed the envelope and disappeared before the mother returned. The young woman did not even realise she had lost her savings until she returned home.[62] Allegorical stories like this one

---

[59] The idea of requiring citizens to save was discussed within the government in the weeks leading up to the war. Göring was rumoured to have been a proponent, but the idea was shelved. See the correspondence among the leadership of the Deutscher Sparkassen- und Giroverband in April 1939 and January 1940 in BArch Berlin, NS25/1388 Kriegssparen.
[60] *Deutsche Sparkassen-Zeitung* 14 (1943), 2.
[61] *Deutsche Sparkassen-Zeitung* 39 (1943), 1.
[62] See 'Das Unglück mit dem Kinderwagen', *Deutsche Sparkassen-Zeitung* 22 (1943), 1.

appeared more frequently in newspapers and magazines, as Germans increasingly chose to keep their money at home, but what is most significant is that the woman was not presented as a bad *Volksgenossin*, a traitor even, to the nation in the crisis that was total war. She was a consumer, out shopping, but there was no shame in that activity, and she was not called a lawbreaker for hoarding cash at home. Rather her loss was recognised simply as unfortunate bad luck for her and her family. Other articles about those who lost savings at home stressed the ignorance of those who believed rumours about the insecurity of the Sparkassen or the regime's plans to confiscate private funds. In general, however, the national cause was rarely raised.[63] Instead, even in the summer of 1943, those who hid their money at home or on their persons were simply missing out on a good investment, who failed to recognise that it was through saving that 'a natural social upward mobility is possible, in that each individual has the same opportunity to raise his or his descendants' personal prosperity and living conditions by the power of his own achievement'.[64]

A chief reason for keeping funds at home was the fear of bombing. Citizens worried that if their banks were hit they would lose all their savings. Germans were reported carrying up to 1,000 RM with them at all times, in case their homes were also lost and they found themselves in need of emergency cash. Privileged Germans, who had greater resources and greater access to consumer goods, sought to invest in land or items that were easily movable, like jewellery, rather than furniture that would more likely be destroyed by fire.[65] The state tried to reassure its citizens that in the case of personal property losses to bombing they would be cared for. Similarly, if bank buildings were hit their personal accounts would not be affected, as long as they continued to safeguard their account booklets. Germans were reminded, for example, to bring these booklets with them to air raid shelters. Account holders were also

---

[63] See report on Reichswirtschaftsminister Funk's speech on the occasion of the 100th anniversary of the Industrie- und Handelskammer München: 'Die große Chance der Sparer', *Deutsche Sparkassen-Zeitung* 48 (1943), 2.

[64] Reichswirtschaftsminister Funk at the Schillertheater in Berlin on the 125th anniversary of the Berliner Sparkasse as quoted in 'Die Aufgaben der Sparkassen', *Deutsche Sparkassen-Zeitung* 52 (1943), 1.

[65] General Gotthard Heinrici berated his wife, Gertrude, in March 1944 for not being as clever as one of his officers' wives who continued to find items to purchase, such as a watch and a fur, that were relatively easy to safeguard against the bombing. In the autumn of 1943, he had also already urged her to seek land, 'even in a destroyed city', that would serve as a wise investment in peacetime; see Johannes Hürter (ed.), *Notizen aus dem Vernichtungskrieg: Die Ostfront 1941/42 in den Aufzeichnungen des Generals Heinrici* (Darmstadt, 2016), here 219 and 229. Many thanks to Johannes Hürter for directing me to this source.

reassured that if they died, their accounts would go to the loved one named by the account holder or next of kin. Importantly, 'the will of the individual' in the matter, and not the needs of the community, was asserted as the paramount concern in deciding the fate of private funds that had been deposited in public banks.[66]

Even when the exigencies of total war were made explicit in the calls for saving, the private dreams of depositors were never ignored, because these were fundamentally tied up with the cause of war. For example, in late October 1943, the annual 'saving-week' propaganda was issued. This time, however, the rationale that was presented for saving insisted that 'the certainty of social mobility in an expanded economic space, which will need all brawn and brains, provides strength in today's difficult times. *Who does not believe in his own future, he has already given up.* He extinguishes all of the bright impulses, each joy that comes from striving.'[67] In other words, when the chips were down, Germans were not only asked to sacrifice for the *Volksgemeinschaft*. They were asked to draw strength, motivation and joy from their own individual lives and dreams for the future.

There were even attempts to entice POWs and foreign workers with the benefits of opening savings accounts on German soil. With nothing to buy and no way to send money home, many of these labourers held on to their cash, which they hid in their barracks or at their work sites during the day. The regime was particularly anxious to get this money off the streets; one official admitted that it 'was understandable' that Polish labourers were hesitant to deposit their earnings in German banks, but insisted these funds fuelled the black market, gambling and other illicit activities.[68] But most importantly, state officials recognised the inconsistency of compelling their own citizens to deposit funds, while permitting POWs and foreign labourers to hold on to their meagre (but mounting) earnings. Despite promotional efforts made through 1944, which included posters and redesigned savings books – but not force, which was considered too risky to production rates – foreign workers preferred to take their chances with their money, rather than handing it back to their overlords.[69] German citizens increasingly made the same decision to 'hoard' cash at home, though in this case seeing their behaviour as a sign of resistance or

---

[66] 'Sparkassenbuch auf fremden Namen', *Deutsche Sparkassen-Zeitung* 24 (1943), 1.
[67] 'Sparsamkeit ein Bekenntnis', S*parkassen-Zeitung zur Deutschen Sparwoche* 23–30 (1943), 1. Emphasis added.
[68] See BArch Berlin, NS6/723, Bericht der Gauleitung Wartheland, 2 Feb. 1942, 'Sparen der Polen'.
[69] See BArch Berlin, NS6/723, SS Report to the Party Chancellery in Munich, 11 Nov. 1942, about attempts to encourage Polish forced labourers to deposit funds in the Warthegau. Here it is noted that forcing them to do so will hurt labour productivity.

a disavowal of the future envisioned by the Nazi movement is less warranted.

Conclusion

So why did the regime encourage people to continue thinking of their savings in personal rather than communal terms? Why was the National Socialist leadership less willing than we might expect to call explicitly on members of the community to contribute their savings *to the nation*? There are a number of well-known reasons, including the desire to distance themselves from the unpleasant recent memories of war bonds, which meant the state never abandoned the pretence that all deposits remained the private property of account holders.[70] State leaders also preferred to maintain the façade that their pre-war planning had been so efficient that they had little need to borrow from their citizenry. Britain, in particular, was frequently lambasted as having to rely on loans for financial solvency.[71] But there seems to be a third point that is worth considering, and that is that the state never got entirely away from seeing its own citizens as liberal subjects (at least when it came to economic decisions), despite the ideological priority placed on the unity of the nation.[72] Historians do this as well when we insist Germans withheld funds in the last stage of the war because of the obvious inflationary pressures. In other words, we assume Germans acted in their economic self-interest, free of ideological considerations. But perhaps ideology was a determining factor. The evidence presented here demonstrates that for years, the propaganda had encouraged the private dreams of Germans as consumers, even if this more often than not meant saving for future spending. Germans listened.

---

[70] According to Tooze, *Wages of Destruction*, 354, policies were also shaped by the 'embarrassing experience with public offerings at the end of 1938'.
[71] See 'Kriegsfinanzierung aus eigener Kraft', *Deutsche Sparkassen-Zeitung* 48 (1941), 1.
[72] Rolf-Dieter Müller makes a related claim when he insists that 'Hitler had no confidence in his own people's willingness to make a sacrifice' and thus 'dodged his responsibility' by hiding the process through which private funds were siphoned toward the war: Rolf-Dieter Müller, 'Albert Speer and Armaments Policy in Total War', in Bernhard R. Kroener, Rolf-Dieter Müller and Hans Umbreit, *Germany and the Second World War*, vol. 5: *Organization and Mobilization of the German Sphere of Power*, part II: *Wartime Administration, Economy and Manpower Resources* (Oxford, 2003), 293–829, here 501. Given the evidence presented here, the assertion that the process of using personal deposits to fund the war was hidden is overblown. There were certainly references to Sparkassen funds being used to finance the war. Müller's better insight is that the leadership did not see sacrifice to the nation as a key selling point.

7 'Hoist the Flag!'
Flags as a Sign of Political Consensus and Distance in the Nazi Period

Karl Christian Führer

The Minister of Propaganda was feeling very pleased with himself. 'Solemn moment. Sirens wail. [One] minute's silence.' This was how Joseph Goebbels described the moment on 27 March 1936 when, with the help of a nationwide radio broadcast, his plans for the climax of the NSDAP's election campaign came to fruition. Voting was to take place on 29 March in elections for the Reichstag and in the retrospective plebiscite on Hitler's re-militarisation of the Rhineland earlier that month. Goebbels had – of course – reserved the main role in this carefully orchestrated spectacle for himself. However, in contrast to other such political spectacles staged by the regime when people had been expected simply to sit and listen to their radios, this time there was also an active role for the majority of the German population to play. Numerous newspaper articles and announcements on the radio had given them detailed instructions about what they were to do. After the sirens had sounded at 3.45 PM, interrupting daily routine throughout Germany and ensuring silence everywhere, Joseph Goebbels came on the radio and, employing the distinctive command used in the navy, issued the order 'Hoist the Flag' ('Heißt Flagge').[1]

Daily newspapers reported that millions of Germans obeyed this command by hoisting swastika flags on the walls outside apartments, in front gardens and on entrance gates. 'Thousands of windows opened, the flags of the movement are fluttering, a billowing army, [...] in the gentle breeze', reported the *Völkischer Beobachter* in Essen. According to the Party newspaper in Berlin: 'Flag after flag appeared at the windows. No more grey frontages in the streets, everything is covered in flags and sprigs of fir, bunting

---

(Translated from German by Kate Tranter)
[1] 'Dr. Goebbels gibt Signal: "Heißt Flagge!"', *Völkischer Beobachter* (*VB*), 28 March 1936. The precise wording of the instructions can be found in Hugo Weidenhaupt (ed.), *Ein nichtarischer Deutscher: Die Tagebücher des Albert Herzfeld 1935–1939* (Düsseldorf, 1982), 55f. On the overall orchestration of this election campaign for propaganda purposes see Marcel Stepanek, *Wahlkampf im Zeichen der Diktatur: Die Inszenierung von Wahlen und Abstimmungen im nationalsozialistischen Deutschland* (Leipzig, 2014), 117–66.

and banners'.[2] The *Berliner Morgenpost* reported that '[t]he next moment there was not a single house without a flag, from East Prussia to the Saar, from Upper Bavaria to the North Sea'. The *Berliner Börsen-Zeitung* wrote, '[t]his moment has turned the whole of Germany into a vast sea of flags'.[3]

Newspapers in small provincial towns reported from their own local perspective in similar vein. In Schwedt, for example, a small town between Berlin and Stettin in the depths of provincial Brandenburg, the local paper reported as follows:

'Hoist the flag' resounded from the loudspeakers at exactly 3.45 and at precisely the same moment flags appeared on all the buildings and at that moment Schwedt was transformed into a sea of flags, to show to the outside world that it is joyfully following the Führer. House after house stood adorned in bright red with black swastikas.[4]

For Goebbels, this moment in which *Volksgenossen* simultaneously responded to a single command was the key to the whole elaborate spectacle. By raising the same flag at their windows or doors at exactly the same time, Germans were each to experience individually the idea that 'we are all united in our thoughts and deeds', and that in the Third Reich under the NSDAP leadership everyone was 'united to form a single giant living organism'.[5]

When investigating the attitude of the large majority of Germans towards the totalitarian demands of the NSDAP during the years of Nazi dictatorship, it is useful to address a ritual like this choreographed hoisting of flags in March 1936. It required individual deeds to be carried out as a collective action so that the integration of individuals into the *Volksgemeinschaft* gained a positive emotional connotation. Since the Nazis were devotees of such ceremonial moments, what happened on 27 March 1936 was also just one link in a whole chain of comparable events.

At first glance all this might seem like the well-known image of German society brought into line and dancing to the Nazis' tune. However, a closer look reveals a different picture. At least in the first years of the dictatorship, between 1933 and 1936/7, it is clear that Germans had some individual room to manoeuvre during the ritualised actions of communal flag-raising, and they used it. Even while conforming, it was still possible to send out particular signals which could express publicly a certain distance towards the Nazi regime. Conversely, precisely an outward

---

[2] In order of citation: 'Das ganze deutsche Volk hörte seinen Führer' (for Essen); 'Die Verkehrsstille in der Reichshauptstadt' (for Berlin), both *VB*, 28 March 1936.
[3] 'Die Nation hört den Führer', *Berliner Morgenpost*, 28 March 1936; 'Eine Stadt hält den Atem an', *Berliner Börsen-Zeitung*, 28 March 1936.
[4] 'Die gestrige Feierstunde', *Schwedter Tageblatt*, 28 March 1936.
[5] 'Dr. Goebbels gibt Signal: "Heißt Flagge!"'.

show of subjugation to the NSDAP could be a strategy to protect an individual's private sphere and to deny the Party power over it.

By looking again at the Nazi staging of public flag-raising in greater depth than has been undertaken hitherto, this chapter sets out to argue that both of these responses were possible.[6] It begins by looking back at the last years of the Weimar Republic, since the flag cult of the NSDAP was connected in several ways with this period of extreme political turbulence: the Party was setting out to overwrite certain images from the time before 1933 which had rendered strikingly visible the political fragmentation of a society racked by crisis. The chapter then considers the first flag ceremonies initiated by the NSDAP in spring 1933 after the Party's takeover of power, and goes on in two further sections to discuss the lengths to which the Party went after 1935 to convert its engineered ritual of communal flag-raising into an absolutely clear and unambiguous political signal.

The Era of Public Political Statements: Privately Flown Flags in the Late Weimar Republic

Flying flags in public as a symbolic action by private individuals was not, of course, an invention of the National Socialists. With the emergence of modern nation states in the nineteenth century, nationalist sentiments intensified while mass politicisation in Western European societies created complex systems of competing political parties and other groupings. As a result, symbols and emblems signifying a nation, a region or a certain political affiliation became increasingly important in everyday life. 'I'm a Prussian, do you recognise my colours?/ The flag is waving black and white before me/ That my fathers died for freedom/ is what – take note! – my colours show': these lines from the *Prussian Song* (*Preussenlied*) of 1830, which refer to the Prussian flag, are just one example of the many political allegiances and messages that flags of all kinds expressed in the nineteenth century. Another obvious example is the international use by socialists of the red flag.[7]

---

[6] These flag rituals are mentioned by various authors including Michael Wildt, 'Self-Assurance in Troubled Times: German Diaries during the Upheavals of 1933', in Alf Lüdtke (ed.), *Everyday Life in Mass Dictatorship: Collusion and Evasion* (Houndmills, 2016), 55–74; Andrew Stuart Bergerson, *Ordinary Germans in Extraordinary Times: The Nazi Revolution in Hildesheim* (Bloomington, IN, 2004), 133–46. See also Janosch Steuwer, *'Ein Drittes Reich, wie ich es auffasse': Politik, Gesellschaft und privates Leben in Tagebüchern 1933–1939* (Göttingen, 2017), 119–24, 129–34, whom I would like to thank for sharing his manuscript with me prior to publication.

[7] See e.g. Peter Häberle, *Nationalflagge: Bürgerdemokratische Identifikationselemente und internationale Erkennungssymbole* (Berlin, 2008); Karlheinz Weißmann, *Schwarze*

The practice of demonstrating affiliation to a certain group or community publicly by means of a flag intensified in the years after the First World War. During the Weimar Republic, public displays of this kind were common. Even on the holiday beaches of the Baltic and North Seas, conservative Germans liked to demonstrate their anti-Republican leanings by flying the black, white and red flag of the Kaiserreich on their beach castles (*Strandburgen*) – a *Strandburg* being a kind of circular wall of sand which staked out territory on the beach and was, according to an unwritten social law, part of the family and private sphere. Anyone who dared to fly the official black, red and gold flag of the Weimar Republic risked the hostility of right-wing bathers.[8]

Flags became even more popular during the crisis years after 1929 when political tension was further fuelled by the electoral successes of the two extremist parties, the NSDAP and the KPD (the German Communist Party). In 1932, political fervour reached a new peak. This was the year Germany experienced two elections to the Reichstag and two different ballots on the new President of the Reich as well as elections to the *Länder* parliaments in Prussia and several other regions. During these election campaigns, the streets of the major German cities were festooned with flags hoisted by private individuals. Shortly before the Reichstag election in July 1932, the liberal Berlin newspaper *Vossische Zeitung* published an article with the headline 'Flags in Every Street', which observed that 'there used to be a time when flags were flown to indicate joy or sadness. [...] Nowadays flags are flown to show political allegiance.'[9] Earlier in the year, in April, during the elections for the Prussian parliament, the same newspaper had reported that Berlin had become 'immersed in a sea of flags. [...] Many buildings are flying all sorts of flags, from the swastika to the Soviet star.' At the same time, it continued, there were 'whole rows of streets', especially in the areas in the north and north-west of the city inhabited by manual workers, white-collar workers and civil servants on lower grades, where practically the only flags to be found hanging from the houses were the black, red and gold colours of the Weimar flag.[10] The paper also observed that even in middle-class suburbs there was a widespread desire to hang 'the symbol of their political convictions, the emblem of their allegiance out of the window'.[11] In

---

Fahnen, Runenzeichen: Die Entwicklung der politischen Symbolik der deutschen Rechten zwischen 1890 und 1945 (Düsseldorf, 1991); Dieter Petzina (ed.), *Fahnen, Fäuste, Körper: Symbolik und Kultur der Arbeiterbewegung* (Essen, 1986).

[8] See Frank Bajohr, '*Unser Hotel ist judenfrei*': *Bäder-Antisemitismus im 19. und 20. Jahrhundert* (Frankfurt a.M., 2003), 99–104.

[9] 'Fahnen in allen Straßen', *Vossische Zeitung* (*VZ*), 30 July 1932.

[10] 'Ruhiger Verlauf in Berlin', *VZ*, 25 April 1932.

[11] F. L., 'Karabiner und Fahnen', *VZ*, 25 April 1932.

early August 1932, one Hamburg newspaper likewise reported that there was 'a sea of flags of every kind and colour' in the city'.[12] The *Vossische Zeitung* reported this image of Germany's second largest city in even more detail:

> There are huge newly-built blocks of flats where there is a flag flying out of literally every window, often the flags of all the political parties are completely mixed up. In the older parts of town there are whole streets loyal to one political party. Alt-Hamburg supports Moscow, St Georg Hitler etc.[13]

However, according to the reports of the *Vossische Zeitung*, there was hardly any sign of the old flag of the Kaiserreich, which had hitherto been very popular as a political statement in conservative and anti-Republican circles: 'Places dominated by black-white-red are no longer to be found.'[14] The rise of the NSDAP, which since 1929 had largely succeeded in draining traditional right-wing parties of their voters, and the resulting polarisation of the political landscape, had a marked effect on the political colouring of the Weimar Republic. Reporting on the 1932 elections, the *Berliner Blatt* spoke of a 'battle of colours between the Republic and the swastika'.[15] In this case the colours supporting the Republic were not only the black, red and gold flag but also the flags and symbols of the *Eiserne Front* and the *Reichsbanner Schwarz-Rot-Gold*. With the help of these two organisations, the SPD, as the strongest party loyal to the Republic, had tried to recruit activists in the fight against the NSDAP and other right-wing elements. In the case of the *Reichsbanner* this also included the support of Republicans from the Centre Party (*Zentrumspartei*) and the *Deutsche Staatspartei*. It was largely as a result of the actions of these organisations close to the SPD that this 'sea of flags', visible so often in German cities during the elections of 1932, was so bright and richly contrasted. Both the *Eiserne Front* and the *Reichsbanner* made a huge effort to prevent the political arena and the public space from being taken over by extremists either from the left or from the right.[16]

These huge displays of political flags showed that voters and sympathisers in every political camp were increasingly self-mobilising because their opponents were so active. It was also a phenomenon found mainly in the

---

[12] 'Der Wahltag in Hamburg', *Hamburger Anzeiger (HA)*, 1 August 1932.
[13] Gustav Kauder, 'Die schwarzen Fahnen der Verschuldung', *VZ*, 30 July 1932.
[14] Ibidem. The report from Berlin quoted earlier also stated that '[t]he old black white and red colours of the Kaiserreich have been completely ousted' ('Fahnen in allen Straßen').
[15] Kauder, 'Die schwarzen Fahnen der Verschuldung'.
[16] See e.g. Marcel Böhles, *Im Gleichschritt für die Republik: Das Reichsbanner Schwarz-Rot-Gold im Südwesten, 1924–1933* (Essen, 2016); Benjamin Ziemann, *Die Zukunft der Republik? Das Reichsbanner Schwarz-Rot-Gold 1924–1933* (Bonn, 2011).

'Hoist the Flag!'

cities. In July 1932 the aforementioned reporter from the *Vossische Zeitung* wrote:

> If you drive out of Hamburg you'll be accompanied by these flags for a short distance into the countryside. [...] You have to drive a long way, to Flensburg or Kiel, to see flags again. There are no flags in between, hardly any election posters, nothing, not even in the small towns, not in Itzehoe, Heide, Husum etc.[17]

It would thus appear that the practice of hoisting a flag to attach a party-political label to one's home – and therefore to oneself and one's family – was not simply a product of the impassioned political climate of 1932. It was also driven by other factors, and it acquired meaning particularly in contexts where most social relations were anonymous and impersonal. By raising a flag precisely on the boundary between the private and public spheres, people were trying to break through this anonymity with a clear political signal. In small towns and villages where more intensive social contact between neighbours was routine and unavoidable, there was no similar need. Most inhabitants probably already knew the political leanings of their neighbours.[18]

Flags flown in the late Weimar Republic served as political propaganda and as a means of demarcation in the anonymous social milieu of large cities. Because of this, the practice became the object of often acrimonious disputes between the political parties. There were frequent attempts to damage opponents' flags. Activists in the NSDAP and in the KPD organised raids to pull down Communist or swastika flags. National Socialists also attacked the black, red and gold Weimar flags and the emblems of the *Eiserne Front*. In July 1932 storm troopers in the Lichtenberg area of Berlin even had the bizarre idea of spraying 'corrosive acid from the roofs' onto the flags hanging in front of the houses 'so that the flags were completely unusable'.[19] This public demonstration of political loyalties probably did nothing to enhance relationships with neighbours, especially in the blocks of rented flats where people lived in

---

[17] Kauder, 'Die schwarzen Fahnen der Verschuldung'.

[18] For this, see the conclusion drawn from biographical interviews in a Swabian village: 'People living in a village environment are not familiar with privacy in the bourgeois sense [...]; there are no secrets': Utz Jeggle and Albert Ilien, 'Die Dorfgemeinschaft als Not- und Terrorzusammenhang: Ein Beitrag zur Sozialgeschichte des Dorfes und zur Sozialpsychologie seiner Bewohner', in Hans-Georg Wehling (ed.), *Dorfpolitik: Fachwissenschaftliche Analysen und didaktische Hilfen* (Opladen, 1978), 38–53, here 46.

[19] 'Lassos und Säure gegen Fahnen', *VZ*, 27 July 1932. For similar reports, see also 'Wirkung des Demonstrations-Verbots', *VZ*, 25 July 1932 (from Braunschweig); 'Kleistertopf und Gummiknüppel', *HA*, 26 July 1932 (from Hamburg); 'Polizei schießt auf Kommunisten', *VZ*, 26 July 1932; 'Haussuchungen [sic] am Abend vor der Wahl', *VZ*, 24 April 1932; 'Gegen die Reichsflagge', *VZ*, 30 July 1932 (these last articles all from Berlin).

close proximity to each other. In April 1932 a journalist from the *Vossische Zeitung* was obviously reporting from his own experience when he wrote of a 'poisonous atmosphere' when people met on the stairs and complained that in Berlin there were 'no longer any neighbours [...], no neighbourly sentiment' because the flags so frequently displayed meant that 'there were only party members and political enemies'.[20]

This may be an overly one-sided view. It ignores the possibility that neighbours might not have realised that they had the same political allegiance until flags were hung out during the election campaigns, and perhaps as a result even developed closer contacts. Apart from such new relationships, however, there must have often been irreconcilable conflict between political opponents. Many neighbourhoods in the cities were socially mixed, and in any case party loyalties, especially enthusiasm for the NSDAP, could not be accurately charted on the basis of social markers.[21] The block of rented flats in Berlin that the *Berliner Morgenpost* reported in July 1932 to be displaying flags and emblems of five different political parties will have been no exception. In any event, across the city as a whole the privately hoisted flags made the political divisions of the later years of the Weimar Republic plain for all to see.

This background is important when analysing the significance and implications of privately hoisted flags during the years of the Nazi dictatorship. Ceremonies like the one on 27 March 1936 were obviously intended by the Nazis to create images of unity and solidarity which would erase the memories of the election campaigns of 1932. Whether they were successful is, of course, a different question.

Conformity and Dissent: Flags in the Propaganda Rituals of the NSDAP during the First Years of the Dictatorship

The NSDAP's first attempts to exploit the tradition of private flag-flying to orchestrate support for its own newly proclaimed 'Third Reich' began on 21 March 1933. This was the 'Day of Potsdam', the elaborately staged opening of the newly elected Reichstag. The NSDAP wanted this carefully choreographed event to be a public demonstration that the new government was connecting with old Prussian-German traditions. This 'reconciliation' had already been symbolically prepared by a 'flag decree' issued by the Reich President. The decree ruled that two flags, the Nazi

[20] F. L., 'Karabiner und Fahnen'.
[21] See e.g. Klaus-Michael Mallmann, *Kommunisten in der Weimarer Republik: Sozialgeschichte einer revolutionären Bewegung* (Darmstadt, 1996), esp. 252–61, and the classic study of NSDAP election successes, Jürgen Falter, *Hitlers Wähler* (Munich, 1991).

'Hoist the Flag!' 163

swastika and the black, white and red flag of the Kaiserreich, were together to replace the black, red and gold flag of the Weimar Republic. In future they were both to be hoisted together at all official events.[22]

It was Joseph Goebbels himself who translated this decree into instructions 'for the people' to participate personally, which were published in all the German daily newspapers.

Men and women! Show how glad and how moved you are by the historic events taking place in Germany these last weeks. Take an active part [...] in the national festivities. Fly the proud black, white and red flag and the swastika flag on your homes and proclaim your support for the rebirth of the German nation.[23]

This was to ensure that the 'Day of Potsdam' contrasted optically with the day of the elections to the Reichstag on 5 March 1933, when the lack of political unity in German society had been evident in the streets due to the variety of privately hoisted flags – including, still, the banners of left-wing and bourgeois-democratic parties and organisations.[24]

Similarly worded appeals to hoist the two official flags privately in order to 'express the solidarity of all sections of the population with the state authorities' were a short time later part of the official preparations for Hitler's birthday on 20 April 1933, which was celebrated like a national holiday, and for 1 May, which was to be a newly introduced 'festival of national labour' and was officially reinterpreted to denote 'the overcoming of class struggle'.[25]

By this time the press had been successfully forced to follow the Party line, so reports on the events of each of these three days were more or less identical. After the 'Day of Potsdam' the *Spandauer Zeitung* spoke of a 'sea of flags' and of the 'flags creating a luxuriating symphony of colour'; after Hitler's birthday the *Berliner Morgenpost* reported that 'countless private houses had put out flags', and after 1 May the same paper stated that 'the mass of flags resembled a forest'.[26] Reports from local communities in the

---

[22] See Weißmann, *Fahnen*, 183–4.
[23] 'Der Tag von Potsdam', *Spandauer Zeitung*, 18 March 1933.
[24] For Hamburg, see the diary of the housewife Luise Solmitz, who on election day could only find black, white and red flags and swastika flags in her own bourgeois neighbourhood, whereas in the streets in the working-class areas there were 'only hammer and sickles, only the three arrows' (the symbols of the *Eiserne Front*). Frank Bajohr, Beate Meyer and Joachim Szodrzynski (eds.), *Bedrohung, Hoffnung, Skepsis: Vier Tagebücher des Jahres 1933* (Göttingen, 2013), 167. Solmitz also discovered numerous flats in a well-to-do bourgeois area that were flying no flags at all, which astonished her: 'What sort of people live there?', 168.
[25] 'Das Festprogramm', *Berliner Morgenpost*, 20 April 1933 (Quote). See also 'Der Feiertag der nationalen Arbeit', *Berliner Morgenpost*, 23 April 1933; 'Aufruf zum 1. Mai', *Berliner Morgenpost*, 28 April 1933.
[26] 'Stadt der Fahnen', *Spandauer Zeitung*, 21 March 1933; 'Die Feier von Hitlers Geburtstag', *Berliner Morgenpost*, 21 April 1933; 'Wie Berlin den 1. Mai feierte', *Berliner Morgenpost*, 2 May 1933.

provinces were no different. In Buckow, a small community of barely 2,500 inhabitants not far from Berlin, which many affluent Berliners since the nineteenth century had used as a summer retreat, the local paper, the *Lokal-Anzeiger*, wrote about the day of 'national celebration' on 21 March 1933 as follows:

> The streets and squares of our town boasted splendid decorations of flags. The black, white and red flag, recently restored to its position of honour, proudly joined the swastika banner and the black and white Prussian flag and they fluttered happy and victorious in the fresh and sunny early spring air. They proclaimed to everyone the importance of this day for our national history.

Many people in Buckow also went to an open-air concert, a torchlight procession in the evening and a final 'freedom bonfire', where they listened to various speeches in praise of Hitler and the new government.[27]

In Baruth, a slightly smaller rural community forty kilometres south of Berlin on the edge of the Spreewald, the local newspaper wrote of 'streets and alleyways decked out with flags. It was a huge declaration of support for the new Reich, a confession of faith in the holy flag of the old, free Germany and in the [...] swastika banner of the national revolution.'[28] Again, on the same day, further north in Brandenburg, in the idyllic little town of Rheinsberg, hundreds of black, white and red flags and swastika flags were on display as the town hosted a torchlight procession and a speech in the market square. 'Nearly everyone in the town was out and about,' according to the local newspaper. 'The overall impression [...] was overwhelming. It was something that hasn't been seen on this scale in Rheinsberg for decades.'[29] A few days earlier storm troopers in Rheinsberg had used their own methods to put an end to the political culture of the Weimar Republic. They had set fire publicly (probably also on the marketplace) to twenty-four black, red and gold Weimar flags that they had confiscated from public offices and private homes.[30]

The celebrations that followed in quick succession in spring 1933 provided the Nazi regime with the formula for subsequent large-scale political events. So, for example, the general hoisting of flags and the marches, parades and torchlight processions were repeated for the pseudo-democratic ballots on Germany's withdrawal from the League of Nations on 12 November 1933, and on the fusion of the offices of the

---

[27] 'Der Tag der Nation', *Buckower Lokal-Anzeiger*, 21 March 1933 (for the programme of events); 'Nationalfeier in Buckow', *Buckower Lokal-Anzeiger*, 23 March 1933 (for the quote about the display of flags).
[28] 'Aus der Heimat', *Baruther Anzeiger*, 23 March 1933.
[29] 'Der National-Feiertag in Rheinsberg', *Rheinsberger Zeitung*, 25 March 1933.
[30] See 'Fahnenverbrennung', *Rheinsberger Zeitung*, 14 April 1933, also an addendum to it without a signature in the 16 March 1933 edition (on the involvement of the SA).

Reich President and the Reich Chancellor on 19 August 1934. Then in March 1936 there were the elections to the Reichstag mentioned earlier, and two years later, on 10 April 1938, the referendum (the so-called *Volksbefragung*) on the annexation of Austria.[31] Since 1933 both 1 May and Hitler's birthday had been integrated into the calendar of annually recurring political festivals.

Many people who kept diaries during the period of the Nazi dictatorship reported how readily a large section of the population responded to the NSDAP's appeals to 'show the flag' as private individuals. 'There are flags and swastika armbands everywhere' was the comment made in Breslau on 1 May 1933 by the Jewish schoolteacher Willy Cohn, who had just been forced by the Nazis into retirement from his position at a *Gymnasium*. On the same day the journalist Lili Hahn wrote that 'there are flags flying from every house' in Frankfurt am Main and the lawyer Fritz Rosenberg in Hamburg remarked on 'flags upon flags'. The banker Cornelius Freiherr von Berenberg-Gossler, who also lived in Hamburg, had already reported on 20 April 1933 that 'today there is a sea of flags everywhere'.[32]

Things were evidently not very different in the German provinces. Immediately after the first 'National Labour Day' Karl Dürkefälden, an engineer in Peine, a small town of about 20,000 inhabitants in Lower Saxony, noted that there were 'swastika flags or at least a black, white and red flag flying on practically every single house'. In Wittlich, an even smaller town situated much further west in the administrative district of Trier, Matthias Joseph Mehs, a local Catholic politician and publican, wrote in his diary on the 'Day of Potsdam', 21 March 1933: 'By lunchtime today there was a black, white and red flag hanging from nearly every house. People are like weather vanes.' On 20 April 1933 he noted, 'Hitler's birthday. Nearly everyone in the town has hung out a flag.'[33]

---

[31] See Stepanek, *Wahlkampf*.
[32] In order of citation, Willy Cohn, *Kein Recht, nirgends: Tagebuch vom Untergang des Breslauer Judentums 1933–1941* (Cologne, 2007), 37; Lili Hahn, *Bis alles in Scherben fällt: Tagebuchblätter 1933–45* (Hamburg, 2007), 10; Bajohr/Meyer/Szodrzynski (eds.), *Bedrohung*, 57 (by this time Fritz Rosenberg had also become a victim of the Nazi persecution of the Jews, since his right to practise as a lawyer had been withdrawn); Bajohr/Meyer/Szodrzynski, *Bedrohung*, 322. For Berlin, see also the letters of Gotthard Heinrici, at that time a colonel in the Reich Ministry of Defence, on 4 March 1933 and 10 March 1933, in Johannes Hürter (ed.), *Notizen aus dem Vernichtungskrieg: Die Ostfront 1941/42 in den Aufzeichnungen des Generals Heinrici* (Darmstadt, 2016), 167 and 168.
[33] In order of citation, Herbert Obenaus and Sybille Obenaus (eds.), *'Schreiben, wie es wirklich war...': Aufzeichnungen Karl Dürkefäldens aus den Jahren 1933–1945* (Hannover, 1985), 47; Matthias Joseph Mehs, *Tagebücher: vol. 1: November 1929 bis Januar 1936*, ed. by Günter Wein and Franziska Wein (Trier, 2011), 253, 265.

It seems, therefore, that the 'sea of flags' so frequently mentioned by contemporary journalists really did keep appearing in Germany after March 1933. What seems to be new is that these displays of flags were now also to be found in smaller towns and villages. In larger cities, as we have seen, many people were motivated to fly flags by the political turmoil around the various elections in 1932 if not before. In smaller communities such as Wittlich there does not seem to have been the same eagerness to display political allegiance. On 2 February 1933 the local National Socialists and the aggressively anti-Republican paramilitary organisation *Stahlhelm* organised slightly belated festivities to celebrate Hitler's appointment as Reichskanzler. All 'nationally minded citizens' were expected to hang flags from their homes, but even then Matthias Mehs only counted seventeen flags in the whole town. As he noted in his diary, there was no doubt that all the other inhabitants were also 'nationally minded', but they did not see the need to 'hang their political sympathies, which can be taken for granted, out of the window'.[34]

This restraint disappeared with the 'Day of Potsdam' in Wittlich and elsewhere. Most Germans also seem to have complied with the Nazis' formal request only to fly the official flags – the black, white and red tricolour of the Kaiserreich and/or the Nazi swastika flag. So it seems that although the regime was still only at the very beginning of its project to transform Germany into a totalitarian dictatorship, by the end of March 1933 the Germans' behaviour as regards flag-flying had already become more or less uniform. The question is what this can tell us about the Germans' attitude to the Nazi regime at this time.

It would be a mistake simply to assume that in the brief period after the elections to the Reichstag on 5 March 1933, when with a result of 43.9 per cent the NSDAP had fallen well short of its target of an absolute majority, Hitler and his Party had managed a huge leap to wholesale popularity. Rather, the Germans were demonstrating that, given the radical changes in the political situation since Hitler came to power and since the Reichstag fire, they were willing to conform publicly to expectations and demands 'from above'. There could, of course, be a number of different reasons for this.

For the smaller communities mentioned earlier, local election statistics can be used to support this analysis. Since many KPD party officials had been arrested after the Reichstag fire and the SA was using terror tactics against Social Democrats and other opponents of the NSDAP, the Reichstag elections on 5 March 1933 certainly cannot be considered truly free. However, even under these circumstances, 31.3 per cent of

[34] Mehs, *Tagebücher, vol. 1*, 240.

the electorate in Buckow had voted SPD or KPD. This was almost exactly the same result as in the elections in 1932. Even in Baruth, a largely agricultural community, at the beginning of March 1933 there were still many supporters of the two main left-wing resolutely anti-Nazi parties, the SPD and the KPD. Their combined votes made up 25 per cent of the total of 1,300. In the city council elections in Rheinsberg on 13 March 1933 they even beat the NSDAP with 781 votes to its 706.[35] The fact that on 21 March 1933 citizens in all three places conformed so uniformly to the Nazi appeal for private displays of flags cannot be the result of a sudden mass political conversion. It is very unlikely that anyone who had not believed the election promises of the NSDAP at the beginning of March would have changed their mind so radically within a few days. They were also such small communities that most adults would have known exactly where those neighbours lived who had just voted against the National Socialists.

Quite a few indications of why even sceptics and opponents of the regime behaved in this way can be found in contemporary diaries. A flag, for instance, also hung on Matthias Mehs' inn in Wittlich on the 'Day of Potsdam'. Mehs was a convinced democrat, a traditionally minded, well-educated, middle-class citizen and a fervent Catholic, and as such he had no time for the NSDAP. He was accordingly minded to withhold his compliance on 21 March 1933. 'We are being silenced, gagged, we aren't allowed to speak or even think what we want – we're considered not "nationally minded", the SA are forbidden to enter our premises and then we're supposed to hang flags out as a sign of gratitude?' However, Mehs did not live alone in his large house and one member of the family who was obviously concerned about the economic future of their family business upset his plans.

And what happened? My father went and secretly hung out a red and white flag [i.e. a flag bearing the colours of the Wittlich municipal coat of arms]. I was so furious I didn't go into the pub all day, even though it was market day [which would have been particularly busy in a rural parish such as Wittlich because of all the farmers from the surrounding countryside coming into the market].

One may assume that it would have been perfectly acceptable for Mehs as the active 'boss' of the family business to exert his authority and put his foot down. However, this did not happen. The fact that his father had hung out the relatively neutral municipal flag of Wittlich to camouflage

---

[35] Figures from 'Reichs- und Landtagswahl', *Buckower Lokal-Anzeiger*, 6 March 1933; 'Aus der Heimat', *Baruther Anzeiger*, 7 March 1933; 'Stadtverordneten-Versammlung', *Rheinsberger Zeitung*, 14 March 1933.

the family's political disengagement with the regime apparently did not seem to him to be worth risking a family dispute.[36]

By November 1933, when Germany voted on whether to withdraw from the League of Nations, Mehs junior had already adopted and adapted his father's attitude. Although the NSDAP in Wittlich appealed to all citizens not to hang out any other flag on the day of the election except the swastika, because the Germans 'owed' this to Adolf Hitler, the Mehs' inn was once again flying the municipal flag, though this time with the accompaniment of the flag of the Kaiserreich. When neighbours warned that the innkeeper and his family might be faced with 'inconveniences' if they did not fly the swastika, Matthias Mehs tried to calm them down. 'I told them black, white and red would be perfectly adequate. [...] Why should anything happen? Afterwards nobody will ever believe how fearful people are.'[37]

It was fear that drove Willy Cohn, the Breslau Jew, to fly a flag on 1 May 1933. In his case it was a much more concrete and justifiable fear, since the boycott of Jewish businesses organised by the Nazi regime on 1 April 1933 had frequently been supported by acts of violence against the Jews. 'We hung out a black, white and red flag so that they didn't come and smash up our apartment!'[38] It is not clear from the diary of Fritz Rosenberg, the lawyer from Hamburg, whether he had complied with the request of the Reich Ministry of Propaganda, but he did write, '[p]eople who don't hang out flags as a matter of principle do it because they are afraid'. He himself was completely indifferent to the NSDAP's orchestration of unity and community, as was his wife. 'We're staying at home and keeping ourselves to ourselves.'[39]

Luise Solmitz, a Hamburg housewife, felt completely differently. She was one of the passionately 'nationally minded' Germans and hated the Weimar Republic. At the same time, however, because her husband's parents had been Jews, the Nazi theory of race categorised him as Jewish, even though he professed the Protestant faith. After 1933 this brought her into serious conflict with her political convictions. On one hand she revered Adolf Hitler, whom she considered a genius, but on the other hand she was worried by the Nazis' 'Jewish policy' which could only be seen as a threat to her family. This conflict led to extremely inconsistent behaviour. On the 'Day of Potsdam' she wept for joy, and when she was in the anonymous crowd watching Party parades she was full of enthusiasm,

---

[36] Mehs, *Tagebücher: vol. 1*, 253f. Mehs' father was not an eager supporter of the NSDAP either. 'Do we have to hang out flags?' he had asked his son. So he obviously did not consider flying the flag to be voluntary.
[37] Ibidem, 360.   [38] Cohn, *Kein Recht*, 37f.
[39] Bajohr/Meyer/Szodrzynski (eds.), *Bedrohung*, 124 and 57.

shouting 'Heil Hitler'. However, when she went into one of the Party offices to collect some propaganda leaflets about Hitler and his Party, she greeted the staff with 'Guten Tag', even though that met with a frosty response. It seems absurd that she insisted on this distancing gesture even when she was passing on to the Party 'compromising material' about her brother. She was shocked that as a journalist in Berlin who had always adopted a resolutely democratic political position, he was trying to obtain a post in the politically subordinated press of the Third Reich.[40]

Frau Solmitz and her husband, who was of similarly strong 'national' leanings, tried to demonstrate their independence of spirit whenever there was an occasion when everyone was expected to hang out flags. Although more and more neighbours were flying the swastika, the Solmitzes kept to the traditional black, white and red flag of the Kaiserreich that they had used before Hitler came to power in order to demonstrate that they were anti-Republican. At the same time, however, the family somehow felt the need to stay abreast of the changes in the political climate, so Herr Solmitz added a small swastika pennant as a sort of extension to the larger flag of the Kaiserreich. Their thirteen-year-old daughter, Gisela, who knew nothing of her father's parentage and would have immediately joined the Hitler Youth if her parents had allowed it, was allowed to fasten some more pennants displaying the Party symbol to the handles of the windows, but these were on the inside rather than the outside of their home.[41]

While Frau Solmitz regarded herself as one of the pioneers of the Nazi Party's cause, she was far from pleased about the 'sea' of swastikas appearing all over Hamburg to mark the political festivals of the Nazi regime. She still had very clear memories of a completely different picture during the election campaigns in the Weimar Republic and even on 5 March 1933, and she suspected that those previous supporters of the democratic parties were now flying the Nazi flag so that they would not stand out.[42] This kind of opportunism made her even more angry because when it came to the 'Jewish question', she herself consciously refused the same demonstration of conformity with the Party.

This analysis of different diaries shows that there was more to the mass ritual of hoisting flags on private homes than its function as propaganda. There were undoubtedly many Germans in 1933 and the subsequent years who were happy to express precisely the enthusiasm the Nazis

---

[40] Ibidem, 165 and 175. Her denunciation of her brother, which at least in retrospect caused her severe pangs of conscience, did not result in any action being taken against him.
[41] Ibidem, 168 and 174. [42] See ibidem, 258.

wished for by hanging out flags. But there were others. So, for example, the flag was hanging on the Mehs' inn in Wittlich on 21 March 1933 because father and son had decided not to disagree openly about the relative value of political convictions and business interests in everyday life. In Breslau Willy Cohn, the Jewish teacher forced into retirement, hung one of the two officially approved flags out of his window on 1 May 1933 to protect himself from attacks by Nazi fanatics. And amidst the general manifestations of solidarity with the NSDAP, the Solmitzes in Hamburg tried to express their own very distinctive relationship to the Party by arranging their individual combination of the swastika and the black, white and red flag of the Kaiserreich.

In all these cases it is important to reiterate that at this point in time the swastika flag was not the only sign of support that the Nazis accepted. In 1933 they were still going to great lengths to establish a line of continuity from the Kaiserreich and the much older Prussian monarchy to the Third Reich. This meant that those who raised the old flag of the Kaiserreich, which the Reich President's 1933 decree had specifically declared as an official flag, or even one of the many traditional local or regional flags were not actually breaking any rules. The three protagonists depicted earlier were making use of precisely this liberty.

Their behaviour provides an example of a paradoxical effect of the totalitarian orchestrations of the Nazi regime, something which the extensive literature on the dictatorship has not yet sufficiently identified and examined. Precisely because the regime attached so much political significance to banal everyday actions and individual aspects of private life, the expressive social power of such actions and choices could be used to demonstrate individuality. During the Weimar Republic the two flags, the black, white and red and the swastika, were very closely associated in their political symbolism, both indicating primarily antidemocratic sentiments. After the Nazi seizure of power this changed. Anyone flying the old imperial flag, for all its official status, might now also be indicating a certain distance towards the NSDAP. The same was now also true for those who flew a local or regional flag, which before 1933 would have expressed no more than a local patriotism that was politically fairly neutral. The flags displayed by private individuals in Nazi Germany were, therefore, by no means a symbol of uniform consent. They should be seen rather as a means used (or that could be used) to take up a more individual position within their immediate social sphere towards the emerging dictatorship.

This could even have been the case when it was the swastika flag that was flown. In November 1933 Matthias Mehs carefully noted the behaviour of one of his neighbours who had been involved in the political struggle for the independence of the Rhineland in the 1920s and so was hardly likely to have any political sympathy with an extreme nationalist party like the NSDAP. This was presumably the reason why, in Mehs' view, he displayed the Nazi flag 'timidly' by 'hanging [it] out of the attic window' rather than right at the front of his house.[43]

This last example shows particularly clearly how important the specific social environment was for an interpretation of the messages conveyed by privately displayed flags – messages that would be understood all the better by those who were well informed about their neighbours. By hanging a flag out of his attic window, the Rhineland separatist in Wittlich would have been giving a clear signal, because his political past would have been well known in such a small town. The Solmitzes, on the other hand, kept their secret so carefully that not even their own daughter knew about it, with the effect that the neighbours could not have known what was behind their particular public gesture. The expressive power of the flags varied, therefore, from case to case. Since the level of familiarity with the neighbours and the relative anonymity of living conditions were crucial in these cases, it was particularly the inhabitants of small towns and villages who were able to send out private signals under the cloak of apparent conformity.

However, the pressure to conform exerted by the NSDAP in such smaller communities did not stop with the general displaying of flags. The examples of Buckow and Rheinsberg show that the Nazis organised many other rituals for their festivals, such as parades, festive gatherings and torchlight processions. In both of these smaller communities practically the whole of the population participated in these events after March 1933, even though many inhabitants were supporters of the SPD or the KPD. In larger communities such as Breslau or Hamburg social control was less strict, so Willy Cohn could feel safe at home in his apartment because he had already sufficiently participated in orchestrating the unity of the *Volksgemeinschaft* by hanging out a flag. At least in the early years of the dictatorship, it was precisely outward conformity that could create a protected sphere. For this reason too, it would be wrong to interpret the fact that Germans were repeatedly prepared to comply with the Nazis' wishes by 'showing their colours' as a straightforward indication of their political consent or submission.

Only those who refused altogether to participate in this ritual aroused suspicion and set themselves clearly apart. Possible consequences were sideways looks from neighbours, sarcastic comments and visits or questioning by the NSDAP block warden (*Blockleiter*, or in popular parlance

---

[43] Mehs, *Tagebücher, vol. 1*, 360.

Blockwart) or one of their helpers. This was particularly the case after 1936/7, by which time the Party had managed to set up a more or less fully comprehensive network of 'house officials' (*Hausbeauftragte*) whose task it was to report any kind of conspicuous behaviour.[44]

At the same time, no actual obligation existed to put out flags and there were no further immediate consequences other than this social pressure. Nevertheless, everyday life could still become quite unpleasant. Years later Heinrich Sellner, who was born in Hamburg in 1928 and whose father was a worker and a committed Social Democrat, could still remember the feeling of being excluded because even in the years immediately preceding the Second World War his father did not completely disguise his political convictions.

> It started with the whole street hanging out swastika flags. There was absolutely no way my father was going to hang out a flag like that. Then they appeared at the door and my father kept cracking jokes to stop them making him hang out that flag.

What Sellner remembered as particularly distressing were the relentless questions his school friends kept asking – 'why haven't you got a flag out' – because he had strict instructions from his father not to say that his parents were anti-Nazi and so had to invent excuses.[45]

We do not know how many Germans behaved as consistently as Heinrich Sellner's father after 1933. However, this type of noncompliance cannot have been so unusual, since the Nazis had a special pre-prepared form at the ready to caution households that had not displayed flags at the time of official festivals. All the block wardens had to do was to fill in the name and the address of the offending household. The wording on the form accused the recipients of being 'indifferent, half-hearted Germans' and also mentioned the possibility of them being in sympathy with the Jews.[46] This kind of accusation could have serious consequences in the Third Reich, because it might under certain circumstances set off the Nazi machinery of persecution. Those individuals who were not willing to run this risk needed the protection of the public demonstration of conformity provided by hoisting flags on the required days. That said, sheer forgetfulness may also have caused some Germans problems – there were after all no fewer than six days a year

---

[44] See Detlef Schmiechen-Ackermann, 'Der "Blockwart": Die unteren Parteifunktionäre im nationalsozialistischen Terror- und Überwachungsapparat', *Vierteljahrshefte für Zeitgeschichte* 48 (2000), 575–602, here 584–7 and 591.
[45] Notes by Heinrich Sellner [pseudonym], *Forschungsstelle für Zeitgeschichte in Hamburg*, Werkstatt der Erinnerung, 422.
[46] Quoted from Cornelia Schmitz-Berning, *Vokabular des Nationalsozialismus* (Berlin, 1998), 297.

after 1937 when the Party expected the national symbol to be visible outside every home.[47]

Bare Islands in the 'Sea of Flags': The Exclusion of the Jews from the Ritual of Public Flag-Flying

In the months following its installation in power, the Party could have been largely satisfied with its flag-flying rituals. Since March 1933 the desired optical effect of a 'sea of flags' had been repeated regularly, because the public had always responded en masse to appeals to participate. On the other hand, there were various reasons why the Party was still dissatisfied with the ritual it had instigated. Party activists were, for example, afraid that the special, festive character of the event was suffering because many Germans were leaving their flags out 'for days and weeks'. This prompted an official statement from the Ministry of Propaganda in December 1933 that such behaviour looked annoyingly like carelessness and was inappropriate for the 'dignity of national symbols'. For this reason private individuals were now required to fly flags only 'on special occasions' when this was 'declared by the authorities to be fitting and desirable'. Always ready to order people about, the Nazi government took great care to be precise: 'On these occasions flags are to be raised as early in the morning as possible and are to be lowered at sunset.'[48]

The leadership was also uneasy about the symbolic support they were receiving on these 'flag days' from an entirely unwelcome quarter, namely from German Jews. In addition, the NSDAP was increasingly concerned about the swastika flag and the old imperial flag being flown together, as had been permitted by the Reich President's initial 'flag decree'. Strict exclusion on one hand, and on the other the coordination (*Gleichschaltung*) of a *Volksgemeinschaft* bonded through the purging of the supposedly 'alien', were in the Nazi world-view inextricably linked. This applied even to an apparently relatively unimportant issue such as private flag-flying. Specifically, the Nazis wanted both to prevent any Jews from participating in the flag-flying ritual and to provide visual evidence of an even more uniform *Volksgemeinschaft* by getting rid of the Kaiserreich's black, white and red flags.

Over the course of a few months in 1935, the regime took action on both of these matters. It began with the exclusion of the Jews. On

---

[47] For more detail, see later in this chapter.
[48] Erlass des Reichspropagandaministeriums über die Beflaggung [Decree of the Reich Propaganda Minister on the Flying of Flags], 5 December 1933, BArch Berlin, R 43 II, 129.

27 April 1935 the Reich Ministry of the Interior issued a directive that in future 'the Reich flags and in particular the swastika flag' were 'not to be flown by Jews'. The Ministry justified this move by maintaining that it was for the sake of preserving public peace and order. It claimed that there had been repeated 'disturbances' because Jewish families and businesses had taken part in the public flag-flying and that it was the aim of this ruling to 'prevent this kind of incident in future'.[49]

It was quite clear, of course, that the regime's real agenda was completely different. 'They want them [the Jews] to be ostracised and clearly identifiable,' noted Matthias Mehs clear-sightedly in his diary, although antisemitism as an almost universally accepted 'cultural code' in German society had left its mark on him as well.[50] The Jewish artist Albert Herzfeld from Düsseldorf observed in his diary that preventing the German Jews from flying the national flag would be only the beginning of a development which was likely to end in them being forced to be identified 'by a particular type of dress, like in the Middle Ages'.[51] Only a few months later in September 1935, the Nuremberg Laws gave legal force to the discriminatory measure to exclude Jews from the ritual of hoisting official flags on private homes. This meant that henceforth every Jewish home was clearly visible during political festivals. Failure to comply with this law could result in a punishment of up to twelve months in jail. A further Nuremberg Law ruled that the swastika was now the only official state symbol of the Third Reich.[52]

The justification the Nazi regime gave for the ministerial decree of 27 April 1935 followed the standard pattern of its antisemitic policies. Official decrees discriminating against Jews were introduced after Jews had been physically attacked by lower-ranking Party members, usually SA, ostensibly acting of their own accord without orders from above.[53] Judging by the numerous enquiries made by members of the Centralverein, the most important Jewish organisation in Germany, many German Jews took part in

---

[49] Rundschreiben des Reichsministeriums des Innern (RMdI) an alle Landesregierungen, 27 April 1935, BArch Berlin, R 43 II, 129.
[50] Mehs, *Tagebücher, vol. 1*, 583. For Mehs' antisemitic tendencies, see e.g. the diary entry for 6 October 1935 (618–19).
[51] Herzfeld, *Ein nichtarischer Deutscher*, 19.
[52] See e.g. Saul Friedländer, *Nazi Germany and the Jews: The Years of Persecution, 1933–1939* (New York, NY, 1997), 142–3. Prohibition and threat of punishment were in the Gesetz zum Schutz des deutschen Blutes und der deutschen Ehre (Law for the Protection of German Blood and German Honour) (§§ 4 and 5), which also criminalised sexual relations and marriage between Jews and 'Aryans'. For more detail on the *Reichsflaggengesetz*, which deprived the black, white and red flag of its status as an official state symbol, as an element of the Nuremberg Laws, see later in this chapter.
[53] See e.g. Michael Wildt, *Volksgemeinschaft als Selbstermächtigung: Gewalt gegen Juden in der deutschen Provinz 1919 bis 1939* (Hamburg, 2007).

the festivals organised by the NSDAP between spring 1933 and April 1935 and hung out flags. Many of them, like Willy Cohn in Breslau, did this so as not to be conspicuous, but others were indeed so 'nationally minded' that they wanted to be personally involved in the celebrations of unity and strength organised by the Nazi regime. On these festivals black, white and red flags were even flown on synagogues.[54]

Precisely this attempt to belong sparked in Nazi Germany aggression and violence against Jews. In Berlin the elders of the Jewish community removed the imperial flag from the major synagogue in the Oranienburgerstrasse after an angry crowd gathered outside, storm troopers marched up threateningly and the police refused to intervene.[55] It seems that attacks on private individuals also took place, although no details of these have so far come to light. Since the attackers in these cases would have had to know exactly where Jews lived, such attacks are more likely to have taken place in smaller communities than in the larger cities.

In any case it is clear that in 1935 there still were Jews in Germany who found it difficult not to be allowed to fly the black, white and red flag of the Kaiserreich. The *Verband nationaldeutscher Juden*, a small organisation of Jews who were culturally particularly well assimilated and politically decidedly conservative, sent a telegram to the Reich Ministry of the Interior protesting emphatically against its ruling of 27 April 1935. It insisted that to be excluded from the rituals of popular national flag-raising was an 'undeserved humiliation', especially for veterans of the First World War. It also stated that the disturbances cited by the Ministry could only be 'isolated incidents caused by particularly undisciplined elements' or possibly even by 'anti-German provocateurs' and called for the police to intervene to prevent such incidents.[56] There was no response to this protest on the part of the Reich Ministry of the Interior, but it illustrates clearly that even in 1935 Jews in conservative nationalist circles were entirely mistaken about the nature of the Nazi dictatorship.

In Hamburg the Solmitzes did not understand the signs of the times either until they experienced the shock of the Nuremberg Laws. Frau Solmitz was emotionally a nationalist who needed the feeling of being at one with the crowd and had accordingly just bought a new black, white and red flag because the old one had faded. In 1935 she felt not only excluded but also emotionally punished and deprived. 'My fatherland, how I have loved you as long as I can remember,' she wrote, and from

---

[54] See Avraham Barkai, *'Wehr Dich': Der Centralverein deutscher Staatsbürger jüdischen Glaubens (C.V.) 1893–1938* (Munich, 2002), 285.
[55] See ibidem and 452 (reference). This incident has no date in Barkai's depiction.
[56] A telegram from the Verband nationaldeutscher Juden 'an den Führer und Reichskanzler', 28 April 1935, BArch Berlin, R 43 II, 129.

what we know of this couple, she as an 'Aryan' would also have been speaking for her Jewish husband.[57] So the popular hoisting of flags on 27 March 1936 described earlier was for Frau Solmitz a traumatic experience. The moment when the windows of her flat appeared for the first time as a bare, empty island in the overall 'sea of flags' felt 'painful and discriminatory for us. We will have to learn to bear it.'[58]

In fact Luise Solmitz had despaired in her own case somewhat too hastily. There was nothing in the wording of the ministerial decree of April 1935 or the relevant paragraphs of the Nuremberg Laws in September 1935 that prohibited her as an 'Aryan' from flying a flag – the prohibition applied to no one except Jews. Frau Solmitz did not, however, take advantage of the loophole that arose from this for the non-Jewish partners of those living in 'mixed marriages'. In accordance with the then current conventions, her self-image depended mainly on her husband, and so it did not occur to her that she could hang out her 'own' swastika flag.

Other couples in similar situations, however, seem to have reacted differently and seized upon precisely this loophole in order to avoid attracting negative attention to their 'unflagged' home. At any rate, the Reich Ministry of the Interior found it necessary to pass a measure in December 1936 banning anyone of 'German blood' who was married to a Jew from flying the national flag in public.[59] A few months later, the Ministry went on to use this particular form of *Sippenhaft*, extending racial discrimination to non-Jews with Jewish family members, as an instrument against civil servants. In April 1937 it was used to justify the removal of 'Aryan' civil servants from their jobs if they were married to Jews and had not succumbed to the constant pressure from their superiors and the Party to seek a divorce. 'Since a situation in which a civil servant is not allowed to fly a flag is not tenable in the long run,' it was maintained that the only solution was to make a swift arrangement for 'civil servants with Jewish spouses' (*jüdisch versippte Beamten*) to be forced to retire.[60]

After December 1936 it was thus possible anywhere in Germany to see exactly where Jews were still living. This was also because – perfidiously – the ban on Jews flying flags affected all Germans indirectly by putting

---

[57] Cited in Steuwer, *'Ein Drittes Reich, wie ich es auffasse'*, 155. On buying a new flag, see ibidem, 131. The diaries show that during political festivals until autumn 1935 the Solmitzes regularly flew the black, white and red flag with the added swastika pennant. See ibidem, 154. There were clearly no problems about this with neighbours or with the SA.
[58] Ibidem, 437.
[59] 'Runderlass vom 7.12.1936', *Ministerialblatt des Reichs- und Preußischen Ministeriums des Innern* 97 (1936), 1631.
[60] Rundschreiben des RMdI, 8 April 1937, BArch Berlin, R 55, 26.

non-Jews under a new form of social pressure. 'If we don't put flags out people will think we're Jews,' was the reaction of an 'Aryan' couple, friends of the Solmitzes, to the Nuremberg Laws in autumn 1935.[61] A further step towards more strictly enforced conformity was taken when after September 1935 the Party wanted the only flag flown for its festivals to be the swastika. For the moment other flags were merely considered undesirable, but in 1937 they were expressly forbidden – as outlined in the following section.

Party Monopoly on the Flagpole: The NSDAP's Campaign against Traditional Flags

Just as we do not know how many Germans after 1933 resisted the pressure to fly flags on the days of political festivals, we also do not know what percentage of households continued to fly the black, white and red flag of the Kaiserreich instead of the swastika. What we do know is that even though it was the Nazis who had reintroduced the old flag as an official national symbol in March 1933, they became more and more irritated by the number of them still being flown. As far as they were concerned, anyone who was still flying the black, white and red flag in 1934 and 1935 was demonstrating their political distance towards the regime. In September 1935 Hermann Göring declared publicly that 'reactionaries were hiding' behind the traditional Kaiserreich tricolour. In the same year, Reich War Minister Werner von Blomberg noted in an internal memo that the old national symbol had 'unfortunately become to some extent the flag of the opposition'.[62]

If one considers the Solmitzes in Hamburg, Matthias Mehs in Wittlich or Willy Cohn in Breslau, these interpretations may seem justified. On the other hand they are a clear indication of National Socialist paranoia and desire for absolute power. It was particularly families who were 'nationally minded' who were likely to have owned a black, white and red flag before 1933, and it may have been for purely economic reasons that many of them decided to stick to it in the new Third Reich. At prices between six and eight Reichmarks (RM) each for a large swastika flag measuring 2 by 1.20 metres, the flags were not cheap. Larger flags could even cost up to 12.50 RM. This would cause quite a hole in the budget of an ordinary working family. Even the 2 RM or 2.70 RM, which was the price of smaller flags measuring 90 by 60 centimetres or 120 by 80 centimetres,

---

[61] Cited in Steuwer, *'Ein Drittes Reich, wie ich es auffasse'*, 155.
[62] Cited in Weißmann, *Fahnen*, 190; Reichskriegsminister von Blomberg an den Chef der Reichskanzlei, 11 December 1935, BArch Berlin, R 43 II, 128 a.

was approximately the equivalent of the hourly wage of an industrial worker.[63] Families who were living quite literally from hand to mouth therefore had good reasons not to buy a new flag.

However, the NSDAP was a totalitarian movement, so by 1935 it no longer wanted to accept the joint display of its own new, specifically Nazi symbolism with the old traditional symbolism that it had supported for domestic political reasons in 1933. Adolf Hitler was personally pressing for political unambiguity, though he also wanted to wait for 'a particularly auspicious moment' to introduce an official ruling against the black, white and red flag.[64] This moment came in September 1935 when the Reichstag was convened in Nuremberg specifically for the elaborately orchestrated announcement of the two rather improvised antisemitic Nuremberg Laws. On 15 September, together with these two laws, the Reichstag passed the *Reichsflaggengesetz* (Reich Flag Decree) which ruled that the swastika flag was to be the sole flag of the Reich. The dictator was evidently intent on making the departure from the traditional flag of the Kaiserreich less painful for traditional *Volksgenossen* by pushing the supposedly 'generous solution to the Jewish problem' conceived by the Third Reich into the political foreground. Most Germans firmly believed that there was indeed a Jewish problem, but many of them found the violent antisemitism of the SA and other lesser groups in the Party suspect. Because this violence was so unpopular, the Party promised that it would be terminated, and so officially the Nuremberg Laws created what was presented as a long-term 'modus vivendi' between *Deutschtum* and *Judentum*, between Germans and Jews.[65]

In spite of this, some sections of the population were unwilling to give up the black, white and red flag. The Gestapo reported that in Lower Saxony, in rural areas and especially in the case of former army officers, there was 'profound regret' that the *Reichsflaggengesetz* had ruled that the only official state symbol still accepted was the swastika

---

[63] Prices cited from advertisements of the companies 'NS-Fahnenfabrik' and 'H. Moeller' or from the 'Reichszeugmeisterei der NSDAP', *VB*, 26./27 February 1933; 28 February 1933 and 13 March 1933. In the early years of the dictatorship typical working-class families had a disposable income of approximately 30–50 RM per week, and the majority of clerks and civil servants earned very little more. For a summary, see Michael Schneider, *Unterm Hakenkreuz: Arbeiter und Arbeiterbewegung 1933 bis 1939* (Bonn, 1999), 602–4.

[64] These are the words of Secretary of State Hans Pfundtner in a memo to Ministerialrat Scholz on 15 August 1935, BArch Berlin, R 1501, 5315.

[65] Staatssekretär Stuckart erläutert die Verordnungen, Meldung des Deutschen Nachrichtenbüros, Erste Mittagsausgabe, 15 November 1935, BArch Berlin, R 43 II, 135. On the disquiet of many Germans about antisemitic violence, see e.g. Peter Longerich, *'Davon haben wir nichts gewusst!' Die Deutschen und die Judenverfolgung 1933–1945* (Munich, 2006), 85–92.

'Hoist the Flag!' 179

flag.[66] The *Reichsverband Deutscher Offiziere* (Reich Association of German Officers) even complained that many of those who had fought at the front were 'extremely distressed' by it, since they had after all 'fought and bled for four years and sacrificed their comrades and close relatives' under the old imperial flag.[67]

There were, of course, many other possible reactions. Matthias Mehs in Wittlich had himself been in the war, but he was completely indifferent to the introduction of the Nazi *Reichsflaggengesetz*: 'I'm not going to get upset about it and will go and get myself a swastika flag. It isn't a party flag any more so hanging it out isn't a political signal.' At the same time he was surprised by the 'idiocy' of the ruling Nazis, who never stopped hoping that they could 'wipe out the deep gulfs [...] by enforcing external uniformity'. If his diary is to be believed, then there was nothing special for Mehs in the fact that he hung the swastika flag outside his inn for the first time for the harvest festival in October 1935. He portrayed it as a simple business strategy alongside other advertising. 'It was also the first time I used light music.'[68] After that, if he mentioned hanging out flags for festivals at all, it was as a matter of pure routine.[69]

By using the *Reichsflaggengesetz* to justify making his own private peace with the swastika flag, Mehs was in fact making it rather easy for himself. In reality the Party and the state were still doing no more than appealing to private individuals to restrict flags on regime holidays to the swastika. There was no actual ban on flying other flags. This state of affairs was clearly laid out in a press release from the Reich Ministry of the Interior.[70]

The dictatorship seems to have avoided absolute clarity in this matter because Adolf Hitler did not want to hurt the sentimental feelings many older citizens had for the imperial flag too deeply. Reich Minister of the Interior Frick privately disagreed with the way it was regulated. He had already argued for a complete ban on all other flags flown by private individuals except the swastika as early as the end of 1935.[71] His desire to create clarity in the question of flags, even in this grey area between the private and the public sphere, seems to have been

---

[66] Klaus Mlynek (ed.), *Gestapo Hannover meldet... Polizei und Regierungsberichte für das mittlere und südliche Niedersachsen zwischen 1933 und 1937* (Hannover, 1986), 423.
[67] Reichsverband Deutscher Offiziere an das Reichsinnenministerium, 21 November 1935, BArch Berlin, R 43 II, 128 a.
[68] Mehs, *Tagebücher, vol. 1*, 617–18.
[69] See e.g. the entry on 20 April 1936: 'Hitler's birthday. People hung flags out, otherwise there was nothing going on here.' Matthias Joseph Mehs, *Tagebücher, vol. 2: January 1936 to September 1946*, 34. Mehs makes no mention of the flag event on 27 March 1936 described at the beginning of this chapter.
[70] See News Release of the RMdI, o. D. [October 1935], BArch Berlin, R 501, 5315.
[71] See RMdI to the director of the RK, 24 December 1935, BArch Berlin, R 43 II, 128 a.

supported by the veterans' organisation, the *Reichsverband Deutscher Offiziere*. In its petition to the Reich Ministry of the Interior in November 1935 it warned of possible 'renewed friction' 'because some Party officials, especially those of a lower rank', could take aggressive measures against citizens who continued to fly one of the traditional flags. They referred expressly to situations 'concerning the question of Jews and non-Aryans' in which the official policy had often judged and acted 'more mildly [...] than the Party'. For this reason 'as much clarity as possible regarding the flag issue' was urgently required, including for private individuals.[72]

Internal memos from summer 1937 show that this kind of 'friction' did indeed take place. With the approval of the Ministry of Propaganda, the Gestapo and the 'Führer's deputy', the Ministry of the Interior had worked out instructions for the implementation of the *Reichsflaggengesetz* because the 'current lack of clarity and information' regarding 'flag-flying by private individuals' was no longer tenable. Unfortunately, no other details of these discussions have come to light.[73] The resulting decree of 28 August 1937 banned Germans completely from flying any other flag in public except the swastika. This even applied to Christian festivals, when Catholics had always decked out their homes with traditional local and regional church flags. The decree also designated six annual 'general flag days' ('*allgemeine Beflaggungstage*'). At least indirectly, therefore, this decree imposed something like a civic duty to participate personally in all these flag rituals.[74]

There was some difficulty in enforcing these new regulations to begin with in many of the Catholic parishes, insofar as many Catholics continued to use the old flags for religious festivals, such as Corpus Christi processions.[75] But during the political festivals of the Third Reich the swastika was now the only flag to be seen. The vast and uniform 'sea of flags' which the Nazis had been talking about since 1933 had finally become a reality.

However, achieving total coordination (*Gleichschaltung*) in German society in the case of the flag-flying rituals so popular with the Nazis had

---

[72] Reichsverband Deutscher Offiziere to the RMdI, 21 November 1935, BArch Berlin, R 43 II, 128 a.

[73] RMdI to the 'Führer's Deputy', 8 July 1937, BArch Berlin, R 43 II, 128 b.

[74] See RGBl. 1937, T. I, 917. The 'general flag days' were 18 January ('anniversary of the founding of the Reich'), 30 January ('anniversary of the national uprising'), 20 April (Hitler's birthday), 1 May and, as moveable feasts, 'Heroes' Memorial Day' (five weeks after Easter) and the harvest festival in the autumn.

[75] This was evidently not the case on the 'general flag days'. From the wealth of literature on conflicts over flags at traditional church festivals, see e.g. Tobias Haaf, *Von volksverhetzenden Pfaffen und falschen Propheten: Klerus und Kirchenvolk im Bistum Würzburg in der Auseinandersetzung mit dem Nationalsozialismus* (Würzburg, 2006), 175–96.

been a long and labourious process. This was because until August 1937 there were sections of the population who, while literally 'showing the flag', stubbornly used the limited room for manoeuvre available to individuals while they conformed. Thus the growing uniformity of German society in the Third Reich, which seems so well illustrated by contemporary photos and newspaper reports of privately flown flags from as early as March 1933, was by no means as clear-cut as it may seem. At the same time, it does not provide adequate evidence for the overarching claim that after 1933 the Germans lived with a 'divided consciousness'.[76]

By allowing *Volksgenossen* for some considerable time to determine their participation in required rituals with at least some degree of individuality, the Nazis made it easier for ideological dissidents like Matthias Mehs to fit into the Third Reich. They could justify their participation by the fact that they were merely continuing the practice, popular in the Weimar Republic, of taking up a clear political position by means of a publicly displayed flag. This was true in any case for supporters of Adolf Hitler and the NSDAP. It meant that instead of enforcement and repression, contemporary actors could speak of personal conviction and national fervour. Political ritual was an integral part of their private life, not its negation. It was not until 1935 (when Jews were excluded) and even more so after 1937 (when all other flags were prohibited) that the popular ritual of flying a flag really became impersonal. However, the paradox that has become evident – that it was precisely this demonstration of conformity that secured the boundary between the public and the private spheres – survived even this transformation. Like all totalitarian regimes, the Nazi dictatorship had to accept the fact that the enforced participation of citizens in public rituals as a sign of personal convictions could mean both very much and nothing at all for those who played their part.

---

[76] See Hans Dieter Schäfer, *Das gespaltene Bewußtsein. Über deutsche Kultur und Lebenswirklichkeit 1933–1945* (Munich, Vienna, 1981).

8 The Vulnerable Dwelling
Local Privacy before the Courts

Annemone Christians

'It is no longer possible to live a private life properly.' This statement was made by a despairing Theodor W. Adorno in American exile at the beginning of the 1940s. It can be found in the early version of one of his major works, *Minima Moralia*, in which he reflects on the 'damaged life' under the conditions of capitalism and fascism.[1] The sentence was originally the conclusion of a paragraph entitled 'Refuge for the Homeless', which dealt with the aesthetic and spiritual aspects of private living. According to Adorno, they were fatally compromised by the excessive demands of the present.

> The predicament of private life today is shown by its arena (*Schauplatz*). Dwelling, in the proper sense, is now impossible. The traditional residences we grew up in have grown intolerable: each trait of comfort in them is paid for with a betrayal of knowledge, each vestige of shelter with the musty pact of family interests.[2]

Adorno goes on to discuss his dislike of the modern style of interior design inspired by New Objectivity (*Neue Sachlichkeit*) and then considers the actual physical impossibility of dwelling which, he claims, results from the current wartime destruction of European cities. He calls the Nazi labour and concentration camps the 'executors' of the contemporaneous development of technology, transforming homes and houses. Finally, he proposes an ultimate exit strategy to counteract this wretched state of affairs, which is to lead a 'private life' without compromise and without convention, albeit 'uncommitted' and 'suspended', knowing that it has lost its bourgeois meaning and is no longer 'socially substantial and individually appropriate'.[3] In the revised and published edition of this farewell to

---

(Translated from German by Kate Tranter)

[1] On the history of the discovery of the early version of *Minima Moralia* in the Adorno Archive in Frankfurt and its analysis, see Martin Mittelmeier, 'Es gibt kein richtiges Sich-Ausstrecken in der falschen Badewanne: Wie Adornos berühmtester Satz wirklich lautet – ein Gang ins Archiv', *Recherche. Zeitung für Wissenschaft*, 31 January 2010, *Recherche. Zeitung für Wissenschaft* 4 (2009), 3.

[2] Theodor W. Adorno, *Minima Moralia: Reflections from Damaged Life* (London, 2005), 38.

[3] Ibidem, 39.

a way of life, however, Adorno does not end with the statement quoted earlier, but with its iconic rhetorical abbreviation: 'Wrong life cannot be lived rightly' ('*Es gibt kein richtiges Leben im falschen*').[4]

Approaches to Spatial Privacy

The private sphere in *Minima Moralia* is a degeneration of real life, a form of existence only one step away from pure consumerism, into which philosophy, now only a 'melancholy science' ('*traurige Wissenschaft*'), has had to retreat as if into exile.[5] Yet this exile was itself endangered. 'The possibility of residence is annihilated by that of socialist society, which, once missed, saps the foundations of bourgeois life.'[6] According to Adorno, the socialist drive for collectivisation has displaced all things bourgeois, including established forms of dwelling. However, he is not concerned with seeking the protection of bourgeois *privacy*. This may stem from the fact that Adorno did not consider it desirable to withdraw into a private sphere with its inherent isolation from the world.

Adorno was forced to transfer his own treasured way of life to America because it had become almost impossible for him to live and work in Germany after the Nazi seizure of power. In 1933 the University of Frankfurt withdrew his right to teach – as the son of a Jewish father, he was one of the first victims of the antisemitic expulsions from the university. He managed to avoid further persecution by emigrating first to Britain in 1934 and then to the United States in 1938.[7] His friend Max Horkheimer helped him to find a suitable house there, for which Adorno and his wife expressed very specific and quite bourgeois requirements. His need to find a certain 'bourgeois comfort' – with a music room and a bathtub – points to a basic ambivalence in Adorno's attitude as well as in the significance of home itself. As a critical theorist, he may have deconstructed private life, but he could not and would not do without its benefits. In his writings, Adorno bemoans the loss of the 'good' private life, but in his own life he invests a great deal to retain at least a vestige of its structures.

The topic of this book is the relationship of the Nazi regime to 'the private'. Adorno's reflections on private life and the 'correct' life, and the

---

[4] Ibidem.
[5] Ibidem, 15. Adorno is referring here to Friedrich Nietzsche's collection of aphorisms, *The Gay Science* (*Die fröhliche Wissenschaft*) (1882/7), in which philosophy is portrayed as a higher discipline than both art and science.
[6] Adorno, *Minima Moralia*, 39.
[7] On Adorno's emigration, see esp. Stefan Müller-Doohm, *Adorno: Eine Biographie* (Frankfurt a.M., 2011), 257–424.

destruction of both by the Nazi dictatorship, speak to one of this volume's key questions. As the philosopher Beate Rössler has suggested in her instructive study *The Value of Privacy*, intimate spatial privacy featured as a classical and defining feature in discourses about 'the private' in modern, liberal societies.[8] Similarly, in his fundamental work *History of Private Life*, Antoine Prost also establishes a structural connection between privacy and space, maintaining that 'the history of private life is initially the history of the space in which it is acted out'.[9] Paul Betts argues that the attitude towards private life played a decisive role in German politics throughout the twentieth century: 'Indeed, the private sphere and the idealized domicile were central to each German government over the course of the last century, not least because decent housing was so closely tied to political legitimacy.'[10]

In this historiography, the private sphere and the home are more or less synonymous. On one hand, home is a place chosen by the individual which offers both distance from the outside world and the public sphere and the opportunity to be alone; on the other hand, home is also a space for familial and intimate interactions. Both of these aspects are generally lived out within a person's own four walls – their flat, house or even a single room. As a result, the space of home is emotionally endowed with the sense of retreat or refuge, reflected linguistically in the use of such phrases as 'my home is my castle' or '*trautes Heim, Glück allein*' ('home sweet home, joy alone'), which suggest that this emotional endowment is closely connected to a subjective sense of security and autonomy.[11] The physical and material boundaries manifested by surrounding walls permit and enable the intimacy of domestic life.[12]

If, as this volume argues, the Nazi regime did not simply dissolve privacy wholesale, then it is worthwhile to explore in more detail how this state dealt with both the tangible boundaries of the home and with the

---

[8] See Beate Rössler, *Der Wert des Privaten* (Frankfurt a.M., 2001), 255; English edition: Beate Rössler, *The Value of Privacy* (Cambridge, 2005).

[9] Antoine Prost, 'Grenzen und Zonen des Privaten', in Antoine Prost and Gérard Vincent (eds.), *Geschichte des privaten Lebens*, vol. 5: *Vom Ersten Weltkrieg zur Gegenwart* (Frankfurt a.M., 1993), 15–151, here 63.

[10] Paul Betts, *Within Walls: Private Life in the German Democratic Republic* (Oxford, 2010), 119.

[11] See also Carmen Keckeis, 'Privatheit und Raum – zu einem wechselbezüglichen Verhältnis', in Eva Beyvers et al. (eds.), *Räume und Kulturen des Privaten* (Heidelberg, 2017), 19–56.

[12] The *Dictionnaire de la langue française* by Émile Littré defines it as early as the end of the nineteenth century: 'La vie privée doit être murée.' Quotation from Sylvie Mesure and Patrick Savidan (eds.), *Dictionnaire des sciences humaines* (Paris, 2006), 431. The quotation is attributed to the French author and publisher Pierre-Jules Hetzel (1814–66). The full version: 'La vie privée doit être murée, c'est un sanctuaire inviolable, c'est le comité secret du moi.'

intangible value of the idea of a domestic retreat. This chapter addresses these questions by adopting a legal historical perspective. It examines private space as a legally protected right, and investigates possible shifts in its lines of demarcation. The legal negotiations of these boundaries in everyday Nazi legal proceedings can shed light on how the regime dealt with conflicting demands and expectations, and what it wished to establish as 'communal (*volksgemeinschaftliche*) normality'. In order to explore these issues, first the legal parameters of local privacy in the Nazi regime are examined and compared with aspects of the subjective perception of a retreat or refuge and its representation in propaganda. Several examples of cases brought before criminal and civil law courts are then used to provide insights into the way in which the spaces of private life and the aspirations they enshrined were evaluated from a legal point of view. This is done, firstly, by examining proceedings on the offence of *Hausfriedensbruch* (breach of domestic peace), prosecution of what is known as *Heimtücke* (treachery or malice towards the state) and on criminal utterances made in domestic contexts. Secondly, I analyse the role of the marital home within family law, and the interpretation of tenancy laws, in order to explore how the Nazi state judged and dealt with conflicts that arose in and about private homes. My analyses of court proceedings are based on legal records preserved from various courts and judgements published in legal journals such as *Juristische Wochenschrift*, *Deutsches Recht* and *Deutsche Justiz*. These were the sources the professional public used to learn about any decisions that might be significant as cases of precedence or as exceptional cases. Examining the practice of sentencing carried out by the relatively low-level judiciary of the District and Regional Courts as well as by the Special Courts allows the historian to challenge historiographical assumptions that are predicated on an imagined stark dichotomy between public and private spheres as opposing concepts.[13] Efforts to either undermine or safeguard private spaces of refuge can only be understood if they are contextualised in terms of the underlying frames of reference and legitimation for the legal negotiations in question. The court proceedings I analyse in this chapter demonstrate that these negotiations were anything but predictable, and that the Nazi judiciary oscillated between protecting and destroying private space.

---

[13] For useful analytical differentiations between the public and private spheres with reference to theories of the state and cultural theory, see esp. Norberto Bobbio, *Democracy and Dictatorship: The Nature and Limits of State Power* (Cambridge, 1989); for a fundamental study of the concept of the public sphere, see also Jürgen Habermas, *The Structural Transformation of the Public Sphere: An Inquiry into a Category of Bourgeois Society* (Cambridge, MA, 1989). For a discussion of the private as an integral and sustaining element of political modes of engagement and citizenship, see also the introduction to this volume and Chapter 2 by Janosch Steuwer.

The Home as a Sanctuary

If local privacy is defined as a value unique to liberal societies and those under the rule of law, notwithstanding all the 'normative difficulties'[14] which this entails here,[15] it would, surely, have lost its significance during the Nazi dictatorship. Just as Adorno suggested, private dwelling would have become invalidated as a side effect of the destruction of a bourgeois way of life. This perception certainly existed. It is evident, for example, in the words of a doctor in 1934, quoted by Detlev Peukert in his seminal study *Inside Nazi Germany*, to illustrate the perception of a total loss of boundaries:

> After my surgery, getting on for 9 in the evening, I want to stretch out peacefully on the sofa with a book about Matthias Grünewald. But the walls of my room, of my whole flat, suddenly vanish. I look around in horror: all of the flats, as far as the eye can see, have lost their walls. I hear the roar of a loudspeaker: 'As per decree abolishing all walls, 17th instant.'[16]

In keeping with the hypothesis set out in the introduction of this volume, I take issue with this quotation. While some areas of Nazi ideology, its programme and the way of life it valorised radically departed from liberal bourgeois concepts of social life, this did not mean that the idea of the home as a domestic retreat disappeared. Nor did it mean that there was a radical change in its emotional charge and significance. Peukert had already identified a paradox between the private and the public spheres under National Socialism, where 'retreating into private space' was viewed with political suspicion, yet simultaneously promised and promoted as a privilege.[17] More recent research has attempted to analyse this ambivalence empirically. Elizabeth Harvey, for example, emphasises the importance of 'normality' at home during wartime as a pivotal but endangered focus of longing: 'Home and the pleasures and comforts of

---

[14] Rössler, *Wert*, 259.
[15] Even in current debates on human rights, the extent to which local safe space can be limited for the sake of free personal development is frequently disputed and has not yet been conclusively defined in constitutional law. However, the jurist Jörg Berkemann has suggested the following approach as one that could find a consensus: 'What is crucial to the spatial private sphere is [...] on the one hand the recognisable desire of the individual that rooms and spaces should only be accessible privately and on the other hand the social acceptance of this individual determination of the spatial private sphere' (Thorsten Kingreen and Ralf Poscher, *Grundrechte: Staatsrecht II*, 29th edn [Heidelberg, 2013], 235).
[16] Cited by Detlev Peukert, *Inside Nazi Germany: Conformity, Opposition and Racism in Everyday Life* (London, 1987), 237. On this example, see also Janosch Steuwer, *'Ein Drittes Reich, wie ich es auffasse': Politik, Gesellschaft und privates Leben in Tagebüchern 1933–1939* (Göttingen, 2017), 497–8.
[17] See Peukert, *Inside Nazi Germany*, esp. 236–42.

the domestic realm were vital but fraught topics on the German wartime home front.'[18] Similarly, the idea of romantic love and attachment to family, explored in this book in the chapters by Umbach (Chapter 5), Seegers (Chapter 9), Usborne (Chapter 12) and Bergerson et al. (Chapter 11), was not just a retreat from political life, but could be drawn upon and mobilised to sustain and nourish a community committed to the ideals of National Socialism, and a nation at war.

The degree to which the domestic and political spheres were intertwined can be illustrated with a passage from a brochure entitled *German Homes*. It came out in 1941 as part of a series called 'Germany of To-Day' published by the German Information Service, a London-based German news agency closely associated with the NSDAP; its several volumes were intended to inform British readers about everyday life and customs in the 'Third Reich'.[19] The author Fritz Alexander Kauffmann describes how:

> German families spend so many hours of the year in their homes that it is their natural desire to make this little world of their own really ideal. They wish to feel absolutely secure within their own four walls and, on returning home after a hard day's work, they like to look forward to a place of rest and peaceful reunion.[20]

The 'German home' is imagined as a family retreat and a place of relaxation and emotional security. The first two of these aspects of having one's 'own four walls' played a significant role in the promises and the political programme of the regime as well as in the real life of the *Volksgemeinschaft* (national community). The idea of one's own home and one's own plot of land (*eigene Scholle*) was a key element of its socio-political plan, and both were promoted in various small-scale housing and development programmes, which were in turn inflated ideologically as 'cells' of the new *Volksgemeinschaft*.[21] Of course, when it came to the home as a safe space, a stark discrepancy existed between the ideal described by Kauffmann,

---

[18] Elizabeth Harvey, 'Housework, Domestic Privacy and the "German Home": Paradoxes of Private Life during the Second World War', in Rüdiger Hachtmann and Sven Reichardt (eds.), *Detlev Peukert und die NS-Forschung* (Göttingen, 2015), 115–31, here 120.

[19] For the German Information Service and its proximity to the Reich Ministry of Propaganda, see Arnd Bauerkämper, *Die 'radikale Rechte' in Großbritannien: Nationalistische, antisemitische und faschistische Bewegungen vom späten 19. Jahrhundert bis 1945* (Göttingen, 1991), 236–7.

[20] Fritz Alexander Kauffmann, *German Homes: Deutsches Wohnen* (= 'Germany of To-Day', vol. 8) (Berlin, 1941), 7.

[21] Ulrike Haerendel, 'Wohnungspolitik im Nationalsozialismus', *Zeitschrift für Sozialreform* 45/10 (1999), 843–79, here 850–60; for the Nazi housing programme, see also Karl Christian Führer, 'Das NS-Regime und die "Idealform des deutschen Wohnungsbaues": Ein Beitrag zur nationalsozialistischen Gesellschaftspolitik', *Vierteljahrschrift für Sozial- und Wirtschaftsgeschichte* 89/2 (2002), 141–66; Tilman Harlander, *Zwischen Heimstätte*

and the legal reality under National Socialism. The introduction of the 'Decree of the President of the German Reich on the Protection of the People and State',[22] the so-called Reichstag Fire Decree (*Reichstagsbrandverordnung*), on 28 February 1933, had erased the guaranteed inviolability of the home, which had originally been enshrined in the constitution of St Paul's Church in Frankfurt in 1849, and had been a basic right that protected the private 'sanctuary' of every German ever since.[23] As a result, the legal right of an individual to decide freely and autonomously to whom access to their private rooms and space should be granted or not was now null and void.[24]

This was also reflected in the lifting of restrictions to police powers, evident in the wide-scale police raids, searches and arrests that were carried out by the new regime as soon as it came to power in the spring of 1933, and that involved a strict clamp-down on supposed 'enemies of the Reich', i.e. potential opponents and those who were thought to be ideologically suspect. This kind of abuse was justified as 'exceptional measures' introduced by the *Reichstagsbrandverordnung* and took place in a space more or less devoid of any judicial control.[25] As the power of the various police organisations increased in relation to the regular judiciary in the course of the 1930s, the codified police law developed into a blurred and baffling mixture of laws, regulations, instructions and decrees.[26] Within this impenetrable mass, any demarcation of a spatial sphere of protection for private lives was effectively lost. According to the established Code of Criminal Procedure, house searches were only permitted by order of a judge, although in the case of 'imminent danger', they could be ordered by the public prosecutor; they were not permitted at night time.[27] In reality, however, during the reign of terror under the Gestapo, they were subject to no restrictions whatsoever.[28]

---

und Wohnmaschine: Wohnungsbau und Wohnungspolitik in der Zeit des Nationalsozialismus (Basel, 1995).

[22] *Reichsgesetzblatt* (RGBl.) I 1 (1933), 83.

[23] § 140 of the Constitution of the German Reich, 28 March 1849; § 115 of the Weimar Constitution, 11 August 1919; see also Eberhard Rhein, *Die Unverletzlichkeit der Wohnung: Eine Spurensuche zwischen Frankfurt und Weimar* (Frankfurt a.M., New York, NY, 2001). On the Reichstag Fire Decree, see also Janosch Steuwer's contribution to this volume (Chapter 2).

[24] See the authoritative work by Rudolf Echterhölter, *Das öffentliche Recht im nationalsozialistischen Staat* (Stuttgart, 1970).

[25] See Andreas Schwegel, *Der Polizeibegriff im NS-Staat* (Tübingen, 2005), esp. 41–120.

[26] See Echterhölter, *Recht*, 277–83.

[27] §§ 104f. of the Code of Criminal Procedure (*Strafprozessordnung*), 1933 edition. In 1934 and 1935 Nazi legislators issued several laws reforming the Code of Criminal Procedure, but the paragraphs mentioned here remained unchanged.

[28] See e.g. Andreas Theo Schneider, *Die geheime Staatspolizei im NS-Gau Thüringen: Geschichte, Struktur, Personal und Wirkungsfelder* (Frankfurt a.M., 2008), 202–311.

Local Privacy in Criminal Law: Domiciliary Rights, Trust and *Heimtücke*

What sentences were passed after the Nazi seizure of power when it came to demarcating the spatial boundaries between private agents? An insight into this can be gained by looking at the judgements made in cases of *Hausfriedensbruch* (breach of domestic peace). In the late 1930s, the University of Munich carried out an analysis of court cases based on paragraph 123 of the penal code, i.e. violation of so-called domiciliary rights, which were still upheld in principle in Nazi law:

> Whoever enters the business premises or enclosed property of another person illegally or whoever likewise enters closed rooms used for public services or communication without permission, or if they do so, refuses to leave when requested to by an authorized person, will be charged with the offence of *Hausfriedensbruch* and subject to a fine or prison sentence of up to 3 months.[29]

This Munich study was based on data from all the cases which came before the Munich District Court (*Amtsgericht*) between 1933 and 1939 relating to this paragraph 123.[30] The results showed that of the approximately 300 trials analysed in the study, more than half pertained to *Hausfriedensbruch* in private flats or houses. Also, in more than half of the cases, the motivation for the crime was given as 'differences of opinion, conflict or hostility regarding private individuals'.[31] What is significant is a change in the sentencing practice. At the beginning of the period in question, the simple offence of *Hausfriedensbruch*, i.e. unauthorised entry into the private space of the plaintiff, was sufficient for an offender to be punished. However, as time passed, the district judges penalised offenders increasingly rarely, particularly in the case of mere intrusion into the flat, house or garden of the plaintiff. It was only when *Hausfriedensbruch* was combined with a further offence such as theft, bodily harm or damage to property that the judges imposed a significant punishment. The Munich study concluded that the occurrences of *Hausfriedensbruch* were partly caused by the lack of adequate housing in large urban centres, but that Nazi housing and house-building policies would result in a (further) reduction of such cases.

It is clear that *Hausfriedensbruch* is due to a great extent to hostility and disputes which are themselves caused by substandard living conditions, especially for

---

[29] Otto Schwarz, *Strafgesetzbuch mit den wichtigsten Nebengesetzen und Verordnungen des Reiches und Preußens*, 2nd edn (München, Berlin, 1934), § 123.

[30] See Walter Reiserer, *Der Hausfriedensbruch: Unter besonderer Berücksichtigung Münchens* (Leipzig, 1939).

[31] Ibidem, 35.

subtenants. There is no doubt that as these are gradually and radically improved or removed, there will be a marked reduction in incidences of *Hausfriedensbruch*.[32]

There were in fact indications of this in the quantitative data of the period studied, since the actual number of cases had sunk by 1939.

The gradual devaluation of the crime of *Hausfriedensbruch* evident in this study was offset by a decision that elevated domiciliary rights to greater legal significance. In late 1937, the Magistrates' Court (*Schöffengericht*) in Leipzig had to try an unusual case. The defendant Z was accused of having made calls to the home of the plaintiff and injured party A in July of that year from various municipal phone boxes, morning, evening and night, a total of twenty-three times. Whenever the plaintiff had answered the phone, the defendant had hung up. However, in this case, the complaint the plaintiff filed did not refer to *Hausfriedensbruch*, but to harassment. The plaintiff evidently felt that the annoyance of frequent phone calls amounted to a personal insult, even though there had been no verbal interaction. The court did not accept the basis of the original complaint, but judged the case in accordance with paragraph 123 of the penal code, reasoning that this was 'a breach of domiciliary law'.[33]

The sole purpose of the telephone calls was to annoy the plaintiff. [...] Such unsolicited phone calls are a breach of domiciliary law, since they violate the legally protected licence for a person to reside undisturbed in their own home, according to their own free will.[34]

However, in order to reach this decision, the judges in Leipzig had to use a method which had only recently been introduced by the Nazi 'reform of the legal system'. In the partial reform of the criminal code in June 1935, the legislators had broken with the legal principle of *nulla poena sine lege* (no penalty without a law), which had been valid until then, and replaced it with the Nazi concept of law, *nullum crimen sine poena* (no crime without a punishment).[35] This meant that 'popular sentiment' or collective gut instinct were now accorded the status of a guiding legal principle. Paragraph 2 of the criminal code now read as follows:

---

[32] Ibidem, 38.
[33] The court records do not contain the final sentence passed in this trial.
[34] Entscheidung des Schöffengerichts Leipzig vom 1. Dezember 1937, *Deutsche Justiz* 100/28, Ausgabe A (1938), 1125.
[35] For Nazi interference in criminal justice, see Peter Salje (ed.), *Recht und Unrecht im Nationalsozialismus* (Münster, 1985); Echterhölter, *Recht*; Lothar Gruchmann, *Justiz im Dritten Reich 1933–1940: Anpassung und Unterwerfung in der Ära Gürtner* (Munich, 1988).

Punishment will be imposed on any person whom the law declares to be worthy of punishment or who deserves punishment in accordance with the basic principles of the criminal code and with popular sentiment. If no specific penal law can be applied directly to the deed, it will be judged according to the law whose principle most closely applies to it.[36]

This break with the so-called prohibition of analogy, the principle of *nulla poena sine lege*, which had previously been the basic principle of a judiciary adhering to the rule of law and acting within the law, made it possible for anyone to be prosecuted arbitrarily for any action whatsoever.[37] Since the boundaries of the home were not physically breached, as was required for the application of paragraph 123, the court turned to the question of whether the deed 'merited punishment', even though there was no true legal basis for this.

The domestic peace of the spouses A was seriously disrupted by these phone calls. It requires no further explanation that the actions of the accused deserve punishment according to popular sentiment. Since no specific penal law can be applied directly to this case, complying with § 2 of the penal code, the deed is to be judged according to the law whose principle most closely applies to it, which in the view of the *Schöffengericht* is § 123 of the penal code. This paragraph protects the home, domestic peace and domiciliary rights in general, and allows occupants and their families to live in their premises undisturbed by any illegal action by an unauthorised third party.

This judgement is remarkable. The decision of the court did not comply with the original request of the plaintiff to sue for harassment, but considered that domestic law had been breached.[38] The court judged that the frequent phone calls constituted an infringement of domestic peace, and conceded to the plaintiff a right to undisturbed time and freedom of movement at home, which were violated by the repeated ringing of the telephone. This meant that the court upheld the right to domestic peace and autonomy for *Volksgenossen* (members of the *Volksgemeinschaft*) as a legitimate claim.

At the same time, this case demonstrates that German law treated violations of the personal sphere differently according to whether they involved a person's tangible or intangible goods. The plaintiff had wanted to prosecute under paragraph 185 of the criminal law, which provided for

---

[36] Gesetz zur Änderung des Strafgesetzbuchs, 28 June 1935, RGBl. I (1935), 839.
[37] See also e.g. Ingeborg Maus, '"Gesetzesbindung" der Justiz und die Struktur der nationalsozialistischen Rechtsnormen', in Ralf Dreier und Wolfgang Sellert (eds.), *Recht und Justiz im 'Dritten Reich'* (Frankfurt a.M., 1989), 80–104.
[38] Both harassment and *Hausfriedensbruch* are cases in criminal law of so-called application offences, meaning that they can be pursued by the law enforcement authorities only if the injured party has made a relevant application.

either a fine or a punishment of up to twelve months in prison.[39] The Leipzig court, however, chose to prosecute for *Hausfriedensbruch*, for which the highest penalty was three months' imprisonment. Since the original implementation of the penal code, the German judiciary had ruled that deliberate degradation and damage to a person's human dignity as a result of an express insult caused a higher level of harm than the violation of the local private sphere. This principle could continue to be upheld in Nazi legal thinking, since it afforded high priority to the *völkisch* concept of human dignity or honour.[40]

In the 1930s, the idea of a personal space that may not be penetrated randomly either by the state or by any other private agent was becoming increasingly irrelevant for criminal law. This is evident in the practices of the Nazi 'Special Courts' (*Sondergerichte*) and particularly in the prosecution of what was known as *Heimtücke*.[41] In December 1934, the Nazi legislators had passed a law 'against malicious attacks on the state and the Party and for the protection of Party officials' (those wearing the uniform). This so-called law against *Heimtücke* (*Heimtückegesetz*) created an all-purpose tool for a politicised judiciary severely to punish any expression of non-conformism as an 'attack on the state and the Party'.[42] Although the law specified that only offensive and inflammatory expressions made in public should be prosecuted, it also included speech acts that were not uttered in public, but that the perpetrator could reasonably expect to penetrate into the public sphere.[43] This meant that the judges had huge leeway for their decisions and, in the majority of cases of *Heimtücke*, this led to the de facto disappearance of non-public space.

This can be evidenced by two sentences passed in short succession at the *Sondergericht* in Hamburg in 1937 and 1938. The court twice brought charges of 'seditious' (*staatsfeindliche*) comments and behaviour against the same defendant. In their own flat and with no one else listening, the defendant had complained to his wife about the government of the Reich, and had smashed a portrait of Adolf Hitler. His wife reported him to the police, and the *Sondergericht* opened proceedings. He was acquitted for the offence committed in July 1937 because the condition of 'being expressed in public' did not apply. But a few months later, his wife reported him again for supposed malice towards the state (*Heimtücke*).

---

[39] See Otto Schwarz, *Strafgesetzbuch: Nebengesetze, Verordnungen, Kriegsstrafrecht*, 11th edn (München, Berlin, 1942), 304.

[40] The level of sentencing for *Hausfriedensbruch* was not raised until 1975 when the German Federal judiciary amended the penal code. After that, it also allowed for a maximum penalty of twelve months' imprisonment.

[41] See Bernward Dörner, *'Heimtücke': Das Gesetz als Waffe. Kontrolle, Abschreckung und Verfolgung in Deutschland 1933–1945* (Paderborn, 1998).

[42] RGBl. I (1934), 1269–71.   [43] See ibidem, 1269.

Just as in the previous case, the accused stated in his defence that that he had had no reason to suspect that a private conversation held in his own home would be made public. He was, therefore, invoking the circumstance of 'not being public' conceded by the law, the *Heimtückegesetz*. This time, however, the court sentenced him to six months' imprisonment. What had changed? In October 1937, the defendant's marriage was breaking down. His wife had already filed for divorce, and she could have hoped for some advantage from her husband's conviction in the pending divorce proceedings. While the court had conceded for the conversation in July 1937 that the defendant had been in the protected space of 'marital trust', these mitigating circumstances were no longer accepted in October. The court claimed that the 'intimate bond of trust' between the spouses had been broken, and that the husband should therefore have foreseen that his comments might be made public.

> The decisive factor is not the name given in public to the relationship between the defendant and the parties concerned, whether it be marriage or friendship, but the private bond of trust between them. [...] In a dysfunctional marriage the perpetrator should be aware that his wife might not keep his comments to herself.[44]

In both rulings the notion of a spatial sphere of safety was completely removed – it was not even mentioned. It was replaced by an abstract notion of a sphere of trust, in which the local dimension of a person's own four walls played no part. The ruling attracted widespread attention in the Reich when it was published in the *Juristische Wochenschrift*, and became a precedent.[45]

A similar tone had already been struck in 1936 by a ruling of the *Sondergericht* in Munich. In proceedings based on the *Heimtückegesetz*, the defendant had been accused of telling his wife about a rumour in a newspaper whose content was considered defamatory. The man was not aware of having committed any crime – he had no sense of any wrongdoing. The *Sondergericht* accepted his argument.

> The defendant is a simple person who lives with his wife in rural seclusion. [...] The rumour, which in a city would probably not have been taken seriously by many, may have seriously alarmed him. So when he returned home from work in the evening and informed his partner of it, he may indeed have been unaware of any wrongdoing.[46]

---

[44] Entscheidung 1 Is Sond. 1473/37 des Sondergerichts Hamburg vom 22. März 1938, in Staatsarchiv Hamburg, Staatsanwaltschaft Landgericht (Strafsachen) 213–11.
[45] See *Juristische Wochenschrift* 67/2 (1938), 1884.
[46] Entscheidung So 218/36 des Sondergerichts München vom 22. März 1936, *Juristische Wochenschrift* 66/4 (1937), 184–5, here 185.

From this the court concluded that a rumour told to one's wife in confidence cannot be expected to be passed on.

The sphere of trust within a family or a marriage enjoyed particular protection in Nazi legal practice, as is demonstrated by a judgement of the Labour Court in Breslau in 1934. The case being tried concerned the question of unlawful dismissal. The plaintiff had been a housekeeper for a well-situated bourgeois family in Breslau, until the defendant dismissed her without notice. She had been offended by an allegedly 'reactionary' remark made over a family dinner by the son of the family. The exact wording was not given by the *Juristische Wochenschrift* when it published the judgement, presumably to prevent it from attracting further attention. Without the knowledge of her employer, the housekeeper had reported the incident to the SA unit to which the son belonged. The Labour Court considered that this was a violation of the employment contract and judged the dismissal to be lawful, quoting in justification the close bond between the housekeeper and the head of the household.

It was [...] their [...] responsibility to see that the family, as a 'cell' of the state, was able to live and flourish in domestic harmony. According to the reformed National Socialist labour law [...], the leaders of a business and their workers are linked by a bond of care and loyalty, which promotes the specific aims of the business and benefits the people and the state. This fundamentally German perception of the moral nature of an employment contract applies to an even higher degree for staff employed in a family home, where the fact that they eat and live together necessitates even more consideration and effort to nourish this primary cell of human and state community.[47]

Although the court conceded that the housekeeper may well have found the son's remarks offensive, it played down their significance.

At the family dinner table any slight disagreement or resentment may escalate. But not all this harmless conversation is intended for outsiders who are inclined to pick up snippets, weigh up every word and exaggerate its political importance.[48]

After hearing the evidence, the court concluded that the remarks in question had been nothing but 'idle chatter'. By reporting them officially without consulting her employer, the housekeeper had severed the (domestic) bond between herself and the family. As a result, the court judged the summary dismissal to be lawful. The court agreed that, in principle, the head of the household and the defendant 'had a natural obligation to ensure that the domestic circumstances did not make it impossible for the plaintiff, as a convinced National Socialist, to hold

---

[47] Entscheidung des Landesarbeitsgerichts Breslau vom 10. August 1934, *Deutsche Justiz* 96/46, Edition Ausgabe A (1934), 1446f., here 1446.
[48] Ibidem, 1447.

a position of trust in his service'.[49] In this case, however, this obligation had not been breached.

When this judgement was published in the legal journal *Deutsche Justiz*, a note was added by a senior prosecutor, Dr Krug, who in his role as a member of the 'Great Criminal Law Commission' (*Große Strafrechtskommission*) had taken part in the consultations on the Nazi reform of the criminal law.[50] He agreed unreservedly with the court that the comments had stemmed from 'nothing more than a temporary vexation that can surface at any time and was vented in the right place within the close family circle'.[51] However, he was not willing to accord this judgement general validity.

> Naturally the above judgement in no way impinges on the duty to neutralize a person who is seditious and to have any seditious comments or behaviour pursued, regardless of how they may come to a person's notice. This is a natural duty which arises from the nature of the National Socialist state and can never be compromised, even if it clashes with less important personal obligations.[52]

He concluded that it was, therefore, necessary to prevent the spirit of this judgement from being applied to other cases, and that judgements would always have to be made taking into consideration the peculiarities of each individual case.

This emphasis on a duty of loyalty can also be found in the case of denunciations by people close to the accused, where the comments in question were indeed considered malicious and offensive. In 1944, for example, the Viennese branch of the Central Army Court (*Zentralgericht des Heeres*) dealt with a case in which the defendant had been denounced by his wife. She claimed that he had made defeatist comments about the war and had maintained, among other things, that anyone who went to the front was an 'idiot'.[53] A 'friend of the family', with whom the wife was evidently conducting an affair, offered to be a witness for the prosecution. Initially the military court instituted proceedings on the grounds of subversion of national defence, but halted them shortly afterwards and merely cautioned the defendant for his 'improper behaviour'. He was also relieved of his post as secretary to a military doctor and transferred to

---

[49] Ibidem, 1447.
[50] See Werner Schubert (ed.), *Protokolle der Großen Strafrechtskommission des Reichsjustizministeriums (1936–1938)* (Berlin, New York, NY, 1991), 538.
[51] Entscheidung des Landesarbeitsgerichts Breslau vom 10. August 1934, *Deutsche Justiz* 96/46, Edition Ausgabe A (1934), 1446f., here 1447.
[52] Anmerkung zum Urteil des Landesarbeitsgerichts Breslau vom 10. August 1934 von Oberstaatsanwalt Dr. Krug, ibidem 1447.
[53] Cited by Ela Hornung, *Denunziation als soziale Praxis: Fälle aus der NS-Militärjustiz* (Vienna, Cologne, Weimar 2010), 130.

a reserve military hospital. Otherwise, however, the court regarded the denunciation as a consequence of private marital conflict, which used the political content purely instrumentally. The defendant had frequently insisted that all these conversations took place within the private sphere of his own home and had never been made public. The *Zentralgericht* considered his statement credible and thus judged that the conditions for the offence, notably a public utterance, were not fulfilled. The view of the court was that the wife and her friend had been conducting an intimate relationship which went beyond the acceptable limits and that it was, therefore, plausible that they were attempting to get rid of the husband and rival in this manner.[54]

Judgements such as this have been cited in recent studies of (military) legal practice and their treatment of denunciations to show that the National Socialist judiciary did indeed respect the limits of spatial privacy in individual cases. They maintain that close familial ties and secluded private space 'did serve a function as a bond or as protection, because there were no or very few witnesses to the events that took place there, and it could be assumed that the people involved enjoyed a certain level of trust'.[55] However, the actual location of these alleged or actual deeds proved to be of secondary importance, if not irrelevant. Whether a confidential conversation that was later denounced had taken place in the marital or family home[56] had little effect on the passing of a lenient sentence or an acquittal.[57] It was not the location that created the legally protected sphere of trust, but the personal relationship of the participants.

---

[54] See ibidem, 131.

[55] Christoph Thonfeld, *Sozialkontrolle und Eigensinn: Denunziation am Beispiel Thüringens 1933–1949* (Vienna, Cologne, Weimar, 2003), 361.

[56] A statistical study around 1975 analysed eighty-nine cases at the People's Court of Justice (*Volksgerichtshof*) in which the defendants were accused of making defeatist comments. It found that in more than 25 per cent of the cases, the scene of the crime was their private or common dwelling. Klaus Kolb, *Fälle defätistischer Äußerungen und deren Anklage vor dem Volksgerichtshof Zersetzung der Wehrkraft betreffend in Bayern von 1940–1945* (Munich, n.d. [1975]), 10.

[57] On privately motivated denunciations, see also Gisela Diewald-Kerkmann, *Politische Denunziation im NS-Regime oder Die kleine Macht der 'Volksgenossen'* (Bonn, 1995), esp. 136–41; see also Peter Hüttenberger, 'Heimtückefälle vor dem Sondergericht München 1933–1939', in Martin Broszat et al. (eds.), *Bayern in der NS-Zeit*, vol. 4 (Munich, 1981), 435–526; John Connelly, 'The Uses of *Volksgemeinschaft*: Letters to the NSDAP Kreisleitung Eisenach, 1939–1940', *Journal of Modern History* 68/4 (1996), 899–930; also Robert Gellately, *The Gestapo and German Society: Enforcing Racial Policy 1933–1945* (Oxford, 1990), esp. 130–58; Robert Gellately, 'Denunciation as a Subject of Historical Research', *Historical Social Research/Historische Sozialforschung* 26/2/3 (2001), 16–29.

Private Households in Civil Law

Analysing civil law disputes turns the spotlight on the everyday structuring of the private sphere. The question here is how the Nazi judiciary approached the home as a space dedicated to private and family life, and as the focus of life and leisure: 'a place of rest and peaceful reunion', as described by Fritz Alexander Kauffmann in the brochure *German Homes*.[58] How did the Nazi judiciary judge and resolve conflicts in which the running of a private home was in dispute? What value did it ascribe to different forms of cohabitation with family members in a home? When and with what effect did the Nazi legislators influence how it was shaped?

By examining the status of the 'marital home', we can trace changing values attributed to spatial privacy in Nazi family law.[59] The marital home was often the object of disputes, particularly in divorce cases, as the emotional and material centre of family life. The participants' domestic circumstances were considered crucial to the proceedings, which often made the participants reveal intimate details. Men filing for divorce frequently quoted deliberate neglect of the home, its cleanliness and the children's upbringing as proof of the breakdown of their marriage. As evidence of this, they were often willing to describe their everyday lives in intimate detail in their written statements, thus allowing the lawyers an inside and in-depth view of their domestic sphere.[60] A peculiarity of the German civil law system came into effect here which allows the parties to act autonomously during proceedings. The law stipulated (and still does) that the 'principle of the presentation of evidence', the *Beibringungsgrundsatz*, is implemented. In contrast to criminal law, where the judge determines the taking of evidence, the *Beibringungsgrundsatz* requires the conflicting parties to present the evidence for their claims or complaints to the court. This could result in a 'voluntary' revelation of intimate details to the court to support allegations about a wife's poor or 'slovenly' housekeeping, or an 'unrestrained' husband's supposedly perverse sexual demands.

This shift in values in family law was the result of a radical intervention by the legislators in the mid-1930s. In connection with the legislation on 'hereditary health', the marriage law was adjusted in 1935 to incorporate

---

[58] Kauffmann, *German Homes*, 7.
[59] For Nazi family policy in general, see Michelle Mouton, *From Nurturing the Nation to Purifying the Volk: Weimar and Nazi Family Policy 1918–1945* (New York, NY, 2007); Paul Ginsborg, *Family Politics: Domestic Life, Devastation and Survival 1900–1950* (New Haven, CT, 2014), 312–95; also Claudia Koonz, *Mothers in the Fatherland: Women, the Family and Nazi Politics* (New York, NY, 1987).
[60] See also Petra Kannapel, *Die Behandlung von Frauen im nationalsozialistischen Familienrecht* (Darmstadt, Marburg, 1999).

the idea of 'racial hygiene' and, with the Nuremberg Law for the Protection of German Blood and German Honour (*Blutschutzgesetz*), charged with a *völkisch* and racial mission. In 1938, the marriage law was completely revised and removed from the German Civil Code. Linked to this was a reform of the divorce law, which some members of the Social Democratic and liberal factions as well as legal lobbyists had been agitating for since the 1920s.[61] In its extended scope the new law now permitted a 'no-fault divorce' on the grounds of 'irretrievable breakdown'. This also permitted the termination of marriages that were no longer 'in the interest of the *Volksgemeinschaft*' for reasons of race or racial hygiene or because they were childless.[62]

The Law for the Unification of Rights of Marriage and Divorce in Austria and the Reich (*Gesetz zur Vereinheitlichung des Rechts der Eheschließung und der Ehescheidung im Lande Österreich und im übrigen Reichsgebiet*), which was passed on 6 July 1938, now also firmly anchored the National Socialist *ordre public* in family law.[63] Marriages between citizens of the German Reich and people who were positioned outside the Nazi *Volksgemeinschaft* could be contested for endangering the racial purity of the people as a whole (*Volksganze*) and declared null and void.[64] The value of a marriage to the racial community (*völkische Gemeinschaft*) came to the fore. This meant, for example, that a divorce could be granted on the grounds of childlessness or an alleged hereditary disease, even if such grounds only played a minor role in legal practice.[65] The principle of a 'no-fault divorce' on the grounds of 'irretrievable breakdown' now took precedence over that of 'culpable marital breakdown',[66] but it was completely separated from its original individualistic liberal tradition.[67] The legislators of this revised marriage law were responding to social changes affecting partnerships and families. The supposedly progressive nature of the divorce law reform, intended as a sign of liberation from the long and

---

[61] See Dirk Blasius, *Ehescheidung in Deutschland 1794–1945* (Göttingen, 1987), 164–87.
[62] See e.g. Kathrin Nahmacher, *Die Rechtsprechung des Reichsgerichts und der Hamburger Gerichte zum Scheidungsgrund des § 55 EheG 1938 in den Jahren 1938 bis 1945* (Frankfurt a.M., 1999).
[63] See RGBl. I (1938), 807.
[64] See e.g. Gabriele Czarnowski, *Das kontrollierte Paar: Ehe- und Sexualpolitik im Nationalsozialismus* (Weinheim, 1991); Hans Wrobel, 'Die Anfechtung der Rassenmischehe: Diskriminierung und Entrechtung der Juden in den Jahren 1933 bis 1935', *Kritische Justiz* 16/4 (1983), 349–74.
[65] See Czarnowski, *Das kontrollierte Paar*, 91–9; Kathrin Kompisch, *Täterinnen: Frauen im Nationalsozialismus* (Cologne, 2008), 26–7.
[66] See e.g. Nahmacher, *Die Rechtsprechung des Reichsgerichts*.
[67] On the position of marital breakdown as grounds for divorce in the legal debate during the Weimar Republic, see Dieter Niksch, *Die sittliche Rechtfertigung des Widerspruchs gegen die Scheidung der zerrütteten Ehe in den Jahren 1938–1944* (PhD, Cologne, 1990).

unsuccessful debates of the Weimar period, gave the general public the illusion that it was in keeping with the times, and ostensibly promised a more autonomous way of life.[68]

The new paragraph in the divorce law referring to 'irretrievable breakdown' made it possible for a marriage to be terminated without either of the spouses being found guilty. If a couple had not been sharing the marital household for a period of more than three years and the marriage was, therefore, profoundly and irretrievably broken, this could now be valid grounds for divorce. The idea of not sharing the household was taken literally to mean living separately, i.e. 'a de facto situation in which personal contact between the spouses is more or less impossible'.[69] However, this did not necessarily mean spatial separation; the spouses could have continued to live in the same house or flat. However, the precedents of the Supreme Court of the Reich (*Reichsgericht*) stipulated that if the spouses continued to live in the same home, they had to have led separate lives in it. This meant not only a separation of bed and board, but also completely separate households and no personal contact beyond matters of organisation or concerning their children.

> There is to be no joint household, for which, for example, the wife is responsible and the husband provides the means. There must be no contact between the spouses except when they occupy the communal domestic space, which they are to set up so as to live their lives in it as independently from each other as possible.[70]

Such living conditions as described here were not rare in court proceedings. In about 30 per cent of the divorce cases heard by the Regional Court (*Landgericht*) in Munich that called on paragraph 55 of the new marriage law, the so-called breakdown paragraph (*Zerrüttungsparagraph*), the spouses did not live apart, but together in their joint home.[71] If, however, it became clear in the course of the proceedings that the couple were sleeping apart but were otherwise 'interacting' with each other, the joint household was considered to be intact.

In a divorce case heard at the *Landgericht* in Berlin in 1939, the claimant gave evidence that the joint household no longer existed, stating that although he had his breakfast in their flat and was occasionally provided with an evening meal by his wife, she did not permit him to speak at these

---

[68] See Blasius, *Ehescheidung*, 157f.
[69] Gustav von Scanzoni, *Das großdeutsche Ehegesetz vom 6. Juli 1938: Kommentar* (Berlin, 1939), 215.
[70] Entscheidung des Reichsgerichts IV in Zivilsachen vom 12. Juni 1939, Az. 164/39, *Deutsches Recht* 9/25 (1939), 1330.
[71] These results stem from a systematic evaluation of the approximately 720 existing records on divorce proceedings between 1938 and 1945 in the Staatsarchiv München, Landgerichte.

times, and their relationship had become totally devoid of feeling. He said he sometimes slept in their flat in a separate room, but had taken his things to his new partner's home, where he spent most nights. However, he still paid his wife housekeeping money, which she used for food for herself and their daughter. His divorce claim was based on the 'breakdown paragraph', but the Berlin *Landgericht* dismissed his case. When he appealed, the Berlin Court of Appeal (*Kammergericht*) ruled in favour of divorce, not on the grounds of marital breakdown, but because the husband was guilty of adultery. After a further appeal, the *Reichsgericht* overturned the decision of the *Kammergericht* and dismissed the case conclusively, ruling that this was not a case of living separate lives.

> The determining factor here is the true state of the domestic arrangements. It is, therefore, not a question [...] of whether the claimant's relationship with the respondent was 'deliberately cool'.[72]

For the *Reichsgericht*, both the joint meals and the husband's financial support served as proof of the continuing existence of a joint household.

In a different case, the *Reichsgericht* accepted the separation within the home even though the couple still had several points of contact. In January 1938, a woman filed for divorce at the Munich *Landgericht*, basing her claim initially on her husband's adultery. The couple had married in 1920 and had a daughter together. When asked, as was obligatory in divorce proceedings, when they had last had sexual intercourse, she had stated December 1936. The husband had left the family for work reasons in 1933, but they spent holidays and days off together. Since the beginning of 1937 they had lived apart. The husband requested the case to be dismissed and for his part put in a claim for his wife to re-establish the conjugal relationship. The *Landgericht* in Munich dismissed the wife's case and ruled in favour of the husband. In the appeal proceedings, the husband now filed for divorce, based on the 'breakdown paragraph'. The appeal court recognised the breakdown of the marriage as a result of various adulterous indiscretions committed by the husband. It did not, however, consider it proven that the couple had not been living in a joint household for at least three years, as required for a divorce by law. They had had recent friendly contact with each other and had occasionally had sexual intercourse in their flat. The court held that it could not be assumed that the joint household no longer existed. This would require not only

---

[72] Entscheidung des Zivilsenats IV des Reichsgerichts vom 4. April 1940, Az. 398/39, Entscheidungen des Reichsgerichts in Zivilsachen (RGZ) 163, 277–80.

that they no longer lived in the same flat and belonged to a joint household, but also that there was no physical or emotional contact, so that all the ties which are the essence of a marriage had been severed.[73]

When it heard the case at the last stage of appeal, the *Reichsgericht* disagreed with the interpretation of the appeal court. It considered that the joint household had indeed been dissolved.

> The joint household can in certain circumstances still have ceased to exist even if the conjugal relationship [...] continues. Thus, a discontinuation of the joint household is not to be ruled out by the fact that the man and wife exchange cordial letters, occasionally visit each other and on these occasions may have sexual intercourse.

The *Reichsgericht* dissolved the marriage on the grounds of its breakdown, particularly since the wife had agreed in the meantime to a no-fault divorce.

What can these cases from Nazi divorce practice show about the legal value of the local private sphere? It is clear that the boundaries of local family space were crumbling. A shared home continued to be of crucial importance as the focus of a person's life, but its use could be seen ambivalently and in different ways. Judgements passed according to the new marriage law no longer necessarily saw cohabitation in the same dwelling as the equivalent of a 'marital relationship'. It was, therefore, no longer the space which determined the intimacy of a family or marriage, but the everyday practices, such as meals, which took place in it. If these took place separately, as they would in a more casual communal household, the divorce courts assumed that everything else was also separate.[74] Judgements passed according to the new marriage law also deemed that amicable or even sexual relations were no longer proof of an intact marriage. If this kind of contact was only sporadic and the spouses had separate households and did not share their everyday lives, the joint household could be said to no longer exist and the marriage could be dissolved.

On one hand, these insights into Nazi divorce practice show that the new divorce law allowed more leeway than before to members of the *Volksgemeinschaft* who were seeking a divorce, and also that the courts were willing to take different modes of living into consideration. On the

---

[73] Entscheidung des Zivilsenats IV des Reichsgerichts vom 22. Mai 1939, Az. IV 16/39, *Deutsches Recht* 9/29 (1939), 1578–9.

[74] Especially after the beginning of the war, the courts began to take into account the fact that the increasing lack of housing in larger and medium-sized cities made it more difficult to live in separate homes. They accepted couples living together in the same space as long as there was proof that they did not run a joint household

other hand, they show that the legal professionals examined the private lives and spaces of the litigants in great detail in order to judge the nature of the marriage and the extent of the necessity for it to be dissolved.

Similar tendencies to judge concrete 'moral' practices inside households can be detected when examining how tenancy laws were applied in the Nazi period. If the judgement was unfavourable, the tenants' rights were generally restricted. So, for example, in May 1941 the *Landgericht* in Berlin ruled in favour of a landlord suing his tenant because of a dispute over subletting. The tenant was not currently living in the flat because he was caring for a sick relative, and wanted to sublet it to an unmarried colleague. The landlord saw this as a transgression of 'moral duty'. The court agreed with him, and cited population policy as justification.

> Significant grounds to prohibit a sub-tenancy are present if a tenant who has no use of a whole flat does not terminate the tenancy but wishes to sub-let it to other unmarried individuals, and as a result, it is not available for families with several children.[75]

At the same time, a tenant's rights could also be upheld against the will of the landlord if the tenant's motives had a positive ideological connotation. In May 1941, the District Court (*Amtsgericht*) Kulmbach granted a tenant the right to let his daughter live in his flat, contrary to the terms of the tenancy agreement. Although the landlord insisted on adherence to the written terms and wanted to evict the daughter from her father's flat, he was unsuccessful. The *Amtsgericht* Kulmbach ruled that:

> It is not against the agreed terms of use for a tenant to permit his married daughter to share his flat when her husband has been called up for military service. This does not, therefore, give the landlord any right to an injunction.[76]

When passing judgement the Nazi judiciary could allow the significance of living space and its usefulness for the furtherance of the *Volksgemeinschaft* to take precedence over other civil law claims and applicable regulations. This can be illustrated by a case brought before the *Amtsgericht* Spandau in autumn 1935, in which a landlord sued for unpaid rent. His tenants, a married couple, had not kept to the agreed period of notice, but had suggested various new tenants to the landlord and had moved out of the flat. The landlord did not accept the offer of new tenants and insisted on the previous tenants fulfilling the terms of the

---

[75] Entscheidung des Landgerichts Berlin vom 19. Mai 1941, cited in Hermann Roquette, 'Die Rechtsprechung zum Mietrecht seit Kriegsbeginn', *Deutsches Recht* 13/3–4 (1943), 50–62, here 56.
[76] Entscheidung des Amtsgerichts Kulmbach vom 2. Mai 1941, cited in Roquette, 'Die Rechtsprechung', 56.

agreement and paying the remaining rent. The court rejected the claim on the following grounds:

> It is highly antisocial for a homeowner to allow his property to remain empty and not to make it generally available, particularly in times like these when there is a shortage of housing. For this reason the claim was rejected as unfounded.[77]

The court decided against the legally regulated period of notice and against the landlord, although he was under no legal obligation to accept the proposed new tenants. The court thus overruled his individual rights in favour of 'public interests'. This meant that the Spandau judges preempted the changes introduced into the commentary or instructions for the implementation of the tenancy law paragraphs of the Civil Code (*Bürgerliches Gesetzbuch*) in 1939, where it then stated:

> The principle of consideration of the community (*Gemeinschaftsdenken*), which is intrinsic to National Socialist ideology, means that the process of letting and renting property can be seen as a kind of community, whereby the signatories enjoy mutual trust and are internally linked contractual partners.[78]

This kind of practice led the legal historian Hans Hattenhauer to diagnose a 'moralisation' of private rights, which had begun to increase in the 1920s, and had become the driving force for practising lawyers when the *Bürgerliches Gesetzbuch* was adapted to take on this *völkisch* turn.[79] This so-called moral principle could have dire consequences for the preservation of private spaces. The legal substance of the walls protecting the private home as a space for an individual to develop freely and to behave relatively unhindered began to crumble when tenants became, in a sense, 'trustees of living space', whose behaviour within that space was expected to meet the demands of the *Volksgemeinschaft*.

Conclusion

The total 'abolition of private walls' experienced in a nightmare of 1934 by the doctor quoted by Detlev Peukert never became a reality in the Nazi state. Nevertheless, after 1933, the private home was no longer legally a place where one could 'live rightly', in the sense of Adorno, nor one which

---

[77] Landesarchiv Berlin, Rep. 49, Acc. 1612, Nr. 10408, 5 C 1009/36 21 October 1936.
[78] Commentary of the *Reichsgerichtsräte* on the *Bürgerliches Gesetzbuch* (BGB), Note 1 proceeding § 535, cited in Philip Hackländer, '*Im Namen des Deutschen Volkes*': *Der allgemein-zivilrechtliche Prozeßalltag im Dritten Reich am Beispiel der Amtsgerichte Berlin und Spandau* (Berlin, 2001), 61, footnote 117.
[79] Hans Hattenhauer, 'Richter und Gesetz (1919–1979): Eine Zwischenbilanz', *Zeitschrift der Savigny-Stiftung für Rechtsgeschichte. Germanistische Abteilung* 106/1 (1989), 46–67, here 46.

provided a place of refuge and autonomy. The Nazi seizure of power ended the guarantee of the inviolability of basic individual rights, including the local private sphere. That did not mean, however, that private and individual rights, needs and demands disappeared from official view after 30 January 1933. It meant that the legal boundaries and the organisation of private spaces had to be negotiated in the gap between the abolition of individual property rights and rights of disposal by the Nazi state, on one hand, and, on the other hand, the need to continue legal regulation of civil life. Sensational anti-privacy rhetoric by legal experts and politicians[80] collided with the parallel promise of private happiness, affluence and 'normality' that was also a defining feature of National Socialist rule.[81]

My analysis of how the law was applied in practice speaks to the central questions of this volume in important ways. It explains how, for 'desirable citizens', National Socialism provided opportunities for enjoying and enhancing domestic life, and for promoting private interests. But it also shows how for those who were excluded on ideological grounds, the very same rights could easily be taken away and denied. The Nazi state permitted the members of the *Volksgemeinschaft* certain degrees of privacy granted by the law in individual cases, but at no point under the dictatorship were they guaranteed. On the contrary, they were considered both as a *volksgenössische* liberty specifically granted by the sentencing judge, and as a collectivist liberty legitimated by reference to the welfare of the whole community. The legitimacy of a claim was now determined by popular sentiment. This meant that legal certainty was forced into a dependency on popular *völkisch* standards, which gave duties precedence over rights. Personal autonomy was legally permitted only when it benefitted the interests of the *Volksgemeinschaft*, or at least had no detrimental effect on them. It may have seemed to anyone who turned to a court to settle a personal dispute that the Nazi legal system was guaranteeing their personal freedom, and they may not have considered it limited in any way. In reality, however, and according to Nazi legal thinking, this freedom was always merely granted as a political privilege, and was never an automatic right.[82] The cases I have discussed, from the domains of

---

[80] At a German Labour Front event in 1937, the *Reichsorganisationsleiter* (Reich Leader of Organisation), Robert Ley, proclaimed, 'No, in Germany nothing is private anymore! [...] The days when everyone could do whatever they wanted are over.' Robert Ley, *Soldaten der Arbeit* (München, 1938), 71. On Ley's speech, see also Chapter 2 by Janosch Steuwer in this volume.

[81] Andreas Wirsching, 'Privatheit', in Winfried Nerdinger et al. (eds.), *München und der Nationalsozialismus: Katalog des NS-Dokumentationszentrums München* (Munich, 2015), 443–9, here esp. 444f.

[82] For more details, see Annemone Christians, 'Privatrecht in der Volksgemeinschaft? Die Eigensphäre im nationalsozialistischen Rechtssystem', in Detlef Schmiechen-

criminal and civil law, show that Nazi jurisdiction used abstract concepts when it had to take up a position towards spatial privacy, and emphasised its immaterial nature. The safe private space which might surround the *Volksgenossen* for the sake of recreation and the family no longer had any physical tangible boundaries: it was defined, instead, by non-spatial concepts such as a sphere of trust or a 'marital bond'. This abstraction seems at first to be paradoxical, because it was precisely at this point that the Nazi legal reform had directed its fierce criticism of the old 'liberalist' bourgeois law, accusing it of being too abstract and out of touch with everyday life because it clung to rigid laws instead of allowing fair judgements.[83] The Nazi legal theorists and practitioners thought it 'fairer' not to apply general norms, but to set the limits of individual freedom in each particular case, and always with reference to the *Volksgemeinschaft*. This meant that although *völkisch* privacy could enjoy legal protection, it was always restrained by the fragile limits of concepts such as 'honour', 'trust' and 'marital sentiments'.

Ackermann et al. (eds.), *Der Ort der 'Volksgemeinschaft' in der deutschen Gesellschaftsgeschichte* (Paderborn, 2017), 274–86.

[83] See also Hans-Jürgen Dickhuth-Harrach, *'Gerechtigkeit statt Formalismus': Die Rechtskraft in der nationalsozialistischen Privatrechtspraxis* (Cologne, 1986); Christian Hilger, *Rechtsstaatsbegriffe im Dritten Reich: Eine Strukturanalyse* (Tübingen, 2003).

9 Walther von Hollander as an Advice Columnist on Marriage and the Family in the Third Reich

Lu Seegers

> I suppose these lines have turned out almost too private, but that is nearly always what happens. You put your unreserved trust in a complete stranger. There are no embellishments or exaggerations.[1]

These words were written in the summer of 1940 by thirty-four-year-old Karla Anders from Hamburg and were addressed to Walther von Hollander, probably to this day the best-known German advice columnist. Born in 1892, he made a name for himself as a writer and journalist in the Weimar Republic, having begun his career in 1917/18 as a war reporter for the *Berliner Tageblatt*.[2] He had earlier studied economics, German and philosophy in Berlin, Munich and Heidelberg under Georg Simmel and others, then served as a volunteer in the First World War and afterwards worked in Munich as the editor of a weekly magazine called *Süddeutsche Freiheit* (*South German Liberty*) and in the editorial office of Georg Müller Publishers.[3] In 1920 he joined the painter Heinrich Vogeler's socialist working group (*Sozialistische Arbeitsgemeinschaft*) in the artist colony in Worpswede and in 1921 founded his own printing business, the Hollander Press. In 1923 he moved to Berlin, where he worked as a bookseller, contributed essays and short stories to the *Vossische Zeitung*, and published his first novel. His political sympathies lay with the Social Democrats. He was married three times. With his third wife, Gertrud, whom he married in the 1920s, he had two daughters, born in 1928 and 1936.[4] Gertrud ran a school for breathing exercises in Berlin,

---

(Translated from German by Kate Tranter)

[1] Forschungsstelle für Zeitgeschichte Hamburg, Archiv (FZH-Archiv), 11/H50, Nachlass Walther von Hollander, Schachtel 40, Mappe 5, Karla Anders to Walther von Hollander, 4 February 1940.

[2] For this and more, see Werner Kayser, *Walther von Hollander* (Hamburg, 1971), 72–5.

[3] See Ben Witter, 'Gespräch mit Walther von Hollander: "Man beschimpft keinen alten Mann"', *Die Zeit*, 17 September 1971.

[4] See FZH-Archiv, 11/H50, Nachlass Walther von Hollander, Schachtel 62, Mappe 8, Walther von Hollander to the Polizeirevier Ahorn-Allee, Berlin, 23 June 1939.

and the couple both became members of the International Mazdaznan Temple Association.[5] In November 1925 Hollander co-founded a group of writers called Gruppe 1925, a loose coalition of thirty-nine mainly leftist writers and artists. Five volumes of Hollander's novels and short stories were published between 1927 and 1931 by Ullstein and other publishing houses; at this point he was mainly writing for the magazines *Uhu* and *Koralle* published by the Ullstein press.

Hollander's career, offering fictional portrayals and expert advice on married life and private happiness, continued successfully after 1933 under very different political conditions. Following the Nazi takeover, Hollander continued working in journalism. He did not become a member of the Nazi Party, but as an author writing on 'unpolitical' popular topics, he did manage to increase his popularity. Between 1933 and 1944, he wrote eleven popular novels and fifteen screenplays (some of them as co-author) for the Universum Film AG (Ufa) and other film companies.[6] Most of them were love stories or stories about the fortunes and misfortunes of women. In an interview years later, Hollander maintained that in spite of some misgivings, Reich Propaganda Minister Joseph Goebbels tolerated him because he needed a continuing supply of sophisticated popular novels.[7] In 1937 his book *Der Mensch über Vierzig. Neuer Lebensstil im neuen Lebensalter* (*Life after Forty. A New Style of Life in a New Phase of Life*) was pre-published in the *Berliner Illustrierte Zeitung* (*BIZ*).[8] His self-help manual *Das Leben zu Zweien. Ein Ehebuch. Geschichten und Betrachtungen* (*Life as a Couple. A Book on Marriage, Stories and Observations*),was also pre-published in the *BIZ* in 1939 and enjoyed similar success.[9] Hollander's publications combined two of the most successful genres in popular women's magazines: serialised

---

[5] See FZH-Archiv, 11/H50, Nachlass Walther von Hollander, Schachtel 67, Mappe 7, Mitgliedskarte Walther von Hollander, 1 June 1929. The Mazdaznan association was a religious society founded by Otto Hanisch, who called himself Otoman Zar Adusht Ha'nish, and whose teachings contained elements of Zoroastrianism, Christianity and Hinduism. Advocating vegetarianism as well as breathing and meditation exercises, the movement aimed to transform customs and attitudes in pursuit of a higher form of culture. On the movement, see Bernd Wedemeyer-Kolwe, '*Der neue Mensch*'. *Körperkultur im Kaiserreich und in der Weimarer Republik* (Würzburg, 2004), 163–4.

[6] See Kayser, *Hollander*, 28ff. Hollander also wrote psychological, instructive but entertaining articles such as Walther von Hollander, 'Keine Angst vor Krisen! Kleine Lebenslehre', in *Bibliothek des Wissens und der Unterhaltung*, vol. 37 (1937), Nr. 61, 71–85; Walther von Hollander, 'Erkenne Dich selbst! Der Blick ins eigene Ich – eine Aufgabe und eine Gefahr', *Koralle, Wochenschrift für Unterhaltung, Wissen, Lebensfreude*, N.F. 9 (1941), 304–7.

[7] See Witter, 'Gespräch'.

[8] See Walther von Hollander, *Der Mensch über Vierzig: Neuer Lebensstil im neuen Lebensalter* (Berlin, 1938).

[9] See Walther von Hollander, *Das Leben zu Zweien: Ein Ehebuch. Geschichten und Betrachtungen* (Berlin, 1940).

novels and advice articles. In the case of illustrated magazines, women's magazines and family magazines, serialised novels were one of the most important means of creating reader loyalty. In the early 1930s, for example, Vicki Baum's novels succeeded in attracting 300,000 new readers to the *BIZ*.[10] This formula for success was retained in the Third Reich. Serialised novels were easy to read and provided colourful characters and a fast-moving plot packed with surprise and emotion. As Karl Christian Führer has shown in his study of serialised novels in the *BIZ* and the successful radio programme magazine *Berlin hört und sieht* (*Berlin Hears and Sees*), it is significant that these novels more or less totally ignored National Socialism: 'Nazi Germany with all the major characteristics of its everyday life was absent.'[11] The genre of advice articles provided practical tips on topics to do with housekeeping and health, but also included psychological advice directed mostly at women, aiming to optimise their private lives.[12] The magazines also tried to communicate directly with their readers. So, for example, in 1939 the magazine *Die junge Dame* (*The Young Lady*) encouraged readers to send written responses to questions such as 'How can I overcome my shyness?' Some of these responses would then be selected and appear in the magazine as readers' letters a few weeks later. Before 1939, various tips on general personal and psychological problems were offered in the advice column *Sie fragen ... Frau Ilse antwortet* (*Frau Ilse Answers Your Questions*).[13] Hollander's career flourished in wartime, and his growing fame following the publication of *Der Mensch über Vierzig* (1938) and *Das Leben zu Zweien* (1940) was reflected in the many letters he received from readers.

Hollander's career continued after 1945 almost without a break, and he now gained a reputation as a particular expert on 'women's issues'. In many of his articles, he argued for women's legal equality and for recognition of the situation of single or so-called unattached women. By the 1950s, as a result of his radio programme *Was wollen Sie wissen: Fragen Sie Walther von Hollander* (*What Do You Want to Know? Ask Walther von Hollander*) and his anonymous advice column *Fragen Sie*

---

[10] On the importance of serialised novels in the *BIZ* for the overall genre of the novels in illustrated magazines, see Wolfgang Langenbucher, *Der aktuelle Unterhaltungsroman: Beiträge zu Geschichte und Theorie der massenhaft verbreiteten Literatur* (Bonn, 1964), 91–2.

[11] Karl Christian Führer, 'Pleasure, Practicality and Propaganda: Popular Magazines in Nazi Germany, 1933–1939', in Pamela E. Swett, Corey Ross and Fabrice d'Almeida (eds.), *Pleasure and Power in Nazi Germany* (New York, NY, 2011), 142–53, 143.

[12] See ibidem, 144–5.

[13] See Sylvia Lott, *Die Frauenzeitschriften von Hans Huffzky und John Jahr: Zur Geschichte der deutschen Frauenzeitschrift zwischen 1933 und 1970* (Berlin, 1985), 272–3. On the magazine *Die junge Dame*, see also the Introduction to this volume.

Frau Irene (*Ask Frau Irene*) in the radio programme magazine *Hörzu*, he had become Germany's most popular 'agony uncle' and expert on marital problems.[14] By the time he died in 1973, he had published numerous further articles on relationships and life skills more generally.[15]

Thus over a period of four decades Walther von Hollander had been read and personally consulted by people seeking orientation and help with their personal problems. From the outset, as he established his brand of writing dealing with marital issues, family relationships, sexuality and lifestyle, Hollander had addressed vital personal questions for individuals, but at the same time tackled matters of intense public and political dispute.[16] Marriage and the family are commonly regarded as the quintessential 'sanctuary of the private',[17] and are positively defined as a space where individuals wish to live their lives together determined as far as possible by themselves. Yet both marriage and the family are institutions associated with societal norms and expectations, and subject to substantial change in different political contexts.[18] While Hollander offered his insights into supposedly universal human attributes, he was at the same time propagating normative ideas of how to live together, accommodating the demands and priorities of different political systems over the course of major historical ruptures.

In exploring the sometimes strange balancing act this involved, this chapter first outlines the views Walther von Hollander adopted towards married life after 1933. This initially involves providing an overview of the genre of self-help manuals that offered life counselling and marriage guidance during the interwar period, disseminating a type of popular psychology easily applicable to individual behaviour known as

---

[14] The fact that it was Walther von Hollander behind this pseudonym was kept a closely guarded secret in the editorial office as long as Eduard Rhein was chief editor, i.e. until 1965. 'Faith' in 'Frau Irene' only began to decline in the mid-1960s when there was a drop in the number of questions received. Lu Seegers, *Hör zu! Eduard Rhein und die Rundfunkprogrammzeitschriften (1931–1965)* (Potsdam, 2001, 2nd edn, 2003), 207, 372.

[15] Walther von Hollander died in 1973. His popularity in Germany can be compared with that of the American advice columnist Ann Landers, who from 1955 onwards published advice on problems to do with the family, morals and sexuality in the *Chicago Sun Times*. See Alfred Messerli, 'Zur Geschichte der Medien des Rates', in Peter-Paul Bänziger et al. (eds.), *Fragen Sie Dr. Sex! Ratgeberkommunikation und die mediale Konstruktion des Sexuellen* (Berlin, 2010), 30–57, here 43.

[16] See Eva Noack-Mosse, 'Uhu', in Joachim W. Freyburg and Hans Wallenberg (eds.), *Hundert Jahre Ullstein*, vol. 2 (Frankfurt a.M., Berlin, Vienna, 1977), 177–208, 198.

[17] Beate Rössler, 'Geschlechterverhältnis und Gerechtigkeit', in Hans-Peter Müller and Bernd Wegener (eds.), *Soziale Ungleichheit und soziale Gerechtigkeit* (Wiesbaden, 1995), 157–72, 185.

[18] See Sandra Seubert, 'Warum die Familie nicht abschaffen? Zum spannungsvollen Verhältnis von Privatheit und politischem Liberalismus', in Sandra Seubert and Peter Niesen (eds.), *Die Grenzen des Privaten* (Baden-Baden, 2010), 89–106, here 89.

Psychowissen.[19] The chapter goes on to examine Hollander's correspondence during the Nazi era with readers who wrote him personal letters.[20] Here, it becomes clear that Hollander's views were articulated but also stimulated through this private correspondence. Analysing these exchanges with his male and female readers offers a glimpse of typical constellations and conditions of private life under the Nazi dictatorship and of the clearly widespread urge to seek advice and orientation on private problems. The readers' letters provide an insight into personal anxieties and hardship, the perception of these problems by those directly affected and the way in which these views were shaped by prevailing social expectations. Hollander's responses, moreover, generic and seemingly common sense though they appear, can also be read as reflecting the political, economic and social context in which he was writing: his advice had to be understood and applied to the situation in which his readers found themselves.

This dual perspective, examining contemporary ideas about the 'purely' personal but also the expectations relating to private life that arose from the political context, may help shed light more generally on the relationship between National Socialism and notions of the private. As Elizabeth Harvey has recently demonstrated, Detlev Peukert was one of the historians who in the 1980s had already begun to look closely at the paradoxes of private life under National Socialism.[21] He emphasised the fact that many Germans were able to retreat 'into the contained and comfortable familiarity of the private sphere' and were thus able to create an illusion of individual integrity and autonomy in spite of or even

---

[19] See Uffa Jensen, 'Die Konstitution des Selbst durch Beratung und Therapeutisierung: Die Geschichte des Psychowissens im frühen 20. Jahrhundert', in Sabine Maasen, Jens Elberfeld, Pascal Eitler and Maik Tändler (eds.), *Das beratene Selbst: Zur Genealogie der Therapeutisierung in den 'langen' Siebzigern* (Bielefeld, 2011), 37–56, here 39. In the twentieth century, the promise of improvement in the socio-political sphere was associated with psychoanalysis and the many other forms of psychology. Uffa Jensen and Maik Tändler define *Psychowissen* as 'all those types of knowledge that enable a secular description and explanation of the psychological structure of the individual self, its inner mental and emotional state and the determinants of its behaviour and combine this with practical advice on how this self can be recognised, treated, modelled, regulated or liberated' (Maik Tändler and Uffa Jensen, 'Psychowissen, Politik und das Selbst. Eine neue Forschungsperspektive auf die Geschichte des Politischen im 20. Jahrhundert', in Maik Tändler and Uffa Jensen [eds.], *Das Selbst zwischen Anpassung und Befreiung: Psychowissen und Politik im 20. Jahrhundert* [Göttingen, 2012], 9–35, here 10).

[20] This correspondence is part of the large collection of Walther von Hollander's personal papers, which I am currently using as the basis for a biographical study of him.

[21] See Elizabeth Harvey, 'Housework, Domestic Privacy and the "German Home": Paradoxes of Private Life during the Second World War', in Rüdiger Hachtmann and Sven Reichardt (eds.), *Detlev Peukert und die NS-Forschung* (Göttingen, 2015), 115–31, here 117–18.

possibly because of the Nazi dictatorship.[22] This withdrawal, he believed, also resulted in the Germans becoming depoliticised and adapting to the barbaric normality of the Nazi dictatorship at the same time as social relations were disintegrating. All this, Peukert claimed, had the effect of stabilising the regime.[23] Moritz Föllmer takes this idea an important step further in his discussion of individuality in National Socialism. He emphasises the fact that the Berlin media under National Socialism promoted promises of individual personal happiness unrelated to any collective ideology just as they had done in the Weimar Republic. At the same time, he argues, these promises of happiness also corresponded with the philosophy of the Nazi regime, which promised to dissolve and to eradicate the ambivalence so often connected to individuality and its expectations and disappointments.[24] This chapter argues that Walther von Hollander's books and letters to his readers, which aimed to optimise personal lives, positioned themselves exactly on this borderline, not committing to either side.

Marriage Guidance and Life Counselling in the Weimar Republic and National Socialism

The dissemination of advice and guidance in written form has a long tradition dating back to the advent of printing around 1450.[25] Handbooks on etiquette and the first books offering advice on sexual matters appeared in the late eighteenth century, and in the nineteenth century they were joined by what was called family doctor literature (*Hausarztliteratur*), which for the first time combined rudimentary psychological advice and medical advice. In the early twentieth century these two fields of practice converged at the interface between scientisation and popular culture. At its centre was *Psychowissen*, which was concerned with the self and its receptivity to advice and therapy. This development, together with the sexual reform movement of the 1920s, also boosted the production of sexual advice literature which offered advice illustrated with everyday situations and fictitious conversations. Marriage guidance manuals similarly became popular after the First World War.[26] This type of advice, based on *Psychowissen* and aiming to optimise private life, also

---

[22] Detlev Peukert, *Volksgenossen und Gemeinschaftsfremde: Anpassung, Ausmerze und Aufbegehren unter dem Nationalsozialismus* (Cologne, 1990), 225.
[23] Ibidem.
[24] See Moritz Föllmer, *Individuality and Modernity in Berlin: Self and Society from Weimar to the Wall* (Cambridge, 2013).
[25] See Messerli, 'Geschichte'.
[26] Advice centres for sexual and marriage guidance also specifically targeted working-class women. See Kristina von Soden, *Die Sexualberatungsstellen der Weimarer Republik*

came to influence other spheres,[27] ranging from education and pastoral care to business and management through the rise of rationalisation, Taylorism and Fordism.[28] A further development of the 1920s was the rise of so-called psychotechnics, which claimed that individuals could be better adapted to modern living and working conditions with the help of psychologically based life coaching and vocational advice.[29]

Michel Foucault has labelled such instructions on practising self-help based on *Psychowissen* 'technologies of the self'.[30] These are techniques that enable individuals to adapt their way of thinking and their behaviour in order to achieve a state of happiness and a sense of completeness.[31] The idea of implementing self-help in order to have a 'good marriage' also played an important role in the manuals on marriage and sexuality in the Weimar Republic. They suggested that even in private and personal relationships, anything could be achieved and that these relationships could be optimised and their efficiency enhanced.[32] Along with a job and good physical health, well-functioning intimate relationships were and still are considered crucial, not only for individuals but also for society.[33] Behind this lies the idea to this day that critical circumstances and difficult situations in life can be overcome, regardless of whether they relate to the individual who is receiving advice or to social and economic problems.[34] Thus the therapeutic and advisory discourses of healing and

---

1919–1933 (West Berlin, 1988), and Atina Grossmann, *Reforming Sex: The German Movement for Birth Control and Abortion Reform 1920–1950* (Oxford, 1995).

[27] In this context 'companionate marriage' came to be regarded as a model. Dagmar Reese, 'Die Kameraden. Eine partnerschaftliche Konzeption der Geschlechterbeziehungen an der Wende vom 19. zum 20. Jahrhundert', in Dagmar Reese et al. (eds.), *Rationale Beziehungen? Geschlechterverhältnisse im Rationalisierungsprozess* (Frankfurt a.M., 1993), 58–74.

[28] For an overview, see Adelheid von Saldern and Rüdiger Hachtmann, 'Gesellschaft am "Fließband": Fordistische Produktion und Herrschaftspraxis in Deutschland', *Zeithistorische Forschungen* 6/2 (2009), 186–208.

[29] For more detail, see Mary Nolan, *Visions of Modernity: American Business and the Modernization of Germany* (New York, NY, Oxford, 1994). This enthusiasm for optimisation and rationalisation was directed not least at housework. See Adelheid von Saldern, 'Social Rationalization of Living and Housework in Germany and the United States in the 1920s', *The History of the Family: An International Quarterly* 2/1 (1997), 73–97.

[30] Michel Foucault, 'Technologien des Selbst', in Michel Foucault, *Schriften*, vol. 4 (Frankfurt a.M., 2005), 966–99.

[31] See Sabine Maasen, 'Das beratene Selbst. Zur Genealogie der Therapeutisierung in den "langen" Siebzigern. Eine Perspektivierung', in Sabine Maasen et al. (eds.), *Das beratene Selbst: Zur Genealogie der Therapeutisierung in den 'langen' Siebzigern* (Bielefeld, 2011), 7–33, here 17.

[32] See Rudolf Helmstetter, 'Der stumme Doktor als guter Hirte. Zur Genealogie der Sexualratgeber', in Peter-Paul Bänziger, Stefanie Duttweiler, Philipp Sarasin and Annika Wellmann (eds.), *Fragen Sie Dr. Sex! Ratgeberkommunikation und die mediale Konstruktion des Sexuellen* (Berlin, 2010), 58–93, here 59.

[33] See Maasen, 'Selbst', 20.   [34] See ibidem, 22.

counselling that were circulating especially after the First World War in the form of advice literature on sexuality, marriage and lifestyle reflected a shift in society but also drove this shift: they were both symptom and cause.[35] As Sabine Maasen points out, these discourses and techniques function not only as individual resources that provide meaning and orientation but also as social institutions for the collective processing of cultural change.[36] As such they moderate the interaction between the public and the private spheres by offering advice in the personal sphere and at the same time adapting it to suit social and therefore indirectly political demands.

The authors of marriage and family advice literature in the Weimar Republic worked on the assumption that the traditional model of marriage was in crisis, that it had been ever since the late nineteenth century and was ever more so now as a result of the First World War and the ensuing socioeconomic and cultural upheaval. During the First World War, women had found themselves taking control of daily life, acting as mediators between the family and social institutions and sometimes even as the family breadwinner.[37] Contemporaries assumed that rising divorce rates and sinking birth rates were caused by the increase in women's independence.[38] In addition, women had also become more publicly conspicuous for two reasons: firstly because of female suffrage, which they formally gained in 1918 and exercised for the first time in the elections to the National Assembly (*Nationalversammlung*) in 1919, and secondly because married women increasingly took up paid employment, doing more jobs particularly in industry, crafts and the service sector.[39] Although in reality society was still determined by the model of women as wives and mothers, in the media the image of mostly single, self-confident young women going out to work became pervasive.[40] The supposed crisis of marriage was, therefore, seen primarily as a crisis of women. The task for the authors of advice literature was, therefore, to preserve the bourgeois institution of marriage while at the

---

[35] See ibidem, 26.
[36] See Sabine Maasen, 'Psycho-Wissen: Eine genealogische Notiz', in Maasen et al. (eds.), *Das beratene Selbst*, 35–6, here 35; Helene Mühlestein, *Hausfrau, Mutter, Gattin: Geschlechterkonstituierung in Schweizer Ratgeberliteratur 1945–1970* (Zurich, 2009), 21.
[37] See Birthe Kundrus, *Kriegerfrauen: Familienpolitik und Geschlechterverhältnisse im Ersten und Zweiten Weltkrieg* (Hamburg, 1995), 418–19.
[38] See Ute Frevert, *Frauen-Geschichte: Zwischen bürgerlicher Verbesserung und neuer Weiblichkeit* (Frankfurt a.M., 1986), 150–2.
[39] See ibidem, 171.
[40] See Günter Schulz, 'Soziale Sicherung von Frauen und Familien', in Hans Günter Hockerts (ed.), *Drei Wege deutscher Sozialstaatlichkeit: NS-Diktatur, Bundesrepublik und DDR im Vergleich* (Munich, 1998), 117–49, here 119.

same time reforming its organisation and inner structure to create a new model of married life.[41]

Up until 1933 there were several types of marriage guidance books: those published by the churches, those directed at the educated middle class, those written specifically for the working class and those to do with medical issues, focusing on sexuality and the body.[42] The Nazi seizure of power caused a certain shift as far as advice literature was concerned. One example of this is a popular book by the educational reformer and Social Democratic politician Heinrich Schulz entitled *Die Mutter als Erzieherin. Zur Praxis der proletarischen Hauserziehung* (*The Mother as Educator: Upbringing in the Proletarian Home*) published in 1908. Although it had already been published under its subtitle, *Ratschläge für die Erziehung im Hause* (*How to Bring Up Children at Home*) in eight editions by 1923, it was no longer reissued.[43] Nevertheless, the majority of advice literature for marriage and the family continued to be sold and/or reissued. In the case of new publications those books were favoured which supported National Socialist principles. There were, however, other books published which followed the tradition of advice literature in that they presented marriage and the family as essentially personal and therefore private matters.[44]

This was the case with Walther von Hollander's self-help manuals such as *Der Mensch über Vierzig* (1938) and *Das Leben zu Zweien* (1940). That said, a review of *Der Mensch über Vierzig*, commissioned by the *Deutsche Verlag* after its publication at the end of 1938, criticised it for containing 'negative attitudes' which were wrong from an 'objectively scientific' point of view or in a 'political sense'. The reviewer referred mainly to the fact that Walther von Hollander had depicted the ageing process in 'repellent detail'.[45] *Das Leben zu Zweien* on the other hand met with very little criticism. Hollander stated in an interview at the beginning of the 1970s that the Reich Literature Chamber (*Reichsschrifttumskammer*) had refused to authorise the provision of any more paper for it to be printed, even though 60,000 copies had already

---

[41] See Regina Mahlmann, *Psychologisierung des 'Alltagsbewusstseins': Die Verwissenschaftlichung des Diskurses über die Ehe* (Opladen, 1991), 118.
[42] Ibidem, 127.
[43] See Markus Höffer-Mehlmer, *Elternratgeber: Zur Geschichte eines Genres* (Baltmannsweiler, 2003), 183. Höffer-Mehlmer's investigations apply primarily to self-help manuals concerning childrearing and the family. A study aimed specifically at marriage guidance literature remains to be carried out.
[44] See ibidem, 184.
[45] FZH-Archiv, 11/H150, Nachlass Walther von Hollander, Schachtel 14, Mappe 4, Vorläufiges Gutachten von Dr. E. Hefter über das Werk von Walther von Hollander, Der Mensch über Vierzig, 30 January 1939, 3.

been sold.[46] However, this can hardly be seen as criticism or censorship, even if that was the impression Walther von Hollander wanted to give in retrospect. On the contrary, excerpts from the book were reproduced in the SS periodical *Das Schwarze Korps* right up to early 1941.[47] Walther von Hollander's views were thus by no means ignored in the political sphere, but, as outlined earlier, his works were seen as popular literature which stood for a private sphere that was considered politically harmless.

Marriage as an Opportunity for Self-Education

Like other authors of advice literature, in *Das Leben zu Zweien*, Walther von Hollander considered marriage problems to be a manifestation of women's independence. His argument was that women had gained self-confidence during the First World War because they had looked after their families on their own and worked in traditionally male jobs. They should, therefore, no longer be judged merely by their relations with the other sex, but seen as independent individuals. In this it was important, he noted, for women to be able to develop freely and to work and to support themselves independently before marrying a suitable man. In his view, relations between the sexes would not be improved by introducing legal measures to protect marriage, or by preventing women from working, or by making sexuality taboo. His book *Das Leben zu Zweien* provides tips and guidelines to enable marriage 'to be felt by everyone as beneficial, experienced as a creative opportunity and sustained through all its ups and downs'.[48] Elsewhere Hollander suggests that in order to be able to do this, people need first and foremost 'techniques for life' which help them to overcome marriage crises and to improve their married life. Problems such as 'sickness, tiredness, lack of success and lack of love' could be resolved by following so-called laws of life, by which he meant the power of regeneration he believed to be inherent in every human being.[49] A 'good' marriage should therefore not depend on moral demands but

---

[46] Walther von Hollander's book *Collected Fates* (*Schicksale gebündelt*), published in 1928, was banned in 1937. See BArch Berlin, R58/910, Gestapo to the Präsident der *Reichsschrifttumskammer*, 17 August 1937. According to an autobiographical account, Hollander was also banned from speaking on the radio between 1933 and 1945. See Walther von Hollander, 'Von ihm selber', *Das Einhorn, Jahrbuch Freie Akademie der Künste* (Hamburg, 1957), 164–7, here 167.

[47] FZH-Archiv, 11/H150, Nachlass Walther von Hollander, Schachtel 26, Mappe 3, 'Das Leben zu Zweien' (II), *Das Schwarze Korps*, 23 January 1941.

[48] Hollander, *Leben*, 12.

[49] Walther von Hollander, 'Vorwort', in Hans Reimann, *Mit 100 Jahren noch ein Kind...* (Berlin, 1940), 2.

on the ability of both marriage partners to be self-aware and self-critical. The basis for this was Hollander's preferred method of 'self-education' which was founded on mutual respect, courtesy and self-discipline.[50] According to Hollander, only those people who engaged in the process of self-education had to 'work so hard on themselves that they have very little time to bother about the faults and weaknesses of others'.[51] He connected the feeling of happiness that was expected to result from this exclusively to the personal sphere. Everyone should feel 'that they can make peace with themselves and with the world through their own efforts'.[52] What is remarkable here is the fact that Hollander did not explicitly refer to National Socialism but merely hinted at it as a context that was simply understood: it required no further elaboration and was not questioned or challenged. Instead, Hollander focussed solely on the envisaged space of the private by referring to the domestic life of man and wife. In fact this reference to the need to provide and to protect a private sphere and space for individual development and self-expression corresponded with Reich Propaganda Minister Goebbels' professed belief that people needed peace and relaxation, achieved for example by listening to popular radio programmes and light music.[53]

The private sphere was of course still categorised by gender. Walther von Hollander assumed that in spite of the independence accorded to women, they remained more responsible for the success of a marriage than men. In a similar way to Georg Simmel, Hollander believed in the 'absolute' nature of women. Simmel maintained that in contrast to men, who required a woman in order to become aware of their masculinity, women were constantly alert to the fact of their femininity. At the same time, Simmel alleged, it was women who were better able to grasp life subjectively and who were therefore better equipped for marriage.[54] In line with Simmel, Hollander also used the category of gender to describe the private sphere as a space largely free from outside influences and so devoted to individual development and self-expression. Thus Hollander left his writing open to a variety of interpretations which could suit both those who were sympathetic towards National Socialism

---

[50] Hollander, *Leben*, 77. [51] Ibidem, 92. [52] Ibidem, 21.
[53] See Monika Pater, 'Rundfunkangebote', in Inge Marszolek and Adelheid von Saldern (eds.), *Radio im Nationalsozialismus: Zwischen Lenkung und Ablenkung* (Tübingen, 1998), 129–241, here 143.
[54] Georg Simmel, 'Das Relative und das Absolute im Geschlechter-Problem' (1911), in Georg Simmel, *Schriften zur Philosophie und Soziologie der Geschlechter*, ed. by Heinz-Jürgen Dahme and Christian Köhnke (Frankfurt a.M., 1985), 200–23, 202; see also Katja Eckhardt, *Die Auseinandersetzung zwischen Marianne Weber und Georg Simmel über die 'Frauenfrage'* (Stuttgart, 2000), esp. 60–2.

and those who were sceptical about it or wished to block it out as a political context.

This openness to different readings is particularly evident in Hollander's book *Das Leben zu Zweien* when he discusses the women's movement.[55] Acknowledging its achievements since the turn of the century, Hollander saw the movement enabling women to find purpose in life not only in terms of their husbands and children but also in their own right as 'all-round personalities'.[56] The women's movement, according to Hollander, had gained civic equality for women, proved that women could do 'almost any job' as well as men and, in the process, endowed women with a new level of self-confidence.[57] Here, Hollander's argument aligned him up to a point with Nazi women's attempts to appropriate the legacy of the German bourgeois women's movement. The National Socialist *Reichsfrauenführung* (Reich Women's Leadership) also used the term *women's movement* to describe itself, promoting the idea of collective female agency which was distinct from men but not opposed to them.[58] In the same vein, Walther von Hollander praised the 'women's movement of today' in general terms for developing the distinctive characteristics of women's thoughts and actions 'the world over'. His views on fundamental gender difference also chimed with those of the *Nationalsozialistische Frauenschaft* (NSF) (National Socialist Women's League) and the *Deutsches Frauenwerk* (DFW) (German Women's Organisation) in that he believed women and men were not 'the same' but were 'worth the same'.[59] Not that this opinion was new or distinctively Nazi – it had been dominant in bourgeois women's circles during the Weimar Republic.[60] Nevertheless, it is striking that Hollander took such a conventional line when he maintained that looking after the family was more suited to women's interests and that women were responsible for choosing the right partner, sustaining a marriage and bringing up children. He even elevated these banal observations to the status of a wisdom supposedly suppressed for centuries and hidden under the 'dust of intellectuals' but lying dormant in women's 'blood, in their instincts'.[61]

---

[55] For the following, see also Lu Seegers, 'Walther von Hollander als Lebensberater im Dritten Reich', in Stephanie Kleiner and Robert Suter (eds.), *Guter Rat: Glück und Erfolg in der Ratgeberliteratur 1900–1940* (Berlin, 2015), 179–207.

[56] Hollander, *Leben*, 23–4.   [57] See ibidem, 26.   [58] See ibidem, 38.

[59] Both organisations were represented by the *Reichsfrauenführung*. The NSF was an explicitly political organisation and devoted itself to training women according to Nazi principles. The DFW in contrast was directed at all women and provided courses and training in home economics, childrearing and racial policies. See Nicole Kramer, *Volksgenossinnen an der Heimatfront: Mobilisierung, Verhalten, Erinnerung* (Göttingen, 2011), 34–5.

[60] See ibidem, 41.   [61] Hollander, *Leben*, 29.

However, Walther von Hollander only partially adopted the stance of the Reich Women's Leadership, whose leader, Gertrud Scholtz-Klink, rejected the movement for women's emancipation, even while claiming to endorse some of what it had achieved.[62] Hollander was admittedly also critical of aspects of women's emancipation, arguing that while enabling women's economic independence, an excessive orientation to the male model had led to 'masculinisation' and 'impoverishment of the work sphere' rather than the emergence of authentic occupations for women.[63] Nevertheless, his conclusions from this differed somewhat from those of the Reich Women's Leadership. Firstly, he argued more emphatically for a variety of models and paths for women's lives. He expressed regret that many women had gone back to being merely wives and mothers;[64] he encouraged women not to get married at all costs but if necessary to live alone;[65] and he argued forcefully that a woman's place in marriage should not be subordinate but alongside her husband as an independent partner,[66] evoking the idea of the *Kameradschaftsehe* (companionate marriage), which had been much discussed in the 1920s. Secondly, in marked contrast to the line taken by the Nazi women's organisations – which also promoted the *Kameradschaftsehe*, but as a wartime partnership between home front and fighting front[67] – Hollander did not explicitly place women's lives or the question of marital relations in the context of their function within the *Volksgemeinschaft*. Stripped of any political or ideological reference in this way, his ideas appeared to stem simply from 'common sense' – a strategy that probably enhanced their appeal.

In this way Walther von Hollander left it up to readers to make connections between his advice and the context of Nazi social and racial policies. Only occasionally did he drop a hint that acknowledged the existence of such a context: he expressed regret, for example, that young women were getting married too early and mentioned more or less in passing that the new 'biologically based education' – in other words based on eugenics – might offer a solution.[68] In other cases Hollander avoided explicit references to contemporary policies altogether: thus when he emphasised that each individual would wish to find the 'right' partner, he may have intended readers to understand this as a sort of personal variation of an official medical certificate of suitability of

---

[62] See Kramer, *Volksgenossinnen*, 38.   [63] Hollander, *Leben*, 25, 27.   [64] See ibidem, 28.
[65] See ibidem, 31. Hollander had already held this view during the Weimar Republic. In 1929 he described his ideal of the independent woman. See Walther von Hollander, 'Autonomie der Frau', in Friedrich M. Huebner (ed.), *Die Frau von Morgen, wie wir sie wünschen* (Leipzig, 1929), 27–37.
[66] Hollander, *Leben*, 33.   [67] Kramer, *Volksgenossinnen*, 41.   [68] Hollander, *Leben*, 64.

marriage promoted by the regime – but he did not spell it out. It was similar in the case of gender-based division of labour in the home. Many women suffered from the burden of housework, according to Hollander, and as a result they were 'miserable, fat, worn-down and dispirited'.[69] He thought that because of this women should take up '4-hour women's jobs', even if they had children, and be able to depend on their husbands to help them in the house with chores like washing up and cleaning.[70] After the world economic crisis the Nazi state used a combination of incentives, coercion and restrictions to try and persuade married women to give up their jobs. Measures included firing married female civil servants and clerks in public employment and reducing the number of female students to 10 per cent. When full employment was reached in 1936, this policy changed and the Nazis not only tolerated female employment but actively encouraged it, especially during the Second World War.[71] As a result there was a huge increase in female students. By 1940 they comprised nearly 30 per cent of all the students in the 'Old Reich'.[72] At the same time the Nazis considered women to be a manoeuvrable mass in the labour market,[73] and there were indeed attempts by the labour administration as the war went on to use part-time jobs to coax more German women into the workforce – but this development is not something with which Hollander engaged explicitly.

Probably both the openness to different interpretations and the 'unpolitical' quality of Hollander's books helped to make them widely accepted and eagerly read. Thus he was in favour of marriage based on partnership and the model of a *Kameradschaftsehe* founded on both equality between the sexes and the differences between them: at the same time, however, he related his advice expressly to the private sphere. This was because, according to Hollander, a good marriage was based first and foremost on the 'self-education' of each individual and only after that on any externally imposed models. This recourse to the private had two advantages from Hollander's point of view: he could refer to supposedly timeless principles of married life and at the same time legitimately ignore the social environment and political events. It was precisely this premise of supposed timelessness in human relationships whose polyvalence contributed to the popularity of Hollander's self-help books after 1945 and

---

[69] Ibidem, 174.   [70] Ibidem, 191.
[71] The number of women in employment rose from 5.89 million in 1937 to 8.82 million in 1939; see Schulz, 'Soziale Sicherung', 119, 124.
[72] See Michael Grüttner, *Studenten im Dritten Reich* (Paderborn, 1995), 119.
[73] Detlev Humann, *'Arbeitsschlacht': Arbeitsbeschaffung und Propaganda in der NS-Zeit 1933–1939* (Göttingen, 2011), 717.

which enabled him to incorporate elements from them into further publications.[74]

Communicating the Private: Readers' Letters to Walther von Hollander

For the period between 1937 and 1945, copies of about 100 readers' letters to Walther Hollander and his replies are available.[75] Most people wrote to him after they had read the advance publication of the self-help manuals *Das Leben zu Zweien* and *Der Mensch über Vierzig* in the *BIZ*. But that was not the only basis for writing to him – some people wrote as a result of reading advice articles in other newspapers and magazines, or reading novels or film scripts. They usually established first contact through the publishers, who passed their letters on to him, after which Hollander corresponded directly with them. There is no evidence of any screening or censorship. Eighty per cent of his correspondents were women, mainly housewives but some skilled and unskilled workers, who first thanked him for his texts and wanted to know something about him as a person. Walther von Hollander answered each of these letters personally and occasionally sent a photo of himself if it was requested. On 28 August 1940, for example, Erica Rückholt from Sonneberg in Thuringia thanked Walther von Hollander enthusiastically as follows:

By sending me your photo as a gift you have given me undescribable pleasure. I'm so happy I don't know what to do with myself. [...] I've never written to a writer before, only to you, because your works have made such a huge impression on me.[76]

Even if he did not send a photo, Walther von Hollander was careful to portray himself to his correspondents as approachable and down to earth. In August 1942, he wrote the following to Fräulein Rossi in Berlin:

You ask who the person behind my novel is? A boring elderly gentleman who spends most of the year sitting around in a small place that's not very grand. He grows cabbages, turnips and potatoes and goes out into the big wide world every now and again to write scripts for films. He's 1.78 metres tall, what hair he has is grey, his posture is not very good, he is polite and only tells people what he thinks if they ask him because he's very busy trying to say a few things that he thinks are important before he dies, an event which he hopes to be able to keep at bay for

---

[74] Even after 1945 readers still referred to Hollander's self-help books from the 1930s. Also large sections of his book *Die Krise der Ehe und ihre Überwindung* (Berlin, 1953) were based on *Das Leben zu Zweien*.
[75] There are many more letters in Walther von Hollander's estate for the post-1945 period.
[76] FZH-Archiv, 11/H50, Nachlass Walther von Hollander, Schachtel 30, Mappe 2, Erica Rückholt, Sonneberg/Thüringen, to Walther von Hollander, 28 August 1940.

another thirty to forty years. So as a person he is neither very interesting nor very attractive.[77]

Walther von Hollander was also popular in Austria, both before but particularly after its annexation. He was highly visible in the Austrian media through his books and frequent newspaper articles. In Graz, for example, Marie-Therese Schwarz was extremely taken with Hollander's advice and wrote to him in May 1939: 'You give such clear and precise answers to the most difficult questions that people wonder why they don't think of them themselves, but they don't.'[78] That said, correspondents occasionally wrote in more critical tones. One was twenty-one-year-old Käthe Harders from Hamburg who in October 1937 complained that his advice on how to cope with the 'crisis of the menopause' was much too vague to be able to help anyone who is too 'despondent and tired of life to endure this dramatic upheaval'. She felt that he was making things too easy for himself by simply advising women to get a job when their children were grown up: a woman who had been managing the home for the past twenty years was not able to just walk into a job. The only thing she could do, according to Käthe Harders, was to be a helper with the National Socialist People's Welfare Organisation (*Nationalsozialistische Volkswohlfahrt* or NSV) – seemingly something she regarded as a routine possibility – and that meant jumping 'out of the frying pan into the fire'. As a result, she wrote, plenty of women had no opportunity to give their lives a new meaning.[79]

Not all Walther von Hollander's correspondents were women. He received many letters from soldiers in the armed forces, especially after the publication of his serialised novel *Der Gott zwischen den Schlachten: Die Geschichte einer Liebe aus unserer Zeit* (*The God between the Battles: A Love Story of Our Time*) in the *BIZ* in 1942. The novel is a love story about the romantic relationship between an actress called Petra Peterson and a young man called Christian Hasselberg who is sent to the Eastern Front in 1941.[80] One reaction came on 5 May 1942 from Private Ewalt Thomas in Russia, who wrote that he read out each instalment to his comrades as soon as he received it because 'we are described here just as we are. What's been done here is what very few are able to do – to strike the right note and the right attitude so that we can find ourselves in what's

---

[77] FZH-Archiv, 11/H50, Nachlass Walther von Hollander, Schachtel 30, Mappe 2, Walther von Hollander to Fräulein Rossi, 20 August 1942.
[78] FZH-Archiv, 11/H50, Nachlass Walther von Hollander, Schachtel 30, Mappe 2, Marie-Therese Schwarz, Graz, to Walther von Hollander, 8 September 1942.
[79] FZH-Archiv, 11/H50, Nachlass Walther von Hollander, Schachtel 48, Mappe 2, Käthe Harders to Walther von Hollander, 5 October 1937.
[80] See Walther von Hollander, *Der Gott zwischen den Schlachten: Die Geschichte einer Liebe aus unserer Zeit* (Berlin, 1942).

there.'[81] Lieutenant Klaus Nienhaber expressed his gratitude even more strongly: 'Here at last are words that are far-removed from patriotic cheering but which talk about things that will have been experienced by many of those who are now in their final resting place.'[82] Walther von Hollander answered by return of post: 'It is immensely gratifying for me to hear from you that my descriptions of young officers correspond with young officers' own perception of themselves.'[83] At the same time he referred to his own experiences in the armed forces:

> I actually served in the previous war from start to finish as a young soldier. So I do know the 'milieu' a little. What I know most is the feeling that for years you are living between two worlds, this world in which we want to stay and the other which we know nothing about but is always beside us and growing in each of us.[84]

Senior Lieutenant Günter Barkow, who was also stationed on the Eastern Front, drew even closer parallels between his personal situation and the book when he wrote on 14 July 1942, 'It is <u>the topic</u> for everyone who has been away from home for 18 months now and for whom everything connected with the idea of home and leave revolves round their young wife, fiancée or lover.'[85] When he was last on home leave, he continued, and had been able to spend five days with his wife and to resume their marriage begun in March 1941, he had been reminded of 'dozens of situations, words and ideas in the book'. 'You can imagine how much I was confronted with and how much I wanted to experience, understand, relish and fulfil in such a short space of time.'[86] These readers' letters and Walther von Hollander's replies are indications of how the war came to a certain extent to be 'privatised'. War experiences were detached from the political sphere and removed entirely into the private world of the senses. Yearning for the familiar world of home was expressed almost poetically, without questioning the war but rather 'normalising' it by concentrating on the exceptional experience of home leave.[87]

---

[81] FZH-Archiv, 11/H50, Nachlass Walther von Hollander, Schachtel 26, Mappe 1, Ewalt Thomas, Ostfront, to Walther von Hollander, 5 May 1942.
[82] FZH-Archiv, 11/H50, Nachlass Walther von Hollander, Schachtel 26, Mappe 1, Klaus Nienhaber, n.p., to Walther von Hollander, n.d. [May 1942].
[83] FZH-Archiv, 11/H50, Nachlass Walther von Hollander, Schachtel 26, Mappe 1, Walther von Hollander to Klaus Nienhaber, 22 May 1942.
[84] Ibidem.
[85] FZH-Archiv, 11/H50, Nachlass Walther von Hollander, Schachtel 26, Mappe 1, Günter Barkow to Walther von Hollander, 14 July 1942.
[86] Ibidem.
[87] On experiences of home leave, see Christian Packheiser's contribution to this volume (Chapter 10).

Wartime Separation

Particularly for women, the war served as a catalyst for letters to Walther von Hollander about concrete personal and relationship problems which could and still can be seen as the essence of the private.[88] Their main focus was the perception and interpretation of separation caused by the war. An example is provided by Karla Anders from Hamburg, mentioned at the outset of this chapter. On 4 February 1940, she wrote to Walther von Hollander stressing that she had spent a lot of time studying his articles, especially because she wanted to be a writer herself. But for now she had taken a job as a shorthand typist to supplement the family's meagre income. Her husband sometimes hated her for this, even though he was happy about the money, and frequently lost his temper. Now that he had been called up, she and her children were leading a much more peaceful life and she could read the classics in the evening 'which gave me so much pleasure as a young girl'.[89] Walther von Hollander replied two days later, sympathising with Karla Anders' situation, and sent her one of his essays entitled *Trennung als Brücke zwischen den Liebenden* (*Separation as a Bridge between Loved Ones*).[90] Karla Anders responded to this on 11 February expressing her ambivalence towards the war.

> I can see that we have had to fight our way through a lot of things so as to free ourselves from all the dregs of subversive literature and degenerate art. There's been a regeneration of whatever is simple and natural, we've been rebuilding, taking on a positive approach to life, but not to the extent that we've forgotten everything! And now we are marching eagerly off to war again without a care! A woman once said to me that she'd rather have a living coward than a dead hero.[91]

In Karla Anders' argument the fight against what she saw as 'degenerate' was of minor importance. What was crucial to her was the general effect of war. She made clear that she was willing to accept or even welcome National Socialism as long as it opposed certain features of modernity. However, the experience of the First World War meant that she was sceptical about a new war. On the other hand, she pointed out that the

---

[88] See Elizabeth Heineman, *What Difference Does a Husband Make? Women and Marital Status in Nazi and Postwar Germany* (Berkeley and Los Angeles, CA, London, 1999, 2nd edn, 2003).
[89] FZH-Archiv, 11/H50, Nachlass Walther von Hollander, Schachtel 40, Mappe 5, Karla Anders, Hamburg, to Walther von Hollander, 4 February 1940.
[90] FZH-Archiv, 11/H50, Nachlass Walther von Hollander, Schachtel 40, Mappe 5, Walther von Hollander to Karla Anders, 6 February 1940.
[91] FZH-Archiv, 11/H50, Nachlass Walther von Hollander, Schachtel 40, Mappe 5, Karla Anders, Hamburg, to Walther von Hollander, 11 February 1940.

war was beneficial to her personally because now that he was separated from her, her husband always wrote her loving letters.[92]

Karla Anders took up her correspondence with Walther von Hollander again in January 1942. She told him that in the meantime she had become a sales representative and had her own typewriter so she was hoping to be able to write literary texts.[93] However, these hopes were shattered, as she wrote nine months later, because her husband was serving in nearby barracks and so was often at home. He never stopped telling her what to do and shouting at her, so he would say, 'make the soup, discipline the children, do the darning', she wrote, so 'I'm no longer my true self [...] there's nothing but criticism whatever I do'.[94] As a result, when she had any spare time she just felt listless and lethargic. She said she cried a lot because of the awful atmosphere and the frequent bombings. Shortly beforehand, Walther von Hollander had written to her sympathising with her wish to have a sphere of her own and expressing hope that she would be able to have a sensible conversation with her husband. He added:

> Sadly it's the case that, if there has been a certain previous development, it's easier to have a sensible conversation with anyone but your partner. You usually can't manage to set anything in motion except the same damned string of words and phrases that keep going round and round in circles and always end up in the same place. [...] You can always call me on the telephone if you're feeling miserable. I'm not far from Hamburg.[95]

This correspondence shows how openly Karla Anders talked about her personal situation. It also suggests that there were social expectations which restricted what she could say to her friends and relations and that presumably made it difficult for her to talk about the hopes raised by the separation from her husband because of the war. On the other hand, it demonstrates how the Second World War came to encroach upon a life that was considered private, determined by changes of mood in the relationship between husband and wife that were themselves influenced by traditional gender norms.[96]

---

[92] See ibidem.
[93] See FZH-Archiv, 11/H50, Nachlass Walther von Hollander, Schachtel 40, Mappe 5, Karla Anders, Hamburg, to Walther von Hollander, 6 January 1942.
[94] FZH-Archiv, 11/H50, Nachlass Walther von Hollander, Schachtel 40, Mappe 5, Karla Anders, Hamburg, to Walther von Hollander, 22 October 1942.
[95] FZH-Archiv, 11/H50, Nachlass Walther von Hollander, Schachtel 40, Mappe 5, Walther von Hollander to Karla Anders, 19 October 1942.
[96] Nicole Kramer has established that German women did not merely passively tolerate the war, but tried to find an active role for themselves in it; see Kramer, *Volksgenossinnen*. The current chapter shows that this was also the case for individual verdicts about the importance of a marriage.

It was also wartime separation from her husband that prompted Magdalene Sabiel from Hannover to confide in Walther von Hollander on 12 April 1943 because he seemed to her to be 'the philosopher of our time'.[97]

I'm thirty-four years old and my husband has been a soldier now for three years. Don't you think we will be growing apart, however much we trust each other? Aren't these the best years of our lives that we're having to live all alone and without any pleasure? I only live for my children and in my home, isn't it hard to have to do without so much of what would make life pleasant? [...] Haven't we got some sort of right to our own individual private lives, to a bit of enjoyment?[98]

In concrete terms, Magdalene Sabiel was afraid that she was going to have to give up her private life as a result of the war, both in terms of her marriage and her personal wishes. When Walther von Hollander replied shortly afterwards, he reminded her that many couples had been separated for years during the First World War and agreed that it was indeed a difficult problem that 'the few years we have in this wonderful world have to be given over to war and fighting'.[99] Even if they were living in turbulent times, in an era lacking in tranquillity, every individual still had the right to their personal life, and this was the case especially for mothers, he said, 'because women are the ones who are literally wearing themselves into the ground and then have quite simply disappeared'.[100] Two months later Magdalena Sabiel's personal situation had seriously deteriorated. On 14 June 1943 she wrote:

Now something has happened that has left my life in ruins [...]. My husband is back from the East and has been in the garrison for over a year. Now he has confessed that he has fallen in love with a girl and that their liaison has not been without consequences. He wants to divorce me. We've been married for nine years, and have two children, an eight-year-old boy and an eighteen-month-old daughter.[101]

She said that all her efforts to get her husband back had been unsuccessful. Now she was faced with the question of whether she should agree to a divorce or refuse for the sake of the children. Walther von Hollander replied that this was a 'common fate in wartime' that had to be seen and

---

[97] FZH-Archiv, 11/H50, Nachlass Walther von Hollander, Schachtel 39, Mappe 7, Magdalene Sabiel, Hannover, to Walther von Hollander, 12 April 1943.
[98] FZH-Archiv, 11/H50, Nachlass Walther von Hollander, Schachtel 44, Mappe 5, Magdalene Sabiel, Hannover, to Walther von Hollander, 12 April 1943.
[99] FZH-Archiv, 11/H50, Nachlass Walther von Hollander, Schachtel 44, Mappe 5, Walther von Hollander to Magdalene Sabiel, 17 April 1943.
[100] Ibidem.
[101] FZH-Archiv, 11/H50, Nachlass Walther von Hollander, Schachtel 48, Mappe 2, Magdalene Sabiel, Hannover, to Walther von Hollander, 14 June 1943

acknowledged. At the same time, he advocated seeing estrangement between married couples as something quite natural that should not be assigned to the category of blame or guilt, especially as men and women could be equally 'unfaithful'. His recommendation to Magdalene Sabiel was to examine objectively whether she was still suited to her husband or not. If she decided that as a couple they were no longer suited to each other, she should agree to the divorce and 'set up a new life for herself as soon as possible'. Magdalene Sabiel thanked him for his 'kind words' and for an article Hollander had sent with them called *Die Dritten! (The Third Ones!)* addressing the question of marital fidelity. She also wrote that she could not prevent herself from blaming her husband, especially as he was intending to take one of the children and not pay any maintenance. She said it was difficult for her that although she had 'shared the good and the bad times with (her husband) for nine long years', he had not even bothered to check on her and the children after the 'terror attack' on Hannover on 26 July 1943.[102] She was sure that the struggle between the sexes would continue 'in spite of the war, perfect upbringing and whatever else'.[103] In the middle of August, Walther von Hollander wrote encouragingly to Magdalene Sabiel, but was sceptical about the meaning of the war.

> I'm glad that you accept the fate you are having to suffer with so much dignity and strength. This is not so easy nowadays because not only is our own fate enough to bear, but on top of that we all bear the heavy burden of our common fate. It's still not yet at all clear where all this misfortune is taking us or what lessons we are supposed to learn from it. It's also not at all clear whether misfortune helps people along the right track or whether its effect is actually to make them completely bewildered.[104]

This exchange shows in how many different ways Walther von Hollander's advice could be interpreted in the context of National Socialism and the Second World War. On the one hand, he tried to alleviate Magdalene Sabiel's individual suffering by suggesting that in the light of the exceptional wartime circumstances, she should try and overcome her feelings of hurt and find a way back to her husband. On the other hand, he put forward the prospect of divorce becoming socially legitimate. In 1938 the Nazi regime had passed a law on marriage and divorce that was driven by considerations of National Socialist population policy.[105] After the annexation of Austria, this 'greater German marriage

---

[102] FZH-Archiv, 11/H50, Nachlass Walther von Hollander, Schachtel 39, Mappe 7, Magdalene Sabiel, Hannover, to Walther von Hollander, 8 August 1943.
[103] Ibidem.
[104] FZH-Archiv, 11/H50, Nachlass Walther von Hollander, Schachtel 39, Mappe 7, Walther von Hollander to Magdalene Sabiel, n.d.
[105] See Michelle Mouton, *From Nurturing the Nation to Purifying the Volk: Weimar and Nazi Family Policy, 1918–1945* (Cambridge, 2007), 85.

law' became valid throughout the enlarged Reich.[106] Among other provisions the law ruled that a marriage could be terminated without any reasons being given if the spouses had been living apart for three years. The introduction of irretrievable breakdown as grounds for divorce was intended to make divorce easier and to enable 'racially valuable people' to remarry and possibly have more children.[107] Although this solution would have been advantageous for Magdalene Sabiel's husband, Walther von Hollander tried to persuade her of its benefits. Hollander also tried to help her by suggesting that in his experience her personal situation was 'a common fate in wartime'.

Conclusion

Walther von Hollander's correspondence with his readers shows that in the 1930s and 1940s there was no established practice of professional or institutionalised counselling. His correspondents approached him initially through their admiration of his work before airing their personal problems. Their letters indicate that there were limits to what it was socially acceptable to talk about since the personal feelings and constellations that were topics in the letters could only be partially expressed in the public sphere. An example of this was mentioning the fact that separation due to the war might also provide the opportunity of leading everyday life without marital conflict. In spite of ambiguities and discreet allusions in his writing, Walther von Hollander stuck to the unspoken rules of what could and could not be said. He portrayed himself as a person who was outside the realm of politics and close to everyday life, but one who did not question the Nazi regime. Indeed, in a sense it could be argued that he helped to stabilise it. Since in his correspondence he was dealing with readers who belonged to the majority of Germans not persecuted on racist or political grounds, by putting their lives in order Hollander ultimately contributed to their being able to come to terms with the Nazi dictatorship. He did not need to deploy Nazi rhetoric in order to do this, even though much of Hollander's advice was in fact compatible with Nazi ideology: he functioned as a defusing and sympathetic ear at the interface

---

[106] Cornelia Essner and Edouard Conte, '"Fernehe", "Leichentrauung" und "Totenscheidung": Metamorphosen des Eherechts im Dritten Reich', *Vierteljahrshefte für Zeitgeschichte* 44/2 (1996), 201–27, here 201–2.

[107] See Frevert, *Frauen-Geschichte*, 229; Gabriele Czarnowski, '"Der Wert der Ehe für die Volksgemeinschaft": Frauen und Männer in der nationalsozialistischen Ehepolitik', in Kirsten Heinsohn, Barbara Vogel and Ulrike Weckel (eds.), *Zwischen Karriere und Verfolgung: Handlungsräume von Frauen im nationalsozialistischen Deutschland*, (Frankfurt a.M., 1978), 78–95, esp. 84–6. For further discussion of the 1938 marriage law and its consequences, see Annemone Christians' contribution to this volume (Chapter 8).

between the world of the media and that of interpersonal relationships, offering solutions for marriage and family problems without referring to or challenging the regime.

To a certain extent, National Socialism can be seen as providing a framework for the expression of individual desire for personal happiness within marital and family relationships as the concrete realisation of the private. This was especially the case for the Second World War, which was seen to a certain extent through the prism of the private. The inferences made by the men writing to Walther von Hollander show that for them the private signified a loving relationship as a location for their longing in the present and a promise for the future. For these men, the war intensified this longing for the private and made it the more attractive since the war itself was portrayed as a predestined external power. For women, by contrast, war was more likely to lead to negotiations and attempts to uphold and defend the private. Some made it clear that the war, which was now also becoming increasingly difficult to ignore in Germany, did not fit into the plans they had made for their lives. These were based on a private life with an intact home and family and, in the words of Magdalene Sabiel, the right to an 'individual personal life'. However, the war also made it possible to renegotiate the private, for example as a result of the freedoms that emerged when wives were separated from their husbands because of the war. Walther von Hollander's advice was tailored to the individual needs of his correspondents when offering solutions to interpersonal conflicts and at the same time supported the acceptance of contemporary circumstances, including the impact of the war. When, for example, he recommended tolerance and understanding in the face of marital infidelity so as to rationalise conflicts, this corresponded with his desire to make each individual problem seem emotionally more bearable for the person concerned.

The circumstances surrounding reader correspondence with Walther von Hollander changed significantly after 1945. For one thing, as a result of the radio programme called *The Round Table* (*Der Runde Tisch*) broadcast by Northwest German Broadcasting (*Nordwestdeutscher Rundfunk*) as well as various articles in the press, in cultural monthly magazines and after 1948 in the women's magazine *Constanze*, Hollander gained a reputation as the leading expert on women's issues in Germany. In addition, readers had become far more inclined to express their views explicitly, regardless of whether it was on the topic of collective guilt or the social consequences of the so-called surplus of women. The latter topic frequently provided Walther von Hollander with the opportunity of promoting the value of women leading independent lives outside marriage and the family. However, readers continued to turn to him with their personal problems, often resulting from their wartime experiences. Walther von Hollander continued to offer them solutions based on a mixture of self-discipline and tolerance, this time within a Western democratic context.

III

The Private at War

10 Personal Relationships between Harmony and Alienation
Aspects of Home Leave during the Second World War

Christian Packheiser

At the beginning of January 1940, the SS newspaper *Das Schwarze Korps* published an article pointedly entitled 'Father on Leave' about reunions between Wehrmacht soldiers and their families.[1] The timing of its publication reflected the fact that many of the men called up at the start of the war the previous September had been granted leave and had returned home for Christmas. Large photographs drove home a straightforward message: visibly relaxed, the homecomer sat in a comfortable armchair while his sons helped him out of his boots, before they did some drills together and with tin soldiers converted 'the living-room table into the frontline'.[2] Holding a wooden cannon in his hand, the uniformed soldier showed his sons the stages of the 'Poland campaign' on a map. The latter part of the evening was depicted as time spent alone together by the parental couple. Alongside the appealing photos, however, the accompanying text sounded a note of warning, alerting soldiers and their families to the fact that this stylised idyll of private domesticity was something they could expect only sporadically in the future. Priority was instead to be given to the 'defensive battle' to secure the future of the German people and following generations. The deeper meaning of home leave, argued the article, lay in its capacity to inspire 'happiness and strength', 'confidence and trust'.[3]

Over the course of the war and using all available media, the regime ever more frequently returned to the topic of home leave. In such features, reports on the few days granted to soldiers to see their families also hinted at the long stretches of time in between. Addressing the political and private implications of lengthy separation, propaganda accounts presented personal deprivations suffered in the present as a sacrifice for the *Volksgemeinschaft*, something that would be compensated for at least in

---

(Translated from German by Paul Bowman)
[1] Archiv des Instituts für Zeitgeschichte (IfZ-Archiv), Z 1012, *Das Schwarze Korps. Zeitung der Schutzstaffeln der NSDAP – Organ der Reichsführung SS*, 'Vater auf Urlaub', 4 January 1940, 11–12.
[2] Ibidem.   [3] Ibidem.

material terms once victory was secured: the vague promise held out was that of improved living standards. In the meantime, the 18 million soldiers who were called up to the Wehrmacht in the course of the war and their relatives had to focus their hopes of family life on the brief spells of leave, with their wishes and expectations concentrated as if placed under a magnifying glass. The intense emotions associated with home leave made the regime all the more interested in influencing and controlling this residue of privacy.

The intentions of those in power can be read up to a point as a subtext of the propaganda targeting soldiers' families. The regime had pragmatic reasons for conceding to soldiers some degree of private life, but this privilege came at a price and was overlaid by the requirement to conform. Given the regime's general readiness to apply coercion in areas of daily life, it is worth asking in this case how far the National Socialist state resorted to force to ensure compliance with its norms and rules.[4] Aside from coercion, however, there were also more subtle strategies through which the regime manipulated the private sphere during home leave. Newspaper articles suggested a range of acceptable scenarios. Men on leave were shown in staged intimate scenes, in the bathtub at home,[5] on a romantic boat trip with a holiday acquaintance[6] or seated at the abundantly laid table with the family.[7] The message was twofold: on the one hand, there were personal moments of privacy and intimacy that would be respected; on the other, certain standards of civility and 'normality' were to be maintained. Such depictions of the pleasures of private life were doubtless at one level intended to appeal to soldiers and their families. Nevertheless, it is worth asking if more complex motives on the part of the regime were in play: whether, for instance, the regime wanted to induce men on leave to withdraw behind their own four walls in order to 'atomise' unwelcome manifestations of waywardness and to prevent potentially deviant behaviour.[8]

The topic of home leave also enables questions to be posed about private relationships in the Second World War. What hopes and wishes did family members have when they met up during home leave, and how

---

[4] See Kerstin Theiss, *Wehrmachtjustiz an der 'Heimatfront': Die Militärgerichte des Ersatzheeres im Zweiten Weltkrieg* (Berlin, 2016), 4–18.

[5] See IfZ-Archiv, Z 1008 a, *Signal*, 5 1941, 'Was braucht ein Soldat, wenn er auf Urlaub kommt?', 4ff.

[6] See Staats- und Stadtbibliothek Augsburg (SuStB Augsburg), Gs 2958–42/60, *Front und Heimat. Soldatenzeitung des Gaues Schwaben*, 'Über den Umgang mit Urlaubern', 29 June 1942, 19.

[7] See IfZ-Archiv, Z 1002, *Illustrierter Beobachter*, 'Hansjürgen kommt auf Urlaub', 21 March 1940.

[8] See Ulrich Heinemann, 'Krieg und Frieden an der "inneren Front". Normalität und Zustimmung, Terror und Opposition im Dritten Reich', in Christoph Kleßmann (ed.), *Nicht nur Hitlers Krieg: Der Zweite Weltkrieg und die Deutschen* (Düsseldorf, 1989), 25–47.

far had such expectations come to diverge during the period of separation? Changing expectations and perceptions regarding home leave are not only evident in the correspondence between home and the front, but are mirrored in the propaganda itself. One telling sign is how the regime increasingly addressed the danger of soldiers becoming alienated from their civilian milieu.[9] Gender norms and roles too were being challenged. It was not always straightforward for fathers simply to resume their position as head of the family, and the classical model of a male-connoted public sphere distinct from a domestic sphere shaped by women looked less compelling under wartime conditions.[10] Meanwhile, the image of drills with the children and re-staging the front on the living-room table suggests that the status of the military had been enhanced vis-à-vis civilian life. Generally, it is worth asking how far the model of the soldier and military life came to influence bourgeois values and ideals.[11]

Investigating these questions raises wider issues concerning the nature of privacy and how private life is negotiated. In making distinctions between different aspects of the private and showing how they interact, the sociologist and philosopher Beate Rössler provides concepts that help to tackle these questions. While, as she shows, it is one's own four walls that provide the conditions for familial reproduction and a much-needed place of retreat, when protecting oneself from unwanted intrusions and limiting information about one's own person, it is control over knowledge and self-determination that are pivotal. Thus in Rössler's model, the 'local' dimension of privacy is joined by 'informational' and 'decisional' dimensions: together, they constitute the preconditions for leading an autonomous life. This model makes sense when examining the National Socialist dictatorship because it allows aspects of performativity and privately motivated action in the public domain to be factored in.[12]

---

[9] See Bundesarchiv, Abteilung Militärarchiv Freiburg (BArch-MA), RHD 69/14, *Das Neueste. Front-Nachrichtenblatt einer Panzer-Armee*, 'Der Probeurlaub', 15 February 1942; BArch-MA, RW 4/v-357, *Mitteilungen für die Truppe*, article 'Urlaub an der Wende vom vierten zum fünften Kriegsjahr', August 1943; SuStB Augsburg, Gs 2958–80/96, *Front und Heimat. Soldatenzeitung des Gaues Schwaben*, 'Keiner kehrt unverwandelt zurück', 5 June 1944.

[10] See Sabina Brändli, '"…die Männer sollen schöner geputzt sein als die Weiber": Zur Konstruktion bürgerlicher Männlichkeit im 19. Jahrhundert', in Thomas Kühne (ed.), *Männergeschichte – Geschlechtergeschichte: Männlichkeit im Wandel der Moderne* (Frankfurt a.M., 1996), 101–18.

[11] See Anette Dietrich and Ljiljana Heise (eds.), *Männlichkeitskonstruktionen im Nationalsozialismus* (Frankfurt a.M., 2013), 7ff.

[12] See Beate Rössler, *Der Wert des Privaten* (Frankfurt a.M., 2001), 19–25 and 134–6; see also Karin Jurczyk and Mechthild Oechsle, 'Privatheit: Interdisziplinarität und Grenzverschiebungen: Eine Einführung', in Karin Jurczyk and Mechthild Oechsle (eds.), *Das Private neu Denken: Erosionen, Ambivalenzen, Leistungen* (Münster, 2008), 8–47, here 34–6; Erika Fischer-Lichte, *Ästhetik des Performativen* (Frankfurt a.M., 2014),

As an intersection point between military and civilian society, home leave thus opens up numerous themes that shed light on how privacy in National Socialism was negotiated in the practice of everyday life. That the topic hitherto has been so neglected is all the more surprising given how much attention was given to it during the war: as a quantitative survey of soldiers' correspondence with their families discovered twenty years ago, home leave was a topic mentioned in around a quarter of all letters between the front and home.[13] While a number of general works have examined the erosion of familial ties during the war, or the problems confronting soldiers returning home after the war,[14] specific studies focusing on home leave are lacking. In the following, some of the lines of enquiry indicated earlier in this chapter are examined in greater detail.[15] Firstly, fundamental aspects of home leave will be discussed, particularly in tandem with the interest in it shown by the National Socialist regime. Secondly, drawing on ego-documents, the strategies pursued by families and couples to stabilise relationships are explored. Thirdly and finally, court records are used to examine how privacy was negotiated during home leave.

Home Leave: Privacy as a Privilege

The soldier on leave [...] is today treated like a treasured guest when back home, and everything is done for him. Back then he wasn't so

---

31–41; Erika Fischer-Lichte, *Performativität: Eine Einführung* (Bielefeld, 2013), 37–52; Ralph Weiß, 'Vom gewandelten Sinn für das Private', in Ralph Weiß (ed.), *Privatheit im öffentlichen Raum: Medienhandeln zwischen Individualisierung und Entgrenzung* (Offenbach, 2002), 27–88, here 27ff.; for the judicially different treatment of offences committed in private, semi-public and public domains, in particular with reference to soldiers on leave, see Ela Hornung, *Denunziation als soziale Praxis: Fälle aus der NS-Militärjustiz* (Vienna, Cologne, Weimar, 2010), 89ff.

[13] See Klaus Latzel, *Deutsche Soldaten – nationalsozialistischer Krieg? Kriegserlebnis – Kriegserfahrung 1939–1945* (Paderborn, 1998), 119; Veit Didczuneit, Jens Ebert and Thomas Jander (eds.), *Schreiben im Krieg – Schreiben vom Krieg: Feldpost im Zeitalter der Weltkriege* (Essen, 2011), 17–23.

[14] See Ela Hornung, *Warten und Heimkehren: Eine Ehe während und nach dem Zweiten Weltkrieg* (Vienna, 2005); Alan Allport, *Demobbed: Coming Home after World War II* (New Haven, CT, London, 2009); Birthe Kundrus, *Kriegerfrauen: Familienpolitik und Geschlechterverhältnisse im Ersten und Zweiten Weltkrieg* (Hamburg, 1995), 364–6; Dagmar Herzog, *Sex after Fascism: Memory and Morality in Twentieth-Century Germany* (Princeton, NJ, 2007), 1–10, 56–8; Hester Vaizey, *Surviving Hitler's War: Family Life in Germany, 1939–48* (Basingstoke, 2010), 89–90; Margarethe Dörr, *'Wer die Zeit nicht miterlebt hat...': Frauenerfahrungen im Zweiten Weltkrieg und in den Jahren danach* (Frankfurt a.M., 1998), 199.

[15] The present chapter draws on my PhD (Munich, 2018): 'Heimaturlaub – Soldaten zwischen Front, Familie und NS-Regime'.

admired. 1918, remember comrades [...] but that won't happen again, and that's why [...] we'll win this war.[16]

This fictionalised narrative by a Great War veteran, printed in a frontline newspaper in 1943, highlights the importance the Nazi regime attached to home leave. The time spent back at home was not only there to reassure soldiers that they still retained an element of privacy; the reference to the defeat of 1918 lent it a meaning that was seen as decisive for the outcome of the war. This raises the question of how often soldiers during wartime were granted leave and on what grounds.

The Wehrmacht regulations on leave set out that every soldier was to receive, at least once a year, a recreational holiday of no less than two weeks' duration at a stretch. Further leave was possible at other times on the condition that the other soldiers in the unit had already had theirs.[17] Wives were usually released from work for the period of their husbands' leave. The terminology reveals that in practice, 'front leave' and 'home leave' were synonyms: usage varied and in discussions of leave there are few signs that people systematically distinguished between those serving on the front line and those stationed in the rear echelons or in the homeland. Nevertheless, when the authorities allocated leave, combat troops and fathers of families were supposed to be favoured over soldiers deployed in the rear echelons. Besides convalescent leave, special or compassionate leave could be granted, depending on the military situation: to attend a wedding, to visit a close relative who was seriously ill, to do agricultural work or if one's home had been bombed. In formal terms, it would thus have been possible to return home several times a year.[18]

---

[16] BArch-MA, RHD 53/54–2, *Die Front*, article 'Urlaub 1918 – Urlaub 1943', 1 December 1943.

[17] Because the Wehrmacht leave regulations were revised several times and adjusted to the necessities of the war, only a greatly simplified description can be given here. Equally complex was the practical handling of these regulations, for this was oriented to local circumstances and to the battle situation. See BArch-MA, RHD 4/208 (Heeresdruckvorschrift [H.Dv.] 17; Marinedruckvorschrift [M.Dv.] 15; Luftwaffendruckvorschrift [L.Dv.] 17), Urlaubsordnung, 28 August 1935; BArch-MA, RHD 4/324 (H.Dv. 75), Bestimmungen für die Erhaltung des Heeres im Kriegszustand, 15 September 1939; IfZ-Archiv, Da. 34.02, Heeresverordnungsblatt 1940 Teil C (374), 133ff., Urlaubsregelung während des Krieges, 20 March 1940; IfZ-Archiv, Da. 34.01, Allgemeine Heeresmitteilungen 1942 (917), 483ff., Bestimmungen über die Gewährung von Urlaub an Soldaten und Wehrmachtbeamte während des Krieges, 25 October 1942; IfZ-Archiv, Da. 34.01, Allgemeine Heeresmitteilungen 1943 (208), 139ff., Neuregelung für den Erholungsurlaub der außerhalb des Heimatkriegsgebietes eingesetzten Teile der Wehrmacht, 5 February 1943; IfZ-Archiv, Da. 34.01, Allgemeine Heeresmitteilungen 1943 (867), 515ff., Bestimmungen über die Gewährung von Urlaub an Soldaten und Wehrmachtbeamte des Feld- und Ersatzheeres während des Krieges, 26 November 1943.

[18] See ibidem.

Division records and pay books show that extensive use was made of these regulations between the so-called *Blitzkrieg* operations. Only after the invasion of the Soviet Union did waiting times lengthen. Despite the regulations stating the contrary, those serving on the front line were often disadvantaged vis-à-vis men in the rear echelons.[19] One key indicator of the importance of home leave is the logistical burden the regime was willing to bear in order to enable soldiers to travel home regularly. In the course of November 1942, for example, around 465,000 soldiers from the *Ostheer* were each granted twenty days' leave,[20] a constant overall quota of around 9 per cent. Even in the spring of 1944, the men on leave numbered some 360,000.[21]

Another propaganda text sheds light on the intra-familial problems the regime associated with leave from the front. The Swabian Gau newspaper *Front und Heimat* published an article in 1942: 'How to Deal with Men on Leave':

> Of course, as always in life, reality can [...] bring disappointments [...]. A man returns from the front who [...] has been close to death so many times that he wouldn't have given a penny for his life. [...] It would be [...] superficial to think that this soldier [...] could quickly metamorphose back into the man he once was [...]. He no longer has any real relationship to the worries here [...]. A new man appears before us, and we have to get to know him all over again. A man who feels strange, who has to bridge an immeasurable abyss [...]. No one can help him to do this better than his wife [...], mother, sister, girlfriend. [...] The devoted woman must [...] realise that every soldier is present only with half of himself, the other half remains back with his comrades [...]. She must put her own self [...] on hold, for ultimately leave is a wellspring that replenishes the emotional reserves.[22]

The reference to a 'disappointing' reality indicated a widespread trend: private longings were powerfully concentrated on leave from the front, and if these often unrealistic expectations were not fulfilled the National Socialist regime regarded them as a threat. The allusion to the soldiers' contempt for death and the notion of metamorphosis expresses the

---

[19] See BArch-MA, RH 26–30/76, Tätigkeitsbericht der Abteilung II b der 30. Infanterie-Division (ID) for the period 1 October 1942 to 30 December 1942; BArch-MA, RH 20–17/543, Stand der Beurlaubungen at 1 April 1943, Bericht der Abtl. II b an das Armee-Oberkommando 17, 14 April 1943.

[20] See Johannes Hürter and Matthias Uhl, 'Hitler in Vinnytsia: A New Document Casts Fresh Light on the Crisis of September 1942', in Elizabeth Harvey and Johannes Hürter (eds.), *German Yearbook of Contemporary History*, vol. 3: *Hitler – New Research* (Berlin, Boston, MA, 2018) 147–210, here 209.

[21] See BArch-MA, RH 2/487 a, Berichte der Heeresabteilung T1 Operationsabteilung des Generalstabs an das Reichskriegsministerium, Lageberichte und Meldungen vom Gesamtkriegsschauplatz und aus den besetzten Gebieten an das OKH im Jahr 1944.

[22] SuStB Augsburg, Gs 2958–42/60, *Front und Heimat. Soldatenzeitung des Gaues Schwaben*, 53, 29 June 1942.

omnipresence of traumatic experiences; feelings of displacement were also not uncommon during leave from the front due to the abrupt spatial switch between the complementarily structured socialisation systems of the military and the family. It is striking that these lines are primarily addressed to the partners of the soldiers. The word 'wellspring' betrays the psychosexual connotation on which the regime based its analysis of soldiers' needs: home was depicted primarily as a female domain into which the fighting man was to let himself fall as if into a refreshing spring, returning to the front reinvigorated.

With regard to the attempts by the Party and the state to intervene in the private sphere during home leave, two aspects can be identified which reveal genuinely National Socialist intentions. Firstly, home leave was to stabilise the morale of wartime society, preventing a repeat of the 1918 revolution. Secondly, home leave was a key instrument in steering population policy. How far either of these goals took precedence over the other is one of the questions this chapter seeks to address. Two further policy considerations were caught in a tense relationship: while on the one hand the regime demanded enormous sacrifices from the soldiers, on the other hand, it acknowledged that there were limits to what wartime society could bear and a corresponding need to accommodate certain personal wishes. Along with discipline, coercion and the terror of Wehrmacht justice,[23] home leave was one of the main instruments for maintaining troop morale.[24]

Those at home were expected to contribute to this goal: family members were seen as having a duty to create the best possible conditions and atmosphere for relaxation, and the authorities imposed sanctions whenever behaviour deviating from this norm was brought to their attention.[25] Private harmony between spouses and within the family was elevated to

---

[23] See Heinemann, 'Krieg und Frieden', 37ff.

[24] See Lothar Burchardt, 'Die Auswirkung der Kriegswirtschaft auf die deutsche Zivilbevölkerung im Ersten und im Zweiten Weltkrieg', *Militärgeschichtliche Mitteilungen* 15 (1974), 65–97; Marlis Steinert, *Hitlers Krieg und die Deutschen: Stimmung und Haltung der deutschen Bevölkerung im Zweiten Weltkrieg* (Düsseldorf, 1970); Bernhard R. Kroener, 'Die personellen Ressourcen des Dritten Reiches im Spannungsfeld zwischen Wehrmacht, Bürokratie und Kriegswirtschaft 1939–1942', in Bernhard R. Kroener, Rolf-Dieter Müller and Hans Umbreit, *Organisation und Mobilisierung des deutschen Machtbereichs: Kriegsverwaltung, Wirtschaft und personelle Ressourcen 1939–1941* (Das Deutsche Reich und der Zweite Weltkrieg, vol. 5/1) (Stuttgart, 1988), 693–1002; Bernhard R. Kroener, '"Menschenbewirtschaftung", Bevölkerungsverteilung und personelle Rüstung in der zweiten Kriegshälfte (1942–1944)', in Bernhard R. Kroener, Rolf-Dieter Müller and Hans Umbreit, *Organisation und Mobilisierung des deutschen Machtbereichs: Kriegsverwaltung, Wirtschaft und personelle Ressourcen 1942–1944/45* (Das Deutsche Reich und der Zweite Weltkrieg, vol. 5/2) (Stuttgart, 1999), 777–995.

[25] See Staatsarchiv München (StAM), Landgerichte München 1, 10024, Az. 4 R 369/1940.

a *raison d'état*, since a soldier's wellbeing affected his combat readiness. The analogy here from the civilian sector, as Wolfhard Buchholz pointed out in an early path-breaking study, was the 'duty to rest' prescribed by the German Labour Front's *Kraft durch Freude* (KdF) organisation.[26] Leisure time and holidays were subordinated to the utilitarian principle of maintaining efficiency in order to serve the *Volksgemeinschaft*. These precepts applied to the wartime military to an even greater degree.

That leave from the front could serve as an instrument of population policy was a matter for discussion in the highest leadership circles: the head of the Party Chancellery, Martin Bormann, noted after a discussion on the future of the German people in the Führer's headquarters on the night of 28 January 1944: 'How many more children would have been born in this war if it had been possible to give our frontline soldiers more leave, or indeed leave at all?'[27] It was largely for this reason that soldiers were granted special leave to get married until well into the second half of the war, if the military situation permitted. With this measure, the regime was seeking to counteract a drastic decline in the population caused by the war and sinking birth rates. At the same time, the regime sought to persuade the population that it was doing everything conceivable to enable the soldiers to continue, or even just establish, a civilian life back home.[28]

There was no precise plan for specific measures and intrusions by the Party into private life during home leave. As a rule, state authorities and the Party acted ad hoc and on a local basis. The Reich Chancellery informed the Reich Ministry of Propaganda in September 1942, responding to an earlier recommendation by Joseph Goebbels for the setting up of a comprehensive 'NSDAP home leave service': 'It is to remain up to the man on leave to decide where and how he wishes to spend his leave [...] but above all else, these measures must not disturb the peace and quiet he wishes. [...] He has to feel that he is free while on leave.'[29] The official newsletter for Party functionaries, *Der Hoheitsträger*, was emphatic on this point: 'Leave serves the private happiness of the soldiers (*Der Urlaub dient dem privaten Glück der Soldaten*). It is thus obvious that the purpose of any

---

[26] Wolfhard Buchholz, *Die Nationalsozialistische Gemeinschaft 'Kraft durch Freude': Freizeitgestaltung und Arbeiterschaft im Dritten Reich* (PhD, Munich, 1976), 90ff.
[27] Bundesarchiv Berlin (BArch Berlin), NS 19/3289, Persönlicher Bestand Reichsführer SS, Abschrift für das Führerhauptquartier, 29 January 1944.
[28] See Lisa Pine, *Nazi Family Policy 1933–1945* (Oxford, 1999), 8ff.
[29] The document infers diverging attitudes on this issue between the Party Chancellery and the Propaganda Ministry, whereby the latter advocated a stronger and more direct instrumentalisation of home leave. BArch Berlin, NS 18/775, Entwürfe zur Ausgestaltung des Urlaubs für Frontsoldaten durch die Partei und zur Einrichtung von Sonderdienststellen 'Fronturlauberdienst der NSDAP' in den Ortsgruppen, Korrespondenz zwischen Parteikanzlei und Propagandaministerium, 15 and 29 September 1942.

assistance provided by Party organisations is to give him and his family as much time as possible for his private life.'[30] Such statements might give the impression that leave was indeed an altruistic concession to soldiers' privacy. However, there were other obvious ways in which those in power sought to influence relationships, marriages and family life. While the Party deliberately kept direct contact during home leave to a minimum,[31] Reich Health Leader Leonardo Conti was blatant in his efforts to boost the birth rate: troop physicians were told to make sure that married childless soldiers coordinated their leave with their wives' ovulation.[32]

Attempts to influence home leave ranged from propaganda and offers of support to informal social pressure and legal sanctions. There were efforts at matchmaking and measures making it easier both to marry and to divorce: a two-track strategy sought to strengthen the stability of the soldiers' relationships while on leave from the front, but also to make it easier formally to end irretrievably broken marriages.[33] To broker new partnerships, the Party set up official marriage bureaux at the home leave service offices which arranged, among other things, informal conversations between 'hostesses' and homecomers.[34] Notices such as the following were placed in newspapers:

During the war a large contingent of worthy and marriageable men are at the front and in the brief weeks of their leave do not have sufficient opportunity to meet a suitable female partner, because she, caught up in an arduous working life, is often resigned and has stopped going out, and cannot make friends because of a lack of company at home or elsewhere. [. . .] For her, a selection [of men] is to be found who are willing to enter into a fruitful marital union.[35]

---

[30] IfZ Archiv, Db 08.01 a, *Der Hoheitsträger* 3 (1942), 'Die Betreuung des Urlaubers'.
[31] See BArch Berlin, NS 18/775, Entwürfe zur Ausgestaltung des Urlaubs für Frontsoldaten durch die Partei und zur Einrichtung von Sonderdienststellen 'Fronturlauberdienst der NSDAP' in den Ortsgruppen, Korrespondenz zwischen Parteikanzlei und Propagandaministerium, 15 and 29 September 1942.
[32] See http://wwii.germandocsinrussia.org/de/nodes/2087-akte-290-ubersetzte-dokumente-zu-fragen-des-sanitats-und-hygienedienstes-zur-fleckfieberbekampfung-zur-beurlaubung-von-ehemannern-usw#page/1/mode/grid/zoom/1, Beuteakten in russischen Beständen, Bestand 500, Findbuch 1248, Akte 290, Abschrift des Armeearztes beim Armeeoberkommando (AOK), 18, 12 October 1943 [accessed 7 March 2017].
[33] See Cornelia Essner and Edouard Conte, '"Fernehe", "Leichentrauung" und "Totenscheidung": Metamorphosen des Eherechts im Dritten Reich', *Vierteljahrshefte für Zeitgeschichte* 44/2 (1996), 201–27.
[34] These service offices ('Betreuungsstellen') for men on leave were usually located at garrison towns or the major railway stations of the Reich. Their primary task was to support the arriving men in completing bureaucratic formalities. For instance, food stamps were distributed or the necessary changes or additions made to where leave was to be spent, noted in the pay book and on the leave pass. They also provided information to men arriving or passing through, such as where food and lodgings could be found, or helped them to find suitable accommodation.
[35] Stadtarchiv München (StdA München), *Münchner Stadtnachrichten*, 'Einrichtung einer amtlichen Ehevermittlung', 18 February 1944.

Meanwhile, family evenings were to strengthen existing ties. The Reich Ministry of Propaganda, which regularly pressed the Party Chancellery and the Führer's headquarters to allow it more influence, proposed that such evenings be held every four to six weeks in local Party branches as well as at the grass-roots levels of 'block' and 'cell'. According to one of its memoranda:

> [T]he war [...] demands that the Party integrate family life more strongly than before into political work. [...] The separation caused by the war leads to estrangement between husband, wife and children. [...] Family evenings become a special [...] occasion when a soldier on leave [...] is present.[36]

Overall, home leave was a contradictory mix of straightforward instrumentalisation and purposeful benevolence: it was a gratification system driven by political and military pragmatism. The utilitarian intentions of the regime were often interpreted by the soldiers as a well-meant concession to their private lives. But in fact the soldiers' wish to 'simply have a bit of peace and quiet' with their families was not incompatible with the goal of the Party and the Wehrmacht: to bolster the morale of a society at war.[37]

At the other end of the spectrum were soldiers who, driven by political but more frequently personal impulses, did not conduct themselves in the manner expected during their leave. The regime sought through various means to fend off potentially deviant behaviour by men on leave and their families – through advice and instruction to men preparing to go on leave, through incentives and benefits during the stay back home and through elaborate monitoring procedures. Reports filed by social workers employed by the National Socialist People's Welfare Organisation (NSV) highlighted widespread complaints about relationship breakdowns and infidelity,[38] while the reports of the *Sicherheitsdienst der SS* (SD) regularly dealt with the dangers of 'married couples drifting apart'.[39] Even as late as January 1945, Propaganda Minister Goebbels was still reacting with concern to a rise in the number of violent acts

---

[36] BArch Berlin, NS 6/346, Memorandum des Propagandaministeriums an das Führerhauptquartier, 16 April 1944 on 'Veranstaltungen für Fronturlauber' and 'Maßnahmen zur Förderung von Eheschließungen'.

[37] National Archives and Records Administration, Washington, DC (NARA), RG 165, Entry 179, Box 474, Room Conversation Goethe – Bornemann, 15 July 1944, 3.10 PM.

[38] See Kundrus, *Kriegerfrauen*, 369–75.

[39] BArch Berlin, R 58/190 Meldungen aus dem Reich, Berichte des Sicherheitsdienstes (SD) der SS, SD-Bericht, 11 November 1943; Heinz Boberach (ed.), *Meldungen aus dem Reich: Die geheimen Lageberichte des Sicherheitsdienstes der SS 1938–1945*, 17 vols. (Herrsching, 1984), SD-Berichte, 27 May 1940, 5 January 1942, 10 June 1943 or 19 November 1943.

committed by men on leave who had 'caught their wives being unfaithful'.[40]

Expectations and Experiences during Home Leave

Ego-documents open up a different perspective on leave from the front. In writing about leave due or spent, men sought reassurance about personal relationships at home. Along with strategies used to maintain relationships over such long distances, letters and diaries also reveal the personal expectations soldiers and their families had of home leave, and how far they saw this private domain threatened by the National Socialist war.

Unsurprisingly, there were many different ideas about how home leave would make up for the deprivations endured during separation. But these were often overshadowed by worries about the strength of basic family ties. 'Will Hano be glad to see his dad? Perhaps he won't even recognise me,' wrote Anton G., who was serving on the Eastern Front. His fear of alienation from the family was shared by many fathers as they waited for their home leave.[41] Of even greater importance was the apprehension about estrangement within a partnership. In warding off such risks, many recognised the need to show empathy with the other's perspective. Writing to her fiancé still at the front, Annemarie H. for example pondered: 'What marks and impressions has the Russian campaign left on you [...]. One has to caress your forehead, ever so gently and sweetly, and wipe away the worst.' With these lines, she sought to dispel his fear that the 'cold indifference' he had begun to feel due to his front-line experiences could have a disconcerting impact on her during his home leave.[42]

Many letter writers hoped that leave would regenerate their private relationships and instil new strength to withstand further privations. Leave could, it was hoped, be a bridge that reunited a couple: '3 weeks of only fondness and happiness' is how Wolfgang B. put it to his fiancée, Maria, in 1943.[43] Annemarie H. dreamt of travelling to the mountains, taking long hikes through the Spessart Range, the Odenwald and along the River Main, and wanted to get a camera to capture the memories – but she was acutely aware of how fragile such private plans were in wartime and described them in the same breath as

---

[40] Elke Fröhlich (ed.), *Die Tagebücher von Joseph Goebbels, Teil II: Diktate 1941–5*, vol. 15: January–April 1945 (Munich, 1995), 29 January 1945.
[41] Deutsches Tagebucharchiv Emmendingen (DTA), 2131, letter by Anton G. dated 16 July 1944.
[42] DTA 1818, letters by Annemarie and Albert H. dated 5 and 31 December 1941.
[43] DTA 491, letter by Wolfgang B. dated 31 May 1943.

a 'castle in the air'.[44] This realisation expressed itself in the uncertainty about whether the short reunion could make up for the long separation. Centa B., for example, wrote to her husband, Franz: 'I want to show you my love even more, but in the short weeks of leave this is simply impossible, they just fly by [...] and one has to draw strength from this time together for so long until the next leave is granted.'[45]

The numerous references to the desire for a sense of emotional security also point to the increasing importance of private refuges during the war. Moreover, there seems to have been a growing need to spend leave with immediate family without any outside intrusions. While serving on the Eastern Front, Herrmann G. vividly described his hopes for his Christmas leave, from tending his stamp collection and playing with his children through to the evening game of *Skat* with his wife on the cosy corner bench. Emphatically he characterised his own four walls as a refuge, longing for its friendly warmth.[46] Maria B. meanwhile wanted to escape with her fiancé, Franz, 'to the woods every single day, roll around in the bushes and just be a girl'.[47] This example is a reminder that unmarried couples were in part forced to pursue their sexual desires in public, albeit somewhere remote and secluded. In such cases, the motivation was even stronger – despite the war – to settle down and set up a home as a way of enjoying the advantages afforded by private space.[48] In this regard, letters between home and front also reveal that couples often found it a burden to have to meet relatives who did not belong to the immediate family or who were part of the same household. In contrast, direct intrusions into home leave by the Nazi regime are rarely discussed.[49] This may or may not reflect fear of the censor: the sources at any rate shed no light on this point.

Material provisions were also a very important aspect of home leave. For a long time, the men were able to uphold their role as family provider

---

[44] DTA 1818, letters by Annemarie H. dated 16 February 1941 and 3 February 1942.
[45] IfZ-Archiv, ED 930, Centa B. to Franz B. dated 30 April 1943.
[46] See DTA 1462, letters by Herrmann and Lore G. dated 27 September, 2 and 30 November 1941.
[47] DTA 491, letter by Maria B. dated 18 April 1943.
[48] See Museum für Kommunikation Berlin, Feldpostarchiv (MfK-FA), 3.2002.0349, letters by Ernst and Irene Guicking dated 27 November 1939, 15 March 1940 and 8 May 1943; around two-thirds of the soldiers deployed in combat units during the Second World War were single. For this reason, it seems necessary to include unmarried or engaged couples in the study. See Christoph Rass, 'Das Sozialprofil von Kampfverbänden des deutschen Heeres 1939 bis 1945', in Jörg Echternkamp (ed.), *Die Deutsche Kriegsgesellschaft 1939 bis 1945* (*Das Deutsche Reich und der Zweite Weltkrieg*, vol. 9/1) (Munich, 2004), 641–742, 682ff.
[49] See DTA 491, diary entry by Maria B. dated 19 May 1944; IfZ-Archiv, ED 930, letter by Centa B. dated 12 May 1943; DTA 1462, letter dated 26 December 1940.

through the largely authorised plundering of other countries. Wives sent wish lists and congratulated the soldiers on their new skills: 'All things considered, you've learnt how to shop rather well,' is how Lore G. put it upon opening a large crate filled with two dozen bottles of wine, fabric for a suit, wool, a fountain pen and other bounty.[50] But here too conditions changed as the war went on. After Herrmann G., transferred to the Eastern Front, complained that 'there's nothing left to loot in this wretched place,' his wife became more modest: 'Onions! [...] If you can requisition some, then don't forget.'[51]

While many men longed for privacy and home comforts, there were countervailing forces too that cast home leave in a less positive light. Ideas of masculinity and military traditions in war continued to exert a powerful dynamic of their own. Seen from this perspective, if a father had gone to war as the protector of the nation and his family, then a longing for privacy, if articulated too strongly, could come across as 'unmanly'.[52] When soldiers wrote to each other expressing reluctance about spending time at home, such thinking may have been in play. At any rate, Sepp B. told his brother Franz things he could never mention to the rest of the family:

I'm not in all that much of a hurry at the moment. At home they naturally ask in every letter, as you can well imagine, they can't wait until I come home. Now I've got several letters full of wailing and moaning [...]. I'm not expecting a lot from leave for myself, it'll be dead boring again, I can see it coming.[53]

Sepp B. did not, at least according to this letter, want to spend his leave with his parents and other siblings: he had his own plans and one could speculate that he prioritised a soldierly identity over bourgeois privacy. Thus, it was not just the traumatising experiences of the soldiers which interacted with relationships back home, but also those experiences which may be characterised as new freedoms. This ranged from contacts with the female civilian population and the relative absence of Party control through to opportunities to indulge in deviant behaviour while protected by the close-knit circle of comrades.[54] Meanwhile, there were family

[50] DTA 1462, letters by Lore to Herrmann G. dated 23 November, 17 and 27 December 1940 and letter by Herrmann G. to his wife, Lore, dated 3 December 1940.
[51] Ibidem, letters dated 4 May and 27 November 1941.
[52] See Frank Werner, '"Noch härter, noch kälter, noch mitleidloser": Soldatische Männlichkeit im deutschen Vernichtungskrieg 1941–1944', in Dietrich/ Heise (eds.), *Männlichkeitskonstruktionen*, 45–64, here 46ff.; Thomas Kühne, *Kameradschaft: Die Soldaten des nationalsozialistischen Krieges und das 20. Jahrhundert* (Göttingen, 2006), 140ff.
[53] IfZ-Archiv, ED 930, letters by Sepp to his brother Franz dated 1 and 7 April 1943.
[54] See Maren Röger, *Kriegsbeziehungen: Intimität, Gewalt und Prostitution im besetzten Polen 1939 bis 1945* (Frankfurt a.M., 2015), 7–27; Kühne, *Kameradschaft*, 113ff. and 131ff.

members who themselves identified with soldierly models of masculinity and affirmed the importance for soldiers of performing one's duty. Maria B. was only one of many letter writers who expressed their pride at a man who proved his worth on the front and showed he was not a coward. It was thus only logical that she felt like a 'war profiteer' when her fiancé was granted four weeks leave in October 1943.[55]

Over the course of the war, some shift in attitudes can be observed with regard to this tension between devotion to military duty and private longings. In the first phase of the war, the wish to earn one's stripes at the front was more pervasive; after the war turned against Germany, soldiers increasingly spoke of home leave more clearly as a compensation for forgoing privacy. Ironically, this was the time when less and less leave was being granted, and soldiers and their families found it increasingly difficult to deal with parting again. Couples started warning each other not to write so much about the prospect of leave, so as to avoid disappointment when – as happened ever more frequently – it was cancelled.[56] But it was hard to resist conjuring up alluring visions of how leave would be when it finally came. Lore G. promised her husband:

> How often you've longed for our cosy bath time! – And even if we have to use up all the wood – when you're back home you can take a bath mornings and evenings, as often as you feel like. And for dinner you can have a leg of venison all to yourself: everything's being saved up for when you arrive – you're to feel as if you're in paradise.[57]

The imaginary scenario conjured up here matched the classic propaganda trope of a wife working selflessly to ensure that a man's fighting strength was restored. Nevertheless, Lore G. did not put aside all her demands and expectations. Running the household alone was becoming increasingly difficult and she was hoping that having her husband at home would ease the burden. Particularly in bringing up the children she was looking forward to 'handing over the reins for a few weeks'.[58] In this case, the expectations the couple pinned to home leave were compatible: Herrmann was also looking forward to taking on household tasks and above all devoting his time to the children. The scene was thus set for a harmonious reunion.[59] However, the growing burden of responsibilities taken on by Lore G. remained an issue, and in the end Herrmann was

---

[55] DTA 491, letter by Maria B. dated 17 October 1943.
[56] See DTA 1462, letters by Lore to Herrmann G. dated 20 March and 14 December 1942; DTA 2108, letters by Werner to Elisabeth K. dated end of October 1943.
[57] DTA 1462, letter by Lore to Herrmann G. dated 30 November 1941.
[58] DTA 1462, letters by Lore G. dated 14 May 1942 and 22 November 1940.
[59] DTA 1462, letter dated 27 September 1941.

moved to hire an 'Eastern worker' (*Ostarbeiterin*) to help in the household.[60]

Maria and Wolfgang B. saw things somewhat differently. Before getting married, Maria had served as a nurse in a military hospital in Warsaw; since then, she had sometimes felt the role of housewife to be a backward step. The narrow confines of family life drove her 'crazy' at times, particularly when decisive defensive battles were raging at the front. Her desire for autonomy was so great that she was only willing to clean her husband's shoes when he was on leave after he had done her shoes first. But no serious conflict ensued: Wolfgang B. accepted Maria's need for breathing space, while she made every effort to ensure that the homecomer's stay was as pleasant as possible.[61]

Miscommunication and taboos surrounding certain topics are common features of personal letters as a genre. Nevertheless, letters written during this period that touched on the topic of fidelity sometimes reflected in specific ways the double sexual standard facilitated by the regime.[62] Many women were under no illusions about the licentious behaviour of soldiers in the occupied territories, and some thus found it far more difficult to accept the role of devoted housewife. This could in turn disrupt harmonious relations during home leave.[63] But conflicts of this kind which flared up during leave are often only hinted at in ego-documents, and when they are discernible, it remains difficult to identify what exactly had eroded the relationship. After his home leave, Carl C. wrote:

You'll certainly be better off now that I'm no longer at home, you were so grumpy a lot of the time, but now you've got peace and quiet for a long time until my next leave. [...] You weren't always that kind to me, but that doesn't matter, I'd imagined that it would have all been much nicer, little Peter didn't leave me disappointed. It's simply that we've already been separated far too long. [...] You also said to me while I was on leave that you'd be glad when I'm gone again – you should know that I've gone through more in this war than you could imagine, when I now think back, I ask myself what you're getting at. But perhaps my little Peter will punish you for such words and won't show you his love.[64]

---

[60] See DTA 1462, letter by Herrmann G. dated 1 October 1942. See also Elizabeth Harvey, 'Housework, Domestic Privacy and the "German Home": Paradoxes of Private Life during the Second World War', in Rüdiger Hachtmann et al. (eds.), *Detlev Peukert und die NS-Forschung* (Göttingen, 2015), 115–31.

[61] See DTA 491, diary entries by Maria B. from the end of January 1944 and 6 September 1944.

[62] See Dörr, *Frauenerfahrungen*, 152.

[63] See IfZ-Archiv, ED 930, letter by Centa B. dated 16 March 1943; MfK-FA, 3.2002.0349, letters by Ernst and Irene Guicking dated 20 January 1940, 16 August 1940, 30 March 1941 and 8 August 1943.

[64] Sammlung Frauennachlässe am Institut für Geschichte der Universität Wien (SFN Wien), NL 57, letters by Carl to Anna C. dated 18, 19 and 21 January 1941.

Quite clearly this couple found the long separation and its seemingly inevitable estrangement an unsurmountable hurdle. Diverging expectations of home leave were a crucial factor: whereas Carl C. wanted to enjoy his free time, relax and go on long walks, his wife faulted his reluctance to help at home and to take on parenting tasks, and she criticised his alcohol consumption.[65] However, lurking suspicions were what really predominated. The tension between the couple dissipated again two years later during another home leave. Carl C. emphasised that he had fallen in love again with his wife, admitting that he had for a while transferred his affections to their son. During other visits back home, he had compensated for the distant relations with his wife by seeking to be even closer to his son, spoiling him unduly. This ultimately led to a vicious circle that had made the estrangement worse.[66]

Despite everything, this family came through the war. The fact that it did raises an intriguing, but ultimately unanswerable question concerning the source base: whether the private family papers available in archives document to a disproportionate extent the relationships within families which remained intact. It certainly seems possible that families who prefer to keep an unhappy or disrupted family history private are less likely to have made personal documents accessible to researchers.

Soldiers' Relationships before the Courts

The records of military and civil courts are a further source that can be used to explore what the Nazi regime considered to be the purpose of home leave and what private behaviour it deemed acceptable on the part of husbands and wives. Quite often, confiscated *Feldpost* letters were part of the documents gathered for divorce proceedings. Such letters point to an intensity and frequency of relationship breakdown that is not found in archive holdings of private family papers: court records can thus serve as something of a corrective to the impressions garnered from personal documents in such collections.

The records of the Wehrmacht judicial system show that many of the offences which at first glance represented violations of military regulations were in fact privately motivated and only gained political significance in wartime. Among the typical offences coming before the military courts were obtaining leave under false pretences and failing to report back for duty on time. Officially, such acts were dealt with as statutory offences

[65] Ibidem, letters dated 16 September 1939, 2 and 25 February 1942.
[66] See ibidem, letter by Carl to Anna C. dated 12 August 1943.

covering 'overstaying' home leave or desertion.[67] In September 1944, the court of the 526th Infantry Division sentenced Private Gottlieb O. to fifteen years' penitentiary (*Zuchthaus*) for 'subversion of the war effort and desertion' in accordance with the Special Wartime Decree on the Criminal Code(*Kriegssonderstrafrechtsverordnung* or KSSVO). The official report of the incident stated that he had conspired with his wife to gain special leave on several occasions.[68] In the record of interrogation, Gottlieb O. claimed:

I have to say that my wife was continually at me to take leave. If I, as described above, told my wife to send a telegram with false details, then this too was because of her. Once, although I would not be able to prove it, my wife started an affair behind my back with a sergeant-major in the air force (*Oberfeldwebel der Flieger*) during a long spell when I had no home leave.[69]

Gottlieb O.'s wife added that she had wanted to speak with her husband about all these things while he was on leave, hoping to improve their relationship.[70] This case shows how the desire for privacy became all the more pressing as familial ties came under strain. For this couple, solving their personal problems took precedence over obeying the rules; taking considerable risks, they sought to force through a reunion to be able to talk things over. They got caught, but it is impossible to guess how often leave was in fact obtained under false pretences.

The case of Private Matthias Z. shows that personal circumstances could sometimes count as mitigating factors. In August 1943, he tampered with his identity papers and overstayed by seventeen days the leave he had been granted when his home was bombed. This amounted to desertion. The court, however, sentenced him to only six weeks' strict detention. It cited the disturbed state of the machine-gunner, who had lost his family during the air raid and 'was panic-stricken by this calamitous blow of fate and thus not aware of the consequences of his actions'.[71]

Anton M., a junior officer, was sentenced to just six months' prison for the attempted manslaughter of his wife. The court took into account three

---

[67] See Manfred Messerschmidt and Fritz Wüllner, *Die Wehrmachtjustiz im Dienste des Nationalsozialismus: Zerstörung einer Legende* (Baden-Baden, 1987), 50–9; Christoph Rass, '*Menschenmaterial*': *Deutsche Soldaten an der Ostfront: Innenansichten einer Infanteriedivision 1939–1945* (Paderborn, Munich, 2003), 166–70.
[68] BArch-MA, RH26/526G 2411, Feldurteil Gericht der Division 526, Zweigstelle Düren, 2 September 1944.
[69] Ibidem, Vernehmungsprotokoll, 19 June 1944.
[70] See ibidem, Protokoll der öffentlichen Sitzung des Feldkriegsgerichts der Division 526, Zweigstelle Düren, 29 August 1944.
[71] BArch-MA, RG 26-526G/791, Gerichtsurteil des Gerichts der 26. Infanteriedivision, 10 December 1943, Stellungnahme des Kompaniechefs der 4. Kompanie des Grenadierregiments 78, 21 November 1943.

months spent in custody awaiting trial. The case documents how a happy marriage crumbled under the weight of alienation and jealousy caused by wartime separation. Anton M. fired the shots during an argument about the couple's furniture, the incident taking place as divorce proceedings were already under way. In passing sentence, the court took into consideration the soldier's decorations for bravery and the fact that his wife had accused him of 'irresponsibility towards the family' because he had again – despite being wounded several times – voluntarily reported for battle duty. As far as the court was concerned, the accused was 'provoked to act in anger by his wife'. The court also referred to her accusations of his infidelity.[72] Along with the bias favouring the soldier, the double standards of the court stand out.

In order to ensure that family differences were resolved, thus enabling soldiers to focus on their wartime duties, the Wehrmacht not only granted recreational leave but also, depending on the military situation at the time, special leave for the 'purpose of clarifying difficult domestic relationships'. Court records show detention being imposed on soldiers who used this leave only half-heartedly. In one such case, a woman respondent from Munich told her husband's company commander through her lawyer that her husband had used his leave for a purpose other than the proposed reconciliation. After the company commander had examined the facts, the petitioner was given several days' detention.[73] It emerged that the soldier while on leave had not travelled to talk things over with his wife at her parents' home, but had instead gone to the couple's flat with his new girlfriend. Despite this, the court dissolved the marriage on the basis of mutual fault, for no children could be expected given the wife's age and she had, before their wedding, 'feigned her ability to bear children'; she had, in fact, lied about her age. The marriage was thus no longer seen as of any value to the *Volksgemeinschaft*.[74] This and the following cases once again illustrate how private refuges and domestic harmony had important functions from the point of view of the Nazi regime. The regeneration of the soldiers and biological reproduction took precedence: if the conditions necessary for fulfilling these dual goals were not given, then the regime insisted that private relationships be rearranged. Against these imperatives, the interests of women tended to be regarded as secondary.

---

[72] BArch-MA, RG 26-526G/347, Feldurteil des Gerichts der Division 526, 1 September 1943, Vernehmungsprotokoll der Wehrmachtskommandantur Dortmund, 19 May 1943.
[73] See StAM, Landgerichte 10201, Urteilsbegründung des Landgerichts München, 20 April 1944.
[74] Ibidem.

A further case from Munich demonstrates the degree to which judges ruled to the advantage of soldiers so as to bolster their fighting morale. In the case of this particular couple, a growing alienation during wartime had led to them exchanging furious insults, followed during a period of home leave by acts of violence. The lawyer justified the divorce petition as follows:

> It is beyond question that a soldier, who since the start of the war has fought on almost all fronts in the foremost line of battle, needs to spend his short leave in comfortable, relaxed surroundings in order to collect his strength for future campaigns. The behaviour of the respondent is in no way conducive to this goal, on the contrary, it only demoralises him. The petitioner thus feels unable, and neither [...] should it be expected of him, to continue this marriage.[75]

The judge accepted this argument because the man repeatedly alluded to his wife's shattered nerves and her 'constant carping' (*querulatorisches Verhalten*), drawing on the evidence of a medical report. Here, the admission that the wife had already been suffering from 'nervous episodes' before the war suggests two general patterns in the erosion of family ties during wartime. On the one hand, private problems were exacerbated by the changed conditions to the point when – combined with other war-related stress factors – they came to be regarded as intolerable. On the other hand, the regime facilitated the dissolution of marriages when it appeared that they were having a detrimental effect on a man's fighting spirit; and if petitioners also conjured up accusations based on racial policy or ideas of biological heredity, they were even more likely to succeed. In this case, the wife countered the accusations levelled against her by claiming that her husband had himself turned his back on her as the war progressed. Instead of examining the validity of these claims, the court followed a logic that prioritised the military and its values over civilian conventions. With several decorations for bravery and promotions, so went the lawyer's argument, the husband had embarked on a 'rapid rise' through the ranks of the Wehrmacht, while his wife, in her passive role at home, had not been able to 'keep pace with him inwardly'. After considering the correspondence between the couple, the court identified a breach of matrimonial duties in how 'the respondent only rarely wrote to him and that her letters were full of trivial matters and did not even congratulate him on being awarded the Knight's Cross in addition to the Iron Cross'. This reproach was considered all the more serious because it was also noted that there had been a neglect of household duties during home leave.[76]

---

[75] StAM, Landgerichte 10170, Verfahrensakte AZ 2 R 554/42, Anklageschrift, 25 November 1942.
[76] Ibidem, Urteilsbegründung, 1 June 1944.

The divorce proceedings between Joseph and Angela Z., opened in Munich at the end of 1944, reveal the distinctive nature of letters sent between the front and home that came to be included in court files:

Dear Sepp [...]. I've already [...] told you that I don't appreciate getting just a couple of hastily jotted down lines. [...] At the moment I'm not worried about you at all, neither the Adriatic nor Ljubljana is the front, I know that much at least and I can picture what life's like there for German soldiers from stories told by German soldiers. [...] If you weren't such an overweening egoist, then maybe you'd remember for a second what my life is like. Working every day from morning to evening, [...] an air raid almost every day, a life surrounded by ruins separated from my child [...]. The child obviously doesn't interest you either. Do you really think that this amount of love and tenderness is enough to make someone who is still young stay with you? [...] When you're able to take leave again [...], then please go directly to Tulbeckstr. Frau P.'s [...] got the key. [...] Despite the war I don't want to completely mess up my young years. Your fall is unfortunate, but as far as I can remember, you also fell over in the Sudetenland and in Regensburg you banged yourself quite badly at the corner of the police headquarters, and it seems likely that we can file all this under the same heading.[77]

This couple proved unable to turn the wartime marriage they had entered into in 1943 into a sustainable relationship. From the wife's perspective, gender roles had been reversed: she claimed to be the one bearing the full brunt of the war, and she reproached her husband, who was stationed in rear areas, with neglecting his soldierly duty and regularly indulging in bouts of heavy drinking. Instead of heroic wounds, he was just suffering embarrassing injuries. The court went to some lengths to ascertain the wife's 'emotional coldness' and contrasted these quoted lines with the 'very obvious love letters' she had written to a new admirer. As that was also a long-distance relationship, it seems that it was not so much the separation itself but the specific dynamics of the wartime relationship that caused the couple's growing indifference towards each other. When it seemed that proceedings were to be adjourned, the petitioner's lawyer objected: he claimed that his client as a 'front-line soldier' with years of service behind him could not possibly be expected to accept a deferral; it was imperative that he be freed from the psychological burden that his wife's 'vile infidelity' had caused him.[78]

Finally, there are divorce files which reveal how some soldiers were mentally destabilised by their experience of combat. For Anna and Karl B., their marital problems began when female neighbours denounced Anna in letters to her husband, accusing her of immoral conduct and

---

[77] StAM, Landgerichte 17420, Verfahrensakte Az 24/45, Protokoll der nichtöffentlichen Sitzung am Landgericht München, 23 March 1945.
[78] Ibidem.

alleging that she regularly received male visitors at night. Anna's response was she had asked her brother-in-law to stay because she was afraid of air raids and did not want to be alone. To investigate the rumours, Karl B. engaged a detective agency while on home leave from the Eastern Front in March/April 1943. A picture emerges from the court records of an intractable situation produced by separation, miscommunication and the sense of sheer helplessness that soldiers often felt when far away. The husband committed suicide while on home leave and it was his parents who filed for a ('post-mortem') divorce, although the relationship had seemed a happy one before its final downturn:

> As B. let himself be provoked into slapping his wife while playing cards on his last [...] home leave [...], she, who in any case was suffering from his changed character, told him that she wanted a divorce. [...] B. had slapped his wife at least twice during his final leave, once after the last marital intercourse. [...] As Frau B., who wished to avoid encountering her husband, lay down to sleep in another room, B. barged in and pleaded with his wife the whole night long to forgive him, [...] and the next morning he brought her a bunch of flowers, asking that she forgive him and saying that his shattered nerves were to blame for everything.[79]

Many court records provide examples of soldiers' relationships where doubts about a spouse's fidelity erupted into sudden and unexpected domestic violence. Jealousy was evidently involved in this case too, but it is striking that both sides during the proceedings cited the man's 'change in character', 'moodiness', use of strange turns of phrase and occasional bouts of apathy. The lawyer of the respondent tried to trace the changed behaviour to a mental problem caused by a brain injury suffered at the front, doubtless in the belief that an emotionally disturbed homecomer would not fit the judge's view of the National Socialist and military ideal of the fighting man. This suggestion was, however, refuted by an excerpt from the muster book containing the man's medical record; it seems, therefore, that traumatic war experiences rather than injury were the decisive factor in this marital estrangement.[80]

Conclusion

The National Socialist regime attached great importance to home leave because it considered the continued existence of a private place of refuge to be decisive for the outcome of the war. A similar logic applied to

---

[79] StAM, Landgerichte München 1, 17353, Aktenzeichen 3 R. 140/44, Vernehmungsprotokoll, 28 May 1943, letter by Rechtsanwalt Dr. K. dated 24 April 1944, Protokoll der Nichtöffentlichen Sitzung, 1 March 1945.
[80] See ibidem.

questions of food supply and distribution: here too, the Nazi leadership sought to learn from the real and imagined mistakes of the First World War. Accordingly, the regime did not simply demand that the population made sacrifices. Instead, the regime's persuasive suggestions that normality could still prevail under wartime conditions inevitably entailed making concessions to family life. The view of the Nazi leadership was that it was crucial to stave off another revolution, a repeat of the alleged 'stab in the back' of 1918, and this meant going to great lengths to maintain the morale of wartime society. It was thus the question of morale above all that guided policy on home leave; other utilitarian considerations, for example increasing the birth rate, remained secondary.

The pragmatic demands that the National Socialist leadership placed on home leave resulted in attempts to manipulate this private space. These efforts were premised on an assumed link between domestic harmony and soldiers' readiness for combat. Such a connection was in turn entwined with gendered role ascriptions: narrowly defined conventions of behaviour were laid down to which soldiers and their relatives during home leave were expected to adhere. In particular, it was seen as the task of women to rejuvenate the fighting spirit of the men: limits were accordingly placed on any aspirations for autonomy on the part of soldiers' wives. Regime goals were clearly in conflict here. On the one hand, the regime exhorted married women in wartime to take on new tasks in addition to running a household; on the other, it demanded that classic roles and behaviour patterns be restored during home leave. War wives were the object of flattering propaganda suggesting that their efforts, whether within or outside the home, elevated them to the status of comrades of their menfolk. But such messages to women amounted essentially to rhetorical compensation which ultimately reaffirmed the primacy of the military ideals.

Above and beyond the purpose of offering soldiers the chance to relax and rekindle their relationships, home leave also fulfilled a bridging function between the military and civilian worlds. For the soldiers, re-establishing their ties to civilian life was supposed to bring with it a renewed sense of purpose and appreciation of what they were fighting for; the reconnection with home thus harboured the promise of a better future, even if this hope faded over time. Up to a point, the authorities realised the importance of leaving soldiers and their families to their own devices during home leave. As long as family members' behaviour remained within the bounds of desired norms, then the influence of the state was largely limited to subtle persuasion and informal pressure exerted before and after leave in the military environment and at home via the neighbourly milieu. However, if soldiers or members of their family overstepped certain boundaries, the National Socialist regime resorted to coercion. Here, again, the authorities upheld the double sexual standard by enforcing legal decisions hostile to women while affording men scope to exercise 'masculine' freedoms. However, for all the power of the authorities to intervene in private matters, court records also indicate that individuals did have some scope for evading control and defending private privileges.

Letters reflecting the wishes and expectations of home leave demonstrate the strategies used to maintain relationships despite wartime separation. Inevitably, the more that partners' experiences diverged, the greater the threat of tension and misunderstandings during home leave. Where partners did succeed in upholding a harmonious relationship, their hopes and desires did not have to coincide with the expectations of the regime. But the widespread desire to use home leave to retreat into a refuge of privacy with one's closest relatives and loved ones nevertheless tended to stabilise the dictatorship. Despite the very different motivations involved, individuals' hopes associated with home leave and the regime's expectations of its function appear to have been commensurable.

Letters and diaries can also offer insights into the complex shifts in roles that took place during the war: alongside instances where conventionally gendered role ascriptions were cemented, there are others where very different dynamics were in play, even if only for the duration of the war. That said, ego-documents, in particular letters, need to be approached with some caution, since they may understate the mechanisms eroding family relationships during the war and shed only limited light on regime intrusions into the private realm. Court records can offer something of a corrective here, since they illuminate more clearly how the claims of the institutions of the military and the family came increasingly into conflict as the war progressed. Such conflicts make visible how far models of behaviour prescribed and enforced by public institutions could collide with the values and codes prevailing in the private realm.

11 Working on the Relationship
Exchanging Letters, Goods and Photographs in Wartime

Andrew Stuart Bergerson, Laura Fahnenbruck and Christine Hartig

Hilde Laube was born in 1920 to a working-class family in rural Saxony. Her family's lack of resources prevented her from pursuing her desired career as an infant nurse or kindergarten teacher; she found work instead in a textile factory. But Hilde wanted more from life, as this criticism of her mother suggests:

[Mother] is so modest; she yields to her fate and does not dare to make any demands of life. [...] Every one of us has the right to be happy. And if we feel courageous and powerful enough to change our fate of our own volition – who can stop us?[1]

Thirteen years her senior, Roland Nordhoff was also dissatisfied. Born in 1907 to a middle-class family, he taught in the lower school (*Volksschule*) in Hilde's village. Both pious Christians, they met in choir at the Protestant church but rarely spoke. Social interactions with women were stressful for Roland. He preferred to spend his free time on his own at home or in nature. By 1938, he had become an inveterate bachelor. Then Roland was suddenly relocated to a village on the other side of Saxony for disciplinary reasons. On 4 May, shortly after his departure, Hilde sent a letter to Roland out of the blue. She confessed her secret affection, requested a rendezvous and utterly destroyed Roland's equanimity.

Making a virtue out of a necessity, Hilde and Roland used this regular exchange of letters as the primary site for their courtship. They took great pains to keep their correspondence a secret, fearing the judgement of neighbours and even their parents. They repeatedly insisted that each must determine for themselves, independent of external influences, if their attraction was true love. They wrote these letters from the intimate spaces of their

---

[1] Andrew Stuart Bergerson et al. (eds.), *Trug und Schein: Ein Briefwechsel*, vols. 1–4: 1938–41 (2013–16), www.trugundschein.org, downloaded spring 2017 (henceforth: T&S). Nr. 380715-2-1. In this signature, the first number refers to the date in reverse order (YrMoDy); the second to the author; and the third to which letter on that day, if the author wrote multiple letters on the same day. '380715-2-1' thus refers to the first letter that day from Hilde on 15 July 1938. The names of both correspondents are pseudonyms.

rooms; shared deep feeling and interests; and developed their own idiolect, nicknames and salutations. Yet their seemingly private relationship as a couple was in fact embedded in broader economic, political and social contexts. As shown in an earlier essay, Hilde and Roland used connections to parents, friends, God and the Führer to bolster their young relationship, just as these microsocial relationships legitimised macrosocial ones.[2] To some degree, both resented the demands for public participation coming from the Nazi Party and feared what might happen if Roland were conscripted. The more they planned a future together, however, the more they imagined it as members of the *Volksgemeinschaft*.

In her latest publication, Christa Hämmerle hints at a paradoxical kind of privacy at work in Austrian love letters during the two world wars.[3] Letter writing re/created 'a space for encounter' that re/invoked familiar emotions of love. Hämmerle admits that this evocation of privacy often held a compensatory and cathartic function for soldiers, but she avoids reducing what she calls a 'couple cosmos' (*Paarkosmos*) to a sphere of privacy distinct from the public. She correctly insists that this performative space served as a primary locus for the 'persistent entanglement' of private and public in terms of language, emotions, materials, relationships and goals. It would also be a mistake to define this space for encounter too rigidly as either factual or fictive, material or conceptual. The exchange of letters, photographs, goods and services was embedded within the war's larger material, emotional and political economies. Already permeated by 'the imagination of presence in absence', a couple cosmos provided a useful medium for authors to adjust their selfhood to the cultural, social, economic and political norms of a *Kriegsgemeinschaft* (war community). Hämmerle concludes convincingly that the practices of letter writing helped ordinary people on both the war and the home fronts to 'persevere' – that is, to commit to the war effort 'often to the very end'.

Hilde and Roland's correspondence illustrates the performative nature of this couple cosmos. For several reasons, Roland bristled at the anticipation of his public wedding ceremony on 13 July 1940. Hilde wrote that her father wanted their pastor to officiate over the wedding, but this pastor was a German Christian – a splinter movement that dejudaised

---

[2] See Andrew Stuart Bergerson, 'Das Sich-Einschreiben in die NS-Zukunft: Liebesbriefe als Quelle für eine Alltagsgeschichte der Volksgemeinschaft', in Detlef Schmiechen-Ackermann et al. (eds.), *Der Ort der 'Volksgemeinschaft' in der deutschen Gesellschaftsgeschichte* (Paderborn, 2018), 223–41.

[3] See Christa Hämmerle, 'Gewalt und Liebe – ineinander verschränkt: Paarkorrespondenzen aus zwei Weltkriegen, 1914/18 und 1939/45', in Ingrid Bauer and Christa Hämmerle (eds.), *Liebe schreiben: Paarkorrespondenzen im Kontext des 19. und 20. Jahrhunderts* (Göttingen, 2017), 171–230.

Christianity for Nazi purposes. On 3 July, Roland protested against this choice philosophically: in the face of a secular society, he did not support any further fragmentation of the Church. But primarily, he did not like outsiders interfering in the decisions of a soon-to-be married couple. In his letters of 5 and 6 July, he braced himself for having to address the needs of their relatives. He only really wanted to celebrate with Hilde in private. 'In your castle, in your room', he wrote on 6 July, they would 'enclose one another in each other's arms and dream away the first days of our life together'.[4] Only after they were 'free from all observation and invasiveness', only after they entered into this '*closed circle*, fully covert and secret', just 'me and you, Dearest, Sweetheart', then 'we will be happy'.[5] Looking forward to performing this closed circle of newlywed bliss in person, Hilde and Roland first performed it in letters – and long before those letters became a war correspondence.

This couple cosmos was never actually isolated from the larger world. The newlywed Nordhoffs were able to purchase their furniture, for instance, only thanks to a marriage loan from the regime. Established in 1933, such loans were only available to German couples if they could prove their 'Aryan' ancestry and eugenic health.[6] The ideological aspects of this policy were largely irrelevant to Hilde and Roland, however. Whereas they enjoyed researching their genealogical histories, they experienced the bureaucratic process of soliciting an 'Aryan' certificate as bothersome. Moreover, Hilde regarded the required gynaecological exam as a radical invasion of her privacy.[7] 'Dearest, you buck every undue demand quite decidedly,' Roland admonished her in advance, 'only to run the risk that our loan will not be granted'.[8] Within the conditions of their everyday lives, Hilde and Roland decided for themselves what was public and what was private.

As these two examples illustrate, their couple microcosmos was intricately entwined in macrohistorical relationships. In the tradition of *Alltagsgeschichte* and microhistory, this chapter seeks to explore the processes by which this intertwining took place in the everyday lives of Hilde and Roland.[9] Their large correspondence is useful for this purpose

---

[4] T&S 400706–1–1.

[5] T&S 400705–1–1, our italics. 'Nun schließt er sich ganz der Kreis voll Heimlichkeit und Traute'.

[6] See Gabriele Czarnowski, '"Der Wert der Ehe für die Volksgemeinschaft": Frauen und Männer in der nationalsozialistischen Ehepolitik', in Kirsten Heinsohn, Barbara Vogel and Ulrike Weckel (eds.), *Zwischen Karriere und Verfolgung: Handlungsräume von Frauen im nationalsozialistischen Deutschland* (Frankfurt a.M., 1997), 78–95.

[7] See T&S 400526–2–1.   [8] T&S 400222–1–1.

[9] See Alf Lüdtke, 'Arbeit, Arbeitserfahrungen und Arbeiterpolitik: Zum Perspektivenwechsel in der historischen Forschung', in Alf Lüdtke, *Eigen-Sinn: Fabrikalltag, Arbeitererfahrungen und Politik vom Kaiserreich bis in den Faschismus* (Hamburg, 1993), 351–440; also Alf Lüdtke, 'Geschichte und Eigensinn', in Berliner Geschichtswerkstatt (ed.), *Alltagskultur, Subjektivität*

precisely because it extends before, during and after the war. After Roland was enlisted in the navy in August 1940, they both revived many of the same epistolary practices from their courtship to maintain their relationship in wartime conditions. In this chapter, we focus on the period from August 1940 to March 1942.[10] To work on the relationship, they re-invoked this closed circle from their honeymoon in the exchange of letters, goods and photographs. Through these exchanges, Hilde and Roland built a minimal degree of consensus between them not only about the future of their private happiness but also about their public integration into the *Kriegsgemeinschaft*. Our argument: the couple cosmos evoked in war correspondence proved an ideal locus for highly political fantasies of privacy.

Basic Training

Hilde left her job at the factory to prepare for the wedding and to adjust to her new role as a teacher's wife. She moved in with Roland's parents after their brief honeymoon, but their newlywed bliss lasted only a few weeks. As Roland described it in September 1940, he was reluctantly conscripted into the navy in August 'from his honeymoon' – which we read in the figurative sense of referring to their early marital bliss.[11] Like many young couples in this era, they spent the vast bulk of the war apart.[12] Bracing for another long separation, they turned back self-consciously to many of the practices established during their courtship. On 27 August 1940, Roland began his very first letter on his way to basic training by returning to their idiolect: 'Dearest Sweetheart, my dear, dear [Hilde]! This salutation from our courtship, from the period of waiting, is going to have to have currency for a while longer.'[13] They even transposed embodied practices of intimacy onto letter writing: kissing their letters, for instance, and

---

und Geschichte: Zur Theorie und Praxis von Alltagsgeschichte (Münster, 1994), 139–53; Thomas Lindenberger, 'Eigen-Sinn, Herrschaft und kein Widerstand', Version: 1.0, in *Docupedia-Zeitgeschichte*, 2 September 2014, http://docupedia.de/zg/lindenberger_eigensinn_v1_2014; Paul Steege et al., 'The History of Everyday Life: A Second Chapter', *Journal of Modern History* 80/2 (2008), 358–78; Sigurður G. Magnússon and István M. Szijártó, *What Is Microhistory? Theory and Practice* (London, 2013).

[10] The correspondence lasted from 1938 to 1946 and consists of more than 4,000 letters. The names and locations of the protagonists have been kept as anonymous as possible. The letters are published on the T&S website seventy-five years or more after the date they were posted. Based on letters released thus far, this chapter is necessarily provisional. Compare to Bärbl Wirrer (ed.), *Ich glaube an den Führer: Eine Dokumentation zur Mentalitätsgeschichte im nationalsozialistischen Deutschland 1942–1945* (Bielefeld, 2003).

[11] T&S 400921-1-2.

[12] See Elizabeth Heineman, *What Difference Does a Husband Make? Women and Marital Status in Nazi and Postwar Germany* (Berkeley, CA, 2003).

[13] T&S 400827-1-1.

reading or writing them in bed. Yet where working on their relationship during their courtship had woven it into the *Volksgemeinschaft*, doing so in basic training embedded it into the *Kriegsgemeinschaft*.[14]

At first, Roland imagined that he could keep his private life apart from his public. He reported the events of his daily life with a matter-of-fact tone in the past tense. Framing this arid prose was an account of his inner experience including the act of writing the letter itself in the present. Roland typically imagined Hilde, or them together, in the home he left behind.[15] That fantasy even included erotic elements encoded in their idiolect such as closed, secret gardens to which Roland held the key.[16] Yet this rhetorical distinction did not stand the test of time, collapsing sometimes even within the same letter. It would be more accurate to say that both tones evoked an epistolary space for encounter between the two, as if they were meeting again at the end of a day's work.

Keeping this microcosmos for just the two of them was next to impossible in a barracks full of recruits. Roland's comrades wondered at the length of his letters.[17] You know,' he wrote on 1 September, 'I cannot always write this loving salutation if the others are standing all around me. But now I am sitting at a table all by myself and I can say what is in my heart.'[18] Roland wrote in bed during lunch break or outside in the sun while his comrades played games or smoked.[19] 'If I had not received a sign from home,' he wrote after receiving her first letter, 'I would have lost all connection to you in this manly environment and atmosphere of the barracks.'[20] But even when they were not directly 'looking over my shoulder longer than appropriate',[21] he was still sensitive to their presence. 'If my comrades saw this,' he wrote on 15 September, after expressing his love for Hilde, 'they would shake their head and laugh at me. Do you understand me? Yes, you, I am quite sure of it!'[22]

Roland defended this space for encounter with Hilde as much with fantasy as memory. 'Sweetheart!' he wrote on 7 September, 'I am so happy to know that you are at home, there where my thoughts hurry away to when I flee from this number- and men-operation to a better existence, to a happier world.'[23] Roland strove to maintain this emotional connection to Hilde throughout the day. 'When I think about the two of us, on the days of our togetherness,' he wrote on 1 September, 'it all seems to me like a dream, so far away, so delicate and finely spun. – And this dream will go along with me,' he continued, 'it stood at the entrance to this life in the barracks and may it become reality again, you!'[24]

[14] See Bergerson, 'Sich-Einschreiben'. [15] See T&S 400915-1-1.
[16] See T&S 400919-1-1. [17] See T&S 400827-1-1. [18] T&S 400901-1-1.
[19] See T&S 400903-1-1, 400915-1-1. [20] T&S 400903-1-1. [21] T&S 401007-1-1.
[22] T&S 400915-1-1, his underlining. [23] T&S 400907-1-1. [24] T&S 400901-1-1.

At the same time, Roland struggled with his new soldierly persona. He admitted to partaking in the jokes and teasing of his comrades, but insisted that he did not smoke or drink; he wrote letters instead.[25] He fantasised that he might be recalled to teach before the war was over and even rewarded with tenure for his brief service. Once he realised that his release from the navy depended on 'how the war developed further',[26] he hearkened closely to the latest reports and rumours for signs that the war might be over soon. A furlough could substitute for more permanent solutions but never wholly replaced them. As late as 4 October, Roland insisted that he was 'not a real soldier'.[27]

Roland did ultimately appropriate this soldierly persona for himself but, ironically, only after his comrades recognised his 'nonconformity'.[28] 'I have already conquered a position in which my peculiarity is respected,' Roland insisted on 13 September. 'I am seen also as a quiet and deep character. I secretly have fun with that.'[29] The way his comrades mocked him for his letter writing was part and parcel of initiating Roland into the Wehrmacht and pressuring him to conform to its organisational culture.[30] Roland also sought validation of his new persona from Hilde. 'Thus I am a comrade,' he continued, 'and still keep to myself, and remain wholly, wholly yours, Sweetheart! That is my great, inner joy, my whole happiness.'[31] Letter writing served as a crucial locus for the cultivation of this new soldierly self.

Notice how Roland's audiences for this role were intertwined through its performance. 'It takes a small dose of courage to claim your particularity,' Roland wrote two days later. 'In the end,' Roland continued, 'I am also really indifferent to what they all think of me if you understand me and trust me, and of that I am certain, Sweetheart!'[32] In fact, he sought a reciprocal kind of validation: from Hilde, supporting his claim to be different from his comrades, and from his comrades, that that difference lay in his attachment to her. Performing this new persona in the porous space of a couple cosmos thus 'authorised' it from both perspectives.[33]

Roland was not alone in trying to preserve his individuality. As Moritz Föllmer has shown, the Third Reich afforded racially fit 'Aryans' the

---

[25] See T&S 400913-1-1. [26] T&S 400915-1-1. [27] T&S 401004-1-1
[28] Andrew Stuart Bergerson et al., 'Nonconformity', in Andrew Stuart Bergerson et al. (eds.), *The Happy Burden of History: From Sovereign Impunity to Responsible Selfhood* (Berlin, 2011).
[29] T&S 400913-1-1.
[30] See Edward B. Westermann, *Hitler's Police Battalions: Enforcing Racial War in the East* (Lawrence, WI, 2005); Thomas Kühne, *Kameradschaft: Die Soldaten des nationalsozialistischen Krieges und das 20. Jahrhundert* (Göttingen, 2006); Thomas Kühne, *Belonging and Genocide: Hitler's Community, 1918–1945* (New Haven, CT, 2010).
[31] T&S 400913-1-1. [32] T&S 400915-1-1.
[33] Andrew Stuart Bergerson, Leonard Schmieding et al., *Ruptures in the Everyday: Views of Modern Germany from the Ground* (Oxford, 2017).

opportunity to cultivate their own selfhood so long as it conformed to the broader framework of the *Volksgemeinschaft* and later its war for living-space (*Lebensraum*).[34] The converse was also true of many Germans: cultivating a 'nonconformist' persona allowed for a sufficient degree of conformity.[35] Roland took pride in both aspects of his persona in his letter of 21 September. While telling Hilde about his fellow recruits, he again described 'Nordhoff' dualistically: as 'a calm, somewhat silent young man, of a deep character!' and as 'a good comrade who always has the same expression, avoids no work, even smiles too when he is detailed to clean the shooting house'.[36]

Commenting on the first photographs he sent home, Roland warned Hilde that basic training has changed his outward appearance. 'The soldierly, the jagged [*das Zackige*], which they are training us for right now, hardens the face.'[37] Through Hilde, Roland was exploring the dominant paradigm for selfhood in the Nazi military – what Frank Werner called 'soldierly masculinity'.[38] Yet the shadow in Figure 11.1 reminds us that Roland was performing this new self for his comrades too. His work on one relationship in his letters was indebted to his work on the other.

In his letters, Roland tended to avoid direct discussions of politics, most likely out of fear of surveillance.[39] Still, we know that Roland had a subscription to an antisemitic publisher and that he actively sought a larger political and spiritual meaning for his military service.[40] He mentioned holding conversations with comrades during basic training in which he struggled to make sense of the war.[41] He stored photos of Hilde for safekeeping in his race-theory book.[42] By 10 November 1941 at least, he seemed to have come to some clarity for himself.

Yesterday, we heard the transmission of Hitler's speech. What daring, fanatic faith inspires this man: 'Fate has chosen me for a new order in Europe!' Anyone else would tremble at the scope and force of the world-transforming events that he set in motion and for which he is responsible. One has to marvel at him, this man! Hope and confidence infused his words. May this man continue to lead the fortunes of our people for a long time![43]

---

[34] See Moritz Föllmer, *Individuality and Modernity in Berlin: Self and Society from Weimar to the Wall* (Cambridge, 2013).
[35] Bergerson et al., 'Nonconformity'. [36] T&S 400921–1-2. [37] T&S 400908–1-1.
[38] Frank Werner, 'Soldatische Männlichkeit im Vernichtungskrieg: Geschlechtsspezifische Dimensionen der Gewalt in Feldpostbriefen 1941–1944', in Veit Didczuneit, Jens Ebert and Thomas Jander (eds.), *Schreiben im Krieg – Schreiben vom Krieg: Feldpost im Zeitalter der Weltkriege* (Essen, 2011), 283–94.
[39] See Christine Hartig, *Briefe als Zugang zu einer Alltagsgeschichte des Nationalsozialismus*, online publication, Hamburg 2018.
[40] See T&S 410527–2-1. [41] See T&S 400930–1-1. [42] See T&S 401005–1-1.
[43] T&S 401110–1-1.

Figure 11.1 Roland in uniform, autumn 1940, *Trug und Schein* (T&S) Ff2.16, reproduced by kind permission of the family.

These facts suggest that Roland was thinking seriously about the ideological goals of the war and had appropriated Nazi principles to some degree like many other enlisted men.[44] Clearly, his outsider persona

---

[44] See Christa Hämmerle, 'Between Instrumentalisation and Self-Governing: (Female) Ego-Documents in the Age of Total War', in François-Joseph Ruggiu (ed.), *The Uses of*

prevented him neither from performing his military duties well nor from identifying with the Nazi war effort.[45]

Their couple cosmos was a primary locus in which Roland adjusted his persona to this new soldierly self. 'Now we must wait patiently with all of the many, many others,' Roland wrote on 19 September.

> They are all full of hope that every day will bring us closer to a better, happier life. Secretly we are building further towards our happiness, Sweetheart, you and I, a[nd] sometime later we will see that it is good that things happened as they did, that this time that challenges us was not wasted.[46]

Through their couple cosmos, Roland and Hilde connected their 'secret' work of 'building' their relationship to a global set of 'challenges' that – they insisted – were taking place for some 'good' reason. These chimeras of future private happiness not only circumscribed the scope of Roland's concern to the members of the *Kriegsgemeinschaft* but also aestheticised the violence of Germany's war for *Lebensraum*.

Managing the Home Economy

During the war, many everyday items were rationed as part of the controlled economy. Still, many Germans were able to expand their opportunities to consume through informal practices. They included: trade for rationed goods (hamstering) or for goods on the street (black market) through money or barter; or the direct barter of ration coupons. Many of these activities were ordinary parts of informal social relationships. The Nazi regime strove to combat such activities with propaganda campaigns and police sanctions, but these practices were often tolerated, especially when the goods were not otherwise available. Germans also supplemented their resources by shipping home loot from the Nazi war of conquest.[47] Hilde and Roland participated in these practices – also before

---

First Person Writings/Les usages des écrits du for privé: Afrique, Amérique, Asie, Europe (Oxford, 2013), 263–84; Klaus Latzel, 'Die Zumutung des Krieges und der Liebe – zwei Annäherungen an Feldpostbriefe', in Peter Knoch (ed.), *Kriegsalltag: Die Rekonstruktion des Kriegsalltags als Aufgabe der historischen Forschung und der Friedenserziehung* (Stuttgart, 1989), 204–21; Inge Marszolek, '"Ich möchte Dich zu gern mal in Uniform sehen": Geschlechterkonstruktionen in Feldpostbriefen', *WerkstattGeschichte* 22 (1999), 41–59; Clemens Schwender, 'Feldpost als Medium sozialer Kommunikation', in Veit Didczuneit, Jens Ebert and Thomas Jander (eds.), *Schreiben im Krieg – Schreiben vom Krieg: Feldpost im Zeitalter der Weltkriege* (Essen, 2011), 127–38.
[45] See Bergerson, Schmieding et al., *Ruptures*, chapter 5. [46] T&S 400919-1-1.
[47] See Götz Aly, *Hitlers Volksstaat: Raub, Rassenkrieg und nationaler Sozialismus* (Frankfurt a.M., 2005).

Roland was conscripted. Many of the goods acquired in these ways became key features and fixtures of their couple cosmos, where they not only generated trust in the war economy but adopted and adapted the war's principles of inclusion and exclusion.

With the exception of an extra allowance for heavy labourers, the German ration system at first ensured a relatively even distribution of foodstuffs and other daily necessities among members of the *Volksgemeinschaft*. 'For the most part, I agree with these measures,' Hilde wrote on 10 November 1939, shortly after the Nazi regime introduced the controlled economy. For the rules 'are being applied equally to everyone'. She also compared the Third Reich's policies to that of the Second. To avoid 'situations like 1914', she continued, the Wilhelmine authorities 'should have distributed grocery and ration cards as soon as the stocks of foodstuffs had begun to decline'. This time, 'these precautionary measures are being taken while the stocks of groceries and other goods are (still) there. There is no opportunity for us to hamster.'[48]

Yet these so-called Unity Cards were cancelled after 25 September 1939. For the rest of the war, this ration system not only reduced the quantity of distributed goods but did so increasingly according to Nazi logic of racial and economic utility.[49] Roland observed these distinctions even in the relatively good provisioning provided in the barracks. In keeping with the Nazi valorisation of the military, soldiers received a rich diet in comparison to civilians. Such preferential treatment must have been particularly noticeable not only to Roland as a lower school teacher but also to working-class men with memories of unemployment in the 1920s and early 1930s.[50]

Hilde and Roland's informal consumption practices actively shaped both the *Kriegsgemeinschaft* and their couple cosmos. Hilde wrote about her first 'hamstering trip' while Roland was in basic training:

Got everything you need. Only no chocolate. I would so very much have liked to sweeten the shipment of paper a bit. But perhaps you will like the gingerbread our

---

[48] T&S 390910–2-1.
[49] See Christoph Buchheim, 'Der Mythos vom "Wohlleben": Der Lebensstandard der deutschen Zivilbevölkerung im Zweiten Weltkrieg', *Vierteljahrshefte für Zeitgeschichte* 58/3 (2010), 299–328.
[50] See Lutz Niethammer, 'Heimat und Front: Versuch, zehn Kriegserinnerungen aus der Arbeiterklasse des Ruhrgebietes zu verstehen', in Lutz Niethammer (ed.), '*Die Jahre weiß man nicht, wo man die heute hinsetzen soll*': *Faschismuserfahrungen im Ruhrgebiet* (Berlin, 1983), 163–232, 168.

baker baked? My Dear! These days we must keep our chin up, not lose our courage!⁵¹

Just two weeks later, Hilde found a shopkeeper who understood her need for chocolate and sold her some without ration coupons: 'Yes, of course dear Mrs. [Nordhoff],' the woman said, 'I already heard that your husband is now also a soldier, so you naturally would like to send him something!'⁵² Hilde decided then and there to continue to buy at her store. Clearly, a large circle of people helped the men to adjust to their new roles as soldiers and the women to adapt to being soldiers' wives. They included, in Hilde's case, not only the 'chocolate lady' but also a shopkeeper who sold Hilde candles before the deadline⁵³ and her father who helped to 'pay' for a particularly well made article of clothing using his 'points'.⁵⁴ Roland encouraged these practices on 13 September: 'Hamster me some letter paper, also some envelopes.'⁵⁵ Not all of Hilde's purchases were for Roland, and these informal consumption practices contradicted the letter of the law, but they validated the underlying principles of the *Kriegsgemeinschaft*. Hilde and Roland overcame the memory of the First World War by showing the strong support of the home front for the war effort while also ensuring that the soldiers on the front received priority.

In these early years of the war, the Nazi command economy deepened Hilde's trust in the *Volksgemeinschaft*, but so too did her informal consumption practices. On 23 July 1941, she explained that potatoes were once again available, so people were standing in line again. 'Yesterday I obtained a ration coupon for them! There is hardly any other way to regulate it; otherwise there is nothing left for the tenth person.'⁵⁶ Even when she began to experience shortages, Hilde continued to emphasise the positive aspects of the rationing system. 'See,' she wrote a few days earlier after a successful hamster trip, 'right when things seem to have reached their worst, a way can be found and everything is fine again'.⁵⁷ To be sure, her thoughts did not always follow the Party line precisely. 'Good that I can stand for a long time,' she added in her letter of July 23. 'For people who have some kind of ailments, it has become a torture.'⁵⁸ Her support for the *Volksgemeinschaft* in this case seemed to run parallel to her Christian love of her neighbour. Similarly, according to the norms of patriarchy, men should provide for women, whether in the form of the father, husband, brother or state. During the war, however, it was women who organised and secured provisions for the family. 'How did I carry all

⁵¹ T&S 400902–2-1. ⁵² T&S 400915–2-1. ⁵³ T&S 401119–2-1.
⁵⁴ T&S 400903–1-1. ⁵⁵ T&S 400913–1-2. ⁵⁶ T&S 410723–2-1.
⁵⁷ T&S 410718–2-1. ⁵⁸ T&S 410723–2-1.

Working on the Relationship   267

of it?' she asked Roland rhetorically. 'With my own strong arms!'[59] At least for the time being, Hilde's pride in managing her home economy meshed smoothly with her concept of the *Volksgemeinschaft*.

Their informal consumption practices were also intertwined with the overarching goals of the war. Consider Hilde's desires for goods from those territories where Roland was stationed. Roland's shipments from the war zone were not limited to items like soap that were hard to find at home. Even before Roland was deployed, Hilde – the former textile worker – had learned at the Leipzig Trade Fair about the 'wonderful leather work' made in Bulgaria.[60] The war now made luxury goods like leather handbags and gloves accessible to her. Thanks to Roland's deployment in Bulgaria – his first – she also learned about 'sought-after' products like embroidered blouses.[61] Once shipped back home, such articles of clothing publicly displayed Hilde's connection and commitment to the soldiers on the front.

The Nazi war of conquest found its way into Hilde's wardrobe more directly after Roland was deployed to Greece. In a single letter dated 20 February 1942, he described both how prices were rising in Greece and that it was causing famine among the Greek people.[62] After a meal one day, he walked around town and immediately found 'a pair of boots for the Love of my Heart'. He shared with Hilde the 'unquestionably distressing news' that the kinds of ration coupons needed for boots were hard to come by and that the boots were twice the cost without them 'because the price of leather has risen rapidly'. The next day, he 'went right out again to invest my money before it loses any more value' by purchasing 'a pair of shoes for my Sweetie'. Then Roland described the Greeks he encountered while shopping:

In town, you see the many haggard, ill-tempered faces. There is little to eat [*beißen*]. A father stood on one corner with 4 children ages one to four years old. He carried the youngest on his arm. The other three crouched next to him – gaunt, emaciated, like ghosts; it is almost certain that two of them cannot be saved from death by starvation. It was a shocking sight.

Their suffering was caused by the systematic plundering of the Greek economy by the Germans. Yet Roland did not make a connection to either his official role in the occupation or his purchases of gifts for Hilde. Rather, he insisted, their suffering:

---

[59] T&S 410728-2-1.   [60] T&S 410407-2-1.   [61] T&S 410404-2-1.
[62] See T&S 420220-1-1, here and following quotes. Also see Mark Mazower, *Inside Hitler's Greece: The Experience of Occupation, 1941–1944* (New Haven, CT, London, 2001).

is an accusation of the Greeks themselves. Should they not be lending a helping hand to the most impoverished, like comrades? Soon the sun will shine more warmly and the lot of many people will become more bearable.

Roland's response ran parallel to the principles and policies of the Nazi war of conquest and extermination. He set narrow limits on his compassion for others by turning his emotional attention back to their couple cosmos.

Oh, my little treasure! How well can we live here and you there in contrast to them [the Greeks]! You! My tongue and palate are not quite accustomed to all of the good things that you serve to me. I have to get used to 'uniform food' again.

Through the practices of both letter writing and consumption, Roland closed ranks with Hilde and the *Kriegsgemeinschaft*.

Hilde's reply on 3 March followed a similar pattern.[63] She expressed her excitement about the shoes, returning to the Greeks a few paragraphs later.

Love of my Heart! It caused me so much pain when you told me in your message [*Bote*] about the poor, half-starved, little children. But you don't see such sorrow here in Germany. Perhaps it cannot ever go so far here at home; after all, the system for supplying the public with foodstuffs functions so well. And the social institutions in the Reich are such that every needy person gets cared for by it.

Hilde's confidence that they will not suffer from starvation was as much a product of her trust in the public system of rationing as in her confidence that she and Roland could expand their consumption informally on both fronts. Like Roland, she limited the scope of her concern for the people suffering from the war to 'Aryans'.

Oh, it is a good deed that gets done that way, for the poor are also just people like us, of German blood, all our neighbours [*Nächsten*]. Purely out of humanitarian feeling, one has to stand by them with aid. But true compassion is as seldom in the world as loyalty and truth.

At first, she too blamed the Greeks for their suffering.

The image provided to you by the city – is it not a grand indictment of the Greeks themselves? Do they not have to step in with aid to ameliorate the lot of the poor? The country itself is poor; it will certainly be a struggle to prevent such scenes, like the one you saw, from arising for the Germans.

An independent thinker, Hilde did then ask herself rhetorically: 'Who should be blamed that the Greek people have been made to suffer so?' But she does not follow this dangerous line of inquiry. 'We must be deeply

---

[63] See T&S 420303–2-1, here and following quotes.

thankful, Dearest, that you can live there so well,' she wrote instead, 'as we can too at home'. Like Roland, Hilde returned to the couple cosmos – constituted as much through the exchange of letters as the consumption of goods – whose political and emotional economy was circumscribed by the logic of the Nazi war for *Lebensraum*.

Lutz Niethammer has emphasised that, in post-war narratives, many Germans depicted the period of the war as 'lost years': as a 'hole of unstructured experiences' in which they could not make plans for the future.[64] Hilde and Roland certainly felt that they had to put their married lives on hold while he was at war, but they viewed it as only temporary. Already during the war, they planned for a secure and stable future none the least in terms of their consumption practices. After his conscription, Hilde had access to her husband's bank account. Although Roland did not demand precise accounting of the money she spent, she regularly reported her expenses to him. Describing a recent purchase, she asked Roland on 9 June 1941: 'Will you chastise? A beautiful lace cloth for our little smoking table, looks totally charming – it cost lots of money, 18 M!!' Hilde purchased many of these goods in anticipation of using them together after the war. 'The money was not wasted,' she insisted.

> It is all serving to decorate our home, You!! Your mother is also of the opinion that I should collect a complete service of Meissner dishes, as long as you are away. She is correct, for later it can be [avoided], since we will have so many other things, more pressing things, that we will need to do.[65]

These newly acquired goods provided inspiration for fantasies of post-war consumption. 'You are right,' Hilde wrote on 7 April, referring to his deployment to Bulgaria. 'We have to take this trip together again sometime and buy everything that we like!'[66] During the war, such purchases reminded Hilde and Roland of their absent partner, while they were designed to serve after the war as a reminder of the first years of their marriage. In both of these temporal dimensions, their informal consumption practices generated a couple cosmos that aligned with all of the most essential principles of the *Kriegsgemeinschaft* – in its social logic, empathic limits and political economy.

Through the exchange of both letters and goods, Hilde and Roland 'settled in'[67] to both their marriage and the war effort. To be sure, Hilde and Roland had their own interpretation of what these terms meant: *Volksgemeinschaft, Kriegsgemeinschaft, Lebensraum*. Our point is that they

---

[64] Niethammer, 'Heimat', 168.   [65] T&S 410609–2–1.   [66] T&S 410407–2–1.
[67] Alf Lüdtke, 'Wo blieb die "rote Glut"? Arbeitererfahrungen und deutscher Faschismus', in Alf Lüdtke (ed.), *Alltagsgeschichte: Zur Rekonstruktion historischer Erfahrungen und Lebensweisen* (Frankfurt a.M., 1989), 224–82.

integrated themselves into them through their couple cosmos. That setting made it easier for them to imagine – both during and after the war – that they were somehow 'retreating' into a private sphere.

Finding Beauty

In November 1941, Roland tried to bring Hilde some joy. It had grown cold in Germany; he knew from experience that Hilde would find few flowers on her walks in the country, so he included a flower in his letter: 'cross-leaved heath – a souvenir from my walk'.[68] Hilde and Roland engaged in a wide variety of practices designed to beautify their and their partner's lives. They exchanged pretty feathers and homemade cakes.[69] They identified certain stars as 'theirs' and thought of each other when they saw them. They discussed the details of films that they saw individually. They even arranged to listen to the same radio programmes at the same time as if they were home together[70] – a practice also encouraged by the regime. These practices seem ancillary to the main goal of letter writing, which was to maintain their relationship; but they created a common realm of aesthetic experience that bridged their vast separation. Along the way, these practices also aestheticised the war.[71]

Unlike during their courtship, the letters themselves became objects for display during the war. Hilde shared Roland's letters with family, though reluctantly with her mother, and she placed them on her bed like an altar.[72] Roland similarly decorated his writing desk at his office in Bulgaria with her letters and photos.[73] Visibly displaying these fetishes of their love for comrades, friends and family blurred the boundary between the personal and the political. When they arranged to listen 'together' to the radio, for instance, that included both the musical request programme (*Wunschkonzert*) and the military report.[74]

To be sure, picking flowers for your beloved, displaying their photos or listening to the radio together were quite ordinary practices for newly-weds. By continuing them during the war, Hilde and Roland arguably sought to create an experience of normalcy – or at least hoped for a return to normalcy sometime in the future. 'I wish that you could be with me now!!' Hilde wrote on 18 May 1941. 'But some things are just not yet

---

[68] T&S 411109–1-1.
[69] See T&S 410327–1-1; 410422–2-1; 410528–2-1; 410613–1-1; 410801–1-1.
[70] See T&S 410409–2-1.
[71] See also Laura Fahnenbruck, *Ein(ver)nehmen: Sexualität und Alltag in den besetzten Niederlanden* (Göttingen, 2017).
[72] See T&S 410519–2-1. [73] See T&S 420509–1-1.
[74] See T&S 410409–2-1; 410427–1-1.

possible. So, she continued, 'we will just have to tell each other about the Spring and our yearning'.[75] Such narratives aestheticised their separation. Calling for them both to 'bear and fight our way through everything', she anticipated that 'the fulfilment [of their yearnings] will then be all the more wonderful and precious to us!'[76] The couple interpreted their separation in war romantically as a test for their marriage that would only strengthen it. On 18 June, Roland wrote of the future: 'When we finally have each other again forever, then an even happier time will begin.'[77] They framed their situation in romantic terms, arguably, to make the present more bearable for the sake of the future.

Like Roland, Hilde sometimes criticised the regime. For instance, she got angry with 'the authorities' for 'their clumsy [dusslichen] decrees'.[78] Yet Hilde could criticise specific policies without abandoning her support for the war effort. 'Patience! That is often a hard word!' she wrote on 18 May. 'And yet we can hardly get by in our times without this word.' Because they had tied the story of their love to the war, losing patience with one would have amounted to giving up on the latter. Instead, they aestheticised their situation with flights of romantic fancy. While waiting for a furlough in the summer of 1941, Roland attested, 'by what darkness could the happiness of our love be vanquished?'[79] Hilde wrote similarly on 20 July, 'love could not be more beautiful or happy for any couple as it is for us – even in a fairy tale!'[80]

Much as Roland did with his comrades, Hilde often described their love not only as beautiful but also as unique. 'Only the thought of you,' she wrote on 1 July, 'of our beautiful, singular love, makes this life bearable for me'.[81] Hilde and Roland were not unique in doing so: they were giving meaning to their relationship using quite common motifs about romantic love. They liked to imagine that the love of these other couples was somehow less intense than theirs. On 9 April, Hilde criticised: 'With silent alienation, I listen as other women complain helplessly about their fate.' She wondered sceptically: 'Is their everyday life not also outshone by the grand happiness of love? Are they not also able to bear this time of anxious waiting thanks to this delightful feeling?'[82] Hilde was not making these comparisons only in her letters to Roland: she was also measuring their love and happiness against other people she encountered in everyday life. Similarly, 'this life' and 'this anxious time of waiting' represented both their separation in particular and the war more

---

[75] T&S 410518–2–1. [76] T&S 410618–2–1. [77] T&S 410618–1–1.
[78] T&S 410518–2–1. [79] T&S 410709–1–1. [80] T&S 410720–2–1.
[81] T&S 410701–2–1. [82] T&S 410409–2–1.

generally. This romantic belief in the singularity of their love aestheticised their relationship as well as its local and global contexts.

Our point is that these practices embedded their relationship both figuratively and interpersonally in its wider context. 'For your sake I can be so strong – ', Hilde wrote on 1 July, 'only for your sake will my courage never falter!'[83] Whether her self-admonition to persevere was referring to the steadfastness of her love or to her commitment to the war effort is ambiguous – and for good reason. It was precisely the relationship between love and war that was obfuscated by beautifying them both.

Collecting Memories

Because of their romantic faith in the singularity of their love, Hilde strove to preserve a record of this important period in their lives. In her letter of 18 May 1941, Hilde looked 'with pride and the happy joy of ownership' at the ever-growing 'document folder' in which she archived their correspondence.[84] She recommended that Roland always write in ink because 'it does not fade as much!' She then gave a particular significance to the letters he was sending from his desk in Bulgaria:

> Your reports, they are witnesses, everlasting witnesses to these dangerous days. And later, when we read them again together, the memory of those days will once again pass just as vividly before our eyes as they do now. [...] Everything that I receive from your hands will be preserved forever.

It was a special time: the joy of being newlyweds, the separation of war, the excitement of grand historical events. With the idea in mind of advising her children, Hilde asked herself whether she should let them read these letters. She decided: when they reach an age when they are thinking of marriage for themselves. She thus framed Roland's wartime service in a larger narrative of marital love that crossed generations. What began as letters reporting on their everyday lives increasingly became an historical record.

The photographs only began to take a larger role in Hilde's collection in their own right during Roland's first foreign deployment in Bulgaria. At first, Roland described his photography as part of his daily activities. On 20 April, he wrote that the day 'was heralded by peeling potatoes, cleaning and brushing, inspection, and a rather meaningless remembrance of the Führer's birthday'.[85] It was in this

---

[83] T&S 410701–2-1. [84] T&S 410518–2-1, here and following quotes.
[85] T&S 410421–1-1.

kind of context that he included reports about snapshots they took at odd times in the day. On 1 April, he wrote: 'I am not so OK with my portrait: 1. I am unshaven, 2. My clothes got a little dishevelled from the steep climb. So, we hope that the next images will be better.'[86] Describing his photography made sense here too in that he often asked Hilde to develop the negatives for him. But photography became an end in itself once Hilde decided that these photos could record their family history. As she wrote on 16 April:

Photography is not too expensive for you, for us. These are irretrievable opportunities – everlasting mementos of a grand time! Of Papa's time in the military! When I consider that our little boys and girls will see these images!! You! : [sic] Preserve them well – we will make a special album![87]

German military authorities actively encouraged soldiers to take pictures of themselves and the countries they occupied.[88] German soldiers not only adapted these popular tropes of tourism to their military activities but also embedded those tropes in their own biographies.[89] Hilde did so in terms of the history of their family.

Around the same time, Roland began to go out intentionally on photo jaunts to capture the scenery, akin to a tourist on a holiday. 'Yesterday at 2 PM, we went on an excursion,' he wrote on 6 April from Plovdiv (Figure 11.2, 11.3). 'We made our way to the mosque through a rather unadulterated Bulgarian quarter – dirty and topsy-turvy. Your Hubo' – Hilde's nickname for Roland – 'climbed it yet again for the sake of taking photographs'.[90]

Such sightseeing tours were also very much in keeping with the way that the German military wanted the men to make sense of the war. The military instructed soldiers about each country and people in order to guide how they made sense of their foreign environment and praised them for their photos when submitted for competitions. Photography was part and parcel of the way the military organised

---

[86] T&S 410401-1-1. [87] T&S 410416-2-1.
[88] See Bernd Boll, 'Das Adlerauge des Soldaten: Zur Fotopraxis deutscher Amateure im Zweiten Weltkrieg', *Fotogeschichte* 85–86/22 (2002), 75–86; Bernd Boll, 'Das Bild als Waffe: Quellenkritische Anmerkungen zum Foto- und Filmmaterial der deutschen Propagandatruppen 1938–1945', *Zeitschrift für Geschichtswissenschaft* 54 (2006), 974–99; Petra Bopp, *Fremde im Visier: Fotoalben aus dem Zweiten Weltkrieg* (Bielefeld, 2009); Bernd Hüppauf, *Fotografie im Krieg* (Paderborn, 2015). On soldiers' photographs, see also Maiken Umbach's contribution to this volume (Chapter 5).
[89] See Alon Confino, 'Dissonance, Normality and the Historical Method: Why Did Some Germans Think of Tourism after May 8, 1945?' in Richard Bessel and Dirk Schumann (eds.), *Life after Death: Approaches to a Cultural and Social History of Europe during the 1940s and 1950s* (Cambridge, 2003), 323–47.
[90] T&S 410406-1-1.

Figure 11.2 Mosque, Plovdiv, Bulgaria, probably 5 April 1941. T&S Ff4.13, reproduced by kind permission of the family.

their free time.[91] Yet Roland deployed his camera, just as he had done with his letters, to re-invoke the closed circle of their marital happiness. 'It was good weather for taking close ups, and Hubo was keenly intent on capturing the most beautiful and unique things in pictures – and while doing so, he thought of his dear [Hilde], who will be the first to see his successes or his failures.'[92]

As we know from the analysis of retrospective interviews with soldiers, framing their military activities in terms of established tropes of tourism not only helped people at home to make sense of the war front; it also helped the soldiers themselves to come to terms with their military activities.[93] Roland's comrades posed for one another, went on photo excursions together, and looked forward to seeing how the photos turned out. Just before departing for Greece, Roland complained that he had difficulties getting enough local currency to develop film there. 'This time only, I will get them developed here because my comrades are all involved and interested; and not only them but also two Bulgarians and a German infantryman who appear in the other images as well.'[94] Roland's photography helped him to build community with his fellow soldiers and allies.

Simply developing the film expanded the scope of their couple cosmos to include informal social relations. 'You took wonderful pictures!' Hilde wrote excitedly on 27 May, after she developed some. 'Even the Optician G. praised you!'[95] We also know that soldiers exchanged photos among themselves, since similar or even identical motifs appear in many military photo albums [96] Once Roland found a steady group of comrades to share his leisure time, he explicitly suggested that Hilde should make copies of his photographs for his comrades. Hilde went further: assuming that other wives would want copies of these photographs – since they too must want to document the history of their families – she assumed the role of quasi-curator for the unit's 'photographic collection' (*Bildvermittlungsstelle*).[97] 'Everyone wants to have not only photos of themselves,' she reported by 16 April, 'but also all of the other images as well'. She began distributing them directly to the other wives. 'I will also order additional copies of all of

---

[91] See Stefan Hördler, 'Sichtbarmachen: Möglichkeiten und Grenzen einer Analyse von NS-Täterfotografien', *Vierteljahrshefte für Zeitgeschichte* 65/2 (2017), 259–71; Fahnenbruck, *Ein(ver)nehmer*; Klaus Latzel, 'Tourismus und Gewalt: Kriegswahrnehmungen in Feldpostbriefen', in Hannes Heer and Klaus Neumann (eds.), *Vernichtungskrieg: Verbrechen der Wehrmacht 1914–1944* (Hamburg, 1994), 447–59; Kerstin Wölki, 'Krieg als Reise: Die Wahrnehmung Frankreichs durch deutsche Soldaten im Zweiten Weltkrieg' (Magisterarbeit Freiburg, 2007).
[92] T&S 410406-1-1.
[93] See Konrad Köstlin, 'Erzählen vom Krieg – Krieg als Reise II', *BIOS. Zeitschrift für Biographieforschung und Oral History* 2/2 (1989), 173–82.
[94] T&S 410401-1-1.   [95] T&S 410527-2-1.   [96] See Bopp, *Fremde*.
[97] T&S 410615-2-1.

the images for K. and H., is that ok?'[98] Hilde even used this 'inside' information to advise Roland about which comrades he should befriend.[99] The circulation of these photos thus helped to build comradeship not only among the men in Roland's unit but also among their wives.

More to the point, this photographic correspondence served as a mechanism for the mutual confirmation of world-views between the home and war fronts. On 20 April, Roland provided an evocative narrative of his explorations that day[100]:

> We walked along the river on the rough, untended path along the river bank. [...] It was a beautiful, Easter-like image; we were reminded of home. [...] Then smells: 6 small slaughter houses along the bank, bladders and intestines drying in the air, garbage heaps in which Gypsy women rummaged for rags.

He described the negative qualities of this foreign country coincidentally.

> The Gypsies: we passed through their quarter on the way home. That such a dissolute, tattered people could exist in God's beautiful world. Every glance from their fellow human beings, every ray of sunshine, one should think, would have had to shame them for this licentiousness.

In this ordinary way, he connected old prejudices with contemporary circumstances.

> The clothing: stink unbelievably [sic]. Why these people endeavour to live so poorly, never employing themselves in some orderly, profitable labour. I wrote already that even the Bulgarians look askance at these Gypsy people.

Through their couple cosmos, Hilde and Roland adopted and adapted motifs of both tourism and racism to their family history.

Photography made this foreign world accessible to them by placing it within established frameworks of meaning. 'We climbed the chapel mountain,' he wrote on 9 November. By then, he was stationed in Thessaloniki. 'This time,' he insisted, 'we will get it to serve as our model'. Like many other travellers, he was referring to the scenery as his muse. Yet he was not a tourist in fact. 'Last time we climbed up,' he continued, 'we had spent all of our ammunition'.[101] Referring to his camera metaphorically as a weapon was not circumstantial.[102] He made this association between capturing the landscape with a camera and conquering it with violence by performing these two roles – the soldier and the tourist – at the same time.

---

[98] T&S 410416–2-1. [99] See T&S 410615–2-1.
[100] T&S 410420–1-1, here and the following quotes. [101] T&S 411109–1-1.
[102] See Rainer Rother and Judith Prokasky (eds.), *Die Kamera als Waffe: Propagandabilder des Zweiten Weltkrieges* (Munich, 2010).

Figure 11.3 Mountain climbers, Plovdiv, Bulgaria, probably 5 April 1941. T&S Ff4.8, reproduced by kind permission of the family.

A similar argument could be made for the goods that Roland purchased for Hilde while abroad. 'I cannot help but be fond of you in all of these pictures!' Roland wrote on 14 August. 'They came out really very well – you!!' He had given his wife that embroidered Bulgarian blouse when he was on leave; now he was in Greece and could still see how it looked on her in a photo. 'How finely it fits you and how fine it looks on you. That makes me so very happy!'[103] For her part, Hilde did more than hope that they would look at these letters and photographs together sometime in the future.[104] She planned that they would someday travel together along the same route that his unit took during the war, just as she was following his path with her finger on the atlas in her lap.[105] Yet Hilde could cross the Balkan peninsula with Roland as a tourist only if the Third Reich actually won its war for *Lebensraum*.

Selected, framed and narrated by the photographer, these images do not depict historical reality. They are the memory artefacts through which Hilde and Roland performed their couple cosmos. By using them to document the history of their love, they embedded that couple cosmos deeply in its cultural, social and political environment. This collaborative effort to memorialise their family history aestheticised the war. By appropriating its motifs, their photographs were another path through which they joined the *Kriegsgemeinschaft*. Thanks to the fact that they preserved these souvenirs of this special time in their lives, this consensus around the war probably survived in their relationship long after the regime had fallen. Still, Hilde and Roland would have no doubt insisted that they took these photographs for wholly private reasons.

Conclusion

Hämmerle's concept of a couple cosmos has helped us to demonstrate that practices designed to produce privacy actually have broad societal anchoring. Privacy is created through social practices that are deeply embedded in their political, economic, social and cultural contexts both near and far as well as past, present and future. In contrast to popular representation and even personal experience, privacy does not operate in everyday life as a space for retreat in any straightforward way. It may seem ironic that the closed circle of letter-writing lovers arises through microsocial interactions beyond the couple per se; but through them, the pair greatly expands their 'room for manoeuvre' (*Handlungsspielraum*).

For Hilde and Roland, imagining a happy and prosperous future for their family became the doorway through which they entered into the

[103] T&S 410814–1-1. [104] See T&S 410808–2-1. [105] See T&S 410404–2-1.

Kriegsgemeinschaft. Their faith in the uniqueness of their love inspired them to persevere through the long years of the war. That faith also convinced them to create these letters, goods and photos as a record of this momentous period in their lives. Rather than a global tragedy, they experienced the early 1940s as an historical achievement for Germany, as a special time in their married life and as beautiful. As Hilde wrote on 18 May 1941:

I am absolutely certain that this station in our life, too, will not pass us by without some deeper meaning. And I will wait to experience what God wants to teach us by it, what he wants to tell us, with patience, courage, and thankfulness.[106]

---

[106] T&S 410518–2-1.

12 Love Letters from Front and Home*
A Private Space for Intimacy in the Second World War?

Cornelie Usborne

In August 1940, Herbert Walter,[1] a young sculptor-recruit wrote from southern Poland to his wife, Katharina, in Berlin:

Dear Heart, my Kinka, my Best of All!

[...] You are a special woman by your very nature. So German and so profound. You've changed so much and for the better. You've become much richer and more resolute and that makes me so happy. You've given me so much love. You're such a wonderful woman. The war has been a process of purification for us both. You'll see that I've become stronger and more decisive. A lot has been made clearer. Oh Kinka, how I'd love to be with you and gaze silently into your beautiful eyes. I can smell your hair and smile at the memory of that time when you splashed me in the waves. [...] Oh when I think of all the happiness that lies ahead of us my heart bursts in expectation. Long live life. Long live heavenly bliss. Oh Kinka, how can I ever thank you for all your love.

I'm all yours for ever. Your madly in love husband

Herbert[2]

Herbert had met his future wife at the Berlin Art Academy. They had married in 1938 despite, as she put it, their 'different social backgrounds': his father was a customs officer originally from Lorraine; her father was a factory owner from Halle, Saxony and 'cultured and socially minded'.[3] When Herbert was called up for military service in May 1940, he had to part from Katharina and his small son, Mickel, in Berlin with another baby on the way. After a brief stay in France, he was stationed in occupied

---

* My thanks to the brilliant 'History Girls', Lucy Bland, Carmen Mangion, Clare Midgley, Alison Oram, Krisztina Robert and Katharina Rowold, for their supportive criticism, to Jenny Willis for expert translations of some of the letters; last not least to the British Academy for supporting research in Germany and Austria.
[1] To protect his privacy, this is a pseudonym, also used for all other correspondents unless they specifically permitted their names to be identified.
[2] Kempowski Biographienarchiv, Berlin (KBA), 0103, Herbert W. to Katharina W., 10 Aug. 1940 from Bad Rymanow.
[3] KBA, 0103, Katharina W. to Walter Kempowski, 20 May 1980.

Poland, then the Soviet Union, where he died two years later near Charkow.

Compare this to a note written at the end of August 1944 by a twenty-year-old railway clerk, Maria Kundera, from near Vienna to her fiancé, Hans Hatschek.[4] He was fighting on the Western Front and she had had no word from him for several weeks.

My Hänschen!

[...] Hänschen, today it all got much too much for me, no, if this goes on longer I can take anything except this appalling anxiety over you, Hänschen, that's the absolute worst. If only I knew if you actually got our letters so that at least you had that comfort but I'm not very hopeful. Hänschen, my dearest, you're probably just as worried about us as we are about you. But, Hänschen, everything's fine with us, don't fret. If we feel frightened from time to time we soon get over it.

My Hanserl, my everything, my love and longing just can't be described. Time to sleep now, then we can be together and happy beyond words.

With all my love and tender kisses

Your Mitzerl[5]

Maria Kundera grew up and continued to live in Kritzendorf, a popular weekend destination for the Viennese. She commuted daily by train along the Danube to Michelhausen, where she worked in the ticket office at the station. She had met Hans, a twenty-two-year-old paratrooper, in mid-November 1943, when he was on leave in Michelhausen, where his father was the station master and Maria's boss. Their whirlwind romance began in the final weeks before he had to rejoin his regiment in early January 1944, first in Germany and then in France. They had become secretly engaged. At the end of August, shortly after his twenty-third birthday, Hans was killed in the 'fortress' Brest in Brittany. News of this did not reach Maria until months later and she continued to write to him long after his death.[6]

Perusing Herbert's optimistic letters to his wife knowing that he would be killed, or Maria's heart-breaking notes to her by now dead fiancé is tricky for the historian. She is vulnerable to the charge of romanticising these epistles, yet she has to show empathy for the emotions expressed

---

[4] I have adopted Christa Hämmerle's fictitious name in her discussion of this correspondence in 'Gewalt und Liebe – ineinander verschränkt. Paarkorrespondenzen aus zwei Weltkriegen: 1914/18 und 1939/45', in Ingrid Bauer and Christa Hämmerle (eds.), *Liebe schreiben: Paarkorrespondenz im Kontext des 19. und 20. Jahrhunderts* (Göttingen, 2017), 171–230.

[5] Sammlung Frauennachlässe, Institute of History, University of Vienna (SFN), papers (NL) 75 II, Maria Kundera to Hans H., 29 Aug. 1944.

[6] See ibidem.

while balancing this with the necessary detachment for an objective critical assessment. A number of questions arise. For example, to what extent can such letters be regarded as 'authentic' traces of the writer's persona? How important were epistolary conventions or conversely, what effect did the lack of writing experience have? Should we conflate intimacy with privacy? Did couples who confided in each other their innermost feelings really live, as they often seemed, in a self-enclosed world, a '*Paarkosmos*', a space sealed off from the outside world, to borrow a phrase from Christa Hämmerle?[7] What social and cultural factors influenced their writing? How did the specific circumstances of life during the Second World War and under the Nazi dictatorship facilitate such entanglement of the 'private' with the 'public'? Were couples inhibited by censorship? Was sexual desire expressed explicitly or only obliquely?

Love letters are no different from other ego-documents, which always combine subjective thoughts and feelings with external influences, and they have to be understood in their historical context. However, historians may still hope to gain insights into the private emotions experienced by their authors. After a brief discussion of the historiography of *Feldpost* (field post), this chapter first makes the case for the importance of outside influences in personal letters and second argues that intimate correspondence could nevertheless constitute a refuge from the horrors of warfare and a regime whose repressions rapidly increased after 1939.

Love Letters and *Feldpost*

Literary and cultural studies scholars rather than historians have until recently led research into love letters, a genre which emerged in the eighteenth century and which was long dominated by the educated middle classes.[8] In the nineteenth century, the new bourgeois ideal of marriage became founded on love rather than chiefly on economic and social considerations, and this new emphasis on personal feelings also promoted the use of love letters, especially during the period of betrothal when the young couple lived apart and sought to strengthen their emotional bond.[9] The First World War created a similar situation when letters helped to bridge the

---

[7] Hämmerle, 'Gewalt und Liebe', 21.
[8] See Niklas Luhmann, *Liebe als Passion: Zur Codierung von Intimität* (Frankfurt a.M., 2001); Wolfgang Müller-Funk, 'Die Erfindung der Liebe aus dem Medium des Briefes', in Ingrid Bauer, Christa Hämmerle and Gabriella Hauch (eds.), *Liebe und Widerstand: Ambivalenzen historischer Geschlechterbeziehungen* (Vienna, Cologne, Weimar, 2009), 89–109.
[9] See Ingrid Bauer and Christa Hämmerle, 'Editorial', *L'Homme. Europäische Zeitschrift für Feministische Geschichtswissenschaft* 24/1, special issue on 'Romantische Liebe' (2013), 5–14, 5; Eva L. Wyss, 'Brautbriefe, Liebeskorrespondenzen, und Online-Flirts: Schriftliche

physical separation between couples; but now all classes took up writing. During the Second World War, writing to a spouse or sweetheart became the universal means for maintaining emotional ties. Correspondence by the well-off and educated strata probably conformed more clearly to the bourgeois concept of the love letter as 'the most intimate of all text genres' which was expected to reveal the self to the loved one in a more transparent fashion than in any other kind of letter, while the less privileged often found it hard to express feelings and concentrated instead on practical issues.[10] References to the mundane constituted, according to literary critics, 'the starting point and the way to maintain love'. Following the example of Bauer and Hämmerle, communications between couples are here considered as love letters even when they contain no explicit messages of affection.[11] The highly emotionally charged letters of my two case studies were almost certainly unrepresentative of many others in that genre. Take the Bavarian lawyer Albert Kremser, stationed with the general command in Trieste, Italy, his tone to his wife near Munich was rather matter of fact. Their affection for each other was more evident in the *Freßpakete*, food parcels, they sent each other.[12] She provided him with Bavarian *Gutzerl* (sweets) and other delicacies, and he in return sent her 'tobacco, little fish, biscuits, flour, rice and a few drops of cooking oil'.[13] Parcels were often vital to ward off hunger or frostbite or, as in this case, to provide luxuries in difficult times, but they also fulfilled an important emotional task.[14] Declarations of love were also in short supply in the letters between the newly wed Ingeborg and her much older officer husband, Wilhelm T. from Berlin. When he left for the front, she wrote that she was 'still like a romantic young girl who expects her first love letter'. Wilhelm replied in a friendly albeit business-like manner; indeed, many of his letters were dominated by his requesting material things: 'Dearest Ingele! Finally I have time to write – please don't be angry if I am brief – Of course we have forgotten something: hand towels!'[15]

Liebeskommunikation vom 19. Jahrhundert bis in die Internet-Ära', in Martin Luginbühl and Daniel Perrin (eds.), *Muster und Variation in Medientexten* (Bern, 2011), 81–123, 92ff.

[10] Ute Jung-Kaiser, 'Vorwort' in Ute Jung-Kaiser (ed.), *Intime Textkörper: Der Liebesbrief in den Künsten* (Bern, Vienna, Brussels, 2004), 7; Reinhard M. G. Nickisch, *Brief* (Stuttgart, 1991), 43, 15.

[11] See Ingrid Bauer and Christa Hämmerle, 'Liebe und Paarbeziehungen im "Zeitalter der Briefe" – ein Forschungsprojekt im Kontext', in Ingrid Bauer and Christa Hämmerle (eds.), *Liebe schreiben: Paarkorrespondenz im Kontext des 19. und 20. Jahrhunderts* (Göttingen, 2017), 9–56, 14.

[12] See KBA, 0020/1–2.

[13] KBA, 0020/1–2, Albert K. to his wife, Gerda, 4 Jan. 1945, 10 Jan. 1945, 1 Feb. 1945.

[14] See Hämmerle, 'Gewalt und Liebe', 194.

[15] Cited in Ingrid Hammer and Susanne zur Nieden (eds.), *Sehr selten habe ich geweint: Briefe und Tagebücher aus dem Zweiten Weltkrieg von Menschen aus Berlin* (Zurich, 1992), 146, Ingrid T. to Wilhelm T., 16 Apr. 1940; ibidem, 149, Wilhelm to Ingrid T., 14 Sept. 1941.

Recently, more historians have turned their attention to *Feldpost* since the two world wars had an explosive effect on personal correspondence to the extent that it has been called a 'democratisation' of the traditional craft of letter writing.[16] In the First World War, an estimated 28.7 billion and in the Second World War between 30 billion and 40 billion letters, marked *Feldpost*, were delivered.[17] The sheer number testifies to the practical and emotional importance of keeping in touch when face-to-face contact was increasingly curtailed as the war progressed.[18] Of course the representativeness of letters can be questioned because of their often haphazard survival, archivists' decisions or researchers' personal selections. Many historians exploring wartime correspondence, myself included, would not want to generalise their findings but rather shine a spotlight on specific life stories at a specific time and place. In this chapter, I indeed select a small sample of love letters, and, like other historians who face the dilemma of selection, I have added to the two case studies other letters by soldiers and, where they survived, their wives or fiancées, and have included letters by individuals from different social and geographical backgrounds.[19]

Only from the 1980s were there serious attempts to evaluate *Feldpost* for everyday lives of rank-and-file soldiers and their morale,[20] the relationship between soldiers and the Nazi regime[21] and, much later, about the experience of separation between couples or relatives.[22] The shift from a focus on soldiers' letters to those written from home, especially by wives

---

[16] Martin Baumeister, '"Feldpostbriefe und Kriegserlebnis": Reviews of Two Books by Klaus Latzel and Bernd Ulrich', *WerkstattGeschichte* 22 (1999), 97–9, 97.

[17] See Klaus Latzel, *Deutsche Soldaten – nationalsozialistischer Krieg? Kriegserlebnis – Kriegserfahrung 1939–1945* (Paderborn, 1998), 26.

[18] See Clemens Schwender, 'Letters between Home and the Front – Expressions of Love in World War II Feldpost Letters', 1, www.feldpost-archiv.de/english/e8-loveletters.html [accessed 10 March 2017].

[19] See Hammer/zur Nieden (eds.), *Sehr selten habe ich geweint*.

[20] See Ortwin Buchbender and Reinhold Sterz (eds.), *Das andere Gesicht des Krieges: Deutsche Feldpostbriefe, 1939–1945* (Munich, 1982); Wolf-Dieter Mohrmann (ed.), *Der Krieg hier ist hart und grausam! Feldpostbriefe an den Osnabrücker Regierungspräsidenten 1941–1944* (Osnabrück, 1984); Joachim Dollwet, 'Menschen im Krieg. Bejahung – und Widerstand? Eindrücke und Auszüge aus der Sammlung von Feldpostbriefen des Zweiten Weltkrieges im Landeshauptarchiv Koblenz', *Jahrbuch für westdeutsche Landesgeschichte* 13 (1987), 279–322; Latzel, *Deutsche Soldaten*; Bernd Ulrich, *Die Augenzeugen: deutsche Feldpostbriefe in Kriegs- und Nachkriegszeit 1914–1933* (Essen, 1997).

[21] See Latzel, *Deutsche Soldaten*.

[22] See Latzel, 'Die Zumutungen des Krieges und der Liebe – zwei Annäherungen an Feldpostbriefe,' in Peter Knoch (ed.), *Kriegsalltag. Die Rekonstruktion des Kriegsalltags als Aufgabe der historischen Forschung und der Friedenserziehung* (Stuttgart, 1989), 204–21; see, for the British experience, Michael Roper, *The Secret Battle: Emotional Survival in the Great War* (Manchester, 2010).

and girlfriends, took longer and was inspired by a new interest in gender and cultural history, including the history of emotions and sexuality.[23] From the early 1990s, pioneering efforts especially by women historians demonstrated the value of wartime correspondence for gendered attitudes and subjective perceptions of wartime circumstances, offering an 'interior view' of the war, as Inge Marszolek put it.[24] Hester Vaizey analysed Second World War correspondence to probe claims by Elizabeth Heineman and others that the war had undermined the institution of the family and fostered women's emancipation.[25] Nicholas Stargardt used to excellent effect the letters of a number of individuals, among them lovers and married couples, to explore why Germans continued to support the Second World War, as did Hämmerle in her most recent magisterial article comparing correspondence between couples during the First and the Second World Wars.[26]

While we are not short of soldiers' letters home, those by their wives or girlfriends are much harder to find. This is due to the more precarious postal service at the front and the loss of letters in combat.[27] Some soldiers took the precaution of taking them back on home leave.[28] The two case studies at the centre of this chapter reflect this gendered unevenness: Katharina Walter treasured every letter Herbert had sent but all hers to him got lost after his death. In 1980, she responded to a newspaper advertisement and donated the majority of Herbert's letters to the archive of the historian and novelist Walter Kempowski.[29]

---

[23] See Detlef Vogel and Wolfram Wette (eds.), *Andere Helme: Heimaterfahrung und Frontalltag im Zweiten Weltkrieg. Ein internationaler Vergleich* (Essen, 1995).

[24] See Hammer/zur Nieden (eds.), *Sehr selten habe ich geweint*; Inge Marszolek, '"Ich möchte Dich zu gern mal in Uniform sehen": Geschlechterkonstruktionen in Feldpostbriefen', *WerkstattGeschichte* 22 (1999), 41–59, here 46ff.; Ulrike Jureit. 'Zwischen Ehe und Männerbund: Emotionale und sexuelle Beziehungsmuster im Zweiten Weltkrieg', *WerkstattGeschichte* 22 (1999), 61–73.

[25] See Hester Vaizey, *Surviving Hitler's War: Family Life in Germany, 1939–48* (Basingstoke, New York, NY, 2010); Hester Vaizey, 'Empowerment or Endurance? War Wives' Experiences of Independence during and after the Second World War in Germany, 1939–1948', *German History* 29/1 (2011), 57–78; for England, see Philomena Goodman, *Women, Sexuality and War* (New York, NY, 2001); Elizabeth Heineman, *What Difference Does a Husband Make? Women and Marital Status in Nazi and Postwar Germany* (London, 1999); Sybille Meyer and Eva Schulze, *Wie wir das alles geschafft haben: Alleinstehende Frauen berichten über ihr Leben nach 1945* (Munich, 1984).

[26] See Nicholas Stargardt, *The German War: A Nation under Arms, 1939–45* (London, 2015), xxviii; Maria Kundera and Hans. H.; Hämmerle, 'Gewalt und Liebe'.

[27] See Hämmerle, 'Gewalt und Liebe', 174, 178; but, as she points out, the SFN in Vienna is evidence that more of women's letters were preserved than previously credited.

[28] See Hammer/zur Nieden (eds.), *Sehr selten habe ich geweint*.

[29] See KBA, 0103, K. W. to Walter Kempowski, 20 May 1980.

Maria and Hans' correspondence is a rare example of a reciprocal exchange, although there is no chronological overlap between the letters that have survived. Hans' seventy-one letters and eleven postcards were written between early January and mid-August 1944 whereas all of Maria's from the same period were lost in the fighting. Her thirty-two letters (plus one birthday card) start roughly where his end, and span the period from late July to late October 1944, two months after his death. They have survived because the military authorities had eventually returned them with the notice 'Return to Sender. Address unknown.'[30] When Maria was in her late seventies and had been married twice, she decided to donate her documents and letters to the Collection of Women's Personal Papers at the University of Vienna. Her letters to Hans which had been sent back to her unopened were still sealed, and those she had received by Hans were neatly tied with coloured ribbons.[31]

The Problem of Authenticity

Klaus Latzel warned against the glib assumption that *Feldpost* offered 'authentic' insights into wartime life as they only conveyed 'small segments' of experiences and emotions and left out much which could not or should not be expressed or was thought to be unspeakable.[32] Some front soldiers found it indeed impossible to admit shameful sensations of panic or to describe scenes of unimaginable brutality.[33] Hans always played down his own danger, probably to save Maria anguish. No doubt many soldiers also felt overwhelmed by the sudden necessity to keep up a flow of letters when writing was not their usual style of communication. One officer wrote to his wife from the front, 'you should not really have reasons to complain that I write too rarely – I think I have never written so much in one go, – and when everything has to be done so quickly. – The great

---

[30] SFN, 75 II.
[31] See SFN, 75 II; my thanks are due to Christa Hämmerle for granting me permission to study this wonderful source and her generous support and to Li Gerhalter for her patient help and information. Maria Kundera never opened her letters again and handed them over to the archive in a parcel tied with coloured ribbons where they were ceremoniously opened one day for research and postgraduate teaching. I owe this information to Li Gerhalter; see *Bestandsverzeichnis der Sammlung Frauennachlässe am Institut für Geschichte der Universität Wien* (Vienna, 2012), 176–7.
[32] Klaus Latzel, 'Feldpostbriefe: Überlegungen zur Aussagekraft einer Quelle', in Christian Hartmann, Johannes Hürter and Ulrike Jureit (eds.), *Verbrechen der Wehrmacht: Bilanz einer Debatte* (Munich, 2005), 171–82, 171–4.
[33] See Christa Hämmerle and Edith Saurer, 'Frauenbriefe – Männerbriefe? Überlegungen zu einer Briefgeschichte jenseits von Geschlechterdichotomien', in Christa Hämmerle and Edith Saurer (eds.), *Briefkulturen und ihr Geschlecht: Zur Geschichte der privaten Korrespondenz vom 16. Jahrhundert bis heute* (Vienna, Cologne, Weimar, 2003), 7–32, here 14ff.

struggle in the north east is still raging.'[34] The cultural historian Rebecca Earle also warns not to regard personal letters as 'windows into the soul of the authors'. Letters are, she argues, not as 'unmediated as a casual conversation' but rather an autobiographical representation of the self, albeit a self which was often unstable and changed according to whom the letter was addressed.[35] Michael Roper, writing about British soldiers' letters in the First World War, similarly suggests that writers adapted their style and sentiment according to whom they wrote.[36]

This is exactly what Maria Kundera did when writing to 'pen friends' in the years before she knew Hans. She adopted a 'cool, independent' persona, reminiscent of the 'New Woman' in Weimar Germany and very different from the passionate lover who bared her soul to her fiancé. Maria had duly complied with the regime's call for young single women to send letters, popularly known as 'love tokens', to as many young unknown and unmarried soldiers as possible to boost morale among the troops.[37] She corresponded with at least eleven young men, mostly village acquaintances but also some complete strangers. Nearly 500 letters from young recruits have survived and a few by her did as well, since they were returned with the stamp 'died in battle for Greater Germany'.[38] The sheer quantity of letters she received from a whole variety of young soldiers is probably proof of the regime's success in orchestrating contact between home and the battle front. However, it also shows soldiers' hunger for female contact and Maria's popularity among young men. Judging from their frequent complaints of her 'laziness' or 'negligence', she seems to have replied to her pen friends much less often or at least less often than they had wished. But she granted their urgent requests for her photograph. To have a young woman's picture in their military quarters was obviously a status symbol for soldiers and may well have been officially encouraged.[39] A young recruit stationed in the Soviet Union wrote to Maria that one of his comrades had come into his room and on seeing her picture with a friend had promptly 'fallen in love with your girlfriend' and was now determined to write to her. Could he ask her for her address?[40] These images provided solace and no doubt facilitated erotic dreams, but they were also a very public status symbol of a soldier's emotional hinterland – and a further sign of the link between

---

[34] Letter written on 16 June 1944, cited in Hammer/zur Nieden (eds.), *Sehr selten habe ich geweint*, 161.
[35] Rebecca Earle, 'Introduction', in Rebecca Earle (ed.), *Epistolary Selves: Letters and Letter-Writers 1600–1945* (London, 1999, repr. 2016), 2–5, 5.
[36] See Roper, *The Secret Battle*, 63, 25.   [37] Stargardt, *The German War*, 422.
[38] SFN Vienna, NL 75 IV, box 6.   [39] See ibidem.
[40] SFN Vienna, 75 IV, box 6, K. S. to Maria Kundera, 10 June 1943.

private and public in the institution of *Feldpost*. Both Hans and Herbert cherished photographs from home. Herbert Walter's reaction was ecstatic on receiving pictures of his toddler son which showed him how much he had changed: 'Finally the photos are here! And so beautiful! I am so happy and I look at them again and again. You, my very best. I'd like to kiss you with all my heart, to embrace you and to tell you that you have given us a magnificent son.'[41] In early January 1944, Hans had to leave Maria to rejoin his unit and he packed a photograph of his new fiancée. This helped him to dream of Maria although, as he admitted in one of his earliest letters, with his memory of her still fresh, the real Maria 'would still be even more wonderful'.[42] In July 1944, Maria sent a holiday snap of her taken during their February outing to the Drachenburg in the Rhineland. Thanking her for this picture, he rhapsodised: 'You look at me so sweetly across your shoulder in the gas light.'[43]

The officially sponsored 'love tokens' campaign functioned almost like a dating agency. Quite a few of Maria's pen friends appear to have hoped for a closer relationship; some addressed her as *mein Schatz* (sweetheart) or *Liebling* (darling). It is not clear whether they were aware of their competition, but their frequent complaints of her tardiness in replying or their vehemently voiced disappointments when she had failed to meet them during their home leave, suggests that they were not. Early in 1944, one pen friend from Maria's village, for example, called her tongue-in-cheek *Sonnenteufel* (sunny devil) and threatened revenge for neglecting him on his next leave home.[44] But by then she had been secretly engaged to Hans. In the correspondence with her pen friends, Maria presented herself as the detached, rational career woman, blasé about marriage and rural conventions. She complained that the railway board had relocated her work back to her home village of Kritzendorf and that she was now expected to go visiting relatives and acquaintances and to listen to 'endless stories at the [train station] counter. [...] I can bear anything except acquaintances, but of course I know everybody here. In one word, Hanserl [another Hans, not her fiancé], I have had it.'[45] In his answer he countered, also flippantly, that Kritzendorf was surely a 'veritable paradise for young girls, now out of danger from procreation', presumably because all the young men had been called up. He begged her for a meeting on his next leave, or was she 'already totally spoken for?' Another young man wrote angrily: 'Now I really want to know what is

[41] KBA, 0103, H. W. to Katharina W., 16 May 1940, 1 July 1940.
[42] SFN, 75 II, Hans H. to Maria Kundera, 11 Jan. 1944.
[43] Ibidem, Hans H. to Maria Kundera, 1944.
[44] See ibidem, H. V. to Maria Kundera, 31 March 1944.
[45] Ibidem, Maria Kundera to H. V., 10 Aug. 1943; H. V. to Maria Kundera, 27 Sept. 1943.

the matter with you! Since I have been in the army you have not written a single letter to me!' When he finally heard from her, he chided her for suggesting that 'love was nothing but a delusion', or even 'complete rubbish [...] I cannot understand what you write about love, you with all your energy and passion'. He mused that it 'really looks as if somebody has disappointed you. Otherwise I cannot imagine that you suddenly have such pessimistic thoughts vis-à-vis love. [...] How will it end if all young girls of your age think like this? If nobody contemplates marriage? [...] Then we soldiers out [at the front] must give up all hope.'[46]

Compare Maria's ironic tone here with her effusive outpourings of love to her fiancé Hans:

A good night *Bussi* (little kiss) and hundred thousand other *Bussis* sends you quickly your Mitzerl! It is already so late [...] but I feel so much love for my Hänschen that I still have to tell you quickly. If you were here tonight with me I would not go to bed yet, it is a wonderful night, and everything longs so for love.[47]

Gone is her sarcasm or ennui.

The notion of the instability of the self was neither new nor confined to letter writing. During the late nineteenth and early twentieth centuries, intellectuals like Sigmund Freud and the theorists of the Frankfurt School Max Horkheimer and Theodor W. Adorno, among others, had considered subjectivity as composed of multiple, socially constructed and context-dependent identities. Friedrich Nietzsche too began to write about his own interpretation and conceptualisation of 'becoming', signalling that everything was in flux, rather than 'being', meaning a fixed reality.[48]

A number of outside influences are, however, evident in love letters. Historians like Ute Frevert, Carol Acton and Aribert Reimann who have explored the relations between public discourse and private feelings have shown how emotions are invariably shaped by the culture in which they are situated.[49] And in Margaretta Jolly's words, love letters like all other epistles are 'pervaded by social, linguistic, and literary codes'. She stresses their unreliability since 'those who write to a lover wrestle with words' inadequacy, exaggerating the awareness in all letter writing of physical

---

[46] Ibidem, F. M to Maria Kundera. 27 Oct. 1941 and 18 June 1943.
[47] SFN, Vienna, 75 II, Maria Kundera to Hans H., 7 Aug. 1944.
[48] See Robin Small, *Time and Becoming in Nietzsche's Thought* (London, New York, NY, 2010); Jennifer Radden, 'Multiple Selves', *The Oxford Handbook of the Self* (Oxford, 2011), 547ff.
[49] See Ute Frevert, *Emotions in History: Lost and Found* (Budapest, New York, NY, 2011); Carol Acton, *Grief in Wartime: Private Pain, Public Discourse* (Basingstoke, 2007); Aribert Reimann, *Der große Krieg der Sprachen: Untersuchungen zur historischen Semantik in Deutschland und England zur Zeit des Ersten Weltkriegs* (Essen, 2000).

absence'.[50] Many couples no doubt found it challenging to express feelings in letters when they may have had little occasion or need to speak about them in everyday life. Even Hans and Maria's intimate confessions adhered to epistolary conventions, like the use of salutations and references modelled on current Austrian predilection for diminutives, pet names and expressions from popular culture. She addressed him as *Schatzi* (little darling), *Hänschen*, *Hansibubi* (little boy Hans), *süßes Schnuckerl* (sweetie) and signed *Mitzi*, *Mitzerl* or *Schmuskatzerl* (cuddly kitten). Hans was less inventive and stuck to *süßes Schatzerl* (sweet little darling), *Herzerl* (little heart) and *Urlaubsengel* (holiday angel). In Austria (and south Germany), diminutives signal affection and echo the maternal relationship of trust and love. Among grown-ups, they are usually reserved for marital or sexual relationships. During the war, mass culture positively promoted terms of endearment and romantic love. Especially Vienna was replete with them and actors in home-grown films spoke them in the Austrian dialect.[51] So it was no surprise that Maria's, like her fiancé's, letters were copiously sprinkled with tender *Bussis* or *Schmusbusserl* (little smooching kisses).

Herbert Walter used fewer diminutives, in keeping with the more restrained habit of north Germany. He also adhered to other social codes: the duplication of phrases for emphasis, as when he addressed Katharina as 'Liebes, liebes Frauchen' or called one of her letters as 'so loving, soooo loving!'[52] or when he frequently referred to *Herz* (heart), *Seele* (soul) and *Tiefe* (depth), staple sites and signifiers of love and truth in bourgeois culture. Interestingly both couples used stars in the night sky as symbols of their union. Maria and Hans' *Sterndl* (little star) transported their kisses and cuddles across Europe's war zone. Shortly before Hans' death in August 1944, Maria wrote:

> Our *Sterndl* glitters and shines so clearly, is this because of the many kisses which we send up every day? Our love is completely mirrored in our *Sterndl*. It is so small and there must never be a cloud over it. We will quickly blow it away, won't we Hänschen? Now good night, tomorrow I will tell you more, much, much more [...].[53]

When she fretted that she had had no letters from Hans for nearly a week, she invoked the power of their special star to reassure herself of his love: 'Everything is alright with my Hanslein, isn't it? My sweet *Schnuckerl*

---

[50] Margaretta Jolly, *In Love and Struggle: Letters in Contemporary Feminism* (New York, NY, 2008), 23, 6.
[51] See Elisabeth Büttner and Christian Dewald, *Das tägliche Brennen: Eine Geschichte des österreichischen Films von den Anfängen bis 1945* (Salzburg, Vienna, 2002).
[52] KBA, 0103, H. W. to K. W., 8 July and 15 Oct. 1940.
[53] SFN, Vienna, 75 II, Maria Kundera to Hans H., 7 Aug. 1944.

(cuddly darling). But our little star tells me that you do think of me, I must quickly go and look at it. And it should bring you many *Bussis*, good night, your Mitzerl.'[54]

One night in France, Herbert used the same trope to tell Katharina of his longing for closeness with her so far away to his east. In keeping with his social pretensions, he wrote that he spotted that 'Cassiopeia stood over your house. Now the east is the land of my dreams.'[55] The symbolic meaning of stars was also popular in other wartime love letters.[56] No doubt they were inspired by German fairy tales and nursery songs in which references to stars abound.[57] When Maria was concerned about the danger Hans might have faced, she evoked the witch in the forest from the Grimms' tale *Hänsel und Gretl*:

> My poor Hänschen has to be awake much more than me and does not cry. He lies hidden in the woods so that the evil witch does not catch him. If only I could search for you I would walk through the woods without fear until I have found you. Then I would never leave you again and my Hänschen would never see anything gruesome in the dark forest.[58]

Significantly, Maria assumed here the role of Hänsel's plucky sister, Gretl, in the fairy tale who managed to free him by pushing the witch into the fire; or Maria might even have assumed a maternal role. She certainly constructs herself as Hans' equal or stronger partner rather than the stereotypically weak woman in need of her man's protection.

Wartime popular culture extolled romantic love as an antidote to the increasing carnage on the battlefield, and this clearly influenced couples' writing. Hans and Maria quite clearly borrowed phrases, images or concepts, whether consciously or not, from contemporary cinema and songs. Especially romantic films like *Die grosse Liebe* (*The Great Love*) (1942) starring Zarah Leander, the sensual superstar of Nazi cinema, or popular songs transmitted by radio as part of the hugely successful *Request Concert* (*Wunschkonzert*) or its successor *Sunday Afternoon* to which both Hans and Maria tuned in, promoted romantic love. For example, one Sunday Hans wrote to Maria that he had just heard Leander sing *Es wird einmal ein*

---

[54] Ibidem, Maria Kundera to Hans H., 7 Aug. 1944.
[55] KBA, 0103, H. W. to K. W., n.d. written end of June 1940.
[56] See letter of Otto Braun to his mistress Julie Vogelstein, March 1916, cited in Dorothee Wierling, *Eine Familie im Krieg: Leben, Sterben und Schreiben 1914–1918* (Göttingen, 2013), 175.
[57] See the Grimms' popular fairy tale, *Der Sterntaler*, where a poor and desolate young girl who has given everything she owns to those who are even more needy than she is rewarded by the stars which fall from the night sky as gold coins; or the folk songs 'Weißt Du wieviel Sternlein stehen?', 'Nun ruhen alle Wälder' and a number of lullabies in which stars have a central place.
[58] SFN, Vienna, 75 II, Maria Kundera to Hans H., 8 Aug. 1944.

Wunder geschehn (*I Know One Day a Miracle Will Happen*) from *Die grosse Liebe* and hoped that she had too.[59] Maria in turn mentioned songs they had listened to together which brought back erotic memories: 'Oh, that song, *Sag mir wieviel Frauenleben* (*Tell Me, How Many Women's Lives*) that we heard in February on your short leave when you came to us on Sunday: *Niemand liebt Dich so wie ich* (*Nobody Loves You as I Do*), Hans, then we kissed and looked deep into each other's eyes.'[60] Or she wrote how she had spent a quiet Sunday with a girlfriend when she suddenly heard Lale Andersen (best known for her interpretation of the song *Lili Marleen* in 1939) on the radio sing her famous *Zum Abschied geb ich Dir die Hände* (*I'll Give You My Hands at Our Farewell*) whereupon she broke down because 'it seemed almost as if you were singing it to me, so full of love and pain'.[61]

It can be argued that most letters are similarly influenced by cultural trends and epistolary conventions: however, in Second World War Germany, these influences became particularly marked as the regime vastly expanded its interference in private communications. The campaign to galvanise young women to write to front soldiers is just one example. Another one is the way in which Nazi wartime propaganda instrumentalised even the most personal feelings of loss for their own ends to ensure that the fighting continued despite mass slaughter on the battlefield.[62] Hämmerle argues that in her wide sample from Austria and Nazi Germany, couples' correspondence during both world wars clearly demonstrated 'participating agreement with the dominant (war) ideologies and power relationships'.[63] This is borne out in my case studies. Herbert's letters to Katharina are ostensible love letters, as Katharina called them and as the opening quotation shows. But on closer inspection, they were imbued by Nazi ideology. He regularly emphasised her role as wife and mother rather than as his lover and partner; this chimed with the Nazi ideology of motherhood. Herbert also had internalised Nazi racism: 'We two belong together, are we not through our children one blood and one soul? We want to confront life directly, work honestly and give value to the victories of our time.'[64] This casual reference to 'blood' resonates, whether consciously or not, with the *völkisch* beliefs in the value of *Blut und Boden* (Blood and Soil); surely 'victories' referred to military as well as racist policies to 'purify' (used in a letter cited later in this chapter) the 'master race' from *Untermenschen* (subhumans), policies he witnessed or possibly assisted to carry out in occupied Poland. Praising Katharina's Germanness and depth, as in the opening letter, also meant denigrating

---

[59] See SFN, 75 II, Hans H. to Maria Kundera, 13 Apr. 1944.
[60] Ibidem, Maria Kundera's letter diary, 2 Oct. 1944. [61] Ibidem.
[62] See Acton, *Grief in Wartime*, 51; Stargardt, *The German War*.
[63] Hämmerle, 'Gewalt und Liebe', 214–15. [64] Ibidem, 21 July 1940, from Poland.

Polish women by comparison. He wrote, they looked 'clean but stink worse than cows. I am always astonished about the degree of primitiveness. [...] Women have a difficult time here! Girls of 18 already have sagging breasts!'[65]

Herbert also trusted Nazi foreign policy and thought war a benevolent force that 'purified' personal traits and reaffirmed traditional gender characteristics: it had, he assured Katharina, rendered her into a 'richer' and stronger persona, meaning probably more of a *Kamerad*[66] and him more virile and closer to the Nazi ideal of 'Aryan' manhood. 'Soldiering has done me good'; it would help him become a proper breadwinner and *pater familias*.[67] And to prove his point, he started sending Katharina epistolary advice on how to measure up to the model 'Aryan' wife.[68]

Censorship, in the Second World War, in Martin Humburg's phrase, 'hung like a sword of Damocles over everyone who did not respect the strict rules' which, he contended, resulted in self-censorship of correspondents, although it was hard to discern how far this was indeed the case.[69] Soldiers were not permitted to reveal their military location, though Hans' reticence concerning the dire situation in which his unit found itself was surely out of concern for Maria than fear of censorship. On his twenty-third birthday and in his last letter, his description of conditions in the besieged fortress Brest was terse: 'We have enough to live. Unfortunately I have lost everything that I did not carry on me, the bundle of letters from you, photos from the last holiday.'[70] His attempts at concealment, however, need not stop the historian (as indeed it almost certainly did not stop Maria) from reading between the lines and detecting terror expressed unconsciously. Clues are in the poor physical quality

---

[65] Ibidem, 29 July 1940.
[66] Thomas Kühne argues that the Nazi regime's 'granting girls and women their own realms of comradeship was meant to harden women and to masculinize traditional notions of femininity, without questioning the superior role of men'; see Thomas Kühne, *The Rise and Fall of Comradeship: Hitler's Soldiers, Male Bonding and Mass Violence in the Twentieth Century* (Cambridge, 2017), 86, 84–8; Dagmar Reese, 'Die Kameraden: eine partnerschaftliche Konzeption der Geschlechterbeziehungen an der Wende vom 19. zum 20. Jahrhundert', in Dagmar Reese et al. (eds.), *Rationale Beziehungen? Geschlechterverhältnisse im Rationalisierungsprozess* (Frankfurt a.M., 1993), 58–74.
[67] Ibidem, 10 Aug. 1940; 8 July 1940. [68] See ibidem, 15 Oct. 1940.
[69] See Martin Humburg, 'Deutsche Feldpostbriefe im Zweiten Weltkrieg', in Martin Humburg, *Das Gesicht des Krieges: Feldpostbriefe von Wehrmachtssoldaten aus der Sowjetunion 1941–1944* (Wiesbaden, 1998), 13–23, 16; Martin Humburg, 'Siegeshoffnungen und "Herbstkrise" im Jahre 1941: Anmerkungen zu Feldpostbriefen aus der Sowjetunion', *WerkstattGeschichte* 22 (1999), 25–30, 25; Bernd Ulrich, 'Feldpostbriefe im Ersten Weltkrieg – Bedeutung und Zensur', in Peter Knoch (ed.), *Kriegsalltag*, 40–83; Benjamin Ziemann, 'Feldpostbriefe und ihre Zensur in den zwei Weltkriegen', in Klaus Beyer and Hans-Christian Täubrich (eds.), *Der Brief: Eine Kulturgeschichte der schriftlichen Kommunikation* (Heidelberg, 1996), 163–70.
[70] SFN, 75 II, Hans H. to Maria Kundera, 16 Aug. 1944.

of his letter, the loose syntax and the hurried scrawl in pencil on a small scrap of pink paper. Maria in turn also downplayed the impact of the Allied bombing raids on Vienna and its vicinity in the summer of 1944 for the same reasons. She admitted that she was tired, 'not surprising since we had an alarm last night. And this morning we spent again in the basement, just for a change'; but immediately sounded cheerful again, 'but it was all very cosy, it was so agreeable that it passed very quickly'.[71] The impact of official censorship on private correspondence is now generally held to have been slight. The task of examining the mountain of daily personal mail by hand (on average an estimated 20 million letters every day) was practically impossible and the authorities could only carry out spot checks.[72] Their main concern was at any rate espionage and attempts of demoralisation among the troops.[73]

But other factors could have influenced *Feldpost*: the habit of issuing model letters to the troops or publishing acceptable norms of wives' letters in the press. Yet letter-writing manuals had a long tradition.[74] Furthermore, as in the First World War, *Jammerbriefe* (misery letters) from home were also castigated.[75] Women's contribution to the war effort, apart from bearing healthy 'Aryan' children, was to care for the home and to shore up soldiers' morale rather than to burden them with their own worries.[76] But in my sample, many women ignored these strictures and instead complained bitterly about sick children, bombing raids and food shortages. The young wife of Wilhelm, her much older army officer husband, never seems to have missed an occasion to complain. In July 1944, she wrote, 'I am so utterly worried: now the Russians are already [...] 150 km from the German border. [...] And if you don't return home in time – I don't want to be raped and/or deported to Russia and neither do my children –, does this mean that now I only have the gas

---

[71] Ibidem, Maria Kundera to Hans H., 22 Aug. 1944.
[72] See Humburg, 'Deutsche Feldpostbriefe', 31, n. 13.
[73] See Latzel, *Deutsche Soldaten*, 25ff.; Buchbender/Sterz, *Das andere Gesicht des Krieges*, 14–15; for French censorship in the First World War, see Martha Hanna, 'A Republic of Letters: The Epistolary Tradition in France during World War I', *American Historical Review* (2003), 1338–61, 1339.
[74] See Humburg, 'Deutsche Feldpostbriefe', 16; Susanne Ettle, *Anleitungen zu schriftlichen Kommunikationen: Briefsteller von 1880 bis 1980* (Tübingen, 1984), 1–2, cited in Hämmerle/Saurer, 'Frauenbriefe – Männerbriefe?', 20–1; Isa Schikorsky, 'Kommunikation über das Unbeschreibbare: Beobachtungen zum Sprachstil von Kriegsbriefen', *Wirkendes Wort* 2 (1992), 295–315, 298, cited in Hämmerle/Saurer, 'Frauenbriefe – Männerbriefe?', 21.
[75] See Benjamin Ziemann, 'Geschlechterbeziehungen in deutschen Feldpostbriefen des Ersten Weltkrieges', in Christa Hämmerle and Edith Saurer (eds.), *Briefkulturen und ihr Geschlecht: Zur Geschichte der privaten Korrespondenz vom 16. Jahrhundert bis heute* (Vienna, Cologne, Weimar, 2003), 261–82, 266.
[76] Marszolek, 'Ich möchte Dich zu gern', 41.

tap?'[77] Despite the 1938 decree which criminalised subversion of the war effort, many soldier-husbands in my sample harshly criticised both the war and the regime. The Bavarian lawyer Kremser, whom we met earlier in this chapter, peppered his letters to his wife with seditious remarks. In January 1945 he told her, 'our *Führungsoffiziere* (officers for ideological instruction)' teach us about '*Volk* and race' while the military situation in the east was 'seriously worrying'. He also criticised diplomats, mocked Goebbels' speeches and was fed up with the war which 'has messed up (*versaut*) everything we had once imagined, nothing good will come of it, often one is inclined to simply chuck it'.[78]

In early July 1940, Herbert Walter still believed that 'the war brings us all closer together,' and believed 'Adolf's message that victory was in sight'; by the end of July, however, even he was disillusioned. He wrote that he had no 'inclination to play soldiers'; he wanted nothing but 'to return home. We all feel the same. Only home!' A month later, 'the longing is shameless and every day eats deeper into the heart. Would that this war finally ended.'[79]

The Importance of Letters

The authorities might well have orchestrated the ritual of mass letter writing to bolster the war effort, but its importance for spouses or sweethearts cannot be overstated. For Hans and Maria, so recently engaged, love letters were vital to keep their new love and passion alive. Since early January 1944, when he rejoined his battalion first in Germany and later in France, Hans wrote to his beloved almost every day, sometime twice, and Maria reciprocated, often writing to him late at night. Herbert's communications were almost as frequent. Especially during the last years of the war, home leave was often postponed at short notice or entirely cancelled and relationships could 'only be lived through writing'.[80] When his leave was cancelled indefinitely, Hans told Maria that they would have to console themselves with epistolary kisses as a 'small compensation'.[81] The utter delight at the recent arrival of a letter was only matched by that of disappointment at being left empty-handed and it dominated every correspondence I have examined. Hans called it a '*Glückstag*', a - lucky day, when he received two letters from his '*Herzl*' Maria and she in

---

[77] Hammer/zur Nieden (eds.), *Sehr selten habe ich geweint*, 159, 163.
[78] KBA, 0020/1–2. Albert K. letters of 25 Jan. 1945, 4 Feb. 1945, 14 Feb. 1945, 14 March 1945.
[79] KBA, 0103, H. W. to K. W., 1 July 1940, 21 July 1940, n.d. (after 8 Aug. 1940).
[80] Marszolek, 'Ich möchte Dich zu gern', 14.
[81] SFN, 75 II, Hans H. to Maria Kundera, 17 Jan. 1944.

turn rewarded him with an epistolary 'special dear *Bussi*' for his letter which arrived on 8 August 1944.[82] A week later, however, and without news, she expressed her profound despondency:

> Absolutely nothing can please me today; I have no peace and I cannot sit quietly doing my work. It is really awful not having heard from you, Hänschen. What is wrong? Oh God, the uncertainty is terrible, Hänschen, when will all this finally end?[83]

My correspondents did not seem to need official encouragement to stay in touch with their loved ones far away. Writing at times even became an obsession, as was the case with Maria. One night, returning from work, she found a letter waiting for her. It was not from him, but her own letter returned from the front. It dashed all her hopes, as she admitted. But she could not stop writing: 'What shall I do now? My best and only enjoyable daily task now makes no longer sense...' So she continued to write daily but did not send it. It became a kind of diary, but one in which she continued to address Hans as if he were still alive. 'You must come back to me. And when you are with me again you'll know in detail what I did every day, everything happens because of you and while thinking of you.'[84] On 21 September, a notice appeared in the press that on 20 September 1944, the Führer had awarded the *Ritterkreuz* of the Iron Cross to General Bernhard Ramcke, of the paratroopers, for his heroic defence of the fortress Brest at the head of his courageous men against the week-long assault by a vastly superior enemy.[85] Maria noted that 'this told us everything. And you are probably there too,' but she still tried to keep her hope alive: 'I have only one wish. Come back to me, I don't care about anything else.' She reminded him of their marriage plans for the following May, 'whether the war is over or not'.[86] Her letter-diary only ended on 25 October with the following entry:

> [Y]es, yesterday I got my marching orders. Tomorrow I have to join the Flak (auxiliary anti-aircraft defence). I'm not going willingly; I want to be the first to welcome you back when you return. [...] Don't worry about me, even if I am joining this outfit (*Verein*) that few decent people respect. [...] I belong only to you always and for all eternity. I am only waiting for the moment when I can be

---

[82] Ibidem.   [83] Ibidem, Maria Kundera to Hans H. 8 Aug. 1944; 15 August 1944.
[84] Ibidem, Maria Kundera, diary-letter, entries 15, 17 and 21 September 1944.
[85] See ibidem, newspaper cutting, no title, 20 September 1944. The siege of Brest lasted twenty-eight days and ended with the German capitulation on 18 Sept. 1944. General Ramcke and more than 37,000 German soldiers were taken prisoner by the American army; more than 4,000 were wounded and at least 1,000 German soldiers were killed, although many bodies were never found.
[86] SFN, Vienna, 75 II, Maria Kundera, letter-diary, 21 Sept. and 23 Oct. 1944.

with you again. [...] I hope it will be very soon. Kisses from me. Sorry to be so unhappy but I'll never lose heart or hope. Yours eternally M.[87]

We have seen to what extent epistolary formulations could be influenced by various outside factors. Both Hans and Maria borrowed phrases from popular culture to convey romantic feelings. However, Hans' use of stock phrases does not render his messages and feelings any less profound. His empathy with her work routine showed his deep affection for her but also how he conjured her up in person from afar. He kept an exact tally of the number of days since their separation: 'and now, two months later, I cannot think you out of my life. My only wish is that situation may never arise, and then I really want to make you completely happy.'[88] Even at the moment of his greatest danger when hiding in the forest, he still wrote that Maria would always be 'at the very centre' of his life.[89] Hans admitted writing to her 'because I simply want to chat to you'. Indeed his letters often resemble informal conversations especially since he often resorted to the vernacular and they seem unmediated and all the more genuine for that. The representation of letters can offer clues of the author's state of mind. When Maria feared the worst, the outward appearance of her letters reveal her emotional turmoil: a broken syntax, a tiny scrawl in pencil and in irregular patterns on rough brown A5 paper, folded into four small sections, to gain more space when paper was in short supply. Her anguish is palpable in her choice of words: 'appalling anxiety', 'absolute worst', 'worried', all of them doom-laden.[90] An analysis of Herbert's writing style is equally revealing: at least until the end of July, his syntax and handwriting were always controlled and his text reflective; his optimistic tone speaks of self-confidence and a belief in the regime which was, however, severely dented as we have seen by the end of July. When no letters arrived from Katharina his tone became cool with stress and his style turned perfunctory.

Sexuality

In 1989, Peter Knoch could still claim that any mention of intimate details would be hard to find in correspondence between front and home. This was, he argued, especially so during the Kaiserreich when erotic and sexual references were generally taboo. If they were mentioned in letters at all, he contended, they were masked by a highly stylised literary language. Erich Maria Remarque wrote in his novel, *All Quiet on*

---

[87] Ibidem, Maria Kundera's letter-diary, 25 Oct. 1944.
[88] Ibidem, Hans H. to Maria Kundera, 17 Jan. 1944. [89] Ibidem, 16 Aug. 1944.
[90] Ibidem, Maria Kundera to Hans H., 16 Aug. 1944.

the Western Front (1928), about a husband who revealed his erotic yearnings to his wife entirely in code.[91] By the Second World War, Knoch claimed, some soldiers were now communicating their sexual desire more explicitly, although most women continued to use the same restrained language as before.[92] Marszolek too found little trace of expressions of physical love in the wartime couple correspondence she examined and suggested that sexual yearning was expressed symbolically in references to hugs, kisses and holding hands which concealed the wish for physicality.[93] This seems at first sight to fit Hans Haschek's letters. He articulated his erotic feelings for Maria obliquely by, for example, mentioning his desire to 'stroke her little head'. He also confined himself to amorous gestures like *Busserl*. By careful reading between the lines, however, Hans' sexual messages emerge in his sensual tone, his seductive empathy which allowed him to share in Maria's actual activity at the moment of writing, and by conjuring up memories of heightened emotions, such as their first affirmation of love. The cumulative effect of tactile words like stroking, kissing or tasting (her kisses) littered throughout his letters renders them passionate. After all, as he reminded her, it was a '*Busserl*' that sealed their love in the first place. Savouring the memories of her 'tasty and tender' kisses seemed to make them real. Hans even bragged about being able to single out Mitzerl straight away 'were a hundred different [women] kissing me while I was blindfolded'.[94] In his imagination he also transformed specific objects associated with Maria into her embodiment. In one letter he remembered blossoms she had put in her décolleté and with which he identified to the point of shapeshifting: 'now I could actually turn into them.' He told Maria, 'the tender blossoms [...] can see you in real life, they feel your breath and are kissed with your lips – very tenderly. I know how tenderly you can kiss. I sense it when they are with you. I sense it as if it was I myself, I sense you always wherever I am and whatever I do.'[95] By July 1944, he had not had any physical contact with her for nearly five months; in his yearning for her, the physicality of Maria's photograph and letters seemed to symbolise her body, as Rebecca Earle put it, in 'a quasi-sexual textual encounter',[96] and thus it could enter into his erotic dreams: 'you yourself

---

[91] See Erich Maria Remarque, *All Quiet on the Western Front* (1928), 103–10, cited in Peter Knoch, 'Kriegsalltag', in Peter Knoch (ed.), *Kriegsalltag: Die Rekonstruktion des Kriegsalltags als Aufgabe der historischen Forschung und der Friedenserziehung* (Stuttgart, 1989), 222–52, here 226.
[92] See Knoch, 'Kriegsalltag', 227; interestingly this historian hides the sexually explicit quotation in a footnote (9).
[93] See Marszolek, 'Ich möchte Dich zu gern', 51.
[94] SFN, 75 II, Hans H. to Maria Kundera, 27 July 1944.
[95] Ibidem, Hans H. to Maria Kundera, 23 July 1944. [96] Earle, 'Introduction', 5.

have come to me!'[97] This symbolic meaning of objects touched by the beloved is also apparent in Maria's writing. A posthumous letter she received did not upset her; on the contrary, seen as an embodiment of him, it gave her solace: 'You had this letter in your hand and Hans, in what state of mind, with what aching heart did you write all this? Thank you for this difficult letter. Every page seems to cut my heart but it is suffused with love.'[98]

Furthermore, Maria frequently wrote to Hans last thing at night and hence often mentioned going to bed, 'then we are together and inexpressibly happy,' surely implying her sexual longing.[99] But she also voiced her desire more explicitly when, despite relying on a well-worn euphemism, she admitted her wish for a baby with him. 'Once we really belong to one another, then you must let the stork come one day. And we will then have such a dear little *Butzerl* (sweetie pie). Hänschen, do you feel excited? Or should we wait a little longer?'[100] This suggests that they had not yet consummated their love affair and that her most tangible hope was starting a family and making a 'really cosy home', echoing the dominant motherhood ideology.[101] Pregnancy was again conjured up obliquely in a letter of mid-August 1944 in which she reported that Hans' father, her boss, had teased her about her 'belly'. This embarrassed her, surely for its underlying assumption that she was pregnant, although she wrote that she did not know what was meant with this remark. But she assured Hans that 'nothing has actually happened'.[102] In another letter she dared to go further. She told him that she wanted to share everything with him, like now her *Betthupferl* (bedtime sweet, literally a 'hop into bed'). Playing on the double meaning, she explained: 'You can now hop happily into bed, I have a green one, the hope. I am not in hope [a euphemism for pregnancy] but have the strong hope that you return to me very soon.'[103]

Herbert too wrote glowing love letters. In his very first communication after he had to take leave in May 1940, he called her his

> best little wife! I kiss you and caress you and send a cuddle to Phoenix II [the second expected baby]. Oh Kinka, I long to be with you, to look into your face and put your dear arms round my neck.[104]

Although one could argue that Herbert simply conformed with the expectations of an absent husband and father, there are other signs that his longing for home was increasing as time went on: his many loving salutations became longer and more expressive the further he was stationed

---

[97] SFN, 75 II, Hans H. to Maria Kundera, 27 July 1944.   [98] Ibidem, 2 Oct. 1944.
[99] Ibidem, Maria Kundera to Hans H., 29 Aug. 1944.   [100] Ibidem, 8 Aug. 1944.
[101] Ibidem, 13 Aug. 1944.   [102] Ibidem, 18 Aug. 1944.   [103] Ibidem, 16 Aug. 1944.
[104] KBA, 0103, H. W. to K. W., 16 May 1940.

from home and the longer he was separated from Katharina. In May 1940, he addressed her as 'dear Kinka', two months later as 'dear, dear little wife',[105] ten days later as 'most beloved little wife', three days on as 'my very best little Kinka!'; but in August, she was his 'beloved heart, my Kinka, my very best!' and in October 1940, 'my dear good most sweetheart little wife'. Herbert's sexual fantasies are revealed in frequent references to his gaze at and touch of her 'beautiful body' – he was after all a sculptor – 'your proud legs were magnificent to perceive', or his stroking her swelling belly, evidence of their sexual union, her fertility and his virility.[106]

In contrast, Ingeborg and her officer husband Wilhelm T.'s upper-middle-class sense of propriety almost certainly hindered a direct mention of erotic yearnings; they may simply have been content knowing that their union had resulted in a steadily increasing family – their third child was born in 1943. In fact, explicit sexual thoughts were rare in all the love letters I have examined. This is surprising given the war was accompanied by greater sexual licence for both men and women because of the geographical and emotional dislocation which frequently encouraged promiscuity at the front but also at home. It was well known that the military had provided brothels for soldiers at the front[107] and the large number of women suspected of and prosecuted for illicit love affairs with prisoners of war is particularly striking evidence of the loosening of sexual moral stricture.[108] Stories of wives at home living it up while their husbands were away at war alarmed many a front soldier and jealousy crept into letters home.[109] Women may have experienced a new level of personal freedom because their fathers or husbands were away on service or because their war work opened up their horizons and gave them an appetite for new adventures, sexual affairs included. It also emboldened women to express their erotic desire in explicit ways as letters exchanged between young women and their prisoner of war lovers testify.[110] Compared to these letters, the reticence displayed by married or engaged couples is remarkable. There are some exceptions, however. The love

---

[105] The German word 'Frau' can mean 'woman' or 'wife'.
[106] KBA, 0103, e.g. H. W. to K. W. n.d. but after 8 Aug. 1940, 8 Oct. 1940.
[107] See Annette Timm, 'Sex with a Purpose: Prostitution, Venereal Disease, and Militarized Masculinity in the Third Reich', in Dagmar Herzog (ed.), *Sexuality and German Fascism* (New York, NY, 2005), 223–55, 224.
[108] See Cornelie Usborne, 'Female Sexual Desire and Male Honor: German Women's Illicit Love Affairs with Prisoners of War in the Second World War', *Journal of the History of Sexuality* 26/3 (2017), 454–88.
[109] See Andreas Heusler, '"Strafbestand Liebe": Verbotener Kontakt zwischen Münchnerinnen und ausländischen Kriegsgefangenen', in Sybille Krafft (ed.), *Zwischen den Fronten. Münchner Frauen in Krieg und Frieden, 1900–1950* (Munich, 1995), 324–41, 335.
[110] See Usborne, 'Female Sexual Desire and Male Honor'.

letters between the Hamburg lawyer Kurt Orgel and the photojournalist Liselotte Purper discussed by Stargardt is one example; the correspondence between a Hamburg baker and his wife analysed by Ulrike Jureit is another.[111] The reason for the disparity between the love letters here considered and the writings between prisoners of war and their German mistresses is difficult to ascertain. One answer maybe the fact that sex was at the centre of and the raison d'être for most of those illicit relationships and hence there was little point to be coy when writing to each other. Furthermore, the decision by young women, often married and with children, to have sex with a foreigner and enemy soldier was such an audacious and risky enterprise, especially since they appreciated it was a crime and that the penalties were very harsh, that all caution of improper behaviour or communication was simply abandoned.

Conclusions

This chapter showed the potential entanglement of public and private with regard to love letters. In Barbara Rosenwein's words, historical actors' emotional experiences are not only influenced by politics but also by the communities that possess 'a common stake, interest, values and goals'.[112] I have attempted here to situate the letters of my two case studies (supplemented by a sample of other correspondence) in the specific 'emotional community' in which they were written. They were liable to replicate, often unconsciously, epistolary conventions and writing styles, often leaning on local vernacular expressions or particular popular songs or films; there was also evidence of an instability of the epistolary self. But the specific conditions of a society living in total war and under the rule of a dictatorship greatly facilitated the intrusion of propaganda or official ideology (for example racist and misogynist policies) and politics (for example the attempt to encourage and orchestrate *Feldpost* to help the war effort). How could such ardent love letters as we have encountered fit their writers' deadly work as soldiers or their wives' and girl friends' complicity or at least tacit awareness? Husbands who assured their wives of their devotion were also engaged in killing or witnessed the slaughter perpetrated by others; wives who wrote lovingly to their husbands at the front may well have supported Nazi war goals. Michael Roper, writing about Britain, suggested that historians 'have found it difficult to write the emotional history of the war because it gave rise to contradictory emotional states: aggression as well as

[111] See Stargardt, *The German War*, 423; Jureit, 'Zwischen Ehe und Männerbund'.
[112] Barbara Rosenwein, *Emotional Communities in the Early Middle Ages* (Ithaca, NY, 2006).

tenderness, cruelty and care, fascination and fear'; he contends that historians 'lacked concepts that can accommodate the contrary character of emotions'. Roper resorted to psychoanalysis.[113] It is the relationships between public discourse and private feeling which prompted Christa Hämmerle to investigate if the 'microcosm of a love relationship' which couples had constructed in their correspondences during both world wars could also have functioned as a 'site of or catalyst for opposition to the often life-threatening circumstances – especially since these endangered the beloved'. But she found that in general the correspondents supported war in both periods and that during the Second World War, they had also accommodated racist as well as sexist policies.[114]

Does all this not suggest that the writing here considered was too infused by public interest and sentiments to be truly private? I have shown that not all the apparent influences should be taken at face value; censorship was not nearly as effective as some historians have suggested, and despite model letters for soldiers and their loved ones, recruits and wives often displayed considerable resistance to official wartime policy or ideology. The sculptor-recruit Herbert, generally supportive of the regime, at times signalled his strong disaffection with 'playing soldier' and his posting to a remote corner of Eastern Europe. Ingrid T., the young officer's wife, ignored Nazi prescriptions against *Jammerbriefe* by repeatedly describing the various vicissitudes she faced first in war-torn Berlin. In contrast, Maria Kundera, the young Viennese clerk, like many other women, subordinated her own problems to those of her paratrooper boyfriend at the Western Front, not in deference to Nazi propaganda but because of her overriding concern for her fiancé.[115]

The sheer hunger for mail from home or front cannot be interpreted merely as a result of the careful orchestration of *Feldpost* by the regime. In my sample, the arrival of letters was universally greeted with enormous pleasure or even childlike excitement just as the failure of letters to arrive could cause extreme dread or anger. Hans and Maria wrote the most intensely intimate and passionate letters to each other. Theirs was first and foremost an epistolary love affair since they were torn apart so soon after it began.

Long periods of separation encouraged or forced couples to find the appropriate written form to express emotional intimacy. While at first glance, many letters appeared unduly influenced by colloquial expressions or samples of popular culture and by a certain coyness to express

---

[113] Roper, *The Secret Battle*, 14.   [114] Hämmerle, 'Gewalt und Liebe', 224ff.
[115] See Ziemann, 'Geschlechterbeziehungen', 270, describing the situation in the First World War.

sexual desire, reading between the lines and exploring changes in handwriting, syntax and salutations brings a richer picture of emotions and sexuality into view. These letters, written at a time of heightened emotional intensity, constituted, I contend, a private space even though it was in many ways entangled with the public sphere. Despite censorship and official propaganda, letters for my four protagonists functioned like a refuge in which to profess their feelings and reveal their dreams, hopes and fears. When they could no longer rely on intimate talks, daily rituals, shared activities or amorous encounters, they had to resort to epistolary narratives, imagining each other's body, touch and scent or conjuring up memories of past happiness. Constructing their own microcosm was their way of coping with enforced separation, confrontations with the enemy and ultimately the fear of a violent death. While it would be wrong to consider letters, as Margaretta Jolly put it, as 'spontaneous outpourings of the true self', it would also be wrong to dismiss them as merely reflecting social, linguistic and literary codes, as many epistolary critics would have put it. Intimate correspondence, Jolly asserts, has been 'an important space' in which to explore and assert 'new selves and desires'.[116] In letters, couples could develop a narrative to help them to discover a better sense of their selves, to understand traumatic circumstances and to transcend pain with language. It was a space which privileged personal feelings and in which subjective thoughts were given the recipient's full attention.

[116] Jolly, *In Love and Struggle*, 6–7, 25.

13 'A Birth Is Nothing Out of the Ordinary Here...'
Mothers, Midwives and the Private Sphere in the 'Reichsgau Wartheland', 1939–1945[*]

Wiebke Lisner

'A birth is nothing out of the ordinary here,' wrote the 'Reich German' midwife Julie Prinz in the National Socialist journal for midwives in 1943: 'Sometimes a calf arrives, sometimes a foal, sometimes a child, not much fuss is made at all.'[1]

Following the German occupation of Poland, Julie Prinz moved with her sister, herself a midwife, from the Altreich ('Old Reich', i.e. Germany in its 1937 borders) to the 'Reichsgau Wartheland' (Warthegau for short). There she worked as a self-employed midwife in the county district (*Kreis*) of Welun/Wieluń.[2] In her article, she recounted her impressions of and experiences with diverse groups of ethnic German resettlers (*Umsiedler* or *Rückwanderer*) from Volhynia, Galicia and Bessarabia as well as with those ethnic German families (usually referred to as *Volksdeutsche*) already living in Wieluń district before the German invasion of Poland who had been incorporated into the *Deutsche Volksliste* (German Ethnic Register).[3] In the quoted passage, Julie Prinz draws an analogy – probably for comic effect – between Volhynian Germans and farm animals, imputing to the resettlers a degree of naïveté and indifference regarding matters of birth.

(Translated from German by Paul Bowman)

[*] This chapter arises out of a project funded by the Deutsche Forschungsgemeinschaft on 'Hebammen im "biopolitischen Laborraum" des "Reichsgaus Wartheland" – Geburtshilfe zwischen Privatheit und staatlichem Zugriff' (RA 806/7–1/2) under the direction of Cornelia Rauh, whom, along with Lu Seegers, Verena Dohrn, Teresa Willenborg and the editors of this volume, I would like sincerely to thank for their valuable comments and suggestions.

[1] Julie Prinz, 'Erlebtes und Erlauschtes einer Hebamme unter den Rücksiedlern im Wartheland', *Die Deutsche Hebamme* 58 (1943), 202. From here onwards, inverted commas for '*Reichsdeutsche*'/'Reich German', and for '*Volksdeutsche*'/'ethnic German' have been omitted for better readability.

[2] See *Reichsadressbuch. Die Ostgebiete* (Berlin, 1942), 197.

[3] For an explanation of the term *volksdeutsch* (ethnic German), see Markus Krzoska, 'Volksdeutsche im Warthegau', in Eckhart Neander (ed.), *Umgesiedelt – Vertrieben: Deutschbalten und Polen 1939–1945 im Warthegau* (Marburg, 2010), 66–82, here 71.

Reich German midwives were recruited to provide health care and advice for the ethnic German resettlers during the resettlement transports and for the resettlement camps in the East.[4] But they also worked, like Julie Prinz, as licenced self-employed midwives in a specific district under the supervision of public medical officers who were in charge of the local health authority.[5] To ensure that there was sufficient obstetric care available to the population, the health administration in the Warthegau, as in the Altreich, relied on a decentralised, midwife-run obstetrics to counter the shortage of hospitals and transport facilities.[6] The place where the midwife carried out her work was thus normally the private dwelling of the woman giving birth. In the Altreich, for example, around 51 per cent of births in 1939 were home births; in Litzmannstadt/Łódź in 1941, the figure was 77 per cent.[7] Obstetric support thus took place mainly in the private sphere and was based on individual consultation between the midwife and the woman giving birth.[8]

At the same time, birth and reproduction were core areas of National Socialist biopolitics, which set out to intervene and to control the body and procreation. Biopolitical measures included practices that sought to discipline the body and to organise and adjust the bodily processes around pregnancy, birth and the postpartum period in order to align them with specific norms. Michel Foucault has described such a complex as an integral part of biopolitics and as characteristic of modernity.[9] In the Warthegau, biopolitics was implemented on the basis of National Socialist racial policy and the campaign to 'Germanise' (*germanisieren* or *eindeutschen*) the annexed territories.[10] The National Socialist state

---

[4] See Nanna Conti, 'Hebammen für die Ansiedlungslager', *Die Deutsche Hebamme* 55 (1940), 121.

[5] See Wiebke Lisner, 'Hebammen im "Reichsgau Wartheland" 1939–45: Geburtshilfe im Spannungsfeld von Germanisierung, Biopolitik und individueller biographischer Umbruchsituation', in Matthias Barelkowski, Claudia Kraft and Isabel Röskau-Rydel (eds.), *Zwischen Geschlecht und Nation: Interdependenzen und Interaktionen in der multiethnischen Gesellschaft Polens im 19. und 20. Jahrhundert* (Osnabrück, 2016), 237–64.

[6] See Bericht über die Sitzung in der Medizinalabteilung der Reichsstatthalterei, 16 January 1940, in Archiwum Państwowe w Poznaniu (APP), Reichsstatthalter (RSH) 299/1923, fol. 29–102.

[7] Łódź in Zahlen, 1941, in Archiwum Państwowe w Łodzi (APŁ), 221/L-15054.

[8] The contract was concluded between the midwife and the pregnant woman. The health insurers defined the scope of services provided. See for example Leni Rahlfs-Wentz, *Mutter werden... Ein Helfer zur Überwindung der Beschwerden dieser Zeit* (Stuttgart, 1941).

[9] See Michel Foucault, *The History of Sexuality*, vol. 1: *An Introduction* (London, 1984); Sebastian Reinfeldt, Richard Schwarz and Michel Foucault (eds.), *Bio-Macht* (Duisburg, 1992).

[10] See Ingo Haar, 'Biopolitische Differenzkonstruktionen als bevölkerungspolitisches Ordnungsinstrument in den Ostgauen: Raum- und Bevölkerungsplanung im Spannungsfeld zwischen regionaler Verankerung und zentralstaatlichem Planungsanspruch', in John/Möller/Schaarschmidt (eds.), *Die NS-Gaue*, 105–22.

expected midwives to 'educate' and control their clientele accordingly. In light of this mission, the interaction between midwife and mother became an act of public significance that was to reinforce the regime's hegemony. The opportunities for autonomous action on the part of individuals were thus in tension with the drive to gain access and to implement control in the name of Germanisation and biopolitics. Such efforts, as Edward Ross Dickinson has emphasised, did not only take the form of a top-down process by experts or state agencies: quoting Foucault, he sees power (including the 'power to manage life') 'coming from everywhere'.[11] Within this contested field, pregnancy, birth and the postpartum period constituted an intersection between the public and private spheres.

As a bourgeois-liberal principle affirming a sphere of freedom for the individual, protected from outside intervention, one pivotal formulation of 'the private' at the end of the nineteenth century was the 'right to be left alone'.[12] As a social and legal category, 'the private' encompasses individual decisions and actions in the sense of autonomy and self-definition. In the sense of 'local' privacy, it refers to spaces of withdrawal and retreat; it also refers to the realm of private ownership and economic freedom. The relationship between 'private' and 'public' is shaped by processes of social negotiation and by historical ruptures.[13] During National Socialism, as has often been pointed out, the private underwent a new degree of politicisation. The regime sought to intervene in all areas of the private, and the household sphere was no exception, including pregnancy, birth and early parenthood.[14] However, privacy – as Andreas Wirsching and Johannes Hürter have observed – was not simply eliminated. On the contrary, the National Socialist regime granted privacy as a privilege and recognised the private as a valuable resource for all those included in the *Volksgemeinschaft*.[15] Under the conditions of dictatorship and war,

---

[11] Edward Ross Dickinson, 'Biopolitics, Fascism, Democracy: Some Reflections on Our Discourse about "Modernity"', *Central European History* 37/1 (2004), 1–48, here 41–2.

[12] See Beate Rössler, 'Zum individuellen und gesellschaftlichen Wert des Privaten', in Sandra Seubert and Peter Niesen (eds.), *Die Grenzen des Privaten* (Baden-Baden, 2010), 41–58.

[13] See ibidem; Sandra Seubert, 'Privat und Öffentlichkeit heute: Ein Problemaufriss', in Seubert/Niesen (eds.), *Die Grenzen des Privaten*, 9–24.

[14] See Andreas Wirsching, '*Volksgemeinschaft* and the Illusion of "Normality" from the 1920s to the 1940s', in Martina Steber and Bernhard Gotto (eds.), *Visions of Community in Nazi Germany: Social Engineering and Private Lives* (Oxford, New York, NY, 2014), 149–56; Johannes Hürter, 'Das Private im Nationalsozialismus', paper given at the conference 'Der Ort der "Volksgemeinschaft"', Hannover, 25–27 June 2015.

[15] See Andreas Wirsching, 'Privacy', in Winfried Nerdinger (ed.), *Munich and National Socialism: Catalogue of the Munich Documentation Centre for the History of National Socialism* (Munich, 2015), 439–45; Hürter 'Das Private'. On the 'private sphere' of the household during the Second World War, see Elizabeth Harvey, 'Housework, Domestic Privacy and the "German Home": Paradoxes of Private Life during the Second World

as Wirsching has outlined, the boundaries between 'private' and 'public' were renegotiated. As a result, the relationship between the sexes changed: particularly in wartime, the assumed, supposedly 'natural', demarcation between gendered spheres became less important, opening up new possibilities, especially for young women.[16] Specifically, as part of the 'civilising mission' of Germanisation in the Nazi-occupied territories of Eastern Europe, women acquired – as Elizabeth Harvey has shown – extensive opportunities and power in the 'female sphere' of housekeeping and childcare.[17]

Against this background, this chapter examines how midwives and mothers came to be involved in negotiations and disputes in the area of pregnancy, birth and early parenthood in occupied Poland. It asks what forms of power were available both to midwives and to mothers, and explores how the boundaries of the private were negotiated. In the Warthegau, the freedom to choose a midwife included, because of a shortage of German midwives, the possibility of calling in a Polish Christian midwife. Given the context of Germanisation policies, racial segregation and racial hierarchies, how far did this possibility open up opportunities to negotiate and defend the private?[18]

In exploring these questions, the specific situation of women giving birth and midwives delivering babies needs to be borne in mind. In this context, the public/private boundary is not a matter of controlling or allowing access merely to private living spaces or private information, but to the most intimately private sphere of the body itself. Arnd Pollmann describes the skin as the physical and sensory boundary between 'private' and 'public', emphasising the crucial importance to the sphere of privacy of controlling and regulating access to the body.[19] Considered from this angle, it is not just wider forms of controlling and influencing behaviour under conditions of Nazi conquest and occupation that need to be examined with respect to how the private was negotiated and defended. The specific physical access to the body of expectant mothers and delivering women was pivotal.

War', in Rüdiger Hachtmann and Sven Reichardt (eds.), *Detlev Peukert und die NS-Forschung: Beiträge zur Geschichte des Nationalsozialismus* (Göttingen, 2015), 115–31.

[16] See Wirsching, 'Privacy', 443–4. See also Julia Paulus and Marion Röwekamp (eds.), *Eine Soldatenheimschwester an der Ostfront: Briefwechsel von Annette Schücking mit ihrer Familie (1941–1943)* (Paderborn, Munich, 2015).

[17] See Elizabeth Harvey, *Women and the Nazi East: Agents and Witnesses of Germanization* (New Haven, CT, London, 2003), 294–301.

[18] On aspects of various configurations of the relationship between 'private' and 'public', see Hürter, 'Das Private'.

[19] Arnd Pollmann, '"Schmerz, lass nach": Die körperliche Hülle als Schauplatz autodestruktiver Privatisierung', in Seubert/Niesen (eds.), *Die Grenzen des Privaten*, 165–80.

This specific quality of interactions in relation to giving birth had a necessary corollary in the sense that permitting such intimate access required a particular degree of trust. This chapter aims to show that due to the intrusion of state agencies, the overarching biopolitical and Germanising objectives as well as deploying midwives in an ideological role, a 'private sphere' in relation to birth was possible only on the basis of very substantial trust between the midwife and the delivering woman. Trust – as Niklas Luhmann describes it – involves the weighing up of two alternatives in a case where the potential damage caused by a breach of trust may be greater than the potential advantages of offering and displaying trust. Trust thus entails the acceptance of risk. At the same time, however, trust opens up a broader spectrum for experience and action, neutralising – in the sense of reducing complexity – certain dangers which, while they cannot be eliminated fully, do not require acting upon. Here Luhmann distinguishes between different levels of trust, such as the 'personal trust' placed in other people within one's own social milieu and 'systemic trust'.[20] Trust, it is argued in this chapter, became a decisive resource in negotiating and defending the private at the bedside of the mother giving birth. It explores how far midwives and mothers succeeded in building and using trust, enabling them to produce a situation-specific realm of the private and to protect it from the intervention of the regime. As an analytical category, the 'private' provides an opportunity to examine the interactions of German and Polish midwives with 'ethnic German' mothers from a perspective that regards social practice as a locus of power and relates this to questions of individuality, identity and autonomy.[21] Focusing on the female profession of the midwife enables, furthermore, a contribution – on a micro level in the female domain of birth and reproduction – to the question as to how the objective of Germanising the annexed territories of Poland was implemented in practice between 'private' and 'public'.

The questions just outlined are examined using reports published from 1939 to 1944 in *Die Deutsche Hebamme*, the organ of the professional midwives' organisation, together with sources from Polish state archives. Under the leadership of Nanna Conti, the mother of Reich Health Leader Leonardo Conti, the professional midwives' organisation called on Reich German midwives to become involved in the work of 'construction' in the

---

[20] Niklas Luhmann, *Vertrauen: Ein Mechanismus der Reduktion sozialer Komplexität* (Stuttgart, 1989), 7, 24–54.
[21] See Hürter, 'Das Private'. For approaches to domination as a social practice, see Alf Lüdtke, *Herrschaft als soziale Praxis: Historische und sozial-anthropologische Studien* (Göttingen, 1991).

conquered East.[22] The motivation behind a decision to respond to this call varied, ranging from the prospect of higher earnings and enthusiasm for the 'work of resettlement' to the wish to escape from burdensome forms of social control back in the Altreich.[23]

The midwife quoted earlier, Julie Prinz, declared: 'We arrived cram full of idealism and with an iron will to do our bit in building the East, and a good thing we did, too.'[24] She painted – like other contributors to the midwives' journal – a picture of midwives actively committed to Germanising occupied Poland who, rolling up their sleeves and armed with 'scrubbing brush and broom', set about getting rid of 'Polish chaos' ('*polnische Wirtschaft*').[25] The published reports reflect primarily the interpretations and self-dramatising accounts of the Reich German midwives active in or closely affiliated with the professional organisation. In their reports they typically reflected the aspirations of midwives as a professional group and propaganda scenarios concerning the 'new Eastern territories' as well as stereotypes of the ethnic German, Polish and Jewish populations. They pursued – in line with Nazi propaganda – the goal of promoting the German 'work of construction' in their field of competence and recruiting others to join them in the conquered territories.[26] The authors identified with their position of authority as Reich Germans, described the prevailing power relations in occupied Poland from that perspective and affirmed the principle of racist hierarchies. Despite their propagandistic intentions, these reports nevertheless provide important evidence on the mentalities as well as the living and working conditions of Reich German midwives in occupied Poland.

The reports of the Reich German midwives are compared with archival sources, above all those of the German health authorities in the Warthegau. Many documents from the state health agencies were

---

[22] Nanna Conti, 'Gebietsneueinteilungen im Reich', *Die Deutsche Hebamme* 54 (1940), 434.
[23] See Lisner, 'Hebammen im "Reichsgau Wartheland"'. Elizabeth Harvey and Franka Maubach have identified similar motivations for female helpers in the war and women involved in the work of 'construction' in the occupied East. See Harvey, *Women and the Nazi East*, 99–118; Franka Maubach, 'Expansionen weiblicher Hilfe: Zur Erfahrungsgeschichte von Frauen im Kriegsdienst', in Sybille Steinbacher (ed.), *Volksgenossinnen: Frauen in der NS-Volksgemeinschaft* (Göttingen, 2007), 93–114.
[24] Prinz, 'Erlebtes', 202.
[25] See Nanna Conti, 'Der Einsatz der Hebamme bei der Großen Heimkehr im Osten', *Die Deutsche Hebamme* 55 (1940), 65–7. A similar style was also evident in accounts given by female students and resettler assistants of the *Nationalsozialistische Frauenschaft* in occupied Poland. See Harvey, *Women and the Nazi East*, 88–90.
[26] For example Ingeborg Morsbach, 'Von der Arbeit in den Ostgebieten', *Die Deutsche Hebamme* 57 (1942), 60–1.

destroyed during the evacuation of the Warthegau in January 1945.[27] This makes the near-complete personnel files of German and Polish midwives which have survived from the holdings of the health offices in Leslau/Włocławek and Litzmannstadt/Łódź all the more valuable. Hitherto unexplored, these files offer – even though they inevitably reflect the perspective of the German occupation authorities – a close-up view of the biographies, working conditions and everyday lives of German and Polish midwives that would otherwise be virtually impossible given the lack of 'ego-documents'. When it comes to the relationships and interactions between midwives and women giving birth and the domestic circumstances of the women and families whom the midwives looked after, the evidence is sparser. Such interactions mostly leave a trace in the files only when conflict arose. That said, petitions and complaints, representations and statements made to the medical officer or in court all provide a glimpse into private domains such as the home, sexuality, interpersonal relations, gender and domestic power relations. Such records offer clues about the outlook and self-perceptions of those in the care of the midwives that were otherwise rarely put down in writing or made public. When people defended themselves against allegations made by neighbours or by the Nazi authorities, they were pursuing particular goals that often concerned vitally important dimensions of their private life.

Obstetrics, Germanisation and Biopolitics in the Warthegau

The Reichsgau Wartheland was created in October 1939 and, like the Reichsgau Danzig-West Prussia and the newly created Regierungsbezirke (districts) of Kattowitz and Zichenau, was incorporated into the German Reich.[28] Julie Prinz largely blanked out the very existence of a Polish population in the Warthegau, creating in her account the impression that Germanisation had already been completed and there was no need even to acknowledge the existence of the Polish and Jewish populations.[29] Of

---

[27] See Johannes Vossen, 'Gesundheitspolitik als Teil der "Volkstumspolitik": Der öffentliche Gesundheitsdienst im "Reichsgau Wartheland"', unpublished final report submitted to the Fritz Thyssen Stiftung, 2005.

[28] See Dieter Pohl, 'Die Reichsgaue Danzig-Westpreußen und Wartheland: Koloniale Verwaltung oder Modell für die zukünftige Gauverwaltung?', in Jürgen John, Horst Möller and Thomas Schaarschmidt (eds.), *Die NS-Gaue: Regionale Mittelinstanzen im zentralistischen 'Führerstaat'* (Munich, 2007), 395–405.

[29] See Doris L. Bergen, Anna Hájková and Andrea Löw, 'Warum eine Alltagsgeschichte des Holocaust?', in Andrea Löw, Doris L. Bergen and Anna Hájková (eds.), *Alltag im Holocaust: Jüdisches Leben im Großdeutschen Reich 1941–1945* (Munich, 2013), 1–12, here 2.

around 4.3 million residents of the Warthegau in 1944, approximately 3.3 million were Polish.[30]

National Socialist expansionist policies aimed at gaining new 'living space' (*Lebensraum*) for Germans.[31] The overriding goal of the German occupiers was the Germanisation of the 'incorporated Eastern territories' through resettlement combined with a large-scale 'ethnic restructuring' (*Umvolkung*) that entailed the inclusion of 'desirable' and the exclusion of 'undesirable' population groups.[32] Around 1 million ethnic German resettlers from South-East and Eastern Europe were transferred to what were designated as German 'areas of interest'.[33] Germanisation policies in the Warthegau under the leadership of Reich Governor Arthur Greiser were particularly radical in the sense that large numbers of the native population were displaced and expelled.[34] The Warthegau accordingly became the main settlement area for the incoming ethnic Germans.[35]

At the same time, a sifting of the resident population of the Warthegau was under way. Introduced in October 1939 by Arthur Greiser, the German Ethnic Register (*Deutsche Volksliste*) divided the resident population into 'Germans' and 'Poles'. Those classified as 'German' were assigned to four different categories, based on judgements about their past commitment to *Deutschtum* ('Germandom'), their ethnic ancestry and their potential social value as 'Germans'.[36] The grouping of the German population in the categories I–IV was linked to the granting of differently graded state citizenship rights tied to specific standards of conduct and special regulations, above all for those in groups III and IV. Those assigned to these groups had to demonstrate their Germanness.[37] Around 12 per cent of the resident

---

[30] The proportion of German population had risen from 7 per cent in 1939 to 23 per cent in 1944. See Krzoska, 'Volksdeutsche im Warthegau', 67–8.

[31] Michael Wildt, 'Völkische Neuordnung Europas', in *clio online* (2016), www.europa.clio-online.de/essay/id/artikel-3748 [accessed 29 December 2016].

[32] See Gerhard Wolf, *Ideologie und Herrschaftsrationalität: Nationalsozialistische Germanisierungspolitik in Polen* (Hamburg, 2012), 90, 97–8.

[33] Maria Fiebrandt, *Auslese für die Siedlergesellschaft: Die Einbeziehung Volksdeutscher in die NS-Erbgesundheitspolitik im Kontext der Umsiedlungen 1939–1945* (Göttingen, 2014), 629–30.

[34] Catherine Epstein, *Model Nazi: Arthur Greiser and the Occupation of Western Poland* (Oxford, 2010).

[35] See Alexa Stiller, 'Germanisierung und Gewalt: Nationalsozialistische Volkstumspolitik in den polnischen, französischen und slowenischen Annexionsgebieten, 1939–1945' (PhD, Bern, 2015), 216–17, 294–300.

[36] According to Wolf, mainly social practices were considered when deciding on the commitment to 'Germandom'. See Wolf, *Ideologie und Herrschaftsrationalität*, 272–3.

[37] See Isabel Heinemann, *Rasse, Siedlung, deutsches Blut: Das Rasse- und Siedlungshauptamt der SS und die rassenpolitische Neuordnung Europas* (Göttingen, 2003); Ingo Haar, 'Vom "Volksgruppen-Paradigma" bis zum "Recht auf Heimat": Exklusion und Inklusion als Deutungsmuster in den Diskursen über Zwangsmigrationen vor und nach 1945', in

population in the Warthegau was entered into the German Ethnic Register.[38] The process of selection and inclusion involved in the administration of the *Volksliste* meant that the ethnicity of German and Poles was thus negotiable within certain limits. One consequence of this was – as Birthe Kundrus has noted – that definitions of 'Germanness' became necessarily more diverse and flexible.[39]

The forced displacement of and use of violence against the Polish and Jewish populations were closely tied to resettling the incoming ethnic Germans and were an integral component of the Germanisation policies pursued in the annexed eastern territories.[40] Up to 1943, some 280,000 persons were forcibly resettled from the Warthegau to the General Government (*Generalgouvernement*) and within the Gau itself, approximately another 254,000 were forcibly removed (*verdrängt*) in order, amongst other things, to create room for ethnic German resettlers.[41]

The Polish midwife Katharina Zalewski, born in 1890 and resident in what became under occupation the county district of Leslau (*Kreis* Leslau), was one of those affected by the forced displacements and dispossession of the Polish and Jewish populations.[42] She had been working in the Leslau (Włocawek) area as a licensed midwife since 1930. Following a motorcycle accident, her husband was an invalid and she became the sole earner. As part of the measures implemented to seize premises and property for the resettlers, here primarily incomers from the Baltic states, Volhynia and Galicia, the family home was confiscated, depriving her husband of his remaining financial security.[43] Unlike some 16,500 Christian Poles from Leslau, however, the family managed to avoid deportation to the General Government and found a new place to live in the district.[44]

Jerzy Kochanowski and Maike Sach (eds.), *Die 'Volksdeutschen' in Polen, Frankreich, Ungarn und der Tschechoslowakei: Mythos und Realität* (Osnabrück, 2006), 17–40.

[38] See Markus Roth, 'Nationalsozialistische Umsiedlungspolitik im besetzten Polen: Ziele, beteiligte Institutionen, Methoden und Ergebnisse', in Neander (ed.), *Umgesiedelt – Vertrieben*, 9–20, here 19.

[39] Birthe Kundrus, 'Regime der Differenz: Volkstumspolitische Inklusionen und Exklusionen im Warthegau und Generalgouvernement 1939–1944', in Frank Bajohr and Michael Wildt (eds.), *Volksgemeinschaft: Neue Forschungen zur Gesellschaft des Nationalsozialismus* (Frankfurt a.M., 2009), 105–23.

[40] See Götz Aly, *'Final Solution': Nazi Population Policy and the Murder of the European Jews* (London, 1995).

[41] See Stiller, 'Germanisierung', 765–6.

[42] On dispossession, see Ingo Loose, *Kredite für NS-Verbrechen: Die deutschen Kreditinstitute in Polen und die Ausraubung der polnischen und jüdischen Bevölkerung 1939–1945* (Munich, 2007).

[43] See personal file of Katharina Zalewski (name altered), in Archiwum Państwowe we Włocławku (APW), 829/44.

[44] Deportation figures taken from Stiller, 'Germanisierung', 765.

With its enactment on 7 October 1940, the Reich Midwifery Law, which had been passed in the Altreich in December 1938, was now introduced into the 'incorporated Eastern territories'.[45] The law supported German midwives financially, legally and professionally, implementing for example a minimum income and a pension scheme, and it ensured that they had a monopoly in obstetrics by introducing their mandatory presence at birth. Pregnant women, relatives and doctors were now obliged to call to every birth or miscarriage a midwife licensed by the Health Office. In this way, the National Socialist state strengthened the position of midwives. At the same time, all midwives considered 'non-Aryan', 'politically unreliable' or 'incompetent' were excluded from accreditation.[46] In the Warthegau, midwives of 'non-German ethnic origin' were able to apply for temporary accreditation. Katharina Zalewski was able to gain permission to continue working as a midwife in *Kreis* Leslau.[47] She was not, however, entitled to full professional status – her licence could be revoked at any time – nor was she included in any measures ensuring her financial security such as the minimum income or pension scheme.[48]

The task of German midwives, meanwhile, was above all to ensure that the German population had obstetric care. Special biopolitical importance was attached to this care,[49] as a report by the Racial Policy Office of the NSDAP in October 1941 made clear:

Faced with the enduring efforts on the part of Poles to continue the struggle deliberately and methodically in the realm of population politics by achieving as high a Polish birth-rate as possible, every single German infant that perishes through improper treatment and every German mother left incapacitated is an irreplaceable loss in the German combat sector (*Kampfabschnitt*)[50]

Birth rates were thus – to continue with the militaristic imagery of the report – a battlefield of Germanisation. Accordingly, care for German mothers and infants as well as measures designed to boost the birth rate, for example financial assistance for mothers and children or restrictive abortion regulations for the German population, became increasingly important. At the

---

[45] 'Verordnung zur Einführung des Hebammengesetzes in den eingegliederten Ostgebieten', 7 October 1940 (RGBl. 178/1940, p. 1333), *Die Deutsche Hebamme* 55 (1940), 227–8.
[46] See Dienstordnung für Hebammen dated 16 February 1943, in RGBl. Nr. 10/43.
[47] See personal file in APW, 829/44.
[48] See Verordnung zur Einführung des Hebammengesetzes, 227–8.
[49] In 1944, around 195,000 Reich Germans (4 per cent) lived in the Warthegau, 319,300 resettlers (*Umsiedler*) (7 per cent) and 500,000 *Volksdeutsche* (11 per cent) registered on the German Ethnic Register. Stiller, 'Germanisierung', 1328.
[50] Bericht Rassenpolitisches Amt der NSDAP, 1 October 1941, in Instytut Pamięci Narodowej (IPN) Łódź, GK 746/95. I would like to thank Robert Parzer for finding and allowing me to use this source.

same time, National Socialist health and biopolitics aimed to break the 'biological potency' of the Polish population, introducing for instance a scaling down of health services justified on 'racial' grounds together with outright anti-natalist measures.[51] A minimum marriage age was set for Poles and the minimum maternity protection granted to Polish women was solely geared to maintaining the capacity of the workforce. In the view of leading health politicians, if miscarriage or premature birth were diagnosed as likely, then remedial intervention was not to be undertaken; instead, the recommendation was to facilitate abortion.[52]

Reich German Midwives: Ethnic German Mothers

The occupation regime never achieved the goal of providing the German population throughout the Warthegau with the services of German midwives. Even though the number of German midwives almost doubled between 1939 and 1942 – rising from 146 to 260 – the German health authorities claimed that an additional 165 German midwives were still needed in order to provide appropriate midwifery care for the German population, which stood at around 850,000 in 1942.[53] In the subsequent years up to 1944, the number of German midwives did not increase significantly, but the number of Polish midwives decreased from 692 in 1942 to 604 in 1944.[54] The German population by contrast reached the 1 million mark – 23 per cent of the total population in the Warthegau – in 1944.[55]

While most German midwives in the Warthegau were Reich German, the majority of the German women and families they cared for belonged to the various categories of *Volksdeutsche*.[56] In the town of Leslau for example, 74 per cent of the German population was classified as ethnic German in 1941. They were either members of the

---

[51] See Vossen, 'Gesundheitspolitik als Teil der "Volkstumspolitik"'; Fiebrandt, *Auslese*, 545–7; Epstein, *Model Nazi*, 215–18.

[52] See Diemut Majer, *'Fremdvölkische' im Dritten Reich: Ein Beitrag zur nationalsozialistischen Rechtssetzung und Rechtspraxis in Verwaltung und Justiz unter besonderer Berücksichtigung der eingegliederten Ostgebiete und des Generalgouvernements* (Boppard am Rhein, 1981), 433. See also Verfügung zum Mutterschutz bei Polinnen, 22 April 1944, in APP, RSH 299/2070, fol. 26; various letters and memos by Leonardo Conti on the question of abortion in BArch Berlin, R 1501/3806.

[53] See report of Abteilung II Reichsstatthalterei, Lagebericht für das 4. Vierteljahr 1942, Medizinalwesen, 20 January 1942, APP, RSH 299/1880.

[54] In 1943, the number of German midwives did rise to nearly 300, but numbers fell again the following year back to 257. See reports 1942–4, in APP, RSH 299/1880, 1882.

[55] See Krzoska, 'Volksdeutsche im Warthegau', 67–8.

[56] In 1943, out of 299 German midwives around 50 were members of the German minority in Poland and 50 were resettlers. See report Stand des Gesundheitswesens, 7 August 1943, in APP, RSH 299/1882.

German minority already living in Poland before 1939 or resettlers from South-East and Eastern Europe.[57] The resettlers were regarded, as Isabel Heinemann has put it, as the 'spearhead of Germanization policy'. They were to settle in the annexed Polish territories, form a 'protective wall' facing the east and 'biologically' supplant the Polish population.[58]

Ethnic Germans were in an ambivalent position. The interactions between Reich Germans, the different categories of *Volksdeutsche* and Poles were characterised by complex relationships involving the interplay of power and powerlessness, trust and betrayal, taboos and contacts.[59] In the racial hierarchy of the Warthegau, the ethnic Germans ranked beneath the Reich Germans but above the Christian Poles and far above the Polish Jews.[60] Depending on their respective classificatory grouping in the German Ethnic Register or the particular community of resettlers to which they belonged, they were subject to diverse constraints: limits were often placed on their freedom of movement and some had to accept restrictions on their choice of employment and marriage partner.[61] Moreover, ethnic Germans had to endure physical examinations, either, in the case of resettlers, as part of the naturalisation process under the authority of the *Einwandererzentralstelle* (Central Immigration Office) attached to the Reich Security Main Office or, in the case of the pre-1939 resident population, as part of the procedures for registering in the German Ethnic Register.[62] At the same time, though, ethnic Germans profited as a group from the dispossession and subordination of the Polish and Jewish populations. They gained flats, homes, farms, businesses and furnishings, and were

---

[57] See Statistik, in APW, 829/ 96.
[58] Heinemann, *Rasse, Siedlung, deutsches Blut*, 188.
[59] See for example Maren Röger, *Kriegsbeziehungen: Intimität, Gewalt und Prostitution im besetzten Polen 1939 bis 1945* (Frankfurt a.M., 2015).
[60] See Maren Röger, 'Sexual Contact between German Occupiers and Polish Occupied in World War II in Poland', in Maren Röger and Ruth Leiserowitz (eds.), *Women and Men at War: A Gender Perspective on World War II and Its Aftermath in Central and Eastern Europe* (Osnabrück, 2012), 135–56.
[61] See 'Anordnung von Greiser', in *Gau-Amtsblatt der NSDAP, Gau Wartheland*, Jg. IV, Lieferung 15/43, 1 August 1943, Ausgabe K, Hoheitsträger.
[62] The *Einwandererzentralstelle* examined resettlers as to their 'racial hygiene' and 'hereditary biology' as part of the naturalisation process for citizenship; in contrast, acceptance in the German Ethnic Register – according to Gerhard Wolf – depended more on the stated commitment to Germandom and its social aspects. See Gerhard Wolf, 'Die deutschen Minderheiten in Polen als Instrument der expansiven Außenpolitik Berlins', in Jerzy Kochanowski and Maike Sach (eds.), *Die 'Volksdeutschen' in Polen, Frankreich, Ungarn und der Tschechoslowakei: Mythos und Realität* (Osnabrück, 2006), 41–78; Fiebrandt, *Auslese*; Andreas Strippel, *NS-Volkstumspolitik und die Neuordnung Europas: Rassenpolitische Selektion der Einwandererzentralstelle des Chefs der Sicherheitspolizei und des SD (1939–1945)* (Paderborn, 2011).

given privileges in all areas of life.[63] They also benefitted by virtue of their position and status from the forced labour of the Polish and Jewish populations. Some meanwhile, took an active part in acts of violence, in plundering, robbery, eviction, rape and murder. The *Volksdeutscher Selbstschutz* ('self-protection' paramilitary unit formed by ethnic Germans) was heavily involved in the murder of many Poles and Jews at the beginning of the occupation – it murdered about 20,000 people on its own account.[64] There were also resettlers and members of the German minority who exploited their new position of power for personal enrichment.[65]

Cultural, religious and linguistic differences, varying traditions, customs, values and norms, together with the gradations of status between the various resettler groups, the German minority in western Poland and the Reich Germans, were all elements in a complex situation harbouring enormous potential for conflict.[66] Through 'cultural engineering' (as Wilhelm Fielitz has put it), the different groups of 'ethnic Germans' were to be adapted to fit in with Nazi society and merge with the Reich Germans to form an 'expanded *Volksgemeinschaft*' with which they were supposed to identify.[67] To achieve this, it was necessary to integrate the various ethnic German groups and to give them a thorough understanding of 'German culture', not least in the female domain of reproduction and housekeeping.[68] Reich German midwives were expected to play their part in this: as the *Regierungspräsident* (district president) in Litzmannstadt stated in 1941,

---

[63] See for example Rainer Schulze, '"Der Führer ruft!" Zur Rückholung der Volksdeutschen aus dem Osten', in Kochanowski and Sach (eds.), *Die 'Volksdeutschen'*, 183–204; Loose, *Kredite*, 445–52.

[64] See Christian Jansen and Arno Weckbecker, *Der 'Volksdeutsche Selbstschutz' in Polen 1939/40* (Munich, 1992); Jochen Böhler, *Auftakt zum Vernichtungskrieg: Die Wehrmacht in Polen 1939* (Frankfurt a.M., 2006), 232. The *Volksdeutsche Selbstschutz* was also involved in killing patients in psychiatric wards. See Volker Rieß, 'Zentrale und dezentrale Radikalisierung: Die Tötungen "unwerten Lebens" in den annektierten west- und nordpolnischen Gebieten 1939–1941', in Klaus-Michael Mallmann and Bogdan Musial (eds.), *Genesis des Genozids: Polen 1939–1941* (Darmstadt, 2004), 127–44; Enno Schwanke, *Die Landesheil- und Pflegeanstalt Tiegenhof: Die nationalsozialistische Euthanasie in Polen während des Zweiten Weltkriegs* (Frankfurt a.M., 2015).

[65] See for example Hans-Jürgen Bömelburg and Marlene Klatt (eds.), *Lodz im Zweiten Weltkrieg: Deutsche Selbstzeugnisse über Alltag, Lebenswelten und NS-Germanisierungspolitik in einer multiethnischen Stadt* (Osnabrück, 2015); Stiller, 'Germanisierung', 1139.

[66] See Wilhelm Fielitz, *Das Stereotyp des wolhyniendeutschen Umsiedlers: Popularisierungen zwischen Sprachinselforschung und nationalsozialistischer Propaganda* (Marburg, 2000), quotes on 154–5. See also Ute Schmidt, *Die Deutschen aus Bessarabien: Eine Minderheit aus Südosteuropa (1814 bis heute)* (Cologne, Weimar, Vienna, 2004).

[67] Fielitz, *Das Stereotyp*, 21; Harvey, 'Der Osten braucht Dich! Frauen und nationalsozialistische Germanisierungspolitik (Hamburg, 2010), 223–4.

[68] Harvey, 'Der Osten braucht Dich!', 413–22.

midwives were to 'teach' their German clientele how to become German mothers.[69]

For Julie Prinz and many other Reich German midwives, the encounter with ethnic German resettlers and the German minority in Poland was a discomfiting experience in which they were faced with a culture that was alien to them and obstetric practices that diverged in fundamental respects from the norms and standards they had been taught in midwifery training.[70] One immediate point of contention between Reich German midwives and ethnic German women was the issue of who should be present at a birth. Above all women from Volhynia clearly regarded giving birth as a 'social event' where neighbours and relatives got together. They accordingly demanded control over who was to enter their private dwellings and who was allowed to have contact with their body. Hildegard Friese, a functionary of the *Bund Deutscher Mädel* (League of German Girls) in the county district (*Kreis*) of Welun, recounted for example a birth in a Volhynian household attended by eight to ten women neighbours. These women refused to leave the room and kept Hildegard Friese – much to her annoyance – away from the birth bed until the child was born.[71] Due to her position of authority as a representative of the National Socialist regime, Hildegard Friese – despite having no expertise in obstetrics – claimed the right to have access to the private sphere of the ethnic German family and to determine how the body of the woman was to be treated during delivery. In this case, however, the Volhynian women prevailed and were able to thwart Hildegard Friese's attempt to exercise control over the birth and the body of the mother, even if they could not prevent her from entering the private dwelling and the room where the birth took place. Like Hildegard Friese, Reich German midwives also preferred births with just a few in attendance. At times they clearly succeeded and were able to regulate who had access to the mother. In a journal article from 1942, one midwife wrote: 'I removed all the neighbours from the room so that they, quite apart from any other harm they might do, would not put my client on edge.'[72] Her comment was revealing: she assumed that her expert knowledge entitled her to pass judgement on the situation and justified her demand for exclusive access

---

[69] Report of Regierungspräsident Litzmannstadt, 4 August 1941, in APP RSH 299/2031.
[70] Regierungspräsident Litzmannstadt, 4 August 1941, in RSH 299/2031. Elizabeth Harvey describes this in relation to the resettler helpers and the *Bund Deutscher Mädel*. See Harvey, '*Der Osten braucht Dich!*', 220–4.
[71] See Dr. Hildegard Friese: Denkschrift über die Siedler im Kreis Welun, 27 September 1944, with additions and abridgements from 1964, in BArch Bayreuth, Ost-Dok. 13/215, fol. 1, fol. 2–40, here fol. 26.
[72] I. S. (full name unknown), 'Bericht einer Hebamme aus dem Gau Westpreußen', *Die Deutsche Hebamme* 57 (1942), 44.

to the birth room and control over the body of her client. She declared the women neighbours to be a danger while at the same time claiming an exceptional position, that of the sole confidante to the woman giving birth.

While Julie Prinz did not send the neighbours out of the room, she did refuse to go along with any obstetric practices she was unfamiliar with and which ran contrary to her ideas of hygiene. Like the midwife quoted earlier, she justified her action and interpretation of the situation with expert knowledge she took to be indisputable and which she described as superior to the practical knowledge and traditions of the ethnic Germans:

> They [the Volhynians] are also familiar with perineum protection. As soon as the head emerges or even before, they actively begin to stretch the vagina apart and push from the anus. That means that during the birth, even if we are not yet at the point of undertaking perineum protection, we always have to watch out that none of those standing by suddenly grab with their dirty hands.[73]

There were also differences in breastfeeding practices. Influenced by self-help books on upbringing and the midwife training she received, Julie Prinz had internalised the Altreich way of dealing with babies, which was oriented towards discipline and control. Fixed feeding, waking and sleeping hours were accordingly regarded as necessary and any 'exaggerated' sentimentality shown towards the infant was seen as damaging. With a view to the needs of the *Volksgemeinschaft*, it was deemed necessary to educate mothers and babies in a way that would optimise health and behaviour.[74] In the Warthegau, Julie Prinz witnessed how the values she had internalised were simply disregarded by the ethnic German mothers and she thus predicted serious consequences for how the infants would behave: 'If the infant screams every hour, it gets something. [...] With cradling and carrying and feeding the infant is more or less kept quiet and so it turns into a little nuisance.'[75] Practices in the care, hygiene and clothing of infants that Julie Prinz characterised as utterly deficient – such as not using an umbilical bandage for new-borns, 'improper' airing in winter or letting infants crawl around on the floor – she also presented as causes of high infant mortality.[76]

Julie Prinz drew a clear distinction, however, between the resident German-speaking population and the Volhynians on one hand, and the

---

[73] Prinz, 'Erlebtes', 203.
[74] See Gudrun Brockhaus, 'Muttermacht und Lebensangst: Zur Politischen Psychologie der NS-Erziehungsratgeber Johanna Haarers', in José Brunner (ed.), *Mütterliche Macht und väterliche Autorität: Elternbilder im deutschen Diskurs* (Göttingen, 2008), 63–77; Miriam Gebhardt, *Die Angst vor dem kindlichen Tyrannen: Eine Geschichte der Erziehung im 20. Jahrhundert* (Munich, 2009).
[75] Prinz, 'Erlebtes', 216.   [76] See ibidem.

Bessarabian Germans, whom she regarded as considerably more 'cultivated', on the other. One could, she opined, see the higher stage of the latter's development in their obstetrical practices, for they treated birth with more respect and did not allow all and sundry to get involved and start meddling.[77] At the same time, though, she argued that there should be some understanding shown for Volhynian women and she explained their 'backward' behaviour with the life 'full of deprivation' they had lived 'under the Poles'.[78] The typical image of the Volhynian presented in the Nazi media portrayed them as poor and modest peasants, members of a downtrodden and uneducated rural underclass, with an 'abundance of children' but lacking a grasp of 'German hygiene' standards.[79] By contrast, Bessarabian Germans were described as the 'most capable farmers'.[80] With her report Julie Prinz cemented these stereotypes and embellished existing prejudices for the field of obstetrics with anecdotes from her practical experience.

Like other Reich German midwives, Julie Prinz reacted to the sense of strangeness separating her from her ethnic German clientele in part with empathy but also with incomprehension and rejection. Above all, though, she took her mission very seriously to educate and instil obstetric standards – through monitoring and regulating the private sphere of her clientele and constraining their autonomy. Her claim to expert status as a midwife and authority as a Reich German was underpinned by a construct of social difference that classified specific groups amongst the ethnic Germans, for example the Volhynians, as 'primitive'. From this construct Julie Prinz then derived a medical-hygienic and cultural superiority.[81] She described the situation she faced: 'It takes a lot of affection and patience, and quite often strictness as well, to prevail here.'[82] Julie Prinz enjoyed her work in the Warthegau and her position of authority. Her enthusiasm is palpable:

> The work brings [...] great satisfaction, after all I'm the midwife, a confidante of the family, medical advisor, household advisor – Girl Friday (*Mädchen für alles*), I can contribute all my skills and knowledge. Above all else, I work independently, and that's something that appeals to every midwife!

From the perspective of her ethnic German clientele, however, the relationship to Julie Prinz, a low-level functionary in the National Socialist

---

[77] See ibidem. [78] See ibidem.
[79] Fielitz, *Das Stereotyp*, 117, 154; Harvey, '*Der Osten braucht Dich!*', 221–3.
[80] See Stiller, *Germanisierung*, 1145. Bessarabian Germans were, moreover, well organised as a group. See Schmidt, *Die Deutschen aus Bessarabien*.
[81] Prinz, 'Erlebtes', 216. On the significance of stereotypes, see Fielitz, *Das Stereotyp*, 153–5, 304–6.
[82] Prinz, 'Erlebtes', 216.

occupation regime, was not necessarily based on trust. Her access to the private, her exploitation of her position of power as an expert and her attempts to reshape traditions and ideas passed on over generations – all this produced on the part of her clients an attitude of wariness. This is something Julie Prinz failed to consider. She interpreted mistrust as proof of backwardness, an aspect that the next section elaborates on.

Trust and the 'Private Sphere' in Obstetrics

To entrust another person with the care of one's own body, particularly in an extreme situation such as giving birth, demands a degree of trust, in combination with an expectation that goodwill is present or at least a sense that one can depend on the other person.[83] The context within which such trust can be generated is not, however, a neutral one: inevitably, it is bound up with the prevailing political and social conditions. In the context of the Nazi dictatorship, as Thomas Kühne has argued, trust was a resource deliberately cultivated within the confines of the Nazi *Volksgemeinschaft*: in Kühne's formulation, trust constituted the very 'emotional foundation' (*seelische Grundlage*) of the *Volksgemeinschaft*. Every relationship of power was to be personal in character as a means to bind every single member of the *Volksgemeinschaft* to the Nazi regime.[84] In the case of the midwives in the Warthegau, the trust that they sought to awaken on the part of their clients was likewise a resource to be mobilised and manipulated for political ends. The health authorities in the Warthegau expected Reich German midwives to be 'access points' (*Zugangspunkte*, to use Ute Frevert's term) for their ethnic German clientele.[85] As experts for pregnancy, childbirth and postpartum care answerable to the local health authority, and as representatives of the National Socialist health system and the occupation regime, they were to utilise their assumed emotional connection to the women in their charge to produce a degree of trust in the Nazi regime and its representatives.[86] They were to organise assistance from the *Nationalsozialistische*

---

[83] Trust can be shown to persons from whom a certain goodwill can be expected. See Ute Frevert, 'Vertrauen: Eine historische Spurensuche', in Ute Frevert (ed.), *Vertrauen: Historische Annäherungen* (Göttingen, 2003), 7–66, here 56.

[84] Thomas Kühne, 'Vertrauen und Kameradschaft: Soziales Kapital im "Endkampf" der Wehrmacht', in Ute Frevert (ed.), *Vertrauen: Historische Annäherungen* (Göttingen, 2003), 245–79.

[85] This is the term Ute Frevert used to describe the function of experts who on one hand build trust in institutions and systems while on the other profiting from the trust placed in these agencies. See Frevert, 'Vertrauen'.

[86] See for example Erich Grossmann quoted in Witte (first name not given), 'Haupttagung der Hebammenschaft im Reichsgau Danzig-Westpreußen', *Die Deutsche Hebamme* 55 (1940), 228–9.

Volkswohlfahrt (NSV), assist at the welfare offices for mothers and children either attached directly to the local health authority or run by the NSV and, if necessary, obtain approval for hospital treatment for mother and/or child.[87] Here the midwives could profit from the authority of the health office as a National Socialist institution, vested with far-reaching powers, and push through their plans with the help of the responsible medical officer or nurse.[88] Conversely, however, ethnic German women could not rely on the goodwill or loyalty of Reich German midwives. Many ethnic German women thus doubted that they would be well cared for by Reich German midwives while giving birth. Lacking the necessary trust, expectant mothers refused to call on their services.

At first, Julie Prinz encountered difficulties finding any work: 'We [Julie Prinz and her sister] approached the women, advised them, drew their attention to possible dangers, and the upshot was: we were only very rarely summoned when the birth took place.'[89] The women and families preferred the help of Polish midwives or women from their particular resettler community, a number of whom had – one can assume – not been granted professional accreditation as a midwife due to the provisions of the Reich Midwifery Law.[90] Midwives classified as *Volksdeutsche* had to take the German midwife examination – a hurdle quite a few women who had previously practised obstetrics clearly failed to overcome.[91]

The enlisting of 'lay midwives' was considered problematic by medical officers and health politicians, for it meant that compliance with obstetrical standards could not be guaranteed, nor the reporting and registering of births and other details that licensed German and Polish midwives were obliged to carry out.[92] But there were good reasons why expectant mothers might have preferred to call on the services of unofficial lay midwives. Besides wishing to avoid the monitoring and control carried out by licensed midwives, they may have been reluctant or unable to pay the comparatively high fees for childbirth and postpartum care

---

[87] See Merkblatt für rußlanddeutsche Mütter, Sept./Oct. 1944 in APP, RSH 299/2073; Vorläufige Dienstordnung für die im Reichsgau Wartheland tätigen Hebammen, 4 September 1942, in *Verordnungsblatt des Reichsstatthalters im Reichsgau Wartheland*, 19 September 1942, 319–26.

[88] See Winfried Süß, *Der 'Volkskörper' im Krieg: Gesundheitspolitik, Gesundheitsverhältnisse und Krankenmord im nationalsozialistischen Deutschland 1939–1945* (Munich, 2003).

[89] Prinz, 'Erlebtes', 203.

[90] Lagebericht Kreis Kalisch, 15 November 1939, in APP, RSH 299/1831; Regierungspräsident Litzmannstadt, 4 August 1941, in APP, RSH 299/2031.

[91] This applied only to resettlers. See Bahmann, 'Fortbildung der rückgewanderten volksdeutschen Hebammen', *Die Deutsche Hebamme* 57 (1942), 195–6; Schreiben Friemert, 6 September 1941 (Eing.), in APP, RSH 299/2070, fol. 71–2.

[92] Schriftwechsel Regierungspräsident Litzmannstadt mit Landräten und Amtskommissaren, 1941–2, in APL, 176/377.

introduced in 1941, mandatory for the services of licensed midwives (whether German or Polish).[93]

The women of the pre-war German minority in Poland had connections with Polish midwives due to long-standing social relationships and a shared language. In many cases, they had gone to school together, grown up in the same place and had similar milieu-specific experiences.[94] This would have been also characteristic for the relationship between resettlers and ethnic German lay obstetricians or non-licenced midwives from their particular community. The basis for developing a relationship of trust, the prerequisite for a sense of privacy to arise – as was the case for midwives and their clientele in the Altreich – was personal familiarity and being rooted in a similar milieu, which also entailed some knowledge of the private life of the midwife or obstetrician.[95] Unlike other expert–client relationships, for example to doctors, the trust in play here was not one-sided but based on reciprocity.[96] This trust was not completely eliminated by Nazi occupation and Germanisation policies, which had ruptured the established social fabric, nor by the complex and shifting categories of Germanness created by the German Ethnic Register. The new social hierarchies and structures created, however, a new set of relationships of domination and power. Polish midwives were now, for example because they were deprived of their rights, dependent to a large degree on the goodwill of their German clientele.

An 'abortion case' heard before the special court (*Sondergericht*) in Litzmannstadt in November 1940 reveals the social connections between members of the *volksdeutsch* minority and Poles, as well as the gendered dynamics between men and women. It shows how relationships of dependency and subordination could enable self-empowerment and generate trust as well as suspicion and mistrust.

Selma Winter, a twenty-nine-year-old *Volksdeutsche* born in the district of Kutno, had worked as a farm servant since she was seven.[97] She had already given birth to two 'illegitimate' children. Now she was pregnant again. The statement and investigation proceedings show that Selma Winter was distraught. She did not know how she could support a third child. The father was her employer at the time, the forty-two-year-old

---

[93] Fees were increased from 5–20 RM to 12–50 RM. See Gebührenordnung für Hebammen im Reichsgau Wartheland, 17 April 1941, in *Verordnungsblatt des Reichsstatthalters im Reichsgau Wartheland*, 1941, 264–5; Schreiben von Bleschke, 8 August 1941, in APP, RSH 299/2070, fol. 117.
[94] See for example personal file of the midwife Bronisława Z., in APW, 829/42.
[95] See Wiebke Lisner, *'Hüterinnen der Nation': Hebammen im Nationalsozialismus* (Frankfurt a.M., New York, NY, 2006); Wiebke Lisner, 'Midwifery and Racial Segregation in Occupied Western Poland 1939–1945', *German History* 35/2 (2017), 229–46.
[96] See Frevert, 'Vertrauen', 58.   [97] The names have been anonymised.

volksdeutsch farmer and local *Amtskommissar* (appointed with authority over a small town or village) Johann Meyer. For Meyer, it was imperative that his wife did not find out about his extramarital fatherhood. He proposed an abortion. The local Polish midwife, Genovefa Karpinska, who was the same age as Selma Winter, refused to carry out the abortion. However, she organised contact with an older Polish midwife, Bronisława Malinowska, in Kutno, who agreed to perform the abortion. By this time, Selma Winter was some six months pregnant. Bronisława Malinowska induced a premature birth. The midwife Genovefa Karpinska was called for assistance. The baby survived the birth. Genovefa Karpinska, however, decided it was too weak and nonviable. She placed it in a corner of the room where Selma Winter lay. Left neglected, the baby died the following morning.[98]

Although the court judged that Johann Meyer had misused his position of authority to get everyone involved to act to his benefit, the main guilt was seen as lying with Bronisława Malinowska, who was labelled a 'professional' abortionist. She was sentenced to eighteen months in a penitentiary (*Zuchthaus*). The sentences handed out to the other accused were lower.[99] In comparison to other abortion trials, the sentence given to Bronisława Malinowska was not particularly severe. In similar cases, midwives were sentenced to several years' incarceration in a penitentiary. The high sentences handed out were to ensure that the prohibition of abortion for German women was observed and the various possibilities available for this, created by the fluid ethnic boundaries and identities as well as the surgical skill of the midwives, were eliminated.[100]

Genovefa Karpinska's judgement on the new-born infant's inability to live was not called into question by the court, probably because it was considered an accepted part of a midwife's area of competence. At the same time, however, it was not a midwife's responsibility to decide on life and death; a midwife's professional duty was to protect the lives of mother and child. Here a grey area existed regarding the action to be taken, one that could extend from failing to undertake life-sustaining measures through to deliberately causing death by failing to provide sufficient care and sustenance. It is obvious, however, that both Polish and German midwives were adjudged to have a discretionary competence in this grey area.[101]

---

[98] See trial 18 November 1940, in APŁ, 196/10888.
[99] Johann Meyer was given a prison sentence of one year, Selma Winter six months and the midwife Karpinska four months. Trial 18 November 1940, in APŁ, 196/10888.
[100] See Lisner, 'Midwifery and Racial Segregation'.
[101] See Benno Ottow, 'Wie hat sich die Hebamme gegenüber einer lebensfähigen Frühgeburt zu verhalten?', *Die deutsche Hebamme* 55 (1940), 146–7; Lisner, '*Hüterinnen*', 330.

Selma Winter had already – before her decision for an abortion – contacted Genovefa Karpinska. The midwife accompanied Selma Winter throughout, even though she did not perform the operation. It seems that a relationship of trust existed between the two women.

The possibility of autonomous, self-determined action on the part of the *Volksdeutsche* involved – as this example suggests – not only trust and goodwill, based for example on long-standing familiarity, but also on Poles' loss of rights and their subordinate position. Poles could hardly do anything to defend themselves against intrusions and infringements by Germans. Every form of insubordination was severely punished.[102] For the Polish midwives Bronisława Malinowska and Genovefa Karpinska, it would have presumably been extremely difficult to refuse help to a German man in the post of *Amtskommissar*, who had various instruments of power in his hands, without fearing disadvantages of some sort. In court, Bronisława Malinowska testified that she had examined Selma Winter only because of the pressure put on her by Johann Meyer.[103] But perhaps Bronisława Malinowska and Genovefa Karpinska saw an opportunity to gain personal benefits and protection from the higher-ranking German and hoped that all involved would keep their silence. For their part, Johann Meyer and Selma Winter could rely on the discretion of the Polish midwives due to the latter's subordinate position.

Unaware of the changes to the law, Bronisława Malinowska obviously assumed that she would be acquitted due to a lack of evidence. But the new judicial practice was geared to cementing 'racial' segregation and ethnic hierarchies. For Poles and Jews, discriminatory special provisions deprived them of legal security. They were not entitled to a defence counsel, nor were they permitted to act as witnesses.[104] Bronisława Malinowska maintained to the very end that she had examined Selma Winter only vaginally, during which the amnion had burst, thus unintentionally triggering the premature birth. However, this statement had hardly any influence on the judgement. The court did not bother to call for a medical expert assessment in order to prove that she had undertaken an operative procedure. Instead, it based its judgement on the statements of those involved and the plausibility of the alleged intervention. A similar reluctance is evident in other abortion cases brought before the special courts: medical expertise was rarely consulted.[105]

---

[102] See Majer, *Fremdvölkische*; Röger, *Kriegsbeziehungen*.
[103] Statement given by the midwife Malinowska, 18 November 1940, in APŁ, 196/10888.
[104] See Holger Schlüter, '*. . . für die Menschlichkeit im Strafmaß bekannt. . .*': *Das Sondergericht Litzmannstadt und sein Vorsitzender Richter* (Recklinghausen, 2014).
[105] See records of the Sondergerichte in Kattowitz and Litzmannstadt, in Archiwum Państwowe w Katowicach (APK), 134 Sondergericht Kattowitz; APŁ, Bestand 196 Sąd Specjalny.

'A Birth Is Nothing Out of the Ordinary Here ...'   325

Given the medical and diagnostic possibilities available at the time, abortions were often scarcely distinguishable from spontaneously occurring miscarriages and premature births.[106] It was difficult for midwives and physicians to determine even whether a woman was pregnant until the baby's movements could be felt.[107] Misdiagnoses were quite frequent.[108]

Controlling Midwives, Mothers and the Private Sphere

As a quality of the relationship between Polish midwives and German mothers, trust, which made possible autonomous, self-determined action within the realm of the private, had the potential to counteract the racial segregation and ban on contact as well as thwart the biopolitical and Germanising objectives of the Nazi regime. Recognising this, the health authorities and occupation regime in the Warthegau thus attempted to gain access to and control over the domestic sphere as well as the areas of pregnancy, childbirth and postpartum care by exploiting various actors, with the Reich German midwives among them. Against this background, two lines of questioning become pertinent: firstly, what were the possibilities for gaining access and controlling the private sphere, and what form did they take; and secondly, what possibilities were available to take action and defend the private in obstetrics practised at home?

Calling on the help of lay obstetricians was made difficult, if not impossible, by the requirement to show an attestation of birth issued by a doctor or midwife. The attestation could be issued by German as well as registered Polish midwives.[109] Julie Prinz refers to her own decisive role in having this procedure introduced to her district and she clung exclusively to German midwives as far as German clients were concerned:

---

[106] See for example Gutachten eines Gefängnisarztes, 15 February 1940, in APK, 134/911. German doctors assumed that the majority of miscarriages were in fact abortions. See Lisner, 'Hüterinnen', 286.
[107] See Barbara Duden, 'Zwischen wahrem Wissen und Prophetie: Konzeptionen des Ungeborenen', in Barbara Duden, Jürgen Schlumbohm and Patrice Veit (eds.), Geschichte des Ungeborenen: Zur Erfahrungs- und Wissenschaftsgeschichte der Schwangerschaft, 17.–20. Jahrhundert (Göttingen, 2000), 11–48; Barbara Duden, Geschichte unter der Haut: Ein Eisenacher Arzt und seine Patientinnen um 1730 (Stuttgart, 1991).
[108] Stellungnahme des Direktors der Landesfrauenklinik Gleiwitz, 28 January 1943, in APK, 117/2143.
[109] See Schreiben, 15 January 1942, in APŁ, 176 Regierungspräsident Litzmannstadt/377.

Thanks to another round of energetic representations to the medical officer and the NSV, it was possible to establish that an official birth registration is only accepted with an attestation issued by a midwife, otherwise no postpartum maternity benefits are paid.[110]

Linking birth registration to the granting of maternity benefits (payable only to German women) created a financial incentive to call on the services of a licensed German midwife.[111]

By placing controls on Polish midwives, the health authorities were attempting to increase the state's ability to intervene and continuously monitor the contact between Polish midwives and German families. To influence the choice of midwife, the medical officer in Leslau, for example, obliged all Polish midwives to assist German women only in emergencies and to notify the health office of all German births.[112] Following his directive, the district branch of the *Nationalsozialistische Frauenschaft* undertook investigations of German women who had enlisted a Polish midwife.[113]

Because the number of German midwives was limited, it was not always feasible to enlist their services. The most frequently named and accepted reason for calling in a Polish midwife was that the birth had taken place so quickly that it had not been possible to reach a German midwife in time.[114] With the introduction of the Reich Midwifery Law, Polish midwives were placed under the control of the *Reichshebammenschaft* (Reich Midwifery League); all Polish midwives (like their German counterparts) were forced to become members. At the same time, they were also subjected to supervision by the local medical officers.[115] To install comprehensive control and surveillance, many Reich German midwives were now given the official function of 'district midwife'; commissioned by the medical officer and the professional association, the 'district midwife' inspected the obstetric instruments and dwellings as well as checked whether the registration requirements of Polish midwives were complied with.[116] However, the

---

[110] Prinz, 'Erlebtes', 203.
[111] Sixty to seventy-five per cent of the last gross salary was paid. In addition, a mother's nursing allowance of 0.50 RM was paid per day and 10 RM delivery allowance, APP, Gauselbstverwaltung/286.
[112] Amtsarzt in Leslau, 10 May 1943, in APW, 829/44.
[113] Amtsarzt an die Kreisfrauenschaftsleitung, 18 April 1944, in APW, 829/44.
[114] See for example Bericht zum Gesundheitsamt Kreis Litzmannstadt, 22 August 1941, in APP, RSH 299/1862; Lisner, 'Hebammen im "Reichsgau Wartheland"'.
[115] See Verordnung zur Einführung des Hebammengesetzes, 227–8.
[116] See Vermerk über Kontrollbesuch einer polnischen Hebamme, in APW, 829/44. In the Altreich, these tasks were reserved for the public medical officer. See Schreiben Reichshebammenschaft Wartheland, 15 June 1941, in APP, RSH 299/2070, 114.

shortage of German midwives gave Polish midwives and ethnic German women some room to manoeuvre, as is indicated by a report from the principal of a maternity school in 1944.

The head of the maternity school visited the former course participant Maria Gerber five days after she gave birth to her third child and noted that she had a fever.[117] Without any further consultation, transportation to the hospital was organised for the woman. The Polish midwife Katharina Zalewski – who was often called to the births of German families[118] – had been responsible for birth and postpartum care.[119] She arrived as Maria Gerber was about to be taken to hospital and indicated that she considered hospital treatment unnecessary. Instead, she proposed calling the local Polish doctor. Her advice was ignored. Maria Gerber spent seventeen days in hospital. A mild mastitis was diagnosed, which evidently cleared up within a few days. Maria Gerber stayed for eight days in the hospital with a normal temperature. Her hospital stay meant separation from her new-born child and her older children. The maternity school head judged the diagnostic assessment given by the Polish midwife to be the sign of a 'guilty conscience' because Katharina Zalewski, at variance with Reich German standards, had cared for Maria Gerber and the baby while not wearing an apron and her skirt was stained. She denied that Katharina Zalewski could possess any medical expertise at all; on the contrary, she judged her to be filthy. To the medical officer, the maternity school head reported that Maria Gerber had admitted to her that the 'dirty Polish midwife' made her feel 'uncomfortable' and she would have most certainly called a German midwife if things had not been so urgent.[120]

This alleged statement given by Maria Gerber fails, however, to tally with a number of details: the midwife Katharina Zalewski was not only called to the birth, but was also entrusted with the postpartum care and asked to assist the mother when the child later fell ill. It seems that Maria Gerber may have spoken to the maternity school head about Katharina Zalewski in derogatory terms so as not to be suspected of having a relationship of trust with the Polish midwife.

Relationships of trust between ethnic German women and Polish midwives were extremely fragile, placed under surveillance and threatened by sanctions.[121] As this example suggests, one strategy to not let the trust become 'public' appears to have been to deny it outwardly. Maria Gerber

---

[117] The names have been anonymised.   [118] See Personalakte in APW, 829/44.
[119] See Krankheitsgeschichte, n.d. gez. Treu, in APW, 829/44.
[120] Amtsarzt in Leslau, 10 May 1943, in APW, 829/44.
[121] See for example the case of a Baltic German senior physician who was given a warning for his 'Pole-friendly' attitude, June 1940, in APP, RSH 299/2131.

thus may have chosen arguments she assumed would meet with the approval of the maternity school head, who would then subsequently – with a similar expectation – pass them on to the medical officer. Maria Gerber claimed that inherent necessity forced her to consult the Polish midwife while at the same time drawing on racial stereotypes, thus denying that there was any bond of trust between herself and Katharina Zalewski. With this pattern of communication she was stabilising racist stereotypes and she exposed the Polish midwife to an investigation by the health authorities, which ended in a reprimand from the medical officer. In this case neither punishment nor banning, nor the involvement of the *Sicherheitsdienst* (SD) or the Gestapo followed.[122]

Conclusions

A birth in the Warthegau was – contrary to what Julie Prinz claimed in the midwives' journal in 1943 – indeed something out of the ordinary, in the sense that all births in the Warthegau were subject to the extreme conditions prevailing there as a result of violently imposed ethnic and racial restructuring. Divisions and alliances between the various population groups were not, however – as Maren Röger, amongst others, has shown – configured one-dimensionally with a clear separation between Poles and Germans. Instead, they crystallised in specific situations, and particularly in the private domain they often ran contrary to the ideas propagated by *Volkstum* policy and the ban on contact.[123] In obstetrics, differences between the various population groups regarded as 'German' emerged, and the boundaries between private and public were negotiated on various levels between the ethnic German women, Polish midwives, Reich German midwives and the National Socialist regime.

The decentralised organisation of obstetric care in the private dwelling of the woman giving birth, together with the self-employed status and self-directed practices of midwives, provided both parties with an array of possibilities to make their own decisions and to define and interpret their actions as they saw fit. Whereas at a hospital physical access to the woman was institutionally controlled on the basis of the rules and regulations in force, the orders of the chief physician and the duty roster, in the domestic sphere women and their families were able to respond to the specifics of a situation, influencing for example who was to be present at a birth. Plans to institutionalise obstetrics for German women in the Warthegau foundered because of the poor roads and lack of infrastructure. Moreover, with respect to

---

[122] See personal file of the midwife Zalewski, in APW, 829/44.
[123] See Röger, *Kriegsbeziehungen*.

extending the scope of institutionalised obstetric services to cover the whole area, differences emerged between the health authorities in the Warthegau and Reich Health Leader Conti, who, in line with the directives issued by his ministry and the exigencies of war, supported midwife assistance at home.[124]

That said, a delivery in a domestic, private sphere could only take place if the woman giving birth was actually living in her own home. In the camps of the *Volksdeutsche Mittelstelle* (Ethnic German Liaison Office) where the ethnic German resettlers were provisionally accommodated, delivery in a private sphere was impossible and took place in either a hospital or a ward run by midwives.[125] Against this background, obstetric care by a midwife and delivery in a domestic setting can also be seen as a privilege granted to those ethnic German women who had successfully passed through the procedure of the *Einwandererzentralstelle* and were thus recognised and officially resettled as 'valuable' members of the *Volksgemeinschaft*. The National Socialist regime conceded to them privacy in the area of pregnancy, birth and postpartum – albeit retaining the right to exercise over them a regulating and controlling influence. Through ever tighter supervision, in tandem with 'education', representatives of the National Socialist regime – and this included Reich German midwives – attempted to control birth and reproduction and to maintain access to the bodies of the women.

In the domestic, private sphere, German midwives were expected to spread ideas about parenting and hygiene in the spirit of social disciplining, for example of the Volhynian Germans who were considered something of an underclass, while at the same time fostering a 'German culture' around pregnancy and birth. These practices of cultural and social engineering entailed access to the body and the private domestic sphere.[126] The goal was the forging of a 'National Socialist-German' identity and the integration of the ethnic Germans into an 'expanded *Volksgemeinschaft*' as well as the 'biological reinforcing' of the German population in pursuit of the overarching objective of Germanising the region, which included reducing maternal and infant mortality. In comparison to the Altreich, here Reich German midwives gained a new position of authority and power, a high degree of autonomy and greater scope for shaping their own working practices. As Julie Prinz indicated, they could create their own domain. Since they did not share the life

---

[124] Tagung der Gesundheitspflegerinnen, 20–21 May 1941, in APP, RSH 299/1923.
[125] See Ermittlungsbögen zu Säuglingssterbefällen, 1944, in APP, RSH 299/1972.
[126] Such an undertaking was able to build on the effort invested in education and upbringing since the nineteenth century, wherein midwives had also played a role as multipliers. See for example Silke Butke and Astrid Kleine, *Der Kampf für den gesunden Nachwuchs: Geburtshilfe und Säuglingsfürsorge im Deutschen Kaiserreich* (Münster, 2004).

experiences or the milieu of the *Volksdeutsche*, the relationship of Reich German midwives to the majority of their clients tended to be a one-sided expert–client relationship analogous to that of doctors and their patients. Reich German midwives, compared to their Polish or *volksdeutsch* counterparts, were much less involved in a relationship of interdependence to their clientele. The options at their disposal were thus more based on their status as experts and relations of power and domination than trust. As privileged representatives of the National Socialist regime, the Reich German midwives represented the regime in their field of competence and made a distinct contribution to implementing National Socialist occupation policy, biopolitics and Germanisation.

The shortage of German midwives, however, helped ethnic German women to gain some freedom of choice. They used this to arrange the birth and its circumstances in line with their own wishes, an assertion of autonomy that, depending on the situation, fended off the intrusion of the National Socialist regime into the private. Trust, based on personal acquaintance, similar biographical experiences, a common language and shifting definitions of 'Germanness', created a degree of autonomy for ethnic German mothers and their Polish midwives as well as unlicensed ethnic German obstetricians to operate in the field of home birth assistance. Trust was the decisive resource enabling the creation of a private sphere in which priority could be given to the wishes and needs of the woman giving birth and her family, defying the imposition of 'German' standards and the state's desire to exercise control. Midwives and mothers were thus acting in accordance with their own specific logic as well as their own interests and need for privacy and autonomy.[127] The circumstances prevailing in the Warthegau did not, however, merely give women defined as *volksdeutsch* a degree of room for manoeuvre: the racist social hierarchy, together with the Polish population's loss of rights, also gave ethnic German women new scope to assert a position of power vis-à-vis Polish midwives.

---

[127] See Alf Lüdtke, 'Eigensinn', in Stefan Jordan (ed.), *Lexikon Geschichtswissenschaft: Hundert Grundbegriffe* (Stuttgart, 2002), 64–6.

14 Transformations of the 'Private'
Proximity and Distance in the Spatial Confinement of the Ghettos in Occupied Poland, 1939–1942

Carlos A. Haas

In the summer of 1941, the young Edmund and his wife, Stefcia, were looking for a flat in the Warsaw ghetto. The ghetto was completely overcrowded and the demand for living quarters so great that their quest seemed hopeless. They were therefore all the more pleased when they at least found a room up for lease. What they had not reckoned with, however, was the business acumen of their new landlady. To double her income, she had leased the room, by no means particularly large, to a second interested party without any further ado – a second couple, Marian and Ada, who were also delighted to have finally brought a frustrating search to an end. And so both couples moved into the room, only to be soon caught up in emotional entanglements and, eventually, new interpersonal constellations. The affairs ignited between Edmund and Ada as well as Marian and Stefcia could not remain undetected for long in the confined space of their shared four walls. Finally, they agreed to swap partners. But the happiness revitalised in such an unconventional way turned out to be short-lived. The flirting of the two women with the head of the house committee harboured new potential for conflict, as did their mounting money worries. Unable to pay the rent, both newly aligned couples were ultimately forced to move out.

This story is too good to be true – and indeed it is not an episode that took place in real life, but the plot of the three-act revue *Miłość szuka mieszkania* (*Love Seeks a Home*) by the author Jerzy Jurandot.[1] In the autumn of 1941, the comedy celebrated a very successful premiere at the Femina Theatre in the Warsaw ghetto, followed by a few further acclaimed performances. Diary entries from the time convey an impression of the play's popularity.[2]

(Translated from German by Paul Bowman)

[1] See Archiwum Ringelbluma (ARG) I 1221 (Ring. I/519). See also Markus Roth and Andrea Löw, *Das Warschauer Getto: Alltag und Widerstand im Angesicht der Vernichtung* (Munich, 2013), 139, as well as Barbara Engelking and Jacek Leociak, *The Warsaw Ghetto: A Guide to the Perished City* (New Haven, CT, 2009), 566–7.

[2] See Mary Berg, *The Diary of Mary Berg: Growing Up in the Warsaw Ghetto* (Oxford, 2007), 101–2.

The script has been handed down for posterity as part of Emanuel Ringelblum's secret archive *Oyneg Shabes*.

For all the exaggeration and hyperbole, the author made a number of apt observations. He realistically described the cramped living conditions in the ghetto. Also accurate is how the massive spatial confinements forced the ghetto residents to change their accustomed ways of life. The home as a place for partners to withdraw to and to enjoy all the different habits and practices that constitute an intimate relationship was no longer readily available. The minimal formula of one couple per bedroom, taken for granted in most Western societies in the twentieth century, was now no longer feasible, bringing with it far-reaching consequences. In the play, the lack of distance between two couples sharing a bedroom is depicted as conducive to emotional constellations which transgressed the boundaries of what had passed for 'normal' behaviour outside the ghetto. For the same reason, in a ghetto, these feelings could not remain hidden for long: moments of closeness and intimacy could no longer go unnoticed. In the play, the physical proximity and the absence of any spatial separation became catalysts for the partner swap. With this reversal, the author created the necessary comedy in the first instance. At the same time, however, the conception of the play indicates that Jerzy Jurandot had attentively followed the spatial changes imposed on the ghetto residents since the start of the war, and understood how they were radically impacting everyday life. The ghetto inmates' positive response to Jurandot's play shows that the author discussed a very common experience by writing about daily life in spatial confinement, a phenomenon everybody could connect to.

Not only relationships between partners but many other, if not all, social practices require space to unfold; indeed, space is a constitutive element of human interaction. Poland's Jewish population experienced massive spatial restrictions from the very first day of the Second World War. During its first weeks, Jewish neighbourhoods were intentionally targeted and destroyed; later, the concentration of Jews in designated areas within towns and cities meant that many lost their homes. The spatial environment in the ghettos erected by the German occupiers over the course of the first year of the war was characterised by confinement and high population density. Drawing on contemporary ego-documents from the ghettos in Warsaw and Tomaschow,[3] this chapter examines examples of how the residents were forced to transform those social practices taking place in relation to space. It does so in terms of broader questions about the transformations that Jewish

---

[3] Under the German occupation, the small city of Tomaszów Mazowiecki in central Poland was part of the Radom district in the *Generalgouvernement*. The occupiers renamed it Tomaschow.

'private' life in the ghettos underwent. How was 'private' space organised and defined under such conditions? How did spatial confinement reshape the relationships between individuals and larger social groups? How was spatial distance or spatial proximity reconfigured? And to what extent did the ghetto residents register and reflect on the changes?

In the following, I begin with some brief comments on methodology and go on to analyse a number of examples from the sources. In doing so, I consider two distinct phases: a short period during which the German occupiers created fundamentally new spatial conditions, and a period of relative stability lasting from around autumn 1940 through to the summer/autumn of 1942. In this latter phase, the population did what it could to adapt to the catastrophic conditions in the ghettos. The mass deportations of 1942 brought this phase to an end.

The 'Private' in the Ghetto: 'Space' as an Analytical Category

When exploring the meanings of the 'private' in National Socialism in relation to its victims, a different concept of privacy is necessary from that which other contributions in this volume employ when analysing the private selves of members of the racially defined *Volksgemeinschaft*. The contrast is particularly stark when examining the experience of the residents of the ghettos in occupied Poland, because during the Second Polish Republic the large Jewish minority of the country had formed several distinct milieus. In the autumn of 1939, heterogeneity was the characteristic feature of this segment of the population, who later comprised the greater majority of the ghetto residents. I therefore take 'privacy' to indicate not a universal norm, but deploy it as an analytical category that takes into consideration the multifaceted social, cultural and political profile of Polish Jewry. In this context, 'privacy' is best understood as a set of social practices which ghetto residents used to permit or negotiate proximity, and also to create distance when required. This approach draws on the work of Beate Rössler and Helen Nissenbaum.[4] Both avoid using 'privacy' as a rigid formula. Rössler distinguishes between decisional, informational and local privacy. She understands decisional privacy as those spaces of action and decision-making closely tied to personal freedom and autonomy. Informational privacy refers to what others know, or are permitted to know, about an individual, which information is publicly accessible and which is not.

---

[4] Beate Rössler, *Der Wert des Privaten* (Frankfurt a.M., 2001); Helen Nissenbaum, *Privacy in Context: Technology, Policy and the Integrity of Social Life* (Stanford, CA. 2009).

A special form of informational privacy relates to what is kept secret. Finally, local privacy refers to tangible places from which the public is excluded. This also entails practices of self-invention and self-presentation, practices through which such spaces take shape beyond a physical framework. Rössler's historical case studies are liberal-democratic societies. However, her analytical categories are sufficiently fluid to be transferred to other historical situations and her considerations on local privacy are of particular relevance for the present chapter.

For Helen Nissenbaum, privacy's meaning is dependent on specific social contexts. The same concept can appear differently in two distinct contexts: as private or as public. While we dislike information about our health being made public at the workplace, we gladly provide our doctor or health insurer with the very same information. When outside influences bring about an impact on (often tacit) agreements that define 'privacy' in a specific context, boundaries are redefined. The actors are forced to develop new strategies to maintain a self-determined 'private sphere'.

My operationalisation of the concept of privacy in relation to the ghettos in occupied Poland is informed by these considerations. I deploy proximity and distance as umbrella terms, each covering a variety of practices, whose classification depends on the specific situation. Taking a meal, for example, could express emotional proximity if it is done within the family circle. But just as frequently, eating was intentionally done alone, mostly as a way of avoiding having to share or having food taken away. Linked to these fields of practice are, as constitutive elements of the 'private', space, time and materiality. Looking at how people responded to and dealt with the spatial, temporal and material restrictions in the ghettos makes the transformations of proximity and distance legible. Thus, measurable time was necessary to experience proximity or distance. Purportedly fixed distinctions between 'public' and 'private' time with a clear-cut beginning and end, for example working time and leisure time, did not exist in the ghettos. Instead, the ghetto residents used fragmented time to claim at least brief moments of mental escape. Dan Diner's concept of *gestaute Zeit* ('jammed time') is helpful in elucidating such experiences, and the narrative structures of perceiving and interpreting the unfolding Holocaust.[5] If someone in the ghetto wished to experience proximity or distance, then a minimum of materiality was also necessary, for instance a couple needed it to be able to dissociate from their surroundings. A vestige of the material was indispensable for the symbols used to put this dissociation into practice. Finally, there

---

[5] See Dan Diner, 'Gestaute Zeit – Massenvernichtung und jüdische Erzählstruktur', in Sigrid Weigel and Birgit R. Erdle (eds.), *Fünfzig Jahre danach: Zur Nachgeschichte des Nationalsozialismus* (Zurich, 1996), 3–16.

is the analytical category 'space' around which this chapter revolves. In most cases, a minimal spatial basis existed in the ghettos, and this was necessary to allow proximity or to create distance. The spatial situation influenced ghetto residents' perception and prompted specific modes of behaviour. Thus, for example, did the lack of partition not automatically cause the surrender of private practices, but led to their transformation. Often these transformation in turn shaped how existing space was organised. Drawing on Martina Löw, I here take 'space' to refer to not only a physically defined setting, but – and above all – as a phenomenon that manifests itself in social interactions, and thus depends on the prevailing social conditions in the ghetto.[6] The ghetto inmates' strategies to adapt to new circumstances by changing accustomed practices offer us an insight into the transformation of lives inside the ghetto walls.

New Foundations of Private Space: The First Year of the War

In the first year of German occupation rule in Poland, numerous anti-Jewish restrictions were imposed, which are generally summarised under the term 'ghettoisation'. Above all, the relocating of Jews to the areas of the later ghettos, ordered by Reinhard Heydrich as early as 21 September 1939, changed the spatial situation enormously.[7] From now on, the local population had to share the 'Jewish residential districts' with 'relocated persons' from other districts of the respective city as well as surrounding towns and villages. The majority of the Jewish population was aware of the consequences of these relocation measures. Noëmi Szac-Wajnkranc, a resident of Warsaw, described how her uncle and aunt felt upon being forced to leave their house on the so-called 'Aryan' side of the city: 'Uncle and aunty had tears in their eyes; for them it was not just moving to the ghetto, for them it was leaving their house, a house they'd bought with the money they'd saved from a lifetime's work, a house that they had renovated, that they had worked on, that was to provide them with security for their old age.'[8] This description of the formerly owned house as the fruit of a life of work and as an investment providing for retirement years conforms to conventional

---

[6] See Martina Löw, *Raumsoziologie* (Frankfurt a.M., 2001).
[7] See Schnellbrief des Chefs des Reichssicherheitshauptamtes, Reinhard Heydrich, an die Chefs der Einsatzgruppen der Sicherheitspolizei, 21 September 1939, in Jüdisches Historisches Institut Warschau (ed.), *Faschismus – Getto – Massenmord: Dokumentation über Ausrottung und Widerstand der Juden in Polen während des zweiten Weltkrieges* (Berlin, 1961), 37–41.
[8] Noëmi Szac-Wajnkranc, 'Im Feuer vergangen', in *Im Feuer vergangen: Tagebücher aus dem Ghetto*, with a foreword by Johann Christoph Hampe (Munich, 1963), 17–149, here 20–1.

bourgeois values of prosperity and security, the loss of which was without doubt an immense shock for the couple.

Having arrived at their new place of residence, the family, like so many others, was confronted with a completely new situation: instead of living in a large multifamily house, they were now forced to share a single small flat with two other parties. The pragmatism Szac-Wajnkranc displayed in dealing with the new living conditions is typical for this ghettoisation phase. Short and to the point, she noted in her diary: 'On the same day, a third family moved into the third room, and I wrote on the door – ring the bell once: Szenberg, twice: Wajnkranc, three times: Ahezojen.'[9]

This kind of response was not an isolated incident, as an artefact in the Ringelblum Archive shows: a handwritten nameplate for the doorbell to a flat in the Warsaw ghetto.[10] Here too different bell signals were assigned to the various parties. The system was even more refined, for here, not just three, but seven parties needed to be taken into account. Anyone wishing to call in on 'Lurie' was to ring once, 'Rotsztajn' twice, 'Rogozińscy' four times, 'Koplewicz' five times. The parties 'Szlengel' and 'Brandsteter' shared the signal of three rings. Visitors for Lunia and Wanda, residents known only by their first names, had to use a combination of twice short and twice long. When members of the *Ordnungsdienst* (the Jewish auxiliary police) or factory security, i.e. ghetto-internal law enforcement agencies, visited the residential community as a whole, then they were to ring six times in quick succession. As in the episode depicted in Szac-Wajnkranc's diary, the instructions on this nameplate structured and organised the consequences of the spatial confinement in the ghetto. The residents arranged anew the crossing of the boundary from public space to private living space. The former separation between the individual living space, alone or in the family unit, and the collective in public space was dissolved by the enforced cohabitation with strangers. For a brief moment at least, the codes on the nameplates revived these spheres to a certain extent. The members of the Ringelblum archive attached a certain value to the item. Far more than a curiosity, they viewed it as collectible because it illustrated the experience of a highly reduced living space. By keeping the nameplate as part of the archive, they signalled that this experience was widespread; the same sense is evident in the reactions to Jerzy Jurandot's revue.

The relocations enforced by the German occupiers in the first year of the war radically affected the living environment of Poland's Jewish population. Immediately upon the outbreak of the war in September 1939, many Jews, and above all Jewish men, had fled eastward, believing that this would

---

[9] Ibidem, 21.   [10] ARG II 558 (RING. II/492).

enable them to avoid the war and its consequences. Fleeing from the German-occupied territories continued until the autumn of 1940. The target destinations of the refugees were by no means always the large urban centres like Warsaw, Łódź or Cracow. Often, they continued from these cities to smaller towns and villages, in particular if they already had family living there. Many of these highly mobile refugees stayed no longer than a few weeks in any one place, be it in reaction to pressure of the occupiers, or (more or less) freely deciding to move on. Many Jews fled from the Reichsgau Wartheland in particular, annexed and incorporated into the German Reich, to the *Generalgouvernement*, because they expected fewer anti-Jewish restrictions there. In retrospect, all these assumptions proved tragically false. Fleeing to the *Generalgouvernement* increased the chances of surviving the war and the Holocaust only in rare cases. In the short or long term, however, it made a difference if one had to live in the ghettos in Warsaw or Litzmannstadt, cut off from the outside world by walls and barbed wire with populations going into the hundreds of thousands, or in a small or medium-sized, semi-open ghetto in Polish provincial towns such as Piotrków Trybunalski/Petrikau or Tomaszów Mazowiecki/ Tomaschow.

The relationships between the local populations and the refugees (or those relocated by the Germans) throw light on the implications of changed spatial situations. The letters of the young Lutek Ohrenbach from Tomaschow provide a good example for how the relationship between individual and collective could be reconfigured under conditions of spatial confinement. Ohrenbach, born in 1920 in nearby Łódź where he grew up, moved to his grandfather in Tomaszów Mazowiecki in September 1939. Just before, he had spent time in Bydgoszcz/ Bromberg as part of his school education. There, he had met two young Jewish women of the same age, Ruth Goldbarth, who was from Bromberg, and Edith Blau, whose maternal family came from Minden in Westphalia, while her father's side were from Danzig. Although the time spent together was relatively short, the three soon bonded in a special relationship. After the Danzig business of Edith's father, Heinrich Blau, was expropriated through 'Aryanisation' in 1938, the family moved to Bromberg, where they remained until December 1939. Mother and daughter finally moved to Minden, where they lived with the family of the mother, until Minden's Jews were deported to the Riga ghetto in 1942. Both survived the Holocaust. Heinrich Blau, who had already disappeared in unclear circumstances in 1939, was murdered by the Germans. The non-Jewish relatives of the Blaus were able to save the more than 200 letters which Edith received from both Lutek Ohrenbach and Ruth Goldbarth between September 1939 and December 1942, and then return them to her after the war. Edith Brandon, as she was now called after marrying an Englishman, handed over the collection to the archive of the United States Holocaust Memorial Museum, Washington, DC, in the mid-1990s.[11]

Lutek Ohrenbach's exact fate once the letters cease is unknown, but in all likelihood he was, like the other residents of the Tomaschow ghetto, transported to Treblinka in 1942 and murdered there. The topics he wrote about in his letters are vast, and yet he consistently returned to what it was like to live with his family. As early as 20 December 1939 he noted:

> I like being alone. There's always lots of people at home (the whole family is living with my grandfather), it's noisy, lots of gossip and chatter, etc. I don't like it one bit, and I just simply head off to be on my own. I go and stay in the fields near the gasworks. Our yard dog Muszka follows me, a dirty, ugly mutt, but I prefer his company to that of the crowd, because he isn't false or devious, he is, paradoxically, more 'human' than they are.[12]

Based on Ohrenbach's description, it would seem that Jews could still move around freely in December 1939, at least for a certain time and within certain limits. Nevertheless, the spatial confinement resulting from German occupation was already noticeable indirectly. The family was not cramped together in his grandfather's house, which was probably anything but spacious, of its own accord. Like many other refugees, they had fled to Tomaschow from various places in Poland, and were forced to live together. It seemed scarcely possible to get out of each other's way and avoid the inevitable by-products when a crowd of people are together, in Ohrenbach's words: the noise, gossip and constant chatter. For a somewhat introverted person like Ohrenbach, this imposed company was obviously unbearable. This source once again reveals the twofold meaning of 'space', as it pertains to the present analysis. On the one hand, there is the physical dimension, the grandfather's house with its limits and

---

[11] United States Holocaust Memorial Museum (USHMM), Washington, DC, Edith Brandon Papers 1939–1994 (bulk 1939–1945), 1996.A.70.1. See Barbara Engelking, 'Miłość i cierpienie w Tomaszowie Mazowieckim', in Barbara Engelking, Jacek Leociak and Dariusz Libionka (eds.), *Zagłada Żydów: Pamięć narodowa a pisanie historii w Polsce i we Francji* (Lublin, 2006), 57–74; Krzysztof Tomasz Witczak, 'Listy z getta tomaszowskiego jako dokument historyczny obrazujący żydowskie życie artystyczne w okresie okupacji', *Rocznik Łódzki* 58 (Łódź, 2011), 161–82. A selection of the letters by Ruth Goldbarth and Lutek Ohrenbach is to be found in Alexandra Garbarini et al. (eds.), *Jewish Responses to Persecution*, vol. 2: *1938–1940* (Lanham, MD, 2011), 453–75, and Jürgen Matthäus et al. (eds.), *Jewish Responses to Persecution*, vol. 3: *1941–1942* (Lanham, MD, 2013), 70–82.

[12] Letter dated 20 December 1939, USHMM 1996.A.70.1-115. Ohrenbach wrote his letters mostly in Polish. Translation in this chapter by the author.

spatial structure, the actual layout; on the other, space is constituted in and through social interaction. The social practices first made the restricted space a tangible experience. That Lutek Ohrenbach not only headed outside, but also took along the yard dog because it was 'better company', underlines this interrelationship.

Unfortunately, at no point did Ohrenbach mention exactly how many people he was forced to live with. At the beginning of April 1940, however, he told Edith Blau about the arrival of further relatives at his grandfather's house:

We haven't any news from my uncle in Romania [...] but we heard that he has moved further away. But me – I'm standing still. No, I'm going backwards! [...] Our cousins from Łódź have arrived – they've also come here to stay with us. It's all very noisy and everyone is worried.[13]

This brief remark shows, firstly, that the stream of refugees had yet to peter out even a few months after the end of fighting. Obviously, Ohrenbach's cousins had succeeded in fleeing Litzmannstadt and thus from Reich territory. Ohrenbach made no mention of the risks they took and the difficulties they most probably encountered on the way. He felt directly affected only by the fact that it was now even more difficult to have some peace and quiet in the house or to find a place to retreat to and be alone. Furthermore, it is striking how he described the worsening of the spatial situation, and associated this description with his own sense of immobility: 'I'm standing still.' In contrast to his uncle and also his cousins, he has not had the opportunity to move away, neither from the overcrowded house of his grandfather nor from Tomaschow, let alone the General Government. The hopelessness of the general situation struck him when he realised the cramped space was a direct consequence of the war and German occupation.

Ohrenbach followed a similar logic in another letter, written just two weeks later on the first day of Pesach. He began it by complaining about unwelcome company, no longer made up of just relatives, but now also joined by friends:

But something terrible is happening here: my friends and all the other devils are sitting around here from morning to evening. The whole of Tomaszow is here! Nothing helps. I hide, I run away and they're still waiting there. I can't have a single minute to myself. They're a disease, damn: a plague. But it's just my luck that every one of them comes to me. Will I finally [*wreszcie*] get any blessed peace?! Will I ever [*kiedyś*] have a minute to myself? Never!!! [*Nigdy*!!!] Today a whole conference was here. I couldn't even count them all.[14]

---

[13] Letter dated 9 April 1940, USHMM 1996.A.70.1–126.
[14] Letter dated 23 April 1940, USHMM 1996.A.70.1–131.

Possibly motivated by Pesach, Ohrenbach makes use of a religious code here, referring to 'devils', the 'plague' and 'blessed peace'. His hyperbole was animated by exaggerating of the temporal framework in phrases such as 'from morning to evening', the use of temporal adverbs such as 'finally' and 'ever', which are then answered with a 'never', underlined with three exclamation marks: all this expressed his pent-up infuriation at the disruptive visitors.

Further on in the letter, he vented his anger about not being able to take the bus to Warsaw, meaning that he could not get away from Tomaschow. Although he did not omit more pleasant episodes of life in this house community – for example his cousins from Litzmannstadt putting on a dance evening – Ohrenbach closed this letter with a pessimistic note. Celebrated on this particular and then the following days, as he saw it, the current circumstances deprived Pesach of any potential to remain a positive exception or reprieve from everyday life:

Everything's always the same. I sit at the table, the candles are lit: it's Pesach. But a different kind of Pesach. 'This night is different to every other night.' There is no difference. This night is just like all the other nights.[15]

Here he took a sentence from the liturgy of the Seder evening and posited it as an antithesis to his assessment of the current situation. In his view, life had become nothing more than a series of indistinguishable days (and nights). Under normal circumstances, meeting family and friends to celebrate an occasion like Pesach would be seen as a positive break from quotidian life, and this would in part define its special allure. Almost eight months after its outbreak, the war had turned everything into a perpetual negative state, leaving Ohrenbach subjected to daily restrictions on his freedom of movement, and constantly confronted with his relatives. An occasion like a religious holiday prompted him to reflect on this development and put it into words. At the same time, he was fully aware that he had no realistic possibility of getting away any time soon. He recognised how threatening the situation was; with none of the ghetto residents able to change the underlying circumstances, everyone was at the mercy of things beyond their control. It is thus by no means a coincidence that in the one and the same letter there is a detailed description of how the arrival of refugees and relocated relatives had changed the spatial foundations of the private, and alongside it a more in-depth interpretation of events.

The authors of the ego-documents quoted thus far, all written during the first year of the war, all emphasised the experience of loss. They found

---

[15] Ibidem.

the spatial changes so radical precisely because they had lived in very different circumstances in the pre-war period. Noëmi Szac-Wajnkranc referred expressly to the multifamily house of her uncle and aunt, and even if Lutek Ohrenbach did not directly mention his parents' home, his letters clearly indicate that he must have lived in a far less cramped house, or at least a family apartment, before the war. Both authors represent the Jews as highly assimilated to the milieu of the urban, non-Jewish bourgeoisie, and as sharing many of their ideas, aspirations and social practices.

A large section of Poland's Jewish population, however, disapproved of assimilation of this kind, and chose, more or less deliberately, to lead a very different lifestyle. The large group of Chassidic Jews, for example, organised their lives around religious commandments and precepts.[16] In this context, proximity, distance and possession were manifested in social practices which were fundamentally distinct from those of assimilated Jews. The arrangement of space in their homes mirrored these differences. Often with many children – six or more were the rule rather than the exception – they frequently lived in two rooms, which fulfilled different functions depending on the time of day. The father spent several hours outside the dwelling, devoting himself to worship and religious studies in the synagogue and prayer room, and was thus not part of life at the family home for this period of time. Meanwhile, the mother not only kept the household running, she also earned the family's livelihood. During the day, the living room and bedroom were frequently used for business. In a way, living in cramped spaces was not unusual. The situation was similar for the mass of Jewish factory workers in the large cities of Łódź and Warsaw. While the spatial situation changed for these groups as well during the first year of the war, the starting point was quite different to that of assimilated Jews like Ohrenbach or Szac-Wajnkranc. In contrast to the latter, members of the lower strata of society initially experienced ghettoisation as a gradual worsening of their situation, for, due to their poverty, confined space was something they were very familiar with. Moreover, in the first half of the war, many lived in a smaller or medium-sized, mostly semi-open ghetto, not in a hermetically closed-off, large ghetto, so that they could, for a few hours at least, still move around relatively freely. This influenced their perception of the spatial conditions, and thus their assessment of the overall situation.

---

[16] See Heiko Haumann, *Geschichte der Ostjuden*, 4th rev. edn (Munich, 1998), particularly 136–46; Esther Farbstein, *Hidden in Thunder: Perspectives on Faith, Halachah and Leadership during the Holocaust* (Jerusalem, 2007).

Private Space in a Phase of Relative Stability, from Autumn 1940 to Autumn 1942

In November 1940, the Germans had largely completed the ghettoisation of the Jewish population in and around Warsaw. They could now erect a wall around the ghetto area and seal it off from the outside world. In January 1941, 400,000 people were living in a built-up area covering a little more than three square kilometres. This corresponded to a population density of more than 130,000 persons per square kilometre. The population was unevenly distributed in the ghetto of the former Polish capital. While in some areas, there was a relatively tolerable distribution, in others, the density was particularly severe. The occupiers formally completed the closing off of the ghettos in the smaller and medium-sized locations from the autumn of 1940, although they maintained their semi-open character. With respect to the living space available, the conditions prevailing here could also only be described as unbearable. Figures for the individual locations are problematic, however, fluctuating strongly depending on the source.[17] The dimensions of the area are often difficult to reconstruct, and the population figures are only roughly estimable. In Tomaschow, 16,000 Jews lived in a total of 250 residential houses, on average sixty-four persons per house.[18] Paradoxically, in many cases, the setting up of the ghettos meant the beginning of a relatively stable phase, stable at least in comparison to the upheavals of the first year of the war. In several ghettos, the population succeeded in putting in place the structures necessary for living together, and even began developing a social and cultural life.[19] Nevertheless, it cannot be emphasised enough just how much life in the ghettos was characterised by catastrophic hygiene and sanitary conditions and the constant undersupply of provisions and malnutrition, and by the permanent existential threat posed by the occupiers. The temporarily 'stable'

---

[17] These difficulties are acutely evident when considering the ghetto in Petrikau. The figures given in the contemporary sources differ by several thousand inhabitants. In mid-1940, depending on the source, between 14,000 and 20,000 were supposedly living there in 182 residential buildings with 4,178 rooms. Thus, on average around five people were living in a room, i.e. 77 to 110 persons in a building.

[18] See Martin Dean and Katrin Reichelt, 'Tomaszów Mazowiecki', in Martin Dean (ed.), *The United States Holocaust Memorial Museum Encyclopedia of Camps and Ghettos 1933–1945*, vol. 2: *Ghettos in German-Occupied Eastern Europe* (Bloomington, IN, 2012), 335–8, here 336.

[19] See the volumes on the history of everyday life in the ghettos e.g. Eric Sterling, *Life in the Ghettos during the Holocaust* (Syracuse, NY, 2005); Imke Hansen, Katrin Steffen and Joachim Tauber (eds.), *Lebenswelt Ghetto: Alltag und soziales Umfeld während der nationalsozialistischen Verfolgung* (Wiesbaden, 2013); Andrea Löw, Doris L. Bergen and Anna Hájková (eds.), *Alltag im Holocaust: Jüdisches Leben im Großdeutschen Reich 1941–1945* (Munich, 2013).

circumstances may have enabled the formation of rudimentary conditions for new forms of privacy, but ultimately, this signified little more than that a catastrophic state of affairs persisted for a particular period of time.

What was life like in this confined space during this phase? The variety of practices within the private living space under analysis here corresponds to a variety of source types. This body of sources is in some ways a mirror image of those analysed in this volume as a whole, primarily with regard to German majority society, notably a range of official records and personal ego-documents. For my analysis, along with the administrative records of the German occupiers and the Jewish self-administration, ghetto newspapers and visual sources, diaries and private correspondence are pivotal. For many, keeping diaries and writing letters was one of the practices which enabled a brief mental respite from the oppressive reality of the ghetto.[20] Given the high population density, the question that immediately springs to mind is where ghetto inhabitants found a space for writing in the first place. Some ego-documents provide clues. The letters of Ruth Goldbarth from Warsaw, the other Polish correspondent of Edith Blau, are an excellent example.[21] In the chaos of the first days of the war, the Goldbarth family fled to Warsaw, from where Ruth Goldbarth then sent more than 100 letters to Minden from the autumn of 1939 through to the autumn of 1942. These letters are ideally suited for direct comparison with those of Ohrenbach. Time and again, Goldbarth reflected on the form and content of her letters, and was self-critical of her habit of composing long letters spread out over several days. In this way, so she once noted, she often lost sight of Edith Blau as the real addressee, and tended to write what were more like diary entries for herself.[22] Given this pronounced reflective faculty, it is hardly surprising that Goldbarth also thought about the practice of writing. In conjunction with her habit of noting the time alongside the date, this makes it possible to reconstruct, to a certain extent, her writing practice.

On Monday, 28 April 1941, at 6.20 AM, she picked up where she had left off writing a letter the day before: 'I'm lying in bed and have an hour to write to you.'[23] Ruth Goldbarth found the necessary privacy to write, where she could remain undisturbed, by waking up an hour earlier than

---

[20] Regarding the social practice of writing ego-documents by members of the *Volksgemeinschaft*, see Janosch Steuwer, '*Ein Drittes Reich, wie ich es auffasse': Politik, Gesellschaft und privates Leben in Tagebüchern 1933–1939* (Göttingen, 2017).
[21] See Klaus-Peter Friedrich, 'Die Brombergerin Ruth Goldbarth im Warschauer Getto, 1940/41', *Jewish History Quarterly* 225 (2008), 35–46.
[22] For example in a letter dated 6 July 1941, USHMM 1996.A.70.1–73.
[23] Letter dated 27 and 28 April 1941, USHMM 1996.A.70.1–60. Ruth Goldbarth's family came from Berlin; the family spoke Polish and German. The letters are written in German.

the other family members she was living with. During the day, she hardly had any time, working in her father's dental practice and contributing greatly to the running of the household. But she could not have used the room she was sharing with her younger sister to sleep during the day in any case. As in all the flats in Warsaw the Goldbarth family inhabited until their deportation in the autumn of 1942, during the day, private rooms were used as waiting and treatment rooms. The bed was the minimal private space afforded to Ruth Goldbarth, where she could write her letters and in this way create a distance to the reality around her, a place of refuge and respite enabling her to reflect on incidents, experiences and feelings, and to put them into words.

Goldbarth described the flats in which she and her family lived in the ghetto several times, and reflected on how better off they were in comparison to the majority of ghetto inhabitants. They were able to rent a whole flat for themselves and did not have to share it with strangers, as in the examples discussed earlier. Only once did she mention that the Jewish ghetto administration had temporarily quartered two women with them; otherwise only Ruth's parents, her younger sister, a grandmother and herself lived in the five-room flat alone. They belonged to the economic elite of the ghetto, and were obviously able to draw on considerable savings from the pre-war period. At the same time, however, Ruth Goldbarth considered life in the ghetto to be a move down the social ladder. Once she told Edith Blau that she called the room where the family washed somewhat euphemistically a 'bathroom', although it had no bath, leading her to conclude: 'But that's by no way the worst (how far we've fallen!).'[24] Despite their privileged position, as time passed, the catastrophic living conditions in the ghetto had a negative impact on Goldbarth and her family as well. The health of both her grandmother and mother seemed precarious on a number of occasions, the disastrous food situation impeding the recovery of those who had fallen ill. The emotional stress, particularly the strain placed on the father, increased continuously, and the atmosphere in the family became more irascible, with outbursts of bad temper. It is astonishing, and only partially explicable in terms of the economic status enjoyed by the family, that Ruth Goldbarth was, nevertheless, able to mostly adopt a positive tone in her letters. She possibly saw them as a means to comfort and encourage both herself and the addressee. Unlike Lutek Ohrenbach in Tomaschow, she proactively tried to adapt to the living conditions in the ghetto. One good example of this strategy is a letter describing the spatial

---

[24] Letter dated 4 November 1940. USHMM 1996.A.70.1–29.

situation in the ghetto. In the already-quoted letter dated 27/28 April 1941, she wrote:

> Our fourth floor was added just a few years ago, and therefore has lots of modern fittings like central heating, wonderful bathrooms, large, wide windows etc. The whole floor is made up of one long corridor, the rooms located on both sides like a hotel. A family lives in each of these 14 rooms, i.e. mostly young married couples [...]. And everyone's very nice to each other. If in the evening you go up and want to speak to someone in particular, then they're never in their own room. There's 2 options: either you run from room to room or you stand in the middle of the corridor and call out the name of the person you're looking for as loud as you can. A door opens somewhere and the person you want sticks their head out.[25]

The somewhat light-hearted tone cannot distract from the fact that the house community was an enforced arrangement. The fact that one family was living in each of the fourteen rooms is testament to the cramped spatial situation in the ghetto. At the same time, the practice of visiting one another at certain times made space available outside one's own room. By temporarily suspending the spatial constraints and thus deliberately forming a house community, the inhabitants negotiated the coerciveness of the situation. Ruth Goldbarth's description of how she dealt with the unusual living conditions reveals two things. Firstly, she could depict the evening visits in such a casual style because her family did not have to live in a single room, but could afford a flat with several rooms on one of the lower floors. Secondly, by portraying the situation to Edith Blau in terms of an entertaining episode, she succeeded in temporarily bracketing the threat immanent to the situation. She not only described the practices of the residents, but actively related them to herself in her letter – although to write it, she had to wake up an hour earlier than usual in order to find the necessary peace and quiet in her own bed.

At first glance, it is the differences between the letters of Ruth Goldbarth and Lutek Ohrenbach which are striking and which were grounded in more than just their different situations in a closed and a semi-open ghetto, respectively. These two correspondents also wrote to one another, but sadly, these letters did not survive. But this makes the occasional remarks both penned about one another in letters to Edith Blau all the more interesting. In a letter dated 12 July 1941, Ruth Goldbarth told of a visitor from Tomaschow, whose stories about life in the ghetto there she found strikingly different from the despairing and despondent tone of Ohrenbach's recent letters. She suggested that 'one

[25] Letter dated 27 and 28 April 1941, USHMM 1996.A.70.1–60.

(above all you) has to give him a stern talking to,'[26] because he had no reason to be so dissatisfied. The economic situation in Tomaschow was much better than in Warsaw, for the ghetto inhabitants were able to have contact with Poles, and could thus find ways of earning some money, an opportunity inconceivable in Warsaw. She also explicitly mentioned the more comfortable living conditions: 'Did you know that Lutek has a small garden?' Moreover, she found out that Ohrenbach had gathered together a 'really nice circle of intelligent friends', with whom he ran a cabaret and earned good money on the side. To conclude, she quoted the visitor from Tomaschow directly: 'All in all, it is like a resort there in comparison to Warsaw, and it is a sin to be dissatisfied.'

Passages like these ostensibly illustrate the different ways Ohrenbach and Goldbarth sought to deal with their respective situations and, above all, the different ways in which they described these situations in their letters. However, the mentioning of Ohrenbach's cabaret activities directs attention to strategies, in principle very similar, for coping with the spatial restrictions in the ghetto. Ruth Goldbarth remained in bed, a place of refuge that allowed her to counter the experiences of spatial confinement and general existential threat in the ghetto with the parlando style of her letters. The artistically gifted Lutek Ohrenbach took similar action by holding soirées together with like-minded friends, reciting poems, singing songs and playing music, and so constructing a counter-world to the ghetto reality. These evenings were not always open to the ghetto public. The young artists and performers frequently retreated to a safe haven. Ohrenbach was aware that their activities in a safe place were subjected to time limits – a further structural parallel to Ruth Goldbarth, who not only in the quoted letter states the time span she had for writing.

The analytical category of 'space' does not only require its analytical pendant 'time' when the correlation between the two is as obvious as in Ohrenbach's descriptions:

> I'm telling you in a nutshell that things are exactly the same here as they are with Ruth in Warsaw. [...] Now and then there is a peaceful moment. A blink of the eye. Then we can arrange an evening, then we can laugh a little (through our tears, through our tears).[27]

Just two months later, the performances once more the topic of discussion, Ohrenbach also mentioned where these were held:

> A smile is the emblem of our theatre group. As often as we can we cast off the yoke of everyday life, meet in Frau Sz's attic and have a bit of fun. Songs, music,

[26] Letter dated 12 July 1941, USHMM 1996.A.70.1–75.
[27] Letter dated 17 December 1940, USHMM 1996.A.70.1–165.

monologues. Recently we had a concert up there, including a performance by famous 'grandma' Makow, formerly the pianist at the Warsaw Opera.[28]

While this concert seems to have been open to others, the attic was usually a safe haven, to which Ohrenbach and his young friends could retreat for a short time. As with Ruth Goldbarth, for Chrenbach there was also a convergence between a space that was shielded from the gaze of others, or the general public, and an activity that could be experienced as an retreat into an interior world.

Lutek Ohrenbach and Ruth Goldbarth were young people, just embarking upon their adult lives. Born after 1918, they represent the large group of ghetto inmates who grew up and were socialised in the Second Polish Republic. For the very same reason, not much is known about their life before the outbreak of the war. But even if, as it likely, they had not yet completed their education and were yet to found a family, their ideas about the future and what they wished for were very clear. Their letters were marked by eloquence, a broad cultural horizon, mental agility and intelligence, and thus attest to the talents and potential of the two letter writers. Over the course of the war, they found different ways of dealing with the spatial confinement of the ghetto. At times, Ohrenbach sought refuge in alcohol to forget the ever-threatening reality; in her last letters of summer 1942, Goldbarth struck an increasingly despairing tone. Both still had so much to look forward to in life as they, together with their families, were murdered by the Germans in Treblinka in the autumn of 1942.

At a very different point in his life was the physician, orphanage director and internationally renowned pedagogue Janusz Korczak, who was also a resident in the Warsaw ghetto during the war.[29] Unlike Ohrenbach and Goldbarth, Korczak was mainly socialised before the First World War, i.e. in Congress Poland under Russian rule. It is useful to take a closer look at two examples from Korczak's ego-documents to broaden the perspective and to compare the strategies employed by the young adults with the views of one man who could look back on an impressive life's work, and who had at his disposal a greater wealth of experience, representing a very different generation. Korczak, born Henryk Goldszmit in 1878 or 1879 and thus already more than sixty years old when the war broke out, wrote a relatively voluminous manuscript between May and the beginning of August 1942, a mixture of autobiographical sketches and

---

[28] Letter dated 6 February 1941, USHMM 1996.A.70.1–169.
[29] There are an enormous number of studies on Korczak's biography and work. See Janusz Korczak, *Gesammelte Werke*, ed. by Friedhelm Beiner and Erich Dauzenroth, 16 volumes and a supplemental volume (Gütersloh, 1996–2010).

a diary.[30] All the differences from his fellow ghetto inmates Ohrenbach and Goldbarth notwithstanding, Korczak wrote about similar topics, including the importance of a private refuge. He repeatedly reflected on the practices of sleeping and of keeping a diary. In this context, it is important to consider the time period. In May 1942, two and a half years after the start of the war, Korczak, like so many others, had adapted to the deceptive calm of a seemingly stable everyday life in the ghetto. For Korczak, a man with extensive experience as an author, this sense of relative security was a precondition for being able to begin writing. At the same time, his disastrous health motivated him to take stock of his life shortly before completing his sixty-fourth year – including detailed descriptions of his serious health problems.

Here too the spatial situation is the starting point for the author's reflections on sleeping and writing. Korczak lived in the Warsaw ghetto together with 200 orphans and a few staff in an orphanage he had founded. His room was adjacent to the large children's dormitory. He did not have the room to himself, however, sharing it with a changing number of particularly ill children as well as the gravely ill father of one of his staff, who passed away during the period in which Korczak kept the diary. At night time, Korczak's roommates usually slept, while he made use of part of this time to write, sleeping for just a few hours. In May 1942, he noted: 'My bed stands in the middle of the room. Under the bed – a bottle of vodka; on the night table, black bread and a jug of water.'[31] And a few days later: 'I am in bed. The bed is in the middle of the room. My subtenants are: Monius, the younger (we have four of them), then Albert and Jerzyk. On the other side against the wall Felunia, Gienia and Haneczka.'[32]

In these short passages, Korczak touched on two subjects. First, how could sleeping and writing be fitted into a daily rhythm predicated on a phase of gainful employment during the day, stretching over several hours, and a sleeping phase at night? Second, how could the sleeping practice be reconfigured to maximise the given spatial (and temporal) possibilities? His mention of vodka under the bed and bread and water on the night table alludes to Korczak's preference to eat and drink not during the day but at night, as he explicitly describes elsewhere.[33] At the same time, he preferred to sleep during the day and to remain awake at night. This reversal was scarcely sustainable for him in his capacity as director of the orphanage, but he arranged his nights at least in part around these

---

[30] Janusz Korczak, *Ghetto Diary*, with an introduction by Betty Jean Lifton (New Haven, CT, 2003).
[31] Ibidem, 10, May 1942. Diary entries with precise dates alternate with longer passages without any date or time given.
[32] Ibidem, 11, exact day not noted.   [33] See ibidem, 23.

wishes, or at least articulated the desire to use his time in this way repeatedly in his notes. He roundly rejected a single sleep phase over several hours, considering it a faulty cultural construct. Instead, he envisaged an unregulated alternation between one or two hours of sleep, eating and drinking and working on his notes. To what extent he succeeded in practising this pattern in the ghetto is difficult to determine with absolute certainty, even if Korczak continuously describes it in his diary. In any case, we should avoid hastily diagnosing this nocturnal activity as a symptom of a sleeping disorder resulting from the living conditions in the ghetto. Korczak's ideal of inverting day and night, and thus the practices linked to this dichotomy, was an expression of his striving for independence and self-determination. In an environment so strongly regulated and controlled by outside influences, individually to determine one's own sleeping practice was one of the last remaining opportunities to enjoy at least a semblance of human autonomy.

The same passages are also concerned with Korczak's sleeping place. Due to the shortage of space in his orphanage, he was forced to share part of his private room with persons suffering from various afflictions. Nevertheless, if we are to believe his notes, he did not consider this lack of distance a problem. Indeed, he understood the deliberate opening of his private domain to be the logical implementation of his pedagogic principles, which were predicated on loving interaction with children as fully fledged persons. This fundamental disposition of affection expressed itself in ways that permitted proximity and renounced distance, as the quote that follows shows. Korczak gave up his own bed for a boy from the dormitory who had slept badly, unsettled by a bad dream, and comforted and reassured him:

> How quickly the hours pass. Just now it was midnight – and already it is three in the morning. I had a visitor in my bed. Mendelek had a bad dream. I carried him to my bed. He stroked my face (!) and went to sleep. He squeals. He's uncomfortable. 'Are you asleep?' 'I thought I was in the dormitory.' He stares surprised with his black monkey-like beads of eyes. 'You were in the dormitory. Do you want to go back to your own bed?' 'Am I in your way?' 'Lie down at the other end. I'll bring you the pillow.' 'Fine.' 'I'll be writing. If you're frightened, come back.' 'O.K.'[34]

Allowing spatial proximity here expresses the solidarity felt with ill orphans, one of the weakest groups amongst the ghetto inhabitants. Necessarily interwoven with Korczak's reflections on sleep are his reflections on keeping a diary, for both were done in the same place and at night, as the end of the quote indicates. It was only through writing that

---

[34] Ibidem, 65.

Korczak was able to create a private sphere in this environment. Even if no actual spatial distance was involved, writing was the only possibility available to Korczak to immerse himself in reflections about his life and the things important to him, a domain of solitude without any other persons needing to be included. With the benefit of hindsight, it is particularly disturbing that this period, after two and a half years of war, during which Korczak had once again found an inner refuge, was simultaneously the time that immediately preceded his deportation and murder in Treblinka. He wrote his last entry on 5 August 1942. A day later he went to his death with 'his' orphans.

Conclusion

This chapter on private life in the spatial confinements of the ghetto has examined the relationship between space and social practices, which are mutually constitutive. The analytical category of 'space' proved helpful for exploring the transformation processes to which privacy in the ghettos of occupied Poland was subject during the Second World War. Over the course of the first year of the war, a phase of radical upheaval having transformed all the conditions that had hitherto framed privacy, ghetto inhabitants developed strategies to negotiate spatial restrictions which were largely pragmatic in character. The two nameplates were prime examples of this attitude, for they reconfigured the crossing from public into private space, which now had to be shared by more parties than usual. How individuals shaped their relationship to a community that was forced to live together, whether in the immediate surroundings of home or in a larger context too, can be deduced from the spatial parameters of social interactions. The letters of Lutek Ohrenbach from Tomaschow are striking in this respect. Despite the relatively favourable spatial situation, particularly in direct comparison to that prevailing in Warsaw, life in the cramped and overcrowded house of Ohrenbach's grandfather was an extremely negative experience for the sensitive young man, a situation he was only very occasionally able to escape. Studying his writings from this period offers insights into the shifting meaning of privacy in the ghetto, and illuminates how living together functioned within the confines of an imposed community.

Ruth Goldbarth's letters from Warsaw show just how variegated strategies for the redefinition of space could be. Of course, this finding is in part the result of focusing on ego-documents as the main source for examining the transformations of the private. And yet such documents show more than just personal whims. The structural parallels between Ohrenbach's and Goldbarth's letters with respect to the connection between space and imagined escape from the reality of the ghetto are striking. The act of writing letters, and artistic pursuits more broadly, helped to configure an inward refuge. For both individuals, spatial distance to one's immediate social surroundings was a decisive component in this construction of counter-worlds. By contrast, in the case of Janusz Korczak, spatial proximity enabled a trace of humanity to be shown in the catastrophic conditions of life in the ghetto. At the same time, Korczak also needed a refuge to be able to assert a remnant of human autonomy, by following his nocturnal sleeping and writing practices.

As I have argued in this chapter, by drawing on contemporary ego-documents, we can explore both the pragmatic strategies deployed during the phase of ghettoisation and the social practices for negotiating proximity and distance that emerged in the period between the establishment of ghettos to the onset of mass deportations. During this time, experiences of proximity and distance changed, and as a result, modes of behaviour did as well. The ghetto inhabitants were acutely aware of these changes. They interpreted these changes by drawing on their experiences and understanding from the pre-war period, and this reservoir of resources still functioned relatively well for some time. It is even plausible to suggest that proximity and distance remained two of the rare categories with which an interpretation of these events was possible at all.

In general, ghetto inhabitants were rarely able to glean insights into the intentions and actions of the German occupiers; nor were such intentions open to conventional interpretations based on rational criteria. In this situation, a 'sensible' or 'reasonable' response was impossible. This was due, in part, to the lack of a clear plan on the part of Germans themselves, so that many of their actions appeared random and ad hoc. But as Dan Diner has shown for the *Judenräte*, an understanding of the unfolding political situation was hardly possible even over a longer period of time. According to Diner, German actions followed a 'counter rationality', a phrase he deploys to characterise the break with civilisation which National Socialism and the Holocaust represented.[35] Diner's thesis can be expanded, yet also modified, with a view to the ghettos: the Jewish population understood full well, in their immediate impact, at least the spatial aspects of German policy. This perception of their predicament engendered concern and fear, and in this way ghetto residents could comprehend, at least to a degree, the dynamics of the indirect, later the direct, extermination. The practices of writing letters and keeping diaries

---

[35] See Dan Diner, 'Die Perspektive des "Judenrats": Zur universellen Bedeutung einer partikularen Erfahrung', in Doron Kiesel (ed.), *'Wer zum Leben, wer zum Tod...': Strategien jüdischen Überlebens im Getto* (Frankfurt a.M., 1992), 11–36, here 25.

were of particular importance in articulating such an understanding.[36] But saving documents such as the play *Love Seeks a Home* or the nameplate with the elaborate signal system was also part of such a process of understanding. Even if the collectors of *Oyneg Shabes* added both of these artefacts to their archive without any explicit comment, the significance they attached to them is obvious. The practices of writing and archiving were like keys with which the ghetto residents could broaden their experiences of dramatic spatial changes to unlock a deeper understanding of what was happening around them.

---

[36] See Janosch Steuwer and Rüdiger Graf (eds.), *Selbstreflexionen und Weltdeutungen: Tagebücher in der Geschichte und der Geschichtsschreibung des 20. Jahrhunderts* (Göttingen, 2015).

Bibliography

Acton, Carol, *Grief in Wartime: Private Pain, Public Discourse* (Basingstoke, 2007).
Adorno, Theodor W., *Minima Moralia: Reflections from Damaged Life* (London, 2005).
Allen, Anita, 'Privacy', in Jaggar, Alison M., and Young, Iris Marion (eds.), *A Companion to Feminist Philosophy* (Oxford, 1998), 456–65.
Allport, Alan, *Demobbed: Coming Home after World War II* (New Haven, CT, London, 2009).
Alltagsgeschichte der NS-Zeit: Neue Perspektive oder Trivialisierung? Kolloqium am 17. November 1983 im Institut für Zeitgeschichte, München (Munich, 1984).
d'Almeida, Fabrice, *High Society in the Third Reich* (Cambridge, 2008).
Aly, Götz, *'Final Solution': Nazi Population Policy and the Murder of the European Jews* (London, 1995).
Aly, Götz, *Hitlers Volksstaat: Raub, Rassenkrieg und nationaler Sozialismus* (Frankfurt a.M., 2005).
Arani, Miriam Y., *Fotografische Selbst- und Fremdbilder von Deutschen und Polen im Reichsgau Wartheland 1939–1945*, 2 vols. (Hamburg, 2008).
Arendt, Hannah, *Elemente und Ursprünge totaler Herrschaft*, 10th edn (Munich, Zurich, 2005).
Arendt, Hannah, *The Origins of Totalitarianism* (Cleveland, OH, New York, NY, 1966).
Auslander, Leora, 'Reading German Jewry through Vernacular Photography: From the Kaiserreich to the Third Reich', *Central European History* 48/3 (2015), 300–34.
Bajohr, Frank, *Arisierung in Hamburg: Die Verdrängung der jüdischen Unternehmer, 1933–1945* (Hamburg, 1997).
Bajohr, Frank, *'Unser Hotel ist judenfrei': Bäder-Antisemitismus im 19. und 20. Jahrhundert* (Frankfurt a.M., 2003).
Bajohr, Frank, 'Die Zustimmungsdiktatur: Grundzüge nationalsozialistischer Herrschaft in Hamburg', in Forschungsstelle für Zeitgeschichte in Hamburg and Schmid, Josef (eds.), *Hamburg im 'Dritten Reich'* (Göttingen, 2005), 69–121.
Bajohr, Frank, Gregor, Neil, Chapoutot, Johann and Hördler, Stefan, 'Podium Zeitgeschichte: *Cultural Turn* und NS-Forschung', *Vierteljahrshefte für Zeitgeschichte* 65 (2017), 219–72.
Bajohr, Frank, Meyer, Beate and Szodrzynski, Joachim (eds.), *Bedrohung, Hoffnung, Skepsis: Vier Tagebücher des Jahres 1933* (Göttingen, 2013).

Bajohr, Frank and Wildt, Michael (eds.), *Volksgemeinschaft: Neue Forschungen zur Gesellschaftsgeschichte des Nationalsozialismus* (Frankfurt a.M., 2009).

Baldwin, Peter (ed.), *Reworking the Past: Hitler, the Holocaust, and the Historians' Debate* (Boston, MA, 1990).

Bankier, David, *The Germans and the Final Solution: Public Opinion under Nazism* (Oxford, 1992).

Baranowski, Shelley, *Strength through Joy: Consumption and Mass Tourism in the Third Reich* (Cambridge, 2004).

Barkai, Avraham, *Vom Boykott zur 'Entjudung': Der wirtschaftliche Existenzkampf der Juden im Dritten Reich, 1933–1945* (Frankfurt a.M., 1988).

Barkai, Avraham, *'Wehr Dich': Der Centralverein deutscher Staatsbürger jüdischen Glaubens (C. V.) 1893–1938* (Munich, 2002).

Bauer, Ingrid and Hämmerle, Christa, 'Editorial', *L'Homme. Europäische Zeitschrift für Feministische Geschichtswissenschaft* 24/1, special issue on 'Romantische Liebe' (2013), 5–14.

Bauer, Ingrid and Hämmerle, Christa, 'Liebe und Paarbeziehungen im "Zeitalter der Briefe" – ein Forschungsprojekt im Kontext', in Bauer, Ingrid and Hämmerle, Christa (eds.), *Liebe schreiben: Paarkorrespondenzen im Kontext des 19. und 20. Jahrhunderts* (Göttingen, 2017), 9–56.

Bauer, Ingrid and Hämmerle, Christa (eds.), *Liebe schreiben: Paarkorrespondenzen im Kontext des 19. und 20. Jahrhunderts* (Göttingen, 2017).

Bauerkämper, Arnd, *Die 'radikale Rechte' in Großbritannien: Nationalistische, antisemitische und faschistische Bewegungen vom späten 19. Jahrhundert bis 1945* (Göttingen, 1991).

Baum, Markus, *Jochen Klepper* (Schwarzenfeld, 2011).

Baumeister, Martin, '"Feldpostbriefe und Kriegserlebnis": Reviews of Two Books by Klaus Latzel and Bernd Ulrich', *WerkstattGeschichte* 22 (1999), 97–9.

Bavaj, Riccardo, *Die Ambivalenz der Moderne im Nationalsozialismus: Eine Bilanz der Forschung* (Munich, 2003).

Bavaj, Riccardo, *Der Nationalsozialismus: Entstehung, Aufstieg und Herrschaft* (Berlin, 2016).

Berg, Mary, *The Diary of Mary Berg: Growing Up in the Warsaw Ghetto* (Oxford, 2007).

Bergen, Doris L., Hájková, Anna and Löw, Andrea, 'Warum eine Alltagsgeschichte des Holocaust?', in Löw, Andrea, Bergen, Doris L. and Hájková, Anna (eds.), *Alltag im Holocaust: Jüdisches Leben im Großdeutschen Reich 1941–1945* (Munich, 2013), 1–12.

Bergerson, Andrew Stuart, *Ordinary Germans in Extraordinary Times: The Nazi Revolution in Hildesheim* (Bloomington, IN, 2004).

Bergerson, Andrew Stuart, 'Das Sich-Einschreiben in die NS-Zukunft: Liebesbriefe als Quelle für eine Alltagsgeschichte der Volksgemeinschaft', in Schmiechen-Ackermann, Detlef et al. (eds.), *Der Ort der 'Volksgemeinschaft' in der deutschen Gesellschaftsgeschichte* (Paderborn, 2017), 223–41.

Bergerson, Andrew Stuart et al., 'Nonconformity', in Bergerson, Andrew Stuart et al. (eds.), *The Happy Burden of History: From Sovereign Impunity to Responsible Selfhood* (Berlin, 2011).

Bergerson, Andrew Stuart, Schmieding, Leonard et al., *Ruptures in the Everyday: Views of Modern Germany from the Ground* (Oxford, 2017).
Bergerson, Andrew Stuart et al. (eds.), *Trug und Schein: Ein Briefwechsel*, vols. 1–4: *1938–41* (2013–16), www.trugundschein.org/.
Berghoff, Hartmut, '"Times Change and We Change with Them': The German Advertising Industry in the Third Reich – Between Professional Self-Interest and Political Repression', *Business History* 45/1 (2003), 128–47.
Bessel, Richard, *Political Violence and the Rise of Nazism: The Storm Troopers in Eastern Germany 1925–1934* (New Haven, CT, London, 1984).
Betts, Paul, *Within Walls: Private Life in the German Democratic Republic* (Oxford, 2010).
Blasius, Dirk, *Ehescheidung in Deutschland 1794–1945* (Göttingen, 1987).
Bobbio, Norberto, *Democracy and Dictatorship: The Nature and Limits of State Power* (Cambridge, 1989).
Boberach, Heinz (ed.), *Meldungen aus dem Reich: Die geheimen Lageberichte des Sicherheitsdienstes des SS 1938–1945*, 17 vols. (Herrsching, 1984).
Bock, Gisela, *Zwangssterilisation im Nationalsozialismus: Studien zur Rassenpolitik und Frauenpolitik* (Opladen, 1986).
Böhler, Jochen, *Auftakt zum Vernichtungskrieg: Die Wehrmacht in Polen 1939* (Frankfurt a.M., 2006).
Böhles, Marcel, *Im Gleichschritt für die Republik: Das Reichsbanner Schwarz-Rot-Gold im Südwesten, 1924–1933* (Essen, 2016).
Boll, Bernd, 'Das Adlerauge des Soldaten: Zur Fotopraxis deutscher Amateure im Zweiten Weltkrieg', *Fotogeschichte* 85–86/22 (2002), 75–86
Boll, Bernd, 'Vom Album ins Archiv: Zur Überlieferung privater Fotografien aus dem Zweiten Weltkrieg', in Holzer, Anton (ed.), *Mit der Kamera bewaffnet: Krieg und Fotografie* (Marburg, 2003), 167–81.
Boll, Bernd, 'Das Bild als Waffe: Quellenkritische Anmerkungen zum Foto- und Filmmaterial der deutschen Propagandatruppen 1938–1945', *Zeitschrift für Geschichtswissenschaft* 54 (2006), 974–99.
Bömelburg, Hans-Jürgen and Klatt, Marlene (eds.), *Lodz im Zweiten Weltkrieg: Deutsche Selbstzeugnisse über Alltag, Lebenswelten und NS-Germanisierungspolitik in einer multiethnischen Stadt* (Osnabrück, 2015).
Bopp, Petra, *Fremde im Visier: Fotoalben aus dem Zweiten Weltkrieg* (Bielefeld, 2012).
Borscheid, Peter, 'Alltagsgeschichte – Modetorheit oder neues Tor zur Vergangenheit?', in Schieder, Wolfgang and Sellin, Volker (eds.), *Sozialgeschichte in Deutschland*, vol. 3 (Göttingen, 1987), 78–100.
Borscheid, Peter, 'Sparsamkeit und Sicherheit: Werbung für Banken, Sparkassen und Versicherungen', in Borscheid, Peter and Wischermann, Clemens (eds.), *Bilderwelt des Alltags* (Stuttgart, 1995), 316–25.
Bracher, Karl Dietrich, 'Die totalitäre Utopie: Orwells 1984', *Psychosozial* 22 (1984), 31–48.
Brändli, Sabina, '"...die Männer sollen schöner geputzt sein als die Weiber": Zur Konstruktion bürgerlicher Männlichkeit im 19. Jahrhundert', in Kühne, Thomas (ed.), *Männergeschichte – Geschlechtergeschichte: Männlichkeit im Wandel der Moderne* (Frankfurt a.M., 1996), 101–18.

Brockhaus, Gudrun, 'Muttermacht und Lebensangst: Zur Politischen Psychologie der NS-Erziehungsratgeber Johanna Haarers', in Brunner, José (ed.), *Mütterliche Macht und väterliche Autorität: Elternbilder im deutschen Diskurs* (Göttingen, 2008), 63–77.

Broszat, Martin, 'Resistenz und Widerstand: Eine Zwischenbilanz des Forschungsprojekts', in Broszat, Martin, Fröhlich, Elke and Grossmann, Anton (eds.), *Bayern in der NS-Zeit*, vol. 4 (Munich, 1981), 691–709.

Broszat, Martin et al. (eds.), *Bayern in der NS-Zeit*, 6 vols. (Munich, 1977–83).

Broszat, Martin, Henke, Klaus-Dietmar and Woller, Hans, 'Einleitung', in Broszat, Martin, Henke, Klaus-Dietmar and Woller, Hans (eds.), *Von Stalingrad zur Währungsreform: Zur Sozialgeschichte des Umbruchs in Deutschland* (Munich, 1988), XXV–XLIX.

Browning, Christopher, *Nazi Policy, Jewish Workers, German Killers* (Cambridge, 2000).

Browning, Christopher, *Ordinary Men: Reserve Police Battalion 101 and the Final Solution in Poland* (New York, NY, 1993).

Buchbender, Ortwin and Sterz, Reinhold (eds.), *Das andere Gesicht des Krieges: Deutsche Feldpostbriefe 1939–1945* (Munich, 1982).

Buchheim, Christoph, 'Der Mythos vom "Wohlleben": Der Lebensstandard der deutschen Zivilbevölkerung im Zweiten Weltkrieg', *Vierteljahrshefte für Zeitgeschichte* 58/3 (2010), 299–328.

Buchheim, Hans, *Totalitarian Rule: Its Nature and Characteristics* (Middletown, CT, 1968).

Buchholz, Wolfhard, *Die Nationalsozialistische Gemeinschaft 'Kraft durch Freude': Freizeitgestaltung und Arbeiterschaft im Dritten Reich* (PhD, Munich, 1976).

Buller, Amy, *Darkness over Germany* (London, 2017; original edition: London, 1943).

Burchardt, Lothar, 'Die Auswirkung der Kriegswirtschaft auf die deutsche Zivilbevölkerung im Ersten und im Zweiten Weltkrieg', *Militärgeschichtliche Mitteilungen* 15 (1974), 65–97.

Burleigh, Michael, *The Third Reich: A New History* (London, 2000).

Burleigh, Michael and Wippermann, Wolfgang, *The Racial State: Germany, 1933–1945* (Cambridge, 1991).

Butke, Silke and Kleine, Astrid, *Der Kampf für den gesunden Nachwuchs: Geburtshilfe und Säuglingsfürsorge im Deutschen Kaiserreich* (Münster, 2004).

Büttner, Elisabeth and Dewald, Christian, *Das tägliche Brennen: Eine Geschichte des österreichischen Films von den Anfängen bis 1945* (Salzburg, Vienna, 2002).

Christians, Annemone, 'Das Private vor Gericht: Verhandlungen des Eigenen im Zivil- und Strafrecht 1933–1945' (manuscript).

Christians, Annemone, 'Privatrecht in der Volksgemeinschaft? Die Eigensphäre im nationalsozialistischen Rechtssystem', in Schmiechen-Ackermann, Detlef et al. (eds.), *Der Ort der 'Volksgemeinschaft' in der deutschen Gesellschaftsgeschichte* (Paderborn, 2017), 274–86.

Cohn, Willy, *Kein Recht, nirgends: Tagebuch vom Untergang des Breslauer Judentums 1933–1941* (Cologne, 2007).

Confino, Alon, 'Dissonance, Normality and the Historical Method: Why Did Some Germans Think of Tourism after May 8, 1945?', in Bessel, Richard, and Schumann, Dirk (eds.), *Life after Death: Approaches to a Cultural and Social History of Europe during the 1940s and 1950s* (Cambridge, 2003), 323–47.

Connelly, John, 'The Uses of *Volksgemeinschaft*: Letters to the NSDAP Kreisleitung Eisenach, 1939–40', *Journal of Modern History* 68/4 (1996), 899–930.

Crew, David, *Germans on Welfare: From Weimar to Hitler* (Oxford, 1998).

Czarnowski, Gabriele, *Das kontrollierte Paar: Ehe- und Sexualpolitik im Nationalsozialismus* (Weinheim, 1991).

Czarnowski, Gabriele, '"Der Wert der Ehe für die Volksgemeinschaft": Frauen und Männer in der nationalsozialistischen Ehepolitik', in Heinsohn, Kirsten, Vogel, Barbara and Weckel, Ulrike (eds.), *Zwischen Karriere und Verfolgung: Handlungsräume von Frauen im nationalsozialistischen Deutschland* (Frankfurt a.M., 1997), 78–95.

Dean, Martin and Reichelt, Katrin, 'Tomaszów Mazowiecki', in Dean, Martin (ed.), *The United States Holocaust Memorial Museum Encyclopedia of Camps and Ghettos 1933–1945*, vol. 2: *Ghettos in German-Occupied Eastern Europe* (Bloomington, IN, 2012), 335–8.

Dickhuth-Harrach, Hans-Jürgen, *'Gerechtigkeit statt Formalismus': Die Rechtskraft in der nationalsozialistischen Privatrechtspraxis* (Cologne, 1986).

Dickinson, Edward Ross, 'Biopolitics, Fascism, Democracy: Some Reflections on Our Discourse about "Modernity"', *Central European History* 37/1 (2004), 1–48.

Didczuneit, Veit, Ebert, Jens and Jander, Thomas (eds.), *Schreiben im Krieg – Schreiben vom Krieg: Feldpost im Zeitalter der Weltkriege* (Essen, 2011).

Dietrich, Anette and Heise, Ljiljana (eds.), *Männlichkeitskonstruktionen im Nationalsozialismus* (Frankfurt a.M., 2013).

Diewald-Kerkmann, Gisela, *Politische Denunziation im NS-Regime oder Die kleine Macht der 'Volksgenossen'* (Bonn, 1995).

Diner, Dan, 'Gestaute Zeit – Massenvernichtung und jüdische Erzählstruktur', in Weigel, Sigrid and Erdle, Birgit R. (eds.), *Fünfzig Jahre danach: Zur Nachgeschichte des Nationalsozialismus* (Zurich, 1996), 3–16.

Dollwet, Joachim, 'Menschen im Krieg. Bejahung – und Widerstand? Eindrücke und Auszüge aus der Sammlung von Feldpostbriefen des Zweiten Weltkrieges im Landeshauptarchiv Koblenz', *Jahrbuch für westdeutsche Landesgeschichte* 13 (1987), 279–322.

Dörner, Bernward, *'Heimtücke': Das Gesetz als Waffe. Kontrolle, Abschreckung und Verfolgung in Deutschland 1933–1945* (Paderborn, 1998).

Dörr, Margarethe, *'Wer die Zeit nicht miterlebt hat...': Frauenerfahrungen im Zweiten Weltkrieg und in den Jahren danach* (Frankfurt a.M., 1998).

Duden, Barbara, *Geschichte unter der Haut: Ein Eisenacher Arzt und seine Patientinnen um 1730* (Stuttgart, 1991).

Duden, Barbara, 'Zwischen wahrem Wissen und Prophetie: Konzeptionen des Ungeborenen', in Duden, Barbara, Schlumbohm, Jürgen and Veit, Patrice (eds.), *Geschichte des Ungeborenen: Zur Erfahrungs- und Wissenschaftsgeschichte der Schwangerschaft, 17.-20. Jahrhundert* (Göttingen, 2000), 11–48.

Earle, Rebecca, 'Introduction', in Earle, Rebecca (ed.), *Epistolary Selves: Letters and Letter-Writers 1600–1945* (London, 1999, repr. 2016), 2–5.

Echterhölter, Rudolf, *Das öffentliche Recht im nationalsozialistischen Staat* (Stuttgart, 1970).

Eckhardt, Katja, *Die Auseinandersetzung zwischen Marianne Weber und Georg Simmel über die 'Frauenfrage'* (Stuttgart, 2000).

Eley, Geoff, 'German History and the Contradictions of Modernity: The Bourgeoisie, the State, and the Mastery of Reform', in Eley, Geoff (ed.), *Society, Culture, and the State in Germany, 1870–1930* (Ann Arbor, MI, 1997).

Eley, Geoff, 'Labor History, Social History, "Alltagsgeschichte": Experience, Culture, and the Politics of the Everyday – A New Direction for German Social History?', *Journal of Modern History* 61/2 (1989), 297–343.

Elias, Norbert, *The Civilizing Process*, vol. I: *The History of Manners* (Oxford, 1978; first published in German 1939).

Elshtain, Jean Bethke, 'The Displacement of Politics', in Weintraub, Jeff and Kumar, Krishan (eds.), *Public and Private in Thought and Practice: Perspectives on a Grand Dichotomy* (Chicago, IL, London, 1997), 166–81.

Emmerich, Norbert-Christian, *Die Deutsche Sparkassenwerbung, 1750–1981* (Stuttgart, 1983).

Engelking, Barbara, 'Miłość i cierpienie w Tomaszowie Mazowieckim', in Engelking, Barbara, Leociak, Jacek and Libionka, Dariusz (eds.), *Zagłada Żydów: Pamięć narodowa a pisanie historii w Polsce i we Francji* (Lublin, 2006), 57–74.

Engelking, Barbara and Leociak, Jacek, *The Warsaw Ghetto: A Guide to the Perished City* (New Haven, CT, 2009).

Epstein, Catherine, *Model Nazi: Arthur Greiser and the Occupation of Western Poland* (Oxford, 2010).

Essner, Cornelia and Conte, Edouard, '"Fernehe", "Leichentrauung" und "Totenscheidung": Metamorphosen des Eherechts im Dritten Reich', *Vierteljahrshefte für Zeitgeschichte* 44/2 (1996), 201–27.

Ettle, Susanne, *Anleitungen zu schriftlichen Kommunikationen: Briefsteller von 1880 bis 1980* (Tübingen, 1984).

Evans, Richard J., *The Third Reich in Power* (London, 2005; German edition Munich, 2006: *Das Dritte Reich*, vol. II/1: *Diktatur*).

Fahnenbruck, Laura, *Ein(ver)nehmen: Sexualität und Alltag in den besetzten Niederlanden* (Göttingen, 2017).

Falter, Jürgen, *Hitlers Wähler* (Munich, 1991).

Farbstein, Esther, *Hidden in Thunder: Perspectives on Faith, Halachah and Leadership during the Holocaust* (Jerusalem, 2007).

Fiebrandt, Maria, *Auslese für die Siedlergesellschaft: Die Einbeziehung Volksdeutscher in die NS-Erbgesundheitspolitik im Kontext der Umsiedlungen 1939–1945* (Göttingen, 2014).

Fielitz, Wilhelm, *Das Stereotyp des wolhyniendeutschen Umsiedlers: Popularisierungen zwischen Sprachinselforschung und nationalsozialistischer Propaganda* (Marburg, 2000).

Fischer-Lichte, Erika, *Ästhetik des Performativen* (Frankfurt a.M., 2014).

Fischer-Lichte, Erika, *Performativität: Eine Einführung* (Bielefeld, 2013).

Föllmer, Moritz, *Individuality and Modernity in Berlin: Self and Society from Weimar to the Wall* (Cambridge, 2013).
Föllmer, Moritz, *Ein Leben wie im Traum: Kultur im Dritten Reich* (Munich, 2016).
Föllmer, Moritz, 'The Subjective Dimension of Nazism', *Historical Journal* 56/4 (2013), 1107–32.
'Forum: Everyday Life in Nazi Germany', *German History* 27/4 (2009), 560–79.
Foucault, Michel, *The History of Sexuality*, vol. 1: *An Introduction* (London, 1984).
Foucault, Michel, 'Technologien des Selbst', in Foucault, Michel (ed.), *Schriften*, vol. 4 (Frankfurt a.M., 2005), 966–99.
Frevert, Ute, *Emotions in History: Lost and Found* (Budapest, New York, NY, 2011).
Frevert, Ute, *Frauen-Geschichte: Zwischen bürgerlicher Verbesserung und neuer Weiblichkeit* (Frankfurt a.M., 1986).
Frevert, Ute, 'Vertrauen: Eine historische Spurensuche', in Frevert, Ute (ed.), *Vertrauen: Historische Annäherungen* (Göttingen, 2003), 7–66.
Friedländer, Saul, *Nazi Germany and the Jews: The Years of Persecution, 1933–1939* (London, 1997).
Friedrich, Carl J., *The Pathology of Politics: Violence, Betrayal, Corruption, Secrecy and Propaganda* (New York, NY, 1972).
Friedrich, Carl J., *Totalitäre Diktatur* (Stuttgart, 1957).
Friedrich, Carl J. and Brzezinski, Zbigniew, *Totalitarian Dictatorship and Autocracy* (Cambridge, 1956).
Fritzsche, Peter, *Germans into Nazis* (Cambridge, MA, 1999).
Fritzsche, Peter, 'Introduction', in Riggs, Thomas (ed.), *Histories of Everyday Life in Totalitarian Regimes*, vol. 2: *Effects of Totalitarianism* (Farmington Hills, MI, 2015), XIII–XVI.
Fritzsche, Peter, *Life and Death in the Third Reich* (Cambridge, MA, 2008).
Fritzsche, Peter, 'Where Did All the Nazis Go? Reflections on Resistance and Collaboration', *Tel Aviver Jahrbuch für deutsche Geschichte* 23 (1994), 191–214.
Fröhlich, Elke (ed.), *Die Tagebücher von Joseph Goebbels, Teil I: Aufzeichnungen 1923–1941*, 9 vols. *Teil II: Diktate 1941–1945*, 15 vols. (Munich, 1993–2006).
Führer, Karl Christian, '"Guter Lebenskamerad, nichtarisch, zw. Ehe ersehnt": Heiratsanzeigen als Quelle für die jüdische Sozial- und Mentalitätsgeschichte im nationalsozialistischen Deutschland 1933–1938', *Historische Anthropologie* 18/3 (2010), 450–66.
Führer, Karl Christian, *Mieter, Hausbesitzer, Staat und Wohnungsmarkt: Wohnungsmangel und Wohnungszwangswirtschaft in Deutschland 1914–1960* (Stuttgart, 1995).
Führer, Karl Christian, 'Das NS-Regime und die "Idealform des deutschen Wohnungsbaues": Ein Beitrag zur nationalsozialistischen Gesellschaftspolitik', *Vierteljahrschrift für Sozial- und Wirtschaftsgeschichte* 89/2 (2002), 141–66.
Führer, Karl Christian, 'Pleasure, Practicality and Propaganda: Popular Magazines in Nazi Germany, 1933–1939', in Swett, Pamela E., Ross, Corey and d'Almeida, Fabrice (eds.), *Pleasure and Power in Nazi Germany* (Basingstoke, 2011), 142–53.

Fulbrook, Mary, 'Bystanders: Catchall Concept, Alluring Alibi or Crucial Clue?', in Fulbrook, Mary, *Erfahrung, Erinnerung, Geschichtsschreibung: Neue Perspektiven auf die deutschen Diktaturen* (Göttingen, 2016), 111–143.

Fulbrook, Mary, *Dissonant Lives: Generations and Violence through the German Dictatorships* (Oxford, 2011).

Fulbrook, Mary, *Reckonings: Legacies of Nazi Persecution and the Quest for Justice* (Oxford, 2018).

Fulbrook, Mary, *Subjectivity and History. Approaches to Twentieth-Century German Society* (London, 2017).

Fulbrook, Mary and Rublack, Ulinka, 'In Relation: The "Social Self" and Ego-Documents', *German History* 28/3 (2010), 263–72.

Garbarini, Alexandra, *Numbered Days: Diaries and the Holocaust* (New Haven, CT, 2006).

Garbarini, Alexandra et al. (eds.), *Jewish Responses to Persecution*, vol. 2: *1938–1940* (Lanham, MD, 2011).

Gebhardt, Miriam, *Die Angst vor dem kindlichen Tyrannen: Eine Geschichte der Erziehung im 20. Jahrhundert* (Munich, 2009).

Gehmacher, Johanna, 'Im Umfeld der Macht: Populäre Perspektiven auf Frauen der NS-Elite', in Fritsch, Elke and Herkommer, Christina (eds.), *Nationalsozialismus und Geschlecht: Zur Popularisierung und Ästhetisierung von Körper, Rasse und Sexualität im 'Dritten Reich' und nach 1945* (Bielefeld, 2009).

Gellately, Robert, *Backing Hitler: Consent and Coercion in Nazi Germany* (Oxford, 2001).

Gellately, Robert, 'Denunciation as a Subject of Historical Research', *Historical Social Research/Historische Sozialforschung* 26/2/3 (2001), 16–29.

Gellately, Robert, *The Gestapo and German Society: Enforcing Racial Policy 1933–1945* (Oxford, 1990).

Gerhardt, Uta and Karlauf, Thomas (eds.), *Night of Broken Glass: Eyewitness Accounts of Kristallnacht* (Malden, MA, 2012).

Geuss, Raymond, *Public Goods, Private Goods* (Princeton, NJ, 2001).

Ginsborg, Paul, *Die geführte Familie: Das Private in der Revolution und Diktatur 1900–1950* (Hamburg, 2014).

Ginsborg, Paul, *Family Politics: Domestic Life, Devastation and Survival 1900–1950* (New Haven, CT, 2014).

Goffman, Erving, *Stigma: Notes on the Management of Spoiled Identity* (Englewood Cliffs, NJ, 1963).

Goldhagen, Daniel, *Hitler's Willing Executioners: Ordinary Germans and the Holocaust* (London, 1996).

Goodman, Philomena, *Women, Sexuality and War* (New York, NY, 2001).

Grau, Günther, 'Persecution, "Re-education" or "Eradication" of Male Homosexuals between 1933 and 1945', in Grau, Günther (ed.), *Hidden Holocaust? Gay and Lesbian Persecution in Germany, 1933–1945* (London, 1995), 1–7.

Gregor, Neil, 'Listening as a Practice of Everyday Life: The Munich Philharmonic Orchestra and Its Audiences in the Second World War', in Thorau, Christian and Ziemer, Hansjakob (eds.), *Oxford Handbook of the History of Music Listening in the 19th and 20th Centuries* (New York, NY, 2019).

von Greyerz, Kaspar, 'Ego-Documents: The Last Word?', *German History* 28/3 (2010), 273–82.
Grossmann, Atina, *Reforming Sex: The German Movement for Birth Control and Abortion Reform 1920–1950* (Oxford, 1995).
Gruchmann, Lothar, *Justiz im Dritten Reich 1933–1940: Anpassung und Unterwerfung in der Ära Gürtner* (Munich, 1988).
Grunberger, Richard, *Das zwölfjährige Reich: Der Deutschen Alltag unter Hitler* (Vienna, Munich, Zurich, 1972).
Grunberger, Richard, *A Social History of the Third Reich* (London, 1971).
Grüttner, Michael, *Studenten im Dritten Reich* (Paderborn, 1995).
Guerin, Frances, *Through Amateur Eyes: Film and Photography in Nazi Germany* (Minneapolis, MN, 2012).
Haaf, Tobias, *Von volksverhetzenden Pfaffen und falschen Propheten: Klerus und Kirchenvolk im Bistum Würzburg in der Auseinandersetzung mit dem Nationalsozialismus* (Würzburg, 2006).
Haar, Ingo, 'Biopolitische Differenzkonstruktionen als bevölkerungspolitisches Ordnungsinstrument in den Ostgauen: Raum- und Bevölkerungsplanung im Spannungsfeld zwischen regionaler Verankerung und zentralstaatlichem Planungsanspruch', in John, Jürgen, Möller, Horst and Schaarschmidt, Thomas (eds.), *Die NS-Gaue: Regionale Mittelinstanzen im zentralistischen 'Führerstaat'* (Munich, 2007), 105–22.
Haar, Ingo, 'Vom "Volksgruppen-Paradigma" bis zum "Recht auf Heimat": Exklusion und Inklusion als Deutungsmuster in den Diskursen über Zwangsmigrationen vor und nach 1945', in Kochanowski, Jerzy and Sach, Maike (eds.), *Die 'Volksdeutschen' in Polen, Frankreich, Ungarn und der Tschechoslowakei: Mythos und Realität* (Osnabrück, 2006), 17–40.
Haas, Carlos A., 'Das Private im Getto: Transformationen jüdischen privaten Lebens in den Gettos von Warschau, Litzmannstadt, Tomaschow und Petrikau 1939 bis 1944' (PhD, Munich, 2018).
Haas, Ernst Joachim, *Stadt-Sparkasse Düsseldorf, 1825–1972* (Berlin, 1972).
Häberle, Peter, *Nationalflagge: Bürgerdemokratische Identifikationselemente und internationale Erkennungssymbole* (Berlin, 2008).
Habermas, Jürgen, *Strukturwandel der Öffentlichkeit: Untersuchungen zu einer Kategorie der bürgerlichen Gesellschaft* (Frankfurt a.M., 1990; orig. 1962).
Habermas, Jürgen, *The Structural Transformation of the Public Sphere: An Inquiry into a Category of Bourgeois Society* (Cambridge, MA, 1989).
Habermas, Rebekka, *Frauen und Männer des Bürgertums: Eine Familiengeschichte (1750–1850)* (Göttingen, 2002).
Hackländer, Philip, *'Im Namen des Deutschen Volkes': Der allgemein-zivilrechtliche Prozeßalltag im Dritten Reich am Beispiel der Amtsgerichte Berlin und Spandau* (Berlin, 2001).
Haerendel, Ulrike, *Kommunale Wohnungspolitik im Dritten Reich: Siedlungsideologie, Kleinhausbau und Wohnraumarisierung am Beispiel München* (Munich, 1999).
Haerendel, Ulrike, 'Wohnungspolitik im Nationalsozialismus', *Zeitschrift für Sozialreform* 45/10 (1999), 843–79.
Haffner, Sebastian, *Defying Hitler: A Memoir* (New York, NY, 2000).

Hahn, Lili, *Bis alles in Scherben fällt: Tagebuchblätter 1933–45* (Hamburg, 2007).
Hammer, Ingrid and zur Nieden, Susanne (eds.), *'Sehr selten habe ich geweint': Briefe und Tagebücher aus dem Zweiten Weltkrieg von Menschen aus Berlin* (Zurich, 1992).
Hämmerle, Christa, 'Between Instrumentalisation and Self-Governing: (Female) Ego-Documents in the Age of Total War', in Ruggiu, François-Joseph,(ed.), *The Uses of First Person Writings/Les usages des écrits du for privé: Afrique, Amérique, Asie, Europe* (Oxford, 2013), 263–84.
Hämmerle, Christa, 'Gewalt und Liebe – ineinander verschränkt: Paarkorrespondenzen aus zwei Weltkriegen, 1914/18 und 1939/45', in Bauer, Ingrid and Hämmerle, Christa (eds.), *Liebe schreiben: Paarkorrespondenzen im Kontext des 19. und 20. Jahrhunderts* (Göttingen, 2017), 171–230.
Hämmerle, Christa, and Saurer, Edith, 'Frauenbriefe – Männerbriefe? Überlegungen zu einer Briefgeschichte jenseits von Geschlechterdichotomien', in Hämmerle, Christa and Saurer, Edith (eds.), *Briefkulturen und ihr Geschlecht: Zur Geschichte der privaten Korrespondenz vom 16. Jahrhundert bis heute* (Vienna, Cologne, Weimar, 2003), 7–32.
Hanisch, Carol, 'The Personal Is Political', www.carolhanisch.org/CHwritings/PIP.html [accessed 19 June 2016].
Harlander, Tilman, *Zwischen Heimstätte und Wohnmaschine: Wohnungsbau und Wohnungspolitik in der Zeit des Nationalsozialismus* (Basel, 1995).
Hartig, Christine, *Briefe als Zugang zu einer Alltagsgeschichte des Nationalsozialismus*, online publication, Hamburg 2018.
Hartmann, Christian, *Wehrmacht im Ostkrieg: Front und militärisches Hinterland 1941/42* (Munich, 2009).
Harvey, Elizabeth, *'Der Osten braucht Dich!' Frauen und nationalsozialistische Germanisierungspolitik* (Hamburg, 2010).
Harvey, Elizabeth, 'Housework, Domestic Privacy and the "German Home": Paradoxes of Private Life during the Second World War', in Hachtmann, Rüdiger and Reichardt, Sven (eds.), *Detlev Peukert und die NS-Forschung* (Göttingen, 2015), 115–31.
Harvey, Elizabeth, *Women and the Nazi East: Agents and Witnesses of Germanization* (New Haven, CT, London, 2003).
Harvey, Elizabeth and Umbach, Maiken (eds.), 'Photography and Twentieth-Century German History', special issue for *Central European History* 48/3 (2015), 287–99.
Hattenhauer, Hans, 'Richter und Gesetz (1919–1979): Eine Zwischenbilanz', *Zeitschrift der Savigny-Stiftung für Rechtsgeschichte, Germanistische Abteilung* 106/1 (1989), 46–67.
Haumann, Heiko, *Geschichte der Ostjuden*, 4th rev. edn (Munich, 1998).
Heim, Susanne, '"Beim Schreiben habe ich immer noch einen Funken Hoffnung": Tagebücher und Briefe verfolgter Juden', in Bajohr, Frank and Steinbacher, Sybille (eds.), *Zeugnis ablegen bis zum letzten: Tagebücher und persönliche Zeugnisse aus der Zeit des Nationalsozialismus und des Holocaust* (Göttingen, 2015), 81–99.
Heineman, Elizabeth, *What Difference Does a Husband Make? Women and Marital Status in Nazi and Postwar Germany* (Berkeley and Los Angeles, CA, London, 1999, 2nd edn, 2003).

Heinemann, Isabel, *Rasse, Siedlung, deutsches Blut: Das Rasse- und Siedlungshauptamt der SS und die rassenpolitische Neuordnung Europas* (Göttingen, 2003).
Heinemann, Ulrich, 'Krieg und Frieden an der "inneren Front": Normalität und Zustimmung, Terror und Opposition im Dritten Reich', in Kleßmann, Christoph (ed.), *Nicht nur Hitlers Krieg: Der Zweite Weltkrieg und die Deutschen* (Düsseldorf, 1989), 25–47.
Helmstetter, Rudolf, 'Der stumme Doktor als guter Hirte. Zur Genealogie der Sexualratgeber', in Bänziger, Peter-Paul et al. (eds.), *Fragen Sie Dr. Sex! Ratgeberkommunikation und die mediale Konstruktion des Sexuellen* (Berlin, 2010), 58–93.
Herbert, Ulrich, *Best: Biographische Studien über Radikalismus, Weltanschauung und Vernunft 1903–1989* (Bonn, 1996).
Herbert, Ulrich, 'Good Times, Bad Times: Memories of the Third Reich', in Bessel, Richard (ed.), *Life in the Third Reich* (Oxford, 1987), 97–110.
Herbert, Ulrich, '"Die guten und die schlechten Zeiten": Überlegungen zur diachroner. Analyse lebensgeschichtlicher Interviews', in Niethammer, Lutz (ed.), *'Die Jahre weiß man nicht, wo man die heute hinsetzen soll': Faschismuserfahrungen im Ruhrgebiet* (Berlin, Bonn, 1983), 67–96.
Herz, Rudolf, *Hoffmann und Hitler: Fotographie als Medium des Führer-Mythos* (Munich, 1994).
Herzog, Dagmar, *Sex after Fascism: Memory and Morality in Twentieth-Century Germany* (Princeton, NJ, 2007).
Heusler, Andreas, '"Strafbestand Liebe": Verbotener Kontakt zwischen Münchnerinnen und ausländischen Kriegsgefangenen', in Krafft, Sybille (ed.), *Zwischen den Fronten. Münchner Frauen in Krieg und Frieden, 1900–1950* (Munich, 1995), 324–41.
Hilberg, Raul, *Perpetrators, Victims, Bystanders: The Jewish Catastrophe 1933–1945* (New York, NY, 1993).
Hilger, Christian, *Rechtsstaatsbegriffe im Dritten Reich: Eine Strukturanalyse* (Tübingen, 2003).
Himmler, Katrin and Wildt, Michael (eds.), *Himmler privat: Briefe eines Massenmörders* (Munich, 2014).
Hirsch, Marianne, *Family Frames: Photography, Narrative and Postmemory* (Cambridge, MA, 1997).
Hirschfeld, Gerhard and Kettenacker, Lothar (eds.), *'Führer State': Myth and Reality. Studies on the Structure and Politics of the Third Reich* (Stuttgart, 1981).
Hirt, Gerulf, *Verkannte Propheten? Zur 'Expertenkultur' (west)deutscher Werbekommunikatoren bis zur Rezession 1966/67* (Leipzig, 2013).
Höffer-Mehlmer, Markus, *Elternratgeber: Zur Geschichte eines Genres* (Baltmannsweiler, 2003).
Hoffmann-Curtius, Kathrin, 'Trophäen und Amulette: Die Fotografien von Wehrmachts- und SS-Verbrechen in den Brieftaschen der Soldaten', *Fotogeschichte* 78/20 (2000), 63–76.
Holzer, Anton (ed.), *Mit der Kamera bewaffnet: Krieg und Fotografie* (Marburg, 2003).
Hong, Young-Sun, *Welfare, Modernity and the Weimar State 1919–1933* (Princeton, NJ, 1998).

Hördler, Stefan, 'Sichtbarmachen: Möglichkeiten und Grenzen einer Analyse von NS-Täterfotografien', *Vierteljahrshefte für Zeitgeschichte* 65/2 (2017), 259–71.

Hornung, Ela, *Denunziation als soziale Praxis: Fälle aus der NS-Militärjustiz* (Vienna, Cologne, Weimar, 2010).

Hornung, Ela, *Warten und Heimkehren: Eine Ehe während und nach dem Zweiten Weltkrieg* (Vienna, 2005).

Horstkotte, Silke and Schmidt, Olaf Jürgen, 'Heil Coca-Cola! Zwischen Germanisierung und Re-Amerikanisierung: Coke im Dritten Reich', in Paul, Heike and Kanzler, Katja (eds.), *Amerikanische Populärkultur in Deutschland* (Leipzig, 2002), 73–87.

Horwitz, Gordon J., *In the Shadow of Death: Living Outside the Gates of Mauthausen* (New York, NY, 1990).

Horwitz, Gordon J., 'Places Far Away, Places Very Near: Mauthausen, the Camps of the Shoah, and the Bystanders', in Berenbaum, Michael, and Peck, Abraham J. (eds.), *The Holocaust and History: The Known, the Unknown, the Disputed, and the Reexamined* (Bloomington, IN, 1998), 409–20.

Hosenfeld, Wilm, *'Ich versuche jeden zu retten': Das Leben eines deutschen Offiziers in Briefen und Tagebüchern*, ed. by Vogel, Thomas (Munich, 2004).

Humann, Detlev, *'Arbeitsschlacht': Arbeitsbeschaffung und Propaganda in der NS-Zeit 1933–1939* (Göttingen, 2011).

Humburg, Martin, 'Feldpostbriefe aus dem Zweiten Weltkrieg: Zur möglichen Bedeutung im aktuellen Meinungsstreit unter besonderer Berücksichtigung des Themas "Antisemitismus"', *Militärgeschichtliche Mitteilungen* 58 (1999), 321–43.

Humburg, Martin, *Das Gesicht des Krieges: Feldpostbriefe von Wehrmachtssoldaten aus der Sowjetunion 1941–1944* (Opladen, Wiesbaden, 1998).

Humburg, Martin, 'Siegeshoffnungen und "Herbstkrise" im Jahre 1941: Anmerkungen zu Feldpostbriefen aus der Sowjetunion', *WerkstattGeschichte* 22 (1999), 25–30.

Hüppauf, Bernd, *Fotografie im Krieg* (Paderborn, 2015).

Hürter, Johannes, *A German General on the Eastern Front: The Letters and Diaries of Gotthard Heinrici, 1941–1942* (Barnsley, 2014).

Hürter, Johannes (ed.), *Notizen aus dem Vernichtungskrieg: Die Ostfront 1941/42 in den Aufzeichnungen des Generals Heinrici* (Darmstadt, 2016).

Hürter, Johannes and Uhl, Matthias, 'Hitler in Vinnytsia: A New Document Casts Fresh Light on the Crisis of September 1942', in Harvey, Elizabeth and Hürter, Johannes (eds.), *German Yearbook of Contemporary History*, vol. 3: *Hitler – New Research* (Berlin, Boston, MA, 2018), 147–210.

Hüttenberger, Peter, 'Heimtückefälle vor dem Sondergericht München 1933–1939', in Broszat, Martin, Fröhlich, Elke and Grossmann, Anton (eds.), *Bayern in der NS-Zeit*, vol. 4 (Munich, 1981), 435–526.

Jansen, Christian and Weckbecker, Arno, *Der 'Volksdeutsche Selbstschutz' in Polen 1939/40* (Munich, 1992).

Jeggle, Utz and Ilien, Albert, 'Die Dorfgemeinschaft als Not- und Terrorzusammenhang: Ein Beitrag zur Sozialgeschichte des Dorfes und zur Sozialpsychologie seiner Bewohner', in Wehling, Hans-Georg (ed.),

Dorfpolitik. Fachwissenschaftliche Analysen und didaktische Hilfen (Opladen, 1978), 38–53.
Jenkins, Jennifer, 'Introduction: Domesticity, Design and the Shaping of the Social', special issue of *German History* 25/4 (2007), 465–89.
Jenkins, Jennifer, *Provincial Modernity: Local Culture and Liberal Politics in Fin-de-Siècle Hamburg* (Ithaca, NY, 2003).
Jensen, Olaf and Szejnmann, Claus-Christian (eds.), *Ordinary People as Mass Murderers: Perpetrators in Comparative Perspectives* (Basingstoke, 2008).
Jensen, Uffa, 'Die Konstitution des Selbst durch Beratung und Therapeutisierung. Die Geschichte des Psychowissens im frühen 20. Jahrhundert', in Maasen, Sabine et al. (eds.), *Das beratene Selbst: Zur Genealogie der Therapeutisierung in den 'langen' Siebzigern* (Bielefeld, 2011), 37–56.
Jesse, Eckhard (ed.), *Totalitarismus im 20. Jahrhundert: Eine Bilanz der internationalen Forschung*, 2nd edn (Baden-Baden, 1999).
Johnson, Eric A., *The Nazi Terror: Gestapo, Jews and Ordinary Germans* (London, 2002; orig. 1999).
Jolly, Margaretta, *In Love and Struggle: Letters in Contemporary Feminism* (New York, NY, 2008).
Joshi, Vandana, *Gender and Power in the Third Reich: Female Denouncers and the Gestapo (1933–45)* (Basingstoke, 2003).
Jüdisches Historisches Institut Warschau (ed.), *Faschismus – Getto – Massenmord: Dokumentation über Ausrottung und Widerstand der Juden in Polen während des zweiten Weltkrieges* (Berlin, 1961).
Jung-Kaiser, Ute (ed.), *Intime Textkörper: Der Liebesbrief in den Künsten* (Bern, Vienna, Brussels, 2004).
Jurczyk, Karin and Oechsle, Mechthild (eds.), *Das Private neu denken: Erosionen, Ambivalenzen, Leistungen* (Münster, 2008).
Jurczyk, Karin and Oechsle, Mechthild, 'Privatheit: Interdisziplinarität und Grenzverschiebungen: Eine Einführung', in Jurczyk, Karin and Oechsle, Mechthild (eds.), *Das Private neu denken: Erosionen, Ambivalenzen, Leistungen* (Münster, 2008), 8–47.
Jureit, Ulrike, 'Zwischen Ehe und Männerbund: Emotionale und sexuelle Beziehungsmuster im Zweiten Weltkrieg', *WerkstattGeschichte* 22 (1999), 61–73.
Kämper, Heidrun, 'Telling the Truth: Counter-Discourses in Diaries under Totalitarian Regimes (Nazi Germany and Early GDR)', in Steinmetz, Willibald (ed.), *Political Languages in the Age of Extremes* (Oxford, 2011), 215–41.
Kannapel, Petra, *Die Behandlung von Frauen im nationalsozialistischen Familienrecht* (Darmstadt, Marburg, 1999).
Kaplan, Marion, *Between Dignity and Despair: Jewish Life in Nazi Germany* (New York, NY, 1998).
Kayser, Werner, *Walther von Hollander* (Hamburg, 1971).
Keckeis, Carmen, 'Privatheit und Raum – zu einem wechselbezüglichen Verhältnis', in Beyvers, Eva et al. (eds.), *Räume und Kulturen des Privaten* (Heidelberg, 2017), 19–56.

Keller, Sven (ed.), *Kriegstagebuch einer jungen Nationalsozialistin: Die Aufzeichnungen Wolfhilde von Königs 1939–1946* (Berlin, Boston, MA, 2015).
Kershaw, Ian, 'Nationalsozialistische und stalinistische Herrschaft: Möglichkeiten und Grenzen des Vergleichs', in Jesse, Eckhard (ed.), *Totalitarismus im 20. Jahrhundert: Eine Bilanz der internationalen Forschung*, 2nd edn (Baden-Baden, 1999), 213–22.
Kershaw, Ian, *The Nazi Dictatorship: Problems and Perspectives of Interpretation* (London, 2000).
Kershaw, Ian, *Der NS-Staat: Geschichtsinterpretationen und Kontroversen im Überblick*, 4th edn (Reinbek bei Hamburg, 2006).
Kershaw, Ian, *Popular Opinion and Political Dissent in the Third Reich: Bavaria 1933–1945* (Oxford, 1983).
Kershaw, Ian, '"Volksgemeinschaft": Potenzial und Grenzen eines neuen Forschungskonzepts', *Vierteljahrshefte für Zeitgeschichte* 59 (2011), 1–17.
Kershaw, Ian, '*Volksgemeinschaft*: Potential and Limitations of the Concept', in Steber, Martina and Gotto, Bernhard (eds.), *Visions of Community in Nazi Germany: Social Engineering and Private Lives* (Oxford, 2014), 29–42.
Kingreen, Thorsten, and Poscher, Ralf, *Grundrechte: Staatsrecht II*, 29th edn (Heidelberg, 2013).
Klemperer, Victor, *Lingua Tertii Imperii: Notizbuch eines Philologen* (Berlin, 1947)
Klemperer, Victor, *Lingua Tertii Imperii: The Language of the Third Reich* (London, 2001).
Klepper, Jochen, *Überwindung: Tagebücher und Aufzeichnungen aus dem Kriege* (Stuttgart, 1958).
Knoch, Peter, 'Kriegsalltag', in Knoch, Peter (ed.), *Kriegsalltag: Die Rekonstruktion des Kriegsalltags als Aufgabe der historischen Forschung und der Friedenserziehung* (Stuttgart, 1989), 222–52.
Kocka, Jürgen, *Sozialgeschichte: Begriff, Entwicklung, Probleme* (Göttingen, 1986).
Kocka, Jürgen, 'Sozialgeschichte zwischen Strukturgeschichte und Erfahrungsgeschichte', in Schieder, Wolfgang and Sellin, Volker (eds.), *Sozialgeschichte in Deutschland*, vol. 1 (Göttingen, 1986), 67–89.
Kolb, Klaus, *Fälle defätistischer Äußerungen und deren Anklage vor dem Volksgerichtshof Zersetzung der Wehrkraft betreffend in Bayern von 1940–1945* (Munich, [1975]).
Kompisch, Kathrin, *Täterinnen: Frauen im Nationalsozialismus* (Cologne, 2008).
König, Wolfgang, *Volkswagen, Volksempfänger, Volksgemeinschaft: 'Volksprodukte' im Dritten Reich. Vom Scheitern einer nationalsozialistischen Konsumgesellschaft* (Paderborn, 2004).
Koonz, Claudia, *Mothers in the Fatherland: Women, the Family and Nazi Politics* (New York, NY, 1987).
Koonz, Claudia, 'A Tributary and a Mainstream: Gender, Public Memory and Historiography of Nazi Germany', in Hagemann, Karen and Quataert, Jean H. (eds.), *Gendering Modern German History: Rewriting Historiography* (New York, NY, 2007), 147–68.
Koselleck, Reinhard, 'Terror and Dream: Methodological Remarks on the Experience of Time during the Third Reich', in Koselleck, Reinhard (ed.),

Futures Past: On the Semantics of Historical Time (Cambridge, MA, 1985), 205–11.

Köstlin, Konrad, 'Erzählen vom Krieg – Krieg als Reise II', *Bios. Zeitschrift für Biographieforschung und Oral History* 2/2 (1989), 173–82.

Kramer, Nicole, *Volksgenossinnen an der Heimatfront: Mobilisierung, Verhalten, Erinnerung* (Göttingen, 2011).

Kratz, Philipp, 'Sparen für das kleine Glück', in Aly, Götz (ed.), *Volkes Stimme: Skepsis und Führervertrauen im Nationalsozialismus* (Frankfurt a.M., 2006), 59–79.

Kreutzmüller, Christoph, *Final Sale in Berlin: The Destruction of Jewish Commercial Activity, 1930–1945* (New York, NY, 2013).

Kroener, Bernhard R., '"Menschenbewirtschaftung", Bevölkerungsverteilung und personelle Rüstung in der zweiten Kriegshälfte (1942–1944)', in Kroener, Bernhard R., Müller, Rolf-Dieter and Umbreit, Hans (eds.), *Organisation und Mobilisierung des deutschen Machtbereichs: Kriegsverwaltung, Wirtschaft und personelle Ressourcen 1942–1944/45* (*Das Deutsche Reich und der Zweite Weltkrieg*, vol. 5/2) (Stuttgart, 1999), 777–995.

Kroener, Bernhard R., 'Die personellen Ressourcen des Dritten Reiches im Spannungsfeld zwischen Wehrmacht, Bürokratie und Kriegswirtschaft 1939–1942', in Kroener, Bernhard R., Müller, Rolf-Dieter and Umbreit, Hans (eds.), *Organisation und Mobilisierung des deutschen Machtbereichs: Kriegsverwaltung, Wirtschaft und personelle Ressourcen 1939–1941* (*Das Deutsche Reich und der Zweite Weltkrieg*, vol. 5/1) (Stuttgart, 1988), 693–1002.

Krzoska, Markus, 'Volksdeutsche im Warthegau', in Neander, Eckhart (ed.), *Umgesiedelt – Vertrieben: Deutschbalten und Polen 1939–1945 im Warthegau* (Marburg, 2010), 66–82.

Kühne, Thomas, *Belonging and Genocide: Hitler's Community, 1918–1945* (New Haven, CT, 2010).

Kühne, Thomas, *Kameradschaft: Die Soldaten des nationalsozialistischen Krieges und das 20. Jahrhundert* (Göttingen, 2006).

Kühne, Thomas, *The Rise and Fall of Comradeship: Hitler's Soldiers, Male Bonding and Mass Violence in the Twentieth Century* (Cambridge, 2017).

Kühne, Thomas, 'Vertrauen und Kameradschaft: Soziales Kapital im "Endkampf" der Wehrmacht', in Frevert, Ute (ed.), *Vertrauen: Historische Annäherungen* (Göttingen, 2003), 245–79.

Kulka, Otto Dov, and Jäckel, Eberhard (eds.), *Die Juden in den geheimen NS-Stimmungsberichten, 1933–1945* (Düsseldorf, 2004).

Kumar, Krishan, 'The Promise and Predicament of Private Life at the End of the Twentieth Century', in Weintraub, Jeff and Kumar, Krishan (eds.), *Public and Private in Thought and Practice: Perspectives on a Grand Dichotomy* (Chicago, IL, London, 1997), 204–36.

Kumar, Krishan and Makarova, Ekaterine, 'The Portable Home: The Domestication of Public Space', in Jurczyk, Karin and Oechsle, Mechthild (eds.), *Das Private neu denken: Erosionen, Ambivalenzen, Leistungen* (Münster, 2008), 70–92.

Kundrus, Birthe, 'Forbidden Company: Romantic Relationships between Germans and Foreigners, 1939 to 1945', in Herzog, Dagmar (ed.), *Sexuality and German Fascism* (New York, NY, 2005), 201–22.

Kundrus, Birthe, *Kriegerfrauen: Familienpolitik und Geschlechterverhältnisse im Ersten und Zweiten Weltkrieg* (Hamburg, 1995).
Kundrus, Birthe, 'Regime der Differenz: Volkstumspolitische Inklusionen und Exklusionen im Warthegau und Generalgouvernement 1939–1944', in Bajohr, Frank and Wildt, Michael (eds.), *Volksgemeinschaft: Neue Forschungen zur Gesellschaft des Nationalsozialismus* (Frankfurt a.M., 2009), 105–23.
Kundrus, Birthe, 'Forbidden Company: Romantic Relationships between Germans and Foreigners, 1939 to 1945', *Journal of the History of Sexuality* 11/1–2 (2002), 201–22.
Lamprecht, Gerald, *Feldpost und Kriegserlebnis: Briefe als historisch-biografische Quelle* (Munich, 2001).
Langenbucher, Wolfgang, *Der aktuelle Unterhaltungsroman: Beiträge zu Geschichte und Theorie der massenhaft verbreiteten Literatur* (Bonn, 1964).
Latzel, Klaus, *Deutsche Soldaten – nationalsozialistischer Krieg? Kriegserlebnis – Kriegserfahrung 1939–1945* (Paderborn, 1998).
Latzel, Klaus, 'Feldpostbriefe: Überlegungen zur Aussagekraft einer Quelle', in Hartmann, Christian, Hürter, Johannes and Jureit, Ulrike (eds.), *Verbrechen der Wehrmacht: Bilanz einer Debatte* (Munich, 2005), 171–82.
Latzel, Klaus, 'Kriegsbriefe und Kriegserfahrung: Wie können Feldpostbriefe zur erfahrungsgeschichtlichen Quelle werden?', *WerkstattGeschichte* 22 (1999), 7–23.
Latzel, Klaus, 'Tourismus und Gewalt: Kriegswahrnehmungen in Feldpostbriefen', in Heer, Hannes and Neumann, Klaus (eds.), *Vernichtungskrieg: Verbrechen der Wehrmacht 1914–1944* (Hamburg, 1994), 447–59.
Latzel, Klaus, 'Die Zumutung des Krieges und der Liebe – zwei Annäherungen an Feldpostbriefe', in Knoch, Peter (ed.), *Kriegsalltag: Die Rekonstruktion des Kriegsalltags als Aufgabe der historischen Forschung und der Friedenserziehung* (Stuttgart, 1989), 204–21.
Liebersohn, Harry and Schneider, Dorothee (eds.), *'My Life in Germany before and after January 30, 1933': A Guide to a Manuscript Collection at Houghton Library, Harvard University* (Philadelphia, PA, 2001).
Limberg, Margarete and Rübsaat, Hubert (eds.), *Germans No More: Accounts of Jewish Everyday Life, 1933–38* (New York, NY, Oxford, 2006).
Limberg, Margarete and Rübsaat, Hubert (eds.), *Nach dem 'Anschluss': Berichte österreichischer EmigrantInnen aus dem Archiv der Harvard University* (Vienna, 2013).
Limberg, Margarete and Rübsaat, Hubert (eds.), *Sie durften nicht mehr Deutsche sein: Jüdischer Alltag in Selbstzeugnissen 1933–1938* (Frankfurt a.M., New York, NY, 1990).
Lindenberger, Thomas, 'Eigen-Sinn, Herrschaft und kein Widerstand', Version: 1.0, in *Docupedia-Zeitgeschichte*, 2 September 2014, http://docupedia.de/zg/lindenberger_eigensinn_v1_2014.
Lisner, Wiebke, 'Hebammen im "Reichsgau Wartheland" 1939–45: Geburtshilfe im Spannungsfeld von Germanisierung, Biopolitik und individueller biographischer Umbruchsituation', in Barelkowski, Matthias, Kraft, Claudia and Röskau-Rydel, Isabel (eds.), *Zwischen Geschlecht und Nation: Interdependenzen und Interaktionen in der multiethnischen Gesellschaft Polens im 19. und 20. Jahrhundert* (Osnabrück, 2016), 237–64.

Lisner, Wiebke, *'Hüterinnen der Nation': Hebammen im Nationalsozialismus* (Frankfurt a.M., 2006).
Lisner, Wiebke, 'Midwifery and Racial Segregation in Occupied Western Poland 1939–1945', *German History* 35/2 (2017), 229–46.
Lixl-Purcell, Andreas (ed.), *Women of Exile: German-Jewish Autobiographies since 1933* (Westport, CT, London, 1988).
Longerich, Peter, *'Davon haben wir nichts gewusst!' Die Deutschen und die Judenverfolgung 1933–1945* (Munich, 2006).
Loose, Ingo, *Kredite für NS-Verbrechen: Die deutschen Kreditinstitute in Polen und die Ausraubung der polnischen und jüdischen Bevölkerung 1939–1945* (Munich, 2007).
Lott, Sylvia, *Die Frauenzeitschriften von Hans Huffzky und John Jahr: Zur Geschichte der deutschen Frauenzeitschrift zwischen 1933 und 1970* (Berlin, 1985).
Löw, Andrea, Bergen, Doris L. and Hájková, Anna (eds.), *Alltag im Holocaust: Jüdisches Leben im Großdeutschen Reich 1941–1945* (Munich, 2013).
Löw, Martina, *Raumsoziologie* (Frankfurt a.M., 2001).
Lüdtke, Alf (ed.), *Alltagsgeschichte: Zur Rekonstruktion historischer Erfahrungen und Lebensweisen* (Frankfurt a.M., 1989).
Lüdtke, Alf, 'Arbeit, Arbeitserfahrungen und Arbeiterpolitik: Zum Perspektivenwechsel in der historischen Forschung', in Lüdtke, Alf, *Eigen-Sinn: Fabrikalltag, Arbeitererfahrungen und Politik vom Kaiserreich bis in den Faschismus* (Hamburg, 1993), 351–440.
Lüdtke, Alf, 'Eigensinn', in Jordan, Stefan (ed.), *Lexikon Geschichtswissenschaft: Hundert Grundbegriffe* (Stuttgart, 2002), 64–6.
Lüdtke, Alf, 'Geschichte und Eigensinn', in Berliner Geschichtswerkstatt (ed.), *Alltagskultur, Subjektivität und Geschichte: Zur Theorie und Praxis von Alltagsgeschichte* (Münster, 1994), 139–53.
Lüdtke, Alf, *Herrschaft als soziale Praxis: Historische und sozial-anthropologische Studien* (Göttingen, 1991).
Lüdtke, Alf, *The History of Everyday Life* (Princeton, NJ, 1995).
Lüdtke, Alf, 'Wo blieb die "rote Glut"? Arbeitererfahrungen und deutscher Faschismus', in Lüdtke, Alf (ed.), *Alltagsgeschichte: Zur Rekonstruktion historischer Erfahrungen und Lebensweisen* (Frankfurt a.M., 1989), 224–82.
Luhmann, Niklas, *Liebe als Passion: Zur Codierung von Intimität* (Frankfurt a.M., 2001).
Luhmann, Niklas, *Vertrauen: Ein Mechanismus der Reduktion sozialer Komplexität* (Stuttgart, 1989).
Maasen, Sabine, 'Das beratene Selbst: Zur Genealogie der Therapeutisierung in den "langen" Siebzigern: Eine Perspektivierung', in Maasen, Sabine et al. (eds.), *Das beratene Selbst: Zur Genealogie der Therapeutisierung in den 'langen' Siebzigern* (Bielefeld, 2011), 7–33.
Maasen, Sabine, 'Psycho-Wissen: Eine genealogische Notiz', in Maasen, Sabine et al. (eds.), *Das beratene Selbst: Zur Genealogie der Therapeutisierung in den 'langen' Siebzigern* (Bielefeld, 2011), 35-6.
Magnússon, Sigurður G. and Szijártó, István M., *What Is Microhistory? Theory and Practice* (London, 2013).

Mahlmann, Regina, *Psychologisierung des 'Alltagsbewusstseins': Die Verwissenschaftlichung des Diskurses über die Ehe* (Opladen, 1991).
Majer, Diemut, *'Fremdvölkische' im Dritten Reich: Ein Beitrag zur nationalsozialistischen Rechtssetzung und Rechtspraxis in Verwaltung und Justiz unter besonderer Berücksichtigung der eingegliederten Ostgebiete und des Generalgouvernements* (Boppard am Rhein, 1981).
Mallmann, Klaus-Michael, *Kommunisten in der Weimarer Republik: Sozialgeschichte einer revolutionären Bewegung* (Darmstadt, 1996).
Mallmann, Klaus-Michael and Paul, Gerhard, 'Omniscient, Omnipotent, Omnipresent? Gestapo, Society and Resistance', in Crew, David (ed.), *Nazism and German Society, 1933–1945* (London, 1994), 166–96.
Marszolek, Inge, '"Ich möchte Dich zu gern mal in Uniform sehen": Geschlechterkonstruktionen in Feldpostbriefen', *WerkstattGeschichte* 22 (1999), 41–59.
Mason, Timothy W., *Arbeiterklasse und Volksgemeinschaft: Dokumente und Materialien zur deutschen Arbeiterpolitik, 1936–1939* (Opladen, 1975).
Mason, Timothy W., *Social Policy in the Third Reich: The Working Class and the 'National Community'* (Providence, RI, 1993).
Mason, Timothy W., *Sozialpolitik im Dritten Reich: Arbeiterklasse und Volksgemeinschaft* (Opladen, 1977).
Matthäus, Jürgen, Kwiet, Konrad and Förster, Jürgen (eds.), *Ausbildungsziel Judenmord? 'Weltanschauliche Erziehung' von SS, Polizei und Waffen-SS im Rahmen der 'Endlösung'* (Frankfurt a.M., 2003).
Matthäus, Jürgen et al. (eds.), *Jewish Responses to Persecution*, vol. 3: *1941–1942* (Lanham, MD, 2013).
Maubach, Franka, 'Expansionen weiblicher Hilfe: Zur Erfahrungsgeschichte von Frauen im Kriegsdienst', in Steinbacher, Sybille (ed.), *Volksgenossinnen: Frauen in der NS-Volksgemeinschaft* (Göttingen, 2007), 93–114.
Maus, Ingeborg, '"Gesetzesbindung" der Justiz und die Struktur der nationalsozialistischen Rechtsnormen', in Dreier, Ralf and Sellert, Wolfgang (eds.), *Recht und Justiz im 'Dritten Reich'* (Frankfurt a.M., 1989), 80–104.
Mazower, Mark, *Inside Hitler's Greece: The Experience of Occupation, 1941–1944* (New Haven, CT, London, 2001).
Mehs, Matthias Joseph, *Tagebücher, vol. 1: November 1929 bis Januar 1936, vol. 2: Januar 1936 bis September 1946*, ed. by Wein, Günter and Wein, Franziska (Trier, 2011).
Messerli, Alfred, 'Zur Geschichte der Medien des Rates', in Bänziger, Peter-Paul et al. (eds.), *Fragen Sie Dr. Sex! Ratgeberkommunikation und die mediale Konstruktion des Sexuellen* (Berlin, 2010), 30–57.
Messerschmidt, Manfred and Wüllner, Fritz, *Die Wehrmachtjustiz im Dienste des Nationalsozialismus: Zerstörung einer Legende* (Baden-Baden, 1987).
Mesure, Sylvie and Savidan, Patrick (eds.), *Dictionnaire des sciences humaines* (Paris, 2006).
Meyer, Beate, 'Grenzüberschreitungen: Eine Liebe zu Zeiten des Rassenwahns', *Zeitschrift für Geschichtswissenschaft* 55 (2007), 916–36.
Meyer, Beate, '"Ich schlüpfe unbeachtet wie eine graue Motte mit durch": Die Wandlungen der Luise Solmitz zwischen 1933 und 1945 im Spiegel ihrer

Tagebücher', in Bajohr, Frank and Steinbacher, Sybille (eds.), *Zeugnis ablegen bis zum letzten: Tagebücher und persönliche Zeugnisse aus der Zeit des Nationalsozialismus und des Holocaust* (Göttingen, 2015), 61–80.

Meyer, Christian, '"... nichts war mehr Privatangelegenheit": Zur Semantik von Politisierungsprozessen in autobiographischen Berichten aus der Zeit des Nationalsozialismus', in Steinmetz, Willibald (ed.), *'Politik': Situationen eines Wortgebrauchs im Europa der Neuzeit* (Frankfurt a.M., New York, NY, 2007), 395–416.

Meyer, Christian, 'Semantiken des Privaten in autobiographischen Deutungen des Nationalsozialismus 1939–1940' (PhD, Bielefeld, 2015).

Meyer, Sybille and Schulze, Eva, *Wie wir das alles geschafft haben. Alleinstehende Frauen berichten über ihr Leben nach 1945* (Munich, 1984).

Meyer-Spacks, Patricia, *Privacy: Concealing the Eighteenth-Century Self* (Chicago, IL, 2003).

Micheler, Stefan, 'Homophobic Propaganda and the Denunciation of Same-Sex-Desiring Men under National Socialism', *Journal of the History of Sexuality* 11/1–2 (2002), 95–130.

Mittelmeier, Martin, 'Es gibt kein richtiges Sich-Ausstrecken in der falschen Badewanne. Wie Adornos berühmtester Satz wirklich lautet – ein Gang ins Archiv', *Recherche. Zeitung für Wissenschaft*, 31 January 2010, www.recherche-online.net/theodor-adorno.html.

Mlynek, Klaus (ed.), *Gestapo Hannover meldet... Polizei und Regierungsberichte für das mittlere und südliche Niedersachsen zwischen 1933 und 1937* (Hannover, 1986).

Mohrmann, Wolf-Dieter (ed.), *Der Krieg hier ist hart und grausam! Feldpostbriefe an den Osnabrücker Regierungspräsidenten 1941–1944* (Osnabrück, 1984).

Mouton, Michelle, *From Nurturing the Nation to Purifying the Volk: Weimar and Nazi Family Policy, 1918–1945* (Cambridge, 2007).

Mühlestein, Helene, *Hausfrau, Mutter, Gattin: Geschlechterkonstituierung in Schweizer Ratgeberliteratur 1945–1970* (Zurich, 2009).

Mühlhäuser, Regina, *Eroberungen: Sexuelle Gewalttaten und intime Beziehungen deutscher Soldaten in der Sowjetunion, 1941–1945* (Hamburg, 2010).

Muller, Jerzy Z., *Capitalism and the Jews* (Princeton, NJ, 2010).

Müller, Rolf-Dieter, 'Albert Speer and Armaments Policy in Total War', in Kroener, Bernhard R., Müller, Rolf-Dieter and Umbreit, Hans (eds.), *Germany and the Second World War*, vol. 5: *Organization and Mobilization of the German Sphere of Power, Part 2: Wartime Administration. Economy and Manpower Resources 1942-1944/5* (Oxford, 2015), 293–829.

Müller-Doohm, Stefan, *Adorno: Eine Biographie* (Frankfurt a.M., 2011).

Müller-Funk, Wolfgang, 'Die Erfindung der Liebe aus dem Medium des Briefes', in Bauer, Ingrid, Hämmerle, Christa and Hauch, Gabriella (eds.), *Liebe und Widerstand: Ambivalenzen historischer Geschlechterbeziehungen* (Vienna, Cologne, Weimar, 2009), 89–109.

Nahmacher, Kathrin, *Die Rechtsprechung des Reichsgerichts und der Hamburger Gerichte zum Scheidungsgrund des § 55 EheG 1938 in den Jahren 1938 bis 1945* (Frankfurt a.M., 1999).

Neitzel, Sönke, *Abgehört: Deutsche Generäle in britischer Kriegsgefangenschaft 1942–1945* (Berlin, 2005).
Neitzel, Sönke and Welzer, Harald, *Soldaten: Protokolle vom Kämpfen, Töten und Sterben* (Frankfurt a.M., 2011).
Nickisch, Reinhard M. G., *Brief* (Stuttgart, 1991).
zur Nieden, Susanne, *Alltag im Ausnahmezustand: Frauentagebücher im zerstörten Deutschland 1943 bis 1945* (Berlin, 1993).
zur Nieden, Susanne, *Homosexualität und Staatsräson: Männlichkeit, Homophobie und Politik in Deutschland 1900–1945* (Frankfurt a.M., 2005).
Niethammer, Lutz, 'Anmerkungen zur Alltagsgeschichte', in Bergmann, Klaus and Schörken, Rolf (eds.), *Geschichte im Alltag – Alltag in der Geschichte* (Düsseldorf, 1982), 11–29.
Niethammer, Lutz, 'Heimat und Front: Versuch, zehn Kriegserinnerungen aus der Arbeiterklasse des Ruhrgebietes zu verstehen', in Niethammer, Lutz (ed.), *'Die Jahre weiß man nicht, wo man die heute hinsetzen soll': Faschismuserfahrungen im Ruhrgebiet* (Berlin, 1983), 163–232.
Niethammer, Lutz et al. (eds.), *Lebensgeschichte und Sozialkultur im Ruhrgebiet*, 3 vols. (Berlin, Bonn, 1983–5).
Niksch, Dieter, *Die sittliche Rechtfertigung des Widerspruchs gegen die Scheidung der zerrütteten Ehe in den Jahren 1938–1944* (PhD, Cologne, 1990).
Nissenbaum, Helen, *Privacy in Context: Technology, Policy and the Integrity of Social Life* (Stanford, CA, 2010).
Noack-Mosse, Eva, 'Uhu', in Freyburg, Joachim W. and Wallenberg, Hans (eds.), *Hundert Jahre Ullstein*, vol. 2 (Frankfurt a.M., Berlin, Vienna, 1977), 177–208.
Nolan, Mary, *Visions of Modernity: American Business and the Modernization of Germany*, (New York, NY, Oxford, 1994).
Nolte, Paul, 'Öffentlichkeit und Privatheit: Deutschland im 20. Jahrhundert', *Merkur* 60 (2006), 499–512.
Nolzen, Armin, 'The NSDAP's Operational Codes after 1933', in Steber, Martina and Gotto, Bernhard (eds.), *Visions of Community in Nazi Germany: Social Engineering and Private Lives* (Oxford, 2014), 87–100.
Obenaus, Herbert and Obenaus, Sybille (eds.), *'Schreiben, wie es wirklich war...': Aufzeichnungen Karl Dürkefäldens aus den Jahren 1933–1945* (Hannover, 1985).
Orłowski, Hubert and Schneider, Thomas F. (eds.), *'Erschießen will ich nicht!' Als Offizier und Christ im Totalen Krieg: Das Kriegstagebuch des Dr. August Töpperwien 3. September 1939 bis 6. Mai 1945* (Düsseldorf, 2006).
Otter, Chris, 'Making Liberalism Durable: Vision and Civility in the Late Victorian City', *Social History* 27/1 (2002), 1–15.
Packheiser, Christian, 'Heimaturlaub: Soldaten zwischen Front, Familie und NS-Regime' (PhD, Munich, 2018).
Palmowski, Jan, 'Mediating the Nation: Liberalism and the Polity in Nineteenth-Century Germany', *German History* 19/4 (2001), 573–98.
Palmowski, Jan, *Urban Liberalism in Imperial Germany: Frankfurt am Main, 1866–1914* (Oxford, 1999).
Pateman, Carole, *The Disorder of Women: Democracy, Feminism, and Political Theory* (Stanford, CA, 1990).

Pater, Monika, 'Rundfunkangebote', in Marszolek, Inge and von Saldern, Adelheid (eds.), *Radio im Nationalsozialismus: Zwischen Lenkung und Ablenkung* (Tübingen, 1998), 129–241.
Paulus, Julia and Röwekamp, Marion (eds.), *Eine Soldatenheimschwester an der Ostfront: Briefwechsel von Annette Schücking mit ihrer Familie (1941–1943)* (Paderborn, Munich, 2015).
Penslar, Derek J., *Shylock's Children: Economics and Jewish Identity in Modern Europe* (Berkeley, CA, 2001).
Perry, Joe, *Christmas in Germany: A Cultural History* (Chapel Hill, NC, 2010).
Petropoulos, Jonathan, *Art as Politics in the Third Reich* (Chapel Hill, NC, 1996).
Petzina, Dieter (ed.), *Fahnen, Fäuste, Körper: Symbolik und Kultur der Arbeiterbewegung* (Essen, 1986).
Peukert, Detlev, *Inside Nazi Germany: Conformity, Opposition and Racism in Everyday Life* (New Haven, CT, London, 1987).
Peukert, Detlev, *Volksgenossen und Gemeinschaftsfremde: Anpassung, Ausmerze und Aufbegehren unter dem Nationalsozialismus* (Cologne, 1982).
Peukert, Detlev and Reulecke, Jürgen (eds.), *Die Reihen fast geschlossen: Beiträge zur Geschichte des Alltags unterm Nationalsozialismus* (Wuppertal, 1981).
Pine, Lisa, *Nazi Family Policy 1933–1945* (Oxford, 1999).
Piorkowski, Jens, *Die deutsche Sparkassenorganisation 1924 bis 1934* (Stuttgart, 1997).
Pohl, Dieter, 'Die Reichsgaue Danzig-Westpreußen und Wartheland: Koloniale Verwaltung oder Modell für die zukünftige Gauverwaltung?', in John, Jürgen, Möller, Horst and Schaarschmidt, Thomas (eds.), *Die NS-Gaue: Regionale Mittelinstanzen im zentralistischen 'Führerstaat'* (Munich, 2007), 395–405.
Pohl, Hans, *Wirtschaft- und Sozialgeschichte der deutschen Sparkassen im 20. Jahrhundert* (Stuttgart, 2005).
Pollmann, Arnd, '"Schmerz, lass nach": Die körperliche Hülle als Schauplatz autodestruktiver Privatisierung', in Seubert, Sandra and Niesen, Peter (eds.), *Die Grenzen des Privaten* (Baden-Baden, 2010), 165–80.
Prost, Antoine, 'Grenzen und Zonen des Privaten', in Prost, Antoine and Vincent, Gérard (eds.), *Geschichte des privaten Lebens*, vol. 5: *Vom Ersten Weltkrieg zur Gegenwart* (Frankfurt a.M., 1993), 15–151.
Prost, Antoine and Vincent, Gérard (eds.), *A History of Private Life: Riddles of Identity in Modern Times*, vol. 5 (Cambridge, MA, 1998).
Przyrembel, Alexandra, *'Rassenschande': Reinheitsmythos und Vernichtungslegitimation im Nationalsozialismus* (Göttingen, 2003).
Raithel, Thomas and Strenge, Irene, 'Die Reichstagsbrandverordnung: Grundlegung der Diktatur mit den Instrumenten des Weimarer Ausnahmezustandes', *Vierteljahrshefte für Zeitgeschichte* 48 (2000), 413–60.
Rapp, Christoph, *Höhenrausch: Der deutsche Bergfilm* (Vienna, 1997).
Rass, Christoph, *'Menschenmaterial': Deutsche Soldaten an der Ostfront. Innenansichten einer Infanteriedivision 1939–1945* (Paderborn, 2003).
Rass, Christoph, 'Das Sozialprofil von Kampfverbänden des deutschen Heeres 1939 bis 1945', in Echternkamp, Jörg (ed.), *Die Deutsche Kriegsgesellschaft 1939 bis 1945* (*Das Deutsche Reich und der Zweite Weltkrieg*, vol. 9/1) (Munich, 2004), 641–742.

Rebentisch, Dieter, 'Die "politische Beurteilung" als Herrschaftsinstitut der NSDAP', in Peukert, Detlev and Reulecke, Jürgen (eds.), *Die Reihen fast geschlossen: Beiträge zur Geschichte des Alltags unterm Nationalsozialismus* (Wuppertal, 1981), 107–28.

Reese, Dagmar, *Growing Up Female in Nazi Germany* (Ann Arbor, MI, 2006).

Reese, Dagmar, 'Die Kameraden: Eine partnerschaftliche Konzeption der Geschlechterbeziehungen an der Wende vom 19. zum 20. Jahrhundert', in Reese, Dagmar et al. (eds.), *Rationale Beziehungen? Geschlechterverhältnisse im Rationalisierungsprozess* (Frankfurt a.M., 1993), 58–74.

Reibel, Carl-Wilhelm, *Das Fundament der Diktatur: Die NSDAP-Ortsgruppen 1932–1945* (Paderborn et al., 2002).

Reichardt, Sven, 'Faschistische Beteiligungsdiktaturen: Anmerkungen zu einer Debatte', *Tel Aviver Jahrbuch für deutsche Geschichte* 42 (2014), 133–60.

Reimann, Aribert, *Der große Krieg der Sprachen: Untersuchungen zur historischen Semantik in Deutschland und England zur Zeit des Ersten Weltkriegs* (Essen, 2000).

Reinfeldt, Sebastian, Schwarz, Richard and Foucault, Michel (eds.), *Bio-Macht* (Duisburg, 1992).

Repp, Kevin, *Reformers, Critics, and the Paths of German Modernity: Anti-Politics and the Search for Alternatives, 1890–1914* (Cambridge, MA, 2000).

Rhein, Eberhard, *Die Unverletzlichkeit der Wohnung: Eine Spurensuche zwischen Frankfurt und Weimar* (Frankfurt a.M., New York, NY, 2001).

Richarz, Monika (ed.), *Jüdisches Leben in Deutschland*, vol. 2: *Selbstzeugnisse zur Sozialgeschichte im Kaiserreich*, vol. 3: *Selbstzeugnisse zur Sozialgeschichte, 1918–1945* (Munich, 1982)

Richarz, Monika (ed.) *Jewish Life in Germany: Memoirs from Three Centuries* (Bloomington, IN, 1991).

Rieger, Bernhard, 'The "Good German" Goes Global: The Volkswagen Beetle as an Icon in the Federal Republic', *History Workshop Journal* 68 (2009), 3–26.

Rieger, Bernhard, *The People's Car: A Global History of the Volkswagen Beetle* (Cambridge, MA, 2013).

Rieß, Volker, 'Zentrale und dezentrale Radikalisierung: Die Tötungen "unwerten Lebens" in den annektierten west- und nordpolnischen Gebieten 1939–1941', in Mallmann, Klaus-Michael and Musial, Bogdan (eds.), *Genesis des Genozids: Polen 1939–1941* (Darmstadt, 2004), 127–44.

Röger, Maren, *Kriegsbeziehungen: Intimität, Gewalt und Prostitution im besetzten Polen 1939 bis 1945* (Frankfurt a.M., 2015).

Röger, Maren, 'Sexual Contact between German Occupiers and Polish Occupied in World War II in Poland', in Röger, Maren and Leiserowitz, Ruth (eds.), *Women and Men at War: A Gender Perspective on World War II and Its Aftermath in Central and Eastern Europe* (Osnabrück, 2012), 135–56.

Römer, Felix, *Kameraden: Die Wehrmacht von innen* (Munich, 2012).

Römer, Felix, *Der Kommissarbefehl: Wehrmacht und NS-Verbrechen an der Ostfront 1941/42* (Paderborn, 2008).

Römer, Felix, *Die narzisstische Volksgemeinschaft: Theodor Habichts Kampf 1914 bis 1944* (Frankfurt a.M., 2017).

Roper, Michael, *The Secret Battle. Emotional Survival in the Great War* (Manchester, 2010).
Rose, Willi, *Shadows of War: A German Soldier's Lost Photographs of World War II*, ed. by Eller, Thomas and Bopp, Petra (New York, NY, 2004).
Rosenwein, Barbara, *Emotional Communities in the Early Middle Ages* (Ithaca, NY, 2006).
Ross, Corey, 'Visions of Prosperity', in Swett, Pamela E., Wiesen, S. Jonathan and Zatlin, Jonathan (eds.), *Selling Modernity: Advertising in Twentieth Century Germany* (Durham, 2007).
Rössler, Beate, 'Geschlechterverhältnis und Gerechtigkeit', in Müller, Hans-Peter and Wegener, Bernd (eds.), *Soziale Ungleichheit und soziale Gerechtigkeit* (Wiesbaden, 1995), 157–72.
Rössler, Beate, *Der Wert des Privaten* (Frankfurt a.M., 2001).
Rössler, Beate, *The Value of Privacy* (Cambridge, 2005).
Rössler, Beate, 'Zum individuellen und gesellschaftlichen Wert des Privaten', in Seubert, Sandra and Niesen, Peter (eds.), *Die Grenzen des Privaten* (Baden-Baden, 2010), 41–58.
Rössler, Beate and Mokrosinska, Dorota (eds.), *Social Dimensions of Privacy: Interdisciplinary Perspectives* (Cambridge, 2015).
Roth, Markus, 'Nationalsozialistische Umsiedlungspolitik im besetzten Polen: Ziele, beteiligte Institutionen, Methoden und Ergebnisse', in Neander, Eckhart (ed.), *Umgesiedelt – Vertrieben: Deutschbalten und Polen 1939–1945 im Warthegau* (Marburg, 2010), 9–20.
Roth, Markus, and Löw, Andrea, *Das Warschauer Getto: Alltag und Widerstand im Angesicht der Vernichtung* (Munich, 2013).
Rother, Rainer, and Prokasky, Judith (eds.), *Die Kamera als Waffe: Propagandabilder des Zweiten Weltkrieges* (Munich, 2010).
Russell, Robert, *Zamiatin's We* (Bristol, 2000).
von Saldern, Adelheid, 'Social Rationalization of Living and Housework in Germany and the United States in the 1920s', *The History of the Family: An International Quarterly* 2/1 (1997), 73–97.
von Saldern, Adelheid, 'Victims or Perpetrators? Controversies about the Role of Women in the Nazi State', in Crew, David (ed.), *Nazism and German Society, 1933–45* (London, 1994), 141–65.
von Saldern, Adelheid and Hachtmann, Rüdiger, 'Gesellschaft am "Fließband": Fordistische Produktion und Herrschaftspraxis in Deutschland', *Zeithistorische Forschungen* 6/2 (2009), 186–208.
Salje, Peter (ed.), *Recht und Unrecht im Nationalsozialismus* (Münster, 1985).
Schäfer, Hans Dieter, *Das gespaltene Bewußtsein: Über deutsche Kultur und Lebenswirklichkeit 1933–1945* (Munich, Vienna, 1981).
Schieder, Wolfgang and Sellin, Volker (eds.) *Sozialgeschichte in Deutschland*, 3 vols. (1986–7).
Schikorsky, Isa, 'Kommunikation über das Unbeschreibbare: Beobachtungen zum Sprachstil von Kriegsbriefen', *Wirkendes Wort* 2 (1992), 295–315.
Schlüter, Holger, '…für die Menschlichkeit im Strafmaß bekannt…': Das Sondergericht Litzmannstadt und sein Vorsitzender Richter* (Recklinghausen, 2014).

Schmidt, Ute, *Die Deutschen aus Bessarabien: Eine Minderheit aus Südosteuropa (1814 bis heute)* (Cologne, Weimar, Vienna, 2004).

Schmidt, Wolfgang, 'Maler an der Front: Zur Rolle der Kriegsmaler und Pressezeichner der Wehrmacht im Zweiten Weltkrieg', in Müller, Rolf-Dieter, and Volkmann, Hans-Erich (eds.), *Die Wehrmacht: Mythos und Realität* (Munich, 1999), 635–84.

Schmiechen-Ackermann, Detlef, 'Der "Blockwart": Die unteren Parteifunktionäre im nationalsozialistischen Terror- und Überwachungsapparat', *Vierteljahrshefte für Zeitgeschichte* 48 (2000), 575–602.

Schmiechen-Ackermann, Detlef, *Nationalsozialismus und Arbeitermilieus: Der nationalsozialistische Angriff auf die proletarischen Wohnquartiere und die Reaktion in den sozialistischen Vereinen* (Bonn, 1998).

Schmiechen-Ackermann, Detlef, '"Volksgemeinschaft": Mythos der NS-Propaganda, wirkungsmächtige soziale Verheißung oder soziale Realität im "Dritten Reich"? – Einführung', in Schmiechen-Ackermann, Detlef (ed.), *'Volksgemeinschaft': Mythos, wirkungsmächtige soziale Verheißung oder soziale Realität im 'Dritten Reich'? Zwischenbilanz einer kontroversen Debatte* (Paderborn, 2012), 13–53.

Schmitz-Berning, Cornelia, *Vokabular des Nationalsozialismus* (Berlin, 1998).

Schneider, Andreas Theo, *Die geheime Staatspolizei im NS-Gau Thüringen: Geschichte, Struktur, Personal und Wirkungsfelder* (Frankfurt a.M., 2008).

Schneider, Michael, *Unterm Hakenkreuz: Arbeiter und Arbeiterbewegung 1933 bis 1939* (Bonn, 1999).

Schneider, Silke, *Verbotener Umgang: Ausländer und Deutsche im Nationalsozialismus: Diskurse um Sexualität, Moral, Wissen und Strafe* (Baden-Baden, 2010).

Schnell, Ralf, *Literarische innere Emigration 1933–1945* (Stuttgart, 1976).

Schubert, Werner (ed.), *Protokolle der Großen Strafrechtskommission des Reichsjustizministeriums (1936–1938)* (Berlin, New York, NY, 1991).

Schulz, Günter, 'Soziale Sicherung von Frauen und Familien', in Hockerts, Hans Günter (ed.), *Drei Wege deutscher Sozialstaatlichkeit: NS-Diktatur, Bundesrepublik und DDR im Vergleich* (Munich, 1998), 117–49.

Schulze, Rainer, '"Der Führer ruft!": Zur Rückholung der Volksdeutschen aus dem Osten', in Kochanowski, Jerzy, and Sach, Maike (eds.), *Die 'Volksdeutschen' in Polen, Frankreich, Ungarn und der Tschechoslowakei: Mythos und Realität* (Osnabrück, 2006), 183–204.

Schwanke, Enno, *Die Landesheil- und Pflegeanstalt Tiegenhof: Die nationalsozialistische Euthanasie in Polen während des Zweiten Weltkriegs* (Frankfurt a.M., 2015).

Schwarz, Angela, *Die Reise ins Dritte Reich: Britische Augenzeugen im nationalsozialistischen Deutschland (1933–1939)* (Göttingen, 1993).

Schwegel, Andreas, *Der Polizeibegriff im NS-Staat* (Tübingen, 2005).

Schwender, Clemens, 'Feldpost als Medium sozialer Kommunikation', in Didczuneit, Veit, Ebert, Jens and Jander, Thomas (eds.), *Schreiben im Krieg – Schreiben vom Krieg: Feldpost im Zeitalter der Weltkriege* (Essen, 2011), 127–38.

Schwender, Clemens, 'Letters between Home and the Front – Expressions of Love in World War II Feldpost Letters', 1, www.feldpost-archiv.de/english/e8-loveletters.html [accessed 10 March 2017].

Seegers, Lu, *Hör zu! Eduard Rhein und die Rundfunkprogrammzeitschriften (1931–1965)* (Potsdam, 2001, 2nd edn, 2003).
Seegers, Lu, 'Walther von Hollander als Lebensberater im Dritten Reich', in Kleiner, Stephanie, and Suter, Robert (eds.), *Guter Rat: Glück und Erfolg in der Ratgeberliteratur 1900–1940* (Berlin, 2015), 179–207.
Semmens, Kristin, *Seeing Hitler's Germany: Tourism in the Third Reich* (Basingstoke, 2005).
Sennett, Richard, *The Fall of Public Man* (New York, NY, 1977).
Seubert, Harald, *'Auch wer zur Nacht geweinet': Jochen Klepper (1903–1942). Eine Vergegenwärtigung* (Wesel, 2014).
Seubert, Sandra, 'Privat und Öffentlichkeit heute: Ein Problemaufriss', in Seubert, Sandra and Niesen, Peter (eds.), *Die Grenzen des Privaten* (Baden-Baden, 2010), 9–24.
Seubert, Sandra, 'Warum die Familie nicht abschaffen? Zum spannungsvollen Verhältnis von Privatheit und politischem Liberalismus', in Seubert, Sandra and Niesen, Peter (eds.), *Die Grenzen des Privaten* (Baden-Baden, 2010), 89–106.
Seubert, Sandra, and Niesen, Peter (eds.), *Die Grenzen des Privaten* (Baden-Baden, 2010).
Shirer, William, *Berlin Diary* (New York, NY, 1942).
Sigmund, Anna Maria, *Die Frauen der Nazis* (Vienna, 1998).
Simmel, Georg, 'Das Relative und das Absolute im Geschlechter-Problem' (1911), in Simmel, Georg, *Schriften zur Philosophie und Soziologie der Geschlechter*, ed. by Dahme, Heinz-Jürgen, and Köhnke, Christian (Frankfurt a.M., 1985), 200–23.
Small, Robin, *Time and Becoming in Nietzsche's Thought* (London, New York, NY, 2010).
von Soden, Kristina, *Die Sexualberatungsstellen der Weimarer Republik 1919–1933* (West Berlin, 1988).
Solove, Daniel, *Understanding Privacy* (Cambridge, MA, 2008).
Spode, Hasso, 'Die NS-Gemeinschaft "Kraft durch Freude" – ein Volk auf Reisen', in Spode, Hasso (ed.), *Zur Sonne, zur Freiheit: Beiträge zur Tourismusgeschichte* (Berlin, 1991), 79–93.
Stargardt, Nicholas, 'Children's Art of the Holocaust', *Past and Present* 161 (1998), 192–235.
Stargardt, Nicholas, *The German War: A Nation under Arms, 1939–1945* (London, 2015).
Stargardt, Nicholas, 'Speaking in Public about the Murder of the Jews: What Did the Holocaust Mean to the Germans?', in Wiese, Christian and Betts, Paul (eds.), *Years of Persecution, Years of Extermination: Saul Friedländer and the Future of Holocaust Studies* (London, 2010), 133–55.
Stargardt, Nicholas, 'The Troubled Patriot: German *Innerlichkeit* in World War II', *German History*, special issue on 'Ego Documents', 28/3 (2010), 326–42.
Stargardt, Nicholas, *Witnesses of War: Children's Lives under the Nazis* (London, 2005).
Starl, Timm, *Knipser: Die Bildgeschichte der privaten Fotografie in Deutschland und Österreich von 1880 bis 1980* (Munich, 1995).

Steber, Martina and Gotto, Bernhard (eds.), *Visions of Community in Nazi Germany: Social Engineering and Private Lives* (Oxford, 2014).
Steber, Martina and Gotto, Bernhard, '*Volksgemeinschaft*: Writing the Social History of the Nazi Regime', in Steber, Martina, and Gotto, Bernhard (eds.), *Visions of Community in Nazi Germany: Social Engineering and Private Lives* (Oxford, 2014), 1–25.
Steege, Paul et al., 'The History of Everyday Life: A Second Chapter', *Journal of Modern History* 80/2 (2008), 358–78.
Steinert, Marlis, *Hitlers Krieg und die Deutschen: Stimmung und Haltung der deutschen Bevölkerung im Zweiten Weltkrieg* (Düsseldorf, 1970).
Steinhoff, William, *George Orwell and the Origins of 1984* (Ann Arbor, MI, 1975).
Stepanek, Marcel, *Wahlkampf im Zeichen der Diktatur: Die Inszenierung von Wahlen und Abstimmungen im nationalsozialistischen Deutschland* (Leipzig, 2014).
Steuwer, Janosch, *'Ein Drittes Reich, wie ich es auffasse': Politik, Gesellschaft und privates Leben in Tagebüchern 1933–1939* (Göttingen, 2017).
Steuwer, Janosch, '"Ein neues Blatt im Buche der Geschichte": Tagebücher und der Beginn der nationalsozialistischen Herrschaft 1933/34', in Bajohr, Frank and Steinbacher, Sybille (eds.), *Zeugnis ablegen bis zum letzten: Tagebücher und persönliche Zeugnisse aus der Zeit des Nationalsozialismus und des Holocaust* (Göttingen, 2015), 42–60.
Steuwer, Janosch, 'Was meint und nützt das Sprechen von der "Volksgemeinschaft"? Neuere Literatur zur Gesellschaftsgeschichte des Nationalsozialismus', *Archiv für Sozialgeschichte* 53 (2013), 487–534.
Steuwer, Janosch, '"Weltanschauung mit meinem Ich verbinden": Tagebücher und das nationalsozialistische Erziehungsprojekt', in Steuwer, Janosch and Graf, Rüdiger (eds.), *Selbstreflexionen und Weltdeutungen: Tagebücher in der Geschichte und der Geschichtsschreibung des 20. Jahrhunderts* (Göttingen, 2015), 100–23.
Steuwer, Janosch and Graf, Rüdiger, 'Selbstkonstitution und Welterzeugung in Tagebüchern des 20. Jahrhunderts', in Steuwer, Janosch and Graf, Rüdiger (eds.), *Selbstreflexionen und Weltdeutungen: Tagebücher in der Geschichte und der Geschichtsschreibung des 20. Jahrhunderts* (Göttingen, 2015), 7–36.
Steuwer, Janosch, and Leßau, Hanne, '"Wer ist ein Nazi? Woran erkennt man ihn?" Zur Unterscheidung von Nationalsozialisten und anderen Deutschen', *Mittelweg 36* 23/1 (2014), 30–51.
Stiller, Alexa, 'Germanisierung und Gewalt: Nationalsozialistische Volkstumspolitik in den polnischen, französischen und slowenischen Annexionsgebieten, 1939–1945' (PhD, Bern, 2015).
Stratigakos, Despina, *Hitler at Home* (New Haven, CT, London, 2015).
Strippel, Andreas, *NS-Volkstumspolitik und die Neuordnung Europas: Rassenpolitische Selektion der Einwandererzentralstelle des Chefs der Sicherheitspolizei und des SD (1939–1945)* (Paderborn, 2011).
Strobl, Gerwin, *The Germanic Isle: Nazi Perceptions of Britain* (Cambridge, 2000).
Strobl, Gerwin, *The Swastika and the Stage: German Theatre and Society, 1933–1945* (Cambridge, 2007).

Strom, Jonathan, 'Pietist Experiences and Narratives of Conversion', in Shantz, Douglas H. (ed.), *A Companion to German Pietism, 1660–1800* (Leiden, 2015), 293–318.

Süß, Dietmar, *Death from the Skies: How the British and Germans Survived Bombing in World War II* (Oxford, 2014).

Süß, Winfried, *Der 'Volkskörper' im Krieg: Gesundheitspolitik, Gesundheitsverhältnisse und Krankenmord im nationalsozialistischen Deutschland 1939–1945* (Munich, 2003).

Swett, Pamela E., 'Mobilizing Citizens and Their Savings: Germany's Public Savings Banks, 1933–1939', in Lindemann, Mary and Poley, Jared (eds.), *Money in the German-Speaking Lands* (New York, NY, 2017), 234–49.

Swett, Pamela E., *Selling under the Swastika: Advertising and Commercial Culture in Nazi Germany* (Stanford, CA, 2014).

Swett, Pamela E., Ross, Corey and d'Almeida, Fabrice (eds.), *Pleasure and Power in Nazi Germany* (Basingstoke, 2011).

Szac-Wajnkranc, Noëmi, 'Im Feuer vergangen', in *Im Feuer vergangen: Tagebücher aus dem Ghetto*, with a foreword by Johann Christoph Hampe (Munich, 1963), 17–149.

Szpilman, Władysław, *The Pianist: The Extraordinary Story of One Man's Survival in Warsaw, 1939–45* (London, 1999).

Tändler, Maik and Jensen, Uffa, 'Psychowissen, Politik und das Selbst. Eine neue Forschungsperspektive auf die Geschichte des Politischen im 20. Jahrhundert', in Tändler, Maik and Jensen, Uffa (eds.), *Das Selbst zwischen Anpassung und Befreiung: Psychowissen und Politik im 20. Jahrhundert* (Göttingen, 2012), 9–35.

Theiss, Kerstin, *Wehrmachtjustiz an der 'Heimatfront': Die Militärgerichte des Ersatzheeres im Zweiten Weltkrieg* (Berlin, 2016).

Thieler, Kerstin, *'Volksgemeinschaft' unter Vorbehalt: Gesinnungskontrolle und politische Mobilisierung in der Herrschaftspraxis der NSDAP-Kreisleitung Göttingen* (Göttingen, 2014).

Thießen, Malte, *Eingebrannt ins Gedächtnis: Hamburgs Gedenken an Luftkrieg und Kriegsende 1943 bis 2005* (Munich, 2007).

Thomes, Paul, 'German Savings Banks as Instruments of Regional Development', in Cassis, Youssef, Feldman, Gerald and Olsson, Ulf (eds.), *The Evolution of Financial Institutions and Markets in Twentieth-Century Europe* (Aldershot, 1995), 143–62.

Thonfeld, Christoph, *Sozialkontrolle und Eigensinn: Denunziation am Beispiel Thüringens, 1933 bis 1949* (Vienna, Cologne, Weimar, 2003).

Timm, Annette, 'Sex with a Purpose: Prostitution, Venereal Disease, and Militarized Masculinity in the Third Reich', in Herzog, Dagmar (ed.), *Sexuality and German Fascism* (New York, NY, 2005), 223–55.

Tooze, Adam, *The Wages of Destruction: The Making and Breaking of the Nazi Economy* (New York, NY, 2006).

Ulrich, Bernd, *Die Augenzeugen: Deutsche Feldpostbriefe in Kriegs- und Nachkriegszeit 1914–1933* (Essen, 1997).

Ulrich, Bernd, 'Feldpostbriefe im Ersten Weltkrieg – Bedeutung und Zensur', in Knoch, Peter (ed.), *Kriegsalltag: Die Rekonstruktion des Kriegsalltags als Aufgabe der historischen Forschung und der Friedenserziehung* (Stuttgart, 1989), 40–83.

Umbach, Maiken, 'The Civilising Process and the Emergence of the Bourgeois Self: Music Chambers in Wilhelmine Germany', in Fulbrook, Mary (ed.), *Uncivilising Processes: Excess and Transgression in German Society and Culture* (New York, NY, 2007), 175–202.

Umbach, Maiken, *German Cities and Bourgeois Modernism, 1890–1924* (Oxford, 2009).

Umbach, Maiken, 'Made in Germany', in Schulze, Hagen and François, Etienne (eds.), *Deutsche Erinnerungsorte*, vol. 2 (Munich, 2003), 405–38.

Umbach, Maiken, 'Selfhood, Place, and Ideology in German Photo Albums, 1933–1945', *Central European History* 48/3 (2015), 335–65.

Umbach, Maiken and Humphrey, Mathew, *Authenticity: The Cultural History of a Political Idea* (Basingstoke, 2018).

Usborne, Cornelie, 'Female Sexual Desire and Male Honor: German Women's Illicit Love Affairs with Prisoners of War in the Second World War', *Journal of the History of Sexuality* 26/3 (2017), 454–88.

Vaizey, Hester, 'Empowerment or Endurance? War Wives' Experiences of Independence during and after the Second World War in Germany, 1939–1948', *German History* 29/1 (2011), 57–78.

Vaizey, Hester, *Surviving Hitler's War: Family Life in Germany, 1939–48* (Basingstoke, 2010).

Valverde, Mariana, 'Despotism and Ethical Liberal Governance', *Economy and Society* 25/3 (1996), 357–72.

Vogel, Detlef and Wette, Wolfram (eds.), *Andere Helme: Heimaterfahrung und Frontalltag im Zweiten Weltkrieg. Ein internationaler Vergleich* (Essen, 1995).

Vollnhals, Clemens, 'Der Totalitarismusbegriff im Wandel', *Aus Politik und Zeitgeschichte* 56/39 (2006), 21–6.

Wachsmann, Nikolaus, *Hitler's Prisons: Legal Terror in Nazi Germany* (New Haven, CT, 2004).

Wacks, Raymond, *Privacy: A Very Short Introduction*, 2nd edn (Oxford, 2015).

Wedemeyer-Kolwe, Bernd, *'Der neue Mensch': Körperkultur im Kaiserreich und in der Weimarer Republik* (Würzburg, 2004).

Wehler, Hans-Ulrich, 'Königsweg zu neuen Ufern oder Irrgarten der Illusionen? Die westdeutsche Alltagsgeschichte: Geschichte "von innen" und "von unten"', in Wehler, Hans-Ulrich (ed.), *Aus der Geschichte lernen?* (Munich, 1988), 130–51.

Weidenhaupt, Hugo (ed.), *Ein nichtarischer Deutscher: Die Tagebücher des Albert Herzfeld 1935–1939* (Düsseldorf, 1982).

Weintraub, Jeff, 'The Theory and Politics of the Public/Private Distinction', in Weintraub, Jeff and Kumar, Krishan (eds.), *Public and Private in Thought and Practice: Perspectives on a Grand Dichotomy* (Chicago. IL, London, 1997), 1–42.

Weintraub, Jeff and Kumar, Krishan (eds.), *Public and Private in Thought and Practice: Perspectives on a Grand Dichotomy* (Chicago. IL, London, 1997).

Weisbrod, Bernd, 'The Hidden Transcript: The Deformation of the Self in Germany's Dictatorial Regimes', *German Historical Institute London Bulletin* 34/2 (2012), 61–72.

Weiß, Ralph, 'Vom gewandelten Sinn für das Private', in Weiß, Ralph (ed.), *Privatheit im öffentlichen Raum: Medienhandeln zwischen Individualisierung und Entgrenzung* (Offenbach, 2002), 27–88.
Weißmann, Karlheinz, *Schwarze Fahnen, Runenzeichen: Die Entwicklung der politischen Symbolik der deutschen Rechten zwischen 1890 und 1945* (Düsseldorf, 1991).
Werner, Frank, '"Noch härter, noch kälter, noch mitleidloser": Soldatische Männlichkeit im deutschen Vernichtungskrieg 1941–1944', in Dietrich, Anette and Heise, Ljiljana (eds.), *Männlichkeitskonstruktionen im Nationalsozialismus* (Frankfurt a.M., 2013), 45–64.
Werner, Frank, 'Soldatische Männlichkeit im Vernichtungskrieg: Geschlechtsspezifische Dimensionen der Gewalt in Feldpostbriefen 1941–1944', in Didczuneit, Veit, Ebert, Jens and Jander, Thomas (eds.), *Schreiben im Krieg – Schreiben vom Krieg: Feldpost im Zeitalter der Weltkriege* (Essen, 2011), 283–94.
Westermann, Edward B., *Hitler's Police Battalions: Enforcing Racial War in the East* (Lawrence, WI, 2005).
Westphal, Uwe, *Werbung im Dritten Reich* (Berlin, 1989).
Weyrather, Irmgard, *Muttertag und Mutterkreuz: Der Kult um die 'deutsche Mutter' im Nationalsozialismus* (Frankfurt a.M., 1993).
Wierling, Dorothee, *Eine Familie im Krieg: Leben, Sterben und Schreiben 1914–1918* (Göttingen, 2013).
Wiesen, S. Jonathan, *Creating the Nazi Marketplace: Commerce and Consumption in the Third Reich* (Cambridge, 2011).
Wildt, Michael, 'Die alltagsgeschichtliche Wende der Zeitgeschichte in den 1970er und 1980er Jahren', in Forschungsstelle für Zeitgeschichte in Hamburg (ed.), *Zeitgeschichte in Hamburg* (Hamburg, 2011), 42–54.
Wildt, Michael, *Die Generation des Unbedingten: Das Führungskorps des Reichssicherheitshauptamtes* (Hamburg, 2002).
Wildt, Michael, *Geschichte des Nationalsozialismus* (Göttingen, 2008).
Wildt, Michael, 'Self-Assurance in Troubled Times: German Diaries during the Upheavals of 1933', in Lüdtke, Alf (ed.), *Everyday Life in Mass Dictatorship: Collusion and Evasion* (Houndmills, 2016), 55–74.
Wildt, Michael, 'Völkische Neuordnung Europas', in *clio online* (2016), www.europa.clio-online.de/essay/id/artikel-3748 [accessed 29 December 2016].
Wildt, Michael, *Volksgemeinschaft als Selbstermächtigung: Gewalt gegen Juden in der deutschen Provinz 1919 bis 1939* (Hamburg, 2007).
Wildt, Michael, *Hitler's Volksgemeinschaft and the Dynamics of Racial Exclusion: Violence against Jews in Provincial Germany, 1919-1939* (New York, NY, and Oxford, 2011).
Wildt, Michael, '"Volksgemeinschaft": Eine Antwort auf Ian Kershaw', *Zeithistorische Forschungen* 8 (2011), 102–9.
Wippermann, Wolfgang, *Totalitarismustheorien: Die Entwicklung der Diskussion von den Anfängen bis heute* (Darmstadt, 1997).
Wirrer, Bärbl (ed.), *Ich glaube an den Führer: Eine Dokumentation zur Mentalitätsgeschichte im nationalsozialistischen Deutschland 1942–1945* (Bielefeld, 2003).

Wirsching, Andreas, 'Privacy', in Nerdinger, Winfried et al. (eds.), *Munich and National Socialism: Catalogue of the Munich Documentation Centre for the History of National Socialism* (Munich, 2015), 439–45.

Wirsching, Andreas, '*Volksgemeinschaft* and the Illusion of "Normality" from the 1920s to the 1940s', in Steber, Martina and Gotto, Bernhard (eds.), *Visions of Community in Nazi Germany: Social Engineering and Private Lives* (Oxford, 2014), 149–56.

Witczak, Krzysztof Tomasz, 'Listy z getta tomaszowskiego jako dokument historyczny obrazujący żydowskie życie artystyczne w okresie okupacji', *Rocznik Łódzki* 58 (Łódź, 2011), 161–82.

Wolf, Gerhard, 'Die deutschen Minderheiten in Polen als Instrument der expansiven Außenpolitik Berlins', in Kochanowski, Jerzy and Sach, Maike (eds.), *Die 'Volksdeutschen' in Polen, Frankreich, Ungarn und der Tschechoslowakei: Mythos und Realität* (Osnabrück, 2006), 41–78.

Wolf, Gerhard, *Ideologie und Herrschaftsrationalität: Nationalsozialistische Germanisierungspolitik in Polen* (Hamburg, 2012).

Wölki, Kerstin, 'Krieg als Reise: Die Wahrnehmung Frankreichs durch deutsche Soldaten im Zweiten Weltkrieg' (Magisterarbeit, Freiburg, 2007).

Wrobel, Hans, 'Die Anfechtung der Rassenmischehe: Diskriminierung und Entrechtung der Juden in den Jahren 1933 bis 1935', *Kritische Justiz* 16/4 (1983), 349–74.

Wyss, Eva L., 'Brautbriefe, Liebeskorrespondenzen, und Online-Flirts: Schriftliche Liebeskommunikation vom 19. Jahrhundert bis in die Internet-Ära', in Luginbühl, Martin and Perrin, Daniel (eds.), *Muster und Variation in Medientexten* (Bern, 2011), 81–123.

Ziegler, Dieter, '"A Regulated Market Economy": New Perspectives on the Nature of the Economic Order of the Third Reich, 1933–1939', in Berghoff, Hartmut, Kocka, Jürgen and Ziegler, Dieter (eds.), *Business in the Age of Extremes: Essays in Modern German and Austrian Economic History* (Cambridge, 2013), 139–52.

Ziemann, Benjamin, 'Feldpostbriefe und ihre Zensur in den zwei Weltkriegen', in Beyer, Klaus and Täubrich, Hans-Christian (eds.), *Der Brief: Eine Kulturgeschichte der schriftlichen Kommunikation* (Heidelberg, 1996), 163–70.

Ziemann, Benjamin, *Die Zukunft der Republik? Das Reichsbanner Schwarz-Rot-Gold 1924–1933* (Bonn, 2011).

Index

Aachen 100
abortion 313, 314, 322, 323, 324, 325
Adorno, Theodor W. 182, 183, 186, 203, 289
adultery 200, *see also* marriage, breakdown of
air raids *see* bombing
air war *see* bombing
Albring, Hans 89, 90, 91, 92, 101
alcohol 248, 247
Allport, Gordon 64
Alltagsgeschichte see everyday life, history of
Altreich ('old Reich') 304, 305, 309, 313, 318, 322, 329
Altrogge, Eugen 89, 90
Andersen, Lale 292
antisemitism 6, 25, 47, 98, 100, 144, 174, 178, 183, 262, *see also* Jews
apartments 4, 14, 30, 31, 34, 47, 69, 156, 160, 161, 162, 168, 171, 176, 184, 186, 189, 192, 199, 200, 201, 202, 250, 315, 331, 336, 341, 344, 345, *see also* tenants
Arendt, Hannah 11, 13, 41, 49, 105
armed forces *see* Wehrmacht
'Aryan' 66, 68, 70, 72, 75, 98, 104, 136, 137, 138, 139, 140, 146, 176, 177, 180, 258, 261, 268, 293, 294, 313, 335, 337
Auschwitz 55, 74, 79, 92
Austria 65, 103, 116, 117, 165, 198, 221, 226, 257, 290, 292
authenticity, concept of 84, 109, 119, 139, 286

Balkans 278
Baltic Sea 159
Baltic states 312
banking, banks 143, 144, 145, 146, 149, 152, 153, 154, *see also* saving, practice of; Sparkassen
Baruth 164, 167
Bäumler, Alfred 24

Bavaria 57, 96, 110, 111, 151, 157, 283, 295
Bayer pharmaceuticals 140
Berenberg-Gossler, Cornelius Freiherr von 165
Berlin 3, 4, 6, 21, 68, 75, 88, 92, 93, 94, 95, 96, 98, 99, 116, 156, 157, 159, 161, 162, 164, 169, 175, 199, 200, 202, 206, 211, 220, 280, 283, 302
Bessarabia 304, 319
Bialystok 120, 123
biopolitics 25, 305, 306, 308, 310, 313, 314, 325, 330, *see also* eugenics
Birkbeck College 113
births 15, 25, 116, 213, 240, 241, 254, 304, 305, 306, 307, 308, 310, 313, 314, 317, 318, 319, 320, 321, 322, 323, 324, 325, 326, 327, 328, 329, 330 *see also* abortion; motherhood
black market 154, 264
Blau, Edith *see* Brandon, Edith
Blitzkrieg 238
Blockleiter, Blockwart (NSDAP block warden) 50, 51, 77, 171, 172
Blomberg, Werner von 177
blood and soil *(Blut und Boden)* 145, 292
Blutschutzgesetz (Law for the Protection of German Blood and German Honour) 198
body 10, 17, 47, 106, 109, 136, 142, 214, 298, 300, 303, 305, 307, 317, 318, 320, 329, 343
Bolshevism 24, 86, 89
bombing 82, 93, 96, 97, 99, 100, 153, 224, 253, 294
Bormann, Martin 138, 240
bourgeoisie 8, 10, 12, 15, 24, 31, 37, 38, 39, 40, 42, 43, 44, 52, 56, 96, 135, 148, 159, 167, 182, 183, 186, 194, 205, 213, 214, 217, 235, 245, 256, 282, 283, 290, 300, 306, 336, 341
boycott 75, 168

383

384 *Index*

Brandeis, Louis 7
Brandenburg 157, 164
Brandon, Edith 337, 338, 339, 343, 344, 345
Breslau 165, 168, 170, 171, 175, 177, 194
Brest 281, 293, 296
Britain 95, 103, 105, 108, 110, 113, 155, 183, 187, 287, 301
Brittany 281
Bromberg *see* Bydgoszcz
Brose, Hanns 142
Buckow 164, 167, 171
Budapest 100, 120
Bulgaria 267, 269, 270, 272, 273, 275, 276, 278
Buller, Amy 103, 105, 107, 108, 109, 110, 111, 112, 113, 114, 115, 119, 130
Bund Deutscher Mädel (BDM) (League of German Girls) 3, 93, 317
Bydgoszcz 337
bystanders 55, 59, 60, 61, 62, 73, 75, 76, 77, 78, 79, 80

capitalism 144, 182
Catholics 74, 75, 86, 87, 89, 95, 100, 107, 110, 111, 165, 167, 180
censorship 20, 140, 215, 220, 282, 293, 294, 302, 303
  self-censorship 20, 66, 91, 293
Centre Party (*Zentrumspartei*) 160
Charkow 281
Christmas 24, 27, 148, 233, 244
cinema 3, 117, 118, 122, 207, 220, 270, 290, 291, 301
citizens 11, 39, 53, 62, 107, 110, 118, 135, 136, 145, 147, 153, 154, 155, 166, 167, 168, 179, 180, 181, 198, 204
citizenship 8, 311
Civil Code 198, 203
civil servants 159, 176, 219
class 74, 86, 139, 140, 163, 283, 319, 329
  middle class *see* bourgeoisie
  working class 13, 47, 108, 214, 256, 265
clubs 56, 76
coercion 11, 13, 58, 59, 149, 219, 234, 239, 255
Cohn, Willy 165, 168, 170, 171, 175, 177
Cold War 11, 33
Communism 33, 73, 74, *see also* KPD
community 5, 11, 14, 17, 21, 24, 27, 28, 35, 46, 51, 52, 58, 61, 62, 63, 67, 74, 79, 107, 139, 154, 155, 159, 168, 187, 194, 198, 203, 204, 275, 301, 315, 321, 322, 350
  house community 340, 345

national community *see* Volksgemeinschaft
comradeship 4, 179, 221, 237, 238, 245, 254, 260, 261, 262, 268, 270, 271, 275, 276, 287
concentration camps 12, 60, 66, 182
concerts *see* music
conformity 29, 59, 61, 62, 75, 76, 130, 162, 169, 171, 172, 177, 181, 262
  non-conformity 81, 261
Congress Poland 347
consent 16, 59, 82, 145, 170, 171
consumers 27, 122, 137, 139, 140, 141, 142, 143, 146, 147, 148, 153, 155, 266
  consumer goods 26, 106, 130, 135, 136, 142, 145, 147, 153
  consumer habits 136
consumerism 183
consumption 10, 13, 26, 27, 80, 106, 135, 136, 137, 138, 139, 140, 142, 145, 146, 147, 248, 265, 266, 267, 268, 269
Conti, Leonardo 241, 308, 329
Conti, Nanna 308
coordination (*Gleichschaltung*) 173, 180
countryside 161, 167
couple cosmos (*Paarkosmos*) 257, 258, 259, 261, 264, 265, 268, 269, 270, 275, 276, 278
courts 6, 24, 25, 236, 248, 249, 250, 251, 252, 253, 255, 310, 323, 324, and Chapter 8
  Central Army Court (*Zentralgericht des Heeres*) 195, 196
  Court of Appeal (*Kammergericht*) 200
  District Court (*Amtsgericht*) 185, 189, 202
  Labour Court (*Arbeitsgericht*) 194
  Magistrates' Court (*Schöffengericht*) 190, 191
  Military Court (*Kriegsgericht*) 195, 248
  Regional Court (*Landgericht*) 185, 199, 200, 202
  Special Court (*Sondergericht*) 185, 192, 193, 322, 324
  Supreme Court of the Reich (*Reichsgericht*) 199, 200, 201
courtship 256, 259, 260, 270
Cracow 337
crime 30, 86, 88, 189, 190, 301
crisis 26, 97, 144, 148, 153, 213, 221
  political 97, 100, 107, 113, 158, 159
  world economic 26, 137, 143, 146, 148, 219
culture 7, 24, 115, 137, 139, 145, 289, 290, 316, 317, 329

commercial 130
military 91, 261
political 164
popular 211, 290, 291, 297, 302

Danube 281
Danzig 337
Denmark 68, 73
denunciation 17, 58, 195, 196
deportation *see* Jews, deportation of
Depression *see* crisis, world economic
design, interior 138, 182
Deutsche Arbeitsfront (DAF) *see* German Labour Front
Deutsche Staatspartei 160
Deutsche Volksliste (German Ethnic Register) 304, 311, 312
Deutsches Frauenwerk (DFW) (German Women's Organisation) 217
dissent 19, 57, 61, 81, 97, 162
divorce 193, 197, 198, 199, 200, 201, 213, 225, 226, 227, 241, 248, 250, 251, 252, 253, *see also* law, marriage and divorce law; marriage
domesticity 106, 233
drawings 22, 115, 120, 122, 126
Dürkefälden, Karl 165
Düsseldorf 174
dwelling 24, 182, 183, 186, 201, 305, 317, 326, 328, 341, *see also* apartments

East Prussia 157
economy 9, 19, 74, 76, 106, 135, 137, 138, 139, 140, 143, 146, 150, 152, 177, 264, 265, 266, 267, 346, *see also* crisis, world economic; employment; Four-Year-Plan; rationalisation; rearmament; unemployment
education 24, 31, 39, 41, 50, 51, 52, 103, 107, 110, 112, 139, 141, 148, 212, 214, 216, 218, 219, 329, 337, 347
ego-documents 17, 18, 22, 29, 44, 63, 75, 102, 103, 104, 105, 114, 120, 130, 236, 243, 247, 255, 282, 310, 332, 340, 343, 347, 350, 351
Einwandererzentralstelle (Central Immigration Office) 315, 329
Eiserne Front 160, 161
Eisernes Sparen 150, 151 *see also* saving
elections 24, 156, 159, 160, 161, 162, 163, 165, 166, 167, 168, 169, 213
elites 10, 86, 120, 138, 139, 141, 344
emigration 66, 71, 138
'inner emigration' 19, 40, 52

emotions 29, 105, 106, 107, 108, 113, 114, 115, 128, 131, 137, 208, 234, 257, 281, 282, 285, 286, 289, 298, 302, 303
employers 194, 322
employment 15, 26, 194, 213, 219, 315, 348, *see also* unemployment
Essen 156
eugenics 15, 218, 258, *see also* biopolitics
evacuation, wartime 94, 97, 119, 310
everyday life, history of 13, 14, 16, 35, 36, 40, 41, 42, 56, 57, 58, 102, 258
exile 64, 65, 84, 182, 183, *see also* emigration
expulsion 140, 183
extermination *see* Jews, extermination of

faith *see* religion
fascism 33, 182
Fay, Sidney B. 64
Feder, Gottfried 143, 144
Federal Republic of Germany 28
Feldpost (field post, forces postal service) 4, 19, 20, 248, 282, 284, 286, 288, 294, 301, 302
femininity 114, 126, 216
fiancé, fiancée 20, 67, 68, 120, 222, 243, 244, 246, 281, 284, 287, 288, 290, 302
fidelity *see* marriage
films *see* cinema
First World War (Great War) 65, 83, 86, 87, 98, 110, 159, 175, 206, 211, 213, 215, 223, 225, 237, 254, 266, 282, 284, 287, 294
flags 25, 53, 63, 129, and Chapter 7, *see also* Reich Flag Decree
Flak (*Flugabwehrkanone*, anti-aircraft defence) 296
flats *see* apartments
food 45, 87, 200, 254, 265, 268, 283, 294, 334, 344
Fordism 212
Foucault, Michel 212, 305, 306
Four-Year-Plan 143
France 89, 90, 280, 281, 291, 295
Frankfurt 75, 165, 183, 188, 289
freedom, concept of 8, 10, 11, 24, 51, 158, 191, 204, 205, 300, 306, 315, 333, 340
Freud, Sigmund 289
Frick, Wilhelm 144, 179
Friedrich, Carl J. 11, 41
Friedrichshagen 94
friendship 9, 13, 73, 74, 75, 76, 77, 111, 193, *see also* Jews, friendships with
Friese, Hildegard 317

front, fighting 4, 22, 114, 119, 120, 179, 195, 218, 266, 267, 275, 283, 285, 286, 287, 289, 292, 296, 297, 300, 301, and Chapter 10, *see also* home front
  Eastern Front 4, 88, 91, 125, 221, 222, 243, 244, 245, 253
  Western Front 281, 302
Führer (Adolf Hitler) 68, 93, 98, 135, 157, 180, 257, 272, 296, *see also* Hitler, Adolf
Führer's Headquarters 240, 242

Galicia 304, 312
gardens 4, 112, 126, 156, 189, 260, 346
Gauleiter (NSDAP Gau leader) 99
gender roles 14, 15, 16, 20, 40, 111, 112, 114, 119, 216, 217, 219, 224, 235, 252, 254, 255, 285, 293, 307, 310, 322, *see also* femininity; masculinity
gender, history of 15, 16, 285
General Government (*Generalgouvernement*) 312, 337, 339
genocide *see* Jews, extermination of
German Democratic Republic (GDR) 12, 74
German Labour Front (*Deutsche Arbeitsfront*) 25, 49, 137, 149, 240
Germanisation 306, 307, 310, 311, 312, 313, 315, 322, 330
Germanness 292, 311, 312, 322, 330
Gestapo 47, 58, 81, 150, 178, 180, 188, 328
ghettos 6, 25, 47, 86, 87, 100, and Chapter 14
Goebbels, Joseph 18, 85, 97, 98, 99, 100, 139, 140, 151, 156, 157, 163, 207, 216, 240, 242
Goffman, Erving 62, 63
Goldbarth, Ruth 337, 343, 344, 345, 346, 347, 348, 350
Göring, Hermann 46, 99, 138, 177
Graz 221
Greece 267, 268, 275, 278
Greiser, Arthur 311
'Gypsies' (Sinti and Roma) 99, 276

Habermas, Jürgen 8
habitus 105, 110
Hahn, Lili 165
Halle 280
Hamburg 47, 67, 72, 75, 76, 96, 97, 100, 151, 160, 161, 165, 168, 169, 170, 171, 172, 175, 177, 192, 206, 221, 223, 224, 301
'hamstering' 264, 265

Hannover 95, 151, 225, 226
Hartshorne, Edward Y. 64
Harvard 7, 18, 64
Hattenhauer, Hans 203
Hausfriedensbruch (breach of domestic peace) 185, 189, 190, 192
health 106, 197, 208, 212, 258, 305, 314, 318, 320, 334, 344, 348
  health authorities 15, 241, 305, 308, 309, 310, 313, 314, 320, 321, 325, 326, 328, 329
Heide 161
Heidelberg 206
Heilbronn 120, 126, 128
Heimat see homeland
Heimtücke (treachery or malice towards the state) 185, 189, 192
Heimtückegesetz 24, 192, 193
Heinrici, Gotthard 21
Herzfeld, Albert 174
Heydrich, Reinhard 335
Himmler, Heinrich 5, 86, 97, 104
Hitler Youth (*Hitlerjugend*) 14, 135, 169, *see also* Bund Deutscher Mädel
Hitler, Adolf 45, 46, 49, 50, 59, 64, 67, 68, 71, 78, 83, 93, 104, 111, 113, 117, 138, 143, 156, 160, 163, 164, 165, 166, 168, 169, 178, 179, 181, 192, 262
holidays 22, 53, 71, 107, 116, 119, 130, 136, 137, 144, 147, 148, 159, 163, 179, 200, 234, 237, 240, 273, 288, 290, 293, 340
Hollander, Walther von 28, and Chapter 9
home front 4, 22, 93, 150, 187, 218, 257, 266, 276
home leave 4, 6, 28, 122, 126, 222, 285, 288, 295, and Chapter 10
homeland 65, 89, 145, 237
homosexuality 16, 26
Horkheimer, Max 183, 289
house search 46, 47, 188
household 13, 16, 67, 144, 148, 172, 177, 194, 197, 199, 200, 201, 202, 244, 246, 247, 251, 254, 306, 317, 319, 341, 344
housekeeper, housekeeping 15, 194, 197, 200, 208, 307, 316
housewives 141, 149, 220
housework 219
Hunke, Heinrich 140, 148
Husum 161
hygiene 318, 319, 329, 342, *see also* race, 'racial hygiene'

ideology, Nazi 16, 29, 41, 46, 61, 102, 103, 104, 106, 110, 115, 119, 130, 131, 135, 136, 146, 155, 186, 203, 227, 292, 299, 301, 302
individuality, concept of 41, 108, 110, 137, 170, 181, 211, 261, 308
information, personal 9, 10, 235, 307, 333, 334
intellectuals 107, 217, 289
intimacy 7, 17, 25, 70, 71, 72, 106, 135, 141, 147, 184, 201, 234, 259, 282, 302, 332
intimate relationships 10, 19, 20, 71, 196, 212, 332
Italy 97, 283
Itzehoe 161

Jews 6, 17, 18, 19, 25, 47, 62, 65, 66, 67, 69, 70, 73, 74, 76, 87, 88, 91, 99, 100, 104, 135, 138, 139, 140, 143, 144, 165, 168, 169, 172, 176, 183, 309, 310, 312, 315, 316, 324, and Chapter 14
'Jew houses' (*Judenhäuser*) 47
and hoisting of flags 25, 170, 173, 174, 175, 176, 178, 180, 181
and religious practice 340, 341
as marital partners 4, 68, 71, 74, 176
attitudes towards regime 175
deportation of 20, 47, 60, 78, 86, 88, 98, 100, 312, 333
extermination of 20, 26, 29, 64, 66, 76, 78, 79, 85, 88, 91, 92, 93, 94, 95, 96, 98, 99, 100, 101, 268, 316
friendships with 67, 70, 71, 74, 75, 76, 77
violence against 47, 78, 82, 86, 168, 174, 175, 178, 312
judiciary 185, 188, 191, 192, 196, 197, 202
Jünger, Ernst 89
Jurandot, Jerzy 331, 332, 336

Kaiserreich 12, 159, 160, 163, 166, 168, 169, 170, 173, 175, 177, 178, 297
Kameradschaftsehe (companionate marriage) *see* marriage
Kant, Immanuel 8
Kattowitz 310
Katyn 99
Kauffmann, Fritz Alexander 187
Kellner, Friedrich 19
Kempowski, Walter 285
Kershaw, Ian 34, 36, 55
Kinderlandverschickung (KLV) (evacuation of children to the countryside) 119
Klemperer, Victor 104
Klepper, Jochen 4

Knight's Cross (*Ritterkreuz*) 251, 296
Kocka, Jürgen 57
Königsberg 92
Korczak, Janusz 347, 348, 349, 350, 351
KPD (German Communist Party) 46, 159, 161, 166, 167, 171
Kraft durch Freude (KdF) (Strength Through Joy) 107, 130, 136, 147, 240
Kraków *see* Cracow
Kreisleiter (NSDAP district leader) 48, 50
Kremser, Albert 283, 295
Kriegsgemeinschaft (war community) 27, 257, 259, 260, 264, 265, 266, 268, 269, 278, 279
Kritzendorf 281, 288
Kulmbach 202
Kutno 322, 323

labour, forced 316
labourers *see* workers
law 7, 48, 69, 143, 159, 266, 324, 336, and Chapter 8, *see also Blutschutzgesetz*; courts; *Heimtückegesetz*; judiciary; Nuremberg Laws; Reich Flag Decree; Reich Midwifery Law; Reichstag Fire Decree
civil law 185, 197, 202, 205
criminal law 189, 191, 192, 195, 197, 205
family law 185, 197, 198
labour law 194
marriage and divorce law 197, 198, 199, 200, 201, 226, 227
police law 188
private law 9
public law 9
rule of law 54, 186, 191
tenancy law 185, 202, 203
Leander, Zarah 291
Lebensraum see living space
Leipzig 190, 192, 267
leisure 10, 76, 106, 107, 116, 197, *see also* holidays
leisure time 14, 106, 122, 240, 275, 334
Leslau *see* Włocławek
Ley, Robert 25, 42, 49, 50
liberalism, liberals 8, 9, 10, 11, 12, 24, 26, 28, 33, 34, 83, 105, 139, 144, 155, 159, 184, 186, 198, 205, 306, 334
Litzmannstadt *see* Łódź
Liverpool 112
living conditions 148, 153, 171, 189, 199, 332, 336, 344, 345, 346, 349
living space (*Lebensraum*) 262, 264, 269, 278, 311
Ljubljana 252

Łódź 305, 310, 316, 322, 337, 339, 340, 341
London 100, 187
Lorraine 280
Lower Saxony 165, 178
loyalty 17, 23, 29, 194, 195, 208, 268, 321
Luftwaffe *see* Wehrmacht
Luhmann, Niklas 308
luxury *see* consumption

magazines 3, 28, 126, 129, 149, 153, 206, 207, 208, 209, 220, 228
Maier, Eugen 48
Majdanek 92
marriage 56, 72, 106, 120, 193, 194, 198, 199, 201, 202, 241, 250, 269, 271, 272, 282, 288, 289, 296, 314, 315, *see also* adultery; courtship; divorce; law, marriage and divorce law; violence, domestic
  advice on Chapter 9
  and wartime separation 250, 252
  breakdown of 193, 197, 200, 201, 241, 250, 251
  fidelity, infidelity 226, 228, 242, 247, 250, 252, 253
  Kameradschaftsehe (companionate marriage) 218, 219
  marriage loans scheme 15, 258
  marriage permit 120
  mixed marriages 74, 176, 198
masculinity 216, 245, 246, 262
media 3, 7, 27, 28, 85, 98, 99, 100, 114, 115, 211, 213, 221, 228, 233, 319, *see also* magazines; newspapers; radio; cinema
Mehs, Matthias Joseph 165, 166, 167, 168, 170, 171, 174, 177, 179, 181
Meyer, Johann 323, 324
Michelhausen 281
midwives 15, and Chapter 13
military service 202, 262, 280, *see also* Wehrmacht
Minden 337, 343
Ministry *see* Reich Ministry
'*Mischlinge*' (of mixed descent) 68
mobilisation 5, 136
  self-mobilisation 16, 17
motherhood 15, 292, 299, *see also* births
Mozart, Wolfgang Amadeus 116
Münchehofe 94
Munich 6, 57, 122, 189, 193, 199, 200, 206, 250, 251, 252, 283
Münster 100
Münsterland 89

music 136, 142, 164, 179, 183, 216, 270, 291, 346, 347
Mussolini, Benito 97

National Assembly (*Nationalversammlung*) 213
Nationalsozialistische Frauenschaft (NSF) (National Socialist Women's League) 326
Nationalsozialistische Volkswohlfahrt (NSV) (National Socialist People's Welfare Organisation) 221, 242, 321, 326
navy *see* Wehrmacht
neighbourhood 13, 14, 77, 162, 332
neighbours 17, 35, 39, 48, 77, 106, 161, 162, 167, 168, 169, 170, 171, 252, 256, 310, 317, 318
newspapers 4, 7, 22, 64, 67, 70, 98, 99, 115, 151, 153, 156, 157, 159, 160, 163, 164, 169, 179, 181, 193, 220, 221, 228, 233, 234, 237, 238, 241, 285, 294, 296, 343
Nietzsche, Friedrich 289
NKVD (Soviet People's Commissariat for Internal Affairs) 99
North Sea 157, 159
Northwest German Broadcasting (NWDR) (*Nordwestdeutscher Rundfunk*) 228
NSDAP 14, 17, 19, 21, 25, 28, 47, 50, 51, 69, 72, 86, 108, 135, 138, 148, 152, 156, 157, 158, 159, 160, 161, 162, 163, 165, 166, 167, 168, 169, 170, 171, 172, 173, 175, 176, 177, 178, 179, 180, 181, 187, 192, 207, 239, 240, 241, 242, 245, 257, 266
  members 50, 67, 72, 75, 87, 174
  officials 15, 17, 18, 42, 48, 49, 50, 51, 67, 137, 144, 171, 180, 192, 240
  organisations 14, 50, 139, 144, 147, 241, 242, 313
Nuremberg 135, 178
Nuremberg Laws 174, 175, 176, 177, 178, 198

occupation 25, 28, 87, 88, 93, 94, 100, 119, 267, 304, 307, 310, 312, 314, 316, 320, 322, 325, 330, 335, 338, 339
occupied territories 16, 18, 20, 23, 114, 247, 307
Odenwald 47, 243
Oder 94, 95
Ohrenbach, Lutek 337, 338, 339, 340, 341, 343, 344, 345, 346, 347, 348, 350
Olympic Games, Olympics 21, 116, 135

opposition to Nazism 23, 38, 59, 61, 62, 111, 177
oral history 44, 57, 77
Ordnungsdienst (Jewish auxiliary police) 336
Orgel, Kurt 301
Orwell, George 30, 31, 32, 33, 34, 37, 38, 39, 40, 42, 43, 54, 90

Pabianice 86
Palestine 71, 73
Party Chancellery (*Parteikanzlei der NSDAP*) 240, 242
Party, Communist *see* KPD
Party, Nazi *see* NSDAP
Party, Social Democratic *see* SPD
patriotism 87, 93, 96, 170
Peine 165
performance 29, 34, 62, 66, 67, 69, 70, 71, 75, 77, 78, 79, 80, 103, 107, 111, 112, 114, 131, 142, 261, 331, 346, 347
perpetrators 60, 78, 79, 81, 102, 192, 193
persecution 13, 29, 61, 79, 172, 183
  of Jews 6, 18, 25, 29, 60, 66, 70, 74
Pesach 339, 340
Pestchana 4
Petrikau *see* Piotrków Trybunalski
photographs 4, 5, 18, 19, 20, 22, 103, 114, 115, 116, 117, 118, 119, 120, 181, 220, 233, 257, 259, 262, 270, 272, 273, 275, 276, 278, 279, 287, 288, 293, 298, 301
  photo albums 22, 29, 114, 118, 119, 120, 122
photography, practice of 7, 22, 115, 142, 272, 273, 275, 276
Piotrków Trybunalski (Petrikau) 337
Plovdiv 273
plundering 60, 245, 267, 316
pluralism 28, 83
poems 22, 91, 95, 115, 117, 346
pogrom of November 1938 47, 48, 86
Poitiers 89
Poland 6, 25, 74, 82, 86, 87, 88, 98, 99, 120, 154, 233, 280, 281, 292, 293, and Chapters 13 and 14, *see also* Congress Poland; General Government; Reichsgau Wartheland; Reichsgau Danzig-West Prussia
police 11, 17, 34, 42, 47, 69, 81, 84, 90, 97, 175, 188, 192, 252, 264, *see also* Gestapo; law, police law; Security Police
postcards 22, 122, 286
Potsdam 162, 163, 165, 166, 167, 168

pregnancy 299, 305, 306, 307, 320, 325, 329, *see also* births; midwives; motherhood
press *see* newspapers
Prinz, Julie 304, 305, 309, 310, 317, 318, 319, 320, 321, 325, 328, 329
prisoners of war (POW) 86, 154, 300, 301
  camps 94, 128
propaganda 13, 21, 30, 83, 97, 98, 100, 106, 107, 117, 118, 120, 122, 130, 145, 154, 155, 161, 162, 169, 185, 233, 234, 235, 238, 241, 246, 254, 264, 292, 301, 302, 303, 309, *see also* Goebbels, Joseph; Reich Ministry of Propaganda
property 9, 10, 19, 105, 135, 148, 153, 155, 189, 203, 204, 312
Protestants 69, 74, 95, 107, 111, 115, 168
Prussia 46, 64, 93, 94, 158, 159, 162, 164, 170
public space 9, 10, 30, 47, 160, 192, 336
public sphere 7, 8, 12, 23, 26, 28, 42, 55, 56, 83, 131, 161, 179, 184, 186, 227, 235, 303
Purper, Liselotte 301

race 5, 25, 28, 66, 70, 72, 73, 74, 76, 77, 82, 98, 107, 140, 145, 198, 227, 261, 265, 295, 314, 328
  'racial defilement' (*Rassenschande*) 73, 78
  racial discrimination 6, 176
  racial hierarchies 6, 17, 23, 52, 70, 307, 315, 324, 333
  'racial hygiene' 198
  racial policies 25, 58, 138, 218, 251, 305
  racial science 66, 111
  racial segregation 307, 325
  racial state 73, 81
  theories of 104, 109, 168, 262
Racial Policy Office (*Rassenpolitisches Amt der NSDAP*) 313
racism 5, 75, 227, 276, 292, 301, 302, 309, 328, 330
radio 26, 68, 92, 142, 150, 156, 208, 209, 216, 228, 270, 291, 292
Ramcke, Bernhard 296
rape 16, 316
rationalisation 212
rearmament 26, 143, 146
Red Army 93, 94, 95
refugees 64, 337, 338, 339, 340
Regensburg 252
Reich Association of German Officers (*Reichsverband deutscher Offiziere*) 179, 180

390 Index

Reich Chancellery (*Reichskanzlei*) 240
Reich Flag Decree (*Reichsflaggengesetz*) 178, 179, 180
Reich Labour Service (*Reichsarbeitsdienst*) 116
Reich Literature Chamber (*Reichsschrifttumskammer*) 214
Reich Midwifery Law (*Reichshebammengesetz*) 313, 321, 326
Reich Ministry of Finance (*Reichsfinanzministerium*) 150, 151
Reich Ministry of Propaganda (*Reichsministerium für Volksaufklärung und Propaganda*) 139, 140, 168, 173, 180, 240, 242
Reich Ministry of the Interior (*Reichsministerium des Innern*) 174, 175, 176, 179, 180, 329
Reich Security Main Office (*Reichssicherheitshauptamt*) 315
Reichsarbeitsdienst see Reich Labour Service
Reichsbanner Schwarz-Rot-Gold 160
Reichsfrauenführung (Reich Women's Leadership) 217
Reichsgau Danzig-West Prussia 310
Reichsgau Wartheland (Warthegau) 337, and Chapter 13
Reichshebammenschaft (Reich Midwifery League) 326
Reichstag 156, 159, 162, 163, 165, 166, 178
Reichstag Fire Decree (*Reichstagsbrandverordnung*) 24, 46, 48, 188
Reinhardt, Fritz 150
religion 78, 89, 90, 104, 110, 111, 168, 180, 316, 340, 341, *see also* Catholics; Jews; Protestants
Remarque, Erich Maria 297
resettlement policies 305, 309, 311
resettlers (*Umsiedler, Rückwanderer*) 304, 305, 312, 315, 316, 317, 321, 322, 329
resistance to Nazism 38, 57, 59, 60, 62, 78, 88, 110, 154, 302
Resistenz 38, 82
revolution 146
  'national revolution' 86, 164
  of 1918 239, 254
Rheinsberg 164, 167, 171
Rhine 95
Rhineland 156, 171, 288
Riefenstahl, Leni 118
Ringelblum, Emanuel 332

ritual 25, 27, 82, 105, 109, 157, 158, 162, 169, 171, 173, 174, 175, 180, 181, 295, 303
Romania 339
Rosenberg, Fritz 165, 168
Rössler, Beate 184, 235, 333, 334
Rothenburg ob der Tauber 96
Ruhr 99
rumours 84, 150, 153, 193, 194, 253, 261
Russia 74, 86, 90, 91, 94, 95, 221, 243, 294, 347

SA (*Sturmabteilung*) 47, 69, 86, 161, 164, 166, 167, 174, 175, 178, 194
Saar 157
Salzburg 116
Sauter, Wilhelm 122
saving, practice of 27, 344, and Chapter 6, *see also Eisernes Sparen*
Saxony 94, 256, 280
Schäfer, Hans Dieter 181
Scheidler, Wilhelm 47
Schering AG 137
Schlüter, Andreas 122, 129
Scholtz-Klink, Gertrud 218
school 45, 56, 66, 68, 75, 77, 86, 87, 89, 94, 107, 110, 144, 165, 172, 206, 256, 265, 322, 327, 328, 337
Schulz, Heinrich 214
Schwedt an der Oder 157
Schweinfurt 96
SD (*Sicherheitsdienst*) 63, 97, 99, 150, 242, 328
security 10, 14, 21, 24, 152, 184, 187, 244, 312, 313, 324, 335, 336, 348
security apparatus 12, 46, 150
Security Police (*Sicherheitspolizei*) 96, 99
seizure of power, Nazi 21, 28, 52, 75, 158, 170, 183, 189, 204, 207, 214
Sennett, Richard 7
sexuality 10, 15, 16, 20, 26, 27, 72, 73, 80, 106, 197, 200, 201, 209, 211, 212, 213, 214, 215, 244, 247, 255, 282, 285, 290, 297, 298, 299, 300, 303, 310
Shirer, William 63
Simmel, Georg 206, 216
sleep 42, 49, 199, 253, 281, 318, 344, 348, 349, 351
social history 36, 41, 57
social practice 19, 27, 42, 58, 278, 308, 332, 333, 339, 341, 350, 351
socialisation 61, 140, 239
soldiers 6, 16, 20, 22, 27, 28, 50, 86, 87, 91, 93, 101, 114, 126, 128, 135, 150, 221, 222, 225, 261, 265, 266, 267, 273,

275, 276, 284, 285, 286, 287, 289, 292, 293, 294, 295, 298, 300, 301, 302, and Chapter 10
Solmitz, Luise 168, 169, 170, 171, 175, 176, 177
Sonneberg 220
Sopade (exile organisation of the SPD) 63
South Africa 113
Southeast Europe 311, 315
Soviet Union 90, 238, 281, 287, *see also* Red Army; Russia; Ukraine
Spandau 202, 203
Sparkassen 143, 144, 145, 146, 148, 149, 150, 151, 152, 153, *see also* banking, banks; saving, practice of
SPD (Social Democratic Party of Germany) 46, 93, 160, 167, 171, 198, 214
Speer, Albert 122
Spessart 243
Spreewald 164
SS *see also* SD (*Sicherheitsdienst*)
SS (*Schutzstaffel*) 69, 71, 86, 87, 98, 110, 111, 114, 215, 233
Stabenow, Gerhard 87
Stalingrad 99
Stalinism 11, 31, 32, 33
sterilisation 15, 95, *see also* biopolitics; eugenics
Stettin 72, 157
storm troopers *see* SA (*Sturmabteilung*)
Strength Through Joy *see* Kraft durch Freude (KdF)
Student Christian Movement (UK) 105
Stuttgart 116
subjectivity 40, 57, 105, 289
Sudetenland 252
suicide 4, 78, 253
surveillance 7, 12, 17, 30, 33, 47, 51, 77, 262, 326, 327
swastika 129, 156, 157, 159, 160, 161, 163, 164, 165, 166, 168, 169, 170, 172, 173, 174, 176, 177, 178, 179, 180
synagogues 175, 341
Szac-Wajnkranc, Noëmi 335, 336, 341
Szpilman, Władysław 87

takeover *see* seizure of power, Nazi
Taylorism 212
telephones 46, 109, 123, 125, 190, 191, 224
Temple, William, Archbishop of Canterbury 113
tenants 202, 203
  subtenants 190, 348

terror 11, 20, 26, 29, 31, 58, 59, 61, 81, 93, 166, 188, 239, 293, *see also* Gestapo; police
Thalau 86
Thamer, Hans-Ulrich 42
Thessaloniki 276
Thuringia 220
Tomaszów Mazowiecki (Tomaschow) 25, 332, 337, 338, 339, 340, 342, 344, 345, 346, 350
Töpperwien, August 94, 95, 101, 104, 115
total war 153, 154, 301
totalitarianism 11, 12, 13, 14, 31, 32, 33, 34, 37, 38, 39, 40, 41, 42, 100, 102, 157, 166, 170, 178, 181
tourism 136, 273, 275, 276, 278
travel 103, 107, 108, 136, 137, 147, 148, 243, 276, 278
Treblinka 86, 87, 88, 338, 347, 350
Trier 165
Trieste 283
trust 3, 17, 25, 63, 66, 67, 70, 71, 76, 140, 141, 142, 143, 145, 189, 193, 194, 195, 196, 203, 205, 206, 225, 233, 261, 265, 266, 268, 290, 293, 308, 315, 320, 321, 322, 324, 325, 327, 328, 330

Ufa (Universum Film AG) 122, 207
Ukraine 4, 89
unemployment 26, 146, 265
uniforms 69, 70, 86, 90, 192, 233
United Kingdom 107
United States Army Air Forces (USAAF) 96
United States of America 93, 95, 100, 182, 183
universities 64, 107, 183, 189, 286

Valverde, Mariana 8
veterans 86, 87, 175, 180, 237
Vienna 116, 281, 286, 290, 294
violence 251, *see also* Jews, violence against; plundering; rape
  against 'enemies' 48, 53, 60, 61, 79, 86, 264, 276, 312, 316
  domestic 253
Vogeler, Heinrich 206
Volhynia 304, 312, 317, 318, 319, 329
Volk (the people) 50, 141, 142, 295
völkisch 144, 192, 198, 203, 204, 205, 292
Volksdeutsche (ethnic Germans) 25, 304, 314, 315, 316, 321, 322, 324, 329, 330
Volksdeutsche Mittelstelle (Ethnic German Liaison Office) 329

Volksdeutscher Selbstschutz (Ethnic German Self-Protection) 316
Volksgemeinschaft 6, 14, 17, 23, 27, 28, 48, 49, 51, 53, 56, 58, 59, 61, 69, 72, 73, 75, 77, 78, 82, 84, 107, 131, 144, 154, 157, 171, 173, 187, 191, 198, 201, 202, 203, 204, 205, 218, 233, 240, 250, 257, 260, 262, 265, 266, 267, 269, 306, 316, 318, 320, 329, 333
Volksgenossen 6, 14, 46, 48, 49, 50, 51, 54, 157, 178, 181, 205
Volkssturm 94, 95
Volkswagen 148

Warren, Samuel 7
Warsaw 25, 86, 87, 88, 89, 95, 247, 331, 332, 335, 336, 337, 340, 341, 342, 343, 344, 346, 347, 348, 350
Warthegau *see* Reichsgau Wartheland
Washington 100
weddings 71, 119, 120, 122, 126, 237, 250, 257, 259, *see also* marriage
Wehler, Hans-Ulrich 57
Wehrmacht 4, 16, 19, 20, 28, 87, 88, 93, 108, 115, 221, 222, 261, and Chapter 10, *see also* Blitzkrieg; *Feldpost*; home leave; Knight's Cross; military service; soldiers; veterans; Volkssturm
Army Group Centre (*Heeresgruppe Mitte*) 91

Luftwaffe 120
navy 156, 259, 261
Weimar Constitution 24
Weimar Republic 12, 26, 28, 31, 38, 45, 46, 141, 148, 158, 159, 160, 161, 162, 163, 164, 168, 169, 170, 181, 206, 211, 212, 213, 217
welfare 13, 15, 26, 204, 321, *see also* Nationalsozialistische Volkswohlfahrt
Westphalia 337
Wieluń (Welun) 304, 317
Wittlich 165, 166, 167, 168, 170, 171, 177, 179
Włocławek 310, 312, 313, 314, 326
women's movement 217
workers 149, 172, 194, 220, 265, *see also* labour, forced
'Eastern workers' (*Ostarbeiter*) 247
factory workers 178
foreign workers 154
Jewish factory workers 341
manual workers 159
social workers 242
textile workers 267
white-collar workers 159
workplace 14, 107, 334
Worpswede 206

Zamyatin, Yevgeny 37
Zichenau 310